Better Homes and Gardens.

All~Time Favorite Recipes

First Edition. Third Printing, 1980.
Library of Congress Catalog Card Number: 79-50869
ISBN: 0-696-00265-5

On the front cover: *Cranberry-Stuffed Cornish Hens, Spring Salad Toss,* and *Red Wine Dressing.* **On the back cover:** *Potatoes and Eggs au Gratin, Strawberry Shortcake, Tetrazzini Crepes, Crusty Water Rolls, Biscuits Supreme,* and *Onion Buns.* (See Index for recipe pages.)

BETTER HOMES AND GARDENS® BOOKS
Editor: Gerald Knox
Art Director: Ernest Shelton
Associate Art Director: Randall Yontz
Production and Copy Editors: David Kirchner,
    Lamont Olson, David A. Walsh
Food Editor: Doris Eby
Senior Associate Food Editor: Sharyl Heiken
Senior Food Editors: Sandra Granseth,
    Elizabeth Woolever
Associate Food Editors: Diane Nelson,
    Joy L. Taylor, Patricia Teberg
Recipe Development Editor: Marion Viall
Senior Graphic Designer: Harijs Priekulis
Graphic Designers: Faith Berven, Linda Ford,
    Richard Lewis, Sheryl Veenschoten, Neoma Alt West

Contents

1   Meat, Fish, and Poultry   6

2   Casserole recipes   66

3   Barbecue recipes   136

4   Vegetable dishes   206

5   Salad favorites   294

6   Bread specialties   366

7   Dessert collection   408

Index   463

Through the years, the editors of Better Homes and Gardens, like all good cooks, have collected a huge recipe file. In *All-Time Favorite Recipes,* we have compiled for you the favorites of all the recipes we've published. Whether you are planning a meal for family or guests, you'll find dishes for the entire meal in these pages. Choose a main dish from the meat, fish, poultry, or casserole pages. Or, for warm weather entrées, turn to the barbecue recipes. Complete your menu with dishes from the vegetable, salad, bread, and dessert sections. From one good cook to another, we give you our favorites.

1 Meat, Fish, & Poultry

Whether you're planning an elegant dinner party or a simple family meal, start by choosing the entrée. In this chapter you'll find a wide variety of meat, fish, and poultry recipes to fit any occasion.

Taco Salad, Cider Stew, and a boneless rib roast (see roasting chart, page 8) with *Crumb-Topped Tomatoes* are a sample of the recipes in this chapter (see index for recipe pages).

Beef

Standing Rib Roast with Yorkshire Pudding

1 4-pound beef rib roast,
   large end
Salt
Pepper
4 eggs
2 cups milk
2 cups all-purpose flour
1 teaspoon salt

Place roast, fat side up, in 15½x10½x2-inch roasting pan. Season with salt and pepper. Insert meat thermometer. Roast, uncovered, at 325° till meat thermometer registers 140° for rare (about 2½ hours); 160° for medium (about 3 hours); and 170° for well done (about 3¼ hours). Remove from pan. Cover; keep warm. Reserve ¼ cup drippings in pan.

Increase oven to 400°. In bowl beat eggs at low speed of electric mixer ½ minute. Add milk; beat 15 seconds. Add flour and salt; beat smooth, 2 minutes. Pour batter into pan. Bake at 400° about 40 minutes. Cut into squares; serve immediately with roast. Makes 8 servings.

Rump Roast with Vegetables

1 4-pound boneless beef round
   rump roast
¼ teaspoon salt
⅛ teaspoon dried marjoram,
   crushed
⅛ teaspoon dried thyme,
   crushed
Dash pepper
8 medium potatoes, peeled
   and halved
8 medium carrots, cut up
¼ cup all-purpose flour
1 tablespoon snipped parsley
¾ teaspoon salt
Dash pepper
Dash dried marjoram, crushed
Dash dried thyme, crushed

Place meat, fat side up, on rack in shallow roasting pan. Combine the ¼ teaspoon salt, the ⅛ teaspoon marjoram, the ⅛ teaspoon thyme, and the dash pepper; rub into meat. Roast, uncovered, at 325° till meat thermometer registers 150° to 170°, about 2¼ hours.

Meanwhile, in separate saucepans cook potatoes and carrots in boiling, salted water 15 minutes; drain. About 45 minutes before roast is done, place vegetables in drippings around roast, turning to coat. When done, transfer meat and vegetables to serving platter; keep warm. Sprinkle vegetables with additional snipped parsley, if desired.

Pour meat juices and fat into large measuring cup. Skim off fat, reserving 3 tablespoons. Add water to juices to make 2 cups; set aside. Return reserved fat to pan. Stir in flour; cook and stir over low heat till blended. Remove from heat. Add meat juices all at once; blend. Stir in snipped parsley, the ¾ teaspoon salt, dash pepper, dash marjoram, and dash thyme. Cook and stir till thickened and bubbly. Simmer 2 to 3 minutes more. Pass gravy with the roast and the cooked vegetables. Makes 8 to 10 servings.

Stuffed Rolled Rib Roast

4 ounces thinly sliced, fully
   cooked ham, chopped (1 cup)
3 slices bacon, snipped
¼ cup chopped onion
2 tablespoons chopped pimiento-
   stuffed green olives
1 clove garlic, minced
1 beaten egg
1 4- to 5-pound boneless beef
   rib roast

In bowl combine chopped ham, snipped bacon, onion, olives, garlic, and beaten egg. Unroll roast; spread ham mixture over meat. Reroll roast; tie securely.

Place roast, fat side up, on rack in shallow roasting pan. Roast, uncovered, at 325° about 3 hours for rare. Let stand about 15 minutes. Remove strings and carve. Makes 12 to 14 servings.

Preparing Beef Roasts

Roast meat at constant oven temperature of 325° unless otherwise indicated.

Cut	Approximate Weight (Pounds)	Internal Temperature on Removal from Oven	Approximate Cooking Time (Total Time)
Rib Roast	4 to 6	140° (rare) 160° (medium) 170° (well done)	2¼ to 2¾ hrs. 2¾ to 3¼ hrs. 3¼ to 3½ hrs.
Rib Roast	6 to 8	140° (rare) 160° (medium) 170° (well done)	2½ to 3 hrs. 3 to 3½ hrs. 3¾ to 4 hrs.
Boneless Rib Roast	5 to 7	140° (rare) 160° (medium) 170° (well done)	3¼ to 3½ hrs. 3¾ to 4 hrs. 4½ to 4¾ hrs.
Boneless Round Rump Roast	4 to 6	150° to 170°	2 to 2½ hrs.
Round Tip Roast	3½ to 4	140° to 170°	2 to 2¾ hrs.
Rib Eye Roast (Roast at 350°)	4 to 6	140° (rare) 160° (medium) 170° (well done)	1½ to 1¾ hrs. 1¾ hrs. 2 hrs.
Tenderloin Roast (Roast at 425°)	4 to 6	140° (rare)	45 min. to 1 hr.

Season the roast by sprinkling with a little salt and pepper. Insert a meat thermometer in center of the roast so that bulb reaches the thickest part of the lean meat. Make sure the bulb does not rest in fat or touch bone. Place roast, fat side up, on rack in a shallow roasting pan. Do not cover, add water, or baste. Except as noted above, roast at 325° till the thermometer registers desired internal temperature. To check, push thermometer into meat a little farther. If temperature drops, continue cooking the roast to desired temperature. Let meat stand 15 minutes for easier carving. (Remove string from rolled and tied roasts.) Carve meat across the grain.

Crumb-Topped Tomatoes (pictured on page 6)

6 small tomatoes
¼ cup sliced green onion
1 tablespoon butter *or* margarine
¼ cup fine dry bread crumbs
½ teaspoon dried dillweed
¼ teaspoon salt
Dash Worcestershire sauce

Cut a thin slice from top of each tomato; sprinkle tomatoes with a little salt and pepper. In small saucepan cook green onion in butter or margarine till tender but not brown; stir in crumbs, dillweed, salt, and Worcestershire sauce.

Sprinkle about 1 tablespoon of the crumb mixture atop each tomato. Place tomatoes in an 8x8x2-inch baking pan. Bake at 325° till heated through, about 25 minutes. Use as garnish with roasts. Makes 6 servings.

Sauerbraten

2½ cups water
1½ cups red wine vinegar
 1 tablespoon sugar
 1 tablespoon salt
¼ teaspoon ground ginger
12 whole cloves
 6 bay leaves
 6 whole black peppercorns
 2 medium onions, sliced
 1 lemon, sliced
 1 4-pound boneless beef round
    rump roast
 2 tablespoons cooking oil
½ cup chopped onion
½ cup chopped carrot
¼ cup chopped celery
 1 cup broken gingersnaps
⅔ cup water
   Hot buttered noodles

In crock or large bowl combine the 2½ cups water, wine vinegar, sugar, salt, ginger, cloves, bay leaves, peppercorns, sliced onion and lemon; add meat. Cover; refrigerate 36 to 72 hours, turning meat occasionally. Remove meat; wipe dry with paper toweling. Strain marinade; reserve.

In Dutch oven brown roast on all sides in hot oil. Add reserved marinade, chopped onion, carrot, and celery. Cover; simmer till meat is tender, about 2 hours.

Transfer meat to platter; keep hot. Reserve 2 cups of the liquid in Dutch oven; stir in gingersnaps and the ⅔ cup water. Cook and stir till thickened and bubbly. Serve meat and gravy with noodles. Makes 8 to 10 servings.

Rump Roast Supreme

 1 4- to 6-pound boneless beef
    round rump roast
 2 tablespoons shortening
 1 cup dry red wine
 1 cup beef broth
½ cup chopped onion
 1 teaspoon salt
¼ teaspoon ground thyme
¼ teaspoon pepper
 1 bay leaf
 1 clove garlic, minced
¼ cup all-purpose flour

In Dutch oven brown meat slowly on all sides in hot shortening. Add ½ *cup* of the dry red wine, the beef broth, onion, salt, thyme, pepper, bay leaf, and garlic. Cover; roast at 325° till meat is tender, 2½ to 3 hours.

Remove strings from roast. Transfer meat to serving platter; keep warm. Discard bay leaf. Skim excess fat from pan juices; add water to juices to make 2 cups.

Return juices to pan. Blend remaining ½ cup wine with flour; stir into juices. Cook and stir till thickened and bubbly. Pass gravy with meat. Makes 8 to 10 servings.

Pot Roast Dip Sandwiches

 1 3-pound beef round rump roast
¼ cup all-purpose flour
 2 tablespoons shortening
   Salt
   Pepper
½ cup water
 2 10½-ounce cans condensed
    beef broth
 2 teaspoons instant minced
    onion
 1 teaspoon Worcestershire sauce
12 hard rolls

Coat meat with flour. In Dutch oven brown meat on all sides in hot shortening. Season with salt and pepper. Remove from heat; add ½ cup water. Cover; return to heat. Simmer till tender, 2 to 2½ hours. Add water, if needed.

Pour off pan juices into measuring cup; skim off fat. Add water to juices, if needed, to make 2 cups. In saucepan combine pan juices, beef broth, onion, and Worcestershire. Bring to boiling; reduce heat. Simmer 5 minutes.

Slice roast as thinly as possible. Split hard rolls lengthwise, cutting almost all the way through. Place a few slices of meat in each roll. Serve each sandwich with about ⅓ *cup* of the hot broth. Makes 12 servings.

Golden Beef Pot Roast

 1 3- to 3½-pound beef chuck
     pot roast
 3 tablespoons all-purpose flour
 1 teaspoon salt
 ¼ teaspoon pepper
 2 tablespoons cooking oil
 ¼ cup water
 ¼ teaspoon celery seed
 ¼ teaspoon dried oregano,
     crushed
 ½ cup water
 ¼ cup frozen orange juice
     concentrate, thawed
1½ pounds sweet potatoes,
     peeled and halved
     (4 medium potatoes)
 2 medium onions, quartered
 ¼ cup cold water
 2 tablespoons all-purpose flour
    Salt
    Pepper
    Parsley sprigs

Trim excess fat from meat. Combine 3 tablespoons flour, 1 teaspoon salt, and ¼ teaspoon pepper; coat meat with flour mixture. In Dutch oven brown meat slowly on all sides in hot oil; drain off excess fat. Add ¼ cup water, celery seed, and oregano. Cover tightly; simmer 1½ hours.

Combine ½ cup water and orange juice concentrate; pour over meat. Add potatoes and onions, pushing vegetables down into liquid. Cover; simmer till meat and vegetables are tender, about 1 hour longer.

Transfer meat and vegetables to platter; keep warm. Pour pan juices into measuring cup; skim off fat. Add enough water to juices to equal 1¼ cups. Blend ¼ cup cold water with 2 tablespoons flour; stir into juices. Cook and stir till thickened and bubbly. Season with salt and pepper.

To serve, spoon a little gravy over meat and vegetables. Garnish platter with parsley sprigs, if desired. Pass remaining gravy. Makes 6 to 8 servings.

Beef and Bean Pot Roast

 1 3-pound beef chuck pot roast
 2 tablespoons cooking oil
 2 cups water
 1 cup chopped onion
 1 cup dry lima beans, rinsed
 ½ cup catsup
 1 teaspoon salt
 ⅛ teaspoon pepper
 1 clove garlic, minced
 2 teaspoons mixed pickling spice
 3 carrots, sliced (about 1½
     cups)

Trim excess fat from meat. In Dutch oven brown meat on all sides in hot oil; remove meat. Drain off fat. In same Dutch oven combine water, chopped onion, dry lima beans, catsup, salt, pepper, and garlic.

Tie mixed pickling spice in cheesecloth bag; add to bean mixture in Dutch oven. Place meat atop beans. Simmer, covered, till meat and beans are almost tender, about 2 hours. Add additional water during cooking, if necessary, to keep beans covered. Add sliced carrots; simmer, covered, 30 minutes more. Discard spice bag. Makes 6 to 8 servings.

Pot Roast Tips

It's easy to make a perfect pot roast when you understand the method. The term "pot roasting" refers to cooking a piece of meat in a covered pan. Since liquid is usually added, braising is another term sometimes used.

The first step is to trim away any excess fat. For a rich brown color, coat the roast on all sides with all-purpose flour. Slowly brown the roast in hot fat using shortening, cooking oil, or drippings from the melted fat trimmings. Add the desired liquid (usually beef broth, tomato juice, or water) and the seasonings. Cover and cook over low heat in a Dutch oven atop the range, *or* in a 325° oven, *or* in an electric skillet set at about 220°.

Vegetable-sauced *Swedish Pot Roast* features cloves and anchovies as the special seasonings. Prepared with chuck pot roast, this dish rates high as a cost-cutting entrée.

Swedish Pot Roast

1 3- to 4-pound beef chuck pot
  roast
1 teaspoon salt
4 whole cloves
2 medium onions, quartered
1 cup chopped carrots
½ cup chopped celery
⅓ cup water
1 tablespoon corn syrup
3 anchovy fillets
¼ cup cold water
2 tablespoons all-purpose flour
  Salt
  Pepper

Trim excess fat from meat. Sprinkle 1 teaspoon salt in Dutch oven; brown meat slowly on all sides in Dutch oven. Stick cloves into onions. Add to meat along with carrots, celery, the ⅓ cup water, corn syrup, and anchovies. Cover and simmer till meat is tender, about 2½ hours.

Transfer meat to serving platter; keep warm. Skim fat from pan juices. Blend the ¼ cup cold water with flour; stir into juices. (Mash carrot if desired.) Cook and stir till thickened and bubbly. Season to taste with salt and pepper; pass with roast. Makes 6 to 8 servings.

Unconventional preparation is a plus for *Peach-Glazed Corned Beef*. Instead of simmering atop the range, the brisket is baked in a covered pan with added water. Preserves make the glaze.

Peach-Glazed Corned Beef

1 3-pound corned beef brisket
    (or 1 3- to 4-pound corned
    beef for oven roasting)
2 cups water
4 small apples
½ cup water
⅓ cup peach preserves
¼ teaspoon ground ginger

Rinse brisket in cold water to remove pickling juices. Place, fat side up, on rack in shallow roasting pan. Add 2 cups water; cover with foil. Roast at 325° for 2 hours. Uncover; drain cooking liquid and discard. (Or prepare corned beef for oven roasting by package directions.)

Cut apples in half lengthwise and core. Arrange apple halves, skin side up, around corned beef in roasting pan; add ½ cup water to pan. Return to oven; continue roasting, uncovered, 30 minutes longer.

Combine peach preserves and ground ginger. Turn apple halves, skin side down. Spoon peach glaze over apple halves and corned beef; return to oven and cook till glaze is hot, about 15 minutes longer. Makes 6 to 8 servings.

New England Boiled Dinner

1 3- to 4-pound corned beef
    brisket
  Water
4 ounces salt pork (optional)
6 small onions
4 medium potatoes, peeled and
    quartered
4 medium carrots, quartered
3 medium parsnips, peeled and
    cut in chunks
2 medium rutabagas, peeled and
    cubed
1 small cabbage, cored and cut
    in wedges
  Salt
  Pepper

Place corned beef in large kettle or Dutch oven; add water to cover meat. Add salt pork, if desired. Bring to boiling; reduce heat and simmer, covered, till corned beef is tender, about 2½ hours.

Remove corned beef and salt pork from kettle. Add onions, potatoes, carrots, parsnips, and rutabagas to cooking liquid. Cover; cook 15 minutes. Add cabbage; cover and cook till cabbage is tender, 15 to 20 minutes more.

Return corned beef to kettle; heat through. Transfer corned beef and vegetables to serving platter. Season to taste with salt and pepper. Makes 6 to 8 servings.

Brisket of Beef with Horseradish Sauce

1 3- to 4-pound fresh beef
    brisket
2 cups water
½ cup chopped onion
2 cloves garlic, minced
2 bay leaves
3 tablespoons grated fresh
    horseradish
2 tablespoons vinegar
1 tablespoon prepared mustard
½ teaspoon salt
  Dash cayenne
  Dash paprika
½ cup whipping cream

Trim excess fat from meat; place meat in 4-quart Dutch oven. Add water, onion, garlic, and bay leaves. Cover; simmer till meat is tender, 2½ to 3 hours. Drain meat; slice.

Meanwhile, in bowl combine horseradish, vinegar, mustard, salt, cayenne, and paprika. Whip cream till soft peaks form; fold in horseradish mixture. Serve sauce with sliced beef brisket. Makes 6 servings.

Rice-Stuffed Steaks

1 **6-ounce package long grain and wild rice mix**
1 **beaten egg**
¼ **cup sliced green onion with tops**
6 **beef top loin steaks, cut 1 inch thick**
¼ **to ½ cup bottled teriyaki sauce**

Cook rice mix according to package directions, about 25 minutes. Cool slightly; stir in egg and onion.

Slash fat edge of steaks at 1-inch intervals. Cut a pocket in the side of each steak; stuff with rice mixture.

Place on cold rack of broiler pan. Broil 4 inches from heat to desired doneness, turning once. Allow 8 to 12 minutes total time for medium-rare. Brush often with teriyaki sauce. Trim with whole fresh mushrooms and watercress, if desired. Makes 6 servings.

Steak with Lobster Tail

4 **beef top loin steaks, cut 1 inch thick**
Salt
Pepper
4 **4-ounce frozen lobster tails**
¼ **cup butter**
2 **teaspoons lemon juice**
¼ **teaspoon salt**
Dash paprika

Slash fat edge of steaks at 1-inch intervals. In skillet cook steaks over medium-high heat to desired doneness; turn occasionally. Allow 9 to 10 minutes total time for rare or 11 to 12 minutes for medium. Season with salt and pepper.

Meanwhile, drop frozen lobster tails in boiling salted water to cover. Return to boiling; reduce heat. Simmer 8 minutes; drain. Snip along each side of thin undershell; remove undershell. Remove meat from shells; cut in chunks. Return to shells; place one atop each steak.

In saucepan melt butter; stir in lemon juice, salt, and paprika. Spoon over lobster. Makes 4 servings.

Broiling Beef Steaks

Thickness of Steak	Rare	Medium	Well Done
	(approximate total time in minutes)		
1 inch	8 to 10	12 to 14	18 to 20
1½ inch	14 to 16	18 to 20	25 to 30
2 inch	20 to 25	30 to 35	40 to 45

Choose a beef porterhouse, T-bone, top loin, sirloin, or tenderloin steak cut 1 to 2 inches thick. Without cutting into the meat, slash the fat edge at 1-inch intervals. Place steak on cold rack of broiler pan.

Broil 1- to 1½-inch-thick steaks so surface of meat is 3 inches from heat. Broil thicker cuts 4 to 5 inches from heat. (Check range instruction booklet.) Broil on one side for about half of the time indicated in chart for desired doneness. Season with salt and pepper, if desired. Turn with tongs and broil for remaining time. Season again.

Doneness test: Slit center; note inside color: red—rare; pink—medium; gray—well done.

Grilling Steaks Outdoors

Thickness of Steak	Temperature of Coals	Open Grill		Covered Grill	
		Rare	Medium	Rare	Medium
		(approximate total time in minutes)			
1 inch	Medium-hot	12 to 18	15 to 20	8 to 10	10 to 15
1½ inch	Medium-hot	18 to 20	20 to 25	10 to 15	15 to 18
	Medium	20 to 25	25 to 30	15 to 18	18 to 22

Choose sirloin, porterhouse, or T-bone steaks. Slash the fat edge at about 1-inch intervals to keep steaks flat on grill. To estimate temperature of coals, hold hand, palm side down, about *4 inches* above coals. Count seconds "one thousand one, one thousand two," and so on. When you can hold your hand comfortably over the coals for 2 to 3 seconds, they have a temperature of *medium-hot;* 3 to 4 seconds indicates *medium.* Grill steaks for about half of the given time. Flip steaks using tongs and pancake turner (piercing with fork wastes good meat juices); grill till desired doneness.

Beef Steaks Wellington

8 5-ounce beef tenderloin
    steaks
Cooking oil
Salt
Pepper
½ pound ground beef sirloin
1 teaspoon snipped parsley
¼ teaspoon garlic salt
    Dash pepper
8 frozen patty shells, thawed
1 slightly beaten egg white
3 egg yolks
½ cup butter *or* margarine,
    melted
2 tablespoons lemon juice
2 tablespoons hot water
¼ teaspoon salt
1 teaspoon snipped parsley
⅛ teaspoon dried tarragon,
    crushed

Brush steaks with oil; sprinkle with a little salt and pepper. In hot skillet brown steaks 5 minutes on *each* side. Transfer to plate; chill.

Combine ground sirloin, 1 teaspoon parsley, ¼ teaspoon garlic salt, and dash pepper. Divide mixture into 8 portions; spoon a mound atop each steak.

Roll each patty shell to a 9x5-inch rectangle. Place steaks, ground sirloin side down, on pastry rectangles. Fold pastry over meat; seal. Place, seam side down, in shallow pan. If desired, top with cutouts from an additional rolled-out patty shell; chill at least 30 minutes.

Before cooking, brush pastry with egg white. Bake at 450° to desired doneness. Allow 18 minutes for rare, 20 minutes for medium-rare, or 22 minutes for medium.

Meanwhile, in top of double boiler (not over water) beat egg yolks with wire whisk till smooth but not fluffy. Add melted butter, lemon juice, hot water, and ¼ teaspoon salt. Place over hot, not boiling water; upper pan should not touch water. Cook and beat till sauce begins to thicken, about 5 minutes. Stir in 1 teaspoon parsley and tarragon. If sauce starts to separate, add a small amount of cold water and beat. Serve sauce with steaks. Makes 8 servings.

Budget Steak Diane

1 **pound beef round steak, cut**
  ½ inch thick
¼ **cup dry sherry**
2 **tablespoons water**
1 **tablespoon snipped chives**
1 **tablespoon bottled steak sauce**
½ **teaspoon dry mustard**
2 **tablespoons cooking oil**
1 **3-ounce can sliced mushrooms**
¼ **cup brandy**

Cut meat into 4 serving-size portions; place in shallow dish. Combine sherry, water, chives, steak sauce, and dry mustard; pour over steak. Cover and refrigerate for several hours or overnight. Spoon marinade over occasionally.

Drain steak; reserve marinade. Pat steak dry with paper toweling. Cook, 2 pieces at a time, in hot oil about 2 minutes; turn and cook 2 minutes more. Transfer to platter; keep warm. Repeat with remaining 2 pieces. Add reserved marinade and mushrooms to skillet. Bring to boiling; pour over steak. Warm brandy in ladle. Ignite; carefully pour over meat. Serve when flame subsides. Makes 4 servings.

Cheese-Stuffed Beef Rounds

2 **pounds beef round steak, cut**
  ½ inch thick
¼ **cup all-purpose flour**
1 **teaspoon salt**
⅛ **teaspoon pepper**
3 **ribs celery, chopped (1 cup)**
1 **medium onion, chopped (½ cup)**
3 **sprigs parsley, snipped**
2 **tablespoons butter**
1 **cup shredded sharp American**
  cheese (4 ounces)
½ **cup soft bread crumbs**
2 **tablespoons cooking oil**
1 **cup water**
1½ **teaspoons instant beef**
  bouillon granules
½ **teaspoon dry mustard**
¼ **teaspoon dried thyme, crushed**
¼ **cup cold water**
2 **tablespoons all-purpose flour**
½ **teaspoon Kitchen Bouquet**
  (optional)

Cut steak into 6 serving-size pieces. Combine the ¼ cup flour, salt, and pepper; with meat mallet, pound flour mixture into meat, pounding each piece to about a 5-inch square.

Cook celery, onion, and parsley in butter till tender but not brown; remove from heat. Stir in cheese and bread crumbs. Spread *about ⅓ cup* of the cheese mixture over each steak; roll up as for jelly roll. Secure steak rolls with wooden picks or tie with string.

In 10-inch skillet slowly brown steak rolls on all sides in hot oil; drain off excess fat. Combine 1 cup water, beef bouillon granules, dry mustard, and thyme; pour over steak rolls in skillet. Cover and cook over low heat till meat is tender, 1 to 1¼ hours.

Transfer meat to serving platter; keep warm. Skim excess fat from pan juices. Blend ¼ cup cold water with 2 tablespoons flour; stir into pan juices. Cook and stir till thickened and bubbly; stir in Kitchen Bouquet, if desired. Serve gravy with steak rolls. Remove picks or string from meat before serving. Makes 6 servings.

Steaks Bertrand

6 **beef cubed steaks**
⅔ **cup dry red wine**
1 **6-ounce can whole mushrooms**
¼ **cup snipped parsley**
  Dash garlic powder
6 **tablespoons butter *or***
  margarine
3 **slices Swiss cheese, halved**

Place steaks in plastic bag; set in deep bowl. Mix wine, mushrooms, parsley, and garlic powder. Pour over meat in bag; close. Marinate ½ hour at room temperature or 2 hours in refrigerator. Drain; reserve marinade.

In skillet, melt butter. Cook meat, half at a time, in butter, about 2 minutes; turn. Cook 2 minutes more; transfer to blazer pan of chafing dish. Repeat. Add reserved marinade to skillet; bring to boiling. Pour over meat. Top with cheese. Cover; place chafing dish on stand. Heat to melt cheese, 2 minutes. Serve sauce with meat. Serves 6.

Rolled Beef Italian-Style

1 1½-pound beef round steak, cut
    about ½ inch thick
1 beaten egg
½ pound ground pork
4 ounces ground fully cooked ham
    (¾ cup)
¼ cup grated Parmesan cheese
    (1 ounce)
¼ cup snipped parsley
1 tablespoon olive oil
1 tablespoon butter *or* margarine
1 large onion, chopped (¾ cup)
1 clove garlic, minced
¼ cup cognac *or* brandy
½ cup dry red wine
1 cup beef broth
¼ cup tomato paste
1 teaspoon dried oregano,
    crushed
Hot cooked noodles

With meat mallet, pound a generous amount of salt and pepper into steak till meat is ¼ inch thick. Combine egg, pork, ham, Parmesan, and parsley. Spread pork mixture evenly over steak; roll up meat as for jelly roll. Press seams together; tie securely with string or skewer.

In skillet, brown meat roll on all sides in mixture of hot olive oil and butter. Add onion and garlic. Cook till onion is tender but not brown; remove from heat.

Add cognac to skillet and ignite. When flame has subsided, return skillet to heat. Add wine; simmer till wine is nearly evaporated. Stir in beef broth, tomato paste, and oregano. Cover and simmer 45 minutes; baste occasionally.

Remove meat from skillet; slice and arrange atop hot cooked noodles on serving platter. (Center of meat roll will have a pink color when sliced.) Skim fat from sauce in skillet; pour sauce over all. Makes 6 to 8 servings.

Vegetable-Stuffed Cubed Steaks

6 beef cubed steaks
    Salt
    Pepper
¼ cup water
¼ teaspoon salt
1½ cups shredded carrot
¾ cup finely chopped onion
¾ cup finely chopped green
    pepper
¾ cup finely chopped celery
⅓ cup French salad dressing
6 slices bacon

Sprinkle meat with a little salt and pepper; set aside. In saucepan bring water and ¼ teaspoon salt to boiling; add vegetables. Simmer, covered, till vegetables are crisptender, 7 to 8 minutes; drain. Stir in *2 tablespoons* of the salad dressing. Place *about ⅓ cup* of the vegetable mixture on each steak; roll up as for jelly roll. Wrap a bacon slice around each meat roll; secure with wooden picks.

Place meat rolls on cold rack of broiler pan. Broil 3 to 4 inches from heat for 20 to 25 minutes; turn rolls about every 5 minutes and brush with remaining salad dressing. (Or, place meat rolls on grill. Cook over *hot* coals 20 to 25 minutes; turn rolls about every 5 minutes and brush with remaining salad dressing.) Remove picks. Makes 6 servings.

Bavarian Supper

4 beef cubed steaks
    (1 to 1¼ pounds)
1 tablespoon cooking oil
⅓ cup chopped onion
2½ cups water
2 envelopes mushroom gravy mix
2 tablespoons brown sugar
2 tablespoons vinegar
1 teaspoon caraway seed
3 cups coarsely shredded cabbage
2 medium potatoes, peeled and
    cubed (2 cups)

In large skillet, quickly brown steaks on both sides in hot oil. Add onion; cook till onion is almost tender, about 5 minutes. Combine water, mushroom gravy mix, brown sugar, vinegar, and caraway; pour over steaks in skillet. Cover; simmer for 15 minutes. Skim off excess fat.

Meanwhile, cook cabbage with potatoes, covered, in boiling salted water till tender, 5 to 7 minutes; drain. Spoon cabbage and potatoes onto serving platter; arrange steaks atop vegetables. Serve with gravy. Makes 4 servings.

Oven Swiss Steak

1½ **pounds beef round steak, cut**
    ¾ inch thick
¼ **cup all-purpose flour**
1 **teaspoon salt**
2 **tablespoons shortening**
1 **16-ounce can tomatoes, cut up**
½ **cup finely chopped celery**
½ **cup finely chopped carrot**
½ **teaspoon Worcestershire sauce**

Cut meat into 6 serving-size portions. Combine flour and salt; pound *2 tablespoons* of the mixture into meat.

Brown meat on both sides in hot shortening. Transfer meat to a 12x7½x2-inch baking dish. Blend remaining 2 tablespoons flour mixture into pan drippings. Stir in undrained tomatoes, celery, carrot, and Worcestershire. Cook and stir till thickened and bubbly; pour over meat.

Bake, covered, at 350° till tender, about 1 hour and 20 minutes. Makes 6 servings.

Deviled Swiss Steak

1 **3-pound beef round steak, cut**
    1 inch thick
2 **teaspoons dry mustard**
1½ **teaspoons salt**
¼ **teaspoon pepper**
2 **tablespoons cooking oil**
1 **4-ounce can mushroom stems**
    and pieces
1 **tablespoon Worcestershire**
    sauce

Trim excess fat from meat; cut meat in half crosswise for easier handling. Mix dry mustard, salt, and pepper; pound seasonings into meat. In heavy 12-inch skillet quickly brown steak on both sides in hot oil; drain off excess fat.

Drain mushrooms, reserving liquid; add water, if needed, to equal ½ cup. Add mushroom liquid and Worcestershire to skillet. Cover; simmer till meat is tender, 1¼ to 1½ hours.

During last few minutes, add mushrooms; heat through. Skim fat from pan juices before serving. Makes 8 servings.

Chicken-Fried Round Steak

1½ **pounds beef round steak, cut**
    ½ inch thick
1 **beaten egg**
1 **tablespoon milk**
1 **cup finely crushed saltine**
    crackers (28 crackers)
½ **teaspoon salt**
¼ **teaspoon pepper**
¼ **cup cooking oil**

Pound steak to ¼-inch thickness; cut in 6 serving-size pieces. Blend egg and milk; combine cracker crumbs, salt, and pepper. Dip meat in egg mixture, then in crumbs.

In 12-inch skillet slowly brown meat in hot oil, turning once. Cover tightly; cook over low heat till meat is tender, 45 to 60 minutes. Makes 6 servings.

Marinated Beef Broil

½ **cup pineapple juice**
1 **envelope meat marinade**
2 **tablespoons lemon juice**
¼ **teaspoon dried basil, crushed**
1 **clove garlic, minced**
1 **2-pound beef round steak, cut**
    1 inch thick
½ **cup water**

Stir pineapple juice into marinade; stir in lemon juice, basil, and garlic. Trim any excess fat from steak; place in shallow pan. Pour marinade over. Pierce steak surfaces deeply with long-tined fork; let stand 15 minutes, turning often. Drain; reserve marinade.

Place steak on cold rack of broiler pan. Broil 3 inches from heat 10 minutes; turn, brushing with some of the reserved marinade. Broil to desired doneness, 8 to 10 minutes more. Stir water into reserved marinade; heat to boiling. Reduce heat; simmer 5 minutes. Pass with steak. Serves 6.

Grilling Hamburgers Outdoors

Thickness of Burger	Temperature of Coals	Open Grill		Covered Grill	
		Rare	**Medium**	**Rare**	**Medium**
		(approximate total time in minutes)			
½ inch	Medium-hot	8 to 10	10 to 12	7 to 9	8 to 10
	Medium	10 to 12	12 to 15	8 to 10	10 to 12
¾ inch	Medium-hot	10 to 12	12 to 15	8 to 10	10 to 12
	Medium	12 to 15	14 to 18	10 to 12	12 to 15

Shape meat mixture into patties as nearly equal in diameter and thickness as possible. To estimate temperature of coals, hold hand, palm side down, about *4 inches* above coals. Count seconds "one thousand one, one thousand two," and so on. When you can hold your hand comfortably over the coals for 2 to 3 seconds, they have a temperature of *medium-hot;* 3 to 4 seconds indicates *medium*. Grill the burgers for about half of the given time; turn and continue grilling to desired doneness.

Bull's-eye Burgers

¾ **cup soft bread crumbs (1 slice)**
¼ **cup milk**
½ **teaspoon onion salt**
¼ **teaspoon garlic salt**
  Dash pepper
1 **pound ground beef**
2 **hard-cooked eggs**
  Hot-style catsup *or* chili sauce

In bowl combine bread crumbs, milk, onion salt, garlic salt, and pepper. Add ground beef; mix well. Shape meat mixture into 4 patties, ¾ inch thick. Cut eggs in half lengthwise. Press one egg half, cut side up, into each meat patty. Place in 8x8x2-inch baking pan. Cover. Bake at 350° for 20 to 25 minutes.

Meanwhile, in small saucepan heat catsup or chili sauce. Serve with burgers. Makes 4 servings.

Planked Chopped Steak

1½ **pounds potatoes**
2 **tablespoons butter**
2 **beaten eggs**
1½ **pounds ground beef sirloin**
½ **teaspoon salt**
⅛ **teaspoon pepper**
8 **small carrots, cooked and buttered**
2 **cups peas, cooked and buttered**
  Snipped parsley

Peel and quarter the potatoes. Cook, covered, in boiling salted water till tender, about 25 minutes. Drain well. Add the butter and eggs to potatoes; beat till fluffy. Add salt and pepper to taste; set aside.

Shape ground beef into 4 oval patties about 1 inch thick. In skillet cook patties till rare, about 5 minutes per side. Place each on a well-buttered seasoned steak plank; sprinkle with the salt and pepper. Place potatoes in pastry bag; pipe onto plank to form border 1-inch larger than patty.

Place 2 planks under broiler, 4 inches from heat; broil till potatoes brown lightly, about 4 minutes. Repeat with remaining planks. Arrange carrots and peas within potato border; sprinkle with parsley. Makes 4 servings.

Taco Salad (pictured on page 6)

1 **pound ground beef**
½ **envelope onion soup mix**
 (¼ cup)
 Few dashes bottled hot pepper
 sauce
1 **small head lettuce, torn in**
 bite-size pieces (4 cups)
1 **cup shredded sharp Cheddar**
 cheese (4 ounces)
1 **large tomato, cut in wedges**
½ **cup sliced pitted ripe olives**
¼ **cup chopped green pepper** *or*
 chopped seeded canned
 green chili peppers
2 **cups corn chips**
 Taco sauce (optional)

In medium skillet brown beef. Drain off excess fat. Sprinkle dry onion soup mix over meat; stir in ¾ cup *water*. Simmer mixture, uncovered, till water cooks away, about 10 minutes. Stir in hot pepper sauce.

Meanwhile, in salad bowl combine lettuce, cheese, tomato, olives, and green pepper; toss well. Divide lettuce mixture onto individual salad plates, if desired. Spoon meat mixture over lettuce; garnish with corn chips. Pass taco sauce. Makes 4 to 6 servings.

Everyday Meat Loaf

2 **beaten eggs**
¾ **cup milk**
½ **cup fine dry bread crumbs**
¼ **cup finely chopped onion**
2 **tablespoons snipped parsley**
1 **teaspoon salt**
½ **teaspoon ground sage**
⅛ **teaspoon pepper**
1½ **pounds ground beef**
¼ **cup catsup**
2 **tablespoons brown sugar**
1 **teaspoon dry mustard**

Combine eggs and milk; stir in crumbs, onion, parsley, salt, sage, and pepper. Add ground beef; mix well. Pat into a 5½-cup ring mold; unmold in shallow baking pan. Bake at 350° for 50 minutes. (Or pat mixture into 8½x4½x2½-inch loaf pan; bake for 1¼ hours.) Spoon off excess fat. Combine catsup, brown sugar, and dry mustard; spread over meat loaf. Return to oven for 10 minutes. Makes 6 servings.

Sicilian Meat Roll

2 **beaten eggs**
½ **cup tomato juice**
¾ **cup soft bread crumbs**
2 **tablespoons snipped parsley**
½ **teaspoon dried oregano,**
 crushed
¼ **teaspoon salt**
¼ **teaspoon pepper**
1 **clove garlic, minced**
2 **pounds ground beef**
4 **to 6 ounces thinly sliced**
 boiled ham
1 **6-ounce package sliced**
 mozzarella cheese

In a bowl combine the eggs and tomato juice. Stir in the bread crumbs, parsley, oregano, salt, pepper, and garlic. Add ground beef; mix well. On foil or waxed paper pat meat to a 10x8-inch rectangle. Arrange ham slices atop meat, leaving a small margin around edges.

Reserve 1 slice of cheese. Tear up remaining cheese; sprinkle over ham. Starting from short end, carefully roll up meat, using foil or paper to lift; seal edges and ends. Place roll, seam side down, in 13x9x2-inch baking pan.

Bake at 350° till done, about 1¼ hours. (Center of roll will be pink because of ham.) Cut reserved cheese slice into 4 triangles; overlap atop meat. Return to oven till cheese melts, about 2 minutes. Makes 8 servings.

Mozzarella cheese and sliced ham are the extra-special fillings in *Sicilian Meat Roll.*
Pat the ground beef mixture on waxed paper to make it easier to roll for the pinwheel effect.

Meat Loaf Puff

  1 beaten egg
 ¾ cup milk
1½ cups soft bread crumbs
      (2 slices)
  1 medium onion, chopped (½ cup)
1½ teaspoons salt
 ⅛ teaspoon pepper
1½ pounds ground beef
  2 medium tomatoes, peeled
  6 slices American cheese
  3 egg whites
 ¾ cup all-purpose flour
  1 cup dairy sour cream
  3 egg yolks
 ½ teaspoon salt
    Dash pepper

In a large bowl combine the 1 egg and milk; stir in soft bread crumbs, onion, the 1½ teaspoons salt, and the ⅛ teaspoon pepper. Add beef; mix well. Pat the meat mixture into an 8x8x2-inch baking dish.

Bake at 350° for 25 minutes. Drain off excess fat. Slice the tomatoes atop partially baked meat loaf; sprinkle with a little salt and pepper. Cover with cheese slices.

Beat the egg whites to soft peaks (tips bend over), 1 minute; set aside. In small mixer bowl combine the flour, sour cream, egg yolks, the ½ teaspoon salt, and the dash pepper. Beat till smooth. Fold beaten egg whites into yolk mixture. Pour egg mixture over cheese-covered meat.

Return to oven till golden brown, about 30 minutes. Let stand 5 minutes before cutting. Spoon some of the sauce in bottom of dish over each serving. Makes 8 or 9 servings.

Meatballs Oriental-Style

1 beaten egg
3 tablespoons milk
¾ cup soft bread crumbs
2 tablespoons finely chopped
   onion
¾ teaspoon salt
   Dash pepper
1 pound ground beef
2 tablespoons shortening
1 5-ounce can water chestnuts
1 cup bias-cut celery
½ cup sliced green onion with
   tops
1 15½-ounce can pineapple chunks
2 tablespoons cornstarch
2 teaspoons instant beef
   bouillon granules
1 cup boiling water
1 tablespoon brown sugar
2 tablespoons soy sauce
1 medium tomato, peeled
1 6-ounce package frozen
   pea pods, thawed
   Chow mein noodles *or* hot
   cooked rice

Combine egg and milk; stir in bread crumbs, chopped onion, salt, and pepper. Add ground beef; mix well. Shape into 24 one-inch balls. In skillet, brown meatballs in hot shortening; drain off excess fat. Drain and slice the water chestnuts; add to skillet with celery and green onion. Cook till celery and onion are crisp-tender, about 5 minutes.

Drain pineapple, reserving syrup; add water to reserved syrup to make 1 cup liquid. Blend cornstarch with syrup mixture. Dissolve bouillon in the 1 cup boiling water; combine with cornstarch mixture, brown sugar, and soy sauce. Add to meat mixture. Cook and stir till mixture is thickened and bubbly.

Cut tomato in eighths; add to skillet with pineapple and pea pods; heat through. Serve over noodles or rice. Makes 4 or 5 servings.

Porcupine Meatballs

1 beaten egg
1 10¾-ounce can condensed
   tomato soup
¼ cup regular rice
2 tablespoons finely chopped
   onion
1 tablespoon snipped parsley
½ teaspoon salt
⅛ teaspoon pepper
1 pound ground beef
½ cup water
1 teaspoon Worcestershire sauce

In bowl combine egg and ¼ *cup* of the tomato soup. Stir in the uncooked rice, chopped onion, parsley, salt, and pepper. Add ground beef and mix well. Shape meat mixture in 20 small balls; place in 10-inch skillet.

Mix remaining soup with water and Worcestershire; pour over meatballs. Bring to boiling; reduce heat. Cover and simmer 35 to 40 minutes; stir often. Makes 4 or 5 servings.

Shaping Ground Beef Mixtures

A light touch is the secret to better burgers, meatballs, and meat loaves. Too much handling gives them a compact texture, so mix carefully. When shaping burgers or meatballs, try to keep them uniform in size. Use a ⅓- or ½-cup measure for each burger. A ¼-cup measure *or* 1 or 2 tablespoons can be used for meatballs. Another shaping trick for burgers is to form the meat into a roll 3 inches in diameter and cut in ½-inch-thick slices. For meatballs, cut a 1-inch diameter roll in 1-inch slices, or pat meat to a 1-inch-thick square and cut in 1-inch cubes.

Olive Spaghetti Sauce

1 pound ground beef
½ pound bulk Italian sausage
1 28-ounce can tomatoes, cut up
2 6-ounce cans tomato paste
1½ cups Burgundy
1 cup water
1 cup chopped onion
¾ cup chopped green pepper
1½ teaspoons Worcestershire
    sauce
1 teaspoon sugar
1 teaspoon salt
½ teaspoon chili powder
⅛ teaspoon pepper
3 bay leaves
2 cloves garlic, minced
1 6-ounce can sliced mushrooms
½ cup sliced pimiento-stuffed
    green olives
20 ounces spaghetti
    Grated Parmesan cheese

In large Dutch oven brown beef and sausage; drain off fat. Stir in undrained tomatoes, tomato paste, Burgundy, water, onion, green pepper, Worcestershire, sugar, salt, chili powder, pepper, bay leaves, and garlic. Simmer, uncovered, for 2 hours; stir occasionally. Remove bay leaves. Stir in mushrooms and olives; simmer 30 minutes longer.

Cook spaghetti according to package directions; drain. Serve with sauce; pass Parmesan. Makes 8 to 10 servings.

Cheeseburger Chowder

1 pound ground beef
2 medium potatoes, peeled and
    cubed (2 cups)
½ cup chopped celery
¼ cup chopped onion
2 tablespoons chopped green
    pepper
1 tablespoon instant beef
    bouillon granules
½ teaspoon salt
2½ cups milk
3 tablespoons all-purpose flour
1 cup shredded sharp Cheddar
    cheese (4 ounces)

In 3-quart saucepan brown beef. Drain off excess fat. Stir in potatoes, celery, onion, green pepper, bouillon granules, salt, and 1½ cups *water*. Cover and cook till vegetables are tender, 15 to 20 minutes.

Blend ½ cup of the milk with the flour. Add to saucepan along with remaining milk. Cook and stir till thickened and bubbly. Add cheese; heat and stir just till cheese melts. Garnish with additional shredded cheese, if desired. Makes 6 to 8 servings.

Sausage and Beef Chili

1½ pounds ground beef
½ pound bulk pork sausage
1 cup chopped onion
2 15½-ounce cans red kidney
    beans, drained
1 28-ounce can tomatoes, cut up
1 cup chopped green pepper
1 cup thinly sliced celery
1 6-ounce can tomato paste
2 cloves garlic, minced
2 teaspoons salt
2 teaspoons chili powder

In Dutch oven cook beef, sausage, and onion till meats are brown; drain off excess fat. Stir in beans, undrained tomatoes, green pepper, celery, tomato paste, garlic, salt, and chili powder. Cover; simmer 1 to 1½ hours, stirring occasionally. Makes 10 to 12 servings.

Note: If a less thick chili is desired, substitute one 8-ounce can tomato sauce for the tomato paste and do not drain the kidney beans.

Manicotti

8 **manicotti shells**
1 **pound ground beef**
2 **6-ounce cans tomato paste**
½ **cup chopped onion**
⅓ **cup snipped parsley**
1 **tablespoon dried basil,
    crushed**
1½ **teaspoons salt**
1 **large clove garlic, minced**
2 **cups water**
2 **beaten eggs**
3 **cups ricotta *or* cream-style
    cottage cheese, drained
    (24 ounces)**
¾ **cup grated Romano *or* Parmesan
    cheese**
¼ **teaspoon salt**

Cook manicotti shells in boiling salted water till just tender, 15 to 20 minutes; drain. Rinse shells in cold water.

Meanwhile, in a 3-quart saucepan brown meat lightly. Drain off excess fat. Stir in tomato paste, onion, *half* of the parsley, the basil, the 1½ teaspoons salt, garlic, and dash *pepper*. Add the 2 cups water; mix well. Simmer, uncovered, for 15 minutes, stirring occasionally.

In bowl combine eggs, ricotta or cottage cheese, ½ *cup* of the Romano or Parmesan cheese, remaining parsley, the ¼ teaspoon salt, and dash *pepper*. Stuff cooked manicotti shells with cheese mixture, using a small spoon (or slit shells lengthwise with scissors and open to fill).

Pour *half* of the tomato-meat sauce into a 12x7½x2-inch baking dish. Arrange stuffed manicotti in dish; top with remaining sauce. Sprinkle with the remaining ¼ cup Romano cheese. Bake, uncovered, at 350° for 40 to 45 minutes. Let stand 10 minutes before serving. Makes 6 to 8 servings.

Texas Beef Skillet

1 **pound ground beef**
¾ **cup chopped onion**
1½ **teaspoons chili powder**
½ **teaspoon salt**
½ **teaspoon garlic salt**
1 **16-ounce can tomatoes, cut up**
1 **15½-ounce can red kidney beans**
¾ **cup quick-cooking rice**
¾ **cup water**
3 **tablespoons chopped green
    pepper**
¾ **cup shredded sharp American
    cheese (3 ounces)**

In skillet cook ground beef and onion till beef is brown and onion is tender; drain off fat.

Sprinkle meat mixture with chili powder, salt, and garlic salt. Stir in undrained tomatoes, undrained beans, uncooked rice, water, and green pepper.

Cover and simmer, stirring occasionally, for 20 minutes. Top with cheese. Cover and heat till cheese melts, about 3 minutes longer. Sprinkle with crushed corn chips, if desired. Makes 6 servings.

Dinner in a Pepper

8 **large green peppers**
1 **pound ground beef**
½ **cup chopped onion**
3 **medium tomatoes, peeled
    and chopped**
1 **8-ounce can whole kernel corn,
    drained**
1 **8-ounce can cream-style corn**
1 **teaspoon salt**
¾ **teaspoon dried basil, crushed
    Dash pepper**
¾ **cup soft bread crumbs (1 slice)**
1 **tablespoon butter, melted**

Cut tops from green peppers; discard seeds and membranes. Chop enough of the tops to make ¼ cup; set aside. Cook the whole green peppers in boiling water for 5 minutes; drain well. Sprinkle insides of peppers lightly with salt.

In skillet cook ground beef, onion, and the ¼ cup chopped green pepper till meat is brown and onion is tender. Add tomatoes; simmer till tomatoes are cooked, about 4 minutes. Drain off liquid. Add whole kernel corn, cream-style corn, salt, basil, and pepper to skillet; mix well.

Stuff peppers with the meat mixture. Toss crumbs with melted butter to combine; sprinkle atop peppers. Place the stuffed peppers in a 13x9x2-inch baking dish. Bake, uncovered, at 350° for 35 to 40 minutes. Makes 8 servings.

Looking for new menu ideas? Plan an Italian-style dinner featuring *Manicotti*. The large pasta tubes are filled with a creamy cheese mixture and baked in a beef-tomato sauce.

Pan Pizza

1 13¾-ounce package hot roll mix
1 cup grated Parmesan cheese
½ pound ground beef
¼ cup chopped onion
¼ cup chopped green pepper
1 clove garlic, minced
1 16-ounce can tomatoes, cut up
⅓ cup tomato paste (half of
    a 6-ounce can)
1 4-ounce can mushroom stems
    and pieces, drained
1 teaspoon sugar
1 teaspoon dried basil, crushed
1 teaspoon dried oregano,
    crushed
½ teaspoon fennel seed (optional)
2 cups shredded mozzarella
    cheese (8 ounces)

In large bowl dissolve yeast from roll mix in 1 cup *warm water*. Stir in flour mixture from mix and ½ *cup* of the Parmesan cheese. Cover and let rest 10 minutes. With greased fingers pat dough out onto bottom and halfway up sides of a greased 15½x10½x1-inch baking pan. Bake at 375° till deep golden brown, 20 to 25 minutes.

Meanwhile, in medium skillet cook ground beef, onion, green pepper, and garlic till meat is brown and onion is tender. Drain off excess fat. Stir in undrained tomatoes, tomato paste, mushrooms, sugar, basil, oregano, fennel, 1 teaspoon *salt,* and ⅛ teaspoon *pepper*.

Spread meat mixture over the hot, baked crust. Sprinkle with mozzarella cheese and the remaining Parmesan cheese. Bake at 375° till bubbly, 20 to 25 minutes. Let stand 5 minutes before cutting. Makes 10 servings.

Tostada Pizza

2 tablespoons yellow cornmeal
2 cups packaged biscuit mix
1 pound ground beef
3 tablespoons chopped seeded
    canned green chili peppers
1 1¼-ounce envelope taco
    seasoning mix
1 16-ounce can refried beans
1 cup shredded sharp American
    cheese (4 ounces)
1 cup shredded lettuce
1 tomato, chopped (1 cup)
½ cup chopped onion
    Taco sauce (optional)

Sprinkle a well-greased 12-inch pizza pan with cornmeal. Combine biscuit mix and ½ cup *water*. Stir with fork till dough follows fork around bowl. Turn dough out on lightly floured surface; knead 5 or 6 times. Roll to 14-inch circle; pat into prepared pizza pan, crimping edges. Bake at 425° till golden brown, about 12 minutes.

Meanwhile, in skillet brown meat; drain. Stir in chili peppers, taco seasoning mix, and ¾ cup *water;* bring to boiling. Reduce heat; simmer, uncovered, 10 to 15 minutes.

Spread refried beans over crust; top with meat mixture. Bake at 425° for 8 to 10 minutes. Top with cheese; bake 2 minutes more. Garnish with fresh chili peppers, if desired. Pass lettuce, tomato, and onion to sprinkle atop. Dash with taco sauce, if desired. Makes 6 servings.

Stroganoff Sandwich

1 pound ground beef
¼ cup chopped green onion
    with tops
1 cup dairy sour cream
1 teaspoon Worcestershire sauce
⅛ teaspoon garlic powder
1 loaf French bread, unsliced
    Butter *or* margarine, softened
2 tomatoes, sliced
1 green pepper, cut in rings
1 cup shredded American cheese

In skillet cook beef and onion till meat is brown; drain off fat. Stir in sour cream, Worcestershire, garlic powder, and ¾ teaspoon *salt;* heat through but *do not boil*.

Meanwhile, cut loaf in half lengthwise. Place cut side up on baking sheet. Broil 4 to 5 inches from heat till toasted, 2 to 3 minutes; spread lightly with butter. Spread half the hot meat mixture on each loaf half. Arrange tomato slices alternately with green pepper rings atop meat. Place on baking sheet; broil 3 minutes. Sprinkle with cheese; broil 2 minutes longer. Makes 8 servings.

Beef Bourguignonne

3 slices bacon, cut in small
    pieces
¼ cup cooking oil
⅓ cup all-purpose flour
2 teaspoons salt
¼ teaspoon pepper
3 pounds boneless beef chuck,
    cut in 1-inch pieces
2 medium onions, chopped
1 clove garlic, minced
¼ cup cognac or brandy
1 cup Burgundy
1 cup beef broth
2 bay leaves
8 small carrots, cut up
½ pound tiny onions
16 medium mushroom caps
    Snipped parsley
    Hot cooked noodles

In 5-quart Dutch oven cook bacon till crisp; remove and set aside. Add oil to bacon drippings. Combine flour, salt, and pepper; toss beef cubes with flour mixture to coat. Cook *half* the beef, the chopped onion, and garlic in the hot oil mixture till beef is brown and onion is tender; remove and set aside. Cook remaining beef in the hot oil mixture till brown. Drain off excess fat. Return beef-onion mixture to Dutch oven. In small saucepan heat cognac or brandy; set aflame and pour over beef. Stir in Burgundy, beef broth, and bay leaves. Bring to boiling; reduce heat. Cover and simmer about 1 hour or till meat is nearly tender. Add carrots and tiny onions. Cook 20 minutes more. Add mushrooms; cook about 10 minutes more or till meat and vegetables are tender. Remove bay leaves. Stir in cooked bacon. Garnish with snipped parsley. Serve with cooked noodles. Makes 8 servings.

Tyrolean Alps Ragout

    Brown Sauce
3 tablespoons butter *or*
    margarine
1 cup sliced fresh mushrooms
1 cup chopped onion
2 pounds beef tenderloin,
    sliced in thin strips
¼ cup dry sherry
¼ teaspoon salt
¼ teaspoon Worcestershire sauce
    Dash pepper
    Hot cooked rice

Prepare Brown Sauce. Meanwhile, in 12-inch skillet melt butter. Add mushrooms and onion; cook and stir over medium heat till tender but not brown. Push vegetables to one side of skillet. Quickly brown meat, ⅓ at a time, in butter. When all meat is browned, stir in Brown Sauce, dry sherry, salt, Worcestershire, and pepper. Heat through, 5 to 10 minutes. Serve over rice. Makes 6 to 8 servings.

Brown Sauce: In saucepan melt 2 tablespoons *butter;* blend in 2 tablespoons all-purpose *flour.* Cook and stir over medium heat till lightly browned, 2 to 3 minutes. Remove from heat; stir in one 10½-ounce can *condensed beef broth* and 1 cup *water.* Cook and stir till thickened and bubbly. Simmer, uncovered, 30 minutes; stir occasionally.

Beef Stroganoff

1 pound beef tenderloin
3 tablespoons cooking oil
1½ cups sliced fresh mushrooms
    (4 ounces)
½ cup dry sherry
¼ cup beef broth
1 cup dairy sour cream
½ teaspoon salt
    Hot cooked fine noodles

Cut tenderloin in ¼-inch-thick strips. In skillet heat oil; brown meat strips quickly in hot oil, 2 to 4 minutes. Remove meat from skillet. Add sliced mushrooms and cook 2 to 3 minutes; remove mushrooms.

Add sherry and beef broth to skillet; bring to boiling. Cook, uncovered, till liquid is reduced to ⅓ cup. Stir in sour cream and salt; stir in meat and mushrooms. Cook slowly till heated through; *do not boil.* Serve over hot cooked noodles. Makes 4 servings.

Pepper Steak, Oriental

1½ pounds boneless beef round
    tip, cut in ½-inch slices
3 tablespoons soy sauce
1 tablespoon cooking oil
    Dash freshly ground pepper
½ teaspoon grated gingerroot *or*
    ground ginger
1 clove garlic, minced
1 tablespoon cooking oil
1 medium green pepper, sliced
2 cups sliced fresh mushrooms,
    (about 5 ounces)
6 green onions with tops, cut in
    ½-inch pieces
½ cup beef broth
1 tablespoon cornstarch
2 medium tomatoes, cut in
    wedges
    Hot cooked rice

Partially freeze beef slices; cut diagonally into ¼-inch strips. In large bowl combine soy sauce, 1 tablespoon oil, and pepper. Add beef; toss to coat well. Let stand several hours in refrigerator. Drain beef, reserving marinade.

In wok or skillet heat ginger and garlic in 1 tablespoon oil. Add beef; stir-fry till beef is browned, about 4 minutes. Remove beef with slotted spoon. Add green pepper, mushrooms, and onions to wok. Cook and stir till vegetables are crisp-tender, about 2 minutes; return beef to wok.

Combine reserved marinade, beef broth, and cornstarch; pour over beef mixture. Cook and stir till thickened and bubbly. Add tomatoes; cover and cook till heated through, about 2 minutes. Serve with rice. Makes 6 servings.

Rainbow Beef

1 pound beef tenderloin *or*
    sirloin
1 egg white
1 tablespoon cornstarch
2 cloves garlic, minced
½ teaspoon grated gingerroot
½ cup peanut *or* cooking
    oil
1 6-ounce package frozen pea
    pods
2 cups sliced fresh mushrooms,
    (about 5 ounces)
2 carrots, cut in thin sticks
    about 3 inches long
2 ribs celery, cut in thin
    sticks about 3 inches long
1 onion, cut in thin wedges
1 red pepper, cut in thin strips
2 teaspoons instant chicken
    bouillon granules
¼ cup soy sauce
¼ cup cold water
3 tablespoons dry sherry
1 tablespoon dark corn syrup
1 tablespoon vinegar
4 teaspoons cornstarch
⅛ teaspoon freshly ground pepper

Slice beef in thin strips. In large bowl combine egg white and 1 tablespoon cornstarch; stir in beef strips. In large wok or skillet stir-fry meat, garlic, and gingerroot in *3 tablespoons* of the hot oil till meat is browned. Remove meat from pan; set aside.

Add remaining oil to pan juices; stir in pea pods, mushrooms, carrots, celery, onion, and red pepper. Sprinkle bouillon granules over vegetable mixture. Cover and simmer till vegetables are crisp-tender, about 10 minutes.

Combine soy sauce, water, sherry, corn syrup, vinegar, 4 teaspoons cornstarch, and ground pepper. Stir mixture into vegetables along with cooked meat; cook and stir till thickened and bubbly. Makes 4 to 6 servings.

Cider Stew (pictured on page 6)

3 tablespoons all-purpose
   flour
¼ teaspoon dried thyme, crushed
2 pounds beef stew meat
3 tablespoons cooking oil
2 cups apple juice *or* cider
½ cup water
2 tablespoons vinegar
4 carrots, quartered
3 potatoes, peeled and
   quartered
2 onions, sliced
1 rib celery, sliced
1 apple, chopped

In paper or plastic bag combine flour, thyme, 2 teaspoons *salt,* and ¼ teaspoon *pepper.* Add meat, ¼ at a time; toss to coat. In Dutch oven brown meat in hot oil. Stir in apple juice or cider, water, and vinegar; cook and stir to boiling. Reduce heat; simmer, covered, till meat is tender, 1½ to 2 hours.

Add vegetables and apple. Cook till vegetables are tender, about 30 minutes. Makes 6 to 8 servings.

Oven-Baked Beef Stew

¼ cup all-purpose flour
1½ pounds beef stew meat, cut
   into 1-inch cubes
3 to 4 medium carrots, cut into
   2-inch strips
4 small onions, quartered
2 cups water
1 6-ounce can tomato paste
1 tablespoon vinegar
1 teaspoon sugar
⅛ teaspoon dried thyme,
   crushed
1 clove garlic, minced
1 bay leaf
1 10-ounce package frozen
   peas, broken apart
1 package refrigerated
   biscuits (6 biscuits)
   Milk
¼ cup crisp rice cereal,
   crushed

In paper or plastic bag combine flour, 2 teaspoons *salt,* and ⅛ teaspoon *pepper.* Add beef cubes, ¼ at a time; shake to coat. Place beef cubes in a 2½- or 3-quart casserole; add carrots and onions. In bowl combine water, tomato paste, vinegar, sugar, thyme, garlic, and bay leaf; pour over meat mixture in casserole. Bake, covered, at 350° for 2 hours.

Stir frozen peas into stew mixture; cover and bake 20 minutes longer. Remove casserole from oven; discard bay leaf. Increase oven temperature to 425°.

Meanwhile, quarter biscuits; dip in milk, then roll in cereal. Place atop hot stew. Bake, uncovered, at 425° till biscuits are done, about 12 minutes. Makes 6 servings.

Cutting Stew Meat

Stretch your meat budget further by cutting round steak or large pot roasts into stew meat and meal-sized roasts. For stew meat, trim away the bone and excess fat; then cut meat into uniform 1- to 2-inch cubes.

If you want to make two meals from one roast, divide a 4- to 5-pound beef blade pot roast. Cut at the end of the bone, separating the square bone-in piece from the triangular boneless piece. Cut the boneless portion for stew meat. Cook the bone-in piece as a pot roast.

Pork and Ham

Pork Crown Roast with Apricot Stuffing

1 5½- to 6-pound pork rib
   crown roast (12 to 16
   ribs)
1 tablespoon sugar
1 teaspoon instant chicken
   bouillon granules
¼ cup snipped dried apricots
4 cups dry whole wheat bread
   cubes (5½ slices)
1 large apple, peeled, cored,
   and chopped
½ teaspoon finely shredded
   orange peel
½ teaspoon salt
½ teaspoon ground sage
¼ teaspoon ground cinnamon
⅛ teaspoon pepper
½ cup chopped celery
¼ cup chopped onion
¼ cup butter *or* margarine
¼ cup orange juice
1 tablespoon light corn syrup
½ teaspoon soy sauce

Place roast, bone tips up, on rack in shallow roasting pan. Season with a little salt and pepper. Make a ball of aluminum foil and press into cavity to hold open. Wrap bone tips with foil. Insert meat thermometer, making sure bulb does not touch bone. Roast at 325° for 2½ hours.

Meanwhile, prepare stuffing. Dissolve sugar and bouillon granules in ¾ cup *hot water;* pour over apricots. Let stand 5 minutes. In large bowl combine bread cubes, apple, orange peel, salt, sage, cinnamon, and pepper. Cook celery and onion in butter or margarine till tender; add to bread mixture. Add apricot mixture; toss lightly to moisten. (If desired, add ¼ cup additional water for a moister stuffing.)

Remove all foil from roast. Pack stuffing lightly into center of roast, mounding high. Combine orange juice, corn syrup, and soy sauce; spoon some over meat. Roast, uncovered, till thermometer registers 170°, 45 to 60 minutes more; baste occasionally with orange juice mixture. Carefully transfer to warm platter. Garnish with canned apricot halves, if desired. Slice between ribs to serve. Serves 12 to 16.

Harvest Pot Roast

1 4-pound pork shoulder roast
2 tablespoons cooking oil
2 cups water
1 medium onion, cut in thin
   wedges
2 teaspoons salt
1 teaspoon dried dillweed
½ teaspoon pepper
1 acorn squash
6 to 8 small potatoes,
   peeled
3 large carrots, sliced
¼ cup all-purpose flour
½ teaspoon Kitchen Bouquet

In Dutch oven brown meat in hot oil. Spoon off fat. Add water, onion, salt, dillweed, and pepper. Bring to boil; reduce heat. Simmer, covered, till meat is nearly tender, about 1 hour. Cut squash crosswise into 1-inch-thick slices; discard seeds. Halve slices. Add squash slices, potatoes, and carrots to meat. Simmer till meat and vegetables are tender, about 30 minutes more; remove to warm platter. Skim fat from juices; reserve 1½ cups juices. Blend ½ cup *cold water* into flour; stir into reserved juices. Cook, stirring constantly, till thickened and bubbly. Stir in Kitchen Bouquet; simmer 2 to 3 minutes, stirring occasionally. Season to taste with salt and pepper. Pass with meat. Makes 6 to 8 servings.

Special Order Roast

A pork rib crown roast is special enough for your most elegant dinner party. Normally, a rib crown roast isn't found in the meat section of your supermarket. You'll have to call ahead and place an order to have it specially cut for you. Specify the number of ribs you want and make sure the fat is trimmed from the center of the roast.

Serve flavorful *Pork Crown Roast* with *Apricot Stuffing* as the star attraction for
your next dinner party. When ordering this special roast, plan at least one rib per serving.

Roasting Fresh Pork

Cut	Approx. Weight (pounds)	Internal Temperature on removal from oven	Approx. Cooking Time (total time)
Roast meat at constant 325° oven temperature.			
Center Loin Roast	3 to 5	170°	2½ to 3 hours
Sirloin Roast	5 to 7	170°	3½ to 4¼ hours
Loin Blade Roast	3 to 4	170°	2¼ to 2¾ hours
Boneless Top Loin Roast	3 to 4	170°	2½ to 3 hours
Tenderloin	1	170°	¾ to 1 hour
Shoulder Blade Boston Roast	4 to 6	170°	3 to 4 hours
Boneless Shoulder Blade Boston Roast	3 to 5	170°	2 to 3 hours
Shoulder Arm Picnic Roast	5 to 8	170°	3 to 4 hours
Leg (fresh ham)	10 to 16	170°	4½ to 6 hours
Leg (fresh ham) rump portion	5 to 7	170°	3½ to 4½ hours

Roasting Directions: *Sprinkle meat with some salt and pepper. Place meat, fat side up, on rack in shallow roasting pan. Insert meat thermometer into center of roast so bulb reaches the thickest part of the lean meat. Make sure bulb doesn't rest in fat or touch bone. Do not cover, add water, or baste. Roast at 325° till meat thermometer registers 170°. To check temperature, push thermometer into meat a little farther. If temperature drops, continue roasting. Remove meat from oven when done. Let meat stand 15 minutes for easier carving. Carve meat across the grain.*

To carve meat successfully, keep the cutting edge of your knife very sharp. For best results, sharpen knives with a hand-held sharpening steel or stone before each use. With steel or stone in one hand, hold knife in the other hand with the blade at a 20° angle to the sharpener. Draw the blade edge over the sharpener, using a motion that goes across and down at the same time. Turn blade over, reverse directions, and sharpen other side an equal number of times.

Pork Steaks with Apple Stuffing

6 **pork shoulder blade steaks,**
  cut ½ inch thick
2 **tablespoons shortening**
  Salt
  Pepper
3 **cups plain croutons**
1½ **cups finely chopped**
  unpeeled apple
½ **cup raisins**
½ **cup finely chopped celery**
½ **cup finely chopped onion**
¾ **teaspoon salt**
½ **teaspoon poultry seasoning**
  Dash pepper
1¼ **teaspoons instant beef**
  bouillon granules
⅔ **cup hot water**

Slowly brown 3 of the steaks on both sides in hot shortening. Season with a little salt and pepper. Place in a 15x10x1-inch baking pan. Repeat with remaining steaks. Combine croutons, apple, raisins, celery, onion, salt, poultry seasoning, and pepper. Dissolve bouillon granules in hot water; toss with crouton mixture. Pack some into ½ cup measuring cup and unmold on one steak; repeat. Cover; bake at 350° about 1 hour. Makes 6 servings.

Chili Barbecued Pork Chops

½ **cup chopped onion**
1 **clove garlic, minced**
2 **tablespoons cooking oil**
½ **cup chili sauce**
¼ **teaspoon finely shredded**
  orange peel
¼ **cup orange juice**
1 **tablespoon brown sugar**
½ **teaspoon salt**
  Dash bottled hot pepper
  sauce
6 **pork loin butterfly chops**

In small saucepan cook onion and garlic in hot oil till tender but not brown. Stir in chili sauce, orange peel, orange juice, brown sugar, salt, and hot pepper sauce; mix well. Bring to boiling; remove from heat.

Sprinkle pork chops with a little salt and pepper. Grill chops over *medium* coals about 15 minutes. Turn meat; brush with some of the chili sauce mixture. Grill 15 to 20 minutes more, brushing with remaining chili sauce mixture occasionally. Makes 6 servings.

Smoky Pork Skillet

1¼ **cups dried whole green**
  peas
4 **cups cold water**
1 **13¾-ounce can chicken**
  broth
½ **cup chopped onion**
1 **teaspoon dried basil,**
  crushed
½ **teaspoon salt**
5 **smoked pork chops, cut**
  ½ inch thick
2 **tablespoons shortening**
1 **tablespoon all-purpose**
  flour

In saucepan bring peas, water, and broth to boiling. Reduce heat; simmer 2 minutes. Remove from heat; cover and let stand 1 hour. (Or, add peas to the cold water; soak overnight.) Add onion, basil, and salt. Cover; simmer till peas are tender but still retain their shape, 3 to 3½ hours. Drain, reserving ¾ cup liquid.

In large skillet brown pork chops in hot shortening. Remove chops. Pour off all but 1 tablespoon of drippings. Blend in flour. Stir in reserved pea liquid. Cook and stir till mixture thickens. Stir in peas; arrange chops atop. Cover and cook over low heat till heated through, about 5 minutes. Makes 5 servings.

Pork Chop Suey

1 **pound boneless pork, cut**
   into ¾-inch cubes
1 **clove garlic, minced**
1 **tablespoon cooking oil**
1½ **cups water**
¼ **cup soy sauce**
2 **teaspoons instant chicken**
   bouillon granules
1½ **cups bias-sliced celery**
1 **medium onion, cut in wedges**
2 **cups fresh bean sprouts** *or*
   1 16-ounce can bean
   sprouts, drained
1 **8-ounce can water chest-**
   nuts, drained and
   thinly sliced
1 **6-ounce package frozen pea**
   pods, thawed and halved
   crosswise
½ **cup thinly sliced fresh**
   mushrooms
2 **tablespoons cold water**
2 **tablespoons cornstarch**
   Hot cooked rice *or* **chow**
   mein noodles, warmed
   Soy sauce

In large skillet brown pork and garlic in hot oil. Add the 1½ cups water, ¼ cup soy sauce, and bouillon granules. Simmer, covered, for 30 minutes. Add celery and onion; cook for 5 minutes, stirring occasionally. Add bean sprouts, water chestnuts, pea pods, and mushrooms. Blend the 2 tablespoons cold water into cornstarch; stir into meat mixture. Cook and stir till vegetables are crisp-tender and mixture is thickened and bubbly. Serve with rice or chow mein noodles. Pass additional soy sauce. Makes 4 to 6 servings.

Pork in Sweet-Sour Sauce

1½ **pounds lean boneless pork,**
   cut into ½-inch cubes
2 **tablespoons cooking oil**
¼ **cup chopped onion**
1 **15¼-ounce can pineapple**
   chunks
¼ **cup packed brown sugar**
2 **tablespoons cornstarch**
¼ **teaspoon ground ginger**
¼ **cup vinegar**
3 **tablespoons soy sauce**
1 **medium green pepper, cut**
   into 1-inch squares
   Hot cooked rice

In large skillet brown the pork, half at a time, in hot oil. Return all meat to skillet. Add onion and ¼ cup *water*. Cover and simmer for 30 to 35 minutes.

Drain pineapple, reserving juice. Combine brown sugar, cornstarch, ginger, and ¼ teaspoon *salt*. Blend in reserved pineapple juice, vinegar, and soy sauce. Add to pork mixture along with green pepper; cook and stir till thickened and bubbly. Stir in pineapple; heat through. Serve over rice. Makes 6 servings.

Compare Prices

You can often find boneless pork cubes prepackaged in supermarket meat counters. However, if you check prices, you may find it is more economical to cut your own pork cubes from lean boneless pork. Some larger cuts to choose from are sirloin end of loin, boneless shoulder roasts, boneless loin roasts, or loin blade roasts.

Oven-Baked Pork Stew

1½ pounds pork stew meat, cut
    into 1-inch cubes
2 tablespoons cooking oil
3 tablespoons all-purpose
    flour
1 16-ounce can tomatoes,
    cut up
1 clove garlic, minced
1 bay leaf
1 teaspoon sugar
1 teaspoon instant beef
    bouillon granules
½ teaspoon dried thyme,
    crushed
½ teaspoon dried oregano,
    crushed
¼ teaspoon bottled hot
    pepper sauce
4 medium sweet potatoes,
    peeled, and sliced ¾
    inch thick (4 cups)
1 large onion, cut in wedges
1 medium green pepper, cut
    into thin strips
1 10-ounce package frozen
    peas, thawed

In large skillet brown meat, half at a time, in hot oil. Remove meat from skillet, reserving drippings. Blend flour into drippings. Add undrained tomatoes, garlic, bay leaf, sugar, bouillon granules, thyme, oregano, pepper sauce, ¼ cup *water,* and ½ teaspoon *salt.* Cook and stir till thickened and bubbly.

In a 3-quart casserole combine meat, sweet potatoes, onion, and green pepper. Add tomato mixture. Bake, covered, at 350° till meat and vegetables are tender, about 1½ hours; stir occasionally. Remove bay leaf. Stir in peas. Bake 5 to 10 minutes more. Makes 6 servings.

Pork Stroganoff for a Crowd

3 pounds pork stew meat, cut
    into ½-inch cubes
2 tablespoons cooking oil
1 cup chopped onion
1 cup water
1 clove garlic, minced
8 ounces medium noodles
    (6 cups)
2 10½-ounce cans condensed
    old-fashioned vegetable
    soup
1 10¾-ounce can condensed
    cream of mushroom soup
2 8-ounce cans imitation
    sour cream (2 cups)
1 8-ounce can mushroom
    stems and pieces, drained
2 teaspoons poppy seed
    (optional)
¼ teaspoon pepper
2 16-ounce cans cut green
    beans, drained
1½ cups soft bread crumbs
2 tablespoons butter *or*
    margarine, melted

In 10-quart Dutch oven brown meat, ⅓ at a time, in hot oil. Return all meat to Dutch oven. Add onion, water, and garlic. Cover; simmer till meat is tender, about 1¾ hours. Meanwhile, cook noodles in large amount of boiling salted water till tender, 7 to 8 minutes; drain. Stir vegetable soup, mushroom soup, imitation sour cream, mushrooms, poppy seed, and pepper into meat; fold in drained noodles and green beans. Divide mixture between two 2-quart casseroles. Toss bread crumbs with melted butter or margarine; sprinkle atop casseroles. Bake at 375° till heated through, about 35 minutes. Makes 12 to 16 servings.

Barbecued Orange-Apricot Ribs

1 teaspoon salt
1 teaspoon ground ginger
1 teaspoon ground
    coriander
½ teaspoon paprika
¼ teaspoon pepper
4 pounds pork loin back ribs
    or spareribs
    Hickory chips
½ cup apricot preserves
¼ cup orange juice
3 tablespoons soy sauce
1 tablespoon lemon juice

Combine salt, ginger, coriander, paprika, and pepper; rub onto meaty side of ribs. Cover and refrigerate for 2 hours. About an hour before cooking time, soak hickory chips in enough water to cover.

Lace ribs accordion-style on spit rod. Secure the ribs with holding fork. Arrange *hot* coals on both sides of a shallow foil drip pan. Drain hickory chips; sprinkle some over coals. Attach spit according to manufacturer's directions; position the foil drip pan under meat. Turn on motor; lower the grill hood or cover grill with foil tent. Grill ribs over *hot* coals till done, about 1 hour. Sprinkle the coals with dampened hickory chips every 20 minutes.

Combine apricot preserves, orange juice, soy sauce, and lemon juice. Brush ribs frequently with orange juice mixture during the last 15 minutes of cooking. Heat and pass the remaining orange juice mixture. Garnish ribs with orange slices, if desired. Makes 4 servings.

Mustard-Glazed Country Ribs

4 pounds pork country-style
    ribs
½ cup sugar
½ cup vinegar
⅓ cup prepared mustard
¼ cup chopped onion
2 cloves garlic, minced
2 teaspoons celery seed
2 teaspoons salt
1 teaspoon ground turmeric
1 medium onion, thinly sliced

In large saucepan or Dutch oven pour enough water over ribs to cover. Bring to boiling; reduce heat. Cover; simmer for 45 minutes. Drain well.

In small saucepan combine sugar, vinegar, prepared mustard, chopped onion, minced garlic, celery seed, salt, and ground turmeric. Bring mixture to boiling, stirring till sugar dissolves. Place ribs, meaty side up, in shallow roasting pan. Brush some of the mustard mixture over ribs. Roast, uncovered, at 350° about 15 minutes. Top with thinly sliced onion and some additional mustard mixture. Roast 15 minutes more, brushing occasionally with mustard mixture. Transfer ribs to warm platter; cut ribs into serving-size pieces. Reheat remaining mustard mixture and pass with ribs. Makes 4 to 6 servings.

Plantation Spareribs

½ cup sorghum *or* molasses
¼ cup prepared mustard
¼ cup vinegar
2 tablespoons Worcestershire
    sauce
½ teaspoon salt
½ teaspoon bottled hot pepper
    sauce
3 pounds pork spareribs

For sauce, in small saucepan blend sorghum or molasses into prepared mustard; stir in vinegar, Worcestershire sauce, salt, and bottled hot pepper sauce. Bring mixture to boiling; set aside. Place pork spareribs, meaty side down, in shallow roasting pan. Roast at 450° for 30 minutes. Remove meat from oven; drain off excess fat. Turn spareribs meaty side up; sprinkle with some salt. Reduce oven temperature to 350°; continue roasting spareribs till tender, about 1 hour more. During the last 30 minutes of roasting, baste frequently with the sorghum sauce. Cut spareribs into serving-size pieces. Makes 4 servings.

Barbecued Orange-Apricot Ribs and meaty, roasted *Mustard-Glazed Country Ribs* make out-of-the-ordinary dining. Their brush-on glazes put these ribs in a class by themselves.

Barbecue-Glazed Ham and Pineapple

1 20-ounce can pineapple
   slices
½ cup chili sauce
¼ cup sugar
2 tablespoons lemon juice
2 teaspoons Worcestershire
   sauce
½ teaspoon chili powder
1 3-pound canned ham
2 tablespoons cold water
1 tablespoon cornstarch

Drain pineapple slices, reserving ¼ cup pineapple syrup. For sauce, in small saucepan combine reserved pineapple syrup, chili sauce, sugar, lemon juice, Worcestershire sauce, and chili powder. Place ham on rack in shallow baking pan. Arrange pineapple slices around ham. Pour sauce over ham and pineapple slices. Bake at 325° about 1½ hours, basting ham and pineapple slices frequently with sauce. Remove ham and pineapple slices to warm platter; keep warm. Measure pan juices; add enough water to make 1¼ cups liquid. Blend the cold water into cornstarch; stir into pan juices. Cook, stirring constantly, till thickened and bubbly. Serve with ham and pineapple slices. Makes 8 to 10 servings.

Curry-Sauced Ham

1 cup water
1 10-ounce package frozen
   mixed vegetables
½ cup chopped celery
⅓ cup chopped onion
3 cups cubed fully cooked
   ham
1 10¾-ounce can condensed
   cream of mushroom soup
1 10¾-ounce can condensed
   cream of potato soup
1 tablespoon curry powder
½ cup dairy sour cream
2 tablespoons milk
3 tablespoons all-purpose
   flour
   Hot cooked rice

In large saucepan combine water, frozen mixed vegetables, celery, and onion. Bring to boiling; reduce heat. Cover; simmer for 10 minutes. Stir in ham, soups, and curry powder. Simmer, covered, for 20 minutes. Combine sour cream and milk; blend into flour. Add to ham mixture. Cook and stir till thickened; *do not boil*. Serve over hot cooked rice. Makes 6 to 8 servings.

Orange-Glazed Smoked Shoulder

1 2-pound smoked pork
   shoulder roll
¼ cup sugar
1 tablespoon cornstarch
¼ teaspoon ground allspice
½ cup orange juice
¼ cup honey
¼ cup butter *or* margarine
1 17-ounce can sweet potatoes,
   drained
1 medium orange, peeled
   and sectioned

Place shoulder roll on rack in shallow baking pan. Insert meat thermometer. Roast at 325° for 1 hour. Meanwhile, in small saucepan combine sugar, cornstarch, and allspice; blend in orange juice and honey. Cook and stir till thickened and bubbly. Cook 1 minute more; stir in butter or margarine. Arrange sweet potatoes and orange sections around roast; spoon orange juice mixture over all. Bake till thermometer registers 170°, about 30 minutes more. Makes 8 servings.

Baking Smoked Pork

Cut	Approx. Weight (Pounds)	Internal Temperature on Removal from Oven	Approx. Cooking Time (Total Time)
Bake meat at constant oven temperature of 325°.			
Ham (cook before eating)			
whole	10 to 14	160°	3¼ to 4 hours
half	5 to 7	160°	2 to 2½ hours
shank or rump portion	3 to 4	160°	2 to 2¼ hours
Ham (fully cooked)			
whole	10 to 14	140°	2½ to 3½ hours
whole, boneless	8 to 10	140°	2 to 2¼ hours
half	5 to 7	140°	1¾ to 2¼ hours
half, boneless	4 to 5	140°	1½ to 2 hours
Arm Picnic Shoulder (cook before eating)	5 to 8	170°	3 to 4 hours
Arm Picnic Shoulder (fully cooked)	5 to 8	140°	2½ to 3¼ hours
Canadian-Style Bacon	2 to 4	160°	1¼ to 2¼ hours

Baking directions: *Place meat, fat side up, on a rack in a shallow baking pan. Do not cover or add water. Score ham fat in diamonds, cutting only ¼ inch deep. Insert whole cloves, if desired. Insert meat thermometer into center of thickest portion of meat, making sure thermometer bulb does not rest in fat or touch bone. Bake meat at 325° till meat thermometer registers the desired internal temperature. To check temperature, push the thermometer into meat a little farther. If temperature drops, continue baking the meat till thermometer registers the desired temperature.*

Lamb

Crown Roast of Lamb with Rice Stuffing

1 6-ounce package long grain
    and wild rice mix
1 pound ground lamb
1 medium onion, chopped
¼ cup raisins
¼ cup toasted slivered
    almonds
¼ cup dry sherry
1 teaspoon salt
¼ teaspoon pepper
¼ teaspoon ground cloves
¼ teaspoon ground cardamom
¼ teaspoon ground ginger
⅛ teaspoon ground cinnamon
1 4-pound lamb rib crown
    roast, containing 2 whole
    rib sections and with fat
    trimmed from center of
    roast (12 to 14 ribs)
3 hard-cooked eggs, sliced

Cook rice mix according to package directions. In skillet cook ground lamb and onion till meat is browned and onion is tender. Drain excess fat. For stuffing, combine cooked rice, raisins, almonds, sherry, salt, pepper, cloves, cardamom, ginger, and cinnamon. Add cooked meat and onion; toss lightly. Place roast on a small piece of foil on rack in shallow roasting pan. Spoon in stuffing till center is half full. Arrange one of the sliced hard-cooked eggs atop stuffing. Spoon additional stuffing atop until mixture mounds. Cover top of roast and stuffing with foil. Place remaining stuffing in a 1-quart casserole, layering another sliced hard-cooked egg in center of mixture.

Insert meat thermometer in meaty portion of roast, not touching bone. Roast lamb at 325° till thermometer registers 175°, 3 to 3¼ hours. Uncover all but stuffing for the last 15 minutes. Bake stuffing in casserole, covered, the last 45 minutes of roasting time. Garnish with remaining sliced egg. Makes 6 or 7 servings.

Seasoned Leg of Lamb

1 6- to 7-pound leg of lamb
    Olive oil
½ cup fine dry bread crumbs
3 tablespoons finely snipped
    parsley
2 tablespoons butter
2 teaspoons finely shredded
    lemon peel
1 clove garlic, minced
1 teaspoon salt
1 teaspoon dried oregano,
    crushed
1 teaspoon dried basil,
    crushed
1 teaspoon dried rosemary,
    crushed
⅛ teaspoon pepper

Have meatman bone leg of lamb, leaving shank bone intact. Remove fell (thin fat covering) from surface of roast. Rub inside and outside of roast with olive oil. Combine bread crumbs, parsley, butter, lemon peel, garlic, salt, oregano, basil, rosemary, and pepper; mix well. Spread mixture as evenly as possible over entire inside cut surface of roast. Skewer roast shut. If necessary, secure with string.

Place roast on rack in shallow roasting pan. Insert meat thermometer in thickest portion of meat. Roast at 325° till thermometer registers 150°, 2 to 2½ hours. Makes 12 servings.

Fresh Mint Sauce

1½ teaspoons cornstarch
¼ cup snipped fresh mint
    leaves
3 tablespoons light corn syrup
1 tablespoon lemon juice
1 drop green food coloring
    (optional)

In small saucepan blend ¼ cup *cold water* into cornstarch; add mint leaves, corn syrup, and lemon juice. Cook, stirring constantly, till thickened and bubbly. Strain. Stir in green food coloring, if desired. Serve with roast lamb. Makes ½ cup.

Lemony Lamb Shoulder Chops

6 **lamb shoulder chops, cut**
    ¾ inch thick
2 **tablespoons cooking oil**
⅓ **cup water**
¼ **teaspoon finely shredded**
    lemon peel (set aside)
¼ **cup lemon juice**
1 **tablespoon Worcestershire**
    sauce
¾ **teaspoon salt**
¼ **teaspoon dried oregano,**
    crushed
¼ **teaspoon dried rosemary,**
    crushed
    Dash freshly ground black
    pepper
1 **tablespoon cornstarch**

In large skillet slowly brown chops on both sides in hot oil about 15 minutes. Combine water, lemon juice, Worcestershire sauce, salt, oregano, rosemary, and pepper; pour over meat. Cover; cook over low heat till tender, about 30 minutes. Remove meat to warm platter.

Pour pan juices into measuring cup; skim off fat. Add water, if necessary, to make 1 cup liquid; return to skillet. Blend 2 tablespoons *cold water* into cornstarch; stir into liquid in skillet. Add lemon peel. Cook and stir till bubbly. Pass with meat. Makes 6 servings.

Herbed Lamb Kabobs

¾ **cup Russian salad dressing**
3 **tablespoons lime juice**
½ **teaspoon dried oregano,**
    crushed
¼ **teaspoon dried tarragon,**
    crushed
1½ **pounds boneless lamb, cut**
    into 1-inch pieces
    Boiling water
2 **cups small fresh mushrooms**
2 **medium green peppers, cut**
    into 1½- to 2-inch squares

For marinade, in bowl combine salad dressing, lime juice, oregano, and tarragon. Add lamb. Cover and let stand 2 hours at room temperature or overnight in refrigerator; stir occasionally. Drain, reserving marinade. Pour some boiling water over mushrooms; drain. Alternately thread lamb, mushrooms, and green peppers on 6 long skewers. Place on unheated rack in broiler pan. Broil 4 inches from heat for 10 to 12 minutes; turn and baste with marinade occasionally. Makes 6 servings.

Spicy Lamb Stew

1½ **pounds boneless lamb, cut**
    into 1-inch cubes
4 **whole cloves**
4 **whole cardamom pods,**
    cracked
1 **inch stick cinnamon**
1 **tablespoon cooking oil**
1 **cup chopped onion**
1 **small clove garlic, minced**
1 **teaspoon grated gingerroot**
1½ **teaspoons ground coriander**
1 **teaspoon ground turmeric**
½ **teaspoon ground cumin**
¼ **teaspoon pepper**
⅛ **teaspoon cayenne**
1 **cup plain yogurt**
2 **tablespoons all-purpose flour**

In saucepan combine meat, ½ cup *water,* and ½ teaspoon *salt.* Cover; simmer 30 minutes. Meanwhile, in skillet cook and stir cloves, cardamom, and cinnamon in hot oil a few seconds. Add onion, garlic, and gingerroot; cook and stir 3 minutes more. Mix coriander, turmeric, cumin, pepper, and cayenne; stir in ¼ cup *water.* Add to onion-spice mixture. Cook and stir 10 minutes. Add onion mixture to lamb in cooking liquid. Stir in ¼ teaspoon *salt.* Cover and simmer till meat is tender, 15 to 20 minutes more. Blend yogurt and flour; stir into lamb mixture. Cook and stir just till thickened and bubbly. Makes 6 servings.

Translated "sauerkraut with all the trimmings," *Choucroute Garni* is a hearty
country dish. Choose from four pork cuts and five types of link sausages for the "trimmings."

Sausage

Choucroute Garni

1 medium onion, sliced
1 tablespoon bacon drippings
   or lard
3 fresh pork hocks (1½ pounds)
   or 2 pounds pork spareribs, cut in 3-rib portions
1 2-pound smoked pork shoulder
   roll *or* 3 or 4 smoked pork
   loin chops, cut ¾ inch
   thick (1½ pounds)
3 16-ounce cans sauerkraut,
   rinsed and drained
2 cooking apples, peeled,
   cored, and cut in wedges
2 tablespoons brown sugar
4 whole cloves
3 juniper berries, crushed
   (optional)
2 small cloves garlic, minced
1 bay leaf
⅛ teaspoon freshly ground
   black pepper
1½ cups rhine wine
1 pound sausage links
   (use desired combination
   of fresh bratwurst, fresh
   bockwurst, fresh
   thuringer, knackwurst
   or frankfurters)
   Boiled potatoes

In 4½- or 5-quart Dutch oven cook onion in bacon drippings or lard till tender; remove from heat. Add pork hocks or spareribs. Cut pork shoulder roll crosswise in ¾-inch slices; add shoulder slices or loin chops to Dutch oven. In large bowl stir together the sauerkraut, apples, brown sugar, cloves, juniper berries, garlic, bay leaf, and pepper. Spoon over meats. Pour wine over all. Cover and bake at 375° till meats are tender, about 2½ hours.

Meanwhile, prepare desired combination of sausages. For bratwurst, bockwurst, and thuringer, place in unheated skillet with 2 to 3 tablespoons *water*; cover and cook over low heat 5 to 8 minutes. Uncover and continue cooking till water has evaporated and sausages are cooked through, 5 to 8 minutes more. For knackwurst and frankfurters, add to boiling water in saucepan; cover and simmer till heated through, 5 to 10 minutes.

Mound sauerkraut mixture on deep, wide serving platter or in large bowl. Arrange meats and sausages around and atop sauerkraut. Add boiled potatoes to platter or pass separately. Makes 6 servings.

Swiss Bratwurst Melt

2 tablespoons butter *or*
   margarine
4 teaspoons all-purpose flour
¼ teaspoon salt
¼ teaspoon dry mustard
¾ cup milk
¾ cup shredded process Swiss
   cheese (3 ounces)
1 8-ounce can sauerkraut
4 cooked bratwurst links
4 large slices pumpernickel
   bread, toasted
4 slices tomato
   Green pepper rings
   Ground nutmeg (optional)

Melt butter or margarine in small saucepan. Stir in flour, salt, and dry mustard; add milk. Cook and stir till thickened and bubbly. Stir in cheese till melted; cover and keep warm. Heat sauerkraut in small saucepan. Meanwhile, halve bratwurst lengthwise; place, cut side down, on broiler pan or baking sheet. Broil 3 to 5 inches from heat for 3 minutes.

Drain sauerkraut. For each sandwich place 2 bratwurst halves on a bread slice. Top with a fourth of the hot sauerkraut and 1 tomato slice; spoon a fourth of the cheese sauce over. Garnish with a green pepper ring and sprinkle with a dash of ground nutmeg, if desired. Makes 4 servings.

Sicilian Pizza Supreme

4 to 4½ cups all-purpose
   flour
1 package active dry yeast
1½ teaspoons salt
1½ cups warm water (110°)
1 beaten egg
2 tablespoons cooking oil
1 pound bulk Italian sausage
½ cup chopped onion
1 15-ounce can tomato sauce
1 teaspoon dried oregano,
   crushed
1 large onion, thinly sliced
   and separated into rings
1 4-ounce can sliced mushrooms,
   drained
2 cups shredded mozzarella
   cheese (8 ounces)
2 medium tomatoes, sliced
1 green pepper, cut into rings
½ cup grated Parmesan cheese
½ teaspoon dried basil,
   crushed

In large mixer bowl combine *2 cups* of the flour, the yeast, and salt. Stir in water, egg, and oil. Beat at low speed of electric mixer for ½ minute, scraping sides of bowl. Beat 3 minutes at high speed. By hand, stir in enough of the remaining flour to make a moderately stiff dough. Turn out onto floured surface and knead till smooth, about 5 minutes. Place in a greased bowl, turning once. Cover; let rise till double (about 1 hour). Divide dough; place in two greased 9x9x2-inch baking pans *or* three 8x1½-inch round baking pans (sprinkle bottoms of pans with cornmeal, if desired). With well-oiled hands, pat dough out to fit pan, making a ½-inch rim around edges. Cover; let rise 30 minutes.

In skillet cook sausage and chopped onion till meat is brown; drain. Stir in tomato sauce, oregano, and dash *pepper.* Simmer, covered, 10 minutes.

When dough has risen, spread with a thin layer of the meat mixture. Arrange onion rings and mushrooms atop; sprinkle with mozzarella cheese. Spoon remaining meat mixture over. Bake at 425° for 25 minutes. Arrange tomato slices and green pepper rings on pizzas; sprinkle with Parmesan cheese and basil. Bake 5 to 10 minutes more. Makes 6 servings.

Chili-Spaghetti Dinner

½ pound bulk pork sausage
¼ cup chopped onion
¼ cup chopped carrot
1¼ cups tomato juice
1 8-ounce can red kidney
   beans, drained
½ teaspoon salt
½ teaspoon chili powder
   Dash pepper
½ cup broken uncooked
   spaghetti

In saucepan cook sausage, onion, and carrot till meat is browned. Drain off fat. Stir in tomato juice, kidney beans, salt, chili powder, and pepper. Place uncooked spaghetti in a 1-quart casserole; stir in meat mixture. Bake at 375° till spaghetti is tender, 55 to 60 minutes; stir twice. Makes 2 or 3 servings.

Corn and Sausage Scallop

1 cup milk
2 eggs
1 tablespoon all-purpose flour
1 16-ounce can cream-style
   corn
1 3-ounce can chopped
   mushrooms, drained
3 cups bite-size shredded
   corn cereal, crushed
   (1½ cups crushed)
1 8-ounce package brown-and-
   serve sausage links

In mixing bowl combine milk, eggs, and flour; beat till smooth. Stir in cream-style corn, mushrooms, and *1 cup* of the crushed corn cereal. Turn into an 8x1½-inch round baking dish. Arrange sausages atop in spoke design. Sprinkle with remaining ½ cup crushed corn cereal. Bake at 350° till knife inserted just off-center comes out clean, 40 to 45 minutes. Makes 4 or 5 servings.

Hot Smoky Potato Salad

4 slices bacon
5 fully cooked smoked
    sausage links, sliced
½ cup chopped onion
1 10¾-ounce can condensed
    cream of celery soup
¼ cup water
2 tablespoons sweet pickle
    relish
2 tablespoons vinegar
¼ teaspoon salt
1 16-ounce package frozen
    French-fried potatoes,
    halved crosswise

In skillet cook bacon till crisp. Drain, reserving 2 tablespoons drippings; set bacon aside. Cook sausage and chopped onion in drippings till meat is browned and onion is tender, about 5 minutes. Stir in cream of celery soup, water, pickle relish, vinegar, and salt. Bring to boiling; add potatoes and cook, covered, for 10 minutes, stirring once or twice. To serve, crumble the reserved bacon over top of potato salad. Makes 4 to 6 servings.

A Soup for All Seasons

10 cups water
1 pound dry lentils
8 ounces pepperoni, thinly
    sliced and halved
1 large onion, chopped
1 6-ounce can tomato paste
2½ teaspoons salt
½ teaspoon dried oregano,
    crushed
¼ teaspoon ground sage
¼ teaspoon cayenne
4 tomatoes, cut up
2 medium carrots, sliced
2 stalks celery, sliced
3 cups water
1½ teaspoons salt
1½ cups bulgur wheat

In Dutch oven combine the 10 cups water, lentils, pepperoni, onion, tomato paste, the 2½ teaspoons salt, oregano, sage, and cayenne. Bring to boiling. Reduce heat; cover and simmer 30 minutes, stirring occasionally. Add tomatoes, carrots, and celery; cover and simmer 40 minutes more.

Meanwhile, in saucepan bring the 3 cups water and the 1½ teaspoons salt to boiling; stir in bulgur wheat. Reduce heat; cover and simmer 25 minutes. To serve, mound the cooked bulgur wheat in soup bowls; spoon the lentil mixture over. Makes 10 to 12 servings.

Golden-Sauced Franks

1 15¼-ounce can pineapple
    chunks
2 17-ounce cans sweet
    potatoes, cut up
1½ pounds frankfurters (12 to
    15), cut in 1-inch pieces
⅓ cup packed brown sugar
2 tablespoons cornstarch
½ teaspoon finely shredded
    orange peel
½ cup orange juice
¼ cup water
2 tablespoons vinegar
2 tablespoons chili sauce

Drain pineapple, reserving syrup. In 3-quart casserole combine pineapple, sweet potatoes, and franks. In small saucepan combine brown sugar and cornstarch. Stir in reserved pineapple syrup, orange peel, orange juice, water, vinegar, and chili sauce. Cook and stir over medium heat till thickened and bubbly. Pour over mixture in casserole. Cover and bake at 350° till heated through, 25 to 30 minutes. Makes 8 servings.

Poultry

Pan-Fried Chicken

¼ cup all-purpose flour
1½ teaspoons salt
1 teaspoon paprika
¼ teaspoon pepper
1 2½- to 3-pound broiler-fryer chicken, cut up
2 tablespoons cooking oil *or* shortening

In a paper or plastic bag combine flour, salt, paprika, and pepper. Add 2 or 3 chicken pieces and shake to coat pieces evenly. Remove chicken pieces; repeat with remaining chicken pieces till all are coated.

In a 12-inch skillet heat oil or shortening. Place meaty chicken pieces toward center and remaining pieces around the edge. *For tender Pan-Fried Chicken,* brown over medium heat about 15 minutes, turning as necessary to brown evenly. Reduce heat; cover tightly. Cook for 30 minutes. Uncover; cook till tender, 5 to 10 minutes. *(For crisp Pan-Fried Chicken,* turn heat to medium-low and cook slowly, *uncovered,* till chicken is tender, 55 to 60 minutes. Turn chicken occasionally. Drain on paper toweling.) Makes 4 servings.

Two-Step Fried Chicken

¼ cup all-purpose flour
1½ teaspoons salt
1 teaspoon paprika
¼ teaspoon pepper
1 2½ to 3-pound broiler-fryer chicken, cut up
2 tablespoons cooking oil *or* shortening

In a paper or plastic bag combine flour, salt, paprika, and pepper. Add 2 or 3 chicken pieces and shake to coat evenly. Remove chicken pieces; repeat with remaining chicken pieces till all are coated.

In a 12-inch oven-going skillet, heat cooking oil or shortening. Brown chicken in hot oil over medium heat about 15 minutes, turning to brown evenly.

Transfer skillet to a 375° oven. *Or,* remove chicken from skillet and place, skin side up, in an ungreased, large shallow baking pan. Bake at 375° till chicken is tender, 35 to 45 minutes. Do not turn. Makes 4 servings.

Bran-Flake Chicken and Peaches

½ cup slightly crushed bran flakes (¾ cup uncrushed)
¼ cup shelled sunflower seed, chopped
½ teaspoon seasoned salt
¼ cup butter *or* margarine, melted
2 tablespoons lemon juice
½ teaspoon salt
3 whole large chicken breasts, halved lengthwise, *or* 6 whole small chicken breasts
1 16-ounce can peach halves, drained

In paper or plastic bag combine bran flakes, sunflower seed, and seasoned salt. Blend melted butter or margarine, lemon juice, and salt. Brush chicken breasts with butter mixture, then shake, one at a time, in bran mixture to coat lightly. (Reserve remaining lemon-butter mixture.)

Place chicken, skin side up, in an ungreased, large shallow baking pan. Bake at 375° for 40 minutes. Do not turn. Brush peaches with reserved lemon-butter mixture. Arrange peaches in pan with chicken; continue baking till chicken is tender, 5 to 10 minutes more. Makes 6 servings.

A crunchy coating and nutty flavor characterize these oven-crisped chicken
breasts. Peach halves bake with *Bran-Flake Chicken and Peaches* the last few minutes.

Oven-Fried Chicken

¼ cup butter *or* margarine, melted
½ teaspoon salt
¼ teaspoon pepper
1 2½- to 3-pound broiler-fryer chicken, cut up
1 cup crushed cornflakes *or* crushed potato chips *or* ½ cup fine dry bread crumbs

Combine butter or margarine, salt, and pepper. Brush chicken with butter mixture, then roll in cornflakes, potato chips, *or* bread crumbs. Place chicken, skin side up, without touching in an ungreased, large shallow baking pan. Bake at 375° till tender, about 1 hour. Do not turn. Season to taste with salt. Makes 4 servings.

Maryland Fried Chicken

1 slightly beaten egg
¼ cup milk
⅔ cup finely crushed crackers
½ teaspoon salt
¼ teaspoon pepper
1 2½- to 3-pound broiler-fryer chicken, cut up
2 tablespoons shortening
1 cup milk
¾ cup milk
3 tablespoons all-purpose flour
1 teaspoon salt
Dash pepper
¾ cup milk

Combine egg and the ¼ cup milk. Combine crackers, the ½ teaspoon salt, and ¼ teaspoon pepper. Dip chicken in egg mixture, then roll in crumbs. In skillet brown chicken in hot shortening about 15 minutes, turning to brown evenly. Add the 1 cup milk. Reduce heat; cover tightly. Simmer for 35 minutes. Uncover; cook till tender, 5 to 10 minutes more. Remove chicken to platter; keep warm.

For gravy, reserve 3 tablespoons drippings in skillet. In screw-top jar combine ¾ cup milk, flour, the 1 teaspoon salt, and dash pepper; shake till well blended. Stir into drippings in skillet. Blend in ¾ cup milk. Cook, stirring constantly, till thickened and bubbly. Cook 2 to 3 minutes more. If necessary, thin with a little additional milk. Serve gravy over chicken. Makes 4 servings.

Southern-Style Fried Chicken

2 2½- to 3-pound broiler-fryer chickens, cut up
2 cups all-purpose flour
2 cups buttermilk
Cooking oil

Season chicken with salt and pepper. Coat with some of the flour, then dip in buttermilk; coat again with remaining flour. Pour cooking oil into deep skillet to depth of 1¼ inches; heat to 350°. Regulate heat so chicken fries at 325°. Fry, a few pieces at a time, in hot oil till tender, 12 to 15 minutes; turn once. Drain well. Serve hot or chilled. Makes 8 servings.

Basic Broiled Chicken

1 2½- to 3-pound broiler-fryer chicken, halved lengthwise *or* quartered
Cooking oil *or* melted butter

Preheat broiler. Break wing, hip, and drumstick joints of chicken so bird will remain flat during broiling. Twist wing tips under back. Brush chicken pieces with oil or melted butter and season with salt and pepper.

Place chicken, skin side down, in broiler pan (rack optional). Broil with surface of chicken 5 to 6 inches from heat till lightly browned, about 20 minutes. Brush occasionally with oil or butter. Turn chicken skin side up and broil till tender, 15 to 20 minutes more, brushing occasionally with oil or butter. Makes 2 to 4 servings.

Fruit-Turkey Kabobs

¾ **pound cooked boneless turkey roast, cut in twelve 1-inch cubes**
1 **orange, cut in wedges**
1 **firm pear, cut in wedges**
1 **green pepper, cut in squares**
4 **small spiced crab apples**
½ **cup jellied cranberry sauce**
½ **cup apricot preserves**
½ **cup light corn syrup**
¼ **cup lemon juice**
2 **tablespoons butter**
¼ **teaspoon ground cinnamon Dash ground cloves**

Thread pieces of turkey, orange, pear, green pepper, and a crab apple onto four 10-inch skewers. In saucepan combine cranberry sauce, apricot preserves, corn syrup, lemon juice, butter, cinnamon, and cloves; bring to boiling, stirring occasionally. Brush cranberry mixture over turkey and fruit. Grill about 4 inches above *medium-hot* coals till meat and fruit are hot and well glazed, 5 to 10 minutes. Turn and brush occasionally with sauce. Pass remaining sauce. Makes 4 servings.

Barbecued Spicy Chicken

¼ **cup finely chopped onion**
1 **clove garlic, minced**
2 **tablespoons cooking oil**
¾ **cup catsup**
⅓ **cup vinegar**
1 **teaspoon grated lemon peel**
1 **tablespoon lemon juice**
1 **tablespoon Worcestershire sauce**
2 **teaspoons sugar**
1 **teaspoon dry mustard**
¼ **teaspoon bottled hot pepper sauce**
2 **2½- to 3-pound broiler-fryer chickens, quartered**

Cook onion and garlic in oil till tender but not brown. Stir in catsup, vinegar, lemon peel, lemon juice, Worcestershire sauce, sugar, dry mustard, hot pepper sauce, ½ teaspoon *salt,* and ¼ teaspoon *pepper.* Simmer, covered, about ½ hour; stir occasionally. Season chicken with salt and pepper. Place, bone side down, over *medium-hot* coals. Grill 25 minutes. Turn skin side down; grill 20 minutes more. Brush onion mixture over chicken. Continue grilling till tender, 10 to 15 minutes, turning frequently and basting with sauce. Makes 8 servings.

Oven-Easy Chicken Croquettes

2 **tablespoons butter *or* margarine**
3 **tablespoons all-purpose flour**
½ **cup milk**
½ **cup chicken broth**
2 **cups ground *or* finely chopped cooked chicken *or* turkey**
1 **tablespoon snipped parsley**
⅛ **teaspoon dried rosemary, crushed**
8 **slices white bread**
1 **beaten egg**
2 **tablespoons butter *or* margarine, melted Cranberry-Claret Sauce**

Melt 2 tablespoons butter or margarine; blend in flour. Add milk and chicken broth; cook and stir till bubbly. Cool slightly. Stir in chicken or turkey, parsley, rosemary, and ¼ teaspoon *salt.* Cover; chill several hours.

Trim crusts from bread; cut bread in ½-inch cubes. Shape chicken mixture into 8 balls, using ¼ cup mixture for each. Dip balls in beaten egg, then coat with bread cubes. Place in greased shallow baking pan. Brush with 2 tablespoons melted butter or margarine. Bake at 375° till hot and toasted, about 30 minutes. Serve croquettes with Cranberry-Claret Sauce. Makes 4 servings.

Cranberry-Claret Sauce: In saucepan combine one 8-ounce can *jellied cranberry sauce* and ¼ cup *claret;* heat through. Beat till mixture is smooth.

Pineapple Hawaiian Chicken

2 2½- to 3-pound broiler-fryer
　　chickens, halved length-
　　wise *or* quartered
　　Cooking oil
2 tablespoons sugar
1 teaspoon cornstarch
1 8¼-ounce can crushed
　　pineapple
2 tablespoons butter *or*
　　margarine
2 tablespoons soy sauce
1 tablespoon finely chopped
　　onion

Preheat broiler. Break joints of chicken. Brush chicken with oil; season with salt and pepper. Place, skin side down, in broiler pan (rack optional). Broil 5 to 6 inches from heat till lightly browned, about 20 minutes. Turn; broil 15 to 20 minutes more.

Meanwhile, in small saucepan combine sugar and cornstarch. Stir in crushed pineapple, butter, soy sauce, and chopped onion. Cook and stir till thickened and bubbly; cook 1 minute more. Spoon pineapple mixture over chicken the last 5 minutes of broiling time. Makes 4 to 6 servings.

Broiled Crab-Chicken Rolls

6 whole medium chicken breasts
¼ cup chopped onion
¼ cup chopped celery
2 tablespoons butter *or*
　　margarine
4 teaspoons all-purpose
　　flour
¼ teaspoon salt
　　Dash white pepper
½ cup milk
1 7½-ounce can crab meat,
　　drained, flaked, and
　　cartilage removed
½ cup snipped parsley
¼ cup dry sherry
¼ cup butter *or* margarine,
　　melted
1 teaspoon paprika

Remove skin and bones from chicken breasts. Place, boned side up, between two pieces clear plastic wrap. Pound out from center with meat mallet to ⅛-inch thickness. Remove wrap. Season both sides of chicken.

Cook onion and celery in the 2 tablespoons butter or margarine. Blend in flour, salt, and white pepper. Add milk; cook and stir till bubbly. Stir in crab, parsley, and sherry. Divide crab mixture among chicken pieces. Fold in sides and roll up. Secure with wooden picks. If desired, wrap and chill up to 24 hours.

Place chicken in broiler pan (rack optional). Brush with mixture of the ¼ cup melted butter and paprika. Broil 5 to 6 inches from heat about 35 minutes; turn once and brush with butter mixture. Makes 6 servings.

Hot Turkey Sandwiches

2 cups chopped cooked turkey
1 cup shredded American
　　cheese (4 ounces)
1 cup chopped, unpeeled apple
½ cup chopped celery
½ cup mayonnaise *or*
　　salad dressing
¼ cup toasted slivered almonds
1 tablespoon lemon juice
1 teaspoon salt
1 teaspoon curry powder
⅛ teaspoon pepper
8 individual French rolls

In mixing bowl combine turkey, cheese, apple, celery, mayonnaise or salad dressing, almonds, lemon juice, salt, curry powder, and pepper. Cut a thin slice from top of each roll. Hollow out bottoms, leaving ½-inch edges (store bread crumbs for other use). Fill each roll with about ½ cup turkey mixture; replace tops. Wrap each in a 12x12-inch piece of foil, twisting ends securely. Grill over *medium* coals till heated through, 15 to 20 minutes, turning several times. Makes 8 sandwiches.

Chicken-Noodle Casserole

1 8-ounce package frozen
   noodles
⅓ cup chopped green pepper
⅓ cup chopped onion
2 tablespoons butter
2 tablespoons all-purpose
   flour
¼ teaspoon dried thyme,
   crushed
1 11-ounce can condensed
   Cheddar cheese soup
1 cup milk
1½ cups chopped cooked chicken
1 4-ounce can mushroom stems
   and pieces, drained
¼ cup chopped pimiento
¼ cup grated Parmesan cheese

Cook frozen noodles in 6 cups rapidly *boiling water;* stir till separated. Cook till tender, 15 to 20 minutes. Drain noodles and set aside.

In saucepan cook green pepper and onion in butter till tender. Blend in flour and thyme. Stir in soup and milk. Cook and stir till thickened and bubbly. Fold in chicken, mushrooms, pimiento, and noodles. Turn into 1½-quart casserole. Sprinkle with cheese. Bake, uncovered, at 350° till heated through, 30 to 35 minutes. Garnish with parsley sprigs, if desired. Makes 6 servings.

Spiced Orange Chicken

3 tablespoons all-purpose
   flour
1 teaspoon salt
¼ teaspoon ground cinnamon
¼ teaspoon ground cloves
   Dash pepper
1 2- to 2½-pound broiler-fryer
   chicken, cut up
2 tablespoons shortening
2 tablespoons butter *or*
   margarine
4 oranges
1 tablespoon brown sugar
1 tablespoon soy sauce

In paper or plastic bag combine flour, salt, cinnamon, cloves, and pepper; add a few pieces of chicken at a time and shake to coat. In large skillet melt together shortening and butter or margarine; add chicken. Brown slowly till golden, about 20 minutes. Peel and section oranges, reserving juice; add enough water to juice to measure ½ cup liquid. Stir in brown sugar and soy. Drain fat from skillet; add juice mixture. Cover; simmer 20 minutes. Add oranges; cover and simmer 2 to 3 minutes more. Transfer chicken and oranges to serving platter. Remove excess fat from pan juices; spoon juices over chicken. Makes 4 servings.

Individual Chicken Pies

½ cup chopped onion
6 tablespoons butter
7 tablespoons all-purpose
   flour
1 teaspoon salt
¼ teaspoon dried rosemary,
   crushed, *or* poultry
   seasoning
⅛ teaspoon pepper
3 cups chicken broth
3 cups cubed cooked chicken
1 10-ounce package frozen
   peas and carrots, cooked
   and drained
¼ cup chopped pimiento
6 refrigerated biscuits

Cook onion in butter till tender; blend in flour, salt, rosemary or poultry seasoning, and pepper. Stir in broth. Cook and stir till thickened and bubbly. Add chicken, peas and carrots, and pimiento; heat till bubbly. Pour into 6 individual casseroles. Quarter biscuits; place 4 pieces atop hot filling in each casserole. Bake at 450° till lightly browned, 8 to 10 minutes. Makes 6 servings.

A crusty-brown batter seasoned with herb wraps tender pieces of chicken in *Popover Chicken Tarragon*. Whisk this dish from oven to table; spoon *Easy Mushroom Sauce* over each serving.

Popover Chicken Tarragon

1 2½- to 3-pound broiler-
   fryer chicken, cut up
2 tablespoons cooking oil
3 eggs
1½ cups milk
1 tablespoon cooking oil
1½ cups all-purpose flour
¾ to 1 teaspoon dried tarragon,
   crushed
¾ teaspoon salt
   Easy Mushroom Sauce

In skillet brown chicken in the 2 tablespoons cooking oil; season with salt and pepper. Place chicken in a well-greased shallow 3-quart casserole or 13x9x2-inch baking dish.

In mixing bowl beat eggs; add milk and the 1 tablespoon oil. Stir together the flour, tarragon, and salt. Add to egg mixture. Beat till smooth. Pour over chicken. Bake at 350° till done, 55 to 60 minutes. Spoon Easy Mushroom Sauce over chicken. Makes 4 servings.

Easy Mushroom Sauce: In saucepan combine one 10¾-ounce can condensed *cream of chicken soup;* ⅓ cup *milk;* one 4-ounce can sliced *mushrooms,* drained; and 2 tablespoons snipped *parsley.* Cook and stir till bubbly.

Chicken Divan

2 10-ounce packages frozen
   cut broccoli
1 10¾-ounce can condensed
   cream of chicken soup
1 tablespoon lemon juice
1 teaspoon Worcestershire
   sauce
   Dash ground nutmeg
½ cup grated Parmesan cheese
2 cups sliced cooked chicken
½ cup whipping cream
½ cup mayonnaise *or*
   salad dressing
   Paprika

Cook broccoli according to package directions; drain well. Arrange in 12x7½x2-inch baking dish. Combine chicken soup, lemon juice, Worcestershire sauce, and nutmeg; pour *half* over broccoli. Sprinkle with *one-third* of cheese. Top with chicken and remaining soup mixture. Sprinkle with *one-third* of cheese. Bake, uncovered, at 350° till heated through, about 20 minutes.

Whip cream till soft peaks form; fold in mayonnaise or salad dressing. Spread over chicken. Top with remaining cheese and paprika. Broil 4 inches from heat till golden, about 2 minutes. Makes 6 servings.

Chicken and Stuffing Scallop

2 cups herb-seasoned stuffing
   mix (½ of an 8-ounce
   package)
2 cups chopped cooked chicken
   or turkey
¼ cup butter *or* margarine
¼ cup all-purpose flour
⅛ teaspoon salt
   Dash pepper
2 cups chicken broth
3 beaten eggs
1 11-ounce can condensed
   Cheddar cheese soup
½ cup milk
2 tablespoons chopped pimiento
   Sliced green olives

Prepare stuffing mix according to package directions for dry stuffing. Spread in a 10x6x2-inch baking dish; top with chopped cooked chicken or turkey. In saucepan melt butter or margarine; blend in flour, salt, and pepper. Add chicken broth; cook and stir till bubbly. Stir moderate amount of the hot mixture into eggs; return to hot mixture. Pour over chicken; bake at 325° till set, about 35 minutes. Let stand 5 minutes. Meanwhile, for sauce, in saucepan combine soup, milk, and pimiento; heat through. Garnish dish with olives; serve with sauce. Makes 6 servings.

Stewed Chicken

1 5- to 6-pound stewing
    chicken, cut up, *or*
    2 3-pound broiler-fryer
    chickens, cut up
4 stalks celery with leaves,
    cut up
1 carrot, sliced
1 small onion, cut up
2 sprigs parsley
1 bay leaf
2 teaspoons salt
¼ teaspoon pepper

Place chicken in a large kettle; add enough *water* to cover (about 8 cups). Add celery, carrot, onion, parsley, bay leaf, salt, and pepper. Cover; bring to boiling. Simmer till chicken is tender, about 1 hour for broiler-fryers or 2 to 2½ hours for stewing chicken. Remove chicken; strain broth. When chicken is cool enough to handle, cut meat from bones; discard skin and bones. Store meat and broth separately in covered containers; chill. Makes 5 cups cooked chicken.

Chicken and Dumplings

Stewed Chicken (see
    recipe above)
½ teaspoon ground sage
    (optional)
1 cup all-purpose flour
2 teaspoons baking powder
½ teaspoon salt
2 tablespoons snipped
    parsley
1 egg
¼ cup milk
2 tablespoons butter *or*
    margarine, melted
1 cup cold water
½ cup all-purpose flour
1½ teaspoons salt
⅛ teaspoon pepper

Prepare Stewed Chicken as directed in recipe *except* add sage to cooking liquid, if desired.

    Prepare dumplings when chicken is almost tender: Stir together the 1 cup flour, baking powder, and the ½ teaspoon salt; add parsley. Stir together egg, milk, and melted butter or margarine. Add to flour mixture, stirring just till blended. Drop dough from tablespoon directly onto chicken in boiling broth. Cover tightly; return to boiling. Reduce heat; *do not lift cover.* Simmer 12 to 15 minutes. Remove dumplings and chicken to platter; keep warm. Strain broth; measure 4 cups broth.

    For gravy, in saucepan bring the 4 cups broth to boiling. Stir cold water into the ½ cup flour; gradually add to broth, mixing well. Cook and stir till thickened and bubbly. Season with the 1½ teaspoons salt and pepper. Pour over chicken and dumplings. Makes 6 to 8 servings.

Chicken Cacciatore

1 2½- to 3-pound broiler-fryer
    chicken, cut up
2 tablespoons cooking oil
2 medium onions, sliced
2 cloves garlic, minced
1 16-ounce can tomatoes,
    cut up
1 8-ounce can tomato sauce
1 teaspoon salt
1 teaspoon dried basil *or*
    oregano, crushed
½ teaspoon celery seed
¼ teaspoon pepper
1 or 2 bay leaves
¼ cup dry white wine

In skillet brown chicken in hot cooking oil. Remove chicken. In same skillet cook onions and garlic till onion is tender but not brown. Return chicken to skillet. Combine undrained tomatoes, tomato sauce, salt, basil or oregano, celery seed, pepper, and bay leaves. Pour over chicken. Cover; simmer 30 minutes. Stir in wine. Cook, uncovered, 15 minutes; turn often. Remove bay leaves; skim fat. Makes 4 servings.

Turkey Chowder

2 medium potatoes, peeled
    and cubed (2 cups)
1 10-ounce package frozen
    baby lima beans
½ cup chopped onion
½ cup sliced celery
¼ teaspoon salt
2 cups water
1 10¾-ounce can condensed
    cream of chicken soup
1 16-ounce can tomatoes,
    cut up
1½ cups chopped cooked turkey
    or chicken
½ teaspoon poultry seasoning
¼ teaspoon garlic salt
⅛ teaspoon pepper
½ cup shredded Cheddar cheese
    (2 ounces)

In 3-quart saucepan combine potatoes, beans, onion, celery, and salt. Blend water into canned soup; add to vegetables. Cook, covered, till vegetables are tender, 35 to 45 minutes. Add undrained tomatoes, turkey or chicken, poultry seasoning, garlic salt, and pepper. Simmer 15 minutes. Sprinkle 1 tablespoon cheese over each serving. Makes 8 servings.

Homemade Corn and Chicken Soup

1 5- to 6-pound stewing
    chicken, cut up
6 cups water
⅓ cup chopped onion
1 bay leaf
2 teaspoons salt
¼ teaspoon pepper
6 medium ears corn *or*
    1 16-ounce can
    cream-style corn
1½ cups uncooked Old-Fashioned
    Egg Noodles (see recipe
    below)
1 cup chopped celery
2 tablespoons snipped parsley

In kettle mix chicken, water, onion, bay leaf, salt, and pepper. Bring to boiling. Simmer, covered, 2 hours.

    For fresh corn, with sharp knife make cuts through center of corn kernels in each row of ears. Cut corn off cobs; scrape cobs. (Should equal 2 cups corn.) Remove chicken from broth; cool. Remove meat from bones; discard bones. Cube meat; set aside. Skim fat from broth. Discard bay leaf. Bring broth to boiling. Add corn, Old-Fashioned Egg Noodles, celery, and parsley. Simmer, covered, till corn and noodles are barely tender, about 8 minutes. Add meat; heat through. Season to taste. Makes 8 servings.

Old-Fashioned Egg Noodles

1 beaten egg
2 tablespoons milk
½ teaspoon salt
    All-purpose flour

Combine the beaten egg, milk, and salt. Stir in enough all-purpose flour to make a stiff dough (about 1 cup). Roll noodles very thin on a floured surface. Let stand 20 minutes. Roll up loosely. Slice ¼ inch wide. Unroll; spread out. Let dry for 2 hours. Store in covered container till needed. Use in recipes as directed *or* cook, uncovered, in boiling salted water till noodles are tender, about 10 minutes. Makes 3 cups cooked or uncooked noodles.

Roasting Domestic Birds

Poultry	Ready-to-Cook Weight	Oven Temp.	Guide to Roasting Time	Special Instructions
Chicken	1½-2 lbs. 2½-3lbs. 3½-4 lbs. 4½-5 lbs.	400° 375° 375° 375°	1-1¼ hrs. 1¼-1½ hrs. 1¾-2 hrs. 2¼-2½ hrs.	Brush dry areas of skin occasionally with pan drippings. Cover chicken loosely with foil.
Capon	4-7 lbs.	375°	2-3 hrs.	Brush the dry areas with pan drippings. Roast as above.
Cornish Game Hen	1-1½ lbs.	375°	1½ hrs.	Cover loosely with foil and roast for ½ hour. Uncover and roast until done, about 1 hour. If desired, baste occasionally the last hour.
Turkey	6-8 lbs. 8-12 lbs. 12-16 lbs. 16-20 lbs. 20-24 lbs.	325° 325° 325° 325° 325°	3½-4 hrs. 4-4½ hrs. 4½-5½ hrs. 5½-6½ hrs. 6½-7½ hrs.	Cover bird *loosely* with foil. Press lightly at the end of drumsticks and neck; leave air space between bird and foil. Baste bird occasionally, if desired. Roast, uncovered, the last 45 minutes or until turkey is done.
Foil-Wrapped Turkey	7-9 lbs. 10-13 lbs. 14-17 lbs. 18-21 lbs. 22-24 lbs.	450° 450° 450° 450° 450°	2¼-2½ hrs. 2¾-3 hrs. 3-3¼ hrs. 3¼-3½ hrs. 3¼-3¾ hrs.	Place turkey, breast up, in the center of greased, wide, heavy foil. Bring ends of foil up over breast; overlap fold and press up against ends of turkey. Place bird in shallow roasting pan (no rack). Open foil the last 20 minutes to brown the turkey.
Domestic Duckling	3-5 lbs.	375°	1½-2¼ hrs.	Prick skin well all over. During roasting, spoon off excess fat. Do not rub with oil.
Domestic Goose	7-9 lbs. 9-11 lbs. 11-13 lbs.	350° 350° 350°	2½-3 hrs. 3-3½ hrs. 3½-4 hrs.	Prick skin well all over. During roasting, spoon off excess fat. Do not rub with oil.
Guinea Hen	1½-2 lbs. 2-2½ lbs.	375° 375°	¾-1 hr. 1-1½ hrs.	Lay bacon over breast. Roast loosely covered with foil. Uncover guinea hen the last 20 minutes.

Preparation for roasting: Rinse bird and pat dry with paper toweling. Rub inside of cavities with salt, if desired. Do not stuff the bird until just before cooking.

To stuff bird, spoon some of the stuffing loosely into neck cavity; pull the neck skin to the back of the bird and fasten securely with a small skewer. Lightly spoon remaining stuffing into the body cavity. If opening has a band of skin across the tail, tuck drumsticks under band; if band of skin is not present, tie legs securely to tail. Twist wing tips under back.

For unstuffed bird, place quartered onions and celery in body cavity, if desired. Prepare and roast. Discard vegetables, if desired.

Roasting directions: Place bird, breast side up, on a rack in a shallow roasting pan. Brush skin of bird, *except* duckling and goose, with cooking oil. If meat thermometer is used, insert in center of inside thigh muscle, making sure bulb does not touch bone.

Roast in uncovered pan (unless specified) according to chart at left. When bird is two-thirds done, cut band of skin or string between legs so thighs will cook evenly. Continue roasting until bird is done. Remove bird from oven; cover loosely with foil to keep warm. Let the bird stand 15 minutes before carving.

Test for doneness: The meat thermometer inserted in thigh should register 185°.

Also, the thickest part of the drumstick should feel very soft when pressed between fingers protected with paper toweling. The drumstick also should move up and down and twist easily in the socket.

Remember, each bird differs in size, shape, or variety. Because of these differences, roasting times can be only approximate.

To roast turkey in a covered roasting pan: Rinse turkey and pat dry. Stuff, if desired; prepare for roasting as directed in chart at left. Place turkey, breast up, on rack in roasting pan. Brush bird with cooking oil or melted butter. Insert meat thermometer in center of inside thigh muscle; make sure bulb

does not touch bone. Do not add water. Cover pan with a lid or cover *tightly* with foil. Roast bird at 350° till about three-quarters done (allow about 3 hours for an 11- to 12-pound turkey). Remove cover; cut band of skin or string between legs. Baste turkey with pan drippings. Continue roasting, uncovered, till done. When done, meat thermometer should register 185° and drumstick should twist easily in socket. Turkey will not be as golden as when roasted loosely covered.

To roast turkey in commercial cooking bag: Rinse turkey and pat dry. Stuff, if desired; prepare for roasting as directed in chart at left. Place 1 tablespoon all-purpose *flour* in the commercial cooking bag; shake to coat interior. Place bag in large roasting pan. Brush turkey with cooking oil or melted butter. Place turkey inside bag, breast side up. Close bag loosely with twist tie. Make six ½-inch slits in top of bag to allow steam to escape. Roast according to manufacturer's directions. About 15 minutes before roasting time is up, cut the bag open. Insert meat thermometer in center of inside thigh muscle of turkey, making sure bulb does not touch bone. When turkey is done, meat thermometer should register 185° and drumstick should move up and down and twist easily in socket.

Carving: 1) Remove bird from oven and let stand 15 minutes before carving; cover to keep warm. Place bird on carving board or on a serving platter protected by a board. Grasp leg with fingers; pull leg away from body. Cut through meat between thigh and body. With the tip of the knife, disjoint thighbone from backbone. 2) Holding leg vertically, large end down, slice meat parallel to bone and under some tendons, turning leg for even slices. *Or,* first separate thigh and drumstick. Slice thigh meat by cutting slices parallel to the bone. 3) Before carving white meat, make a deep horizontal cut into breast close to wing. Note that the wing tips have been twisted under the back before roasting so that carving can be done without removing wings. 4) Cut thin slices from top of breast down to horizontal cut. Final smaller slices can follow curve of breastbone. Turn bird and repeat each step to carve the other side of the bird.

Cranberry-Stuffed Cornish Hens

⅔ **cup chopped cranberries**
2 **tablespoons sugar**
1 **teaspoon shredded orange peel**
½ **teaspoon salt**
⅛ **teaspoon ground cinnamon**
3 **cups toasted raisin bread cubes**
2 **tablespoons butter** *or* **margarine, melted**
4 **teaspoons orange juice**
4 **1- to 1½-pound Cornish game hens**
Salt
Cooking oil
¼ **cup orange juice**
2 **tablespoons butter** *or* **margarine, melted**

In bowl combine chopped cranberries, sugar, orange peel, the ½ teaspoon salt, and cinnamon. Add raisin bread cubes; sprinkle with 2 tablespoons melted butter or margarine and the 4 teaspoons orange juice. Toss lightly to mix.

Season cavities of hens with salt. Lightly stuff birds with cranberry mixture. Pull neck skin to back of each bird and fasten securely with a small skewer. Tie legs to tail; twist wing tips under back. Place Cornish game hens, breast side up, on a rack in shallow roasting pan. Brush hens with cooking oil; cover loosely with foil. Roast at 375° for 30 minutes.

Combine the ¼ cup orange juice and 2 tablespoons melted butter or margarine. Uncover birds; baste with orange juice mixture. Roast, uncovered, till done (drumstick can be twisted easily), about 1 hour longer; baste once or twice with orange juice mixture. Makes 4 servings.

Apricot-Sauced Duckling

1 **small orange**
1 **4- to 5-pound domestic duckling**
1 **medium onion, cut in wedges**
1 **small apple, halved and cored**
1 **12-ounce can apricot nectar**
2 **teaspoons instant chicken bouillon granules**
1 **tablespoon cornstarch**

Peel orange; scrape white membrane from peel. Cut outer portion of peel into thin strips; set aside. Quarter orange. Lightly salt cavity of duckling. Stuff loosely with orange, onion, and apple. Skewer neck skin to back; tie legs to tail and twist wings under back. Prick skin all over with fork. Place, breast up, on rack in shallow roasting pan. Roast in uncovered pan at 375° for 1¾ to 2 hours; spoon off fat.

Meanwhile, stir nectar, bouillon granules, and reserved peel into cornstarch in saucepan. Cook and stir till bubbly. Brush duckling with nectar mixture; roast till done, about 15 minutes more. Discard stuffing, if desired. Pass remaining nectar mixture. Makes 3 or 4 servings.

Roast Sweet-Sour Chickens

1 **8¼-ounce can crushed pineapple**
4 **cups dry bread cubes**
½ **cup flaked coconut**
½ **cup chopped celery**
½ **teaspoon salt**
¼ **teaspoon poultry seasoning**
¼ **cup butter** *or* **margarine, melted**
2 **2½- to 3-pound whole broiler-fryer chickens**
Cooking oil
2 **tablespoons cornstarch**
2 **tablespoons brown sugar**
¼ **teaspoon salt**
1 **tablespoon lemon juice**

Drain crushed pineapple, reserving 1 tablespoon syrup. Combine pineapple, dry bread cubes, coconut, chopped celery, the ½ teaspoon salt, and poultry seasoning. Drizzle with melted butter or margarine; toss lightly. For moist stuffing, add the reserved syrup.

Rub neck and body cavities of broiler-fryer chickens with salt. Stuff loosely with bread mixture. Skewer neck skin to back. Tie legs to tail; twist wing tips under back. Place chickens, breast up, on rack in shallow roasting pan. Rub skin with cooking oil. Roast in uncovered pan at 375° till done, 1¼ to 1½ hours, brushing often with pan drippings. Remove to platter; keep warm.

Skim off fat from pan drippings. Measure drippings; add water to make 1½ cups liquid. In small saucepan blend cornstarch, brown sugar, and the ¼ teaspoon salt. Add drippings. Cook and stir till bubbly. Stir in lemon juice. Pass lemon juice mixture with chickens. Makes 6 to 8 servings.

When a special occasion calls for just the right entrée, serve *Cranberry-Stuffed Cornish Hens.* Garnish the birds with parsley, cranberry-centered kumquat roses, and a lemon twist.

Old-Fashioned Bread Stuffing

½ cup chopped onion
½ cup butter *or* margarine
1 teaspoon poultry seasoning
  or ground sage
½ teaspoon salt
⅛ teaspoon pepper
8 cups dry bread cubes
1 cup chicken broth *or* water

Cook onion in butter or margarine till tender; add poultry seasoning or sage, salt, and pepper. Combine with bread cubes. Drizzle with broth; toss to mix well. Use to stuff a 10-pound turkey (or two 4- to 5-pound roasting chickens) *or* bake, covered, in a 2-quart casserole at 325° for 40 to 45 minutes. Makes 6 to 7 cups.

Corn Bread Stuffing Loaf

1 cup chopped celery with
  leaves
½ cup chopped onion
¾ cup chicken broth
2 beaten eggs
⅓ cup mayonnaise *or* salad
  dressing
1 teaspoon poultry seasoning
½ teaspoon ground sage
¼ teaspoon salt
  Chopped cooked giblets
  (optional)
6 cups coarsely crumbled corn
  bread

In small saucepan cook chopped celery and onion, covered, in chicken broth till vegetables are tender, about 5 minutes. Do not drain.

In large bowl combine eggs, mayonnaise or salad dressing, poultry seasoning, sage, salt, giblets, and vegetables with broth. Add corn bread; toss lightly to mix. If desired, add extra ¼ cup broth for a moist stuffing.

In a 10x6x2-inch baking dish shape mixture into a loaf. Cover with foil. Bake at 400° till heated through, 25 to 30 minutes; uncover the last 5 minutes to brown slightly. Garnish with celery leaves, if desired. Makes 8 to 10 servings.

Bread and Butter Stuffing

8 slices bread
6 tablespoons butter *or*
  margarine
¼ cup chopped onion
¼ cup chopped celery
¾ cup chicken broth *or* water
½ teaspoon ground sage
¼ teaspoon dried thyme,
  crushed
¼ teaspoon salt
¼ teaspoon pepper

Toast bread; spread with butter. Cut into cubes. In covered saucepan cook onion and celery in broth or water about 5 minutes. Stir in sage, thyme, salt, and pepper. Combine with toast cubes; toss lightly. If desired, add extra ¼ cup broth for moist stuffing. Use to stuff a 5-pound roasting chicken *or* bake, covered, in greased 1-quart casserole at 375° about 30 minutes. Makes about 4 cups.

Rice and Vegetable Stuffing

1 cup grated carrot
½ cup chopped green onion
½ cup snipped parsley
2 tablespoons butter *or*
  margarine
1 cup regular rice
3 cups chicken broth
½ teaspoon salt
  Dash pepper

In saucepan cook carrot, onion, and parsley in butter or margarine for 10 minutes, stirring frequently. Add uncooked rice; stir to mix well. Add broth, salt, and pepper. Cook, covered, over low heat till rice is done, about 20 minutes. Use to stuff two 3- to 4-pound roasting chickens (or one 6- to 7-pound capon). *Or* bake, covered, in a 1½-quart casserole at 375° for 20 to 25 minutes. Makes about 5 cups.

Fish and Seafood

Corn-Stuffed Whitefish

1 3-pound fresh *or* frozen
   dressed whitefish or other
   fish, boned
1 tablespoon butter *or*
   margarine
¼ cup chopped onion
3 tablespoons chopped green
   pepper
1 12-ounce can whole kernel
   corn, drained
1 cup soft bread crumbs (1½
   slices)
2 tablespoons chopped pimiento
½ teaspoon salt
⅛ teaspoon dried thyme,
   crushed
2 tablespoons cooking oil

Thaw fish, if frozen; pat dry with paper toweling. Place fish in a well-greased shallow baking pan; sprinkle cavity generously with salt.

To make stuffing, in a medium saucepan melt butter or margarine. Add onion and green pepper; cook till vegetables are tender, about 5 minutes. Stir in drained corn, bread crumbs, pimiento, salt, and thyme; mix well.

Stuff fish cavity loosely with the corn mixture. Brush skin with the cooking oil. Cover fish loosely with foil. Bake at 350° till fish flakes easily when tested with a fork, 45 to 60 minutes. Use two large spatulas to transfer the whole fish to a serving platter. Makes 6 servings.

Pan-Fried Fish

3 10- to 12-ounce fresh *or* frozen
   pan-dressed trout *or* other
   fish
1 beaten egg
2 tablespoons water
¾ cup fine dry bread crumbs
   or finely crushed saltine
   crackers (21 crackers) *or*
   cornmeal
½ teaspoon salt
   Dash pepper
   Shortening *or* cooking oil
   for frying

Thaw fish, if frozen. Rinse and pat dry. In a shallow dish beat egg; stir in water. Dip fish in egg mixture to coat on both sides. Combine bread crumbs or crushed crackers or cornmeal with the salt and pepper. Roll fish in crumb mixture, coating evenly.

In large skillet heat ¼ inch shortening or cooking oil. Add fish in single layer to hot oil. Fry fish on one side till brown, 4 to 5 minutes. Turn and fry fish 4 to 5 minutes more. Fish is done when both sides are brown and crisp, and when it flakes easily when tested with a fork. Drain fish on paper toweling. Makes 3 servings.

Trout Amandine

4 to 6 8-ounce fresh *or* frozen
   pan-dressed trout
1 slightly beaten egg
¼ cup light cream *or* milk
¼ cup all-purpose flour
2 tablespoons cooking oil
2 tablespoons butter *or*
   margarine
¼ cup slivered almonds
¼ cup butter *or* margarine,
   melted
2 tablespoons lemon juice

Thaw fish, if frozen; rinse and pat dry. Season trout with salt and pepper. Combine egg with cream or milk. Dip trout in flour, then in egg mixture.

In large skillet heat oil and the 2 tablespoons butter or margarine. Fry fish till golden, 8 to 10 minutes; turn once. Drain; transfer to platter.

In another skillet cook almonds in the ¼ cup melted butter or margarine till golden. Remove from heat; stir in lemon juice. Pour almond mixture over fish; serve at once. Makes 4 to 6 servings.

Bouillabaisse

1 **pound small fresh** *or* **frozen lobster tails**
1 **pound fresh** *or* **frozen red snapper** *or* **sole fillets**
1 **pound fresh** *or* **frozen cod** *or* **haddock fillets**
12 **ounces fresh** *or* **frozen scallops**
12 **clams in shells**
2 **large onions, chopped (2 cups)**
⅓ **cup olive** *or* **cooking oil**
6 **cups water**
1 **28-ounce can tomatoes, cut up**
2 **small cloves garlic, minced**
2 **sprigs parsley**
2 **bay leaves**
1½ **teaspoons dried thyme, crushed**
½ **teaspoon thread saffron, crushed**
French bread slices

Thaw shellfish and fish, if frozen. When lobster is partially thawed, split tails in half lengthwise; cut crosswise to make 6 to 8 portions. Cut fish fillets into 2-inch pieces. Cut large scallops in half. Wash clams well. Cover clams with salted water (⅓ cup salt to 1 gallon cold water); let stand 15 minutes; rinse. Repeat twice. Set seafood aside.

In large saucepan or Dutch oven cook onions in hot oil till tender but not brown. Add water, undrained tomatoes, garlic, parsley, bay leaves, thyme, saffron, 1 tablespoon *salt*, and ⅛ teaspoon *pepper*. Bring to boiling. Reduce heat; cover and simmer 30 minutes. Strain tomato mixture into a large kettle; discard vegetables and herbs.

Bring strained mixture to boiling; add lobster and fish and cook 5 minutes. Add scallops and clams; boil till clams open, about 5 minutes. Discard any clams that do not open. Serve in shallow bowls with French bread. Serves 6 to 8.

Broiled Fish

2 **pounds fresh** *or* **frozen trout** *or* **other fish fillets,** *or* **halibut** *or* **other fish steaks**
2 **tablespoons butter** *or* **margarine, melted**
1 **teaspoon salt**
Dash pepper

Thaw fish, if frozen. Cut into 6 serving-size pieces. Arrange fish in a single layer on greased, unheated rack in a broiler pan or in a greased baking pan. Tuck under any thin edges. Brush *half* the melted butter or margarine over the fish. Season with the salt and pepper.

Place fish 4 inches from the heat. Broil for 5 to 8 minutes; turn thick pieces. Brush fish with the remaining melted butter. Broil 5 to 8 minutes more. Fish is done when it flakes easily when tested with a fork. Serves 6.

Salmon Croquettes

1 **16-ounce can salmon**
3 **tablespoons butter**
¼ **cup all-purpose flour**
½ **cup milk**
1 **tablespoon snipped parsley**
2 **teaspoons lemon juice**
1 **teaspoon grated onion**
Dash paprika
Dash ground nutmeg
1 **cup fine dry bread crumbs**
1 **beaten egg**
Shortening *or* **cooking oil for deep-fat frying**
1 **10-ounce package frozen peas in cream sauce**

Drain salmon, reserving ½ cup liquid. Remove bones and skin; flake meat. Melt butter in saucepan. Blend in flour. Add milk and reserved salmon liquid. Cook and stir till thickened and bubbly. Cook and stir 1 minute more. Add parsley, lemon juice, onion, paprika, nutmeg, ¼ teaspoon *salt,* and dash *pepper.* Stir in salmon; chill.

With wet hands, shape salmon mixture into 8 balls, using about ¼ cup for each. Roll in crumbs. Shape balls into cones, handling lightly so crumbs remain on outside. Dip into mixture of beaten egg and 2 tablespoons *water;* roll in crumbs again.

Fry a few at a time in deep, hot fat (350°) till brown and hot, about 2½ to 3 minutes. Drain on paper toweling. Prepare peas in cream sauce according to package directions; spoon over croquettes or pass as a sauce. Serves 4.

French-inspired *Bouillabaisse* incorporates lobster, scallops, clams, and two kinds
of fish. One sample and you'll agree that the time it took to prepare was put to good use.

Tuna-Broccoli Bake

2 10-ounce packages frozen
  cut broccoli
¼ cup butter *or* margarine
¼ cup all-purpose flour
¾ teaspoon salt
⅛ teaspoon pepper
2 cups milk
½ cup mayonnaise *or* salad
  dressing
1 9¼-ounce can tuna, drained
  and broken into chunks
3 hard-cooked eggs, cut
  into wedges
  Paprika

Cook broccoli according to package directions; set aside. In saucepan melt butter or margarine; blend in flour, salt, and pepper. Add milk. Cook and stir till thickened and bubbly. Remove from heat. Stir in mayonnaise or salad dressing. Carefully stir in cooked broccoli, tuna, and hard-cooked eggs. Turn into 2-quart casserole. Sprinkle with paprika. Bake at 400° till mixture is heated through, 20 to 25 minutes. Makes 6 servings.

Shrimp and Tuna Bake

⅔ cup long grain rice
1 9-ounce package frozen
  cut green beans
1 10½-ounce can condensed
  cream of celery soup
½ cup milk
2 tablespoons chopped
  pimiento
¼ teaspoon dried thyme,
  crushed
  Dash cayenne
1 6½- *or* 7-ounce can tuna,
  drained and broken into
  chunks
1 4½-ounce can shrimp, drained
½ of a 3½-ounce can French-
  fried onions (about 1 cup)

Cook rice according to package directions. Cook green beans according to package directions. Drain; set aside. Combine cream of celery soup, milk, pimiento, thyme, and cayenne. Stir till smooth. Stir *half* of the soup mixture into cooked rice. Fold tuna into rice mixture. Turn into a 1½-quart casserole.

Spread cooked and drained green beans over rice. Top with shrimp. Pour remaining soup mixture over all. Bake, covered, at 325° till heated through, 25 to 30 minutes. Uncover and sprinkle with onions. Bake till onions are crisp, about 5 minutes longer. Makes 6 servings.

Halibut with Dill Topping

6 fresh *or* frozen halibut steaks
  or other fish steaks
3 tablespoons lemon juice
½ teaspoon salt
¼ teaspoon paprika
  Dash pepper
½ cup finely chopped onion
2 tablespoons butter *or* margarine
¼ cup dairy sour cream
2 tablespoons mayonnaise *or*
  salad dressing
1 teaspoon dried dillweed

Thaw fish, if frozen. Arrange fish in a single layer in 13x9x2-inch baking dish. Combine lemon juice, salt, paprika, and pepper; brush mixture over both sides of fish. Let stand 30 minutes at room temperature. Meanwhile, in saucepan cook onion in butter or margarine till tender. Top fish with onion and butter. Bake, uncovered, at 325° till fish flakes easily when tested with fork, 20 to 25 minutes. Combine sour cream, mayonnaise or salad dressing, and dillweed; serve over fish. Makes 6 servings.

French-Fried Shrimp

1 cup all-purpose flour
½ teaspoon sugar
½ teaspoon salt
1 beaten egg
1 cup cold water
2 tablespoons cooking oil
2 pounds fresh or frozen
   shrimp in shells
   All-purpose flour
   Shortening or cooking oil
   for deep-fat frying

For batter, stir together the 1 cup flour, the sugar, and salt. Make a well in center. Combine beaten egg, cold water, and the 2 tablespoons oil; pour into the well. Beat with a rotary beater till smooth.

Thaw shrimp, if frozen. Peel shrimp leaving last section and tail intact. With a sharp knife, remove the sandy black vein. To butterfly shrimp, make a deep slit in shrimp's back cutting almost all the way through. Pat dry with paper toweling. Dip shrimp in flour to coat. Dip flour-coated shrimp into batter.

In saucepan or deep-fat fryer, heat shortening or cooking oil to 375°. Fry a few shrimp at a time in the hot fat till golden, 2 to 3 minutes. Remove from fat with a slotted spoon; drain on paper toweling. Makes 6 to 8 servings.

Delaware Crab Cakes

1 beaten egg
½ cup finely crushed saltine
   crackers (14 crackers)
⅓ cup milk
½ teaspoon dry mustard
⅛ teaspoon white pepper
⅛ teaspoon cayenne
1 7½-ounce can crab meat,
   drained, flaked, and
   cartilage removed
1 tablespoon snipped parsley
3 tablespoons lard or
   shortening
   Lemon wedges

In a bowl combine egg, crushed crackers, milk, mustard, white pepper, and cayenne. Stir in crab meat and parsley. Shape into patties using ⅓ cup mixture for each. Cover and chill patties at least 30 minutes.

In skillet heat lard or shortening. Add crab patties and cook over medium heat till golden brown, 6 to 8 minutes; turn patties once. Drain and serve at once with lemon wedges. Makes 5 crab cakes.

Crab or Lobster Newburg

6 tablespoons butter or
   margarine
2 tablespoons all-purpose
   flour
1½ cups light cream
3 beaten egg yolks
1 7½-ounce can crab meat or
   1 5-ounce can lobster,
   drained and broken into
   large pieces
3 tablespoons dry white wine
2 teaspoons lemon juice
¼ teaspoon salt
   Pastry Petal Cups or toast
   points
   Paprika

Melt butter or margarine in saucepan; blend in flour. Add cream all at once. Cook, stirring constantly, till mixture thickens and bubbles. Stir small amount of hot mixture into egg yolks; return to remaining hot mixture. Cook, stirring constantly, till thickened and bubbly. Add crab or lobster; heat through. Stir in wine, lemon juice, and salt. Serve in Pastry Petal Cups or over toast points. Sprinkle with paprika. Makes 4 or 5 servings.

Pastry Petal Cups: Prepare 1 stick *piecrust mix* according to package directions. Roll ⅛ inch thick; cut in 2¼-inch rounds. In each of 5 muffin cups, place one round in bottom and overlap 4 rounds on sides; press together. Prick. Bake at 450° for 10 to 12 minutes. Cool.

2 Casserole recipes

Whether you're planning a family meal or a gala celebration, a casserole is the perfect answer to the question "What's for dinner?" In this section, you'll find everything from quick-to-fix casseroles to international specialties.

Hearty casseroles featuring family-pleasing ingredients: *Sunday Chicken-Rice Bake*, *Biscuit-Topped Stew* made with leftovers (see page 103), and *Tuna Salad Bake* (see page 89).

Home-Style Casseroles

Sunday Chicken-Rice Bake

1 10¾-ounce can condensed
   cream of mushroom soup
1 cup milk
1 envelope onion soup mix
1 3-ounce can chopped
   mushrooms
1 cup regular rice
1 10-ounce package frozen peas
   and carrots, thawed
1 2½- to 3-pound ready-to-cook
   broiler-fryer chicken, cut up
   Paprika

In bowl stir together mushroom soup, milk, dry onion soup mix, and undrained mushrooms. Reserve ½ cup of the soup mixture and set aside. Stir uncooked rice and thawed vegetables into remaining soup mixture.

Turn rice mixture into a 12x7½x2-inch baking dish; arrange chicken pieces atop. Pour reserved soup mixture over chicken. Sprinkle chicken pieces with paprika. Cover tightly with foil. Bake at 375° till rice is tender, 1¼ to 1½ hours. Makes 4 to 6 servings.

Carolina Chicken Pie

1 4½- to 5-pound stewing
   chicken
8 cups water
1 medium onion, sliced
2 celery stalks with leaves
2 parsley sprigs
2 teaspoons salt
¼ teaspoon pepper
3 hard-cooked eggs, chopped
½ cup all-purpose flour
   Plain Pastry (see recipe, page
   72)

In 5-quart kettle combine chicken, water, onion, celery, parsley, salt, and pepper; bring to boiling. Reduce heat; simmer, covered, till chicken is tender, about 2½ hours. Drain chicken; reserve broth and ¼ cup chicken fat. Strain and refrigerate broth. Cool chicken enough to handle. Remove meat from bones; discard skin and bones. Cube meat; place in 13x9x2-inch baking pan. Sprinkle chopped hard-cooked eggs atop.

In saucepan combine reserved chicken fat and the flour. Stir in *4 cups* of the reserved broth. Cook and stir till bubbly; pour over chicken.

Prepare Plain Pastry for a double-crust pie. Roll pastry to 14x12-inch rectangle. Place pastry over chicken; seal and flute edges. Cut slits; bake at 375° till filling bubbles and pastry browns, about 45 minutes. Makes 6 to 8 servings.

Chicken and Onion Bake

1 2½- to 3-pound ready-to-cook
   broiler-fryer chicken,
   cut up
1 10¾-ounce can condensed
   cream of chicken soup
1 tablespoon snipped parsley
½ teaspoon poultry seasoning
1½ cups frozen small whole
   onions
   Paprika

Place chicken pieces, skin side up, in a 12x7½x2-inch baking dish. Stir together soup, parsley, and poultry seasoning; stir in onions. Spoon over chicken. Bake, covered, at 350° till chicken is tender, about 1 hour. Stir sauce; sprinkle with paprika. Serve with mashed potatoes or hot cooked rice, if desired. Makes 4 servings.

Microwave cooking directions: Cut large pieces of chicken in half. In a 12x7½x2-inch nonmetal baking dish combine soup, parsley, and poultry seasoning; stir in onions. Place chicken, skin side down, in sauce. Turn skin side up, coating with sauce. Cook, covered, in a countertop microwave oven till chicken is tender, about 25 minutes, rearranging chicken and stirring sauce every 10 minutes. Stir sauce again before serving; sprinkle with paprika.

Chicken-Spaghetti Bake

4 **ounces spaghetti**
3 **slices bacon, chopped**
½ **cup chopped onion**
1 **clove garlic, minced**
3 **tablespoons all-purpose**
   flour
1 **16-ounce can tomatoes,**
   cut up
1 **10¾-ounce can condensed**
   cream of mushroom soup
½ **cup milk**
1 **cup shredded American cheese**
   (4 ounces)
2 **cups cubed cooked chicken**
1 **10-ounce package frozen peas,**
   thawed
¼ **cup grated Parmesan cheese**

Break spaghetti pieces in half. Cook according to package directions; drain (should have about 2 cups).

In large saucepan cook bacon, onion, and garlic till bacon is crisp; blend in flour. Add undrained tomatoes, soup, and milk. Cook and stir till thickened and bubbly. Add shredded American cheese; stir till melted. Stir in cooked spaghetti, cubed chicken, and thawed peas.

Turn into a 2½-quart casserole; top with Parmesan. Bake, uncovered, at 350° for 45 minutes. Makes 8 servings.

Potato-Ham Scallop

2 **cups cubed fully cooked ham**
6 **medium potatoes (2 pounds),**
   peeled and thinly sliced
¼ **cup finely chopped onion**
⅓ **cup all-purpose flour**
2 **cups milk**
3 **tablespoons fine dry bread**
   crumbs
1 **tablespoon butter *or***
   margarine, melted
2 **tablespoons finely snipped**
   parsley

Place *half* the ham in a 2-quart casserole. Cover with *half* the potatoes and *half* the onion. Sift *half* the flour over; season with salt and pepper. Repeat layering ham, potatoes, and onion. Season with additional salt and pepper. Sift remaining flour atop. Pour milk over all.

Bake, covered, at 350° till potatoes are nearly tender, 1 to 1¼ hours. Uncover. Combine bread crumbs and melted butter; sprinkle atop casserole. Top with parsley. Bake 15 minutes longer. Makes 4 to 6 servings.

Ham and Mac Bake

3½ **ounces elbow macaroni**
    (1 cup)
¼ **cup butter *or* margarine**
¼ **cup all-purpose flour**
2 **tablespoons brown sugar**
2 **tablespoons prepared**
   mustard
¼ **teaspoon salt**
   Dash pepper
2 **cups milk**
2 **cups cubed fully cooked ham**
2 **medium apples, peeled and**
   thinly sliced (2 cups)
1½ **cups soft bread crumbs**
    (2 slices)
2 **tablespoons butter *or***
   margarine, melted

Cook macaroni in boiling salted water just till tender, 8 to 10 minutes; drain. In large saucepan melt the ¼ cup butter; blend in flour, brown sugar, mustard, salt, and pepper. Add milk all at once; cook and stir till thickened and bubbly. Stir in cooked macaroni, ham, and apple slices. Turn mixture into a 2-quart casserole.

Combine bread crumbs and the 2 tablespoons melted butter; sprinkle over casserole. Bake, uncovered, at 350° for about 35 minutes. Makes 6 servings.

Pork Chop-Fried Rice Casserole

1¾ **cups water**
1½ **cups Minute Rice**
 2 **slices bacon**
 2 **beaten eggs**
 2 **tablespoons water**
 ¼ **cup sliced green onion
        with tops**
 3 **tablespoons soy sauce**
 4 **pork rib chops**
      Soy sauce

In saucepan bring the 1¾ cups water to boiling. Remove from heat; stir in rice. Cover; set aside. In skillet cook bacon till crisp. Remove bacon and crumble, reserving 2 tablespoons drippings. Set aside.

In bowl combine eggs and the 2 tablespoons water. In skillet cook eggs in *1 tablespoon* of the reserved drippings till set, stirring occasionally. Cut eggs in narrow strips. Add rice, bacon, onion, and the 3 tablespoons soy sauce to eggs; mix well. Turn into a greased 1½-quart casserole.

In skillet brown chops on both sides in remaining 1 tablespoon drippings. Arrange chops atop rice mixture; brush with additional soy sauce. Bake, covered, at 350° till chops are tender, about 40 minutes. Makes 4 servings.

Microwave cooking directions: In a 1-quart glass bowl heat the 1¾ cups water, covered, in a countertop microwave oven till boiling, 4 minutes. Stir in rice. Cover; set aside.

Place bacon in a 10x6x2-inch nonmetal baking dish; cover with paper toweling. Micro-cook till crisp, 1½ to 1¾ minutes. Crumble bacon; set aside. Reserve 1 tablespoon bacon drippings in baking dish.

In glass bowl combine eggs and the 2 tablespoons water. Micro-cook till eggs puff, 1½ minutes; cut into narrow strips. Into reserved drippings stir rice, bacon, eggs, onion, and the 3 tablespoons soy sauce. Arrange chops atop rice mixture; brush with additional soy sauce.

Micro-cook, covered, for 5 minutes. Turn chops; micro-cook till chops are done, about 6 minutes.

Sweet-Sour Kraut and Chops

 4 **medium baking potatoes, peeled
        and thinly sliced (4 cups)**
 ½ **cup chopped onion**
 6 **pork rib chops,
        cut ¾ inch thick**
 2 **tablespoons cooking oil**
 1 **27-ounce can sauerkraut,
        rinsed and drained**
 1 **20-ounce can crushed pineapple**
 2 **tablespoons brown sugar**
 ½ **teaspoon salt**
      Dash pepper

In a 12x7½x2-inch baking dish combine potato slices and onion. Add ¼ cup water. Bake, covered, at 350° till nearly tender, about 45 minutes.

Meanwhile, in a skillet brown pork chops on both sides in hot oil. In bowl combine sauerkraut, undrained pineapple, and brown sugar; spoon over potato mixture. Place chops atop. Season with salt and pepper. Bake, covered, 45 minutes longer. Makes 6 servings.

*Use Your
Oven
Wisely*

Save both energy and money by planning to bake foods together that require the same oven temperature. For example, when cooking a main dish casserole or a roast, bake potatoes or other vegetables, a bread, or a dessert to serve at the same meal or even for the following day. Avoid overcrowding the oven, though, or cooking may be uneven. And check for doneness before removing from the oven, as some foods will require additional baking time.

Frank Tamale Pie

1 cup chopped onion
½ cup chopped green pepper
2 tablespoons butter
½ pound frankfurters (4 or 5)
1 16-ounce can pork and beans
   in tomato sauce
1 12-ounce can whole kernel
   corn, drained
1 8-ounce can tomato sauce
¼ cup chopped pitted ripe olives
1 clove garlic, minced
1 tablespoon sugar
2 to 3 teaspoons chili powder
1½ cups shredded American cheese
¾ cup yellow cornmeal

In a large skillet cook onion and green pepper in butter till tender but not brown.

Cut franks in ½-inch pieces. Stir into skillet along with beans, corn, tomato sauce, olives, garlic, sugar, chili powder, and dash pepper. Simmer, uncovered, till thickened, about 30 minutes. Add cheese; stir till melted. Turn mixture into a greased 12x7½x2-inch baking dish.

Place 2 cups cold water in saucepan. Stir in cornmeal and ½ teaspoon salt. Cook and stir till very thick (½ to 1 minute after mixture comes to boiling). Spoon over *hot* frank mixture, forming a lattice design as shown in photo at right. Bake, uncovered, at 375° for about 25 minutes. Makes 6 to 8 servings.

Frank-Vegetable Bake

½ cup yellow cornmeal
½ cup all-purpose flour
1 tablespoon sugar
1½ teaspoons baking powder
½ teaspoon salt
1 beaten egg
⅓ cup milk
4 tablespoons cooking oil
½ cup chopped carrot
¼ cup chopped onion
¼ cup chopped green pepper
¼ cup chopped celery
1 11½-ounce can condensed bean
   with bacon soup
¾ cup milk
2 teaspoons prepared mustard
1 pound frankfurters, sliced

Stir together cornmeal, flour, sugar, baking powder, and salt. Combine egg, the ⅓ cup milk, and *2 tablespoons* of the cooking oil. Add to dry ingredients; beat smooth.

In saucepan heat remaining 2 tablespoons oil; add vegetables. Cook, covered, 10 minutes. Blend in soup, the ¾ cup milk, and mustard; stir in franks. Bring to boiling. Turn into a 2-quart casserole. Spoon batter atop *hot* mixture. Bake, uncovered, at 425° for 20 to 25 minutes. Serves 6.

Microwave cooking directions: Prepare cornmeal batter as above. In a 2-quart glass casserole combine remaining 2 tablespoons oil and vegetables. Cook, covered, in a counter-top microwave oven till crisp-tender, 4 minutes, stirring once. Stir in soup, the ¾ cup milk, and mustard; stir in franks.

Micro-cook, covered, till bubbly, 9 to 10 minutes, stirring 3 times. Drop spoonfuls of batter in a ring atop *hot* mixture; cook, uncovered, till topping is done, about 5 minutes; give dish a quarter turn every 2 minutes.

Frankfurter-Cheese Casserole

¾ cup macaroni
6 frankfurters
⅓ cup chopped onion
⅓ cup chopped green pepper
2 tablespoons butter
3 tablespoons all-purpose flour
1 teaspoon Worcestershire sauce
½ teaspoon prepared mustard
1 cup milk
1½ cups cream-style cottage
   cheese (12 ounces)

Cook macaroni according to package directions; drain well. Thinly slice *four* of the frankfurters; set aside.

Cook onion and green pepper in butter till tender but not brown. Blend in flour, Worcestershire, mustard, ¼ teaspoon salt, and dash pepper; add milk all at once. Cook and stir till thickened and bubbly. Stir in the sliced franks, cooked maca-roni, and cottage cheese; mix well.

Turn into a 1½-quart casserole. Bake, uncovered, at 350° for 20 minutes, stirring once. Cut remaining 2 franks diago-nally into thirds; arrange atop casserole. Bake till heated through, 15 minutes more. Makes 6 servings.

Sporting a cornmeal topper in a lattice design, *Frank Tamale Pie* offers south-of-the-border flavor in a one-dish meal. Vary the amount of chili powder to suit family preferences.

Hot Frank and Rice Salad

¾ **cup regular rice**
1½ **cups chicken broth**
2 **tablespoons butter *or***
    margarine
2 **tablespoons all-purpose flour**
2 **tablespoons prepared mustard**
2 **teaspoons sugar**
⅛ **teaspoon pepper**
1 **cup chicken broth**
1 **pound frankfurters, cut in**
    1-inch pieces (8 to 10)
4 **slices bacon, crisp-cooked,**
    drained, and crumbled
½ **cup chopped celery**
½ **cup sliced pitted ripe olives**
¼ **cup sliced green onion**
    with tops
¼ **cup sweet pickle relish**

In a saucepan prepare rice according to package directions, *except* substitute the 1½ cups chicken broth for the water and omit the salt.

In small saucepan melt butter or margarine; blend in flour, mustard, sugar, and pepper. Add the 1 cup chicken broth all at once; cook and stir till thickened and bubbly. Stir into rice with franks, bacon, celery, olives, onion, and pickle relish. Turn into a 2-quart casserole.

Bake, uncovered, at 375° till mixture is heated through, about 30 minutes. Garnish with more bacon and sliced pitted ripe olives, if desired. Makes 6 servings.

Salami-Cheese Pie

    Plain Pastry (see below)
1 **tablespoon all-purpose flour**
⅛ **teaspoon pepper**
1 **cup evaporated milk**
½ **cup shredded American cheese**
    (2 ounces)
½ **pound salami, chopped**
    (1½ cups)
1 **cup cubed cooked potato**
¼ **cup chopped onion**
2 **tablespoons chopped**
    pimiento

Prepare Plain Pastry for a single-crust pie. Prick bottom and sides well with fork. Reroll trimmings; cut with decorative cutter for pie top. Place cutouts on baking sheet. Bake cutouts and pie shell at 400°, 5 minutes for cutouts and 10 minutes for pie shell. Remove from oven; set aside. Reduce oven temperature to 350°.

In saucepan combine flour and pepper; blend in milk. Cook and stir till thickened and bubbly; remove from heat. Stir in cheese till melted. Stir in salami, potato, onion, and pimiento. Turn into pie shell; top with baked cutouts.

Bake at 350° till center is nearly set, 35 to 40 minutes. Let stand 5 minutes. Makes 6 servings.

Plain Pastry (enough for one 9-inch piecrust)

1 **cup all-purpose flour**
½ **teaspoon salt**
⅓ **cup shortening**
3 **to 4 tablespoons cold water**

Stir together flour and salt; cut in shortening till pieces are the size of small peas. Sprinkle *1 tablespoon* water over part of the mixture. Gently toss with fork; push to side of bowl. Repeat till all is moistened. Form dough into a ball. Continue as directed in recipe.

For single-crust pie: Flatten dough on lightly floured surface. Roll from center to edge till ⅛ inch thick. Fit pastry circle into a 9-inch pie plate. Trim ½ to 1 inch beyond edge of pie plate. Fold under and flute edge. Continue as directed in recipe.

For double-crust pie: Prepare dough as directed above, *except* double the recipe. Form into two balls. Flatten each ball on a lightly floured surface. Roll each from center to edge till ⅛ inch thick. Fit one pastry circle into a 9-inch pie plate. Trim crust even with rim of plate. Continue as directed in recipe.

Puffed Potatoes and Sausage

¼ cup sliced green onion
  with tops
2 tablespoons butter *or*
  margarine
3 medium potatoes,
  peeled and cubed
  (1 pound)
1 cup shredded American
  cheese (4 ounces)
3 egg yolks
⅓ cup milk
½ teaspoon salt
3 stiffly beaten
  egg whites
1 8-ounce package
  brown-and-serve
  sausage links

Cook onion in butter or margarine till tender but not brown. Cook potatoes in boiling salted water till tender, about 10 minutes; drain and mash (should have about 2 cups mashed). Beat in cooked onion and cheese.

Beat together egg yolks, milk, and salt; blend into potato mixture. Fold in beaten egg whites.

Turn into a 2-quart casserole. Arrange sausage links over potato mixture. Bake, uncovered, at 375° till set, about 45 minutes. Makes 4 or 5 servings.

Lamb-Lentil Stew

1 pound boneless lamb shoulder,
  cut in ½-inch cubes
2 tablespoons cooking oil
4 medium carrots, thinly sliced
  (2 cups)
1½ cups chopped onion
1 cup chopped celery
1 cup dry lentils
  (8 ounces)
1 tablespoon instant chicken
  bouillon granules
3 cloves garlic, minced
2 bay leaves
1 teaspoon dried oregano,
  crushed
½ teaspoon salt
⅛ teaspoon pepper
3 cups hot water

In large skillet brown lamb cubes in hot oil; drain off fat. Stir in carrots, onion, celery, lentils, bouillon granules, garlic, bay leaves, oregano, salt, and pepper.

Turn mixture into a 2- or 2½-quart casserole; add hot water. Bake, covered, at 350° till meat and vegetables are tender, about 1¾ hours, stirring once or twice. Add more water during cooking, if needed. Makes 6 servings.

Yankee Bacon Bake

½ pound sliced bacon
½ cup yellow cornmeal
1 cup milk
½ cup all-purpose flour
1 tablespoon sugar
1 teaspoon baking powder
½ teaspoon salt
1 cup milk
3 beaten egg yolks
3 stiffly beaten
  egg whites

Cook bacon till crisp; drain and coarsely crumble. Set bacon aside. In saucepan stir cornmeal into the 1 cup milk; cook, stirring constantly, till mixture is thickened and bubbly. Remove from heat.

Stir together flour, sugar, baking powder, and salt; blend into cornmeal mixture. Stir in the remaining 1 cup milk and egg yolks; fold in the beaten egg whites and crumbled bacon. Turn into a greased 1½-quart casserole or soufflé dish. Bake, uncovered, at 325° for 55 to 60 minutes. Makes 6 servings.

Beef Stew Bake

1½ pounds beef stew meat, cut in
    1-inch cubes
  2 tablespoons cooking oil
  1 10½-ounce can mushroom gravy
  1 cup tomato juice
  ½ cup water
  ½ envelope onion soup mix
    (¼ cup)
  1 teaspoon prepared horseradish
  4 medium potatoes,
    peeled and quartered
    (1¼ pounds)

In a heavy skillet brown meat in hot oil; drain off excess fat. Combine gravy, tomato juice, water, soup mix, and horseradish; stir into meat. Simmer, covered, 5 minutes.

Place potatoes in a 2-quart casserole. Top with meat mixture. Bake, covered, at 350° till meat and potatoes are tender, 1½ to 1¾ hours, stirring once or twice during baking. Makes 6 servings.

Zippy Mostaccioli

  1 pound beef chuck blade roast,
    cut in 1-inch cubes
  1 tablespoon shortening
  1 16-ounce can tomatoes, cut up
  2 carrots, halved lengthwise,
    then cut crosswise into
    1-inch pieces
  ½ cup sliced celery
  ½ cup coarsely chopped onion
1½ teaspoons salt
  1 teaspoon paprika
  ½ teaspoon chili powder
  ⅛ teaspoon pepper
1½ cups water
  3 ounces mostaccioli
    (1 cup)

In large skillet brown meat in hot shortening. Add undrained tomatoes, carrots, celery, onion, salt, paprika, chili powder, and pepper. Cover; cook over low heat 30 minutes.

Stir in water and uncooked mostaccioli. Bring to boiling. Turn into a 2-quart casserole. Bake, covered, at 350° till mostaccioli and meat are tender, 40 to 45 minutes, stirring occasionally. Makes 4 to 6 servings.

Layered Corned Beef Bake

  4 medium potatoes, peeled and
    sliced ¼ inch thick
    (4 cups)
  4 cups coarsely shredded
    cabbage
  3 tablespoons butter *or*
    margarine
  2 tablespoons all-purpose flour
  ¼ teaspoon salt
1¼ cups milk
  2 tablespoons Dijon-style
    mustard
  1 12-ounce can corned beef,
    chilled and sliced
    Paprika

Cook potato slices, covered, in large amount of boiling salted water till nearly tender, about 15 minutes. Add cabbage; cook 5 minutes more. Drain; set aside.

In saucepan melt butter; blend in flour and salt. Add milk all at once; cook and stir till thickened and bubbly. Remove from heat; stir in mustard. Add drained potatoes and cabbage; mix well.

Turn *half* of the vegetable mixture into a 2-quart casserole; top with corned beef slices. Spoon remaining vegetable mixture over all. Bake, covered, at 350° till casserole is heated through, 25 to 30 minutes. Sprinkle with paprika, if desired. Makes 6 servings.

Two-layered *Cheesy Hash-Spinach Pie* is tasty as well as thrifty. Lined with corned beef hash, the pastry boasts a colorful spinach, mushroom soup, cheese, and pimiento filling.

Cheesy Hash-Spinach Pie

Plain Pastry (see page 72)
2 **10-ounce packages frozen chopped spinach**
2 **beaten eggs**
1 **10¾-ounce can condensed cream of mushroom soup**
¼ **cup all-purpose flour**
1 **tablespoon prepared horseradish**
1 **teaspoon prepared mustard**
1 **15-ounce can corned beef hash**
1 **cup shredded American cheese (4 ounces)**
2 **tablespoons chopped pimiento**

Prepare Plain Pastry for a single-crust pie. Prick bottom and sides well with fork. Bake at 450° for 10 to 12 minutes. Remove from oven; reduce oven temperature to 350°.

Cook spinach according to package directions, *except* omit salt. Drain well, pressing out excess water. Combine eggs, mushroom soup, flour, horseradish, and mustard; stir in drained spinach.

Spread hash in baked pastry shell; spoon spinach mixture over. Bake, uncovered, at 350° for 45 minutes. Combine cheese and pimiento; sprinkle over pie. Bake 2 to 3 minutes longer. Let stand 5 minutes. Makes 6 servings.

Round Steak Louisiana

4   **medium sweet potatoes *or* yams, peeled and cut ¾ inch thick**
1   **large onion, sliced**
1   **medium green pepper, cut in wedges**
1½ **pounds beef round steak, cut about ¾ inch thick**
    Salt
2   **tablespoons cooking oil**
1   **clove garlic, minced**
3   **tablespoons all-purpose flour**
1   **16-ounce can tomatoes, cut up**
½   **cup beef broth**
1   **teaspoon sugar**
½   **teaspoon salt**
½   **teaspoon dried thyme, crushed**
⅛   **teaspoon pepper**
    Several dashes bottled hot pepper sauce

Layer sweet potato slices, onion slices, and green pepper wedges in a 2-quart casserole. Cut meat in 6 serving-size pieces; pound to about half the original thickness. Sprinkle with a little salt. In skillet quickly brown meat in hot oil. Transfer meat to casserole atop sweet potato mixture; reserve drippings in skillet.

Cook garlic in reserved drippings till tender but not brown. Blend in flour. Add undrained tomatoes, beef broth, sugar, the ½ teaspoon salt, thyme, pepper, and hot pepper sauce. Cook and stir till thickened and bubbly; pour over meat and vegetables in casserole.

Bake, covered, at 350° till meat and vegetables are tender, about 1½ hours; occasionally spoon sauce over meat and vegetables. Makes 6 servings.

Stuffed Cabbage Rolls

1   **beaten egg**
½   **cup milk**
¼   **cup finely chopped onion**
1   **teaspoon Worcestershire sauce**
¾   **teaspoon salt**
    Dash pepper
1   **pound ground beef *or***
    ½ pound ground beef and ½ pound ground pork
¾   **cup cooked rice**
6   **large *or* 12 medium cabbage leaves**
1   **10¾-ounce can condensed tomato soup**
1   **tablespoon brown sugar**
1   **tablespoon lemon juice**

In mixing bowl combine egg, milk, onion, Worcestershire sauce, salt, and pepper; mix well. Add ground meat and cooked rice; mix thoroughly.

Remove center vein of cabbage leaves, keeping each leaf in one piece. Immerse leaves in boiling water till limp, about 3 minutes; drain. Place ½ cup meat mixture on each large leaf *or* ¼ cup mixture on each medium leaf; fold in sides. Starting at unfolded edge, roll up each leaf making sure folded sides are included in roll. Arrange in a 12x7½x2-inch baking dish.

Stir together condensed tomato soup, brown sugar, and lemon juice; pour sauce mixture over cabbage rolls. Bake, uncovered, at 350° for 1¼ hours, basting once or twice with sauce. Makes 6 servings.

Oven-Baked Beef-Lima Stew

1   **cup large dry lima beans**
¼   **cup all-purpose flour**
1   **8-ounce can tomatoes, cut up**
1   **cup sliced celery**
1   **cup sliced carrot**
½   **cup chopped onion**
1½ **teaspoons salt**
¼   **teaspoon Worcestershire sauce**
1   **bay leaf**
1   **pound ground beef**

Place beans in a large saucepan or Dutch oven; add 4½ cups water. Soak overnight. (Or, bring beans to boiling; reduce heat and simmer 2 minutes. Remove from heat; cover and let stand 1 hour.) *Do not drain.* Blend ½ cup cold water slowly into flour; stir into beans. Cook and stir till bubbly.

Stir in undrained tomatoes, celery, carrot, onion, salt, Worcestershire, and bay leaf. Crumble ground beef into beans. Bring mixture to boiling. (If desired, turn into a 2½-quart casserole.) Bake, covered, at 350° for about 1½ hours, stirring occasionally.

Discard bay leaf. Skim off fat. Season to taste with additional salt and pepper. Makes 6 servings.

Hamburger Pie

1 **pound ground beef**
½ **cup chopped onion**
1 **15½-ounce can cut green
   beans, drained**
1 **10¾-ounce can condensed
   tomato soup**
¼ **cup water**
¾ **teaspoon salt**
⅛ **teaspoon pepper**
3 **medium potatoes, peeled and
   quartered (1 pound)***
1 **beaten egg
   Milk**
½ **cup shredded American cheese
   (2 ounces)**

In large skillet cook meat and onion till meat is lightly browned and onion is tender; drain off fat. Stir in green beans, tomato soup, water, salt, and pepper; turn mixture into a 1½-quart casserole.

Cook potatoes in boiling salted water till tender, about 20 minutes; drain. Mash potatoes while hot; blend in egg. Add enough milk to make potatoes fluffy, yet stiff enough to hold their shape. Season to taste with salt and pepper.

Drop potatoes in mounds atop meat mixture. Sprinkle with cheese. Bake, uncovered, at 350° till heated through, 25 to 30 minutes. Makes 4 to 6 servings.

*Or prepare packaged instant mashed potatoes (enough for 4 servings) according to package directions, *except* omit the milk. Add 1 beaten egg; stir in a little milk, if necessary, to make potatoes fluffy, yet stiff enough to hold their shape. Season to taste with salt and pepper.

Spaghetti Pie

6 **ounces spaghetti**
2 **tablespoons butter *or*
   margarine**
2 **beaten eggs**
⅓ **cup grated Parmesan cheese**
1 **cup cream-style cottage cheese
   (8 ounces)**
1 **pound ground beef *or* bulk
   pork sausage**
½ **cup chopped onion**
¼ **cup chopped green pepper**
1 **8-ounce can tomatoes, cut up**
1 **6-ounce can tomato paste**
1 **teaspoon sugar**
1 **teaspoon dried oregano,
   crushed**
½ **teaspoon garlic salt**
½ **cup shredded mozzarella cheese
   (2 ounces)**

Cook spaghetti according to package directions; drain (should have about 3 cups). Stir butter or margarine into hot spaghetti; stir in beaten eggs and Parmesan cheese. Form spaghetti mixture into a "crust" in a greased 10-inch pie plate. Spread with cottage cheese.

In skillet cook ground meat, onion, and green pepper till meat is brown and vegetables are tender. Drain off fat. Stir in undrained tomatoes, tomato paste, sugar, oregano, and garlic salt; heat through.

Turn meat mixture into spaghetti crust. Bake, uncovered, at 350° for 20 minutes. Sprinkle with mozzarella cheese; bake till melted, about 5 minutes. Makes 6 servings.

Containers for Casseroles

The wrong baking container can ruin a good casserole. So, for best results, use the dish the recipe recommends. If you do substitute, remember that food may bubble over if baked in too small a dish; if the container is too large, food can dry out. Also keep in mind that food prepared in a deep casserole requires more cooking time than that cooked in a shallower one.

A *baking dish* is shallow and usually square or rectangular. To determine its dimensions, measure across the top from the inside edges. When you need a cover, use foil.

A *casserole* is deeper and often has a fitted cover. To find its volume, fill to the top with water, measuring as you fill.

Herb-seasoned stuffing mix makes a crispy coating for perch fillets in *Fish and Chip Bake.* The fish bakes atop a bed of instant mashed potatoes, chopped spinach, and sour cream.

Fish and Chip Bake

Packaged instant mashed
   potatoes (enough for
   4 servings)
1 10-ounce package frozen
   chopped spinach, cooked
   and well drained
½ cup dairy sour cream
   Dash pepper
1 16-ounce package frozen
   perch fillets,
   thawed
¼ cup milk
½ cup herb-seasoned
   stuffing mix,
   crushed
2 tablespoons butter *or*
   margarine, melted
   Lemon slices

Prepare potatoes according to package directions, *except* reduce water by ¼ cup. Stir in drained spinach, sour cream, and pepper. Turn into a 10x6x2-inch baking dish.

Skin fish fillets. Dip one side of each fillet in milk, then in crushed stuffing mix. Fold fillets in half, coating side out. Place atop potato mixture; drizzle with melted butter. Bake, uncovered, at 350° till fish flakes easily when tested with a fork, 30 to 35 minutes. Serve with lemon slices. Makes 4 or 5 servings.

Clam Chowder Pie

2 cups chopped potato
¼ cup chopped onion
2 7½-ounce cans minced clams
2 tablespoons butter
2 tablespoons snipped parsley
4 teaspoons all-purpose flour
¼ teaspoon salt
Dash pepper
¾ cup milk
Plain Pastry (see page 72)

Cook potato and onion in 1 cup water till tender; drain. Drain clams, reserving ½ cup liquid. In saucepan melt butter; stir in parsley, flour, salt, and dash pepper. Add reserved clam liquid and milk all at once; cook and stir till thickened and bubbly. Stir in cooked potato mixture and clams. Turn into a 9-inch pie plate.

Prepare Plain Pastry. Roll out to a 10-inch circle; place atop filling. Turn edges under and flute; cut slits for escape of steam. Bake, uncovered, at 425° for 25 to 30 minutes. Let stand 5 minutes before serving. Makes 6 servings.

Shaker Fish Pie

1 pound fresh *or* frozen fish
Plain Pastry (see page 72)
1 cup chopped onion
½ cup chopped celery
3 tablespoons butter
1 tablespoon snipped parsley
½ teaspoon dried marjoram,
   crushed
2 tablespoons all-purpose flour
1 teaspoon salt
Dash pepper
1 cup light cream
⅓ cup fine dry bread crumbs
2 tablespoons butter, melted

Thaw frozen fish. Cook the fish in boiling salted water to cover till fish flakes easily when tested with a fork. Drain; break fish into chunks.

Prepare Plain Pastry for a single-crust pie. Do not prick. Bake pastry shell at 450° for 15 minutes. Remove from oven; set aside. Reduce oven temperature to 325°.

Meanwhile, cook onion and celery in the 3 tablespoons butter till onion is tender. Stir in parsley and marjoram. Blend in flour, salt, and pepper. Add cream; cook and stir till thickened and bubbly. Remove from heat; stir in fish. Turn mixture into partially baked 9-inch pastry shell.

Toss together bread crumbs and melted butter; sprinkle over pie. Bake, uncovered, at 325° for 30 to 35 minutes. Let stand 5 minutes. Makes 6 servings.

Tuna-Noodle Casserole

6 cups water
1 8-ounce package frozen noodles
1 cup chopped celery
¼ cup chopped onion
2 tablespoons butter *or*
   margarine
2 tablespoons all-purpose flour
1 11-ounce can condensed
   Cheddar cheese soup
¾ cup milk
1 9¼-ounce can tuna, drained
   and flaked
¼ cup chopped pimiento
¼ cup thinly sliced pitted ripe
   olives
¼ cup grated Parmesan cheese

In saucepan bring water to boiling; add frozen noodles, stirring till separated. Boil rapidly till tender, 15 to 20 minutes. Drain and set aside.

Meanwhile, in saucepan cook celery and onion in butter till tender. Blend in flour; stir in cheese soup. Gradually stir in milk. Cook and stir till thickened and bubbly. Stir in tuna, pimiento, olives, and cooked noodles.

Turn into a 2-quart casserole; top with Parmesan. Bake, uncovered, at 375° for 25 minutes. Makes 6 servings.

Microwave cooking directions: On range top cook and drain noodles as directed above. Meanwhile, in a 1½-quart nonmetal casserole cook celery and onion in butter, covered, in a countertop microwave oven till tender, 3½ to 4 minutes, stirring twice. Blend in flour; stir in soup and milk.

Micro-cook, uncovered, till thickened and bubbly, about 4 minutes, stirring after each minute. Fold in tuna, pimiento, and cooked noodles. Micro-cook, uncovered, till heated through, 3 to 4 minutes, stirring after 2 minutes. Stir; sprinkle with olives and Parmesan.

Tuna-Macaroni Casserole

  4 ounces small shell macaroni
  1 10¾-ounce can condensed
     cream of celery soup
  ⅓ cup milk
  ¼ cup mayonnaise *or* salad
     dressing
  ½ teaspoon dry mustard
  1 cup shredded American cheese
  1 6½- *or* 7-ounce can tuna,
     drained and flaked
  ¼ cup chopped pimiento
  ¼ cup fine dry bread crumbs
  1 tablespoon butter, melted
  ½ teaspoon paprika

Cook macaroni according to package directions; drain. In bowl blend together soup, milk, mayonnaise, and mustard. Stir in cheese, tuna, and pimiento. Gently fold in cooked macaroni. Turn into a 1½-quart casserole.

Combine crumbs, melted butter, and paprika; sprinkle atop casserole. Bake, uncovered, at 350° till heated through, 45 to 50 minutes. Garnish casserole with parsley sprig, if desired. Makes 4 or 5 servings.

Curried Seafood Bake

  3½ ounces elbow macaroni (1 cup)
  ¼ cup sliced green onion
     with tops
  ½ teaspoon curry powder
  3 tablespoons butter
  3 tablespoons all-purpose flour
  ½ teaspoon salt
  1¾ cups milk
  1 cup dairy sour cream
  1 5-ounce can lobster *or* one
     7½-ounce can crab meat,
     drained, flaked, and
     cartilage removed
  1 4½-ounce can shrimp, drained
  ½ cup coarsely crushed rich
     round crackers
  1 tablespoon butter, melted

Cook macaroni according to package directions; drain. Cook onion and curry in the 3 tablespoons butter till onion is tender. Stir in flour and salt. Add milk; cook and stir till thickened and bubbly. Remove from heat; stir in sour cream. Stir in macaroni and seafood. Turn into a 2-quart casserole. Mix crumbs and melted butter; sprinkle around edge. Bake, uncovered, at 350° for 30 minutes. Serves 4 to 6.

Microwave cooking directions: On range top cook macaroni according to package directions; drain. In a 2-quart nonmetal casserole cook onion and curry in the 3 tablespoons butter, covered, in a countertop microwave oven till onion is tender, about 2 minutes. Blend in flour and salt; stir in milk. Micro-cook, uncovered, 1½ minutes; stir. Micro-cook, uncovered, 3 minutes more, stirring after every minute. Stir in sour cream; gently stir in macaroni and seafood. Micro-cook, uncovered, till hot, about 7 minutes, stirring twice. Toss crumbs with melted butter; sprinkle atop.

Shrimp and Noodle Bake

  4 ounces wide noodles
  1 7-ounce package frozen
     shelled shrimp
  ¼ cup chopped onion
  3 tablespoons butter
  3 tablespoons all-purpose flour
  ½ teaspoon salt
  ½ teaspoon dried dillweed
  2 cups milk
  ⅓ cup grated Parmesan cheese
  ½ of a 3-ounce can French-fried
     onions

Cook noodles according to package directions; drain and set aside. Cook frozen shrimp according to package directions; drain and set aside.

In saucepan cook chopped onion in butter till tender but not brown. Stir in flour, salt, and dillweed. Add milk all at once; cook and stir till thickened and bubbly. Stir in Parmesan. Gently stir in cooked noodles and shrimp.

Turn mixture into a 1½-quart casserole. Bake, covered, at 350° till heated through, about 30 minutes. Sprinkle French-fried onions around edges of casserole. Bake, uncovered, 5 minutes longer. Garnish with a sprig of dill, if desired. Makes 5 or 6 servings.

Tuna-Macaroni Casserole, Curried Seafood Bake, and *Shrimp and Noodle Bake* go together in a jiffy with pull-from-the-shelf ingredients. These cupboard casseroles are great for busy families.

Macaroni and Cheese

6 ounces elbow macaroni
  (1½ cups)
3 tablespoons butter *or*
  margarine
¼ cup finely chopped onion
  (optional)
2 tablespoons all-purpose flour
½ teaspoon salt
  Dash pepper
2 cups milk
2 cups cubed sharp American
  cheese (8 ounces)
1 medium tomato, sliced
  Salt

Cook macaroni according to package directions; drain. In saucepan melt butter or margarine. If using onion, cook it in butter till tender but not brown. Blend in flour, the ½ teaspoon salt, and pepper. Add milk all at once; cook and stir till thickened and bubbly. Add cubed cheese to sauce; stir till melted.

Stir cheese sauce into macaroni. Turn mixture into a 1½-quart casserole. Sprinkle tomato slices with a little salt; arrange atop macaroni. Bake, uncovered, at 350° till heated through, 30 to 35 minutes. Makes 6 servings.

Classic Cheese Strata

8 slices day-old bread
6 ounces sharp American cheese
  or Swiss cheese, sliced
4 eggs
2½ cups milk
¼ cup finely chopped onion
1½ teaspoons salt
½ teaspoon prepared mustard
  Dash pepper
  Paprika

Trim crusts from *4 slices* of the bread. Cut trimmed slices in half diagonally to make 8 triangles; set aside. Arrange trimmings and remaining 4 slices untrimmed bread to cover bottom of a 9x9x2-inch baking pan.

Place cheese slices over bread in baking pan. Arrange the 8 bread triangles in 2 rows over cheese. (Points should slightly overlap bases of preceding triangles.)

Beat eggs; blend in milk, chopped onion, salt, mustard, and pepper. Pour over bread and cheese layers. Sprinkle with paprika. Cover and let stand 1 hour at room temperature or several hours in the refrigerator.

Bake, uncovered, at 325° till knife inserted off-center comes out clean, about 1 hour. Let stand 5 minutes before serving. Makes 6 servings.

Acapulco Bean Casserole

1 cup chopped celery
½ cup chopped onion
2 tablespoons butter *or*
  margarine
1 15-ounce can chili with beans
1 8¾-ounce can whole kernel
  corn, drained
2 3⅛-ounce cans jalapeño
  bean dip
1 4-ounce can taco sauce
⅛ teaspoon salt
6 corn tortillas, torn
½ cup shredded sharp American
  cheese *or* sharp Cheddar
  cheese (2 ounces)

In saucepan cook celery and onion in butter or margarine till tender, about 10 minutes. Stir in chili with beans, drained corn, bean dip, taco sauce, and salt.

Arrange *half* the torn tortillas in an 8x1½-inch round baking dish; top with *half* the chili mixture. Repeat layers using remaining torn tortillas and chili mixture.

Bake, covered, at 350° for 35 to 40 minutes. Sprinkle with shredded cheese. Bake, uncovered, till cheese melts, 2 to 3 minutes more. Makes 4 servings.

Microwave cooking directions: In glass bowl combine celery, onion, and butter. Cook, covered, in a countertop microwave oven till tender, about 5 minutes, stirring once. Stir in chili, corn, bean dip, taco sauce, and salt. Micro-cook, covered, till hot, 7 to 8 minutes, stirring twice.

Arrange *half* the torn tortillas in an 8x1½-inch round non-metal baking dish; top with *half* the chili mixture. Repeat layers using remaining torn tortillas and chili mixture.

Micro-cook, covered, till hot, about 4 minutes, giving dish a half turn after 2 minutes. Top with cheese.

How to Freeze Casseroles

Your freezer can be a big help to you in planning and preparing meals. First, it allows you to stock up on bargain-priced and in-season foods (freeze a batch of stew when stew meat is on sale, a zucchini casserole when zucchini's at its best). Second, it affords you the flexibility of making casseroles ahead (if you're serving one tonight, fix twice as much as you need and freeze the extra for that busy day when supper is the last thing you want to think about).

To prepare foods for freezing:
- Freeze most casseroles before baking, especially when all the ingredients are already cooked. Exceptions to this are dishes that contain uncooked rice, raw vegetables, or uncooked meat that has been frozen and thawed.
- Do not freeze mixtures containing hard-cooked egg whites, raw vegetables, mayonnaise, or sour cream.
- Undercook starchy ingredients such as beans, rice, and noodles, as they can become mushy when frozen. Potatoes become especially soft.
- Freeze casserole toppings separately to keep them from becoming soggy. Keep a supply of plain or buttered crumbs in the freezer to use on frozen casseroles.
- Do not freeze baked pastry; add fresh or frozen *unbaked* pastry during reheating.
- Season foods lightly before freezing, then add more when reheating. Cloves, pepper, garlic, and celery become stronger on freezing; onion, salt, and chili powder weaken.
- Freeze casseroles either in quantities just right for your family or in individual servings.

To freeze:
- Chill hot casseroles rapidly. Set pan of hot food in ice water; cool to room temperature. Wrap, label, and freeze.
- When possible, use shallow baking dishes to speed freezing and thawing of casseroles.
- Allow some headspace to permit expansion of food.
- Cover casseroles with moisture-vaporproof material such as freezer paper, heavy foil, plastic wrap, or a tight-fitting lid. Fix tape around the edges to make a tight seal. Label contents, number of servings, and date of freezing.
- One handy way to freeze a casserole is to line the dish with heavy foil, leaving a long overhang; prepare casserole as directed. Seal foil over food; freeze. When frozen, remove wrapped casserole from dish. Label and store in the freezer. Reheat in the same casserole dish.

To serve:
- Use frozen casseroles within 2 or 3 months for best quality.
- The size of the frozen casserole affects baking time. Shallow dishes and smaller quantities of food require less reheating time than deeper, larger casseroles.
- To reheat casserole without thawing, bake, uncovered, at 400° till heated through, 1 to 2 hours for most casseroles.
- To thaw casserole before reheating, let it stand overnight in the refrigerator. Then, cook as directed in the recipe, baking an additional 15 to 30 minutes.
- If gravies or sauces separate on freezing, stirring may help return them to their original consistency.

Step-Saving Combinations

Sour Cream-Chili Bake

1 pound ground beef
1 15-ounce can pinto beans, drained
1 10-ounce can hot enchilada sauce
1 8-ounce can tomato sauce
1 cup shredded sharp American cheese (4 ounces)
1 tablespoon instant minced onion
1 6-ounce package corn chips
1 cup dairy sour cream
½ cup shredded sharp American cheese (2 ounces)

In skillet brown ground beef; drain off fat. Stir in drained beans, enchilada sauce, tomato sauce, the 1 cup shredded cheese, and instant minced onion.

Set aside *1 cup* of the corn chips; coarsely crush remaining chips. Stir crushed chips into meat mixture. Turn into a 1½-quart casserole. Bake, covered, at 375° for 30 minutes.

Spoon sour cream atop casserole; sprinkle with the ½ cup cheese. Sprinkle reserved chips around edge of casserole. Bake, uncovered, 2 to 3 minutes. Makes 6 servings.

Enchilada Squares

1 pound ground beef
¼ cup chopped onion
4 eggs
1 8-ounce can tomato sauce
1 5⅓-ounce can evaporated milk (⅔ cup)
1 1½-ounce envelope enchilada sauce mix
⅓ cup sliced pitted ripe olives
2 cups corn chips
1 cup shredded Cheddar cheese (4 ounces)

In skillet cook beef and onion till meat is brown and onion is tender. Drain off fat. Spread meat mixture in a 10x6x2-inch baking dish.

Beat together eggs, tomato sauce, evaporated milk, and enchilada sauce mix; pour over meat. Sprinkle with olives; top with chips. Bake, uncovered, at 350° till set in center, 20 to 25 minutes. Sprinkle with cheese. Bake till cheese melts, 3 to 5 minutes. Makes 6 servings.

Meat and Potato Pie

1 package piecrust mix (for 2-crust pie)
½ cup milk
½ envelope onion soup mix (¼ cup)
Dash pepper
Dash ground allspice
1 pound ground beef
2 tablespoons snipped parsley
1 tablespoon butter *or* margarine, melted
½ teaspoon salt
1 12-ounce package frozen loose-pack hash brown potatoes, thawed (3 cups)
Warmed catsup

Prepare piecrust mix according to package directions; roll out for a 2-crust 9-inch pie. Line a 9-inch pie plate with *half* of the pastry. Set aside.

In bowl combine milk, dry onion soup mix, pepper, and allspice. Add ground beef; mix thoroughly. Lightly pat meat mixture into pastry-lined pie plate.

Combine parsley, melted butter, and salt; add thawed hash brown potatoes, stirring to coat. Spoon potatoes over meat mixture. Adjust top crust; seal and flute edges. Cut slits for escape of steam.

Bake, uncovered, at 350° till crust is golden, about 1 hour. Serve with warmed catsup. Makes 6 servings.

Quick-mix casseroles such as *Sour Cream-Chili Bake* make excellent use of convenience foods. To complete this speedy supper, thaw frozen avocado dip to spoon over a tossed salad.

Beef-Noodle Bake

4 **ounces medium noodles (3 cups)**
1 **pound ground beef**
½ **cup chopped onion**
¼ **cup chopped green pepper**
1 **15-ounce can tomato sauce**
½ **teaspoon seasoned salt**
¼ **teaspoon pepper**
2 **cups cream-style cottage cheese (16 ounces)**
1 **3-ounce package cream cheese, softened**

Cook noodles according to package directions; drain. In skillet cook beef, onion, and green pepper till meat is brown and vegetables are tender; drain off fat. Stir in tomato sauce, seasoned salt, and pepper.

Blend together cottage cheese and cream cheese till fluffy. Spoon the cooked noodles into a greased 10x6x2-inch baking dish. Spread cheese mixture over noodles; pour meat sauce over all. Bake, uncovered, at 350° till heated through, 30 to 40 minutes. Makes 6 servings.

Macaroni and Meatballs

2 **beaten eggs**
¾ **cup soft bread crumbs (1 slice)**
2 **tablespoons finely chopped onion**
2 **tablespoons finely chopped green pepper**
2 **tablespoons snipped parsley**
1 **teaspoon dried oregano, crushed**
¼ **teaspoon garlic salt**
1 **pound ground beef**
1 **7¼-ounce package macaroni and cheese dinner mix**
1 **2½-ounce envelope sour cream sauce mix**
2 **cups milk**

In medium bowl combine eggs, bread crumbs, onion, green pepper, parsley, ½ *teaspoon* of the oregano, garlic salt, and dash pepper. Add ground beef; mix well. Shape into 24 meatballs. Place in shallow baking pan. Bake, uncovered, at 375° for about 20 minutes.

Meanwhile, cook macaroni from dinner mix in boiling salted water according to package directions; drain. Combine dry cheese mix from packaged dinner, sour cream sauce mix, and the remaining ½ teaspoon oregano; beat in milk. Stir in cooked macaroni.

Turn mixture into a 12x7½x2-inch baking dish. Arrange meatballs atop. Bake, uncovered, at 375° till heated through, 20 to 25 minutes. Makes 6 servings.

Festive Hash and Eggs

1 **15-ounce can corned beef hash**
4 **eggs**
½ **cup milk**
½ **cup shredded Swiss cheese**
Paprika

Spread hash in 4 individual casseroles. Make a depression in each with back of spoon. Break *one* egg into each; do not season. Spoon *2 tablespoons* milk over each; top with cheese. Bake, uncovered, at 350° till almost set, 18 to 20 minutes. Top with paprika; let stand 5 minutes. Makes 4 servings.

Make Your Own Bread Crumbs

Soft crumbs: Tear slices of fresh bread into quarters. Place a few at a time in blender container; cover and blend till coarsely chopped. Or, tear bread into crumbs. Each slice makes about ¾ cup soft crumbs.
Fine dry crumbs: Oven-toast stale bread at 300° till crisp and dry. Crush with a rolling pin. Or, add to blender container a little at a time; cover and blend till finely crushed. Each slice makes about ¼ cup fine dry crumbs.
Buttered crumbs: Add 1 tablespoon melted butter to ¾ cup soft crumbs *or* ¼ cup fine dry crumbs; toss to combine.

Corned Beef-Macaroni Pie

3½ **ounces elbow macaroni (1 cup)**
1 **beaten egg**
1 **8-ounce can tomato sauce**
¼ **cup chopped onion**
½ **teaspoon prepared mustard**
½ **teaspoon prepared**
   horseradish
1 **12-ounce can corned beef,**
   finely flaked
¾ **cup shredded sharp American**
   cheese (3 ounces)
1 **beaten egg**
½ **teaspoon dried basil, crushed**
¾ **cup soft bread crumbs**
   (1 slice)
1 **tablespoon butter *or***
   margarine, melted

Cook macaroni in large amount of boiling *unsalted* water till tender, about 10 minutes; drain and set aside.

Meanwhile, combine 1 beaten egg, ¼ *cup* of the tomato sauce, onion, mustard, and horseradish. Add corned beef; mix well. Press mixture into bottom and sides of a 9-inch pie plate, forming a shell; set aside.

Combine cooked macaroni with shredded cheese, the remaining tomato sauce, 1 beaten egg, and basil. Turn mixture into the corned beef shell.

Toss bread crumbs with melted butter or margarine; sprinkle atop macaroni mixture. Bake, uncovered, at 350° till heated through, 25 to 30 minutes. Makes 6 servings.

Frank and Corn Crown

½ **cup chopped green pepper**
¼ **cup chopped onion**
2 **tablespoons butter *or***
   margarine
2¾ **cups soft bread crumbs**
   (about 4 slices)
1 **17-ounce can cream-style corn**
1 **12-ounce can whole kernel**
   corn, drained
2 **beaten eggs**
1 **teaspoon salt**
1 **tablespoon butter *or***
   margarine, melted
1 **pound frankfurters, halved**
   crosswise (8 to 10)

Cook green pepper and onion in the 2 tablespoons butter till tender but not brown. Add *2 cups* of the bread crumbs, cream-style corn, whole kernel corn, eggs, and salt; mix lightly. Spoon mixture into an 8x1½-inch round baking dish.

Combine the remaining ¾ cup bread crumbs and the 1 tablespoon melted butter or margarine; sprinkle atop corn mixture. Bake, uncovered, at 350° for 30 minutes.

Stand franks, cut end down, around edge of baking dish to form crown. Bake, uncovered, till franks are hot and knife inserted in corn mixture comes out clean, 10 to 15 minutes longer. Makes 5 or 6 servings.

Savory Frank-Noodle Bake

1 **cup medium noodles**
½ **cup chopped onion**
1 **tablespoon butter *or* margarine**
3 **beaten eggs**
1 **8-ounce can imitation sour**
   cream (1 cup)
½ **cup cream-style cottage**
   cheese
½ **pound frankfurters, thinly**
   sliced (4 or 5)
½ **teaspoon salt**
   Dash pepper
½ **cup cornflake crumbs**
1 **tablespoon butter *or***
   margarine, melted

Cook noodles according to package directions; drain. In small skillet cook onion in the 1 tablespoon butter or margarine till tender but not brown.

Combine eggs, imitation sour cream, cottage cheese, frankfurters, cooked onion, cooked noodles, salt, and pepper. Turn mixture into a 1-quart casserole.

Toss cornflake crumbs with the melted butter or margarine; sprinkle atop casserole. Bake, uncovered, at 350° till heated through, 40 to 45 minutes. Makes 4 servings.

Substantial *Salmon-Macaroni Pie* is an easy put-together that even young cooks can
master. This flavor-packed casserole features salmon, shredded cheese, and canned macaroni.

Salmon-Macaroni Pie

4 **beaten eggs**
2 **15-ounce cans macaroni in cheese sauce**
1 **16-ounce can salmon, drained, bones and skin removed, and broken into chunks**
1½ **cups soft bread crumbs (2 slices)**
1 **cup shredded sharp American cheese (4 ounces)**
¼ **teaspoon salt**

In large bowl stir together beaten eggs, macaroni in cheese sauce, salmon chunks, soft bread crumbs, shredded American cheese, and salt.

Turn mixture into a greased 10-inch oven-going skillet or a 10x6x2-inch baking dish. Bake, uncovered, at 350° till set in center, 40 to 45 minutes. Cut in wedges or squares; garnish each serving with a parsley sprig, if desired. Makes 6 to 8 servings.

Fish Florentine

6 **frozen breaded fish portions**
1 **10-ounce package frozen chopped spinach**
1 **10-ounce package frozen Welsh rarebit, thawed**
1 **5-ounce can water chestnuts, drained and chopped (½ cup)**
6 **slices bacon, crisp-cooked, drained, and crumbled**

Fry fish according to package directions. Meanwhile, cook spinach according to package directions; drain.

In medium saucepan stir together spinach, rarebit, water chestnuts, and bacon; heat through. Spread spinach mixture in a 10x6x2-inch baking dish. Top with fish portions.

Bake, uncovered at 350° till heated through, about 10 minutes. Garnish with lemon slices, if desired. Serves 6.

Tuna Salad Bake (pictured on page 66)

1 **package refrigerated crescent rolls (8 rolls)**
1 **9¼-ounce can tuna, drained and flaked**
½ **cup chopped celery**
¼ **cup green goddess salad dressing**
2 **cups chopped lettuce**
2 **medium tomatoes, sliced**
4 **slices American cheese, halved diagonally (4 ounces)**

Unroll dough and separate into 8 triangles. Place in a greased 9-inch pie plate, pressing edges together to form a pie shell. Bake, uncovered, at 350° for 10 minutes.

Meanwhile, toss tuna and celery with salad dressing; spread mixture over partially baked shell. Sprinkle with chopped lettuce; arrange tomato slices atop. Bake, uncovered, 10 minutes longer. Top with cheese halves; bake 10 minutes more. Makes 6 servings.

Tuna-Rice Soufflé

1 **10 ¾-ounce can condensed cream of mushroom soup**
1 **6½- or 7-ounce can tuna, drained and flaked**
1 **cup cooked rice**
¼ **cup chopped pimiento**
2 **tablespoons snipped parsley**
4 **eggs, separated**

In saucepan heat and stir condensed soup. Stir in tuna, cooked rice, pimiento, and parsley; heat through.

Beat egg whites to stiff peaks; set aside. Beat yolks till thick and lemon-colored; slowly stir in tuna mixture. Fold into beaten egg whites; turn into an ungreased 2-quart soufflé dish. Bake, uncovered, at 350° till set in center, 30 to 35 minutes. Serve immediately with a cheese sauce, if desired. Makes 6 servings.

Creamy Chicken Casserole

3½ ounces elbow macaroni (1 cup)
¾ cup milk
1 10¾-ounce can condensed cream of chicken soup
2 cups chopped cooked chicken
1 cup shredded sharp American cheese (4 ounces)
1 4-ounce can mushroom stems and pieces, drained
¼ cup chopped pimiento

Cook macaroni according to package directions; drain. In a bowl stir milk into soup. Add chicken, *half* the cheese, the mushrooms, pimiento, and cooked macaroni; mix well.

Turn mixture into a 2-quart casserole. Bake, covered, at 350° for 50 minutes. Uncover and stir. Top with the remaining cheese; bake till cheese melts, 2 to 3 minutes longer. Makes 6 servings.

Deep-Dish Chicken Pie

1 cup packaged biscuit mix
½ teaspoon dried sage, crushed
1 10½-ounce can chicken gravy
1 4-ounce can mushroom stems and pieces, drained
2 tablespoons sliced pimiento-stuffed green olives
Dash pepper
2 5-ounce cans boned chicken

In bowl combine biscuit mix and sage. Prepare biscuit dough according to package directions for biscuits, *except* substitute ¼ cup of the chicken gravy for the liquid. Roll out on waxed paper to an 8-inch circle; set aside.

In saucepan combine remaining gravy with mushrooms, olives, and pepper; stir in chicken with its broth. Bring to boiling; turn into an 8x1½-inch round baking dish. Invert dough onto *hot* sauce; remove paper. Bake, uncovered, at 450° till topper is done, 12 to 15 minutes. Makes 6 servings.

Maple-Glazed Meat and Beans

1 12-ounce can luncheon meat
¼ cup maple-flavored syrup
1 21-ounce can pork and beans in tomato sauce
¼ cup finely chopped onion
1 tablespoon all-purpose flour
1 teaspoon prepared mustard
¼ cup shredded sharp American cheese (1 ounce)

Cut luncheon meat into 8 slices; brush each slice with some of the syrup, reserving remaining syrup. Arrange meat around edge of a 9-inch pie plate, overlapping slightly.

In saucepan combine beans, the remaining syrup, onion, flour, and mustard. Cook and stir till thickened and bubbly; pour boiling bean mixture into pie plate. Sprinkle with cheese. Bake, uncovered, at 350° till meat is lightly browned, about 20 minutes. Makes 4 servings.

How to Make Croutons

Brush bread slices lightly with oil or melted butter, if desired. Cut into ½-inch cubes. For seasoned croutons, sprinkle with garlic powder or crushed dried herbs.

In the oven: Spread bread cubes in a shallow baking pan. Bake at 300° till dry, 20 to 25 minutes, stirring once.

In the microwave oven: Spread bread cubes in a shallow baking dish. Micro-cook, uncovered, till crisp and dry, about 6 minutes for 4 cups croutons; stir every 2 minutes.

Cheese croutons: Make croutons, using butter or margarine. Sprinkle with grated Parmesan cheese while hot; cool.

You'll save double the time when you make *Pork and Apples with Stuffing* and freeze half to serve later. For a quick garnish, poach apple slices two minutes in a little water.

Pork and Apples with Stuffing

3 **pounds pork tenderloin**
2 **tablespoons cooking oil**
2 **20-ounce cans pie-sliced apples, drained**
½ **cup packed brown sugar**
6 **cups herb-seasoned stuffing mix**
½ **cup chopped celery**
¼ **cup butter *or* margarine, melted**
3 **tablespoons instant minced onion**
1 **teaspoon salt**
½ **teaspoon ground sage**
2 **cups beef broth**

Have your meatman cut the pork tenderloin into 12 slices and flatten each slice. Sprinkle meat slices with a little salt and pepper. In a skillet brown meat well on both sides in hot cooking oil. Divide the pork tenderloin slices between two 12x7½x2-inch baking dishes.

Combine apples and brown sugar. Spoon over tenderloin slices. Combine stuffing mix, celery, melted butter or margarine, onion, salt, and sage; toss with beef broth till moistened. Press stuffing into ½ cup measure; unmold a stuffing mound onto each tenderloin slice.

Bake, uncovered, at 375° till pork is done, about 1 hour. Garnish with parsley and poached fresh apple slices, if desired. Makes 2 casseroles, 6 servings each.

To freeze: Omit baking casseroles; wrap securely, label, and freeze. Bake frozen casseroles, covered, at 400° till pork is done, about 1¼ hours.

Sauerkraut and Sausage Bake

1½ **pounds bulk pork sausage**
  1 **27-ounce can sauerkraut,
    rinsed, drained, and snipped**
  1 **tablespoon sliced green onion
    with tops
    Packaged instant mashed
    potatoes (enough for
    4 servings)**
  4 **tablespoons grated Parmesan
    cheese**

In skillet brown sausage; drain off fat. Stir together sauerkraut and green onion; turn into a 1½-quart casserole. Spoon sausage over sauerkraut mixture.

Prepare mashed potatoes according to package directions. Stir 2 *tablespoons* of the cheese into potatoes. Spread potatoes over sausage; sprinkle with remaining 2 tablespoons cheese. Bake, uncovered, at 400° till heated through, 35 to 40 minutes. Makes 6 servings.

Red-Ribbon Cheese Casserole

  1 **7-ounce package macaroni
    (2 cups)**
  1 **10¾-ounce can condensed
    tomato soup**
  1 **10¾-ounce can condensed
    cream of chicken soup**
  ½ **cup milk**
  8 **slices American cheese
    (8 ounces)**
  7 **tomato slices**
1½ **cups soft bread crumbs
    (2 slices)**
  2 **tablespoons butter *or*
    margarine, melted**

Cook macaroni according to package directions; drain. Stir together soups and milk; stir in cooked macaroni.

Turn mixture into a 12x7½x2-inch baking dish. Alternate cheese and tomato slices down center of casserole. Toss crumbs with melted butter; sprinkle atop. Bake, uncovered, at 350° for 30 minutes. Serves 6 to 8.

Triple-Cheese Pie

  1 **package piecrust mix
    (for 2-crust pie)**
  ¼ **cup all-purpose flour**
  1 **egg yolk**
1½ **cups dry cottage cheese
    (12 ounces)**
  3 **eggs**
  ⅓ **cup grated Parmesan cheese**
  ⅛ **teaspoon pepper**
  1 **cup finely chopped fully
    cooked ham**
  1 **4-ounce can mushroom stems
    and pieces, drained**
  1 **6-ounce package sliced
    mozzarella cheese**

Combine piecrust mix and flour; stir in water according to package directions. Roll out *half* the dough; fit into a 10-inch pie plate. Flute edges. Combine egg yolk and 1 tablespoon water; brush *half* the mixture over pastry shell. Prick lightly with a fork. Roll out remaining pastry dough to an 8½-inch circle. Cut into 6 wedges; place on an ungreased baking sheet. Bake pastry shell and wedges at 450° till lightly browned, 8 to 10 minutes. Remove from oven; reduce oven temperature to 375°.

In mixing bowl beat dry cottage cheese, eggs, Parmesan cheese, and pepper at medium speed of electric mixer till fluffy, 3 to 4 minutes. Stir in ham and mushrooms.

Arrange *half* the mozzarella cheese slices in baked pastry shell; pour *half* the ham mixture over cheese-lined pastry. Repeat layers.

Place pastry wedges atop pie. Brush wedges with remaining egg yolk mixture. Bake, uncovered, at 375° till set, about 35 minutes. (Center will look slightly watery.) Let stand 10 minutes before serving. Makes 6 servings.

Microwave Know-How

Your microwave oven can save you plenty of time when you prepare casseroles, regardless of whether you use the conventional or the microwave oven for the final heating. It's ideal for melting butter or margarine, cooking onion in butter, cooking ground beef or bacon, and preparing sauces.

Use the timings in the chart below to help make meal preparation easy. And read the information at the bottom of the page for help in choosing containers and timing recipes. Then, check the index to find several recipes with complete microwave directions as well as conventional methods.

Step	Amount	Special Directions	Cooking Time
Melt butter	2 tablespoons	Uncovered	30 to 40 seconds
Toast nuts	¼ cup	Use shallow dish; stir frequently	3 minutes

Cook onions in
  butter or oil
	½ cup chopped onion
	1 tablespoon butter
	  or cooking oil
		Cover; stir once	2 to 3 minutes

Cook ground beef	1 pound	Crumble into bowl; cover; stir several times	5 minutes

Cook bacon	4 slices	Cook between layers
		  of paper toweling
		  in a shallow dish
			2½ to 3½ minutes

Make white sauce	2 tablespoons butter	Melt butter	30 to 40 seconds
	2 tablespoons flour ¼ teaspoon salt 1 cup milk	Stir in flour and salt; then stir in milk	1 minute
		Stir every 30 seconds till thickened	2 to 3 minutes

Special Helps

Use heat-resistant glass and glass-ceramic containers—no metals—in the microwave oven. For short-time cooking you can cook on paper or in plastic dishes. To cover casseroles, use a fitted lid, waxed paper, or a dinner plate.

Because so many variables enter into microwave cooking, times given here are only approximate. For this book, recipes were tested at the high power setting of countertop microwave ovens rated at 600 to 700 watts. If yours has a lower wattage, expect to increase the cooking time. For an oven with a higher wattage, shorten the cooking time.

Other factors such as the starting temperature, the shape, and the amount of food in the oven can affect the timing, too, so be sure to watch the food carefully.

Make the Most of Leftovers

Ham-Potato Bake

2 15- or 16-ounce cans sliced
    potatoes, drained, *or* 4 cups
    sliced cooked potatoes
2 medium carrots, shredded
    (1 cup)
1½ cups cubed fully cooked ham
1 10¾-ounce can condensed
    cream of mushroom soup
½ cup shredded sharp American
    cheese (2 ounces)
¼ cup milk
1 tablespoon instant minced
    onion
⅛ teaspoon pepper
¾ cup soft bread crumbs
    (1 slice)
½ cup shredded sharp American
    cheese (2 ounces)
1 tablespoon butter *or*
    margarine, melted

Layer *half* the potatoes and *half* the carrots in a 2-quart casserole. Stir together cubed ham, condensed mushroom soup, the ½ cup shredded cheese, milk, instant minced onion, and pepper. Pour *half* the ham mixture over potatoes and carrots in casserole. Repeat layers.

Combine soft bread crumbs, the ½ cup shredded cheese, and melted butter; sprinkle over casserole. Bake, uncovered, at 350° till heated through, about 45 minutes. Garnish with parsley sprigs, if desired. Makes 4 to 6 servings.

Ham and Vegetables Mornay

2¼ pounds potatoes,
    peeled and cut up
    (7 medium)
1 beaten egg *or*
    2 beaten egg yolks
2 tablespoons snipped chives
    or sliced green onion
    with tops
    Paprika
1 10-ounce package frozen mixed
    vegetables *or* 2 cups
    leftover cooked vegetables
3 tablespoons butter *or*
    margarine
3 tablespoons all-purpose
    flour
½ teaspoon salt
⅛ teaspoon white pepper
⅛ teaspoon ground nutmeg
1½ cups milk
½ cup shredded Swiss cheese
    (2 ounces)
1 tablespoon grated Parmesan
    cheese
2 cups cubed fully cooked ham
1 tablespoon butter *or*
    margarine, melted

In saucepan cook potatoes in boiling salted water to cover till tender, 15 to 20 minutes; drain. Mash with potato masher or electric mixer on lowest speed. Stir beaten egg or egg yolks and chives or green onion into potatoes; season to taste with a little salt and pepper. Spread potato mixture on bottom and sides of a 2-quart casserole to form a shell; sprinkle top edges with paprika.

Cook frozen mixed vegetables according to package directions; drain and set aside.

In saucepan melt the 3 tablespoons butter or margarine; blend in flour, salt, white pepper, and nutmeg. Add milk all at once. Cook and stir till thickened and bubbly. Add Swiss and Parmesan cheeses; stir till melted. Stir in cubed ham and cooked vegetables.

Spoon sauce mixture into potato-lined casserole, being sure mixture is below edge of potato shell. Brush exposed surface of potatoes with the melted butter.

Bake, uncovered, at 375° till mixture is heated through and potatoes are lightly browned, 30 to 35 minutes. Makes 6 to 8 servings.

Next time you plan a ham dinner, buy enough extra to prepare *Ham-Potato Bake.* Sprinkled with cheesy bread crumbs, this delicious casserole makes the most of leftover ham and potatoes.

Ham Pot Pie

½ **cup chopped onion**
3 **tablespoons butter *or*
    margarine**
⅓ **cup all-purpose flour**
½ **teaspoon dried basil, crushed**
¼ **teaspoon salt**
2¼ **cups milk**
2 **to 3 cups cubed fully cooked
    ham**
1½ **to 2 cups cooked *or* canned
    cut green beans**
1½ **to 2 cups cooked *or* canned
    whole kernel corn**
2 **tablespoons snipped parsley
    Plain Pastry (see page 72)**

In saucepan cook onion in butter or margarine till tender but not brown. Stir in flour, basil, and salt. Add milk all at once; cook and stir till thickened and bubbly.

Add ham, green beans, corn, and parsley to sauce; mix well. Turn mixture into a 12x7½x2-inch baking dish. Bake, uncovered, at 350° till hot, 35 to 40 minutes.

Meanwhile, prepare Plain Pastry. Roll out ¼ inch thick. Cut into wedges or other shapes. Place cutouts on baking sheet; prick well with a fork. Place baking sheet in oven with casserole the last 20 to 25 minutes. Bake till pastry is golden brown. Arrange the baked pastry cutouts atop casserole. Makes 6 servings.

Stuffed Pepper Cups

1 **10½-ounce can condensed
    beef broth**
1 **soup can water (1¼ cups)**
1 **cup regular rice**
½ **teaspoon salt**
6 **large green peppers**
½ **cup finely chopped onion**
¼ **cup chopped celery**
2 **tablespoons butter *or*
    margarine**
1½ **cups chopped fully cooked ham**
¾ **cup soft bread crumbs
    (1 slice)**
1 **tablespoon butter *or*
    margarine, melted**

In saucepan bring first 4 ingredients to boiling; stir. Cover; cook slowly till rice is done, 15 to 20 minutes.

Cut tops from peppers; discard seeds and membranes. Chop tops; set aside. Cook peppers in boiling salted water for 5 minutes; drain. Arrange in a 12x7½x2-inch baking dish.

Cook onion, celery, and chopped pepper in the 2 tablespoons butter; stir in ham. Toss with rice; spoon into peppers. Mix crumbs and the melted butter; sprinkle atop peppers. Bake, uncovered, at 350° for 20 to 25 minutes. Serves 6.

Microwave cooking directions: On range top cook first 4 ingredients as directed above.

Cut tops from peppers; discard seeds and membranes. Chop tops; set aside. Place peppers in a 12x7½x2-inch non-metal baking dish; sprinkle insides with salt. Cook, covered, in a countertop microwave oven till nearly tender, about 7 minutes, giving dish a half turn after 4 minutes.

In glass bowl micro-cook onion, celery, and the chopped pepper, covered, in the 2 tablespoons butter for 2 to 3 minutes. Stir in ham; toss with rice. Spoon into peppers. Combine crumbs and the melted butter; sprinkle atop peppers. Micro-cook, uncovered, for 8 to 10 minutes, giving dish a half turn after 4 minutes.

Fruit and Vegetable Garnishes

The most colorful garnish you'll find for a casserole may be an ingredient in the dish itself. Save a few cooked carrot or olive slices, mushrooms, or snipped parsley to sprinkle over the casserole just before serving. Or, slice an extra tomato or green pepper to arrange atop the dish during the last few minutes of baking.

Slices of lemon or avocado perk up a seafood casserole, while pineapple or poached apple slices complement ham and pork dishes. Use your imagination and the available produce to create casseroles that look as good as they taste.

Cranberry-Pork Bake

1 8-ounce can whole cranberry
  sauce
2 tablespoons light corn
  syrup
1 17-ounce can sweet potatoes,
  drained
2 tablespoons butter *or*
  margarine, melted
1 tablespoon brown sugar
1 teaspoon salt
¼ teaspoon ground ginger
2 cups coarsely chopped cooked
  pork

Stir together cranberry sauce and corn syrup; set aside. In mixing bowl beat together sweet potatoes, melted butter, brown sugar, salt, and ginger with electric mixer till well blended. Stir in chopped pork.

Turn sweet potato mixture into a 1-quart casserole. Bake, uncovered, at 350° for 35 minutes. Spread cranberry sauce mixture over top; return to oven till heated through, 5 to 10 minutes longer. Makes 4 servings.

Pork Florentine

2 10-ounce packages frozen
  chopped spinach
1 10¾-ounce can condensed
  cream of chicken soup
¼ cup shredded Swiss cheese
  (1 ounce)
2 tablespoons mayonnaise
  or salad dressing
1 teaspoon lemon juice
½ teaspoon Worcestershire
  sauce
1½ cups chopped cooked pork
1½ cups soft bread crumbs
  (2 slices)
2 tablespoons butter *or*
  margarine, melted

Cook spinach according to package directions, *except* use unsalted water; drain. In saucepan stir together condensed soup, Swiss cheese, mayonnaise, lemon juice, and Worcestershire sauce; bring to boiling. Stir ¾ *cup* of the soup mixture into drained spinach.

Pat spinach mixture into 6 individual casseroles. Sprinkle chopped pork over spinach in casseroles. Spoon remaining soup mixture over all.

Toss together bread crumbs and melted butter or margarine; sprinkle atop casseroles. Bake, uncovered, at 350° till heated through, about 25 minutes. Makes 6 servings.

Apple and Pork Casserole

¼ cup chopped onion
1 tablespoon shortening
1 10½-ounce can chicken
  gravy
3 tablespoons brown sugar
¼ teaspoon ground cinnamon
3 cups cubed cooked pork
2 tart apples, peeled
  and chopped
  Packaged instant mashed
  potatoes (enough for
  4 servings)
¼ cup milk
  Dash pepper
1 beaten egg
½ cup shredded American
  cheese (2 ounces)

In saucepan cook onion in shortening till tender. Stir in gravy, sugar, and cinnamon. Add pork and apples; mix well. Spoon mixture into a 8x1½-inch round baking dish.

Prepare potatoes according to package directions, *except* use ¼ cup milk and dash pepper. Blend egg into potatoes. Spoon potatoes in 6 mounds atop pork mixture.

Bake, uncovered, at 350° for 25 minutes. Sprinkle with shredded cheese; return to oven till cheese melts, about 5 minutes longer. Makes 6 servings.

The family won't mind eating last night's roast beef when you prepare spicy *Beef-Macaroni Italiano.* This popular casserole will find its way into your meal plans frequently.

Beef-Macaroni Italiano

¾ **cup elbow macaroni**
1 **tablespoon butter *or* margarine**
2 **tablespoons all-purpose flour**
1 **16-ounce can stewed tomatoes, cut up**
1 **8-ounce can tomato sauce**
¼ **cup dry red wine**
½ **envelope onion soup mix (¼ cup)**
½ **teaspoon dried oregano, crushed**
¼ **teaspoon salt**
   Dash pepper
2 **cups cubed cooked beef**
½ **cup shredded mozzarella cheese (2 ounces)**
   Green pepper rings

Cook macaroni according to package directions; drain. In saucepan melt butter; blend in flour. Stir in undrained stewed tomatoes, tomato sauce, red wine, onion soup mix, oregano, salt, and pepper. Cook and stir till thickened and bubbly. Stir in cubed beef and cooked macaroni.

Spoon mixture into a 1½-quart casserole. Bake, uncovered, at 350° for 20 minutes. Sprinkle with cheese; top with green pepper rings. Return to oven till cheese melts, about 5 minutes more. Makes 4 or 5 servings.

Beefy Onion Pie

2 recipes Plain Pastry
    (see page 72)
1½ cups thinly sliced onion
    (3 medium)
¼ cup chopped green pepper
¼ cup butter *or* margarine
2 cups chopped cooked beef
1 cup dairy sour cream
2 tablespoons all-purpose flour
¾ teaspoon salt
⅛ teaspoon pepper
1 beaten egg
2 tablespoons snipped parsley
2 tablespoons chopped pimiento

Prepare Plain Pastry for a double-crust pie. Set aside. In skillet cook onion and green pepper in butter till tender. Stir in beef; remove from heat. Combine sour cream, flour, salt, and pepper; blend in egg, parsley, and pimiento. Stir into onion-beef mixture; mix well.

Turn beef mixture into pastry-lined 9-inch pie plate. Adjust top crust. Seal and flute edges; cut slits for escape of steam. Bake, uncovered, at 375° till crust is golden, about 40 minutes. Makes 6 servings.

Oven Beef Hash

2 cups finely chopped
    cooked potato
1 13-ounce can evaporated milk
1½ cups finely chopped
    cooked beef
1¼ cups finely crushed rich
    round crackers
    (about 30 crackers)
½ cup shredded carrot
⅓ cup finely chopped onion
⅓ cup snipped parsley
1 tablespoon Worcestershire
    sauce
¾ teaspoon salt
⅛ teaspoon pepper
⅛ teaspoon dried oregano,
    crushed
1 tablespoon butter *or*
    margarine, melted

Lightly stir together potato, evaporated milk, beef, *1 cup* of the crushed crackers, carrot, onion, parsley, Worcestershire sauce, salt, pepper, and oregano. Turn mixture into a 1½-quart casserole.

Combine remaining ¼ cup cracker crumbs and melted butter; sprinkle atop casserole. Bake, covered, at 350° till heated through, 35 to 40 minutes. Makes 4 to 6 servings.

Mexican-Style Hash

2 cups chopped cooked beef
⅓ cup chopped onion
2 tablespoons shortening
1½ cups finely chopped raw
    potato
1 12-ounce can whole kernel
    corn, drained
1 10¾-ounce can condensed
    tomato soup
1½ teaspoons chili powder

In 10-inch oven-going skillet cook beef and onion in shortening till onion is tender, about 5 minutes. Sprinkle with salt and pepper. Add potato, corn, soup, and chili powder; stir to combine. Bake, covered, at 350° for 35 to 40 minutes. Makes 4 servings.

Chicken Puff Casserole

¼ **cup butter** *or* **margarine**
¼ **cup all-purpose flour**
½ **teaspoon salt**
   Dash pepper
1½ **cups milk**
 1 **cup chicken broth**
 2 **cups cubed cooked chicken**
   or **turkey**
 1 **cup frozen peas, cooked and**
   drained
 2 **tablespoons chopped**
   pimiento
 3 **egg whites**
 3 **egg yolks**
½ **cup all-purpose flour**
 1 **teaspoon baking powder**
½ **teaspoon salt**
½ **teaspoon paprika**
½ **cup milk**
 1 **tablespoon cooking oil**

In saucepan melt butter or margarine; blend in the ¼ cup flour, the ½ teaspoon salt, and pepper. Add the 1½ cups milk and chicken broth all at once. Cook and stir till thickened and bubbly. Stir in chicken or turkey, peas, and pimiento; heat through. Cover and keep hot.

Beat egg whites till stiff peaks form, about 1½ minutes on medium speed of electric mixer; set aside. In small bowl beat egg yolks till thick and lemon-colored, about 5 minutes on high speed of electric mixer.

Stir together the ½ cup flour, baking powder, the ½ teaspoon salt, and paprika. Combine the ½ cup milk and cooking oil. Stir flour mixture into beaten yolks alternately with milk mixture. Fold in beaten egg whites.

Turn hot chicken mixture into an 11x7½x1½-inch baking pan. Spread batter over all. Bake, uncovered, at 425° for 20 to 25 minutes. Makes 4 or 5 servings.

Turkey Soufflé

 3 **tablespoons butter** *or*
   margarine
 3 **tablespoons all-purpose**
   flour
 1 **teaspoon salt**
¼ **teaspoon paprika**
   Dash pepper
 1 **cup milk**
 1 **cup finely chopped**
   cooked turkey
   or **chicken**
 1 **tablespoon snipped**
   parsley
 1 **teaspoon grated onion**
 3 **egg yolks**
 3 **stiffly beaten**
   egg whites
 1 **tablespoon chopped**
   onion
 1 **tablespoon butter** *or*
   margarine
 1 **tablespoon all-purpose**
   flour
⅛ **teaspoon dried dillweed**
⅛ **teaspoon salt**
   Dash pepper
⅔ **cup milk**
 1 **2-ounce can mushroom**
   stems and pieces,
   drained

In saucepan melt the 3 tablespoons butter or margarine. Stir in the 3 tablespoons flour, the 1 teaspoon salt, paprika, and the dash pepper. Add 1 cup milk all at once; cook and stir till mixture is thickened and bubbly.

Remove from heat. Stir in finely chopped turkey or chicken, snipped parsley, and grated onion. Set aside.

Beat egg yolks till thick and lemon-colored, about 5 minutes on high speed of electric mixer; slowly add turkey mixture to beaten egg yolks, stirring constantly. Cool mixture slightly, about 5 minutes.

Gradually add turkey mixture to stiffly beaten egg whites, folding together thoroughly. Turn into an ungreased 1-quart soufflé dish. Bake, uncovered, at 325° till knife inserted off-center comes out clean, about 50 minutes.

Meanwhile, prepare mushroom-dill sauce. In small saucepan cook chopped onion in the 1 tablespoon butter or margarine till onion is tender but not brown.

Stir the 1 tablespoon flour, dillweed, the ⅛ teaspoon salt, and the dash pepper into cooked onion. Add the ⅔ cup milk all at once; stir in mushroom stems and pieces. Cook and stir till thickened and bubbly. Keep warm till serving time.

When soufflé is done, serve immediately with mushroom-dill sauce. Makes 4 servings.

Curried Turkey Pie

¼ **cup light raisins**
  Boiling water
1½ **cups herb-seasoned**
  stuffing mix
¼ **cup butter *or* margarine,**
  melted
2 **tablespoons water**
½ **cup milk**
1 **10¾-ounce can condensed**
  cream of celery soup
1½ **cups cubed cooked turkey**
  ***or* chicken**
1 **cup cooked *or* canned peas**
1 **2-ounce can chopped**
  mushrooms, drained
1 **tablespoon finely chopped**
  onion
1 **to 2 teaspoons curry powder**

In small bowl cover raisins with boiling water. Let stand 5 minutes; drain and set aside.

Combine herb-seasoned stuffing mix, melted butter or margarine, and the 2 tablespoons water. Reserving ⅓ cup of the mixture, press remaining stuffing mixture into a 9-inch pie plate to form a pie "shell".

Blend milk into soup; stir in turkey or chicken, peas, mushrooms, onion, curry powder, and drained raisins. Turn mixture into stuffing-lined pie plate.

Sprinkle reserved stuffing mixture over pie. Bake, uncovered, at 375° till pie is heated through, 30 to 35 minutes. Makes 6 servings.

Turkey-Broccoli Bake

2 **10-ounce packages frozen**
  chopped broccoli
1 **tablespoon lemon juice**
2 **tablespoons butter *or***
  margarine
2 **tablespoons all-purpose flour**
½ **teaspoon salt**
2 **cups milk**
½ **cup shredded Swiss cheese**
  (2 ounces)
2 **cups cooked turkey cut in**
  strips
¾ **cup soft bread crumbs (1 slice)**
¼ **cup grated Parmesan cheese**
1 **tablespoon butter *or***
  margarine, melted

Cook broccoli according to package directions; drain thoroughly. Place broccoli in an 8x1½-inch round baking dish. Sprinkle with lemon juice.

In saucepan melt the 2 tablespoons butter or margarine. Blend in flour and salt. Add milk all at once. Cook and stir till thickened and bubbly. Remove from heat; stir in Swiss cheese till melted. Stir in turkey strips.

Spoon turkey mixture over broccoli in baking dish. Combine bread crumbs, Parmesan, and the melted butter or margarine. Sprinkle over casserole. Bake, uncovered, at 350° till hot, 20 to 25 minutes. Makes 6 servings.

Pastry and Biscuit Tips

For best results every time, keep these tips in mind when topping a casserole with pastry or biscuits:

• Quarter refrigerated biscuits, or cut your favorite biscuit dough (with cheese or herbs, if you like) into 1½-inch rounds to make a mini-biscuit topper.

• To prevent a doughy topper, be sure the casserole mixture is bubbling hot when you add the pastry or biscuit dough.

• Bake pastry cutouts separately, if desired. Place cutouts on a baking sheet; prick with a fork. Bake at 450° till brown, about 12 minutes (time depends on dough's thickness). Arrange atop casserole just before serving.

• To ensure a golden brown color, brush pastry or biscuit dough with a little milk before baking.

Create a Casserole

Contemporary Strata

5 **cups cubed day-old bread***
  (about 7 slices)
2 **cups finely chopped or ground**
  cooked meat**
¼ **cup chopped green pepper**
2 **tablespoons very finely**
  chopped onion
4 **eggs**
1 **10¾-ounce can**
  condensed soup***
1 **soup can milk (1¼ cups)**
½ **cup mayonnaise**
  Seasoning (optional)****
  Dash cayenne
2 **tablespoons butter, melted**

Place *2 cups* of the bread cubes in an 8x8x2-inch baking dish. Combine meat, green pepper, and onion; sprinkle over bread in dish. Top with another *2 cups* bread cubes.

Beat eggs; combine with soup, milk, mayonnaise, seasoning, and cayenne. Pour evenly over ingredients in baking dish. Cover and chill for 1 to 3 hours.

Toss remaining 1 cup bread cubes with melted butter; sprinkle atop. Bake, uncovered, at 325° till knife inserted just off-center comes out clean, 50 to 60 minutes. Let stand 5 minutes before serving. Sprinkle with snipped parsley, if desired. Makes 6 servings.

*Bread Suggestions	**Meat Suggestions	***Soup Suggestions	****Seasoning Suggestions
white bread	beef	cream of celery	¼ teaspoon dried thyme, crushed (with beef)
whole wheat bread	pork	cream of mushroom	¼ teaspoon caraway seed (with ham)
rye bread	ham	cream of chicken	½ teaspoon dried sage, crushed (with chicken or turkey)
	chicken or turkey	Cheddar cheese	
	tuna (9¼-ounce can)		

Individual Pot Pies

½ **cup chopped celery**
½ **cup chopped onion**
¼ **cup chopped green pepper**
3 **tablespoons butter or**
  margarine
½ **cup all-purpose flour**
¼ **teaspoon salt**
  Seasoning*
⅛ **teaspoon pepper**
3 **cups broth****
2½ **cups chopped cooked meat*****
1 **cup cooked vegetables******
¼ **cup chopped pimiento**
2 **recipes Plain Pastry (see**
  page 72)
  Milk

Cook celery, onion, and green pepper in butter till tender. Blend in flour, salt, seasoning, and pepper. Stir in broth all at once; cook and stir till thickened and bubbly. Stir in meat, vegetables, and pimiento. Divide mixture into eight 4¼x1-inch round pie pans (about ¾ cup each).

Prepare Plain Pastry; divide into 8 equal parts. On floured surface roll each part into a 5-inch circle. Place one circle atop each pie; seal to edge of pan. Cut slits in top for escape of steam. Brush with a little milk. Bake, uncovered, at 425° till golden, 25 to 30 minutes. Cover edges with foil last few minutes of baking, if needed, to prevent overbrowning. Makes 8 servings.

To freeze: Do not cut slits or brush with milk until ready to bake. Wrap, label, and freeze unbaked pies. Bake frozen pies at 425° for 45 minutes. *Or,* thaw in refrigerator 5 hours; bake at 425° for 35 minutes.

*Seasoning Suggestions	**Broth Suggestions	***Meat Suggestions	****Vegetable Suggestions
¼ teaspoon dried rosemary, crushed (with beef, pork, or ham)	chicken broth	beef	peas
¼ teaspoon dried dillweed (with chicken, turkey, or tuna)	turkey broth	pork	green beans
	beef broth	ham	sliced carrots
		chicken or turkey	corn
		tuna (two 7-ounce cans)	mixed vegetables

Biscuit-Topped Stew (pictured on page 66)

1 **cup packaged biscuit mix**
   Biscuit variation (optional)*
¼ **cup milk**
¼ **cup chopped onion**
¼ **cup chopped green pepper**
1 **clove garlic, minced**
2 **tablespoons cooking oil**
2 **tablespoons all-purpose flour**
1 **teaspoon sugar**
¾ **teaspoon salt**
   Seasoning (optional)**
⅛ **teaspoon pepper**
1 **16-ounce can tomatoes, cut up**
2 **cups cubed cooked meat*****
1½ **to 2 cups cooked vegetables******
1 **teaspoon instant chicken or**
   beef bouillon granules
1 **teaspoon Worcestershire sauce**

Stir together biscuit mix and biscuit variation, if desired. Add milk; stir till well blended. On floured surface roll dough to a 5-inch circle. Cut into 6 wedges; set aside.

In saucepan cook onion, green pepper, and garlic in hot oil till onion is tender but not brown. Stir in flour, sugar, salt, seasoning, and pepper. Blend in undrained tomatoes, meat, vegetables, bouillon granules, and Worcestershire sauce. Cook and stir till thickened and bubbly. Turn boiling meat mixture into a 1½-quart casserole. Immediately top with biscuit wedges. Bake, uncovered, at 400° till biscuits are golden, 18 to 20 minutes. Makes 4 to 6 servings.

*Biscuit Variations	**Seasoning Suggestions	***Meat Suggestions	****Vegetable Suggestions
¼ teaspoon dry mustard	¼ teaspoon dried basil, crushed	beef	green beans
½ cup shredded	(with beef, pork, or lamb)	pork	corn
Swiss cheese	¼ teaspoon dried sage, crushed	lamb	peas
½ cup shredded	(with chicken or turkey)	chicken or turkey	mixed vegetables
American cheese		sliced frankfurters	

Meat and Rice Bake

1 **10¾-ounce can**
   condensed soup*
½ **cup dairy sour cream**
½ **cup milk**
1½ **cups chopped cooked meat****
1½ **cups cooked rice**
1 **cup cooked or canned peas**
1 **2-ounce can chopped**
   mushrooms, drained
   Seasoning (optional)***
   Crumbs****
1 **tablespoon butter, melted**

In bowl stir together soup, sour cream, and milk till smooth. Stir in meat, rice, peas, mushrooms, and seasoning. Turn mixture into a 1½-quart casserole. Combine crumbs and melted butter; sprinkle over casserole. Bake, uncovered, at 350° till heated through, 55 to 60 minutes. Makes 4 to 6 servings.

Microwave cooking directions: Prepare casserole as directed above, *except* do not sprinkle with crumbs. Cook, covered, in a countertop microwave oven till heated through, about 12 minutes, stirring once. Stir again before serving; sprinkle with buttered crumbs.

*Soup Suggestions	**Meat Suggestions	***Seasoning Suggestions	****Crumb Suggestions
cream of mushroom	beef	1 tablespoon snipped parsley	¾ cup soft bread crumbs
cream of celery	pork	(with any meat)	(1 slice)
Cheddar cheese	ham	¼ to ½ teaspoon chili powder	½ cup crushed crackers
cream of chicken	chicken or turkey	(with beef or ground beef)	(14 crackers)
	cooked ground beef	¼ teaspoon caraway seed	½ cup crushed pretzels
		(with pork or ham)	(omit butter)

Small-Scale Casseroles

Reuben Casserole

1 8-ounce can sauerkraut
⅛ teaspoon caraway seed
1 small tomato, cut in thin
    wedges
2 tablespoons thousand island
    salad dressing
1 3- *or* 4-ounce package thinly
    sliced corned beef, cut up
¼ cup shredded Swiss cheese
¼ cup soft rye bread crumbs
2 teaspoons butter, melted

Drain sauerkraut; place in 3-cup baking dish. Sprinkle with caraway; top with tomato wedges, salad dressing, and beef. Top with Swiss cheese. Toss bread crumbs with butter; sprinkle over casserole. Bake at 375° till heated through, 25 to 30 minutes. Makes 2 servings.

Good things do come in small packages. And *Frank-Stuffed Tomatoes* and *Beef-Stuffed Acorn Squash* are among the better ones. Both feature a tasty meat mixture tucked inside edible shells.

Baked Eggs and Ham

¼ **cup plain croutons**
2 **teaspoons butter, melted**
1 *or* 2 **eggs**
  Dash pepper
1 **tablespoon shredded cheese**
2 **tablespoons fully cooked**
    ham strips

Toss croutons with melted butter; set aside. Break eggs into a buttered individual casserole. Sprinkle with pepper. Top with cheese; arrange ham atop. Place buttered croutons around edge of dish.

Bake, uncovered, at 350° till eggs are done, 15 to 18 minutes. Makes 1 serving.

Beef-Stuffed Acorn Squash

1 **medium acorn squash**
    (1 pound)
½ **pound ground beef**
2 **tablespoons chopped onion**
2 **tablespoons chopped celery**
2 **tablespoons all-purpose flour**
¼ **teaspoon salt**
¼ **teaspoon ground sage**
¾ **cup milk**
½ **cup cooked rice**
¼ **cup shredded sharp American**
    cheese (1 ounce)

Cut squash in half; discard seeds. Sprinkle squash with a little salt. Bake, cut side down, in 10x6x2-inch baking dish at 350° till tender, 45 to 50 minutes. Cook beef, onion, and celery till meat is brown. Drain off fat. Stir in flour, salt, and sage. Add milk. Cook and stir till thickened and bubbly. Stir in rice. Turn squash cut side up in dish; fill. Bake, uncovered, at 350° for 30 minutes. Top with cheese; bake 3 minutes. Makes 2 servings.

Microwave cooking directions: Pierce whole squash with a cooking fork several times. Place on paper toweling. Cook in a countertop microwave oven till tender, 7 to 8 minutes; turn after 4 minutes. Set aside.

Crumble meat in a 1-quart glass casserole; add onion and celery. Micro-cook, covered, till vegetables are tender, 4 minutes, stirring twice. Drain off fat. Stir in flour, salt, and sage. Add milk; micro-cook, uncovered, till bubbly, 2 to 3 minutes, stirring every 30 seconds. Stir in rice.

Halve squash; discard seeds. Fill squash halves with meat mixture. Place in a 10x6x2-inch glass baking dish or individual bakers. Micro-cook, uncovered, till hot, about 4 minutes. Top with cheese; micro-cook 30 seconds longer.

Frank-Stuffed Tomatoes

2 **large tomatoes**
2 **tablespoons chopped onion**
2 **tablespoons chopped celery**
1 **tablespoon butter *or***
    margarine
1 **tablespoon all-purpose flour**
⅛ **teaspoon salt**
½ **cup milk**
½ **cup shredded sharp American**
    cheese (2 ounces)
2 **frankfurters *or* fully cooked**
    smoked sausage links,
    sliced
½ **cup plain croutons**

Cut tops off tomatoes; scoop out pulp and reserve for another use. Invert tomatoes on paper toweling to drain.

In saucepan cook onion and celery in butter till tender but not brown. Stir in flour and salt. Add milk all at once; cook and stir till thickened and bubbly. Add cheese and franks; cook and stir till cheese melts. Stir in croutons.

Spoon into tomato shells; place in small baking dish. Bake, uncovered, at 350° for 30 minutes. Serves 2.

Microwave cooking directions: Prepare tomatoes as above. In a small glass bowl cook onion and celery in butter, covered, in a countertop microwave oven till tender, about 1½ minutes. Stir in flour and salt. Add milk; micro-cook, uncovered, till thickened and bubbly, about 1½ minutes, stirring every 30 seconds. Stir in cheese and frankfurters. Micro-cook, uncovered, till cheese melts, about 1 minute, stirring after 30 seconds. Stir in croutons.

Spoon mixture into tomato shells. Place in small glass baking dish or 2 individual casseroles. Micro-cook till mixture bubbles and tomatoes are cooked, about 2 minutes.

A cottage cheese filling sparked by chopped chili peppers is the star attraction
in *Chili Manicotti.* Three or four of the large pasta shells will make two generous servings.

Oven Stew for Two

1 **tablespoon all-purpose**
  flour
¾ **teaspoon salt**
  Dash pepper
¾ **pound boneless beef chuck,**
  cut in 1-inch cubes
1 **tablespoon shortening**
1 **10¾-ounce can condensed**
  tomato soup
1 **soup can water (1¼ cups)**
¾ **cup chopped onion**
¼ **teaspoon dried basil, crushed**
2 **medium potatoes, peeled and**
  cubed (2 cups)
2 **medium carrots, cut in 1-inch**
  pieces (1 cup)
¼ **cup dry red wine *or* water**

Combine flour, salt, and pepper; coat meat cubes with the seasoned flour. In a small Dutch oven brown meat in hot shortening. Add tomato soup, the soup can of water, chopped onion, and basil.

Bake, covered, at 375° for 1 hour. Add potatoes, carrots, and wine; cover and bake till meat and vegetables are tender, about 1 hour longer. Makes 2 servings.

Chili Manicotti

2 tablespoons chopped onion
1 small clove garlic, minced
1 tablespoon cooking oil
1 11¼-ounce can condensed
   chili beef soup
3 *or* 4 manicotti shells
1 beaten egg
¾ cup cream-style cottage
   cheese, drained
½ cup shredded sharp American
   cheese (2 ounces)
2 tablespoons chopped canned
   green chili peppers

Cook onion and garlic in oil till tender; stir in soup. Cook manicotti in boiling salted water till tender, 15 to 20 minutes. Drain. Cut shells in half crosswise, if necessary, to fit two individual baking dishes or a 6½x6½x2-inch baking dish.

Combine egg, cottage cheese, *half* the American cheese, and chili peppers. Spoon cheese mixture into manicotti. Pour *half* the soup mixture into the two individual baking dishes or the 6½x6½x2-inch baking dish. Top with stuffed manicotti. Pour remaining soup mixture over, being sure manicotti are coated. Bake, covered, at 350° for 35 to 40 minutes. Uncover; sprinkle with remaining cheese. Bake 2 or 3 minutes more. Let stand 5 minutes. Makes 2 servings.

Macaroni and Cheese for Two

½ cup elbow macaroni
2 tablespoons chopped onion
1 tablespoon butter *or* margarine
4 teaspoons all-purpose flour
1 cup milk
½ teaspoon Worcestershire sauce
¾ cup shredded Cheddar *or*
   American cheese (3 ounces)
¼ cup crushed rich round
   crackers (6 crackers)
1 tablespoon butter, melted

Cook macaroni according to package directions. Drain; set aside. In saucepan cook onion in the 1 tablespoon butter till tender but not brown. Blend in flour. Add milk and Worcestershire sauce all at once; cook and stir till thickened and bubbly. Stir in cheese till melted. Stir in cooked macaroni. Turn mixture into two 10-ounce casseroles.

Combine crushed crackers and the 1 tablespoon melted butter; sprinkle atop casseroles. Bake, uncovered, at 350° for 20 to 25 minutes. Makes 2 servings.

Meatball Meal-in-One

⅓ cup soft bread crumbs
   (½ slice)
2 tablespoons milk
⅛ teaspoon salt
   Dash garlic salt
   Dash dried basil, crushed
¼ pound ground beef
1 small potato, peeled and sliced
1 medium carrot, sliced (½ cup)
1 tablespoon butter *or* margarine
1 tablespoon all-purpose flour
⅛ teaspoon salt
   Dash pepper
½ cup milk
   Paprika

Combine first 5 ingredients. Add meat; mix well. Shape into 4 meatballs; set aside. Combine potato and carrot in a 2½-cup casserole; sprinkle with salt and pepper.

In saucepan melt butter. Stir in flour, the ⅛ teaspoon salt, and the dash pepper. Add the ½ cup milk; cook and stir till thickened and bubbly. Pour over vegetables; top with meatballs. Bake, covered, at 350° for 30 minutes. Uncover; bake 10 minutes longer. Sprinkle with paprika. Makes 1 serving.

Microwave cooking directions: Prepare meatballs as above; place in a 2½-cup glass casserole. Cook, covered, in a countertop microwave oven 3 minutes; remove meatballs. Wipe out dish. In same dish combine potato, carrot, and ¼ cup water. Season with salt and pepper. Micro-cook, covered, 5 minutes. Drain off liquid.

In 1-cup glass measure micro-melt butter 30 to 40 seconds. Stir in flour, the ⅛ teaspoon salt, and the dash pepper. Add the ½ cup milk. Micro-cook, uncovered, 1½ minutes, stirring every 30 seconds. Pour over vegetables; top with meatballs. Micro-cook, covered, 2 minutes. Sprinkle with paprika.

Enchiladas Dos

½ **pound ground beef**
¼ **cup chopped onion**
½ **teaspoon salt**
4 **6-inch flour tortillas**
1 **4-ounce can taco sauce**
½ **cup shredded Cheddar cheese**
2 **tablespoons butter**
2 **tablespoons all-purpose flour**
1 **teaspoon instant chicken bouillon granules**
⅔ **cup water**
2 **tablespoons chopped canned green chili peppers**
⅓ **cup dairy sour cream**

Cook beef and onion till meat is browned and onion is tender; drain off excess fat. Stir in salt. Divide meat onto tortillas; top *each* with about ¼ of the taco sauce and 1 tablespoon of the cheese. Roll up. Place seam side down in a 10x6x2-inch baking dish.

In saucepan melt butter. Blend in flour and chicken bouillon granules. Stir in water. Cook and stir till thickened and bubbly. Stir in chili peppers. Gradually stir about half the hot mixture into sour cream; return to remaining hot mixture in saucepan. Pour over tortillas in baking dish.

Bake, uncovered, at 350° till heated through, about 15 minutes. Sprinkle with remaining cheese. Bake till cheese melts, about 2 minutes longer. Makes 2 servings.

Shrimp Rockefeller

2 **tablespoons butter *or* margarine**
½ **teaspoon celery seed**
½ **teaspoon Worcestershire sauce**
¼ **teaspoon salt**
2 **tablespoons sliced green onion with tops**
1 **small clove garlic, minced**
1 **10-ounce package frozen chopped spinach, thawed**
½ **cup chopped lettuce**
½ **cup light cream**
1 **beaten egg**
4 **ounces fresh *or* frozen shelled shrimp, cooked**
2 **tablespoons fine dry bread crumbs**
2 **tablespoons grated Parmesan cheese**
1 **tablespoon butter, melted**

In medium saucepan combine the 2 tablespoons butter, celery seed, Worcestershire, and salt. Stir in the green onion and garlic. Cook, covered, 2 to 3 minutes. Drain the spinach thoroughly; stir into mixture in saucepan with lettuce, cream, and beaten egg. Cook and stir till mixture just begins to bubble.

Divide *half* the shrimp between two 8-ounce individual casseroles or baking shells. Divide hot spinach mixture between the casseroles; top with remaining shrimp.

Combine the bread crumbs, cheese, and the melted butter; sprinkle evenly over the casseroles. Bake, uncovered, at 375° for 15 minutes. Makes 2 servings.

Scallops Mornay

½ **cup dry white wine**
¼ **teaspoon salt**
    Dash white pepper
8 **ounces fresh *or* frozen scallops**
½ **cup sliced fresh mushrooms**
2 **tablespoons chopped onion**
1 **tablespoon butter *or* margarine**
4 **teaspoons all-purpose flour**
⅓ **cup milk**
¼ **cup shredded process Swiss cheese (1 ounce)**
2 **tablespoons snipped parsley**

In saucepan combine wine, salt, pepper, and ¾ cup water; bring to boiling. Add scallops and mushrooms; return to boiling. Cover; simmer till scallops are tender, about 5 minutes. Remove scallops and mushrooms; set aside. Boil liquid, uncovered, till reduced to ½ cup, 10 to 15 minutes.

In another saucepan cook onion in butter till tender; blend in flour. Add the ½ cup scallop liquid and milk. Cook and stir till thickened and bubbly. Stir in cheese till melted. Season with more salt and pepper, if needed. Remove from heat; stir in scallops and mushrooms. Turn into two 8- to 10-ounce individual casseroles. Bake, uncovered, at 375° for 15 to 20 minutes. Sprinkle with parsley. Serve with hot cooked rice, if desired. Makes 2 servings.

Tuna with Rice for One

1 small cucumber, seeded and
  chopped (½ cup)
1 3¼-ounce can tuna, drained
  and flaked *or* ½ cup flaked
  cooked fish
¼ cup quick-cooking rice
¼ cup water
1 teaspoon lemon juice
  Dash garlic salt
¼ cup shredded sharp American
  cheese (1 ounce)

In a 12-ounce casserole combine cucumber, tuna or fish, uncooked rice, water, lemon juice, and garlic salt. Bake, covered, at 350° till rice is cooked, about 25 minutes. Top with cheese. Bake, uncovered, till cheese melts, 2 to 3 minutes more. Makes 1 serving.

Microwave cooking directions: In a 12-ounce nonmetal casserole combine cucumber, tuna or fish, uncooked rice, water, lemon juice, and garlic salt. Cook, covered with waxed paper, in a countertop microwave oven till rice is done, about 3 minutes. Sprinkle with cheese; micro-cook, uncovered, about 45 seconds longer.

Fiesta Salmon

½ of an 11-ounce can condensed
  Cheddar cheese soup
3 tablespoons milk
3 tablespoons chopped canned
  green chili peppers
2 teaspoons instant minced
  onion
1 7¾-ounce can salmon *or* 1 6½-
  or 7-ounce can tuna, drained
  and broken into chunks
¾ cup coarsely crushed
  tortilla chips

In a saucepan combine soup, milk, chili peppers, and onion. Heat and stir till bubbly. Stir in salmon or tuna and ½ *cup* of the corn chips. Turn mixture into two 8-ounce individual casseroles. Top with remaining tortilla chips. Bake, uncovered, at 375° till heated through, about 30 minutes. Makes 2 servings.

Stuffed Zucchini for One

1 small zucchini (6 inches long)
2 ounces bulk pork sausage
  (¼ cup)
1 tablespoon chopped onion
1 tablespoon chopped celery
¼ cup plain *or* garlic croutons
¼ cup shredded mozzarella *or*
  Monterey Jack cheese

Trim ends of zucchini; cook zucchini in boiling salted water till crisp-tender, about 8 minutes; drain. Cut in half lengthwise; scoop out centers and chop.

Cook sausage, onion, and celery till meat is done; drain off fat. Stir in croutons, *half* the cheese, and the chopped zucchini. In a small baking dish mound mixture in zucchini shells. Bake, uncovered, at 350° for 20 minutes. Top with remaining cheese. Bake 5 minutes more. Makes 1 serving.

Pork Chop Supper

2 pork chops, cut ¾ inch thick
⅓ cup regular rice
2 tablespoons chopped onion
1 cup water
1 teaspoon instant chicken
  bouillon granules
½ cup chopped apple
1 tablespoon butter, melted
1 tablespoon brown sugar
¼ teaspoon ground cinnamon
½ cup sliced apples

Trim fat from chops; cook trimmings in skillet till 2 tablespoons fat accumulates. Discard trimmings. Brown chops slowly in hot drippings. Set chops aside; reserve drippings.

In same skillet cook rice and onion in reserved drippings till rice is golden, stirring constantly. Stir in water and bouillon granules. Bring to boiling; stir in chopped apple. Turn mixture into a 6½x6½x2-inch baking dish; arrange chops atop. Bake, covered, at 350° for 30 minutes. Combine butter, sugar, and cinnamon. Brush sliced apples with mixture; arrange around chops. Bake, uncovered, till apples and pork are tender, about 20 minutes. Serves 2.

Casseroles for Company

Delicatessen Casserole

¼ cup butter *or* margarine
8 slices rye bread
¾ cup grated Parmesan cheese
1½ cups sliced cooked beef
8 ounces sliced salami
2 beaten eggs
1 16-ounce carton cream-style
    cottage cheese
1 cup shredded mozzarella
    cheese (4 ounces)
½ cup sliced dill pickle
½ cup milk

Soften butter or margarine. Spread one side of each bread slice with butter or margarine; sprinkle bread with ¼ *cup* of the Parmesan cheese. Cut bread into ½-inch cubes. Cut beef and salami into bite-size strips. In bowl combine eggs, cottage cheese, mozzarella cheese, dill pickle, milk, meat, and remaining ½ cup Parmesan cheese. Spread *half* of the bread cubes in a 12x7½x2-inch baking dish. Spread with cottage cheese mixture. Top with the remaining bread cubes. Bake at 375° for 45 to 50 minutes. Makes 8 servings.

Plan a party around a festive casserole. *Mandarin Ham Rolls, Fruited Beef Stew,* and *Chicken Breasts Florentine* are three flavorful, attractive, and easy-to-serve choices.

Chicken Breasts Florentine

2 **10-ounce packages frozen chopped spinach**
3 **whole large chicken breasts, skinned, boned, and halved**
1 **rib celery, cut up**
½ **medium onion, cut up**
½ **teaspoon salt**
¼ **cup butter** *or* **margarine**
¼ **cup all-purpose flour**
   Dash white pepper
1 **cup light cream**
½ **cup grated Parmesan cheese**
   Dash ground nutmeg

Cook spinach according to package directions; drain well.

Place chicken in saucepan with celery, onion, salt, and 1 cup water. Bring to boil; reduce heat and simmer till meat is tender, about 20 minutes. Remove chicken from broth. Strain broth; reserve 1 cup. Discard vegetables.

In saucepan melt butter; blend in flour and pepper. Stir in reserved broth and cream. Cook and stir till thickened and bubbly. Remove from heat; stir ½ *cup* of the sauce into drained spinach along with *half* the cheese and the nutmeg; spread in a 10x6x2-inch baking dish. Arrange chicken atop. Pour remaining sauce over all. Sprinkle with remaining cheese and more nutmeg, if desired. Bake, uncovered, at 375° till lightly browned, 25 to 30 minutes. Serves 6.

Mandarin Ham Rolls

1 **11-ounce can mandarin orange sections, drained**
1½ **cups cooked rice**
⅓ **cup mayonnaise** *or* **salad dressing**
2 **tablespoons chopped pecans**
2 **tablespoons snipped parsley**
1 **tablespoon sliced green onion with tops**
8 **slices boiled ham (8 ounces)**
¼ **cup orange marmalade**
1 **tablespoon lemon juice**
¼ **teaspoon ground ginger**

Reserve 8 orange sections; chop remainder and combine with cooked rice, mayonnaise, pecans, parsley, and onion. Divide mixture among ham slices. Roll up ham around filling. Place seam side down in 10x6x2-inch baking dish.

Combine marmalade, lemon juice, and ginger; brush some over ham rolls. Bake, uncovered, at 350° for 25 to 30 minutes, brushing occasionally with remaining sauce. Garnish with reserved orange sections. Makes 4 servings.

Fruited Beef Stew

1½ **pounds boneless beef chuck, cut in 1-inch cubes**
2 **tablespoons cooking oil**
3 **medium sweet potatoes, peeled and quartered (3 cups)**
1 **16-ounce can tomatoes, cut up**
1 **cup chopped onion**
½ **cup chopped green pepper**
2 **inches stick cinnamon** *or*
   ¼ **teaspoon ground cinnamon**
1 **clove garlic, minced**
1 **teaspoon salt**
⅛ **teaspoon pepper**
2 **ears corn, cut crosswise in 2-inch pieces**
2 **medium zucchini, sliced**
1 **16-ounce can peach slices**

In a Dutch oven brown meat, ⅓ at a time, in hot cooking oil. Drain off excess fat. Add sweet potatoes, undrained tomatoes, onion, green pepper, cinnamon, garlic, salt, pepper, and ½ cup water. (If desired, transfer mixture to a 3-quart casserole.) Bake, covered, at 350° for 1¼ hours. Stir in corn and zucchini; bake 45 minutes longer.

Drain peaches; reserve liquid for another use. Add peach slices to stew; season to taste with additional salt and pepper. Makes 6 to 8 servings.

Club Chicken Casserole

2 cups chicken broth
⅔ cup regular rice
1 10-ounce package frozen
  chopped broccoli
3 tablespoons butter *or*
  margarine
3 tablespoons all-purpose flour
1½ teaspoons salt
  Dash pepper
2 cups milk
2 cups cubed cooked chicken
  or turkey
1 4½-ounce jar sliced mushrooms,
  drained
¼ cup toasted slivered almonds

In saucepan bring chicken broth and rice to boiling. Reduce heat; cook, covered, for 15 minutes. Remove from heat; let stand, covered, for 10 minutes. Meanwhile, cook broccoli according to package directions; drain well.

In saucepan melt butter or margarine. Stir in flour, salt, and pepper. Add milk all at once; cook and stir till thickened and bubbly. Stir in chicken, cooked rice, drained broccoli, and mushrooms. Turn into a 2-quart casserole. Bake, covered, at 350° till heated through, 30 to 35 minutes. Sprinkle with almonds. Makes 6 servings.

Saucy Turkey Manicotti

6 manicotti shells
2 tablespoons water
1 tablespoon instant minced
  onion
1 3-ounce package cream cheese,
  softened
1 1¼-ounce envelope sour
  cream sauce mix
¼ cup milk
1 4-ounce can chopped
  mushrooms, drained
1 tablespoon snipped parsley
¼ teaspoon salt
⅛ teaspoon pepper
2 cups chopped cooked turkey *or*
  chicken
1 1½-ounce envelope cheese
  sauce mix
¼ cup grated Parmesan cheese

Cook manicotti shells in boiling salted water till tender, 15 to 20 minutes; drain. Combine water and instant minced onion; let stand 5 minutes.

Combine cream cheese and sour cream sauce mix; blend in milk. Stir in softened onion, mushrooms, parsley, salt, and pepper. Add turkey or chicken; mix well. Spoon mixture into cooked manicotti shells. Arrange stuffed manicotti in a single layer in a 10x6x2-inch baking dish.

Prepare cheese sauce mix according to package directions. Pour sauce over manicotti. Sprinkle with Parmesan cheese. Bake, covered, at 350° till heated through, 35 to 40 minutes. Makes 6 servings.

Chicken Curry Soufflés

3 eggs, separated
1 cup cream-style cottage cheese
¼ cup finely chopped onion
1 clove garlic, minced
2 tablespoons butter *or*
  margarine
2 tablespoons all-purpose flour
1 teaspoon curry powder
½ teaspoon salt
¼ teaspoon ground ginger
½ cup milk
1 cup coarsely chopped cooked
  chicken *or* turkey

Beat egg whites till stiff peaks form; set aside. In another bowl beat together egg yolks and cottage cheese.

In a heavy saucepan cook onion and garlic in butter or margarine till onion is tender but not brown. Combine flour, curry, salt, and ginger; add to butter mixture, mixing well. Add milk all at once. Cook and stir till thickened and bubbly. Stir half the hot mixture into egg yolk mixture; return to pan. Cook and stir till thickened. Remove from heat; stir in chicken. Fold in beaten egg whites.

Turn mixture into four 8-ounce casseroles (or individual soufflé dishes with foil collars). Bake, uncovered, at 300° till a knife inserted off-center comes out clean, 40 to 45 minutes. Serve immediately. Makes 4 servings.

Crab-Stuffed Chicken

4 **whole large chicken breasts, skinned, boned, and halved lengthwise**
3 **tablespoons butter** *or* **margarine**
¼ **cup all-purpose flour**
¾ **cup milk**
¾ **cup chicken broth**
⅓ **cup dry white wine**
¼ **cup chopped onion**
1 **tablespoon butter** *or* **margarine**
1 **7½-ounce can crab meat, drained, flaked, and cartilage removed**
1 **4-ounce can chopped mushrooms, drained**
½ **cup coarsely crumbled saltine crackers (10 crackers)**
2 **tablespoons snipped parsley**
½ **teaspoon salt**
Dash pepper
1 **cup shredded Swiss cheese**
½ **teaspoon paprika**

Place one chicken piece, boned side up, between 2 pieces of waxed paper. Working from the center out, pound chicken lightly with meat mallet to make cutlet about ⅛ inch thick. Repeat with remaining chicken.

In saucepan melt the 3 tablespoons butter or margarine; blend in flour. Add milk, chicken broth, and wine all at once; cook and stir till thickened and bubbly. Set aside.

In skillet cook onion in the 1 tablespoon butter or margarine till tender but not brown. Stir in crab, mushrooms, cracker crumbs, parsley, salt, and pepper. Stir in *2 tablespoons* of the sauce. Top each chicken piece with about ¼ cup of the crab mixture. Fold sides in; roll up.

Place seam side down in a 12x7½x2-inch baking dish. Pour remaining sauce over all. Bake, covered, at 350° till chicken is tender, about 1 hour. Uncover; sprinkle with Swiss cheese and paprika. Bake till cheese melts, about 2 minutes longer. Makes 8 servings.

Chicken-Asparagus Divan

2 **8-ounce packages frozen cut asparagus**
1 **10¾-ounce can condensed cream of chicken soup**
1 **teaspoon Worcestershire sauce**
Dash ground nutmeg
½ **cup grated Parmesan cheese**
2 **cups sliced cooked chicken**
½ **cup whipping cream**
½ **cup mayonnaise** *or* **salad dressing**

Cook asparagus according to package directions; drain. Arrange in a 12x7½x2-inch baking dish.

Stir together soup, Worcestershire sauce, and nutmeg; pour *half* over asparagus. Sprinkle with ⅓ of the cheese. Top with chicken and remaining soup mixture. Sprinkle with another ⅓ of the cheese. Bake, uncovered, at 350° till heated through, about 20 minutes.

Whip cream just till soft peaks form; fold in mayonnaise. Spread mixture over chicken; sprinkle with remaining ⅓ of the cheese. Broil 3 to 4 inches from heat till topping is golden, 1 to 2 minutes. Makes 6 servings.

Wild Rice-Chicken Casserole

1 **6-ounce package long grain and wild rice mix**
½ **cup chopped onion**
½ **cup chopped celery**
2 **tablespoons butter**
1 **10¾-ounce can condensed cream of mushroom soup**
½ **cup dairy sour cream**
⅓ **cup dry white wine**
½ **teaspoon curry powder**
2 **cups cubed cooked chicken** *or* **turkey**
¼ **cup snipped parsley**

Prepare rice mix according to package directions. Meanwhile, cook onion and celery in butter till tender. Stir in soup, sour cream, wine, and curry. Stir in chicken and cooked rice; turn into a 12x7½x2-inch baking dish. Bake, uncovered, at 350° for 35 to 40 minutes. Stir before serving; garnish with snipped parsley. Makes 4 to 6 servings.

Microwave cooking directions: On range top prepare rice mix according to package directions. Place onion, celery, and butter in 2-quart nonmetal casserole. Cook, covered, in countertop microwave oven till tender, 2 to 2½ minutes. Blend in soup, sour cream, wine, and curry. Stir in chicken and rice. Micro-cook, covered, till hot, 8 to 10 minutes; turn dish after 5 minutes. Top with parsley.

Rice and Tuna Pie

1 **beaten egg**
2 **cups cooked rice**
2 **tablespoons butter** *or*
   margarine, melted
2 **tablespoons finely chopped**
   onion
½ **teaspoon dried marjoram,**
   crushed
1 **9¼-ounce can tuna, drained**
   and flaked
3 **beaten eggs**
1 **cup milk**
1 **cup shredded Swiss cheese**
   (4 ounces)
¼ **teaspoon salt**
   Dash pepper

Combine the 1 egg, cooked rice, melted butter, *1 tablespoon* of the chopped onion, and ¼ *teaspoon* of the marjoram. Press onto bottom and sides of a lightly buttered 10-inch pie plate or 10x6x2-inch baking dish. Place tuna atop.

Combine the 3 beaten eggs, milk, Swiss cheese, salt, pepper, remaining 1 tablespoon onion, and remaining ¼ teaspoon marjoram. Pour over tuna. Bake, uncovered, at 350° till a knife inserted just off-center comes out clean, 40 to 45 minutes. Garnish with chopped pimiento or snipped parsley, if desired. Makes 6 servings.

Curried Eggs with Shrimp

8 **hard-cooked eggs**
⅓ **cup mayonnaise**
½ **teaspoon salt**
½ **teaspoon paprika**
¼ **teaspoon curry powder**
¼ **teaspoon dry mustard**
2 **tablespoons butter** *or*
   margarine
2 **tablespoons all-purpose flour**
¼ **teaspoon curry powder**
1 **10¾-ounce can condensed**
   cream of celery soup
¾ **cup milk**
1 **cup frozen cooked shrimp**
½ **cup shredded sharp Cheddar**
   cheese (2 ounces)
¾ **cup soft bread crumbs**
1 **tablespoon butter** *or*
   margarine, melted

Cut eggs in half lengthwise; remove and mash yolks. Mix mashed yolks with mayonnaise, salt, paprika, the ¼ teaspoon curry powder, and dry mustard. Stuff egg whites with yolk mixture. Arrange egg halves in a 10x6x2-inch baking dish.

Melt the 2 tablespoons butter; blend in flour and the ¼ teaspoon curry powder. Add soup and milk; cook and stir till thickened and bubbly. Add shrimp and cheese; stir till cheese melts. Pour sauce over eggs in baking dish.

Toss bread crumbs with the melted butter to combine; sprinkle around edge of mixture. Bake, uncovered, at 350° till heated through, 15 to 20 minutes. Makes 6 to 8 servings.

Menu-Planning Reminders

Menu planning is easy when you serve a casserole. Since a casserole is a combination of foods, you can keep accompaniments simple—serve a plain vegetable or salad with a casserole entrée, a vegetable casserole with a simple entrée.

Use a variety of colors, flavors, textures, and temperatures to make a menu more interesting. Choose attractive foods; and remember that a garnish of parsley or toasted almonds can transform a plain dish into an elegant one.

When your budget won't allow you to stage a spectacular party with all the trimmings, invite a few friends over for *Highbrow Haddock*. And don't tell them how inexpensive it is.

Highbrow Haddock

1 **pound frozen haddock fillets**
¼ **cup finely chopped onion**
¼ **cup butter *or* margarine**
2 **tablespoons all-purpose flour**
¼ **teaspoon salt**
⅛ **teaspoon pepper**
1½ **cups milk**
1 **cup shredded sharp American cheese (4 ounces)**
1 **1¼-ounce envelope sour cream sauce mix**
1 **cup frozen peas, thawed**
1 **4-ounce can mushroom stems and pieces, drained**
1½ **cups soft bread crumbs**

In large skillet barely cover haddock with water. Simmer gently till fish flakes with a fork, 12 to 15 minutes; drain. Break fish into large chunks; set aside.

Meanwhile, in large saucepan cook onion in *2 tablespoons* of the butter or margarine till tender but not brown. Blend in flour, salt, and pepper. Add *1 cup* of the milk all at once. Cook and stir till thickened and bubbly. Remove from heat. Add cheese; stir till melted.

Using the remaining ½ cup milk, prepare sauce mix according to package directions. Stir in cheese sauce, fish, peas, and mushrooms. Turn into six 8-ounce shallow casseroles. Melt remaining 2 tablespons butter; toss with bread crumbs to combine. Sprinkle atop casseroles. Bake, uncovered, at 400° for 15 to 20 minutes. Garnish each with parsley and paprika, if desired. Makes 6 servings.

After a day of skiing or sledding, you're bound to be cold and weary. Take the chill
off with corn bread and *Easy Cassoulet,* a hearty mixture of ham, beans, wine, and seasonings.

Shrimp Tartlets

Plain Pastry (see page 72)
3 eggs
1½ cups cream-style cottage
cheese (12 ounces)
1 8½-ounce can peas, drained
½ teaspoon salt
Dash pepper
1 4½-ounce can shrimp, drained
and rinsed (about 1 cup)

Prepare Plain Pastry; divide into four parts. On floured surface roll out into four 7-inch circles. Fit pastry rounds into four 5-inch tart pans; flute edges. Set aside.

Beat eggs till foamy; stir in cottage cheese, peas, salt, and pepper. Reserve 4 shrimp for garnish; stir remaining into egg mixture. Turn into prepared pastry shells. Bake, uncovered, at 350° till a knife inserted off-center comes out clean, about 40 minutes. Let stand 5 minutes. Garnish with reserved shrimp and parsley, if desired. Makes 4 servings.

Hot Crab Bake

6 tablespoons butter or
margarine
¼ cup all-purpose flour
2 cups milk
1 7½-ounce can crab meat,
drained, flaked, and
cartilage removed
2 hard-cooked eggs, chopped
½ cup chopped pimiento
½ cup fine dry bread crumbs
¼ cup slivered almonds

In skillet melt 4 tablespoons of the butter; blend in flour. Add milk all at once; cook and stir till thickened and bubbly. Stir in crab meat, chopped eggs, pimiento, 1 teaspoon salt, and ⅛ teaspoon pepper. Spoon mixture into 6 individual casseroles or baking shells.

Melt remaining 2 tablespoons butter; toss with bread crumbs to combine. Sprinkle crumbs atop crab mixture. Top with slivered almonds. Bake, uncovered, at 350° for 20 to 25 minutes. Makes 6 servings.

Easy Cassoulet

½ pound bulk pork sausage
1 small onion, sliced (½ cup)
1 clove garlic, minced
1½ cups cubed fully cooked ham
2 tablespoons snipped parsley
1 bay leaf
2 15-ounce cans navy beans
¼ cup dry white wine
Dash ground cloves

In skillet cook sausage, onion, and garlic till meat is lightly browned and onion is tender; drain off fat.

Add ham, parsley, and bay leaf; mix well. Stir in undrained beans, wine, and cloves. Turn into a 1½-quart casserole. Bake, covered, at 325° for 45 minutes. Uncover and bake 40 to 45 minutes longer, stirring occasionally. Remove bay leaf. Serve in bowls with hot corn bread, if desired. Makes 6 servings.

Shallot-Bacon Quiche

6 slices bacon
¼ cup sliced shallots (4 medium)
Plain Pastry (see page 72)
1 cup shredded Swiss cheese
3 beaten eggs
1 cup light cream
½ teaspoon salt
½ teaspoon dry mustard
Dash ground nutmeg

In skillet cook bacon till crisp; drain, reserving 1 tablespoon drippings. Cook shallots in reserved drippings till tender.

Prepare Plain Pastry. Roll out and fit into an 8-inch pie plate or quiche dish; flute edges. Bake at 450° for 5 minutes; set aside. Reduce oven temperature to 325°.

Sprinkle cheese over pastry. Crumble bacon over cheese; top with shallots. Combine remaining ingredients; pour over mixture in pastry. Bake, uncovered, at 325° till set, 40 to 45 minutes. Let stand 10 minutes. Makes 6 servings.

Cauliflower-Ham Bake

1 **large head cauliflower**
2 **tablespoons butter** *or*
   margarine
3 **tablespoons all-purpose**
   flour
1½ **cups milk**
1½ **cups shredded sharp American**
   cheese (6 ounces)
2 **cups cubed fully cooked ham**
1 **4-ounce can mushroom stems**
   and pieces, drained
¼ **cup fine dry bread crumbs**
1 **tablespoon butter** *or*
   margarine, melted

Break cauliflower into flowerets (should have about 5 cups); cook in boiling salted water till tender, about 10 minutes. Drain thoroughly; set aside.

In saucepan melt the 2 tablespoons butter or margarine. Stir in flour; add milk all at once. Cook and stir till thickened and bubbly. Add cheese and stir till melted. Stir in cooked cauliflower, ham, and mushrooms. Turn into a 2-quart casserole. Combine crumbs and the melted butter; sprinkle over top. Bake, uncovered, at 350° till heated through, 30 to 35 minutes. Makes 6 servings.

Gold Rush Brunch

1 **5½-ounce package dry hash**
   brown potatoes with onion
¼ **cup butter** *or* **margarine**
¼ **cup all-purpose flour**
½ **teaspoon salt**
⅛ **teaspoon pepper**
2 **cups milk**
1 **cup dairy sour cream**
2 **tablespoons snipped parsley**
8 **slices Canadian-style bacon,**
   cut ¼ inch thick
8 **eggs**

Prepare potatoes according to package directions; set aside. In 3-quart saucepan melt butter; blend in flour, salt, and pepper. Add milk all at once; cook and stir till thickened and bubbly. Remove from heat. Stir in sour cream, parsley, and potatoes.

Turn mixture into a 13x9x2-inch baking dish. Arrange Canadian-style bacon in a row down center, overlapping slices slightly. Bake, uncovered, at 350° for 20 minutes.

Remove from oven. Make 4 depressions in potato mixture on *each* side of the row of bacon; slip 1 egg into each depression. Sprinkle with salt and pepper. Return to oven; bake till eggs are set, 10 to 12 minutes more. Makes 8 servings.

Pizza Quiche

2 **recipes Plain Pastry**
   (see page 72)
1 **cup ricotta** *or* **cream-style**
   cottage cheese (8 ounces)
3 **eggs**
4 **ounces Italian sausage, cooked**
   and drained
1 **cup shredded mozzarella**
   cheese (4 ounces)
½ **cup sliced pepperoni, halved**
   (2 ounces)
½ **cup cubed prosciutto** *or*
   fully cooked ham
½ **cup sliced salami, cut in**
   strips (2 ounces)
¼ **cup grated Parmesan cheese**
1 **beaten egg**
2 **tablespoons milk**

Prepare Plain Pastry. Divide dough in half. Roll out half; fit into a 9-inch pie plate. Reserve remaining dough. Crimp edges of pastry shell; *do not prick.* Bake at 450° for 5 minutes. Remove from oven; reduce oven temperature to 350°.

Beat together ricotta or cottage cheese and the 3 eggs; fold in Italian sausage, mozzarella, pepperoni, prosciutto or ham, salami, and Parmesan cheese. Turn into partially baked pastry shell.

Roll out remaining pastry dough to an 8-inch circle; cut in 6 to 8 wedges. Arrange wedges atop filling. Bake, uncovered, at 350° for 20 minutes.

Combine the 1 egg and milk; brush over pastry wedges. Continue baking till golden brown, about 20 minutes more. Let stand about 10 minutes before serving. Makes 6 to 8 servings.

Spinach and Cheese Soufflé

1 10-ounce package frozen
   chopped spinach
¼ cup butter *or* margarine
¼ cup all-purpose flour
½ teaspoon salt
1 cup milk
1 cup shredded sharp American
   cheese (4 ounces)
4 egg yolks
4 stiffly beaten egg whites
½ cup milk
   Dash white pepper
¼ cup dairy sour cream

Cook spinach according to package directions; drain well. In saucepan melt butter. Blend in flour and salt. Add the 1 cup milk all at once. Cook and stir till thickened and bubbly. Remove from heat. Add cheese; stir till melted. Reserve ¾ *cup* of the sauce; stir spinach into remaining sauce.

Beat egg yolks till thick and lemon-colored, about 5 minutes. Slowly stir in spinach mixture; gradually pour over beaten egg whites, folding together well. Turn into a 1½-quart soufflé dish. Bake, uncovered, at 350° till knife inserted just off-center comes out clean, 30 to 35 minutes. Just before serving, in saucepan combine reserved sauce, the ½ cup milk, and pepper; heat till bubbly. Slowly stir hot sauce into sour cream. Pass with soufflé. Makes 4 to 6 servings.

Party Eggplant Parmesan

¾ cup soft bread crumbs
   (1 slice)
⅓ cup milk
1 teaspoon seasoned salt
½ teaspoon seasoned pepper
1 pound ground beef
½ pound ground veal
   Cooking oil
1 medium eggplant
¼ cup all-purpose flour
2 8-ounce cans tomato sauce
   with mushrooms
¼ cup water
¼ teaspoon dried oregano,
   crushed
½ cup grated Parmesan cheese

Combine crumbs, milk, salt, and pepper. Add beef and veal; mix well. Shape into 8 patties. Brown on both sides in a small amount of cooking oil. Remove from skillet.

Peel eggplant; cut into eight thick slices. Brush lightly with oil; coat with flour. Brown eggplant slices in same skillet. Arrange slices in a 13x9x2-inch baking pan; top each slice with a meat patty.

Combine tomato sauce, water, and oregano; pour over all. Sprinkle with Parmesan cheese. Bake, uncovered, at 350° for 20 to 25 minutes. Makes 8 servings.

Beef-Broccoli Pie

1 pound ground beef
¼ cup chopped onion
2 tablespoons all-purpose flour
¾ teaspoon salt
¼ teaspoon garlic salt
1¼ cups milk
1 3-ounce package cream
   cheese, softened
1 beaten egg
1 10-ounce package frozen
   chopped broccoli, cooked
   and well drained
2 recipes Plain Pastry (see
   page 72)
4 ounces Monterey Jack cheese,
   sliced
   Milk

In a skillet brown beef and onion; drain off fat. Stir in flour, salt, and garlic salt. Add 1¼ cups milk and the softened cream cheese; cook and stir till smooth and bubbly. Stir about 1 cup of the hot mixture into the beaten egg; return to mixture in skillet. Cook and stir over medium heat till mixture is thickened, 1 to 2 minutes. Stir in cooked chopped broccoli; set aside.

Prepare Plain Pastry as for a double-crust pie. Spoon the hot meat mixture into the pastry shell. Arrange cheese slices atop the meat mixture. Adjust remaining pastry over filling to form the top crust; crimp edges to seal. Cut slashes for escape of steam.

Brush top crust with a little milk. Bake, uncovered, at 350° for 40 to 45 minutes. If the pastry browns too quickly, cover edges of crust with foil during last 20 minutes of baking. Let stand 10 minutes. Makes 6 servings.

Sherried Beef Stroganoff

2 **pounds beef stew meat, cut**
   in 1-inch cubes
¼ **cup all-purpose flour**
2 **tablespoons cooking oil**
1 **10¾-ounce can condensed**
   cream of mushroom soup
½ **cup dry sherry**
1 **1½-ounce envelope stroganoff**
   sauce mix
1 **tablespoon instant minced**
   onion
1 **4-ounce can sliced mushrooms,**
   drained
½ **cup dairy sour cream**

Toss beef cubes with flour to coat. In large skillet brown meat in hot cooking oil. Drain off excess fat.

Combine soup, sherry, dry stroganoff sauce mix, and instant minced onion; stir into meat along with mushrooms. Turn mixture into a 2-quart casserole. Bake, covered, at 350° till meat is tender, about 1½ hours. Stir in sour cream. Serve over hot cooked white or brown rice, if desired. Makes 6 to 8 servings.

Beef Burgundy Pies

1½ **pounds beef stew meat, cut in**
   1-inch cubes
2 **tablespoons cooking oil**
1½ **cups water**
1 **beef bouillon cube**
1 **cup sliced carrot**
¾ **cup chopped onion**
2 **cloves garlic, minced**
½ **cup Burgundy**
¼ **cup all-purpose flour**
1 **teaspoon Worcestershire sauce**
½ **teaspoon salt**
½ **teaspoon mixed salad herbs**
½ **teaspoon Kitchen Bouquet**
⅛ **teaspoon pepper**
1 **cup packaged biscuit mix**
⅓ **cup water**

In a 3-quart saucepan brown meat in hot cooking oil. Drain off fat. Add the 1½ cups water and bouillon cube. Bring to boiling. Cover; reduce heat and simmer over low heat for 30 minutes.

Add sliced carrot, chopped onion, and minced garlic; simmer till meat is tender, about 20 minutes longer. Blend Burgundy into flour; slowly stir into hot meat mixture. Add Worcestershire sauce, salt, mixed salad herbs, Kitchen Bouquet, and pepper to beef mixture. Cook and stir till thickened and bubbly. Turn into four 8-ounce casseroles.

Stir together biscuit mix and the ⅓ cup water; drop from a spoon atop the *hot* meat mixture in each casserole. Bake, uncovered, at 375° till biscuits are golden brown, 15 to 20 minutes. Makes 4 servings.

Curried Beef Bake

2 **tablespoons all-purpose flour**
½ **teaspoon salt**
   Dash pepper
1 **pound beef stew meat, cut in**
   ½-inch cubes
2 **tablespoons cooking oil**
1 **tablespoon instant minced**
   onion
1 **5½-ounce package noodles with**
   sour cream mix
1 **8-ounce can tomato sauce**
2 **tablespoons butter *or***
   margarine
1½ **teaspoons curry powder**
⅓ **cup finely crushed rich round**
   crackers (8 crackers)

In paper or plastic bag combine flour, salt, and pepper. Add beef cubes, a few at a time; shake to coat. In a large skillet brown meat in hot oil. Remove from heat. Drain off excess fat. To skillet add instant minced onion and 2¼ cups water; cover and simmer for 30 minutes.

Meanwhile, cook noodles from the mix in large amount boiling salted water for 5 minutes; drain. In same saucepan blend sauce mix, tomato sauce, butter, and curry. Stir in meat mixture; fold in cooked noodles.

Turn mixture into a 1½-quart casserole. Bake, covered, at 350° for 30 minutes. Uncover and sprinkle with cracker crumbs; bake till crumbs are lightly browned, about 10 minutes longer. Makes 4 servings.

Tetrazzini Crepes

12 **Crepes (see recipe below)**
5 **ounces fresh mushrooms,**
   halved (2 cups)
6 **tablespoons butter *or***
   margarine
⅓ **cup all-purpose flour**
1¼ **cups chicken broth**
¾ **cup light cream**
½ **cup shredded sharp Cheddar**
   cheese (2 ounces)
¼ **cup dry sherry**
2 **cups cubed cooked chicken**
   ***or* turkey**
2 **tablespoons chopped pitted**
   ripe olives
2 **tablespoons snipped parsley**

Prepare Crepes. Brown mushroom halves in *3 tablespoons* of the butter or margarine.

In saucepan melt the remaining 3 tablespoons butter; stir in flour. Add chicken broth and cream. Cook and stir till mixture is thickened and bubbly. Add cheese and sherry; stir till cheese melts.

Combine chicken, olives, mushrooms, and *1 cup* of the sauce. Spoon about ¼ cup filling on unbrowned side of each crepe; roll up. Place crepes seam side up in a 13x9x2-inch baking dish or two 10x6x2-inch baking dishes; pour remaining sauce over. Bake, uncovered, at 375° till heated through, about 25 minutes for the 13x9x2-inch dish or 20 minutes for the two 10x6x2-inch dishes. Sprinkle with parsley. Serves 6.

Salmon-Broccoli Crepes

12 **Crepes (see recipe below)**
¼ **cup chopped onion**
¼ **cup butter *or* margarine**
¼ **cup all-purpose flour**
¼ **teaspoon salt**
2¼ **cups milk**
2 **cups shredded sharp American**
   cheese (8 ounces)
1 **10-ounce package frozen**
   chopped broccoli
1 **7¾-ounce can salmon, drained,**
   boned, and flaked

Prepare Crepes; set aside. In saucepan cook onion in butter till tender but not brown. Stir in flour and salt. Add milk; cook and stir till thickened and bubbly. Add cheese; stir till melted. Remove from heat.

Cook broccoli according to package directions; drain. Cut up any large pieces; fold in salmon and ¾ *cup* of the sauce. Spoon about 3 tablespoons salmon mixture onto unbrowned side of each crepe; roll up. Place crepes seam side down in a 12x7½x2-inch baking dish; pour remaining sauce over crepes. Bake, covered, at 375° till heated through, 20 to 25 minutes. Makes 4 to 6 servings.

Crepes

1 **cup all-purpose flour**
1½ **cups milk**
2 **eggs**
1 **tablespoon cooking oil**
¼ **teaspoon salt**

In a bowl combine flour, milk, eggs, oil, and salt; beat with a rotary beater till blended. Heat a lightly greased 6-inch skillet; remove from heat. Spoon in about 2 tablespoons batter; lift and tilt skillet to spread evenly. Return to heat; brown on one side only. To remove, invert pan over paper toweling. Repeat with remaining batter to make 12 crepes, greasing skillet occasionally.

Make Casseroles Ahead

Shorten the time you'll spend in the kitchen after your guests arrive—prepare a casserole the day before.

Assemble the casserole as directed, but omit the final heating step. Cover the dish tightly and store it in the refrigerator. Be sure to use within one or two days. When you heat the casserole, remember to allow an extra 15 to 20 minutes of baking time for the chilled food to heat through.

Casseroles for a Crowd

Hamburger-Noodle Bake

4 pounds ground beef
3 large onions, chopped (3 cups)
1 cup chopped green pepper
16 ounces medium noodles
3 10¾-ounce cans condensed
    tomato soup
4 cups shredded American cheese
1 12-ounce bottle chili sauce
¼ cup chopped pimiento
2 teaspoons salt
2 teaspoons chili powder
½ teaspoon pepper
4½ cups soft bread crumbs
¼ cup butter, melted

In a large skillet cook beef, onion, and green pepper, half at a time, till meat is brown. Drain off fat.

Cook noodles according to package directions; drain well. Return drained noodles to kettle. Stir in meat mixture, tomato soup, cheese, chili sauce, pimiento, salt, chili powder, pepper, and 2 cups water; mix well. Divide mixture between two 13x9x2-inch baking dishes.

Toss bread crumbs with melted butter; sprinkle atop casseroles. Bake, uncovered, at 350° till heated through, about 45 minutes. Garnish with green pepper rings, if desired. Makes 2 casseroles, 12 servings each.

Layered Supper

4 pounds potatoes, peeled and
    thinly sliced (12 cups)
2 17-ounce cans whole kernel
    corn, drained
1 cup chopped green pepper
2 cups chopped onion (2 large)
4 cups sliced carrot (8 medium)
3 pounds ground beef
1 15-ounce can tomato sauce
2 cups shredded sharp American
    cheese (8 ounces)

Divide potatoes between two 12x7½x2-inch baking dishes. Season with salt and pepper. Arrange corn and green pepper over potatoes in each casserole. Layer the onion, then the carrot in each. Crumble beef evenly over the vegetables; sprinkle with more salt and pepper. Pat gently to smooth. Top each casserole with tomato sauce.

Bake, covered, at 350° for 2 hours. Uncover; sprinkle with cheese. Let stand 10 to 15 minutes before serving. Makes 2 casseroles, 8 or 9 servings each.

Barbecued Beans and Meatballs

3 beaten eggs
⅔ cup milk
2 tablespoons instant minced
    onion
3 cups soft bread crumbs
3 pounds ground beef
2 31-ounce cans pork and beans
    in tomato sauce
1 28-ounce can tomatoes, cut up
2 12-ounce cans whole kernel
    corn, drained
1 8-ounce can tomato sauce
¼ cup packed brown sugar
¼ cup light molasses
2 tablespoons prepared mustard
8 fully cooked smoked sausage
    links or frankfurters
2 cups shredded American cheese

In a large bowl combine eggs, milk, and instant minced onion; let stand 5 minutes. Stir in bread crumbs, 1½ teaspoons salt, and ¼ teaspoon pepper. Add ground beef; mix well. With wet hands, shape mixture into 48 two-inch meatballs. Place meatballs in two 15½x10½x1-inch baking pans. Bake, uncovered, at 375° for 20 minutes. Drain off fat.

Meanwhile, in a large Dutch oven combine pork and beans, tomatoes, corn, tomato sauce, brown sugar, molasses, and mustard. Heat till boiling.

Cut sausages or frankfurters crosswise into thirds. Divide sausages and meatballs between two 3-quart casseroles. Turn *half* the bean mixture into *each* casserole. Stir to combine. Bake, uncovered, at 375° for 1½ hours, stirring occasionally. Sprinkle with cheese. Bake till cheese melts, 2 to 3 minutes longer. Makes 2 casseroles, 12 servings each.

Next time it's your turn to serve two football teams (or six tables of bridge), don't panic. Put *Hamburger-Noodle Bake* in the oven about 45 minutes before you plan to eat, then relax.

Ham and Broccoli Bake

2 20-ounce packages frozen
    cut broccoli
1 large onion, chopped (1 cup)
¼ cup butter *or* margarine
2 10¾-ounce cans condensed
    cream of mushroom soup
2 10¾-ounce cans condensed
    cream of celery soup
2 soup cans milk (2½ cups)
2 cups shredded sharp American
    cheese (8 ounces)
6 cups cubed fully cooked ham
4 cups quick-cooking rice
1 tablespoon Worcestershire
    sauce

Cook frozen broccoli according to package directions; drain well. In saucepan cook onion in butter or margarine till tender but not brown.

In a large mixing bowl stir together mushroom soup, celery soup, milk, and cheese. Add drained broccoli, cooked onion, ham, uncooked rice, and Worcestershire sauce; mix well. Divide mixture between two 2½-quart casseroles.

Bake, covered, at 350° till rice is done, 45 to 50 minutes. Garnish each with a sprig of watercress, if desired. Makes 2 casseroles, 10 servings each.

Peppy Lasagna

1 pound bulk Italian sausage
½ cup chopped onion
½ cup chopped celery
½ cup chopped carrot
1 16-ounce can tomatoes, cut up
1 6-ounce can tomato paste
1 teaspoon sugar
½ teaspoon dried oregano,
    crushed
10 ounces lasagna noodles
2 beaten eggs
2 cups ricotta *or* cream-style
    cottage cheese (16 ounces)
½ cup grated Parmesan cheese
2 tablespoons snipped parsley
16 ounces mozzarella cheese,
    thinly sliced

In a large skillet cook sausage, onion, celery, and carrot till meat is lightly browned. Drain off excess fat. Stir in tomatoes, tomato paste, sugar, oregano, 1 teaspoon salt, and ¼ teaspoon pepper. Simmer, uncovered, for 20 minutes, stirring occasionally.

Meanwhile, cook lasagna noodles according to package directions; drain well. Combine eggs, ricotta, Parmesan cheese, parsley, and ¼ teaspoon pepper.

Arrange *half* the lasagna noodles in a greased 13x9x2-inch baking dish. Spread with *half* the cheese filling; add *half* the mozzarella cheese and *half* the meat sauce. Repeat layers. Bake, uncovered, at 375° till bubbly, about 40 minutes. Let stand 10 to 15 minutes. Makes 12 servings.

Sausage au Gratin

4 pounds potatoes (12 medium)
2 8-ounce jars cheese spread
2 cups dairy sour cream
2 tablespoons instant minced
    onion
1 tablespoon dried parsley flakes
1 12-ounce package fully cooked
    smoked sausage links, sliced
1½ cups soft bread crumbs
1 tablespoon melted butter
¼ teaspoon paprika

In covered kettle cook potatoes in boiling salted water to cover till tender, about 30 minutes. Drain and cool. When cool enough to handle, peel and slice potatoes.

Meanwhile, in a large bowl blend together cheese spread and sour cream. Stir in instant minced onion, parsley flakes, and 1 teaspoon salt. Fold in sliced potatoes and sliced sausages. Turn into a 13x9x2-inch baking dish. Bake, uncovered, at 350° for 40 to 45 minutes.

Toss together bread crumbs, melted butter, and paprika. Sprinkle atop casserole. Bake till lightly browned, about 10 minutes longer. Makes 12 servings.

Rich and creamy *Ham and Broccoli Bake* is ideal for a spur-of-the-moment get-together.
Share it with as many as 20 friends and relatives, or halve the recipe to serve a smaller group.

Casserole Chop Suey

5 **pounds boneless pork, cut in**
  ½-inch cubes
2 **tablespoons cooking oil**
1 **teaspoon salt**
4 **10¾-ounce cans condensed**
  cream of mushroom soup
4 **cups milk**
1 **16-ounce can bean sprouts,**
  drained
1½ **cups chopped celery**
1½ **cups chopped onion**
1½ **cups chopped green pepper**
1½ **cups regular rice**
1 **8-ounce can water chestnuts,**
  drained and sliced
⅔ **cup soy sauce**
2 **3-ounce cans chow mein noodles**

In a large kettle or Dutch oven brown meat, about ⅓ at a time, in hot oil. Return meat to pan; sprinkle with salt. Stir in soup, milk, bean sprouts, celery, onion, green pepper, uncooked rice, water chestnuts, and soy sauce. Divide mixture between two 13x9x2-inch baking dishes.

Bake, covered, at 350° till rice is done, about 1½ hours, stirring after 1 hour. Uncover; stir each casserole. Sprinkle *each* with 1 can of chow mein noodles. Bake 5 minutes longer. Pass additional soy sauce with casseroles. Makes 2 casseroles, 12 servings each.

Spinach Squares Hollandaise

3 10-ounce packages frozen
   chopped spinach
½ cup finely chopped onion
2 tablespoons butter *or*
   margarine
4 beaten eggs
2 cups milk
3 cups soft bread crumbs
3 cups chopped fully cooked ham
½ teaspoon seasoned salt
2 1⅛-ounce envelopes
   hollandaise sauce mix
4 hard-cooked eggs, chopped

Cook frozen spinach according to package directions; drain well. Cook chopped onion in butter or margarine till onion is tender but not brown. Combine beaten eggs and milk. Add bread crumbs, ham, cooked onion, spinach, and seasoned salt; mix well. Spread evenly in a 12x7½x2-inch baking dish. Bake, uncovered, at 350° till set, 40 to 45 minutes.

Meanwhile, prepare hollandaise sauce mix according to package directions; stir in chopped hard-cooked eggs.

To serve, cut casserole into squares; spoon sauce over each serving. Makes 12 servings.

Ham Potluck Supper

½ cup chopped onion
½ cup chopped green pepper
¼ cup butter *or* margarine
⅓ cup all-purpose flour
2 10½-ounce cans condensed
   chicken with rice soup
1 cup milk
3 cups cubed fully cooked ham
7 hard-cooked eggs, sliced
1½ cups soft bread crumbs
2 tablespoons butter, melted

Cook onion and green pepper in the ¼ cup butter or margarine till tender but not brown. Blend in flour; stir in soup and milk. Cook and stir till thickened and bubbly. Fold in ham and *six* of the sliced hard-cooked eggs. Turn mixture into a 12x7½x2-inch baking dish.

Toss bread crumbs with melted butter to combine. Sprinkle around edges of baking dish. Bake, uncovered, at 350° for 25 minutes. Top with remaining egg slices. Makes 10 servings.

Seafood Lasagna

8 lasagna noodles
1 large onion, chopped (1 cup)
2 tablespoons butter
1 8-ounce package cream
   cheese, softened
1½ cups cream-style cottage
   cheese (12 ounces)
1 beaten egg
2 teaspoons dried basil, crushed
½ teaspoon salt
⅛ teaspoon pepper
2 10¾-ounce cans condensed
   cream of mushroom soup
⅓ cup milk
⅓ cup dry white wine
1 pound fresh *or* frozen shelled
   shrimp, cooked and halved
1 7½-ounce can crab meat,
   drained, flaked, and
   cartilage removed
¼ cup grated Parmesan cheese
½ cup shredded sharp American
   cheese (2 ounces)

Cook lasagna noodles according to package directions; drain well. Arrange 4 noodles to cover bottom of a greased 13x9x2-inch baking dish.

Cook onion in butter till tender but not brown; blend in cream cheese. Stir in cottage cheese, egg, basil, salt, and pepper; spread *half* atop noodles.

Combine soup, milk, and wine. Stir in shrimp and crab; spread *half* over cottage cheese layer.

Repeat layers of noodles, cheese mixture, and seafood mixture. Sprinkle with Parmesan cheese. Bake, uncovered, at 350° for 45 minutes. Top with shredded American cheese. Bake till cheese melts, 2 to 3 minutes more. Let stand 15 minutes before serving. Makes 12 servings.

Crowd-Size Chicken Bake

16 **ounces medium noodles**
½ **cup butter** *or* **margarine**
½ **cup all-purpose flour**
1½ **teaspoons salt**
¼ **teaspoon white pepper**
7 **cups milk**
4 **10½-ounce cans chicken gravy**
8 **cups chopped cooked chicken**
    or **turkey**
1 **2-ounce jar diced pimiento,**
    drained (¼ cup)
1 **cup fine dry bread crumbs**
¼ **cup butter** *or* **margarine,**
    melted

Cook noodles according to package directions; drain well. In a large kettle melt the ½ cup butter or margarine. Blend in flour, salt, and pepper. Add milk all at once. Cook and stir till thickened and bubbly; stir in chicken gravy. Stir in chicken or turkey, pimiento, and cooked noodles. Divide mixture between two 13x9x2-inch baking dishes. Bake, covered, at 350° about 35 minutes.

Toss together bread crumbs and the melted butter to combine; sprinkle atop casseroles. Bake, uncovered, 10 minutes longer. Makes 2 casseroles, 12 servings each.

Buffet Chicken Scallop

1 **cup regular rice**
1 **large onion, chopped (1 cup)**
1 **cup chopped green pepper**
2 **tablespoons butter** *or*
    margarine
1 **16-ounce package herb-**
    seasoned stuffing mix
4 **cups chicken broth**
6 **beaten eggs**
3 **10¾-ounce cans condensed**
    cream of celery soup
8 **cups chopped cooked chicken**
    or **turkey**
1 **4-ounce jar diced pimiento,**
    drained (½ cup)
2 **10¾-ounce cans condensed**
    cream of chicken soup
½ **cup milk**
1 **cup dairy sour cream**

Cook rice according to package directions. Meanwhile, cook chopped onion and green pepper in butter or margarine till tender but not brown.

In large mixing bowl combine stuffing mix with broth; stir in eggs and celery soup; add chicken, cooked rice, onion-green pepper mixture, and pimiento. Mix well. Divide between two greased 13x9x2-inch baking dishes. Bake, uncovered, at 325° for 30 to 40 minutes.

In saucepan combine chicken soup and milk; heat and stir till smooth. Stir in sour cream; heat through but *do not boil.* To serve, cut casserole into squares; spoon sauce over each serving. Makes 2 casseroles, 12 servings each.

Turkey with Fruited Stuffing

1 **2½-pound frozen boneless**
    turkey roast
1 **cup chopped celery**
½ **cup butter** *or* **margarine**
1 **cup pitted dried prunes,**
    chopped
½ **cup water***
½ **teaspoon ground sage**
1 **8-ounce package corn bread**
    stuffing mix
1 **cup orange juice**
¼ **cup water**
1 **tablespoon cornstarch**
1 **tablespoon soy sauce**

Cook turkey roast according to package directions. In large saucepan cook celery in butter or margarine till tender. Stir in prunes, the ½ cup water, and sage. Add stuffing mix; toss to coat. Turn mixture into a 12x7½x2-inch baking dish.

Cut turkey roast into 10 slices; arrange atop stuffing mixture. Bake, covered, at 350° for 30 to 35 minutes.

Meanwhile, in saucepan slowly stir orange juice and the ¼ cup water into cornstarch. Stir in soy sauce; cook and stir till thickened and bubbly. Pour orange sauce over turkey. Makes 10 servings.

*Increase water to ¾ cup if moister stuffing is desired.

International Casseroles

Armenian Pilaf

¾ cup fine noodles
2 tablespoons cooking oil
2 cups chopped cooked lamb
   or beef
¾ cup long grain rice
½ cup raisins
1 tablespoon instant beef
   bouillon granules
½ teaspoon dried mint, crushed
¼ cup toasted slivered
   almonds

In skillet brown *uncooked* noodles in hot oil till golden. Stir in meat, *uncooked* rice, raisins, bouillon granules, mint, 3 cups water, and 1 teaspoon salt. Bring to boiling; turn into 2-quart casserole. Bake, covered, at 325° till liquid is absorbed, 30 to 40 minutes; stir once after 20 minutes. Sprinkle with almonds. Makes 6 servings.

Of French origin, *Quiche Lorraine* is a main-dish custard tart flavored with Swiss cheese and bacon. Serve it as an entrée, or cut the pie in smaller wedges to use as an appetizer.

Quiche Lorraine (French)

Plain Pastry (see page 72)
4 slices bacon
1 cup shredded Swiss cheese
  (4 ounces)
2 teaspoons all-purpose flour
¼ teaspoon salt
  Dash ground nutmeg
1 cup milk
2 beaten eggs

Prepare Plain Pastry as for a single-crust pie, *except* fit pastry into a 7½-inch quiche dish. Bake at 450° for 5 minutes. Set aside; reduce oven temperature to 325°.

Cook bacon till crisp. Drain; crumble. Reserve 1 tablespoon bacon; sprinkle remaining in pastry shell. Top with cheese. Mix flour, salt, and nutmeg; stir in milk and eggs. Carefully pour over cheese in pastry shell.

Bake, uncovered, at 325° for 30 minutes. Sprinkle with reserved bacon. Bake till knife inserted off-center comes out clean, 5 to 10 minutes more. Let stand 10 minutes before serving. Trim with parsley, if desired. Serves 3 or 4.

Cheese Soufflé (French)

¼ cup butter *or* margarine
¼ cup all-purpose flour
½ teaspoon salt
  Dash cayenne
1 cup milk
8 ounces sharp Cheddar cheese,
  thinly sliced
4 egg whites
4 egg yolks

In saucepan melt butter; blend in flour, salt, and cayenne. Add milk all at once; cook and stir till thickened and bubbly. Remove from heat; stir in cheese till melted.

Beat egg whites till stiff peaks form, about 1½ minutes on medium speed of electric mixer; set aside. In small bowl beat egg yolks till thick and lemon-colored, about 5 minutes on high speed of electric mixer. *Slowly* add cheese mixture, stirring constantly; cool slightly. Gradually pour yolk mixture over beaten egg whites; fold together well. Turn into an ungreased 1½-quart soufflé dish or casserole.

Bake at 300° till knife inserted off-center comes out clean, about 1¼ hours. Serve immediately. Makes 4 servings.

Dilled Lamb Ragout (French)

⅓ cup all-purpose flour
1½ teaspoons salt
½ teaspoon dried dillweed
  Dash pepper
2 pounds boneless lamb, cut
  in ¾-inch cubes
¼ cup cooking oil
1 10-ounce package frozen peas
1 cup sliced celery
½ cup rosé wine
1 cup dairy sour cream

In paper or plastic bag combine flour, salt, dillweed, and pepper. Add lamb cubes, ¼ at a time; shake to coat.

In Dutch oven brown lamb in hot oil. Stir in any flour mixture remaining in bag; blend in 2 cups water. Bake, covered, at 375° for 45 minutes.

Stir in peas, celery, and wine; cover and bake till meat is tender, about 45 minutes longer. Skim off excess fat. Just before serving, stir in sour cream. Heat through *but do not boil.* Makes 6 servings.

Toad in the Hole (British)

2 slices bacon
½ pound fresh pork sausage
  links, cut in ½-inch pieces
1 cup all-purpose flour
1 teaspoon baking powder
1 teaspoon salt
1½ cups milk
3 beaten eggs

Cook bacon till crisp. Drain; set aside 2 tablespoons drippings. Crumble bacon; set aside. In same skillet brown sausage; drain off fat. Stir together flour, baking powder, and salt. Add milk and eggs; beat till smooth.

Spread reserved bacon drippings in a 10x6x2-inch baking dish. Place sausage pieces in dish; sprinkle with crumbled bacon. Pour batter over all. Bake, uncovered, at 400° till set, 30 to 35 minutes. Makes 4 servings.

Steak and Kidney Pie (British)

1 beef kidney (about 1 pound)
1 tablespoon salt
1 pound beef round steak, cut
   in ½-inch cubes
¼ cup all-purpose flour
3 tablespoons shortening
1 medium onion, sliced
1 teaspoon Worcestershire sauce
   Plain Pastry (see page 72)
¼ cup all-purpose flour
1 teaspoon salt
   Dash pepper
2 tablespoons snipped parsley
   Milk

Remove membrane and fat from kidney. Let kidney stand for 1 hour in solution of the 1 tablespoon salt and 4 cups water; drain. Cover with cold water. Bring to boiling; simmer, covered, 20 minutes. Drain; cut into ½-inch cubes. Set aside.

Toss beef with ¼ cup flour. In skillet brown beef in shortening. Add onion, Worcestershire, and 2 cups water. Cover, simmer till meat is tender, about 30 minutes.

Meanwhile, prepare Plain Pastry. Roll out to a circle ½ to 1 inch larger than a 1½-quart casserole; set aside.

Combine ¼ cup flour, the 1 teaspoon salt, and pepper; blend in ½ cup cold water. Stir into hot beef mixture. Cook and stir till slightly thickened and bubbly. Stir in cubed kidney and parsley; heat mixture to boiling.

Pour hot meat mixture into a 1½-quart casserole. Place pastry atop meat mixture. Turn under edges and flute; cut slits for escape of steam. Brush top with milk. Bake, uncovered, at 450° for 20 to 25 minutes. Makes 6 servings.

Cipâte (French-Canadian)

2 whole large chicken breasts
1½ pounds cubed boneless pork,
   veal, *or* beef
3 tablespoons cooking oil
1 13¾-ounce can chicken broth
1 cup chopped onion
1 cup chopped celery
1 cup chopped raw potato
1 cup sliced carrot
1 cup sliced fresh mushrooms
2 tablespoons snipped parsley
1 teaspoon salt
⅛ teaspoon pepper
⅛ teaspoon dried savory, crushed
1 cup all-purpose flour
1½ teaspoons baking powder
¼ teaspoon salt
6 tablespoons butter
¼ cup milk
2 tablespoons all-purpose flour

Remove skin and bones from chicken; cube chicken. In saucepan brown chicken and meat in hot oil. Stir in broth, vegetables, parsley, the 1 teaspoon salt, pepper, and savory. Cook, covered, till meat is tender, 1¼ to 1½ hours.

Meanwhile, to prepare pastry topper stir together the 1 cup flour, baking powder, and the ¼ teaspoon salt. Cut in butter till size of small peas. Add milk; mix well. On lightly floured surface roll out pastry to a circle ½ to 1 inch larger than a 2-quart casserole; set aside.

Blend ⅓ cup cold water into the 2 tablespoons flour. Stir into hot meat mixture. Cook and stir till thickened and bubbly. Turn hot meat mixture into a 2-quart casserole. Place pastry atop meat mixture. Turn under edges and flute; cut slits for escape of steam. Bake, uncovered, at 350° till crust is golden brown, 30 to 35 minutes. Makes 8 to 10 servings.

Tourtière (French-Canadian)

1 pound lean ground pork
1 cup water
½ cup finely chopped onion
½ cup fine dry bread crumbs
1 teaspoon salt
⅛ teaspoon ground sage
   Dash pepper
   Dash ground nutmeg
2 recipes Plain Pastry
   (see page 72)

In skillet brown ground pork; drain off excess fat. Stir in water, chopped onion, dry bread crumbs, salt, sage, pepper, and nutmeg. Simmer, covered, till onion is tender, about 20 minutes, stirring often.

Meanwhile, prepare Plain Pastry as for a double-crust pie. Fill pastry-lined 9-inch pie plate with hot meat mixture. Adjust top crust; seal and flute edges. Cut slits in top for escape of steam. Bake, uncovered, at 400° till golden brown, about 30 minutes. Cover edges of pastry with foil, if necessary, to prevent overbrowning. Makes 6 servings.

Greek Spinach Pie

½ cup sliced green onion
    with tops
½ teaspoon dried dillweed
1 tablespoon cooking oil
1 10-ounce package frozen
    chopped spinach, thawed
¼ cup butter *or* margarine
¼ cup all-purpose flour
½ teaspoon salt
1½ cups milk
2 beaten eggs
1 cup cream-style cottage cheese
½ cup crumbled feta cheese
    (2 ounces)
¼ teaspoon baking powder
2 16x16-inch sheets fillo dough
2 tablespoons butter, melted

In skillet cook onion and dill in hot oil till onion is tender. Squeeze excess water from spinach; add to skillet. Cook till heated through; keep warm.

In large saucepan melt the ¼ cup butter; blend in flour and salt. Stir in milk all at once. Cook and stir till thickened and bubbly; cook and stir 1 minute more. Stir *half* the hot sauce mixture into eggs; return to saucepan. Stir in cheeses, spinach mixture, and baking powder. Set aside.

Brush *half* of *one* sheet of fillo dough with some of the melted butter; fold in half. Butter half of this dough rectangle and fold again, forming an 8-inch square. Place in greased 8x8x2-inch baking pan. Pour in spinach mixture.

Repeat buttering and folding remaining fillo dough. Place atop spinach mixture; tuck in edges. Bake, uncovered, at 325° till mixture is set and top is browned, 35 to 40 minutes. Let stand 10 minutes. Makes 4 servings.

Pasticchio (Greek)

6 ounces pasticchio macaroni *or*
    elbow macaroni (1½ cups)
⅓ cup grated Parmesan cheese
¼ cup milk
1 beaten egg
¾ pound ground beef
½ cup chopped onion
1 8-ounce can tomato sauce
¾ teaspoon salt
½ teaspoon ground cinnamon
⅛ teaspoon ground nutmeg
⅛ teaspoon pepper
3 tablespoons butter
3 tablespoons all-purpose flour
¼ teaspoon salt
1½ cups milk
1 beaten egg
¼ cup grated Parmesan cheese

Cook macaroni according to package directions; drain. Stir in the ⅓ cup Parmesan, the ¼ cup milk, and 1 egg; set aside.

In skillet cook ground beef and chopped onion till meat is lightly browned and onion is tender; drain off excess fat. Stir in tomato sauce, the ¾ teaspoon salt, the cinnamon, nutmeg, and pepper; set aside.

In saucepan melt butter; blend in flour and the ¼ teaspoon salt. Stir in the 1½ cups milk; cook and stir till thickened and bubbly. Cook and stir 1 minute more. Stir *half* the hot sauce mixture into 1 beaten egg; return all to saucepan. Stir in the ¼ cup Parmesan cheese.

Layer *half* the macaroni mixture in an 8x8x2-inch baking pan. Spoon meat mixture atop, then remaining macaroni. Spread cream sauce over all. Bake, uncovered, at 350° for 45 to 50 minutes. Let stand 10 minutes. Makes 6 servings.

Pasta Pointers

When you cook macaroni, spaghetti, or noodles, use a large pot with plenty of water. (During cooking, macaroni and spaghetti generally double in volume, while the measure of noodles remains about the same.) Add 1 teaspoon of salt for each quart of water and a teaspoon of cooking oil, if desired, to prevent sticking and to prevent boiling over.

Add the pasta to vigorously boiling water, leaving the pan uncovered. Stir a moment to separate pieces. Making sure the water continues to boil, cook without stirring till pasta is barely tender. Drain at once. If you need to hold the pasta before serving, stir in a little butter or oil to keep it from sticking.

Moussaka (Greek)

2 **medium eggplants, peeled and
cut into ½-inch slices
(2 pounds)**
1 **pound ground lamb** *or*
ground beef
1 **cup chopped onion**
¼ **cup dry red wine**
¼ **cup water**
2 **tablespoons snipped parsley**
1 **tablespoon tomato paste**
1 **teaspoon salt
Dash pepper**
¾ **cup soft bread crumbs (1 slice)**
½ **cup shredded sharp American
cheese (2 ounces)**
2 **beaten eggs**
¼ **teaspoon ground cinnamon**
3 **tablespoons butter** *or*
margarine
3 **tablespoons all-purpose flour**
½ **teaspoon salt**
⅛ **teaspoon ground nutmeg
Dash pepper**
1½ **cups milk**
1 **beaten egg
Cooking oil**

Sprinkle eggplant slices with a little salt; set aside. In skillet cook meat and onion till meat is brown; drain off excess fat. Stir in wine, water, parsley, tomato paste, the 1 teaspoon salt, and dash pepper. Simmer till liquid is nearly evaporated, about 4 minutes. Cool slightly.

Stir *half* the bread crumbs, *half* the cheese, the 2 eggs, and cinnamon into meat mixture. Set aside.

In saucepan melt butter; stir in flour, the ½ teaspoon salt, nutmeg, and dash pepper. Add milk all at once; cook and stir till thickened and bubbly. Stir *half* the hot sauce mixture into the 1 beaten egg; return all to saucepan. Cook and stir over low heat 2 minutes. Set aside.

Brown eggplant slices in a little hot oil. Sprinkle bottom of a 12x7½x2-inch baking dish with remaining bread crumbs. Cover with *half* the eggplant.

Spoon meat mixture over eggplant layer. Arrange remaining eggplant atop; pour milk-egg sauce over all. Sprinkle with remaining ¼ cup cheese. Bake, uncovered, at 350° till set, about 45 minutes. Makes 6 to 8 servings.

Paella Casserole (Spanish)

½ **pound chorizos** *or* **Italian
sausage links, sliced**
1 **2½- to 3-pound ready-to-cook
broiler-fryer chicken,
cut up**
1 **medium onion, chopped
(½ cup)**
1 **medium sweet red pepper,
chopped (½ cup)**
1 **medium green pepper, chopped
(½ cup)**
2 **cloves garlic, minced**
1½ **cups regular rice**
2 **medium tomatoes, peeled and
chopped (1½ cups)**
2 **teaspoons salt**
¼ **teaspoon saffron, crushed**
4 **cups boiling water**
1 **pound fresh** *or* **frozen shelled
shrimp**
10 **small clams in shells**
1 **10-ounce package frozen peas**

In large skillet cook sausage over medium heat till done. Drain sausage, reserving drippings in skillet; set aside.

Season chicken pieces with a little salt and pepper. Brown chicken in reserved drippings; remove chicken, reserving drippings in skillet.

Add chopped onion, red pepper, green pepper, and garlic to reserved drippings; cook till onion is tender but not brown. Stir in uncooked rice, chopped tomatoes, salt, and saffron. Stir in boiling water; bring mixture to boiling. Stir in cooked sausage.

Turn rice mixture into a paella pan *or* a 4-quart casserole *or* a Dutch oven; arrange chicken pieces atop mixture. Bake, covered, at 375° for 30 minutes.

Meanwhile, thaw frozen shrimp. Thoroughly scrub clams. Place clams in a saucepan with ½ inch of boiling water; cover and cook till shells open, 3 to 5 minutes. Drain; discard any clams that do not open.

Place peas in a colander or strainer; rinse with hot water to thaw. Arrange peas, clams, and shrimp atop rice mixture. Bake, covered, till chicken and rice are done, 15 to 20 minutes longer. Garnish with lemon slices, if desired. Serves 8.

Paella Casserole, a Spanish specialty, offers a festival of flavors in a single
dish. This colorful entrée includes sausage, chicken, shrimp, clams, peas, and saffron rice.

Chicken Enchiladas (Mexican)

  1 **cup chopped onion**
  1 **clove garlic, minced**
  2 **tablespoons cooking oil**
  1 **tablespoon all-purpose flour**
  1 **16-ounce can tomatoes, cut up**
  1 **15-ounce can tomato sauce**
  1 **4-ounce can green chili**
      peppers, drained, seeded,
      and chopped
  1 **teaspoon sugar**
  1 **teaspoon ground cumin**
  ¼ **teaspoon salt**
  2 **cups chopped cooked chicken**
1½ **cups shredded sharp American**
      cheese (6 ounces)
  ¼ **cup finely chopped onion**
  ¼ **cup chopped pitted ripe olives**
  ¾ **teaspoon salt**
 12 **frozen corn tortillas, thawed**
      Cooking oil
  ¼ **cup sliced pitted ripe olives**

Cook the 1 cup chopped onion and garlic in the 2 tablespoons oil till onion is tender but not brown; stir in flour. Add undrained tomatoes, tomato sauce, chili peppers, sugar, cumin, and the ¼ teaspoon salt. Cook and stir till thickened and bubbly; set aside.

Combine chicken, *half* the cheese, the ¼ cup onion, the chopped olives, and the ¾ teaspoon salt. Set aside.

In skillet dip tortillas briefly in small amount of hot oil till limp but not crisp; drain. Spoon ¼ *cup* of the chicken mixture onto each tortilla; roll up.

Place filled tortillas in a 13x9x2-inch baking dish. Pour tomato mixture over all. Bake, covered, at 350° about 15 minutes. Uncover; bake till heated through, about 15 minutes more. Sprinkle with remaining shredded cheese; return to oven till cheese melts, 2 or 3 minutes. Top with the sliced olives. Makes 6 servings.

Brunch Eggs Ranchero (Mexican)

  5 **slices bacon, cut up**
  1 **16-ounce can tomatoes, cut up**
  2 **tablespoons chopped canned**
      green chili peppers
      (about 2 peppers)
  1 **clove garlic, minced**
  4 **eggs**
      Salt
      Pepper
  4 **slices bacon**

In skillet cook the cut-up bacon slices till crisp; drain off fat. Stir in undrained tomatoes, chili peppers, and garlic; heat through. Divide among 4 individual casseroles.

Carefully break one egg atop tomato mixture in *each* casserole. Season eggs lightly with salt and pepper. Bake, uncovered, at 325° till eggs are set, 20 to 25 minutes.

Cook the 4 bacon slices till done *but not crisp;* drain. Insert tines of fork into one end of each bacon slice; turn fork to wind bacon around it. Remove fork. Garnish each casserole with a bacon curl. Makes 4 servings.

Pastel de Chocolo (South American)

  2 **tablespoons raisins**
  1 **pound ground beef**
  2 **cups chopped onion**
  ½ **small clove garlic, minced**
  1 **tablespoon ground cumin**
1½ **teaspoons paprika**
  1 **teaspoon salt**
  ⅛ **teaspoon pepper**
  ½ **cup chopped pitted ripe olives**
  1 **2½- to 3-pound ready-to-cook**
      broiler-fryer chicken,
      cut up
  2 **tablespoons olive oil**
  1 **10-ounce package frozen corn**
  1 **cup dry white wine**

Soak raisins in ¼ cup hot water till plump; set aside. Cook beef, onion, and garlic till meat is brown and onion is tender; drain off fat. Stir in raisins with their liquid, cumin, paprika, salt, and pepper; turn into a 3-quart casserole. Spread chopped olives evenly over meat mixture; set aside.

Brown chicken lightly in the olive oil about 15 minutes. Arrange chicken atop meat mixture. Top with corn; season with more salt and pepper. Pour wine over all.

Bake, covered, at 350° for 45 minutes. Spread corn evenly over casserole, if necessary. Bake, uncovered, 15 minutes more. Serve over hot cooked rice, if desired. Makes 8 servings.

Veal Parmesan Casserole (Italian)

  6 ounces spaghetti
1½ pounds boneless veal round
     or sirloin steak, cut in
     6 serving-size pieces
  ¼ cup all-purpose flour
  ½ teaspoon salt
     Dash pepper
  1 beaten egg
  2 tablespoons milk
  ⅓ cup fine dry bread crumbs
  ⅓ cup grated Parmesan cheese
  3 tablespoons cooking oil
  1 large green pepper,
     finely chopped
     (1 cup)
  1 large onion, finely chopped
     (1 cup)
  2 cloves garlic, minced
  2 15-ounce cans tomato sauce
  ¼ cup water
  1 teaspoon dried basil,
     crushed
  1 cup shredded mozzarella
     cheese (4 ounces)
  ¼ cup grated Parmesan cheese

Break spaghetti pieces in half. Cook spaghetti according to package directions; drain and set aside. Pound veal pieces to ¼-inch thickness.

In shallow dish combine flour, salt, and pepper. In another dish combine egg and milk; in a third dish mix crumbs and the ⅓ cup Parmesan. Coat veal with flour mixture; dip in egg mixture, then in crumbs. In large skillet brown meat on both sides in hot oil, 2 or 3 pieces at a time; remove meat, reserving drippings in skillet.

In reserved drippings cook green pepper, onion, and garlic till onion is tender. Stir in tomato sauce, water, and basil. Set aside ½ *cup* of the sauce; stir remaining sauce into cooked spaghetti. Turn spaghetti mixture into a 13x9x2-inch baking dish; arrange veal atop.

Spoon reserved sauce over meat. Bake, covered, at 350° for 40 minutes. Sprinkle with mozzarella and the ¼ cup Parmesan. Bake, uncovered, 10 minutes more. Makes 6 servings.

Pizza Siciliana (Italian)

4½ cups all-purpose flour
  1 package active dry yeast
1½ teaspoons salt
1½ cups *warm* water (110°)
  2 tablespoons cooking oil
  1 cup chopped onion
  1 clove garlic, minced
  2 tablespoons olive oil
  1 16-ounce can tomatoes,
     cut up
  1 6-ounce can tomato paste
1½ teaspoons dried basil,
     crushed
1½ teaspoons dried oregano,
     crushed
  1 teaspoon salt
  ½ teaspoon sugar
  ⅛ teaspoon pepper
  ½ cup chopped onion
  ½ cup sliced pitted
     ripe olives
  1 medium green pepper,
     cut in strips
  2 cups shredded mozzarella
     cheese (8 ounces)
  ¼ cup grated Parmesan cheese

Combine *2 cups* of the flour, yeast, and the 1½ teaspoons salt. Add water and cooking oil. Beat at low speed of electric mixer for ½ minute, scraping bowl. Beat 3 minutes at high speed. By hand, stir in enough of the remaining flour to make moderately stiff dough. On floured surface, knead till smooth. Place in greased bowl; turn once. Cover; let rise till double (about 1 hour).

Cook the 1 cup chopped onion and garlic in olive oil till onion is tender. Add undrained tomatoes, tomato paste, basil, oregano, salt, sugar, and pepper. Bring mixture to boiling; cover and simmer for 10 minutes.

Pat dough from center to edges in a greased 15½x10½x1-inch baking pan. Cover; let rise 45 minutes. Spoon sauce over dough. Bake, uncovered, at 475° for 25 minutes.

Sprinkle pizza with the ½ cup onion and olives. Top with green pepper; sprinkle mozzarella and Parmesan cheese over. Bake 10 to 15 minutes longer. Makes 6 servings.

3 Barbecue recipes

There's nothing like the smell of sizzling steaks, ribs, or other meats wafting through the air. And this chapter abounds with over-the-coals favorites. You'll also find pointers on equipment, grills, and charcoal cooking.

Cornish Hens with Rice Stuffing, Beef-Yam Kobobs, Steak and Shrimp Kabob Dinner, and *Halibut Kabobs.* (See index for pages.)

Beef Off the Grill

Steak and Bacon Tournedos

1 1- to 1½-pound beef flank
  steak
  Instant unseasoned meat
  tenderizer
10 slices bacon
1 teaspoon garlic salt
½ teaspoon freshly ground
  pepper
2 tablespoons snipped parsley
1 1¾-ounce envelope hollandaise
  sauce mix
¼ teaspoon dried tarragon,
  crushed

Pound flank steak evenly about ½ inch thick. Apply meat tenderizer according to package directions. Meanwhile, cook bacon till almost done, but not crisp.

Sprinkle flank steak with garlic salt and pepper. Score steak diagonally, making diamond-shaped cuts. Place bacon strips lengthwise on flank steak. Sprinkle with parsley. Roll up as for jelly roll, starting at narrow end. Skewer with wooden picks at 1-inch intervals. Cut into eight 1-inch slices with serrated knife.

Grill over *medium* coals for 8 minutes. Turn; grill 7 minutes more for rare. Meanwhile, in saucepan prepare hollandaise sauce mix according to package directions, adding tarragon to dry mix. Remove picks from meat slices. Serve hollandaise sauce with meat. Makes 4 servings.

Vegetable-Beef Rolls

1 beaten egg
1½ pounds ground beef
½ cup shredded carrot
¼ cup finely chopped onion
¼ cup finely chopped green
  pepper
¼ cup finely chopped celery
½ teaspoon salt
  Dash pepper
12 slices bacon
½ cup Italian salad dressing

Combine egg and ground beef; mix well. Divide meat mixture into six portions. On waxed paper flatten each meat portion into a 6×4-inch rectangle. Combine carrot, onion, green pepper, celery, salt, and pepper. Divide vegetable mixture into six portions. Pat one vegetable portion onto each meat rectangle. Roll up each rectangle as for jelly roll. Wrap two slices of bacon around each of the rolls and secure with wooden picks.

Place rolls in shallow baking dish. Pour salad dressing over; let stand at room temperature about 1 hour, turning occasionally to moisten all sides. Remove meat rolls from dressing, reserving marinade. Grill rolls over *medium* coals for 20 to 25 minutes, turning to grill all sides and brushing with reserved dressing occasionally. Remove picks before serving. Makes 6 servings.

Lemon Pepper Flank Pinwheels

2 1-pound beef flank steaks
½ cup Burgundy
¼ cup cooking oil
¼ cup soy sauce
1 tablespoon lemon pepper
1 tablespoon Worcestershire
  sauce
  Few drops bottled hot pepper
  sauce
8 cherry tomatoes *or* mushroom
  caps

Pound each flank steak to a 10×8-inch rectangle. Cut each rectangle into four 10×2-inch strips.

In bowl combine Burgundy, cooking oil, soy sauce, lemon pepper, Worcestershire, and pepper sauce. Place meat strips in plastic bag; set in a deep bowl. Pour wine mixture over meat; close bag. Marinate 4 to 6 hours or overnight in refrigerator, turning twice.

Drain meat; reserve marinade. Loosely roll each strip around a cherry tomato or mushroom cap, starting with short side. Skewer securely with wooden picks.

Grill pinwheels over *medium* coals for 15 minutes. Turn meat; grill about 10 minutes more for rare. Baste with marinade often. Remove picks. Makes 8 servings.

Smoked French Pepper Steak

Hickory chips
2 tablespoons cracked
 pepper
1 2-pound beef sirloin steak,
 cut 1½ inches thick
¼ cup butter *or* margarine
2 tablespoons lemon juice
1 teaspoon Worcestershire
 sauce
½ teaspoon garlic powder
¼ teaspoon salt

About an hour before cooking time, soak hickory chips in enough water to cover. Drain.

Press cracked pepper into both sides of steak, using the heel of your hand or the flat side of a cleaver.

In saucepan over coals melt butter; stir in lemon juice, Worcestershire, garlic powder, and salt. Remove from coals.

Add damp hickory chips to *medium-hot* coals; place steak on grill and lower smoke hood. Grill steak for 17 to 20 minutes, brushing occasionally with lemon sauce. Turn meat; grill, covered, 15 to 17 minutes more for rare to medium-rare. Heat reserved lemon sauce. Slice steak; spoon sauce over slices. Makes 6 servings.

Peppy Chuck Steak Grill

1 2- to 3-pound beef chuck steak,
 cut 1 inch thick
½ cup cooking oil
½ cup dry red wine
2 tablespoons catsup
2 tablespoons molasses
2 tablespoons finely snipped
 candied ginger
1 clove garlic, minced
1 teaspoon salt
¼ teaspoon pepper

Slash fat edges of steak, being careful not to cut into meat. Place in shallow baking dish. Combine cooking oil, wine, catsup, molasses, ginger, garlic, salt, and pepper. Pour over steak. Cover; let stand 3 hours at room temperature or 6 hours, in refrigerator, turning several times.

Drain steak, reserving marinade. Pat excess moisture from steak with paper toweling.

Grill steak over *medium* coals for about 20 minutes on each side for rare; about 25 minutes on each side for medium-rare. Brush occasionally with reserved marinade.

Remove meat to serving platter. Carve across grain in thin slices. Makes 4 to 6 servings.

Lemon-Marinated Chuck Roast

1 4-pound beef chuck pot roast,
 cut 1½ inches thick
1 teaspoon grated lemon
 peel
½ cup lemon juice
⅓ cup cooking oil
2 tablespoons sliced green
 onion with tops
4 teaspoons sugar
1½ teaspoons salt
1 teaspoon Worcestershire
 sauce
1 teaspoon prepared mustard
⅛ teaspoon pepper

Score fat edges of roast. Place meat in shallow baking dish. Combine lemon peel and juice, cooking oil, green onion, sugar, salt, Worcestershire, mustard, and pepper. Pour over roast. Cover; let stand 3 hours at room temperature or overnight in the refrigerator, turning roast several times.

Remove roast from marinade, reserving marinade. Pat excess moisture from roast with paper toweling.

Grill roast over *medium-hot* coals 17 to 20 minutes. Turn; cook 17 to 20 minutes more for rare to medium-rare. Heat reserved marinade on grill.

Remove roast to serving platter. Carve across the grain into thin slices. Spoon marinade over. Serves 6 to 8.

At your next backyard party, impress your guests by serving savory *Lemon-Marinated Chuck Roast*. The tangy lemon marinade tenderizes the beef roast and adds flavor distinction.

Onion-Stuffed Steak

2 1¼- to 1½-pound porterhouse
   steaks, cut 1½ inches thick
   or 1 2-pound sirloin steak,
   cut 1½ inches thick
½ cup chopped onion
1 large clove garlic, minced
1 tablespoon butter
   or margarine
   Dash celery salt
   Dash pepper
¼ cup dry red wine
2 tablespoons soy sauce
1 cup sliced fresh mushrooms
2 tablespoons butter
   or margarine

Slash fat edges of steak at 1-inch intervals, being careful not to cut into meat. Slice pockets in each side of meat, cutting almost to bone.

In skillet cook onion and garlic in the 1 tablespoon butter. Add celery salt and pepper. Stuff pockets with onion mixture; skewer closed. Mix wine and soy sauce; brush on steak. Grill over *medium-hot* coals for 15 minutes; brush often with soy mixture. Turn; grill 10 to 15 minutes more for rare. Brush often with soy mixture. In small skillet cook mushrooms in the 2 tablespoons butter till tender. Slice steak across grain; pass the mushrooms, and spoon atop steak. Makes 4 servings.

Rice-Stuffed Flank Steak

1 1- to 1¼-pound beef flank
   steak
½ teaspoon unseasoned meat
   tenderizer
¼ cup chopped onion
¼ cup chopped celery
2 tablespoons butter *or*
   margarine
½ cup water
1 tablespoon curry powder
1 teaspoon instant beef
   bouillon granules
¼ cup quick-cooking rice

Score meat diagonally on both sides; pound to an 11×9-inch rectangle. Sprinkle with tenderizer, salt, and pepper.

In saucepan cook onion and celery in butter till tender. Add water, curry, and bouillon; stir in rice. Bring to boiling; cover. Remove from heat; let stand 5 minutes.

Spread mixture on meat; roll up as for jelly roll, starting at short side. Tie with string both lengthwise and crosswise.

Insert spit rod lengthwise through center of steak. Adjust holding forks; test balance. Place *medium* coals on both sides of drip pan. Attach spit; position drip pan under meat. Turn on motor: lower hood or cover with foil tent. Roast over *medium* coals till done, about 50 minutes. Remove strings. Makes 4 servings.

Spit-Roasted Châteaubriand

1 2- to 2½-pound beef
   tenderloin
1 cup crumbled blue cheese
   (4 ounces)
1 tablespoon brandy

Trim fat from surface of roast. Make a slanting cut, 2 inches deep, the full length of the roast with a sharp, narrow-bladed knife held at a 45-degree angle. Make another cut, just as before, along opposite side.

Blend blue cheese and brandy together. Spread cheese mixture in the two slashed openings. Securely tie string around the roast at both ends and the middle.

Insert spit rod lengthwise through center of roast. Adjust holding forks; test balance. Insert meat thermometer near center of roast, not touching metal rod. Place *hot* coals on both sides of drip pan. Attach spit; position drip pan under meat. Turn on motor; lower hood or cover with foil tent. Grill over *hot* coals till thermometer registers 130° for rare (about 45 minutes), 150° for medium-rare (about 50 minutes), and 160° for medium to medium well (55 to 60 minutes). Remove string. Makes 6 to 8 servings.

Marinated Hickory-Smoked Chuck Roast

1 2-pound beef chuck pot roast,
   cut 1¼ inches thick
5 cloves garlic, peeled
¼ cup cooking oil
¼ cup wine vinegar
1 tablespoon Worcestershire
   sauce
½ teaspoon salt
½ teaspoon dried basil, crushed
¼ teaspoon pepper
   Several dashes bottled
     hot pepper sauce
   Hickory chips

Stud roast with garlic by inserting tip of knife in meat and pushing cloves into meat as you remove knife. Make sure garlic cloves are evenly spaced.

In bowl mix oil, vinegar, Worcestershire, salt, basil, pepper, and hot pepper sauce. Place meat in plastic bag; set in shallow baking dish. Pour marinade over meat; close bag. Marinate 6 to 8 hours or overnight in refrigerator; turning roast occasionally.

About an hour before cooking soak hickory chips in enough water to cover; drain chips. Drain meat, reserving marinade. Pat excess moisture from meat with paper toweling. Arrange *medium-slow* coals around drip pan. Add hickory chips to coals. Place roast over drip pan on grill. Lower hood. Grill 25 minutes. Brush occasionally with marinade and add additional hickory chips. Turn roast; grill 20 minutes more for medium, brushing with marinade. Season to taste; remove garlic. Serves 6.

Rib Roast Barbecue

1 5- to 6-pound boned and rolled
   beef rib roast
½ cup Burgundy
½ cup vinegar
¼ cup cooking oil
¼ cup finely chopped onion
2 tablespoons sugar
1 tablespoon Worcestershire
   sauce
1½ teaspoons salt
½ teaspoon dry mustard
¼ teaspoon pepper
¼ teaspoon chili powder
¼ teaspoon dried thyme, crushed
1 clove garlic, minced
   Several drops bottled hot
     pepper sauce

Place meat in plastic bag; set in deep bowl. Combine remaining ingredients. Pour over meat; close bag. Marinate 6 to 8 hours or overnight in refrigerator; turn several times.

Drain meat; reserve marinade. Pat excess moisture from meat with paper toweling. Insert spit rod through center of roast. Adjust holding forks; test balance. Insert meat thermometer near center of roast but not touching metal rod. Place *medium* coals around drip pan. Attach spit; position drip pan under meat. Turn on motor; lower hood or cover with foil tent. Roast over *medium* coals till meat thermometer registers 140° for rare (2 to 2½ hours), 160° for medium, and 170° for well-done. Brush frequently with marinade during the last 30 minutes of roasting. Let stand 15 minutes before slicing. If desired, heat remaining marinade and pass with meat. Makes 15 to 20 servings.

Hot-Style Eye of Round

1 3-pound beef eye of round
   roast
   Instant unseasoned meat
     tenderizer
1 cup hot-style catsup
½ cup water
2 tablespoons Worcestershire
   sauce
1 clove garlic, minced
½ teaspoon chili powder
¼ teaspoon salt

Sprinkle all sides of roast evenly with tenderizer, using ½ teaspoon per pound of meat. To ensure penetration, pierce all sides deeply at ½-inch intervals with long-tined fork. In saucepan combine catsup, water, Worcestershire, garlic, chili powder, and salt. Simmer 5 minutes.

Insert spit rod through center of roast. Adjust holding forks; test balance. Insert meat thermometer near center of roast, not touching metal rod. Place *medium-hot* coals around drip pan. Attach spit; position drip pan under meat. Turn on motor; lower hood or cover with foil tent. Roast over *medium-hot* coals till thermometer registers 140° for rare, about 1½ hours. Brush with sauce during last 30 minutes. Heat sauce; pass with meat. Serves 8.

Prepare a wintertime cookout the easy way—on a covered grill. You'll find that *Corned Beef Barbecue Dinner* needs little tending, and has a special taste that will satisfy appetites.

Corned Beef Barbecue Dinner

1 3-pound piece corned beef for
  oven roasting
6 medium baking potatoes
1 envelope dry onion soup mix
½ cup butter *or* margarine,
  softened
½ cup sugar
¼ cup vinegar
3 tablespoons prepared mustard
  Dash salt
1 cup dairy sour cream
¼ cup milk
2 tablespoons prepared mustard

Unwrap and rinse corned beef. Arrange *medium* coals around edge of grill. Place beef on heavy-duty foil drip pan on grill. Close hood; grill for 1½ hours. Scrub potatoes but do not peel. Cut each in 3 or 4 lengthwise slices. Set aside 3 tablespoons soup mix. Blend together remaining soup mix and butter. Spread mixture over potato slices. Reassemble potatoes. Wrap each in a square of heavy-duty foil. Place at edges of grill. Grill, hood down, along with meat for 45 to 60 minutes more; turn potatoes once.

Meanwhile, in saucepan mix sugar, vinegar, 3 tablespoons mustard, and salt. Bring to boiling; stir till sugar dissolves. Brush over meat during last few minutes of grilling. Just before serving, mix sour cream, milk, reserved soup mix, and 2 tablespoons mustard. Heat through, stirring occasionally. *Do not boil.*

Unwrap potatoes. Arrange meat and potatoes on serving platter. Serve with sour cream sauce. Makes 6 servings.

Brazilian Barbecued Beef

1 4-pound beef chuck pot roast,
  cut 2 to 2½ inches thick
1 cup catsup
⅓ cup vinegar
¼ cup cooking oil
2 tablespoons instant coffee
  crystals
1 teaspoon salt
1 teaspoon chili powder
1 teaspoon celery seed
½ teaspoon pepper
⅛ teaspoon garlic powder
3 or 4 dashes bottled hot
  pepper sauce

Slash fat edges of meat, being careful not to cut into meat. Place roast in shallow baking dish. In small bowl combine catsup, vinegar, oil, coffee crystals, salt, chili powder, celery seed, pepper, garlic powder, hot pepper sauce, and ½ cup water; pour over roast. Cover; refrigerate 6 to 8 hours or overnight, turning roast several times. Remove roast from marinade, reserving marinade. Remove excess moisture from roast with paper toweling. Grill roast over *medium* coals for 20 to 25 minutes. Turn roast; grill 10 minutes. Brush roast with marinade. Grill for 10 to 15 minutes more for rare to medium rare, brushing occasionally with marinade. Heat remaining marinade.

To serve, carve meat across the grain in thin slices. Pass heated marinade. Makes 6 to 8 servings.

Wined-and-Dined Beef Roast

1 clove garlic, minced
3 tablespoons cooking oil
½ cup dry red wine
2 tablespoons lemon juice
1 teaspoon dried basil, crushed
½ teaspoon dry mustard
1 3-pound beef chuck pot roast,
  cut 1½ inches thick
2 tablespoons bottled steak
  sauce

Cook garlic in oil; remove from heat. Add wine, lemon juice, basil, dry mustard, and ½ teaspoon salt. Prick roast on both sides with long-tined fork; place in plastic bag and set in deep bowl. Pour in marinade; close bag. Marinate overnight in refrigerator, turning roast in bag or pressing marinade against roast occasionally. Drain meat, reserving marinade. Remove excess moisture from roast with paper toweling. Add steak sauce to reserved marinade. Grill over *medium* coals 25 to 30 minutes on each side for medium doneness. Brush with marinade. Serves 6 to 8.

Avoid Flare-Ups with a Drip Pan

When grilling large pieces of meat, use a drip pan to catch meat juices. Make your own pan as follows: (A) Tear off a piece of 18-inch-wide heavy-duty foil twice the length of your grill and fold it in half for a double thickness. Turn up all edges of the foil 1½ inches. (B) Miter corners securely and fold tips toward the inside for added strength. (C) Set the drip pan under the meat to catch drippings, and arrange the coals around the pan. Position the pan in place either before or after you ignite the charcoal. Carefully empty the drip pan after each use.

A

B

C

Horseradish-Stuffed Rump Roast

¼ cup prepared horseradish
2 cloves garlic, minced
1 5-pound boneless beef rump
    roast, rolled and tied
1 clove garlic, halved

Combine horseradish and minced garlic. Unroll roast; make a lengthwise cut slightly off-center going almost to but not through other side. (Leave center area uncut for spit to go through.) Spread cut area with horseradish mixture. Reroll roast and tie securely. Insert spit rod through center of roast. Adjust holding forks; test balance. Rub outside of roast with the additional clove of garlic. Insert meat thermometer. Place *medium* coals on both sides of drip pan. Attach spit; position drip pan under meat. Turn on motor; lower hood or cover with foil tent. Roast till thermometer registers 140° for medium-rare, about 1½ hours. Let stand 15 minutes before carving. Serves 10.

Wine-Basted Short Ribs

½ cup dry red wine
1 teaspoon dried thyme, crushed
½ teaspoon garlic salt
½ teaspoon lemon pepper
2 pounds beef plate short ribs,
    cut in serving-size pieces

In large Dutch oven combine wine, thyme, garlic salt, lemon pepper, and ½ cup water. Add rib pieces. Cover and simmer just till tender, 1¼ to 1½ hours. Drain, reserving liquid. Place ribs over *slow* coals. Grill till done, 15 to 20 minutes, turning ribs occasionally and brushing with wine mixture. Makes 4 servings.

Smoked Short Ribs

  Hickory chips
4 pounds beef plate short ribs,
    cut in serving-size pieces
1 10¾-ounce can condensed
    tomato soup
¾ cup dry red wine
¼ cup finely chopped onion
2 tablespoons cooking oil
1 tablespoon prepared mustard
2 teaspoons chili powder
1 teaspoon paprika
1 teaspoon celery seed

Soak hickory chips in enough water to cover about an hour before cooking time. Drain chips. In covered grill place *slow* coals on both sides of drip pan. Sprinkle coals with some dampened hickory chips. Place ribs, bone side down, on grill. Lower grill hood. Grill ribs till done, about 1½ hours, adding more hickory chips every 20 minutes.

   Meanwhile, in saucepan mix tomato soup, wine, onion, cooking oil, mustard, chili powder, paprika, celery seed, and ¼ teaspoon salt. Heat sauce at side of grill. Brush ribs with sauce. Grill, uncovered, about 20 minutes more; brush ribs frequently with sauce. Serves 4 or 5.

Be Sure with a Meat Thermometer

Using a meat thermometer helps you make sure your roasts are cooked the way you want them—to perfection. Insert thermometer in center of raw roast so tip reaches thickest part of meat and does not touch fat, bone, or metal spit rod. When thermometer registers the doneness you like (see charts, pages 202–205), push it into meat a little farther. If temperature drops below the desired temperature, continue cooking till it rises again.

Enjoy the tang of horseradish and the savory flavor of barbecued beef with *Horseradish-Stuffed Rump Roast*. To round out the meal, add your favorite cooked vegetables.

Quick Garlic Cubed Steaks

¼ cup butter *or* margarine
2 tablespoons Worcestershire
    sauce
2 tablespoons lemon juice
1 teaspoon finely snipped
    parsley
½ teaspoon celery salt
1 clove garlic, minced
6 beef cubed steaks
6 Vienna *or* French bread slices,
    toasted

In saucepan melt butter or margarine; stir in Worcestershire sauce, lemon juice, snipped parsley, celery salt, and garlic. Brush butter mixture on both sides of steaks. Place the steaks in wire grill basket. Grill over *hot* coals for 1 to 2 minutes. Turn basket over and grill for 1 to 2 minutes more. Season steaks with salt and pepper. Place each steak atop a slice of toasted bread. Spoon remaining butter mixture over steaks. Serves 6.

Smoked Beef and Cheese Soup

4 cups milk
1 10¾-ounce can cream of
    potato soup
1 4-ounce package sliced smoked
    beef, snipped (1 cup)
1 cup shredded Muenster cheese
¼ cup finely chopped onion
2 tablespoons snipped parsley
½ teaspoon caraway seed

In heavy 3-quart saucepan gradually stir milk into soup. Add smoked beef, cheese, onion, parsley, and caraway seed. Cook and stir over *hot* coals till mixture is heated through, about 30 minutes, stirring often. Serves 6 to 8.

Beef and Bean Ragout

2 tablespoons cooking oil
2 pounds beef for stew, cut
    in ½-inch pieces
3½ cups water
3 medium potatoes, peeled and
    cubed (3 cups)
2 cups chopped peeled
    tomatoes *or* 1 16-ounce can
    tomatoes, cut up
2 medium onions, chopped
1 6-ounce can tomato paste
1 medium green pepper, chopped
¼ cup snipped parsley
1 tablespoon instant beef
    bouillon granules
1½ teaspoons salt
1 teaspoon sugar
½ teaspoon dried basil,
    crushed
½ teaspoon dried thyme,
    crushed
¼ teaspoon pepper
1 bay leaf
1 15½-ounce can red kidney
    beans, drained
¾ cup dry red wine
¼ cup all-purpose flour

Heat oil in heavy 4-quart Dutch oven over *hot* coals; brown half the meat at a time in the hot oil. Add *3 cups* of the water, potatoes, tomatoes, onions, tomato paste, green pepper, parsley, beef bouillon granules, and seasonings. Cover and heat to boiling (will take about 1¼ hours), stirring occasionally. Add coals as necessary. Boil till meat and vegetables are tender, about 1 hour more, stirring occasionally. Stir in beans and wine. Cover and heat to boiling. Blend the remaining ½ cup water into the flour; stir into bean mixture. Cook, stirring constantly, till mixture thickens and bubbles. Remove bay leaf. Makes 6 servings.

Beef and Mushroom Kabobs

½ cup cooking oil
⅓ cup soy sauce
¼ cup lemon juice
2 tablespoons prepared
  mustard
2 tablespoons Worcestershire
  sauce
1 clove garlic, minced
1 teaspoon coarsely cracked
  pepper
1½ pounds lean beef round *or*
  chuck, cut in 1-inch pieces
  Boiling water
12 to 16 mushroom caps

Mix oil, soy sauce, lemon juice, mustard, Worcestershire, garlic, pepper, and 1½ teaspoons salt. Add beef pieces. Cover and refrigerate overnight; turn meat occasionally. Pour boiling water over mushrooms. Let stand a few minutes; drain. Thread meat and mushrooms on skewers. Grill over *hot* coals till meat is desired doneness; allow 15 minutes for medium-rare; turn often. Makes 4 or 5 servings.

Steak and Shrimp Kabob Dinner (pictured on page 136)

½ cup catsup
¼ cup water
¼ cup finely chopped onion
1 tablespoon brown sugar
3 tablespoons lemon juice
2 tablespoons cooking oil
2 teaspoons prepared mustard
2 teaspoons Worcestershire
  sauce
½ teaspoon chili powder
1 pound beef sirloin steak, cut
  in 1-inch pieces
½ pound fresh *or* frozen shrimp,
  shelled
2 zucchini, cut diagonally in
  1-inch pieces
2 ears corn, cut in 1-inch pieces
2 small onions, cut in wedges
1 green pepper *or* red sweet
  pepper, cut in squares
6 cherry tomatoes

In small saucepan combine catsup, water, chopped onion, and brown sugar. Stir in lemon juice, cooking oil, prepared mustard, Worcestershire sauce, and chili powder. Simmer, uncovered, 10 minutes, stirring once or twice.

On six short skewers thread steak pieces alternately with shrimp, zucchini, corn, onion wedges, and pepper squares. Grill kabobs over *medium-hot* coals till meat is desired doneness; allow 15 to 17 minutes for medium-rare. Turn kabobs often, brushing with sauce. Garnish end of each skewer with a cherry tomato. Makes 3 or 4 servings.

How to Turn Barbecued Steaks

Every time a drop of meat juice falls to its sizzling end on the coals, you're losing a little bit of the flavor that makes barbecued steak so delicious. To prevent this flavor loss, be sure to use tongs when turning the meat. Or, if you don't have tongs, insert a fork into a strip of fat and flip steak with a turner.

Plan a barbecue menu around a variety of tasty kabobs such as *Skewered Beef Bundles,* a selection of your favorite vegetables, and *Glazed Pork Kabobs* (see recipe, page 163).

Beef-Yam Kabobs   (pictured on page 136)

4 medium yams *or* sweet potatoes *or* 1 8-ounce can syrup-packed sweet potatoes
¼ cup packed brown sugar
1 teaspoon cornstarch
½ cup orange juice
¼ cup chili sauce
1 tablespoon prepared mustard
1 pound beef sirloin steak, cut ½ inch thick
1 orange, cut into 8 wedges

Cut off woody portion of fresh yams or sweet potatoes. In saucepan cook fresh yams or sweet potatoes, covered, in enough boiling salted water to cover till potatoes are tender, 25 to 30 minutes. Drain; cool potatoes. Peel and cut into 1-inch pieces. (If using canned sweet potatoes, drain; cut sweet potatoes into 1-inch pieces.)

Meanwhile, prepare sauce. In small saucepan stir together brown sugar and cornstarch; stir in orange juice, chili sauce, and mustard. Cook, stirring constantly, till thickened and bubbly. Simmer, uncovered, 5 minutes; stirring once or twice. Sprinkle steak with salt and pepper; cut steak into 1-inch pieces. On four skewers alternately thread steak pieces, yam or sweet potato pieces, and orange wedges. Grill over *medium* coals till meat is desired doneness; allow 12 to 14 minutes for medium-rare. Turn kabobs occasionally and brush frequently with some of the sauce; pass remaining sauce. Makes 4 servings.

Skewered Beef Bundles

⅓ cup soy sauce
2 tablespoons sugar
¼ teaspoon ground ginger
1 pound beef round tip steak,
  cut 1 inch thick
½ pound fresh whole green beans
4 large carrots, cut into
  3-inch-long sticks
2 tablespoons butter *or*
  margarine, melted

In medium bowl combine soy sauce, sugar, and ginger. Cut steak into thin strips. Cover; marinate meat in soy mixture for 2 to 3 hours at room temperature, stirring occasionally. Meanwhile, cook beans and carrots separately in boiling salted water till barely tender; drain well and cool. Wrap half the meat strips around bundles of four beans; repeat with remaining meat and carrot sticks. Secure with wooden picks. Thread bundles ladder fashion on two parallel skewers (see photo at left). Brush with melted butter. Grill over *medium* coals about 4 minutes. Turn and grill for 3 to 4 minutes more. Brush with melted butter once or twice more during cooking. Serves 4 or 5.

Skewered Cherry Tomato Meatballs

1 beaten egg
¾ cup soft bread crumbs
  (1 slice)
¼ cup milk
¼ cup finely chopped onion
¾ teaspoon salt
½ teaspoon dried oregano,
  crushed
⅛ teaspoon pepper
1 pound ground beef
15 cherry tomatoes
2 dill pickles, cut into
  ½-inch chunks
  Bottled steak sauce

In bowl combine egg, bread crumbs, milk, onion, salt, oregano, and pepper. Add ground beef; mix well. Shape 3 tablespoons of the meat mixture around each cherry tomato to form meatballs. On five large skewers thread meatballs and dill pickle chunks. Grill over *medium* coals for 15 to 20 minutes, turning 3 or 4 times to cook evenly; brush meatballs occasionally with steak sauce. Makes 5 servings.

Hawaiian Kabobs

½ cup soy sauce
¼ cup cooking oil
1 tablespoon dark corn
  syrup
2 cloves garlic, minced
1 teaspoon dry mustard
1 teaspoon ground ginger
2½ pounds beef sirloin steak, cut
  in 1½-inch pieces
3 green peppers, cut in
  1-inch squares
5 small firm tomatoes,
  quartered

In large bowl combine soy sauce, oil, corn syrup, garlic, dry mustard, and ginger. Add meat; cover and refrigerate several hours or overnight. Drain meat, reserving marinade. Alternate meat, green pepper, and tomato on skewers. Grill over *medium-hot* coals till desired doneness; allow about 15 minutes for rare. Baste the kabobs occasionally with reserved marinade. Makes 8 servings.

Burgers and Sandwiches

Burgers O'Brien

1 12-ounce package frozen
   loose-pack hash brown
   potatoes (3 cups)
¼ cup chopped onion
¼ cup chopped green pepper
2 tablespoons melted butter
1 beaten egg
2 tablespoons chopped pimiento
1½ teaspoons salt
¼ teaspoon pepper
1½ pounds ground beef
8 hamburger buns, split,
   toasted, and buttered

Chop potatoes slightly; sprinkle with salt. In skillet combine potatoes, onion, green pepper, and butter. Cover and cook till potatoes are tender, stirring occasionally. Combine egg, pimiento, 1½ teaspoons salt, and pepper; stir in potato mixture. Add ground beef; mix well. Shape meat mixture into 8 patties, about ½ inch thick. Grill over *medium-hot* coals for 5 minutes. Turn and grill 3 to 4 minutes more. Serve patties on toasted buns; place green pepper ring atop burger, if desired. Serves 8.

Beef and Carrot Burgers

1 beaten egg
2 tablespoons milk
¼ cup wheat germ
½ cup grated carrot
¼ cup finely chopped onion
¾ teaspoon salt
¼ teaspoon dried marjoram,
   crushed
⅛ teaspoon pepper
1 pound ground beef
4 slices Monterey Jack cheese
4 whole wheat hamburger buns,
   split, toasted, and buttered
4 lettuce leaves
4 tomato slices

Combine egg, milk, and wheat germ; stir in carrot, onion, salt, marjoram, and pepper. Add ground beef; mix well. Shape into four patties. Grill over *medium-hot* coals for 5 to 6 minutes; turn and grill 4 to 5 minutes more. During last minute of cooking time, place a slice of cheese atop each patty. Serve patties on toasted buns with lettuce and tomato. Makes 4 servings.

Burgers Extravaganza

1 beaten egg
¼ cup water
¼ cup fine dry bread crumbs
¼ teaspoon dried oregano,
   crushed
¼ teaspoon fennel seed
¼ teaspoon garlic salt
¼ teaspoon onion salt
   Dash pepper
1½ pounds ground beef
½ pound bulk pork sausage
8 slices American cheese
8 onion slices
8 hamburger buns, split,
   toasted, and buttered

In bowl combine egg, water, bread crumbs, oregano, fennel, garlic salt, onion salt, and pepper. Add ground beef and sausage; mix well. Form into 8 patties, ½ inch thick. Grill burgers over *medium* coals for 6 to 7 minutes. Turn and cook 6 to 7 minutes more. Top each patty with a cheese and onion slice; serve on toasted buns. Makes 8 servings.

Hash brown potatoes, onion, and green pepper qualify *Burgers O'Brien* as a grilled
burger to appreciate. These tasty burgers will rank high on your family's list of all-time favorites.

Bacon Burger Squares

8 **slices bacon**
2 **pounds ground beef**
2 **tablespoons lemon juice**
1 **tablespoon Worcestershire**
   sauce
   Salt
   Pepper
8 **hamburger buns, split and**
   toasted

Cook bacon till almost done, but not crisp. Cut bacon strips in half crosswise. Pat ground beef to a 12×6-inch rectangle; cut into 8 squares. Combine lemon juice and Worcestershire; brush over the beef patties. Sprinkle with salt and pepper. Arrange squares in greased wire grill basket. Place 2 half-slices of bacon crisscrossed atop each burger to form an "X". Close basket. Grill burgers over *medium-hot* coals turning often, till desired doneness, about 20 minutes. Serve on hamburger buns. Serves 8.

Chili Burger Patties

2½ **pounds ground beef**
¾ **cup chili sauce**
4 **teaspoons prepared mustard**
4 **teaspoons prepared horseradish**
4 **teaspoons Worcestershire sauce**
1 **tablespoon chopped onion**
2 **teaspoons salt**
   Dash pepper
12 **hamburger buns, split**
   and toasted

In mixing bowl thoroughly combine ground beef, chili sauce, prepared mustard, horseradish, Worcestershire sauce, chopped onion, salt, and pepper; mix well. Form into 12 patties. Grill over *medium-hot* coals for 5 minutes. Turn patties and grill till desired doneness, about 3 minutes longer. Serve grilled patties on hamburger buns. Serves 12.

Basic Grilled Burgers

1 **pound ground beef**
½ **teaspoon salt**
   Dash pepper

Mix ground beef, salt, and pepper. Form into four 4-inch patties. Grill over *medium-hot* coals for 5 to 6 minutes; turn and grill 4 to 5 minutes more. Serves 4.

For variety add any one of the following to basic meat mixture: 2 tablespoons chopped green onion with tops, 2 tablespoons drained sweet pickle relish, 2 tablespoons chopped pimiento-stuffed olives, 1 tablespoon prepared horseradish, or ¼ teaspoon instant minced garlic.

Barbecued Beef Burgers

1 **beaten egg**
2 **tablespoons milk**
2 **tablespoons catsup**
¼ **cup finely crushed saltine**
   crackers (7 crackers)
½ **teaspoon salt**
1 **pound ground beef**
4 **thin slices onion**
4 **slices sharp American cheese**
¼ **cup chopped onion**
¼ **cup butter *or* margarine**
¼ **cup catsup**
2 **tablespoons brown sugar**
½ **teaspoon prepared horseradish**
½ **teaspoon salt**

Combine egg, milk, and 2 tablespoons catsup; stir in cracker crumbs and ½ teaspoon salt. Add ground beef; mix well. Form into four patties; place each on a 12-inch square of heavy-duty foil. Top each patty with 1 slice onion and 1 slice cheese.

Cook chopped onion in butter till tender but not brown. Add ¼ cup catsup, brown sugar, horseradish, and ½ teaspoon salt; simmer, uncovered, 5 minutes. Spoon over burgers. Wrap foil loosely around meat, sealing edges well. Cook the bundles over *medium* coals, onion side down, for 15 minutes. Turn burgers over; grill till desired doneness, about 10 minutes more. Makes 4 servings.

Vegetable Burgers

2 **slightly beaten eggs**
¾ **cup soft bread crumbs**
¼ **cup finely chopped onion**
¼ **cup catsup**
1½ **pounds ground beef**
1 **6-ounce can chopped**
   mushrooms, drained
6 **slices American cheese**
6 **hamburger buns**
6 **slices onion**
6 **slices tomato**

In bowl combine eggs, crumbs, onion, catsup, 1 teaspoon salt, and dash pepper. Add beef; mix well. Form into 12 patties. Top *half* of the patties with mushrooms to within ³/₄ inch of edge. Top with remaining patties, sealing edges. Grill over *medium* coals for 5 to 6 minutes. Turn and grill till desired doneness, 5 to 6 minutes more. Top with cheese; heat just till melted. Split and toast hamburger buns. Serve burgers on buns with onion and tomato slices. Makes 6 servings.

Cheese-Stuffed Patties

1 **pound ground beef**
½ **teaspoon salt**
  Dash pepper
  American cheese, shredded
  Chopped onion
  Bottled barbecue sauce

Mix ground beef, salt, and pepper. Between sheets of waxed paper, roll out patties ¼ inch thick. Center half of patties with small amount of cheese, onion, and barbecue sauce. Top with remaining meat patties; press around edges to seal. Grill over *medium-hot* coals about 7 minutes. Turn meat; grill 6 to 7 minutes more. Makes 3 burgers.

Burrito Burgers

1 **cup refried beans**
   (½ of 15-ounce can)
1 **4-ounce can mild green chili**
   peppers, drained, seeded,
   and chopped
¼ **cup chopped onion**
1½ **pounds ground beef**
4 **slices sharp American cheese**
8 **flour tortillas**
1 **cup chopped lettuce**
1 **medium tomato, chopped**

Combine beans, *2 tablespoons* of the chili peppers, onion, and ³/₄ teaspoon salt. Add beef; mix well. Form into eight 5-inch patties. Cut cheese slices in half; place ½ cheese slice on each beef patty. Fold to seal cheese inside, forming semicircle. Grill over *medium* coals for 5 to 6 minutes; turn and grill 4 to 5 minutes more. Heat the tortillas on grill. Serve burgers in hot tortillas. Add the lettuce, chopped tomato, and remaining chili peppers as desired. Makes 8 servings.

Don't Do without a Wire Grill Basket

Wire grill baskets are indispensable when you grill foods that need frequent turning or are difficult to turn, such as burgers, frankfurters, bite-size rib appetizers, chops, or shrimp. A hinged grill basket is the best buy, since you can adjust it to hold small fish, thick burgers, thin steaks, or chicken halves, quarters, or cut-up pieces.

People with hearty appetites will appreciate a generous wedge of *Giant Stuffed Grillburger.*
Layered between the ground beef is a tasty herb-seasoned stuffing mix and mushroom filling.

Mini Pineapple Meat Loaves

1 15¼-ounce can crushed
   pineapple (juice pack)
2 beaten eggs
1½ cups soft bread crumbs
   (2 slices)
2 tablespoons finely chopped
   onion
2 tablespoons chopped green
   pepper
½ teaspoon salt
⅛ teaspoon pepper
1½ pounds ground beef
1 tablespoon cornstarch
2 teaspoons prepared mustard
¼ cup catsup
2 tablespoons soy sauce
4 drops bottled hot pepper sauce

Drain crushed pineapple; reserve juice. Add water to juice, if necessary, to make 1 cup; set aside for use in sauce. In bowl combine eggs, bread crumbs, pineapple, onion, green pepper, salt, and pepper. Add beef; mix well. Form into five 4×2-inch loaves. Place meat loaves in wire grill basket. Grill over *medium-hot* coals for 20 to 25 minutes. Turn and grill till done, about 20 minutes more.

Meanwhile, in small saucepan blend together cornstarch and mustard. Stir in reserved pineapple juice, catsup, soy sauce, and hot pepper sauce. Cook over *medium-hot* coals, stirring constantly, till thickened and bubbly. Pass with the meat loaves. Makes 5 servings.

Giant Stuffed Grillburger

1 beaten egg
1¼ cups herb-seasoned
    stuffing mix, crushed
1 4-ounce can chopped
    mushrooms, drained
⅓ cup beef broth
¼ cup sliced green onion
    with tops
¼ cup snipped parsley
2 tablespoons butter *or*
    margarine, melted
1 teaspoon lemon juice
2 pounds ground beef
1 teaspoon salt

Mix together the egg, stuffing mix, drained mushrooms, beef broth, green onion, parsley, butter or margarine, and lemon juice; set aside. Combine meat and salt; divide mixture in half. On sheets of waxed paper, pat each half to an 8-inch circle. Spoon stuffing over one circle of meat to within 1 inch of edge. Top with second circle of meat; peel off top sheet of paper and seal edges of meat.

Invert meat patty onto well-greased wire grill basket; peel off remaining paper. Grill over *medium* coals for 10 to 12 minutes. Turn and grill till desired doneness, 10 to 12 minutes more. Cut the burger into wedges; serve with warmed catsup, if desired. Makes 8 servings.

Chili Meat Loaf

2 slightly beaten eggs
1 8-ounce can tomatoes, cut up
1 8-ounce can red kidney beans,
    drained
1 cup crushed corn chips
¼ cup finely chopped green onion
    with tops
2 tablespoons snipped parsley
1½ teaspoons salt
1 teaspoon chili powder
2 pounds lean ground beef
1 10-ounce can mild enchilada
    sauce
½ cup shredded sharp American
    cheese (2 ounces)

Combine eggs, undrained tomatoes, beans, corn chips, green onion, parsley, salt, and chili powder; mash beans slightly. Add ground beef; mix well. Shape into two 7×3×2-inch loaves. Tear off two 18-inch lengths of 18-inch-wide heavy-duty foil. Place loaves on foil pieces; wrap foil around each loaf and seal securely. Grill over *medium* coals 30 minutes. Turn and grill 20 minutes longer.

Meanwhile, in saucepan heat enchilada sauce. Open foil and fold down to make "pan". Continue cooking meat till done, about 10 minutes more, brushing frequently with enchilada sauce. Pass remaining sauce and cheese to top each serving. Makes 8 servings.

Stuffed Steak Sandwiches

2 1-pound beef flank steaks
    Instant unseasoned meat
    tenderizer
2 tablespoons prepared
    horseradish
⅓ cup chopped onion
⅓ cup chopped celery
2 tablespoons butter *or*
    margarine, melted
½ teaspoon seasoned salt
1 cup dairy sour cream
12 slices French bread, toasted
    and buttered

Score steaks diagonally on both sides. Use tenderizer according to directions. Spread one side of steaks with horseradish. Combine onion, celery, butter, and seasoned salt; spread on steaks. Roll up as for jelly roll. Fasten with skewers and tie with string. Insert spit rod through center of meat rolls. Adjust holding forks; test balance. Place *medium* coals on both sides of drip pan. Attach spit; position drip pan under meat. Turn on motor. Grill over *medium* coals till done, about 45 minutes. Let stand a few minutes; remove strings and skewers.

In small saucepan heat sour cream over low heat; *do not boil*. Carefully carve meat rolls into thin slices and place on bread. Spoon warm sour cream atop meat. Serves 6.

Pizza-Frank Sandwiches

1 beaten egg
¼ cup milk
¾ cup soft bread crumbs
¼ cup grated Parmesan cheese
2 tablespoons snipped parsley
½ teaspoon garlic salt
    Dash pepper
½ pound bulk pizza sausage
½ pound ground beef
6 frankfurters
1 8-ounce can pizza sauce
2 tablespoons chopped onion
2 tablespoons sliced pimiento-
    stuffed green olives
6 frankfurter buns, split and
    toasted
⅓ cup shredded mozzarella
    cheese

Combine egg and milk; stir in crumbs, Parmesan cheese, parsley, garlic salt, and pepper. Add sausage and beef; mix thoroughly. Divide into 6 equal portions. Shape meat around frankfurters, leaving ends open; roll each between waxed paper to make uniform thickness. Chill.

In saucepan combine pizza sauce, chopped onion, and green olives. Simmer, uncovered, 5 minutes; stir occasionally. Grill frankfurters over *medium* coals till meat is set, about 5 minutes. Turn and grill till meat is done, about 10 minutes more. Brush with pizza sauce mixture during the last 5 minutes. Serve on toasted buns. Spoon remaining pizza sauce atop sandwiches and sprinkle with shredded mozzarella cheese. Makes 6 servings.

Spiced Ham Patties

1 slightly beaten egg
¼ cup milk
1½ cups soft bread crumbs
    (2 slices bread)
1 tablespoon finely chopped
    green onion with tops
    Dash pepper
1 pound ground cooked ham
    (3 cups)
⅓ cup packed brown sugar
¼ cup honey
1 teaspoon dry mustard
¼ cup reserved spiced apple
    syrup
4 spiced apple rings

Combine the egg and milk; stir in bread crumbs, onion, and pepper. Add ham; mix well. Shape mixture into four 4-inch patties. In saucepan combine brown sugar, honey, dry mustard, and the spiced apple syrup; heat through. Grill patties over *medium-hot* coals for 5 minutes. Turn; brush with glaze. Place an apple ring atop each patty; brush with glaze. Grill ham patties till done, 5 to 6 minutes more. Pass remaining glaze with patties. Serves 4.

Corned Beef-Turkey Heroes

8 Kaiser rolls *or* hamburger
    buns, split
    Tartar sauce
    Russian, Italian, *or* blue
    cheese salad dressing
2 3- or 4-ounce packages thinly
    sliced smoked corned beef
8 thin onion slices
4 slices Swiss cheese,
    cut in half
2 3- or 4-ounce packages thinly
    sliced smoked turkey

Lightly spread cut surfaces of Kaiser rolls or buns with tartar sauce and salad dressing. Layer slices of the corned beef, onion, Swiss cheese, and turkey on rolls. Replace tops of rolls; place each sandwich on an 18×12-inch rectangle of heavy-duty foil. Wrap foil around sandwiches, sealing edges well. Grill over *medium* coals till heated through, about 25 minutes, turning several times. Serves 8.

Bratwursts in Beer

1 12-ounce can beer (1½ cups)
2 tablespoons brown sugar
2 tablespoons soy sauce
1 tablespoon prepared mustard
1 teaspoon chili powder
2 cloves garlic, minced
  Several drops hot pepper sauce
6 bratwursts
6 individual French rolls
  Zesty Sauerkraut Relish
    (see recipe, page 192)

Combine beer, brown sugar, soy sauce, mustard, chili powder, garlic, and hot pepper sauce. Place brats in shallow baking dish; pour marinade over. Cover; refrigerate several hours or overnight, spooning marinade over occasionally. Remove brats, reserving marinade. Grill over *medium-hot* coals about 4 minutes. Turn and grill till done, 3 to 4 minutes more. Brush often with reserved marinade. Cut rolls in half lengthwise; hollow out rolls, leaving a ¼ inch wall. Fill each roll bottom with about ¼ cup drained relish. Add bratwurst and top with roll top. (Refrigerate remaining relish until needed.) Makes 6 servings.

Oriental Pork Wrap-Ups

3 tablespoons chopped green
    onion with tops
4 teaspoons soy sauce
⅛ teaspoon garlic powder
1 pound ground pork
  Sweet-Sour Sauce
8 leaf lettuce leaves *or*
    lettuce cups
  Parsley Rice

Combine green onion, soy sauce, and garlic powder. Add ground pork; mix well. Shape mixture into eight 3×1-inch logs. Grill over *medium* coals for 4 to 5 minutes; turn and brush with Sweet-Sour Sauce. Grill logs till done, 3 to 4 minutes more. In center of each leaf lettuce place about 1 tablespoon Parsley Rice. Place a grilled log horizontally atop rice. Fold two opposite edges of lettuce crosswise so they overlap atop logs. Dip the bundle in Sweet-Sour Sauce for each bite. (Or, place rice in lettuce cups; top with pork log. Drizzle sauce over.) Serves 4.

Sweet-Sour Sauce: In saucepan combine ½ cup packed brown sugar and 1 tablespoon cornstarch. Stir in ⅓ cup red wine vinegar, ⅓ cup chicken broth, ¼ cup finely chopped green pepper, 2 tablespoons chopped pimiento, 1 tablespoon soy sauce, ¼ teaspoon garlic powder, and ¼ teaspoon ground ginger. Place over *medium* coals, stirring occasionally, till thickened and bubbly. Makes 1¼ cups sauce.

Parsley Rice: In saucepan combine ⅔ cup water, ⅓ cup regular rice, and ¼ teaspoon salt. Cover with tight-fitting lid. Bring to boiling over *medium* coals, about 15 minutes. Move to edge of coals; cook 10 minutes more (do not lift cover). Remove from heat; let stand, covered, 10 minutes. Stir in 2 tablespoons snipped parsley.

Grilled Crab and Cheese Rolls

1 cup shredded Monterey Jack
    cheese (4 ounces)
¼ cup finely chopped celery
2 tablespoons mayonnaise *or*
    salad dressing
2 tablespoons chopped pimiento
2 teaspoons lemon juice
1 teaspoon prepared mustard
1 7½-ounce can crab meat,
    drained, flaked, and
    cartilage removed
4 individual French rolls

Stir together cheese, celery, mayonnaise or salad dressing, pimiento, lemon juice, and prepared mustard. Fold in crab. Split French rolls; spread crab mixture over bottom halves and replace tops. Wrap heavy-duty foil loosely around roll; fold edges of foil to seal tightly. Grill over *medium* coals for 10 minutes. Turn; grill till heated through, about 10 minutes more. Makes 4 servings.

Barbecued Pork and Ham

Apple-Orange Stuffed Pork Chops

6 pork loin chops, cut
    1½ inches thick
½ cup chopped celery
½ cup chopped unpeeled apple
    (1 medium)
2 tablespoons butter
1 beaten egg
1½ cups toasted raisin bread
    cubes (2½ slices)
½ teaspoon grated orange peel
1 orange, sectioned and chopped
    (⅓ cup)
¼ teaspoon salt
⅛ teaspoon ground cinnamon

Make a slit in each chop by cutting from fat side almost to bone. Season cavity with a little salt and pepper.

In small saucepan cook celery and apple in butter till tender but not brown. Combine egg, bread cubes, orange peel, chopped orange, salt, and cinnamon. Pour cooked celery and apple over bread cube mixture; toss lightly. Spoon about ¼ cup stuffing into each pork chop. Securely fasten pocket opening with wooden picks.

Grill chops over *medium* coals about 20 minutes. Turn meat and grill till done, 15 to 20 minutes more. Before serving, remove the picks. Makes 6 servings.

Corn-Stuffed Pork Chops

6 pork loin chops, cut
    1½ inches thick
¼ cup chopped green pepper
¼ cup chopped onion
1 tablespoon butter *or*
    margarine
1 beaten egg
1½ cups toasted bread cubes
½ cup cooked whole kernel corn
2 tablespoons chopped pimiento
½ teaspoon salt
¼ teaspoon ground cumin
    Dash pepper

Make a slit in each chop by cutting from fat side almost to bone. Season cavity with a little salt and pepper.

In small saucepan cook green pepper and onion in butter till tender but not brown. Combine egg, bread cubes, corn, pimiento, salt, cumin, and pepper. Pour cooked pepper and onion over bread cube mixture; toss lightly. Spoon about ¼ cup stuffing into each pork chop. Securely fasten pocket opening with wooden picks.

Grill chops over *medium* coals about 20 minutes. Turn meat and grill till done, 15 to 20 minutes more. Before serving, remove the picks. Makes 6 servings.

Roast Pork Chops

1 cup chopped onion
1 clove garlic, minced
2 tablespoons cooking oil
¾ cup catsup
¼ cup lemon juice
3 tablespoons sugar
2 tablespoons Worcestershire
    sauce
1 tablespoon prepared mustard
1 teaspoon salt
¼ teaspoon bottled hot pepper
    sauce
    Salt
6 pork loin chops *or* rib chops,
    cut 1¼ to 1½ inches thick

In saucepan cook onion and garlic in hot oil till tender but not brown. Stir in catsup, lemon juice, sugar, Worcestershire sauce, prepared mustard, 1 teaspoon salt, and bottled hot pepper sauce. Simmer, uncovered, 5 minutes, stirring once or twice. Sprinkle chops with salt.

Place chops in wire grill basket. Grill chops over *medium* coals about 25 minutes. Turn meat and grill about 20 minutes more, brushing with sauce occasionally. Serves 6.

Broccoli and parslied French bread warm at the edge of the grill while *Apple-Orange Stuffed Pork Chops* and *Chinese Smoked Ribs* (see recipe, page 162) finish cooking.

Gypsy Pork Steaks

2 whole pork tenderloins
  (1½ pounds)
4 teaspoons paprika
1 teaspoon salt
⅛ teaspoon pepper

Cut tenderloin into six 3-inch pieces. Resting each piece on cut side, flatten with side of cleaver or meat mallet to ¾-inch thickness. Stir together paprika, salt, and pepper. Coat meat on both sides with seasoning mixture. Grill pork over *medium* coals about 10 minutes. Turn meat and grill till done, about 10 minutes more. Serves 6.

Apple-Peanut Buttered Pork Steaks

½ cup apple butter
2 tablespoons peanut butter
¼ teaspoon finely shredded
  orange peel
2 tablespoons orange juice
4 pork blade steaks,
  cut ¾ inch thick

Blend apple butter into peanut butter; add orange peel and juice. Season steaks with salt and pepper. Grill over *medium* coals for about 15 minutes. Turn steaks; brush with apple butter mixture. Grill till done, 15 to 20 minutes more. Brush on remaining apple butter mixture. Serves 4.
  Note: If desired, use 1½-inch-thick steaks. Grill 25 minutes. Turn; grill till done, about 25 minutes. Serves 8.

Marinated Pork Loin Roast

1 5-pound boneless pork loin
  roast, rolled and tied
¼ cup water
3 tablespoons Dijon-style mustard
2 tablespoons cooking oil
1 tablespoon soy sauce

Pierce pork loin in several places with long-tined fork; place in shallow baking dish. Blend water, mustard, oil, and soy; brush over meat. Cover; let stand at room temperature 1 hour. Drain meat; reserve sauce. Insert spit rod through center of roast. Adjust holding forks; test balance. Insert meat thermometer near center of roast, not touching rod. Place *medium-hot* coals on both sides of drip pan. Attach spit; position drip pan under meat. Turn on motor. Grill till thermometer registers 170° for well-done, 2 to 2½ hours.
  During last 30 to 45 minutes, brush meat with mustard sauce. Heat remaining sauce; pass with meat. Serves 8.

Company Pork Loin Roast

1 cup catsup
¼ cup cooking oil
¼ cup wine vinegar
2 tablespoons instant minced
  onion
2 tablespoons Worcestershire
  sauce
1 tablespoon brown sugar
1 teaspoon mustard seed
1 teaspoon dried oregano,
  crushed
1 bay leaf
½ teaspoon salt
½ teaspoon cracked pepper
¼ teaspoon chili powder
1 5-pound boneless pork loin
  roast, rolled and tied

In saucepan combine catsup, cooking oil, wine vinegar, onion, Worcestershire sauce, brown sugar, mustard seed, oregano, bay leaf, salt, pepper, chili powder, and ½ cup water. Simmer the mixture 20 minutes; remove bay leaf.
  Insert spit rod through center of roast. Adjust holding forks and test balance. Insert meat thermometer near center of roast, not touching spit rod. In covered grill place *medium-hot* coals on both sides of drip pan. Attach spit; position drip pan under meat. Turn on motor; lower grill hood or cover with foil tent. Grill till meat thermometer registers 170° for well-done, 2 to 2½ hours. Brush with sauce frequently during last 30 minutes. Serves 8.

Hickory-Smoked Royal Ribs

Hickory chips
¾ **cup catsup**
½ **cup finely chopped onion**
¼ **cup olive oil** *or* **cooking oil**
¼ **cup tarragon vinegar**
¼ **cup water**
3 **tablespoons lemon juice**
2 **tablespoons Worcestershire sauce**
1 **tablespoon brown sugar**
2 **teaspoons dry mustard**
2 **teaspoons paprika**
2 **teaspoons chili powder**
2 **cloves garlic, minced**
2 **bay leaves**
1 **teaspoon cumin seed, crushed**
1 **teaspoon dried thyme, crushed**
½ **teaspoon salt**
¼ **teaspoon pepper**
4 **pounds pork loin back ribs** *or* **spareribs**

Soak hickory chips in enough water to cover for about 1 hour before cooking time; drain. In saucepan stir together catsup, onion, oil, vinegar, water, lemon juice, Worcestershire sauce, brown sugar, dry mustard, paprika, chili powder, garlic, bay leaves, cumin seed, thyme, salt, and pepper; simmer 10 minutes.

Lace ribs accordion-style on spit; secure with holding forks. In covered grill place *hot* coals on both sides of foil drip pan. Sprinkle coals with some dampened hickory chips. Attach spit; position drip pan under meat. Turn on motor; lower the grill hood or cover with foil tent. Grill the ribs over hot coals till done, about 1 hour. Sprinkle the coals with chips every 20 minutes. Brush ribs frequently with sauce mixture during the last 15 minutes of cooking. Pass the remaining sauce. Serves 4 to 6.

Luau Spareribs

1 **cup pineapple preserves**
2 **tablespoons vinegar**
2 **tablespoons chopped pimiento**
1 **tablespoon lemon juice**
2 **teaspoons Dijon-style mustard**
1 **teaspoon Kitchen Bouquet**
3 **to 4 pounds pork spareribs**
Salt
1 **fresh pineapple, peeled and cut into lengthwise wedges**
1 **green pepper, cut into lengthwise strips**

In a bowl combine the pineapple preserves, vinegar, pimiento, lemon juice, mustard, and Kitchen Bouquet; set aside.

Sprinkle the ribs with salt. Lace ribs, pineapple wedges, and green pepper strips accordion-style on spit; secure with holding forks. In covered grill place *slow* coals on both sides of foil drip pan. Attach spit; position drip pan under meat. Turn on motor; lower grill hood or cover with foil tent.

Grill the ribs over *slow* coals till done, about 1 hour. During the last 15 minutes of cooking time, brush the meat, pineapple wedges, and green pepper occasionally with the pineapple glaze. Makes 3 or 4 servings.

For smoke flavor sprinkle coals with dampened hickory chips during the last 30 minutes of cooking.

How to **Barbecue Ribs**

If your grill has a spit attachment, try using it to barbecue long strips of pork spareribs or pork loin back ribs. Simply lace the ribs on the spit accordion-style. Secure the ribs with holding forks so they'll stay in position while rotating over the coals.

Chinese Smoked Ribs (pictured on page 159)

6 **pounds pork loin back ribs**
   ***or* spareribs**
2 **tablespoons sugar**
1 **teaspoon salt**
½ **teaspoon paprika**
½ **teaspoon ground turmeric**
¼ **teaspoon celery seed**
⅛ **teaspoon dry mustard**
   Hickory chips
½ **cup catsup**
½ **cup packed brown sugar**
3 **tablespoons soy sauce**
1 **tablespoon grated fresh**
   gingerroot *or* 2 teaspoons
   ground ginger
1 **clove garlic, minced**

Thoroughly rub the ribs with mixture of sugar, salt, paprika, turmeric, celery seed, and dry mustard; cover and let stand 2 hours. About an hour before cooking time soak hickory chips in enough water to cover; drain.

In covered grill place *slow* coals on both sides of drip pan. Sprinkle coals with dampened hickory chips. Place ribs, bone side down, on grill; lower grill hood. Grill ribs over *slow* coals about 30 minutes. Turn meat and grill about 30 minutes more. Sprinkle coals with chips every 20 minutes. (If the thin end of spareribs cooks too quickly, place foil under thin end of ribs and continue cooking.)

Meanwhile, in saucepan combine catsup, brown sugar, soy sauce, ginger, and garlic. Cook and stir till sugar is dissolved. Brush mixture on both sides of ribs and grill, uncovered, till done, 10 to 15 minutes more. Heat any remaining sauce and serve with ribs. Makes 6 servings.

Country-Style Barbecued Ribs

4 **pounds pork country-style**
   ribs
1 **cup chopped onion**
1 **clove garlic, minced**
¼ **cup cooking oil**
1 **8-ounce can tomato sauce**
½ **cup water**
¼ **cup packed brown sugar**
¼ **cup lemon juice**
2 **tablespoons Worcestershire**
   sauce
2 **tablespoons prepared mustard**
1 **teaspoon salt**
1 **teaspoon celery seed**
¼ **teaspoon pepper**

In large saucepan or Dutch oven cook ribs, covered, in enough boiling salted water to cover till ribs are tender, 45 to 60 minutes; drain well.

Meanwhile, in saucepan cook onion and garlic in hot oil till tender but not brown. Stir in tomato sauce, water, brown sugar, lemon juice, Worcestershire sauce, mustard, salt, celery seed, and pepper. Simmer, uncovered, 15 minutes; stir once or twice.

Grill ribs over *slow* coals till done, about 45 minutes, turning every 15 minutes. Brush with sauce till ribs are well coated. Makes 6 servings.

Apricot Glazed Ribs

4 **pounds pork loin back ribs,**
   cut in serving-size pieces
1½ **cups water**
1 **cup snipped dried apricots**
½ **cup packed brown sugar**
2 **tablespoons vinegar**
1 **tablespoon lemon juice**
1 **teaspoon ground ginger**
½ **teaspoon salt**

In large saucepan or Dutch oven cook ribs, covered, in enough boiling salted water to cover till ribs are tender, 45 to 60 minutes. Drain well; season the ribs with a little salt and pepper.

Meanwhile, in a small saucepan combine the 1½ cups water, apricots, brown sugar, vinegar, lemon juice, ginger, and salt. Bring the mixture to boiling. Reduce heat; cover and simmer 5 minutes. Pour mixture into blender container. Cover and blend till smooth.

Brush the glaze over the ribs. Grill ribs over *medium-slow* coals for 10 to 15 minutes. Turn ribs and grill till done, 10 to 15 minutes more; brush occasionally with the apricot glaze. Makes 4 servings.

Glazed Pork Kabobs (pictured on page 148)

4 large carrots
½ cup apricot preserves
½ of an 8-ounce can tomato sauce
¼ cup packed brown sugar
¼ cup dry red wine
2 tablespoons lemon juice
2 tablespoons cooking oil
1 teaspoon onion juice
1½ pounds lean boneless pork
  Fresh pineapple chunks

Cut carrots into 1-inch pieces. In small saucepan cook, covered, in small amount boiling salted water for 15 to 20 minutes; drain. In saucepan combine apricot preserves, tomato sauce, brown sugar, wine, lemon juice, oil, and onion juice. Cook, uncovered, 10 to 15 minutes; stir occasionally. Cut pork into 1-inch cubes.

Thread pork, carrots, and pineapple chunks on six skewers; season with salt and pepper. Grill over *medium* coals about 10 minutes; turn frequently. Brush with sauce; grill till done, about 5 minutes more. Makes 6 servings.

Korean Kabobs

1½ pounds lean boneless pork
½ cup unsweetened pineapple
  juice
¼ cup soy sauce
¼ cup sliced green onion
  with tops
4 teaspoons sesame seed
1 tablespoon brown sugar
1 clove garlic, minced
⅛ teaspoon pepper
1 teaspoon cornstarch
1 green pepper

Cut pork into 18 pieces. In large bowl combine pineapple juice, soy sauce, green onion, sesame seed, brown sugar, garlic, and pepper; add meat pieces. Cover; refrigerate overnight or let stand 2 hours at room temperature, turning meat occasionally in the marinade.

Drain meat; reserve marinade. In saucepan blend cornstarch and 2 tablespoons water; stir in reserved marinade. Cook and stir till thickened. Cut green pepper into 1-inch squares. Thread pepper on six skewers alternately with meat. Grill over *medium* coals 6 to 8 minutes. Turn kabobs; grill till done, 6 to 8 minutes more, brushing with sauce occasionally. Pass remaining sauce. Serves 6.

How to Spit-Roast a Pig

Obtain a small dressed pig. (Plan on 60 to 70 servings from a 60-pound dressed pig—live weight, 90 to 100 pounds.)

Rent a large barbecue or follow these general guidelines for making a barbecue pit. In a grassless place, dig a pit 12 inches deep and as wide and long as the pig. Arrange charcoal in two lengthwise rows, 12 to 15 inches apart. Drive notched pipes into ground to hold spit about 16 inches above coals. Rig up motor-driven rotisserie. (Or plan to turn spitted pig by hand throughout roasting period.)

Insert spit rod through center cavity of dressed pig; test balance. Secure pig well with wires and/or wire mesh. Tie legs together; cover tail and ears with foil. Place drip pan between rows of *hot* coals. Balance spit on pipes. Position drip pan under pig. Start motor or begin turning.

Pig will shrink as it roasts; have tools handy to tighten wires. Use a water-filled sprinkler to put out any flare-ups. (Fires are more frequent during first or second hour.) Do not baste pig. Add *hot* coals to maintain constant heat.

Allow about 8 hours for 60-pound pig to be done. Time varies with heat of coals and size of pig. Check doneness by placing meat thermometer in center of thigh of hind leg; make sure it doesn't touch bone or spit rod. Roast till meat thermometer registers 170° to 185°. Have large, clean surface available for carving. Generally, meat will be so thoroughly cooked that it will fall off the bones.

Charcoal cooking gives a flavorful turn to pineapple slices barbecued alongside *Orange-Ginger Ham Grill.* And a hint of mustard and wine accents the delicate flavor of the meat's glaze.

Orange-Ginger Ham Grill

¼ cup frozen orange juice
    concentrate, thawed
¼ cup dry white wine
1 teaspoon dry mustard
¼ teaspoon ground ginger
1 1½- to 2-pound fully cooked
    ham slice, cut 1 inch thick
6 canned pineapple slices
    Orange slices (optional)

Combine orange juice concentrate, wine, mustard, and ginger. Slash fat edge of ham slice. Brush sauce over ham. Grill over *medium* coals for 10 to 15 minutes, brushing with sauce occasionally. Turn ham and grill till done, 10 to 15 minutes more, brushing with sauce. Grill pineapple slices alongside the ham, brushing frequently with sauce. Place pineapple atop ham during last 5 to 10 minutes of grilling. Garnish with orange slices, if desired. Makes 6 servings.

Ham Slice with Cranberry Sauce

1 8-ounce can jellied cranberry
    sauce
2 tablespoons bottled steak
    sauce
1 tablespoon cooking oil
2 teaspoons brown sugar
1 teaspoon prepared mustard
1 1½-pound fully cooked ham
    slice, cut 1 inch thick

Combine jellied cranberry sauce, steak sauce, cooking oil, brown sugar, and prepared mustard. Beat with electric mixer or rotary beater till smooth.

Slash fat edge of ham slice. Grill over *medium* coals for 10 to 15 minutes, brushing with sauce occasionally. Turn ham and grill till done, 10 to 15 minutes more, brushing with sauce. Heat remaining sauce on edge of grill; serve with ham. Makes 4 or 5 servings.

Fruit-Glazed Ham

    Apricot Glaze *or*
    Grape Glaze
1 1½-pound fully cooked center
    cut ham slice, cut 1 inch
    thick

Prepare one of the fruit glazes. Slash fat edge of ham slice to prevent curling. Place ham slice in shallow dish; pour glaze mixture over ham. Cover; refrigerate overnight or let stand at room temperature for 2 hours, spooning glaze over ham several times. Remove ham, reserving glaze.

Grill ham slice over *medium* coals for 10 to 15 minutes, brushing with glaze occasionally. Turn ham and grill till done, 10 to 15 minutes more, brushing with glaze. Heat the remaining glaze in small saucepan on edge of grill. To serve cut the ham into slices and pass heated fruit glaze. Makes 6 servings.

Apricot Glaze: In saucepan combine ½ cup apricot preserves, 2 tablespoons prepared mustard, 1 tablespoon water, 2 teaspoons lemon juice, 1 teaspoon Worcestershire sauce, and ⅛ teaspoon ground cinnamon. Heat, stirring occasionally, till preserves melt.

Grape Glaze: In saucepan combine ½ cup grape jelly, 2 tablespoons prepared mustard, 1½ teaspoons lemon juice, and ⅛ teaspoon ground cinnamon. Heat, stirring occasionally, till jelly melts.

Orange-Sauced Ham

1 5-pound boneless fully cooked
    canned ham
1 10-ounce jar currant jelly
¼ cup light corn syrup
2 tablespoons cornstarch
1 teaspoon grated orange peel
⅓ cup orange juice
¾ teaspoon ground nutmeg
    Orange slices
    Parsley sprigs

Insert spit rod through center of ham. Adjust holding forks; test balance. Insert meat thermometer near center of ham, not touching rod. In covered grill place *medium* coals on both sides of drip pan. Attach spit; position drip pan under ham. Turn on motor; lower grill hood or cover with foil tent. Grill ham over *medium* coals till done and meat thermometer registers 140°, 1 to 1¼ hours. (If grill does not have spit, see Note.) Meanwhile, in saucepan combine jelly, corn syrup, cornstarch, orange peel and juice, and nutmeg. Cook, stirring constantly, till sauce is thickened. Brush over ham frequently during last 15 minutes of cooking. Heat remaining sauce; pass with ham. Garnish ham with orange slices and parsley. Serves 12.

   Note: If grill does not have spit, place ham directly on grill over drip pan. Lower hood or tent grill with heavy-duty foil. Grill ham over *medium* coals for 1 hour. Lift foil tent; turn ham. Insert meat thermometer and brush with sauce. Re-cover grill with foil tent. Roast ham till thermometer registers 140°, about 30 minutes more.

Sweet-Sour Ham

1 5-pound boneless fully cooked
    canned ham
1 20-ounce can pineapple slices
¼ cup dry sherry *or* dry white
    wine
3 tablespoons vinegar
2 tablespoons soy sauce
2 tablespoons honey
1 tablespoon cooking oil
1 clove garlic, minced
    Dash salt
2 small green peppers, cut in
    1½-inch squares
12 cherry tomatoes
2 limes, cut in wedges

Insert spit rod through center of ham. Adjust holding forks; test balance. Insert meat thermometer near center of ham, not touching rod. In covered grill place *medium* coals on both sides of drip pan. Attach spit; position drip pan under meat. Turn on motor; lower grill hood or cover with foil tent. Grill ham over *medium* coals till done and meat thermometer registers 140°, 1 to 1¼ hours. (If grill does not have spit, see Note above.) Meanwhile, drain pineapple, reserving ⅔ cup syrup. Set drained pineapple aside. In saucepan combine the reserved syrup, dry sherry, vinegar, soy, honey, cooking oil, garlic, and salt. Boil mixture down to equal ⅔ cup (about 10 minutes); stir occasionally. During last 30 minutes of cooking, brush ham often with sauce; pass remaining sauce. Before serving, quarter each pineapple slice. Thread 12 small bamboo skewers with green pepper, pieces of pineapple, cherry tomato, and lime wedge. Serve with ham. Serves 12.

Skewered Ham and Fruit Kabobs

1 8-ounce can pineapple slices
½ cup extra-hot catsup
⅓ cup orange marmalade
2 tablespoons finely chopped
    onion
1 tablespoon cooking oil
1 to 1½ teaspoons dry mustard
2 pounds fully cooked boneless
    ham, cut into 1-inch cubes
2 oranges, cut in wedges
1 16-ounce jar spiced crab apples

Drain pineapple slices, reserving ⅓ cup syrup. Quarter each pineapple slice and set aside. In saucepan stir together the pineapple syrup, catsup, orange marmalade, onion, oil, and dry mustard. Simmer, uncovered, for about 5 minutes, stirring once or twice.

   On six skewers thread ham cubes and orange wedges. Grill over *medium* coals about 15 minutes, turning frequently and brushing with sauce. Thread crab apples and pineapple pieces on ends of skewers. Grill till meat and fruits are hot, 5 to 10 minutes longer, turning the kabobs often and brushing with the sauce. Makes 6 servings.

Pineapple-Glazed Luncheon Meat

⅔ cup pineapple preserves
⅓ cup packed brown sugar
¼ cup lemon juice
¼ cup prepared mustard
 Whole cloves
3 12-ounce cans luncheon meat

Combine preserves, brown sugar, lemon juice, and mustard. Score each piece of meat in diamonds, cutting only ¼ inch deep. (A strip of heavy paper makes an easy guide for cutting parallel lines.) Stud meat with cloves. Insert spit rod lengthwise through center of each luncheon meat. Secure with holding forks; test balance. In covered grill arrange *hot* coals on both sides of drip pan. Attach spit; position drip pan under meat. Turn on motor; lower grill hood or cover with foil tent. Grill meat over *hot* coals till done, 35 to 40 minutes. During last 10 minutes baste meat often with sauce. Pass remaining sauce. Serves 10 to 12.

Meat and Potato Bake

4 large baking potatoes
 Cooking oil
1 12-ounce can luncheon meat
4 slices American cheese, cut in
  half diagonally (3 ounces)
 Grated Parmesan cheese
 Butter *or* margarine

Rub potatoes with oil. Wrap each potato in 18×12-inch rectangle of heavy-duty foil; seal edges well. Grill over *medium* coals for 1½ hours; turn frequently. (Or, cook on covered grill over *medium-slow* coals for 1½ to 2 hours.)
 Remove from grill; unwrap. Slice each potato crosswise into four pieces. Cut meat in half crosswise; cut each half into six slices crosswise. Insert slices of meat between potato pieces. Reassemble potato; rewrap in foil, closing top. (Or, skewer potato together and omit foil.)
 Grill till heated through, 10 to 15 minutes more; turn twice. Remove foil; place 2 cheese triangles atop each potato. Sprinkle with Parmesan; serve with butter. Serves 4.

Vegetable-Meat Kabobs

3 medium yams *or* sweet
  potatoes
1 9-ounce package frozen
  Brussels sprouts
1 12-ounce can luncheon meat
½ cup cooking oil
¼ cup vinegar
½ teaspoon celery seed
1 envelope French salad
  dressing mix
4 to 8 cherry tomatoes

Cook yams, covered, in enough boiling salted water to cover for 25 to 30 minutes, drain. Cool; peel and cut into 1-inch chunks. Cook sprouts in boiling salted water 5 minutes; drain. Cut meat in 1-inch cubes. In bowl mix oil, vinegar, celery seed, dressing mix, and dash pepper; blend well. Stir in meat and sprouts. Cover; refrigerate 4 to 6 hours, stirring often. Drain; reserve marinade. Thread meat, Brussels sprouts, and yams on four skewers. Grill over *hot* coals for 5 minutes. Turn; add tomatoes to skewers. Grill till meat is heated through, about 5 minutes more. Baste often with reserved marinade. Serves 4.

Super-Simple Skillet Supper

1 12-ounce can luncheon meat
1 16-ounce can cut green beans
1½ cups water
1 5½-ounce package dry hash
  brown potatoes with onion
1 5⅓-ounce can evaporated milk
1 5-ounce jar cheese spread
  with hickory smoke flavor

Cut luncheon meat into strips. In skillet combine luncheon meat, undrained green beans, water, dry potatoes, milk, cheese spread, and dash pepper. Cover; cook over *medium* coals, stirring occasionally. Heat till mixture is bubbly and potatoes are tender, about 10 minutes. Serves 4.

Barbecued Poultry

Hickory-Smoked Turkey

Hickory chips
1 12-pound turkey
1 tablespoon salt
¼ cup cooking oil

Soak hickory chips in enough water to cover, about an hour before cooking. Drain chips. Rinse bird and pat dry; rub cavity with salt. Skewer neck skin to back. Tuck wing tips behind shoulder joints. Push drumsticks under band of skin or tie to tail.

In covered grill arrange *medium-slow* coals around edge of grill. Sprinkle coals with some of dampened chips. Center foil pan on grill, not directly over coals. Place bird, breast side up, in foil pan; brush with oil. Insert meat thermometer in center of inside thigh muscle without touching bone. Lower grill hood. Grill over *medium-slow* coals till thermometer registers 185°, 3½ to 4½ hours. Sprinkle hickory chips over coals every 20 to 30 minutes. Brush bird often with additional oil. Add more coals, if needed. Let the turkey stand 15 minutes before carving. Makes 12 servings.

Barbecued Lemon Turkey

1 6- to 7-pound turkey
¼ cup cooking oil
¼ cup soy sauce
¼ cup finely chopped onion
1 teaspoon sugar
1 teaspoon ground turmeric
1 teaspoon ground ginger
½ teaspoon grated lemon peel
2 tablespoons lemon juice

Have meatman cut frozen turkey in half lengthwise. At home thaw turkey. Cut into pieces: 2 wings, 2 drumsticks, 2 thighs, 4 breast pieces, and 2 back pieces.

In large plastic bag combine oil, soy sauce, onion, sugar, turmeric, ginger, lemon peel, and juice. Place turkey pieces in bag; close bag.

Marinate turkey in the refrigerator 6 hours or overnight. Drain, reserving marinade. In covered grill place thighs and breast pieces over *slow* coals. Lower hood and grill about 30 minutes, turning pieces occasionally. Add drumsticks, wings, and back pieces. Lower hood; grill about 1 hour more, turning pieces occasionally. During the last 15 minutes, brush turkey pieces with the reserved marinade. Serves 6 to 8.

Smoked Turkey Roast

Hickory chips
1 3½- to 4-pound frozen boneless turkey roast, thawed
¼ cup cooking oil
1 tablespoon snipped parsley
2 teaspoons dried sage, crushed
¼ teaspoon lemon pepper marinade

Soak the hickory chips in enough water to cover, about an hour before cooking. Drain chips. Insert spit rod through center of turkey roast. Adjust holding forks; test balance. Insert meat thermometer in center of roast, not touching metal rod. In covered grill place *slow* coals on both sides of drip pan. Attach spit; position drip pan directly under roast. Turn on motor. Place a small pan of water at one end of firebox for moisture. Sprinkle coals with some dampened chips; lower grill hood or cover with foil tent. Grill roast over *slow* coals till thermometer registers 185°, 2½ to 3 hours. Brush roast occasionally with mixture of oil, parsley, sage, and lemon pepper. Sprinkle chips over coals every 20 minutes. Let roast stand 10 minutes before carving. Serves 8 to 10.

Turkey is more than a traditional holiday bird. It's an anytime treat when prepared as *Hickory-Smoked Turkey* and served with grilled potatoes topped with cheese and green onion.

Rotisserie-Roast Turkey

6 tablespoons butter *or*
   margarine, melted
¼ cup dry white wine
1 clove garlic, minced
½ teaspoon dried rosemary,
   crushed
1 5- to 6-pound frozen boneless
   turkey roast, thawed
   Salt
   Pepper

Combine *4 tablespoons* of the butter, the wine, garlic, and rosemary. Keep at room temperature to blend flavors.

Insert spit rod through center of turkey roast. Adjust holding forks; test balance. Insert meat thermometer in center of roast, not touching metal rod. Brush roast with remaining 2 tablespoons butter; season with salt and pepper. Place *hot* coals on both sides of foil drip pan. Attach spit; position drip pan directly under roast. Turn on motor. Grill turkey over *hot* coals till thermometer registers 185°, 2½ to 3 hours. During the last 30 minutes, baste roast with wine sauce. Makes 16 to 18 servings.

Sweet-Sour Cornish Hens

4 1- to 1½-pound Cornish game
   hens
   Salt
   Pepper
¼ cup butter *or* margarine,
   melted
1 10-ounce jar sweet and sour
   sauce
1 8-ounce can tomatoes, cut up
1 teaspoon soy sauce
6 thin slices lemon, halved

Season cavity of each hen with a little salt and pepper. Skewer neck and tail openings closed. Run spit rod through each hen crosswise, below breastbone. With four 18-inch cords, use one cord to tie each tail to crossed legs. Bring cord around to back, cross and bring around and across breast securing wings to body. Tie knot, cut off loose ends. Space birds about 1 inch apart on rod; secure with holding forks. Test balance. Place *hot* coals on both sides of drip pan. Attach spit; position drip pan under hens. Turn on motor. Grill hens till leg joints move easily, about 45 minutes. Baste hens often with melted butter.

Meanwhile, in saucepan combine sweet and sour sauce, tomatoes, soy sauce, and lemon slices; heat just to boiling. Grill hens about 15 minutes more, basting often with sauce. Pass extra sauce. Makes 4 servings.

Cornish Hens with Rice Stuffing (pictured on page 136)

1 6-ounce package long grain
   and wild rice mix
¼ cup light raisins
2 tablespoons butter *or*
   margarine
2 tablespoons blanched slivered
   almonds
½ teaspoon ground sage
   Salt
4 1- to 1½-pound Cornish game
   hens
¼ cup butter *or* margarine, melted

Cook rice mix according to package directions; stir in raisins, 2 tablespoons butter, almonds, and sage. Rub cavities of each hen with salt. Skewer neck skin to back. Fill each body cavity with about ¾ cup rice stuffing; cover opening with foil. Tie legs to tail; twist wing tips under back. Brush hens with ¼ cup melted butter. Arrange *medium-hot* coals around edge of grill. Center foil pan on grill, not directly over coals. Place birds in foil pan, allowing space between each bird. Grill hens over *medium-hot* coals till tender, 1½ to 1¾ hours. Brush occasionally with the drippings on foil. Serves 4.

Poultry lovers will savor *Sweet-Sour Cornish Hens*. Grill several birds at a time by inserting the spit rod crosswise through them, then secure with holding forks and cord.

Kowloon Duckling

Hickory chips
1 4- to 5-pound duckling
6 to 8 green onions with tops, cut up
6 sprigs parsley
1 clove garlic, minced
½ cup soy sauce
2 tablespoons honey
2 tablespoons lemon juice
Plum Sauce

Soak the hickory chips in enough water to cover, about an hour before cooking. Drain chips. Stuff cavity of duckling with onion, parsley, and garlic. Skewer neck and body cavities closed; tie legs to tail securely with cord. In saucepan heat soy sauce, honey, and lemon juice. In covered grill arrange *slow* coals around edge of grill. Sprinkle coals with some of the dampened chips. Center foil pan on grill, not directly over coals. Place duck, breast up, in foil pan. Lower grill hood. Grill for 2¼ to 2½ hours. Sprinkle chips over coals every 30 minutes. Brush duck often with soy mixture. Remove drippings from pan as needed. Serve with Plum Sauce. Serves 2 or 3.

Plum Sauce: Drain one 16-ounce can purple plums, reserving ¼ cup syrup. Force plums through a sieve. In saucepan combine the sieved plums, plum syrup, ¼ teaspoon grated orange peel, 3 tablespoons orange juice, 2 tablespoons sugar, ½ teaspoon Worcestershire sauce, and ¼ teaspoon ground cinnamon. Heat the mixture to boiling; reduce heat and simmer 10 minutes.

Grilled Island Chicken

1 8¼-ounce can crushed
    pineapple
¾ cup packed brown sugar
3 tablespoons lemon juice
1 tablespoon prepared mustard
2 2½- to 3-pound ready-to-cook
    broiler-fryer chickens,
    split in half lengthwise
½ cup cooking oil
1½ teaspoons salt

Drain pineapple and reserve 2 tablespoons syrup. Combine pineapple, reserved syrup, sugar, lemon juice, and mustard. Break wing, hip, and drumstick joints of chickens; twist wing tips under back. Brush chickens well with oil; season with salt and ¼ teaspoon pepper. Grill chickens over *slow* coals, bone side down, till bone side is well browned, 20 to 30 minutes. Turn chicken; grill till tender, about 30 minutes more. Turn and brush chickens often with glaze last 10 minutes. Serves 4.

Corn-Stuffed Chicken Breasts

8 whole chicken breasts
¼ cup chopped onion
¼ cup chopped celery
2 tablespoons butter
1 8¾-ounce can whole kernel
    corn, drained (1 cup)
1 cup herb-seasoned stuffing mix
1 slightly beaten egg
½ teaspoon poultry seasoning
¼ teaspoon salt
¼ cup butter, melted

Cut breasts through white cartilage at V of neck. Using both hands, grasp the small bones on either side. Bend each side back, pushing up with fingers to snap out breastbone, keeping meat in one piece. Do *not* remove skin. Sprinkle cut side with salt. In skillet cook onion and celery in the 2 tablespoons butter till tender. Add corn, stuffing mix, egg, poultry seasoning, and salt; mix well. Spoon some corn mixture on cut side of each chicken breast. Fold over and skewer or tie closed. Grill chicken over *medium-hot* coals till tender, 30 to 35 minutes, turning often. Brush with the ¼ cup melted butter during the last 10 minutes. Serves 8.

Chicken Teriyaki

½ cup packed brown sugar
½ cup soy sauce
2 tablespoons sweet sake, mirin,
    or dry sherry
1 tablespoon grated onion
1 clove garlic, minced
4 whole large chicken breasts,
    split, skinned, and boned
  Nonstick vegetable spray
    coating *or* cooking oil

In saucepan stir together brown sugar, soy, sake, onion, and garlic. Cook and stir over low heat till sugar dissolves. Cook, uncovered, till like thin syrup, about 5 minutes more; cool. Place chicken in shallow baking dish. Pour soy mixture over chicken. Cover; refrigerate 4 to 6 hours or overnight, occasionally spooning marinade over.

Remove chicken; reserve marinade. Coat grill with nonstick spray coating or cooking oil. Grill chicken over *medium-hot* coals for 15 to 20 minutes; turn often. Brush frequently with reserved marinade. Serves 8.

Sausage-Stuffed Chicken Roll-Ups

6 whole large chicken breasts,
    skinned and boned
2 tablespoons chopped green
    onion with tops
6 fully cooked smoked sausage
    links
½ cup butter, melted
¼ cup white wine *or* dry sherry
¼ cup snipped parsley
½ teaspoon paprika
  Cooking oil

Place chicken breasts one at a time between two sheets of waxed paper. Working out from center, pound to form 8×8-inch cutlets. Remove paper; sprinkle each cutlet with a little salt and *1 teaspoon* of the green onion. Place a sausage link at the end of each cutlet. Tuck in sides; roll up as for jelly roll. Press end to seal well; secure with wooden picks. Blend next four ingredients. Coat grill with cooking oil. Grill chicken, seam side down, over *medium-hot* coals about 15 minutes, turning often and brushing with butter mixture. Grill till done, 8 to 10 minutes more, turning and brushing with butter mixture. Serves 6.

Chicken with Zucchini Stuffing

2 2½- to 3-pound whole ready-to-
    cook broiler-fryer chickens
1½ cups chicken broth
⅔ cup regular rice
2 cups chopped zucchini
1 cup shredded carrot
½ cup chopped onion
¾ teaspoon salt
⅛ teaspoon pepper
½ cup chicken broth
¼ cup grated Parmesan cheese
1½ teaspoons dried chervil,
    crushed
    Cooking oil

Sprinkle cavity of birds with salt. In saucepan combine 1½ cups chicken broth and rice. Bring to boiling; cover. Reduce heat; cook 14 minutes. *Do not drain.* In another saucepan combine zucchini, carrot, onion, salt, pepper, and remaining ½ cup broth. Cook, covered, just till tender, about 10 minutes. *Do not drain.* Stir in Parmesan cheese and chervil. Fold in rice. Spoon mixture loosely into bird cavities. Skewer neck skin to back of chickens. Mount one chicken on spit rod (see tip below). Repeat with second fork and chicken. Add a third holding fork, pressing tines into meat; test balance. Place *medium* coals around drip pan under meat. Turn on motor; lower hood or cover with foil tent. Brush birds with cooking oil. Grill over *medium* coals till done, about 2 hours. Serves 8.

Herb-Glazed Chickens

2 2½- to 3-pound whole ready-to-
    cook broiler-fryer chickens
½ cup cooking oil
¼ cup light corn syrup
¼ cup finely chopped onion
1 tablespoon lemon juice
1 teaspoon dried oregano,
    crushed
1 teaspoon caraway seed
½ teaspoon salt

Salt chicken cavities. Skewer neck skin to back of chickens. Mount one chicken on spit rod (see tip below). Repeat with second fork and chicken. Add a third holding fork, pressing tines into meat; test balance. Place *medium-hot* coals around drip pan. Attach spit; position drip pan under meat. Turn on motor; lower hood or cover with foil tent. Grill chickens over *medium-hot* coals till tender, 1½ to 1¾ hours. Position drip pan under meat. Meanwhile, combine remaining seven ingredients. Brush over chicken occasionally last 30 minutes. Serves 6 to 8.

How to Mount Birds for Spit Roasting

Proper balance and correct timings are the keys to success when spit-roasting. (A) Place one holding fork on spit rod, tines toward point. Insert rod through bird lengthwise. Pinch fork tines together; push into breast. (B) Tie wings, using 24 inches of cord. Start cord at back; loop around each wing. Wrap around wings again. Tie in center of breast. Loop an 18-inch cord around tail, then around crossed legs; tie tightly to hold bird securely. (C) Pull together cords attached to wings and legs; tie tightly. Secure bird with second holding fork.

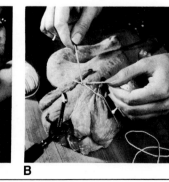

A   B

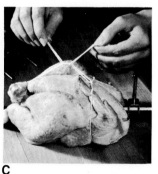

C

Curry Barbecued Chicken

2 2½- to 3-pound ready-to-cook
    broiler-fryer chickens
½ cup cooking oil
1 teaspoon grated lime peel
¼ cup lime juice
1 tablespoon grated onion
1 clove garlic, minced
2 teaspoons curry powder
½ teaspoon salt
½ teaspoon ground cumin
½ teaspoon ground coriander
¼ teaspoon ground cinnamon
¼ teaspoon pepper
    Lime slices
    Parsley

Quarter chickens. Break wing, hip, and drumstick joints of chickens so pieces will remain flat. Twist wing tips under back. Combine cooking oil, lime peel and juice, onion, garlic, curry powder, salt, cumin, coriander, cinnamon, and pepper. Place chickens in large plastic bag set in deep bowl. Pour marinade mixture over chickens. Close bag; refrigerate 4 to 6 hours, turning bag occasionally to coat chickens evenly.

Remove chickens, reserving marinade. Place chicken pieces, bone side down, over *medium-hot* coals. Grill chickens about 25 minutes. Turn, bone side up, and grill till done, 15 to 20 minutes more. Brush chickens with marinade frequently last 10 minutes. Garnish with lime twists and parsley. Makes 8 servings.

Chicken and Vegetable Bundles

4 chicken drumsticks, skinned
4 chicken thighs, skinned
2 large potatoes, peeled and
    cubed
1 8-ounce can sliced carrots,
    drained
1 8-ounce can cut green beans,
    drained
1 small onion, sliced and
    separated into rings
4 tablespoons butter *or*
    margarine
½ teaspoon dried tarragon,
    crushed
½ teaspoon hickory-smoked salt

Tear off four 18×18-inch pieces of heavy-duty foil. On each piece of foil, place one chicken leg and one thigh; sprinkle chicken with salt and pepper. Top each serving with a *few pieces* of potato, carrots, green beans, and onion. Place 1 tablespoon butter in each bundle; sprinkle each with some of the tarragon and hickory-smoked salt. Bring 4 corners of foil to center, twist securely, allowing room for expansion of steam. Grill the chicken bundles over *slow* coals till chicken is tender, about 1 hour. Makes 4 servings.

Spicy Barbecued Chicken

¼ cup finely chopped onion
1 clove garlic, minced
2 tablespoons cooking oil
¾ cup catsup
⅓ cup vinegar
1 teaspoon grated lemon peel
1 tablespoon lemon juice
1 tablespoon Worcestershire
    sauce
2 teaspoons sugar
1 teaspoon dry mustard
½ teaspoon salt
¼ teaspoon pepper
¼ teaspoon bottled hot pepper
    sauce
2 2½- to 3-pound ready-to-cook
    broiler-fryer chickens

Cook onion and garlic in oil till tender but not brown. Stir in catsup, vinegar, lemon peel and juice, Worcestershire sauce, sugar, dry mustard, salt, pepper, and bottled hot pepper sauce. Simmer, covered, about 30 minutes; stir occasionally. Quarter chickens. Break wing, hip, and drumstick joints of chickens so pieces will remain flat. Twist wing tips under back. Season chicken pieces with additional salt and pepper.

Place chicken pieces, bone side down, over *medium-hot* coals. Grill chickens about 25 minutes. Turn, bone side up, and grill till done, 15 to 20 minutes more. Brush chickens with sauce often last 10 minutes. Makes 8 servings.

Lemonade Chicken

2 2½- to 3-pound ready-to-cook
   broiler-fryer chickens
1 6-ounce can frozen lemonade
   concentrate, thawed
⅓ cup soy sauce
1 teaspoon seasoned salt
½ teaspoon celery salt
⅛ teaspoon garlic powder

Cut the chickens into serving pieces. In small bowl combine thawed lemonade concentrate, soy sauce, seasoned salt, celery salt, and garlic powder. Stir mixture to blend well. Dip chicken pieces in lemonade mixture. Place chicken, bone side down, over *medium-hot* coals. Grill about 25 minutes. Turn, bone side up, and grill till done, 15 to 20 minutes more. Brush chicken with lemonade mixture frequently last 10 minutes. Makes 8 servings.

Japanese-Style Chicken

4 whole large chicken breasts
¼ cup peanut oil *or* cooking
   oil
¼ cup soy sauce
¼ cup dry sherry
1 tablespoon brown sugar
1 tablespoon grated fresh
   gingerroot *or* 1 teaspoon
   ground ginger
1 clove garlic, minced
½ teaspoon salt
18 fresh mushroom caps
3 medium zucchini, cut in 1-inch
   slices (about 18 pieces)

Cut breasts through white cartilage at V of neck. Using both hands, grasp the small bones on either side. Bend each side back, pushing up with fingers to snap out breastbone. To split breast, cut in two lengthwise pieces. Working out from center, pound each to form 5×5-inch cutlet. Cut into strips about 1 inch wide. Combine next seven ingredients. Place chicken in shallow baking dish; pour marinade over. Cover; refrigerate 4 to 6 hours, spooning marinade over occasionally. Remove chicken, reserving marinade. Pour some boiling water over mushrooms in bowl. Let stand 1 minute; drain. On long skewers thread chicken accordion-style alternately with zucchini and mushrooms. Grill over *medium hot* coals for 12 to 15 minutes; turning and basting often with marinade. Serves 6.

Chicken and Beef Kabobs

1 pound beef sirloin steak
1 14¼-ounce can pineapple slices
½ cup catsup
3 tablespoons vinegar
2 teaspoons instant beef
   bouillon granules
¼ cup finely chopped onion
1 teaspoon celery seed
½ teaspoon ground cinnamon
¼ teaspoon ground allspice
1 bay leaf
12 small whole chicken wings

Cut beef in 1-inch pieces. Drain pineapple; reserve syrup. Cover and refrigerate pineapple. Add water to syrup, if necessary, to measure ¾ cup liquid; combine with catsup, vinegar, bouillon, onion, celery seed, cinnamon, allspice, and bay leaf. Add meat pieces to marinade. Cover; refrigerate several hours, stirring occasionally. Drain meat, reserving marinade. Quarter each pineapple slice; place 2 pieces together. Thread on skewers alternately with beef and chicken. Grill over *hot* coals till done, about 20 minutes, turning and brushing occasionally with reserved marinade. Heat remaining marinade; pass with kabobs. Makes 6 servings.

Microwave Helps to Shorten Grilling Time

Yes, it is possible to get barbecued-flavored chicken in a hurry. The secret: precook chicken pieces in a countertop microwave oven before putting them on grill. For example, place a single layer of chicken pieces in a 10×6×2-inch baking dish and micro-cook, covered, about 15 minutes. Then grill over *medium-hot* coals till tender, 10 to 15 minutes more; turn chicken till evenly browned.

Grilled Fish and Seafood

Wine-Sauced Trout

1 15-ounce can tomato sauce
½ cup dry red wine
½ cup butter *or* margarine
2 tablespoons lemon juice
2 tablespoons chopped green
  onion with tops
1 teaspoon sugar
1 teaspoon dried salad herbs
½ teaspoon salt
  Few drops bottled hot pepper
  sauce
6 whole pan-dressed lake *or*
  brook trout *or* perch
  (about 8 ounces each)

In small saucepan combine tomato sauce, wine, butter, lemon juice, green onion, sugar, salad herbs, salt, and hot pepper sauce. Simmer, uncovered, 10 to 15 minutes. Grill fish over *hot* coals 10 to 12 minutes. Turn fish and grill till done, 10 to 12 minutes more. Brush fish with sauce during last few minutes of grilling. Pass the warm sauce. Makes 6 servings.

Skillet-Fried Fish

6 fresh *or* frozen pan-dressed
  trout *or* other fish (about 6
  ounces each)
⅔ cup yellow cornmeal
¼ cup all-purpose flour
2 teaspoons salt
1 teaspoon dried parsley flakes
½ teaspoon paprika
1 5⅓-ounce can evaporated
  milk (⅔ cup)
  Cooking oil

Thaw fish, if frozen. Thoroughly stir together cornmeal, flour, salt, dried parsley, and paprika. Dip fish in evaporated milk, then coat with seasoned cornmeal mixture.

Heat a small amount of cooking oil in a large skillet over *hot* coals till oil is hot. Cook fish, a few at a time, in hot oil till lightly browned, 4 to 5 minutes. Turn and cook till fish flakes easily with a fork, 4 to 5 minutes more. Add more oil as needed. Drain the fish on paper toweling before serving. Makes 6 servings.

Hickory-Smoked Stuffed Trout

  Hickory chips
¼ cup chopped onion
2 tablespoons butter *or*
  margarine
¼ cup snipped dried apricots
3 tablespoons orange juice
1 teaspoon sugar
1 teaspoon instant chicken
  bouillon granules
¼ teaspoon celery salt
2 cups dry bread cubes
  (2½ slices bread)
2 tablespoons toasted slivered
  almonds
1 4- to 5-pound whole lake
  trout *or* walleyed pike,
  dressed
  Cooking oil

About 1 hour before cooking, soak the hickory chips in enough water to cover; drain. In skillet cook onion in butter till tender but not brown. Stir in apricots, orange juice, sugar, bouillon granules, and celery salt. Heat and stir to dissolve bouillon granules. Remove from heat. Add bread cubes and almonds; toss lightly. Spoon stuffing into fish cavity. Brush outside of fish with a little oil.

In covered grill arrange *slow* coals around edge of grill. Sprinkle some of the dampened hickory chips generously over coals. Center foil pan on grill, not directly over coals. Place the fish in foil pan. Close grill hood. Grill till fish flakes easily with fork, about 1¼ hours. Sprinkle hickory chips over the coals every 20 minutes. Makes 8 servings.

Show off your next catch in *Wine-Sauced Trout*. Trout or perch cooks quickly as you baste it with an herbed tomato-wine sauce. Serve with corn on the cob roasted in the husks.

Barbecued Fish

1½ **pounds fresh** *or* **frozen fish**
       fillets *or* **steaks,** *or*
       4 pan-dressed fish (about
       8 ounces each)
 ½ **cup cooking oil**
 1 **tablespoon Worcestershire**
       sauce
 ½ **teaspoon onion salt**
 ⅛ **teaspoon pepper**
       Lemon wedges

Thaw fish, if frozen. Cut fish fillets or steaks into 4 portions. (For pan-dressed fish, wrap tails in greased foil. Sprinkle fish cavities with salt and pepper.) Combine the oil, Worcestershire sauce, onion salt, and pepper; mix well. Place fish in well-greased wire grill basket. Brush fish with oil mixture.

Grill fish over *medium-hot* coals for 5 to 8 minutes. Brush with oil mixture; turn and brush second side. Grill till fish flakes easily when tested with a fork, 5 to 8 minutes more. Serve with lemon wedges. Serves 4.

Crispy-Grilled Fish Fillets

 ¾ **cup finely crushed**
       cornflakes
 ⅓ **cup sesame seed, toasted**
       (1⅞-ounce container)
 1 **16-ounce package frozen fish**
       fillets, thawed
 2 **tablespoons soy sauce**
       Salt
       Pepper
 ½ **cup dairy sour cream**

Combine cornflake crumbs and sesame seed. Brush fish with soy sauce. Season with salt and pepper. Spread one side of each fillet with sour cream; press coated side in crumb mixture. Repeat spreading with sour cream and coating other side of fillets. Place the coated fish fillets in well-greased wire grill basket. Grill fish over *medium-hot* coals about 8 minutes. Turn fish and grill till fish flakes easily with a fork, about 8 minutes more. Makes 4 servings.

Soy-Marinated Perch Fillets

 2 **pounds fresh** *or* **frozen perch**
       fillets
 ⅓ **cup cooking oil**
 3 **tablespoons soy sauce**
 2 **tablespoons wine vinegar**
 2 **tablespoons finely chopped**
       onion

Thaw fish, if frozen. Place fish fillets in plastic bag set in deep bowl. Combine the cooking oil, soy sauce, wine vinegar, and finely chopped onion; mix well. Pour mixture over fish fillets in bag; close bag. Marinate fish for 30 to 60 minutes at room temperature; turn bag occasionally. Drain fish, reserving marinade.

Place fish in well-greased wire grill basket. Grill over *hot* coals for 8 to 9 minutes. Turn fish and brush with marinade. Grill till fish flakes easily when tested with a fork, 6 to 8 minutes more. Makes 6 servings.

Fish in a Basket

 ⅓ **cup all-purpose flour**
 ½ **teaspoon salt**
 ⅛ **teaspoon pepper**
 4 **whole pan-dressed lake** *or*
       brook trout *or* **perch (about**
       12 ounces each)
 ¼ **cup butter** *or* **margarine,**
       melted

In a bowl combine flour, salt, and pepper. Dip fish in seasoned flour, coating thoroughly. Place the coated fish in a well-greased wire grill basket.

Grill fish over *hot* coals about 10 minutes. Turn fish and baste with melted butter. Grill till fish flakes easily when tested with a fork, about 10 minutes more; baste often with butter. Makes 4 servings.

Wild Rice-Stuffed Salmon

Hickory chips
2 cups chicken broth
¼ cup finely chopped onion
1 cup wild rice, rinsed
1 tablespoon butter *or*
   margarine
1 tablespoon snipped parsley
1 6-pound whole dressed salmon
   Butter, melted

Soak the hickory chips in enough water to cover about 1 hour before grilling. Drain chips. In saucepan combine chicken broth and onion; bring to boiling. Add wild rice to saucepan and reduce heat. Cover; simmer till the liquid is absorbed, about 40 minutes. Stir in the 1 tablespoon butter and snipped parsley. Spoon stuffing into cavity of salmon; skewer or tie.

In covered grill arrange *slow* coals around edge of the grill. Sprinkle some of the dampened chips generously over coals. Center foil pan on grill, not directly over coals. Place fish in foil pan.

Close the grill hood. Grill till fish flakes easily when tested with a fork, 1¼ to 1½ hours. Brush fish occasionally with melted butter. Sprinkle the hickory chips over coals every 20 minutes. Makes 10 servings.

Stuffed Smoked Salmon

Hickory chips
½ cup finely chopped celery
¼ cup chopped onion
3 tablespoons butter *or*
   margarine
4 cups herb-seasoned stuffing
   croutons
2 tablespoons snipped parsley
½ teaspoon grated lemon peel
1 tablespoon lemon juice
½ teaspoon salt
   Dash pepper
1 8-pound whole dressed
   salmon
½ cup butter *or* margarine,
   melted

Soak hickory chips in enough water to cover about 1 hour before grilling. Drain chips. In saucepan cook celery and onion in the 3 tablespoons butter till tender. Pour over stuffing croutons. Add parsley, lemon peel and juice, salt, and pepper. Toss together till well combined. Spoon into cavity of salmon; skewer or tie closed.

In covered grill arrange *slow* coals around edge of grill. Sprinkle some of the dampened chips over coals. Center foil pan on grill, not directly over coals. Place fish in foil pan. Close grill hood. Grill till fish flakes easily when tested with fork, 1¼ to 1½ hours. Brush fish occasionally with melted butter. Sprinkle hickory chips over coals every 20 minutes. Serves 10 to 12.

Halibut Kabobs (pictured on page 136)

1 12-ounce package frozen
   halibut steaks, thawed
¼ cup cooking oil
¼ cup dry vermouth
¼ cup lemon juice
1 teaspoon salt
1 teaspoon dried oregano,
   crushed
1 small clove garlic,
   minced
6 mushroom caps
1 large green pepper
12 cherry tomatoes

Cut fish into 1-inch pieces. In bowl combine oil, vermouth, lemon juice, salt, oregano, and garlic. Place fish pieces in marinade. Cover; marinate at room temperature for 1 hour. Drain fish, reserving marinade. Pour some boiling water over mushrooms in bowl. Let stand 1 minute; drain. Cut green pepper into 1-inch squares. On six skewers alternate fish, green pepper, and cherry tomatoes; end with mushroom caps. Grill the kabobs over *medium* coals for 8 to 10 minutes, turning and basting frequently with marinade. Makes 6 servings.

Charcoaled Halibut Steaks

½ cup shredded unpeeled
    cucumber
½ cup dairy sour cream
¼ cup mayonnaise *or*
    salad dressing
1 tablespoon snipped chives
2 teaspoons lemon juice
¼ teaspoon salt
    Dash pepper
2 pounds fresh *or* frozen halibut
    steaks *or* other fish
¼ cup butter *or* margarine
1 teaspoon salt
⅛ teaspoon pepper
    Paprika

Blend shredded cucumber with sour cream, mayonnaise or salad dressing, chives, lemon juice, the ¼ teaspoon salt, and the dash pepper. Mix well and chill sauce.

Thaw fish, if frozen. Cut into 6 portions. Place in well-greased wire grill basket. In saucepan melt butter; stir in the 1 teaspoon salt and ⅛ teaspoon pepper.

Grill fish over *medium-hot* coals for 5 to 8 minutes, brushing with butter mixture occasionally. Turn and baste with remaining butter mixture. Grill till fish flakes easily when tested with a fork, 5 to 8 minutes more. Sprinkle fish with paprika and serve with chilled cucumber sauce. Makes 6 servings.

Charcoal-Grilled Shrimp

2 pounds fresh *or* frozen large
    shrimp, shelled and deveined
½ cup olive *or* cooking oil
½ cup finely chopped onion
½ cup dry white wine
¼ cup lemon juice
¼ cup finely snipped parsley
1 tablespoon Worcestershire
    sauce
1 teaspoon dillweed
½ teaspoon salt

Thaw shrimp, if frozen. Combine oil, onion, wine, lemon juice, parsley, Worcestershire, dillweed, and salt. Place shrimp in plastic bag set in deep bowl. Pour marinade mixture over shrimp. Close bag. Marinate 3 to 4 hours in the refrigerator. Drain shrimp, reserving marinade.

Place shrimp in well-greased wire grill basket *or* on 24×18-inch piece of heavy-duty foil. Grill over *hot* coals for 15 to 20 minutes, turning basket or individual shrimp often and basting with marinade. Makes 6 servings.

Barbecued Shrimp Kabobs

1 8-ounce can tomato sauce
1 cup chopped onion
½ cup water
¼ cup packed brown sugar
¼ cup cooking oil
¼ cup lemon juice
3 tablespoons Worcestershire
    sauce
2 tablespoons prepared mustard
2 teaspoons salt
¼ teaspoon pepper
1 pound fresh *or* frozen large
    shrimp, shelled and deveined
1 15¼-ounce can pineapple
    chunks
1 green pepper, cut in 1-inch
    squares
2 cups cold water
1 cup regular rice
½ teaspoon salt
2 tablespoons snipped parsley

In saucepan combine tomato sauce, onion, the ½ cup water, brown sugar, cooking oil, lemon juice, Worcestershire, mustard, the 2 teaspoons salt, and pepper. Simmer, uncovered, 15 minutes, stirring once or twice; set aside. Thaw shrimp, if frozen. Drain pineapple, reserving 2 tablespoons syrup. Combine syrup with sauce mixture.

Place shrimp in plastic bag set in a deep bowl. Pour sauce mixture over shrimp; close bag. Marinate at room temperature for 2 to 3 hours. Drain, reserving sauce.

On four skewers alternately thread the shrimp, 2 pineapple chunks, and green pepper squares. Grill over *hot* coals for 5 to 8 minutes. Turn kabobs and brush with marinade. Grill till shrimp are done, 5 to 8 minutes more, basting occasionally with sauce.

Meanwhile, prepare the rice. In a saucepan combine the 2 cups cold water, rice, and ½ teaspoon salt; cover with tight-fitting lid. Bring to a rolling boil; reduce heat. Continue cooking 14 minutes (do not lift cover). Remove from heat; let stand, covered, 10 minutes. Stir in the parsley. Serve hot shrimp kabobs over rice. Pass remaining sauce, if desired. Makes 4 servings.

Foil-Barbecued Shrimp

2 pounds fresh *or* frozen
   large shrimp, shelled
   and deveined
6 tablespoons butter *or*
   margarine
½ cup snipped parsley
¾ teaspoon curry powder
1 clove garlic, minced
½ teaspoon salt
   Dash pepper

Thaw shrimp, if frozen. In saucepan melt butter; stir in parsley, curry powder, garlic, salt, and pepper. Add shrimp; stir to coat. Divide shrimp mixture equally among six 12×18-inch pieces of heavy-duty foil. Fold foil around shrimp, sealing the edges well.

Grill shrimp over *hot* coals about 8 minutes. Turn and grill till done, 7 to 8 minutes more. Serve in foil packages, if desired. Makes 6 servings.

Skewered Scallops and Bacon

8 ounces fresh *or* frozen
   unbreaded scallops
   (about 24)
3 tablespoons butter *or*
   margarine, melted
2 tablespoons lemon juice
   Dash pepper
12 bacon slices, halved crosswise
   (12 ounces)
   Paprika

Thaw scallops, if frozen. Remove any shell particles and wash thoroughly. Combine butter, lemon juice, and pepper. Pour marinade over scallops. Cover; let stand at room temperature for 30 minutes. Drain scallops; reserve marinade. In skillet partially cook bacon. Drain on paper towels and cool. Wrap each scallop with a half slice of partially cooked bacon. On six skewers thread bacon-wrapped scallops, securing bacon with skewer and allowing some space between each scallop. Sprinkle with paprika. Grill over *hot* coals, bacon side down, about 5 minutes. Turn, using spatula; baste with marinade. Grill till bacon is crisp and brown, about 5 minutes more. Serves 6.

Foil-Wrapped Clambake

48 soft-shelled clams
   in shells
4 quarts cold water
⅓ cup salt
2 2- to 2½-pound ready-to-cook
   broiler-fryer chickens,
   quartered
   Salt
   Pepper
8 whole ears of corn
   Rockweed *or* large bunch
   parsley
8 frozen lobster tails, thawed
   (about 2 pounds)
1 16-ounce package frozen fish
   fillets, thawed and cut in
   8 pieces
1 pound butter, melted

Thoroughly wash clams in shells. In a large kettle combine cold water and ⅓ cup salt. Place clams in salt-water mixture; let stand 15 minutes. Rinse well. Repeat salt-water soaking and rinsing twice more.

Break drumstick, hip, and wing joints of chickens so pieces will remain flat on grill. In covered grill place chicken pieces, skin side down, over *hot* coals. Grill about 10 minutes. Season with salt and pepper. Turn back husks of corn. Use a stiff brush to remove silk. Lay husks back in place.

Tear off sixteen 36×18-inch pieces of heavy-duty foil. Place 1 sheet crosswise over a second sheet. Repeat, making a total of 8 sets. Lay a handful of rockweed or parsley in center of each foil set. Cut eight 18-inch squares of cheesecloth; place 1 square atop rockweed.

For each package arrange the following on cheesecloth: 6 clams in shells, 1 precooked chicken quarter, 1 ear of corn, 1 lobster tail, and 1 piece of fish. Securely tie opposite ends of cheesecloth together. Seal opposite ends of foil together, sealing edges well.

Place foil packages, seam side up, on grill. Lower the grill hood. Grill over *hot* coals about 45 minutes.

To test for doneness: the chicken drumstick should move up and down easily in socket. Serve with individual cups of hot, melted butter. Makes 8 servings.

Grilled Rock Lobster Tails

4 medium frozen rock lobster
    tails
¼ cup butter *or* margarine,
    melted
2 teaspoons lemon juice
1 teaspoon grated orange peel
    Generous dash *each* ground
    ginger, aromatic bitters,
    and chili powder

Thaw rock lobster tails. Cut off thin undershell membrane with kitchen scissors. Bend tail back to crack shell or insert long skewers lengthwise between shell and meat to prevent curling. (To butterfly rock lobster tails, partially thaw tails; snip through center of hard top shell with kitchen scissors. With sharp knife cut through the meat, but *not through undershell.* Spread open.)

Combine melted butter or margarine, lemon juice, orange peel, ginger, aromatic bitters, and chili powder; brush over lobster meat. With meat side up, grill lobster tails over *hot* coals for about 5 minutes. Turn, shell side up, and brush with sauce, grill till meat has lost its transparency and is opaque, 5 to 10 minutes more. Makes 4 servings.

Barbecued King Crab Legs

¼ cup butter *or* margarine, melted
¼ cup snipped parsley
¼ cup lemon juice
1 tablespoon prepared mustard
2 pounds frozen cooked king crab
    legs, thawed and shelled

Combine butter, parsley, lemon juice, mustard, and ¼ teaspoon salt. Brush the mixture on crab meat. Place crab on grill about 4 inches from *medium* coals. Brush the crab with butter mixture and turn occasionally till heated through, 5 to 8 minutes. Makes 6 servings.

Grilled Salmon Steaks

6 fresh *or* frozen salmon steaks
    or other fish steaks
½ cup salad oil
¼ cup snipped parsley
¼ cup lemon juice
2 tablespoons grated onion
½ teaspoon dry mustard
¼ teaspoon salt
    Dash pepper

Thaw fish, if frozen. Place fish in shallow dish. Combine oil, parsley, lemon juice, onion, mustard, salt, and pepper. Pour over fish. Let stand at room temperature 2 hours, turning occasionally. (*Or,* marinate, covered, in refrigerator 4 to 6 hours.) Drain, reserving marinade. Place fish in well-greased wire grill basket. Grill over *medium-hot* coals till fish is lightly browned, 5 to 8 minutes. Baste with marinade and turn. Brush again with marinade; grill till fish flakes easily when tested with a fork, 5 to 8 minutes more. Serves 6.

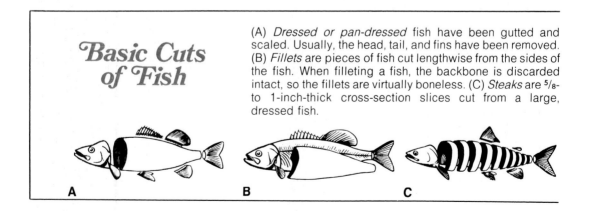

Basic Cuts of Fish

(A) *Dressed or pan-dressed* fish have been gutted and scaled. Usually, the head, tail, and fins have been removed. (B) *Fillets* are pieces of fish cut lengthwise from the sides of the fish. When filleting a fish, the backbone is discarded intact, so the fillets are virtually boneless. (C) *Steaks* are ⅝- to 1-inch-thick cross-section slices cut from a large, dressed fish.

A   B   C

Sausages and Frankfurters

Mustard-Brushed Bologna Kabobs

1 **pound chunk bologna, cut into 1-inch cubes**
1 **15¼-ounce can pineapple chunks, drained**
¼ **cup butter** *or* **margarine, melted**
2 **tablespoons Dijon-style mustard**
1 **tablespoon snipped parsley**
2 **teaspoons lemon juice Dash pepper**

On four skewers alternately thread bologna cubes with pineapple chunks. Combine melted butter, mustard, parsley, lemon juice, and pepper. Brush over skewered bologna and pineapple. Grill kabobs over *medium* coals, turning frequently till heated through, 8 to 10 minutes. Brush the kabobs frequently with the butter mixture. Serves 4.

Quick Frank Kabobs

8 **frankfurters, cut into thirds**
1 **16-ounce can whole new potatoes, drained**
2 **medium green peppers, cut in pieces**
¼ **cup horseradish mustard**
¼ **cup catsup**
½ **envelope taco seasoning mix (about 2 tablespoons)**
2 **tablespoons water**
2 **tablespoons cooking oil Several drops bottled hot pepper sauce**

Thread frank pieces on skewers alternately with potatoes and pepper pieces. In small bowl stir together horseradish mustard, catsup, taco seasoning mix, water, oil, and hot pepper sauce. Grill kabobs over *medium* coals for 10 minutes, turning often and brushing frequently with mustard mixture. Makes 4 to 6 servings.

Tangy Barbecued Franks

1 **medium onion, thinly sliced**
¼ **cup chopped celery**
¼ **cup chopped green pepper**
1 **clove garlic, minced**
¼ **cup butter** *or* **margarine**
1 **10¾-ounce can condensed tomato soup**
⅓ **cup water**
¼ **cup packed brown sugar**
2 **tablespoons vinegar**
2 **tablespoons prepared mustard**
1 **tablespoon Worcestershire sauce**
¼ **teaspoon bottled hot pepper sauce**
1 **pound frankfurters (8 to 10)**

In heavy 10-inch skillet over *hot* coals cook sliced onion, celery, green pepper, and garlic in butter or margarine till tender but not brown, about 10 minutes. Stir in tomato soup, water, brown sugar, vinegar, mustard, Worcestershire, and hot pepper sauce. Cover; bring to boil, allowing 15 to 20 minutes. Score franks on bias; add to hot mixture. Cook till heated through, about 10 minutes more, stirring occasionally. Makes 4 or 5 servings.

Jiffy Frank and Cabbage Skillet

2 tablespoons butter *or*
   margarine
2 16-ounce jars sweet-sour red
   cabbage, drained
1 12-ounce package frankfurters,
   cut in 1-inch pieces
2 medium apples, cored and
   chopped
1 small onion, chopped

In heavy skillet over *medium* coals melt butter or margarine; stir in drained cabbage, frankfurters, chopped apple, and onion. Cover; simmer mixture till onion is tender and cabbage and meat are heated through, about 20 minutes. Makes 4 servings.

Skewered Bratwurst

1 pound bratwurst (6 brats)
¼ cup light cream
2 tablespoons prepared mustard
½ teaspoon instant minced onion
¼ teaspoon coarsely cracked
   pepper
   Dash paprika
1 16-ounce can sauerkraut,
   drained

Cut each brat into thirds. Thread the bratwurst pieces on four skewers. For sauce, combine light cream, mustard, instant minced onion, pepper, and paprika.

Grill brat pieces over *medium-hot* coals till heated through, 7 to 8 minutes; turning and brushing often with sauce. In saucepan heat sauerkraut. Serve grilled meat and sauce over hot sauerkraut. Makes 4 servings.

Polish Sausage-Krauters

8 slices bacon
8 Polish sausage *or* large
   frankfurters
1 8-ounce can sauerkraut,
   drained and snipped
¼ cup chili sauce
2 tablespoons finely chopped
   onion
1 teaspoon sugar
1 teaspoon caraway seed

Partially cook bacon. Drain; set aside. Slit sausages or frankfurters lengthwise, cutting almost to ends and only ¾ of the way through.

Combine sauerkraut, chili sauce, onion, sugar, and caraway seed. Stuff about 2 tablespoons of the mixture into slit of each sausage or frankfurter. Wrap each with a strip of bacon; secure with wooden picks.

Grill over *hot* coals for 10 to 12 minutes, turning frequently so bacon cooks crisp on all sides. Serves 8.

Frank and Bean Skillet

1 1¼-ounce envelope sour cream
   sauce mix
¾ cup milk
   Few drops bottled hot pepper
   sauce
1 22-ounce jar baked beans
4 or 5 frankfurters, bias-sliced
1 3-ounce can French-fried
   onions

In heavy skillet blend together sour cream sauce mix, milk, and hot pepper sauce. Stir in baked beans and frank pieces. Cook over *medium* coals, stirring occasionally, till mixture is heated through. Before serving, stir in about ¾ of the French-fried onions. Sprinkle remaining onions atop each serving. Makes 4 servings.

Barbecued Lamb

Marinated Leg of Lamb

1 5- to 6-pound leg of lamb
⅓ cup lemon juice
½ cup cooking oil
¼ cup finely chopped onion
2 tablespoons finely snipped
    parsley
1 teaspoon salt
½ teaspoon dried thyme, crushed
½ teaspoon dried basil, crushed
¼ teaspoon dried tarragon,
    crushed

Have meatman bone leg of lamb and slit lengthwise so you can spread it flat on grill like a thick steak. Combine lemon juice, oil, onion, parsley, salt, thyme, basil, and tarragon. Place lamb in large plastic bag set in deep bowl. Pour lemon juice mixture over lamb; close bag. Refrigerate 4 to 6 hours, turning bag occasionally to coat lamb evenly. Drain lamb, reserving marinade.

Insert two long skewers through meat at right angles making a +, *or* place meat in a wire grill basket. (This makes for easy turning of meat and keeps meat from curling during cooking.) Grill over *medium* coals, turning every 15 minutes, till desired doneness, about 1½ hours for medium or 2 hours for well-done. Baste frequently with reserved marinade. Place lamb on carving board; remove from basket or remove skewers. Cut lamb across grain into thin slices. Makes 8 to 10 servings.

Note: This marinade is equally good on bone-in leg of lamb such as pictured below in the tip box (see chart on pages 204–205 for timings).

Apricot Lamb Kabobs

½ cup chopped onion
1 small clove garlic, minced
2 tablespoons cooking oil
1 17-ounce can apricot halves
3 tablespoons vinegar
2 tablespoons brown sugar
½ teaspoon curry powder
    Dash bottled hot pepper sauce
1½ pounds boneless lamb, cut in
    1½-inch cubes

In saucepan cook onion and garlic in hot oil till onion is tender but not brown. Place cooked onion, garlic, oil, apricots, vinegar, brown sugar, curry powder, hot pepper sauce, and 1 teaspoon salt in blender container. Cover; blend till smooth. Return mixture to saucepan; simmer, covered, 10 minutes. Cool. Pour mixture over lamb; cover and refrigerate overnight, turning meat occasionally. Drain, reserving marinade. Thread meat on six skewers; grill over *hot* coals for 15 to 20 minutes, turning often. Heat marinade; pass with kabobs. Makes 6 servings.

Balancing Meat on a Spit

Meat "done to a turn" on the rotisserie is easy once you learn how to balance the meat. To mount boneless roasts, insert the spit rod

through the center of the roast and secure with holding forks. Test the balance by holding one end of rod in the palm of each hand and turning gently. If the meat flops or turns unevenly, re-adjust holding forks or rod as necessary. Bone-in meat is harder to balance. To off-set the bone's weight, insert the rod diagonally as shown at left. Adjust the holding forks and test the balance as above.

Let *Herbed Lamb-Vegetable Kabobs,* which combine marinated lamb with onion wedges
and green and red pepper squares, make your next barbecue one that guests will long remember.

Saucy Lamb Riblets

3 to 4 pounds lamb riblets, cut
   in serving-size pieces
½ cup chopped onion
1 tablespoon cooking oil
¾ cup catsup
¼ cup water
3 tablespoons Worcestershire
   sauce
2 tablespoons brown sugar
2 tablespoons vinegar
¾ teaspoon salt
   Dash bottled hot pepper sauce

Trim excess fat from riblets. Cook riblets, covered, in boiling salted water till tender, 1 to 1¼ hours. Drain. Meanwhile, cook onion in oil till tender. Add catsup, water, Worcestershire, brown sugar, vinegar, salt, and hot pepper sauce; heat through.

Grill riblets over *medium-hot* coals for 10 to 15 minutes; turn. Grill 10 to 15 minutes. Brush riblets with catsup mixture; continue grilling till riblets are hot and glazed, 10 to 15 minutes more. Reheat catsup mixture. Brush on riblets before serving; pass with meat. Makes 4 servings.

Herbed Lamb-Vegetable Kabobs

½ cup cooking oil
½ cup chopped onion
¼ cup snipped parsley
¼ cup lemon juice
1 teaspoon salt
1 teaspoon dried marjoram,
   crushed
1 teaspoon dried thyme, crushed
1 clove garlic, minced
½ teaspoon pepper
2 pounds boneless lamb, cut in
   1-inch cubes
   Onion wedges
   Green pepper squares
   Sweet red pepper squares

Combine cooking oil, onion, parsley, lemon juice, salt, marjoram, thyme, garlic, and pepper; stir in lamb. Cover; refrigerate 6 to 8 hours, stirring occasionally. Drain lamb, reserving marinade. Cook wedges of onion in water till tender; drain.

Thread six skewers with lamb cubes, onion wedges, green pepper squares, and sweet red pepper squares. Grill over *hot* coals for 10 to 12 minutes; turn and brush often with reserved marinade. Serves 6.

Armenian-Italian Lamb Chops

1 cup tomato juice
½ cup finely chopped onion
⅓ cup lemon juice
¼ cup finely chopped dill
   pickle
¼ cup finely chopped
   green pepper
2 tablespoons sugar
1 teaspoon salt
1 teaspoon ground cumin
1 teaspoon dried marjoram,
   crushed
4 teaspoons cornstarch
2 tablespoons cold water
6 lamb shoulder chops, cut
   1 inch thick

In saucepan combine tomato juice, onion, lemon juice, pickle, green pepper, sugar, salt, cumin, marjoram, and ¼ teaspoon pepper. Simmer, covered, till onion and green pepper are tender, about 10 minutes. Blend cornstarch and cold water; stir into sauce. Cook and stir till thickened.

Grill lamb chops over *medium* coals for 10 to 12 minutes. Turn chops and grill till done, 10 to 12 minutes more, brushing frequently with sauce. (Keep sauce warm by placing it in small saucepan on grill.) Pass the remaining sauce with the lamb chops. Makes 6 servings.

Barbecue Sauces and Relishes

Wine Barbecue Sauce

 1 **2-ounce jar sliced pimiento**
¼ **cup thinly sliced green onion with tops**
½ **teaspoon dried oregano, crushed**
¼ **teaspoon dried tarragon, crushed**
 2 **tablespoons cooking oil**
 1 **tablespoon Worcestershire sauce**
 1 **tablespoon cornstarch**
½ **cup dry white wine**

Drain and chop pimiento. In small saucepan cook pimiento, green onion, oregano, tarragon, and ¼ teaspoon pepper in oil till onion is tender. Blend Worcestershire and ⅓ cup cold water into cornstarch; stir into onion mixture. Cook, stirring constantly, till thickened and bubbly. Stir in wine. Use to baste beef, lamb, or pork during last 10 to 15 minutes of barbecuing. Pass remaining sauce. Makes about 1 cup.

Sample the flavor makers: *Big-Batch Barbecue Sauce* with chicken, *Cucumber Relish,*
Seasoned Butter Log on steak, and *Zesty Sauerkraut Relish* on a sandwich. (See index for pages.)

Snappy Barbecue Sauce

1 cup catsup
1 cup water
¼ cup vinegar
1 tablespoon sugar
1 tablespoon Worcestershire
    sauce
1 teaspoon salt
1 teaspoon celery seed
2 or 3 dashes bottled hot
    pepper sauce

In saucepan combine catsup, water, vinegar, sugar, Worcestershire, salt, celery seed, and bottled hot pepper sauce. Bring the mixture to boiling; reduce heat and simmer, uncovered, for 30 minutes. Use to baste pork or beef ribs during last 15 to 20 minutes of barbecuing. Pass remaining sauce. Makes about 2 cups.

Easy Barbecue Sauce

1 14-ounce bottle hot-style
    catsup
3 tablespoons vinegar
2 teaspoons celery seed
1 clove garlic, halved

Combine catsup, vinegar, celery seed, and garlic. Refrigerate, covered, for several hours. Remove garlic. Use to baste hamburgers or beef during last 10 minutes of barbecuing. Makes about 1½ cups sauce.

Western Hot Sauce

½ cup catsup
¼ cup water
¼ cup finely chopped onion
3 tablespoons red wine vinegar
2 tablespoons cooking oil
2 teaspoons brown sugar
2 teaspoons Worcestershire
    sauce
2 teaspoons whole mustard seed
1 teaspoon paprika
½ teaspoon dried oregano,
    crushed
½ teaspoon chili powder
¼ teaspoon salt
⅛ teaspoon ground cloves
1 bay leaf
1 clove garlic, minced

In saucepan combine catsup, water, onion, vinegar, oil, brown sugar, Worcestershire, mustard seed, paprika, oregano, chili powder, salt, cloves, bay leaf, and garlic. Bring mixture to boiling; reduce heat and simmer, uncovered, for 10 minutes, stirring once or twice. Discard bay leaf. Use to baste hamburgers or ribs during last 10 to 15 minutes of barbecuing. Makes about 1½ cups.

Durango Sauce

1 16-ounce can pork and beans
    in tomato sauce
1 8-ounce can tomato sauce
½ cup water
1 1¼-ounce envelope chili
    seasoning mix
1 teaspoon Worcestershire sauce

In blender container combine pork and beans in tomato sauce, tomato sauce, water, chili seasoning mix, and Worcestershire sauce. Cover and blend the mixture till smooth. Use sauce to baste pork chops, steaks, or hamburgers during last 5 minutes of barbecuing. Heat remaining sauce to pass. Makes 2½ cups.

Easy-to-make *Chili Barbecue Sauce* doubles as a marinade and basting sauce. Marinate shrimp in the sauce, then skewer, adding extras to make a kabob. (See page 180 for timings.)

Molasses-Orange Barbecue Sauce

1　**10¾-ounce can condensed tomato soup**
1　**8-ounce can tomato sauce**
½　**cup light molasses**
½　**cup vinegar**
½　**cup packed brown sugar**
¼　**cup cooking oil**
1　**tablespoon instant minced onion**
1　**tablespoon seasoned salt**
1　**tablespoon dry mustard**
1　**tablespoon Worcestershire sauce**
1　**tablespoon finely shredded orange peel**
1½　**teaspoons paprika**
½　**teaspoon pepper**
¼　**teaspoon garlic powder**

In medium saucepan combine soup, tomato sauce, molasses, vinegar, brown sugar, oil, onion, salt, mustard, Worcestershire, peel, paprika, pepper, and garlic powder. Bring to boiling; reduce heat and simmer, uncovered, for 20 minutes. Use to baste poultry or beef during last 15 minutes of barbecuing. Makes about 3½ cups sauce.

Chili Barbecue Sauce

½ cup chili sauce
2 tablespoons cooking oil
2 tablespoons pineapple *or*
    orange juice
1 tablespoon brown sugar
    Dash bottled hot pepper sauce

Combine chili sauce, oil, pineapple or orange juice, brown sugar, and pepper sauce; mix well. Use as a marinade or brush over seafood, chicken, or pork during last 5 to 10 minutes of barbecuing. Makes about ¾ cup.

Big-Batch Barbecue Sauce (pictured on page 188)

½ cup finely chopped celery
½ cup finely chopped green
    pepper
1 clove garlic, minced
¼ cup butter *or* margarine
4 cups catsup
1 10½-ounce can condensed
    onion soup
1 10½-ounce can condensed
    chicken gumbo soup
2 tablespoons vinegar
½ teaspoon bottled hot
    pepper sauce
1 cup dry white wine

In large saucepan cook celery, green pepper, and garlic in butter or margarine till tender. Stir in catsup, soups, vinegar, hot pepper sauce, and ½ cup water. Simmer mixture 30 minutes, stirring occasionally. Stir in wine. Pour into 1- or 2-cup freezer containers. Seal, label, and freeze. To use, thaw the sauce. Use to baste chicken, frankfurters, ribs, or steaks the last 10 to 15 minutes of barbecuing. Heat the remaining sauce to pass, if desired. Makes 8 cups sauce.

Pineapple-Orange Glaze

½ of a 6-ounce can frozen
    pineapple juice concentrate
¼ cup orange marmalade
2 tablespoons bottled
    steak sauce

In saucepan combine pineapple concentrate, marmalade, and steak sauce. Cook and stir the mixture till heated through. Use to baste poultry or pork during the last 10 to 15 minutes of barbecuing. Makes about ⅔ cup.

Tarragon-Cider Basting Sauce

½ cup apple cider *or* juice
¼ cup vinegar
¼ cup sliced green onion
    with tops
2 tablespoons butter *or*
    margarine
2 tablespoons bottled steak
    sauce
2 tablespoons honey
1 teaspoon salt
1 teaspoon dried tarragon,
    crushed
¼ teaspoon pepper

In a 1½-quart saucepan combine cider, vinegar, onion, butter, steak sauce, honey, salt, tarragon, and pepper. Bring to boiling; simmer, uncovered, for 20 minutes, stirring mixture occasionally. Use as a meat marinade or use to baste chicken, beef, pork, or fish during last 15 to 20 minutes of barbecuing. Heat and pass the remaining sauce. Makes about ¾ cup sauce.

Coffee-Soy Glaze

½ **cup packed brown sugar**
1 **tablespoon cornstarch**
⅔ **cup cold strong coffee**
¼ **cup soy sauce**
3 **tablespoons wine vinegar**

In a small saucepan blend together the brown sugar and cornstarch. Add coffee, soy sauce, and vinegar; mix well. Cook and stir mixture till thickened and bubbly. Use to baste spareribs or pork chops during the last 15 minutes of barbecuing. Makes about 1 cup sauce.

Soy-Lemon Basting Sauce

1 **tablespoon brown sugar**
1 **teaspoon cornstarch**
2 **tablespoons lemon juice**
2 **tablespoons soy sauce**
2 **tablespoons water**
2 **tablespoons sliced green**
   onion with tops
1 **tablespoon butter** *or* **margarine**
1 **clove garlic, minced**

In saucepan blend brown sugar and cornstarch. Stir in lemon juice, soy sauce, and water. Add onion, butter, and garlic. Cook and stir till thickened and bubbly. Use to baste poultry or fish during last 15 minutes of barbecuing. Makes about ⅓ cup.

Seasoned Butter Log (pictured on page 188)

¼ **cup butter, softened**
2 **tablespoons braunschweiger**
2 **teaspoons lemon juice**
¼ **teaspoon dried basil, crushed**
   Paprika

Blend together softened butter, braunschweiger, lemon juice, and basil. Shape into a 4-inch log on waxed paper. Roll log in paprika to coat. Chill till firm. Slice butter log and serve with grilled steaks.

Caraway-Cheese Spread

1 **3-ounce package cream**
   cheese, softened
1 **tablespoon butter, softened**
1 **teaspoon caraway seed**
1 **teaspoon prepared mustard**

In a small bowl blend together cream cheese and softened butter. Stir in caraway seed and mustard. Spread atop grilled hamburgers. Makes about ½ cup.

Zesty Sauerkraut Relish (pictured on page 188)

½ **cup sugar**
½ **cup vinegar**
1 **teaspoon prepared mustard**
¼ **teaspoon garlic powder**
¼ **teaspoon pepper**
1 **16-ounce can sauerkraut,**
   drained
⅓ **cup chopped sweet red** *or*
   green pepper
⅓ **cup chopped onion**
⅓ **cup chopped cucumber**

In saucepan heat sugar and vinegar till sugar is dissolved; stir occasionally. Stir in mustard, garlic powder, and pepper. Cool. Combine drained sauerkraut, red or green pepper, onion, and cucumber; stir together with the vinegar mixture. Cover and chill the relish till needed. Makes about 3 cups relish.

Cucumber Relish (pictured on page 188)

3 large tomatoes, chopped
1 medium cucumber, peeled,
    seeded, and chopped (1 cup)
¼ cup chopped fresh coriander
    leaves
3 tablespoons finely chopped
    onion
¼ teaspoon finely chopped
    canned green chili peppers
1 tablespoon lemon juice
½ teaspoon salt

Combine tomatoes, cucumber, coriander leaves, onion, and chili peppers. Stir together lemon juice and salt. Add to the vegetable mixture and mix well. Cover and chill till needed. Makes about 2⅔ cups relish.

Sandwich Coleslaw

2 cups finely shredded cabbage
⅓ cup thinly sliced green onion
    with tops
¼ cup snipped parsley
2 tablespoons sugar
3 tablespoons vinegar
1 teaspoon salt
½ teaspoon celery seed
    Dash bottled hot pepper sauce

Combine the shredded cabbage, green onion, and parsley. Stir together sugar, vinegar, salt, celery seed, and hot pepper sauce. Pour over cabbage mixture and toss. Cover and chill till needed. Makes about 2 cups relish.

Ratatouille Relish

2 medium green peppers, stems
    and seeds removed
2 tomatoes, cored
1 medium onion
1 medium zucchini
½ of a small eggplant, peeled
2 tablespoons salt
1 cup sugar
1 cup vinegar
1 cup water
1 teaspoon whole mustard seed
¾ teaspoon celery seed
¼ teaspoon fines herbs

Using coarse blade of food chopper, grind peppers, tomatoes, onion, zucchini, and eggplant. Stir salt into vegetables. Cover; refrigerate and let stand overnight. Rinse and drain vegetables. In saucepan combine sugar, vinegar, water, mustard seed, celery seed, and fines herbs. Stir in vegetables. Bring mixture to boiling; reduce heat and simmer 5 minutes, stirring frequently. Cool. Cover and chill till needed. Makes about 4 cups relish.

Red Pepper Relish

6 sweet red peppers
    (about 1½ pounds)
2 medium onions, quartered
¾ cup sugar
¾ cup vinegar
1½ teaspoons salt

Remove stems and seeds from red peppers. Using coarse blade of food chopper, grind peppers and onions, reserving juices. In Dutch oven or large saucepan combine peppers and onions and reserved juices. Stir in sugar, vinegar, and salt. Bring to boiling; boil gently, uncovered, for 20 to 25 minutes. Cool; cover and chill till needed. Makes about 2 cups relish.

Barbecue Marinades

Armenian Herb Marinade

½ cup olive oil *or* cooking oil
½ cup chopped onion
½ cup tomato juice
¼ cup lemon juice
¼ cup snipped parsley
1 teaspoon salt
1 teaspoon dried marjoram, crushed
1 teaspoon dried thyme, crushed
½ teaspoon pepper
1 clove garlic, minced

Combine oil, chopped onion, tomato juice, lemon juice, parsley, salt, marjoram, thyme, pepper, and garlic. Place lamb, pork, or chicken in a plastic bag set in a deep bowl or a shallow baking dish. Pour marinade mixture over meat. Close bag or cover dish; refrigerate 4 to 6 hours or overnight. Turn the bag or spoon marinade over the meat occasionally to coat evenly. Makes 1¾ cups (enough for 3 to 4 pounds meat).

Savory Wine Marinade

1 small onion
½ cup cooking oil
½ cup white wine
¼ cup lime juice *or* lemon juice
2 tablespoons snipped parsley
½ teaspoon salt
¼ teaspoon bottled hot pepper sauce

Thinly slice the onion; separate into rings. Combine oil, wine, lime juice, parsley, salt, and pepper sauce; add onion. Place fish or chicken in a plastic bag set in a deep bowl or a shallow baking dish. Pour marinade mixture over meat. Close bag or cover dish; refrigerate for 4 to 6 hours or overnight. Turn the bag or spoon marinade over the meat occasionally to coat evenly. Makes about 1½ cups (enough for 3 pounds meat).

Teriyaki Marinade

¼ cup cooking oil
¼ cup soy sauce
¼ cup dry sherry
1 tablespoon grated fresh gingerroot *or* 1 teaspoon ground ginger
1 clove garlic, minced
2 tablespoons molasses

Combine oil, soy sauce, dry sherry, ginger, and garlic. Place chicken, beef, or pork in plastic bag set in deep bowl or a shallow baking dish. Pour marinade mixture over meat. Close bag or cover dish; refrigerate 4 to 6 hours or overnight. Turn bag or spoon marinade over meat occasionally to coat evenly. Drain, reserving marinade. Stir in molasses. Use to baste meat during last 10 minutes of barbecuing. Makes about 1 cup (enough for 2 pounds meat).

Herb-Seasoned Marinade

¼ cup cooking oil
¼ cup wine vinegar
¼ cup finely chopped onion
1 tablespoon Worcestershire sauce
½ teaspoon dried basil, crushed
½ teaspoon dried rosemary, crushed
¼ teaspoon pepper
⅛ teaspoon bottled hot pepper sauce

Combine oil, vinegar, onion, Worcestershire, basil, rosemary, pepper, hot pepper sauce, and ½ teaspoon salt. Place beef, pork, or chicken in a plastic bag set in a deep bowl or a shallow baking dish. Pour marinade mixture over meat. Close bag or cover dish; refrigerate 4 to 6 hours or overnight. Turn bag or spoon marinade over meat occasionally to coat evenly. Makes about ¾ cup (enough for 2 pounds meat).

Marinating a roast in *Armenian Herb Marinade* allows the meat to take on a subtle flavor from the well-seasoned liquid. Basting with the marinade reinforces the goodness.

Equipment for Cookouts

Small Equipment

After purchasing the grill, limit your selection of other tools to small essentials that simplify barbecuing. Listed below are items that every serious barbecuer should purchase, and also some optional gear. Not illustrated but equally necessary to have on hand are long skewers, salt and pepper shakers, a carving knife, and heavy-duty foil.

(1) Long-handled tongs—no chef does without two pairs, one for food, and one for the coals; (2) a basting brush to swish on sauces; (3) a fork to help keep a grip on the food; and (4) a multi-purpose turner. (All with long handles to keep you a safe distance from the coals.)

Other good investments for outdoor chefs include (5) a wire grill basket that adjusts to the thickness of the food; (6) spit basket that attaches to a spit rod; (7) rib rack; (8) potholders and asbestos mitts; and (9) a meat thermometer to help ensure that the internal temperature or meat and poultry is done to your liking. (A thermometer is especially useful in outdoor cooking where meat may look done on the outside and be undercooked on the inside.)

Also, keep (10) a plant sprinkler or a pump-spray bottle filled with water to put out flare-ups, and don't forget to have (11) a supply of extra coals ready to use.

Barbecue Grills

It's unbelievable the amount of outdoor cooking equipment that's available for today's barbecue enthusiast. Grills come in many sizes, styles, and prices with features to suit the needs of experienced backyard chefs and novices alike. The more expensive models offer the added conveniences of motor-driven rotisseries and skewers, storage drawers, utensil racks, and cutting boards. The following pointers will help you decide which type and model of grill are right for you.

Best buys for the beginner

Start your barbecuing career with a small brazier or a lightweight folding unit. Either style is easy to use, convenient to store, and inexpensive. Experiment with using foil drip pans, placement of coals, and different types of food cooked over a variety of coal temperatures. After a season or two of barbecuing, you'll know whether you are an avid barbecue fan or only an "occasional backyard chef."

Selecting the right grill

After you learn the basic techniques of barbecuing on a small brazier grill, you may want to consider buying a more elaborate model. Which type of grill you purchase depends on the amount of money you want ot invest and how much barbecuing you want to do. If you barbecue infrequently or only with small groups, there's no need to invest in an expensive model. You may decide the grill you started with does everything desired. But even if you need a more elaborate unit, don't cast aside the old one. The first grill makes a handy unit for grilling appetizers, breads, or hot desserts. Even use the unit to store hot coals for supplementing long cooking on the main grill.

Types of barbecue grills

Brazier grills—Lightweight, inexpensive, and easy to use, the brazier is the most popular grill on the market. Options available include models ranging from simple fold-up units to elaborate three-legged ones on wheels with half hoods, rotisseries, and air dampers. Large braziers have a lever or crank that regulates the distance between the grate and coals. This aids in controlling the heat.

Hibachis—Apartment dwellers or anyone cramped for space who need a small outdoor grill will find the sturdy hibachis just the thing. These small, efficient grills come complete with adjustable grates, air dampers, and coal racks to let ashes sift to the bottom. Even backyard chefs with elaborate equipment find this well-designed grill great for the appetizer table or an intimate dinner for two.

Kettle and wagon grills—Although relatively expensive compared to the lighter-weight braziers, the kettle and wagon grills are far more versatile and usually constructed with heavier materials. The kettle, semispherical in shape, features a coal rack near the bottom and grate in the middle. The lid then is the top half of the sphere. Wagons,

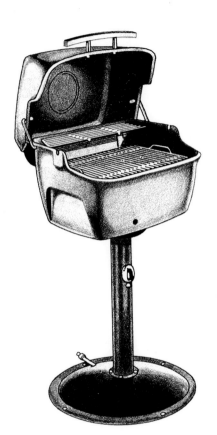

Pedestal mount gas grill

Barbecue Grills *continued*

Tabletop propane gas grill

on the other hand, are rectangular in shape, with options such as full hoods, smoke chambers, warming ovens or racks, cutting boards, and built-in fire starters.

The shape of kettles and wagons differs from brand to brand, but they all feature important air dampers both in the bottom and in the lid to control ventilation. Open these dampers when you need a hot fire or close them partway to cool down the coals.

Similar cooking techniques are available in kettle and wagon grills. Lid up, the kettles and wagons become braziers, even offering motor-driven rotisseries and skewers. Lid down, these grills are effective ovens, with heat controlled by air dampers. If you desire a smoky taste, set the grill up as for an oven and add dampened hickory chips to the hot coals.

Smokers—As their name implies, smokers give foods an appetizing smoky flavor after many hours of cooking. Like all barbecue equipment, the various smokers range from the relatively simple to elaborate units. A popular style is the small portable domed smoke oven. The meat cooks directly over a bed of smoldering coals, similar to smoking in covered kettle or wagon grills.

Another portable model is completely open at the bottom, providing good air circulation. A tray of coals supported by pegs heats the meat and dampened hickory chips plus a small pan of water between it and the grate. The heated water adds moisture to the smoke and keeps the meat moist during the long hours of cooking.

There's another, more elaborate unit, the Chinese smoker. Whether the unit is a permanent brick structure or a movable metal one, the smoker is L-shaped with an upright chimney. The meat hangs on racks or hooks in the chimney away from the bed of coals and the food cooks slowly in the hot smoke.

Remember, smokers only cook the food—they are not food curing and preserving equipment. Refrigerate any food leftover from smoker cooking.

Gas and electric grills—The newest in barbecue grills feature gas or electricity as the heat source instead of charcoal. Gas and most electric models work on the principle of radiant heat. Volcanic pumice or ceramic briquets, placed on racks between the heat source and grate, heat to a desired temperature. It's the heat radiating from them that actually cooks the food producing an appetizing flavor and appearance.

Gas and electric models are convenient versions of the kettle and wagon grills. Quick and easy to start plus better heat control are factors contributing greatly to their increasing popularity. Permanently installed gas grills use natural or LP gas. Portable gas grills use only LP gas, which comes in tanks of various sizes.

Gas and electric grills differ greatly from brand to brand, it's important to understand how your particular model works. Read all the manufacturer's instructions.

Charcoal Cooking Know-How

You undoubtedly know an outdoor chef who barbecues delightful meals atop the grill. The food smells tantalizing and tastes even better. And everything always remains under control—never a flare-up, never a burnt pork chop. This expertise doesn't happen by accident. Chances are, the backyard barbecue expert you know has taken the time to master the techniques involved in barbecuing.

Following are some pointers that will help you get the most out of your equipment and the food you barbecue.

A To start briquets, mound the coals in a foil-lined firebox

B For spit-roasting, spread the hot coals in a circle

Preparing the firebox
Before you go out and fire up the grill, no matter what type of equipment it is, always read the manufacturer's instructions. The firebox may need a foundation for the charcoal fire. (A) Protect the brazier grill's firebox with a lining of heavy-duty foil, then top with 1 inch of pea gravel, coarse grit, or expanded mica insulation pellets. This bedding foundation allows some air in under the briquets so the coals will burn better. It also protects the firebox from the intense heat of the coals, distributes the heat more evenly, and reduces flare-ups by absorbing dripping fats and the meat juices.

After you've used the grill a dozen times, the liner will be full of greasy drippings. Gravel or grit bedding can be washed, dried thoroughly, and used again. If you have used insulation pellets, discard and replace with new.

Keep the briquets to a minimum
Beginning chefs often overdo it and build too big a bed of coals. Estimate how many briquets you'll need for the size of the grill and the type and amount of food to be grilled. It's unnecessary to cover the entire grill area for a few frankfurters. Large thick cuts of meat require more charcoal than do thin steaks and burgers.

If you plan to barbecue for more than one hour, extra briquets need to be added to the bed of coals to maintain its proper cooking temperature. Place a dozen cold briquets around the outer edge of the hot bed of coals. Then, as needed, rake them into the other coals. Or, have a metal bucket or small portable brazier of glowing coals ready at the side of your barbecue unit.

Getting the charcoal started
Pile the number of briquets needed into a pyramid or mound in the center of the firebox. Drizzle liquid lighter or jelly fire starter over the whole surface of the charcoal. Wait 1 minute, then ignite with a match. (Never use gasoline or kerosene to start charcoal. Gasoline is much too dangerous, and kerosene adds an unpleasant taste to your food.) For faster starting, use an electrical fire starter (see photo, page 200). Place the briquets over the coil, plug in the starter, and in 5 to 15 minutes the coals will be ready. Remove the coil to a heatproof location, and distribute coals around the firebox to suit the kind of food you'll be cooking.

Charcoal Cooking Know-How *continued*

Electrical fire starters provide glowing coals quickly, only 5 to 15 minutes, and
they are odorless. Equipped with one of these, you can eliminate fussing with liquid fuel.

C For covered grilling, pile the
charcoal on both sides of drip pan

Don't start barbecuing too soon; the coals need to burn
about 20 to 30 minutes. The charcoal is ready for grilling
when it dies down to a glow and no areas of black show.
Live coals look ash-gray by day and glow red after dark. A
thin layer of gray ash smothers the coals. You'll need to tap
the coals frequently to loosen ashes so the coals can
breathe and burn properly.

Arranging the hot coals

When the coals are ready, use a fire rake or long-handled
tongs to spread the coals in a single layer. The arrangement
of the hot coals depends on the kind of grill used and the
type of food being barbecued.

(B) For spit-roasting spareribs, roasts, leg of lamb, or
poultry, use a ring of coals to grill. Position the foil drip pan
directly under the meat, and then spread the coals in a
circle all around the firebox.

D For grilling steaks, burgers, and chops, rake coals over firebox

E To test the coals, hold your hand palm-side down

(C) In a covered grill for barbecuing large pieces of meat, make a foil drip pan a little larger than the meat. Place drip pan in center of firebox and pile coals on both sides of pan. Replace the grate and set meat directly over the drip pan. Lower the hood.

(D) Barbecue steaks, chops, and other foods that are grilled flat by raking coals over the entire firebox. Place the coals about 1/2 inch apart for even heat.

Grill kabobs by lining up hot coals in parallel rows in the firebox plus coals around edge of grill. Stagger skewers on the grate directly above spaces between briquet rows so meat fats will not drip on coals.

Determine cooking temperature of the coals

(E) Hold your hand palm-side down just above hot coals at the height the food will be cooking. Begin counting "one thousand one, one thousand two;" if you need to withdraw your hand after two seconds the coals are hot, three seconds for medium-hot coals, four seconds for medium coals, and five or six seconds for slow coals.

Adjusting the heat for the right temperature

When the coals are too hot, either raise the grill's grate, lower the firebox, close the air vents, or simply remove some of the hot briquets. Increase the temperature of the coals in the grill's firebox by tapping the ashes off the burning coals with tongs, moving the coals closer together, lowering the grate, raising the firebox, or opening the vents to allow more air to circulate through the grill.

Controlling the flare-ups

Reduce flare-ups when meat fat drips on the coals by spacing farther apart or removing a few to cut down on the heat. Keep a pump-spray bottle filled with water handy. Sprinkle a little water on the flare-ups—don't soak the coals.

Save and reuse the charcoal

After barbecuing don't let briquets just burn away. If using a covered grill, lower hood and close air vents. Or, if you own an open-type unit, use tongs to transfer hot coals to a metal pail half full of water. Drain and spread the charcoal onto a stack of papers to dry. The charcoal must be absolutely dry or it will not relight.

Cleaning up the barbecue grill

It's easiest to clean the grates right after barbecuing. Read all the cleaning, care, and storage directions supplied with your equipment before using any cleaning products or abrasives. Fill sink with hot, sudsy water and put the grill's grate in to soak. Later, a few swipes with a wet cloth will clean the grate.

If the grate is too large to fit in a sink, cover with wet paper towels or wet newspapers while you eat. Place the hot grate on one stack of well-soaked papers, then cover with second. Burned-on food usually washes right off with a wet cloth. Use scouring or abrasive-type pads and/or a stiff grill brush for the stubborn spots.

Grilling Over the Coals

Type of food	Cut or portion (placed 4 inches above coals)	Weight or thickness	Temperature of coals*	
BEEF	Burgers	½ inch	Medium-hot Medium	
		¾ inch	Medium-hot Medium	
	Porterhouse, T-bone, or sirloin steak	1 inch	Medium-hot	
		1½ inches	Medium-hot Medium	
	Chuck blade steak	1 inch	Medium	
		2½ inches	Medium	
LAMB	Rib chops	1 inch	Medium	
		1½ inches	Medium	
	Shoulder chops	1 inch	Medium	
		1½ inches	Medium	
PORK	Loin chops	1 inch	Medium	
		1½ inches	Medium	
	Blade steak	¾ inch	Medium	
	Loin back ribs or spare ribs	5–6 pounds	Medium	
HAM	Fully cooked slice	½ inch	Medium-hot	
		1 inch	Medium	
	Canned	5 pounds	Medium	
CHICKEN	Broiler-fryer halves	2½–3 pounds	Medium-hot	
	Roasting chicken, unstuffed	3–4 pounds	Medium	
TURKEY	Unstuffed	6–8 pounds	Medium	
		12–16 pounds	Medium	
FISH	Salmon or halibut steaks	¾ inch	Medium	
		1–1½ inches	Medium-hot	
	Trout, snapper, or whitefish fillets	6–8 ounces each	Medium-hot Medium	
SEAFOOD	Shrimp (large)	2 pounds	Hot	

*Estimate by holding hand, palm down, about 4 inches above hot coals. Count seconds you can hold position. Figure 2 seconds as Hot coals; 3 seconds for Medium-hot coals, 4 seconds for Medium coals, and 5 or 6 seconds for Slow coals.

A handy guide for barbecuing your favorite foods

	Approximate total cooking times				Comments
	Open grill		**Covered grill**		
	Rare	Medium	Rare	Medium	
	8–10 min. 10–12 min.	10–12 min. 12–15 min.	7–9 min. 8–10 min.	8–10 min. 10–12 min.	Four burgers per pound
	10–12 min. 12–15 min.	12–15 min. 14–18 min.	8–10 min. 10–12 min.	10–12 min. 12–15 min.	Three burgers per pound
	12–18 min.	15–20 min.	8–10 min.	10–15 min.	Check doneness by cutting a slit in meat near bone
	18–20 min. 20–25 min.	20–25 min. 25–30 min.	10–15 min. 15–18 min.	15–18 min. 18–22 min.	
	12–18 min.	15–20 min.	8–10 min.	12–18 min.	
	50–60 min.	55–65 min.	45–55 min.	50–60 min.	Use foil tent on open grill
		20–25 min.		20–25 min.	Check doneness by cutting a slit in meat near bone
	25–30 min.	28–32 min.	20–25 min.	23–28 min.	
		22–28 min.		18–22 min.	
	28–32 min.	30–35 min.	20–25 min.	25–30 min.	
		Well-done		**Well-done**	
		22–25 min.		18–22 min.	A wire grill basket aids in turning
		30–35 min.		25–30 min.	
		15–20 min.		15–20 min.	
				1¼–1½ hrs.	
		10–15 min.		10–15 min.	Slash fat edge of ham slice
		25–35 min.		20–30 min.	
		1½–1¾ hrs.		1¼–1¾ hrs.	Use foil tent on open grill
		45–50 min.		40–45 min.	
				2–2½ hrs.	
				3–3¾ hrs.	Meat thermometer inserted in thigh should register 185°
				3½–4½ hrs.	
		17–22 min.		15–20 min.	Use a wire grill basket
		10–17 min.		10–15 min.	
		10–17 min. 17–20 min.		10–15 min. 15–17 min.	Use a wire grill basket
		15–18 min.		15–18 min.	

Rotisserie Specialties

Type of food	Cut	Weight	Temperature of coals*	
BEEF	Rolled rib roast	5–6 pounds	Medium	
	Tenderloin roast	2½ pounds	Medium-hot	
	Eye of round	3–4 pounds	Medium-hot	
	Boneless rump roast	3–4 pounds	Slow	
LAMB	Leg	5–7 pounds	Medium	
PORK	Boneless loin roast	5–6 pounds	Medium	
	Loin back ribs or spareribs	3–4 pounds	Slow	
HAM	Boneless piece	9–10 pounds	Medium	
	Canned	5 pounds	Medium	
CHICKEN	Whole	2½–3 pounds	Medium-hot	
			Medium	
CORNISH HENS	4 birds	1–1½ pounds each	Medium-hot	
DUCKLING	Whole domestic	4–6 pounds	Medium-hot	
TURKEY	Unstuffed	6–8 pounds	Medium	
	2 rolled turkey roasts	28 ounces each	Medium-hot	
	Boneless turkey roast	5–6 pounds	Medium-hot	

Smoker Cooking

Type of food	Cut or portion	Size or weight
PORK	Boneless loin roast	4–5 pounds
	6–8 loin chops	1½ inches thick (1 pound each)
	Loin back ribs or spareribs	4–5 pounds
TURKEY	Ready-to-cook frozen bird, completely thawed	12–15 pounds
FISH	Salmon (fillets or red snapper)	3–4 pounds

*Estimate by holding hand, palm down, about 4 inches above hot coals. Count seconds you can hold position. Figure 2 seconds as Hot coals; 3 seconds for Medium-hot coals; 4 seconds for Medium coals, and 5 or 6 seconds for Slow coals.

Guidelines for cooking meats and poultry on a spit

	Approximate roasting time			Comments
	Covered grill			
	Rare	**Medium**	**Well-done**	
	2–2½ hrs.	2½–3 hrs.		
	40–45 min.	45–50 min.		
	1¼–1½ hrs.	1½–2 hrs.		
		1¼–1¾ hrs.	1½–2 hours	Have meat rolled and tied
	1 hr.	1½–2 hrs.	1¾–2¼ hours	Have shank cut off short / Balance diagonally on spit
			4–4½ hours	Have meat rolled and tied
			1–1¼ hours	Thread on spit accordion fashion
			2–2¼ hours	
			1¼–1½ hours	Tie securely after mounting on spit
			1½–1¾ hours	
			1½–2 hours	
			1½–1¾ hours	
			1½–1¾ hours	Deep foil drip pan is essential
			3¼–4½ hours	Push holding forks deep in bird
			1¾–2¼ hours	Purchase frozen; thaw completely
			2½–3½ hours	

Approximate timings when using a portable smoker**

Approximate smoking time	Doneness	Comments
4–5 hours	well-done	170° on roast meat thermometer
2–2½ hours	well-done	Cut slit in chop near bone to check doneness of meat
4–5 hours	well-done	
8–9 hours	185° (internal temperature)	Check internal temperature at thigh with meat thermometer
2–3 hours	fully cooked	Fish will flake easily with a fork

**Check manufacturer's directions for placement of charcoal, hickory chips, and water pan.

4 Vegetable dishes

Show your family the difference between ordinary and vibrant vegetables with the recipes in this section. From dishes you've requested to some of our own favorites, we've cooked up a collection of specialties to tempt even the reluctant vegetable fan.

A seasonal treat that's well worth waiting for is a dish of garden-fresh green peas. Serve them as delicately seasoned *Creamed Peas and Onions* or tomato-studded *Pea-Cheese Salad*.

Artichokes

Selecting: *Although most plentiful during the spring months, Globe artichokes are available year-round. Look for compact green artichokes with tightly closed leaves. You can store them, unwashed, in your refrigerator several days.*

Preparing: *Wash, trim stems, and remove loose outer leaves. Cut off 1 inch of tops; snip off sharp leaf tips. Brush cut edges with lemon juice.*

Cooking: *In large covered kettle simmer in boiling salted water till a leaf pulls out easily, 20 to 30 minutes. Drain upside down.*

Serving: *Offer cooked whole artichokes, hot or cold, with a favorite sauce. To eat, pull off a leaf and dip the base of the leaf in sauce. Draw through teeth, eating only the tender flesh. Discard rest of leaf. Continue till a cone of young leaves appears. Pull away the cone, eating the little bit of soft flesh, then scoop out and discard the fuzzy "choke." Eat the remaining heart with a fork, dipping each piece in sauce.*

Jerusalem Artichokes: *These tuberous vegetables resemble Globe artichokes in flavor. Serve raw in salads, or baked or boiled as a cooked vegetable.*

Artichoke-Crab Entrée

4 artichokes
1 tablespoon finely chopped green onion with tops
1 clove garlic, minced
2 small bay leaves, crushed
¼ cup butter *or* margarine
¼ cup all-purpose flour
Dash pepper
1 12-ounce can clam juice
1 7½-ounce can crab meat, drained, flaked, and cartilage removed
¼ cup grated Parmesan cheese
¼ cup dry white wine
1 1-ounce triangle Gruyère cheese

Prepare, cook, and drain artichokes as directed above. Cut off and discard remaining top fourth of artichokes, trim stems so artichokes sit flat, and remove center leaves and chokes. Place artichokes in an 8x8x2-inch baking dish.

In medium skillet cook green onion, garlic, and bay leaves in butter or margarine till onion is tender but not brown. Blend in flour and pepper. Add clam juice; cook quickly, stirring constantly, till mixture thickens and bubbles. Stir in crab meat, Parmesan cheese, and dry white wine. Spoon crab mixture into the artichokes. Slice Gruyère cheese into 4 triangles; place 1 triangle atop each artichoke. Pour boiling water into baking dish around artichokes to depth of ½ inch. Cap loosely with foil. Bake at 375° till heated through, 25 to 30 minutes. Makes 4 servings.

Sunburst Artichoke

1 **medium artichoke**
½ **cup mayonnaise *or* salad dressing**
1 **teaspoon dry mustard**
½ **teaspoon Worcestershire sauce**
3 **hard-cooked eggs**

Prepare, cook, and drain artichoke as directed on page 207. Chill thoroughly. Pull off leaves. Combine mayonnaise, mustard, and Worcestershire. Halve hard-cooked eggs crosswise; cut each half into 8 wedges. Dollop about ½ teaspoon mayonnaise mixture at base of each artichoke leaf; place an egg wedge atop mixture on each leaf. Arrange leaves sunburst fashion on a plate. Makes about 48.

Italian-Dipped Artichokes (pictured on page 210)

2 **artichokes**
1 **8-ounce container sour cream dip with French onion**
2 **tablespoons finely chopped green pepper**
1 **tablespoon snipped parsley**
1 **teaspoon lemon juice**
½ **teaspoon dried oregano, crushed**

Prepare, cook, and drain artichokes as directed on page 207. Remove center leaves and chokes. Chill thoroughly.

Meanwhile, combine sour cream dip, green pepper, parsley, lemon juice, oregano, and dash pepper; chill well. Serve sauce with chilled artichokes. Makes 1 cup sauce.

Artichokes Parmesan

8 **small artichokes**
1 **tablespoon sliced green onion with tops**
1 **clove garlic, minced**
3 **tablespoons butter *or* margarine**
1½ **cups soft bread crumbs**
¼ **cup grated Parmesan cheese**
2 **tablespoons snipped parsley**

Prepare artichokes as directed on page 207, trimming stems so they sit flat. Remove center leaves and chokes. Do not cook. Cook onion and garlic in butter till tender. Combine bread crumbs, Parmesan, and parsley. Add onion mixture; mix lightly. Spoon into artichokes. Place stuffed artichokes in large saucepan, making sure artichokes won't tip over. Pour water around artichokes in saucepan to a depth of 1 inch. Bring to boiling; reduce heat. Cover tightly; simmer till artichokes are done, about 30 minutes. Add a little additional water during cooking, if necessary. Makes 8 servings.

Artichokes with Lemon Butter Sauce

Artichokes
¼ **cup butter *or* margarine**
1 **tablespoon snipped parsley**
1 **tablespoon lemon juice**

Prepare, cook, and drain artichokes as directed on page 207. Meanwhile, melt butter or margarine; stir in snipped parsley, lemon juice, and dash pepper. Serve butter sauce with cooked artichokes. Makes ⅓ cup sauce.

Jerusalem Artichokes with Parslied Cream Sauce

1 **pound Jerusalem artichokes**
2 **tablespoons butter**
2 **tablespoons all-purpose flour**
½ **teaspoon salt**
Dash white pepper
1 **cup light cream *or* milk**
¼ **cup finely snipped parsley**

Wash and peel Jerusalem artichokes; slice. In covered pan cook in a small amount of boiling salted water till tender, 10 to 15 minutes. Drain well. Melt butter in a saucepan; blend in flour, salt, and white pepper. Add cream or milk all at once. Cook and stir till thickened and bubbly. Remove from heat. Stir in snipped parsley. Serve sauce over cooked Jerusalem artichokes. Makes 4 to 6 servings.

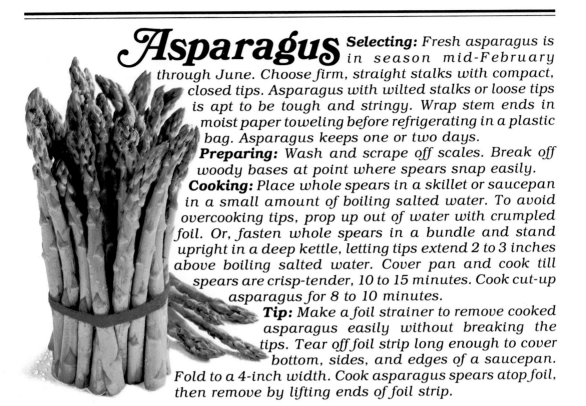

Asparagus

Selecting: *Fresh asparagus is in season mid-February through June. Choose firm, straight stalks with compact, closed tips. Asparagus with wilted stalks or loose tips is apt to be tough and stringy. Wrap stem ends in moist paper toweling before refrigerating in a plastic bag. Asparagus keeps one or two days.*

Preparing: *Wash and scrape off scales. Break off woody bases at point where spears snap easily.*

Cooking: *Place whole spears in a skillet or saucepan in a small amount of boiling salted water. To avoid overcooking tips, prop up out of water with crumpled foil. Or, fasten whole spears in a bundle and stand upright in a deep kettle, letting tips extend 2 to 3 inches above boiling salted water. Cover pan and cook till spears are crisp-tender, 10 to 15 minutes. Cook cut-up asparagus for 8 to 10 minutes.*

Tip: *Make a foil strainer to remove cooked asparagus easily without breaking the tips. Tear off foil strip long enough to cover bottom, sides, and edges of a saucepan. Fold to a 4-inch width. Cook asparagus spears atop foil, then remove by lifting ends of foil strip.*

Asparagus Omelet Tarragon (pictured on page 210)

½ **pound asparagus, bias-sliced
    into 1-inch pieces**
6 **eggs**
2 **tablespoons water**
¼ **teaspoon salt**
    Dash pepper
2 **tablespoons butter *or*
    margarine**
    Golden Tarragon Sauce

Cook cut-up fresh asparagus as directed above. Drain well; keep warm. Beat eggs, water, salt, and pepper with fork till blended but not frothy. In 10-inch skillet or omelet pan heat butter or margarine till it sizzles and browns slightly. Tilt pan to grease sides. Add egg mixture and cook slowly. Run spatula around edge, lifting egg to allow uncooked portion to flow underneath. Spoon asparagus across center of omelet; top with ½ cup Golden Tarragon Sauce. Tilt pan to fold omelet and roll onto hot platter. Serve with remaining Golden Tarragon Sauce. Makes 4 servings.

Golden Tarragon Sauce: In small saucepan cook ¼ cup sliced green onion with tops in 1 tablespoon butter till tender. Stir in 3 tablespoons dry white wine and 1 tablespoon white wine vinegar. Simmer till liquid is reduced by half, 3 to 5 minutes. In another saucepan melt 1 tablespoon butter; blend in 4 teaspoons all-purpose flour. Add 1¼ cups milk. Cook, stirring constantly, till thickened and bubbly. Remove from heat; stir in ¼ teaspoon salt and ¼ teaspoon dried tarragon, crushed. Return to low heat and slowly stir in onion mixture. Heat through, but *do not boil.*

Start with spring vegetables to create *Italian-Dipped Artichokes* (see page 208), *Asparagus with Orange Hollandaise Sauce,* and elegant *Asparagus Omelet Tarragon* (see page 209).

Asparagus Vinaigrette

¾ **pound asparagus *or***
   1 8-ounce package frozen
     asparagus spears
½ **cup salad oil**
2 **tablespoons vinegar**
2 **tablespoons lemon juice**
2 **teaspoons sugar**
½ **teaspoon salt**
½ **teaspoon paprika**
½ **teaspoon dry mustard**
   Dash cayenne
2 **tablespoons finely chopped**
   pimiento-stuffed green
     olives
1 **hard-cooked egg, finely**
   chopped
2 **small tomatoes, chilled**
   Lettuce leaves

Cook the fresh asparagus spears as directed on page 209. (Or, cook frozen asparagus according to package directions.) Drain. In screw-top jar combine salad oil, vinegar, lemon juice, sugar, salt, paprika, dry mustard, and cayenne. Add the pimiento-stuffed olives and chopped hard-cooked egg; cover and shake well. Arrange asparagus in a shallow dish; top with vinegar mixture. Cover and refrigerate for several hours or overnight, spooning vinegar mixture over asparagus occasionally.

To serve, drain asparagus, reserving vinegar mixture. Slice tomatoes. On each of 4 salad plates, arrange a few asparagus spears atop lettuce. Top each salad with a few tomato slices. Spoon a little of the reserved vinegar mixture over each salad. Makes 4 servings.

Asparagus with Orange Hollandaise Sauce

1 pound asparagus
¼ cup butter *or* margarine, softened
2 egg yolks
¼ teaspoon finely shredded
    orange peel
1 teaspoon orange juice
    Dash salt
    Dash white pepper
¼ cup dairy sour cream

Cook fresh asparagus as directed on page 209. Drain well. Meanwhile, divide butter into 3 portions. In small heavy saucepan combine egg yolks and 1 portion of the butter. Cook and stir over *low* heat till butter melts. Add another portion of the butter and continue stirring. As mixture thickens and butter melts, add remaining butter, stirring constantly. When butter is melted, remove from heat. Stir in orange peel, orange juice, salt, and white pepper. Return to *low* heat. Cook and stir till thickened, 2 to 3 minutes. Remove from heat at once. Blend hot mixture into sour cream. Spoon over asparagus. Garnish with more finely shredded orange peel, if desired. Makes 4 or 5 servings.

Sesame Asparagus

2 8-ounce packages frozen cut
    asparagus
1 2½-ounce jar sliced mushrooms,
    drained
2 tablespoons butter *or*
    margarine
1 teaspoon lemon juice
1 teaspoon sesame seed, toasted

Cook frozen asparagus according to package directions. Drain well. Season to taste with salt and pepper. Gently stir in mushrooms, butter, and lemon juice. Cook until heated through. Turn mixture into serving bowl; sprinkle with sesame seed. Makes 6 servings.
Microwave cooking directions: Place frozen asparagus in 1½-quart nonmetal casserole. Cook, covered, in countertop microwave oven till tender, about 10 minutes, stirring twice. Drain well. Season. Gently stir in mushrooms, butter, and lemon juice. Micro-cook, covered, till heated through, about 2 minutes, stirring once. Serve as above.

Stir-Fry Beef with Asparagus

1 pound beef flank steak,
    partially frozen
2 tablespoons soy sauce
1 tablespoon cooking oil
1 tablespoon cornstarch
12 asparagus spears
3 tablespoons cooking oil
1 teaspoon sugar
2 tablespoons dry sherry
2 tablespoons chicken broth

Using a sharp knife, cut flank steak across grain into very thin slices. Blend soy sauce and the 1 tablespoon oil into the cornstarch; pour over beef slices, stirring to coat. Bias-slice asparagus into 1-inch pieces. Drop asparagus into a pan of boiling water. Simmer for 1 to 2 minutes; drain. In wok or skillet heat the 3 tablespoons oil till sizzling. Sprinkle sugar over oil. Add beef; cook and stir for 1 minute. Add asparagus; cook and stir 1 minute longer. Add sherry and chicken broth; cook ½ minute longer. Arrange meat and asparagus on serving platter. Serve with hot cooked rice, if desired. Serves 4.

Chilled Asparagus Soup

¾ pound asparagus, cut up, *or*
    1 8-ounce package frozen
    cut asparagus
1 thin slice onion
½ cup boiling water
1 cup milk
½ cup light cream
½ teaspoon salt
    Dash pepper

In covered pan cook fresh or frozen asparagus and the onion slice in the boiling water till crisp-tender; do not drain. Cool slightly. In blender container combine the undrained asparagus and onion, milk, light cream, salt, and pepper. Cover and blend until smooth, 15 to 20 seconds. Chill for 3 to 4 hours (chill in blender container, if desired). Stir or blend before serving. Makes 4 to 6 servings.

Beans

Selecting: *Green and wax beans are grown for the tender, fleshy pod. Choose long, straight pods that snap crisply when bent. Lima and fava beans are usually cultivated for the seed. Select dark green, crisp, full pods (fava pods are lima-like in shape, but thicker and slightly larger). The shelled beans should be plump with a tender green or greenish-white skin. You can store unshelled fresh beans in the refrigerator for a few days. Dry beans are available in numerous varieties. When selecting, discard beans that are wrinkled or discolored. Store in tightly covered container in cool, dry place.*

Preparing: *Wash green and wax beans; remove ends and strings. Leave whole, or cut in 1-inch pieces. For French-style, slice diagonally end to end. Shell limas or favas and wash. Rinse dry beans; place in heavy saucepan or kettle with about 3 times as much water as beans. Cover pan; soak overnight. (Or, bring to boiling; simmer for 2 minutes. Remove from heat. Cover pan; soak at least 1 hour.) Do not drain.*

Cooking: *In covered pan cook whole or cut fresh beans in small amount of boiling salted water till crisp-tender, 20 to 30 minutes. Cook French-style beans 10 to 12 minutes. Cover and simmer dry beans till tender.*

Green Beans Supreme

1 pound green beans *or*
   2 9-ounce packages frozen
   French-style green beans
1 small onion, sliced
1 tablespoon snipped parsley
3 tablespoons butter
2 tablespoons all-purpose flour
½ teaspoon finely shredded lemon
   peel
½ cup milk
1 cup dairy sour cream
½ cup shredded American cheese
¼ cup fine dry bread crumbs

Cut fresh beans French-style and cook as directed above. (Or, cook frozen beans according to package directions.) Drain. Cook onion and parsley in *2 tablespoons* of the butter till onion is tender. Blend in flour, lemon peel, ½ teaspoon salt, and dash pepper. Add milk; cook and stir till thickened and bubbly. Stir in sour cream and cooked beans; heat till just bubbly. Spoon into 1-quart casserole. Sprinkle with cheese. Melt the remaining 1 tablespoon butter; toss with bread crumbs and sprinkle atop beans. Broil 4 to 5 inches from heat till cheese melts and crumbs brown, 1 to 2 minutes. Makes 8 servings.

Creamy Lima Beans

1 pound lima beans, shelled
  (2 cups), *or* 1 10-ounce
  package frozen lima beans
2 tablespoons sliced green
  onion with tops
1 tablespoon butter *or* margarine
1 tablespoon all-purpose flour
½ cup milk
2 tablespoons brown sugar
½ cup dairy sour cream

Cook fresh lima beans as directed on page 212. (Or, cook frozen limas according to package directions.) Drain well. In medium saucepan cook green onion in butter or margarine till tender but not brown. Blend in flour, ¼ teaspoon salt, and dash pepper. Add milk and brown sugar. Cook, stirring constantly, till thickened and bubbly. Stir sour cream and drained cooked limas into sauce mixture. Heat through, but *do not boil*. Makes 4 servings.

Mustard Beans

1 pound wax beans *or* 1 15½-ounce
  can whole wax beans, drained
½ cup sugar
½ cup vinegar
¼ cup prepared mustard
2 tablespoons finely chopped
  onion
¼ teaspoon salt

Cook the whole fresh wax beans as directed on page 212. Drain. In saucepan combine sugar, vinegar, mustard, onion, salt, and ⅓ cup water. Bring mixture to boiling, stirring till sugar dissolves. Add drained cooked fresh beans or the drained canned beans. Simmer, uncovered, for 5 minutes; cool. Cover and refrigerate several hours or overnight, stirring occasionally. Makes 2 cups relish.

Two-Bean Fritters

1 cup green beans cut
  in ½-inch pieces
1 cup wax beans cut
  in ½-inch pieces
1½ cups all-purpose flour
1 tablespoon baking powder
1 beaten egg
1 cup milk
  Fat for deep-fat frying

Cook green and wax beans as directed on page 212. Drain well. Stir together flour, baking powder, and ¾ teaspoon salt. Combine egg, milk, and cooked beans. Add to dry ingredients, mixing just till moistened. Drop batter by tablespoonfuls into deep hot fat (375°). Fry, several at a time, till golden brown, 3 to 4 minutes. Drain on paper toweling. Makes about 24 vegetable fritters.

Baked Bean Cassoulet

1 pound dry navy beans (2⅓ cups)
1 cup chopped celery
1 cup chopped carrot
2 teaspoons instant beef
  bouillon granules
1 teaspoon salt
1 2½- to 3-pound ready-to-cook
  broiler-fryer chicken with
  giblets, cut up
½ pound bulk pork sausage
1 cup chopped onion
1½ cups tomato juice
1 tablespoon Worcestershire
  sauce
½ teaspoon paprika

Soak dry beans, using 8 cups water, as directed on page 212. Stir in celery, carrot, bouillon granules, and salt. Add giblets from chicken (refrigerate remaining chicken). Bring to boil; reduce heat. Cover; simmer 1 hour. Shape sausage into small balls; brown in large skillet. Remove sausage; set aside. Reserve drippings in skillet. Season chicken generously with salt and pepper; brown in reserved drippings. Remove chicken; set aside. In same skillet cook onion till tender. Stir in tomato juice and Worcestershire.

Drain bean mixture, reserving liquid. Combine bean mixture, sausage, and tomato mixture. Turn into 6-quart Dutch oven. Top with chicken; add 1½ cups of the reserved liquid. Sprinkle with paprika. Cover; bake at 325° for 1 hour, adding more bean liquid for moistness, if needed. Makes 8 servings.

New England Baked Beans

1 **pound dry navy beans (2⅓ cups)**
8 **cups water**
½ **teaspoon salt**
½ **cup light molasses**
¼ **cup packed brown sugar**
1 **teaspoon dry mustard**
½ **teaspoon salt**
⅛ **teaspoon pepper**
4 **ounces salt pork, cut in small
    pieces (1 cup)**
1 **large onion, chopped**

Soak dry navy beans, using 8 cups water, as directed on page 212. Add the ½ teaspoon salt. Bring to boiling; reduce heat. Cover and simmer till beans are tender, about 1 hour. Drain, reserving bean liquid.

Combine molasses, brown sugar, mustard, the remaining ½ teaspoon salt, and pepper. Stir in 2 cups of the reserved bean liquid. In 2-quart bean pot or casserole combine cooked beans, salt pork, onion, and molasses mixture. Cover and bake at 300° for 3½ hours. Stir beans occasionally. Stir in a little of the reserved bean liquid or water for moistness, if necessary. Makes 6 to 8 servings.

Crockery cooker directions: Rinse beans. In large heavy saucepan combine beans, water, and ½ teaspoon salt. Bring mixture to boiling; reduce heat. Cover and simmer for 1½ hours. Pour into a bowl. Cover and refrigerate overnight. Drain beans, reserving 1 cup liquid.

Place beans in an electric slow crockery cooker. Combine molasses, brown sugar, mustard, ½ teaspoon salt, pepper, and reserved liquid. Add to beans with salt pork and onion; mix well. Cover and cook on low-heat setting for 12 to 14 hours. Stir before serving.

Green Beans Amandine

1 **pound green beans**
2 **tablespoons slivered almonds**
2 **tablespoons butter**
1 **teaspoon lemon juice**

Cut green beans French-style and cook as directed on page 212. Drain. Meanwhile, cook slivered almonds in butter over low heat, stirring occasionally, till golden. Remove from heat; add lemon juice. Pour over beans. Makes 4 servings.

Green Bean Bake with Onion

2 **9-ounce packages frozen** *or*
  2 **16-ounce cans French-style
    green beans**
1 **10¾-ounce can condensed cream
    of mushroom soup**
2 **tablespoons chopped pimiento**
1 **teaspoon lemon juice**
½ **of a 3-ounce can French-fried
    onions**

Cook frozen beans according to package directions; drain. (Or, drain canned beans.) Combine the cooked frozen or the canned beans, mushroom soup, pimiento, and lemon juice. Turn mixture into a 1-quart casserole. Bake, uncovered, at 350° for 35 minutes. Sprinkle with French-fried onions. Continue baking, uncovered, till onions are heated through, about 5 minutes longer. Makes 6 servings.

Micro-cooking Vegetables

Microwave cooking is an excellent way to prepare colorful, flavorful, and nutritious vegetables. The countertop microwave oven will also save you time, as you'll see in selected recipes throughout the book.

When preparing vegetables, micro-cook them on high power just till almost done; they'll finish cooking with stored heat. Season with salt after cooking to avoid drying out. For basic vegetable cookery, follow your owner's manual.

Spanish String Beans

1 **pound green beans, cut in
     1-inch pieces (3 cups)**
½ **cup chopped green pepper**
¼ **cup chopped onion**
1 **tablespoon olive oil** *or*
     cooking oil
2 **medium tomatoes, peeled and
     chopped**
1 **teaspoon salt**
½ **teaspoon dried basil, crushed**
¼ **teaspoon dried rosemary,
     crushed**

Cook fresh cut-up green beans as directed on page 212; drain. Meanwhile, cook chopped green pepper and onion in hot olive oil or cooking oil till tender but not brown. Add chopped tomatoes, salt, basil, rosemary, and ⅛ teaspoon pepper. Stir in cooked green beans; heat through. Season to taste with salt and pepper. Makes 8 servings.

Marinated Three-Bean Salad

1 **8½-ounce can lima beans**
1 **8-ounce can cut green beans**
1 **8-ounce can red kidney beans**
1 **medium sweet onion, sliced and
     separated into rings**
½ **cup chopped green pepper**
⅔ **cup vinegar**
½ **cup salad oil**
¼ **cup sugar**
1 **teaspoon celery seed**

Drain canned beans. In large bowl combine lima beans, green beans, red kidney beans, onion rings, and green pepper. In a screw-top jar combine vinegar, salad oil, sugar, and celery seed; cover and shake well. Pour vinegar mixture over vegetables and stir lightly. Cover and refrigerate for 8 hours or overnight, stirring occasionally. Drain before serving. Makes 8 servings.

Easy Baked Beans

4 **slices bacon**
½ **cup chopped onion**
2 **16-ounce cans pork and beans
     in tomato sauce**
2 **tablespoons brown sugar**
2 **tablespoons catsup**
1 **tablespoon Worcestershire
     sauce**
1 **tablespoon prepared mustard**

Cook bacon till crisp. Remove bacon, reserving about 3 tablespoons drippings in skillet. Crumble bacon and set aside. Cook onion in reserved drippings till tender. Stir in pork and beans, brown sugar, catsup, Worcestershire, and mustard. Turn into 1½-quart casserole. Bake, uncovered, at 350° for 1½ to 1¾ hours. Stir; top with bacon. Let stand a few minutes before serving. Makes 6 servings.

Mexican Lima Beans

1 **pound large dry lima beans
     (2½ cups)**
1 **15-ounce can tomato sauce**
1 **medium onion, sliced**
⅓ **cup chili sauce**
¼ **cup chopped green pepper**
1 **teaspoon salt**
1 **teaspoon chili powder**
1 **cup dairy sour cream**
¼ **cup shredded American cheese**
½ **cup crushed corn chips**

Soak dry lima beans, using 8 cups water, as directed on page 212. Bring mixture to boiling; reduce heat. Cover and simmer till lima beans are just tender, 30 to 40 minutes. Drain, reserving 1 cup of the bean liquid.

In 2-quart casserole combine beans, reserved liquid, tomato sauce, onion, chili sauce, green pepper, salt, and chili powder. Cover; bake at 300° for 2½ hours. Spread sour cream over top; sprinkle with cheese. Sprinkle chips around edge. Bake for 5 minutes more. Makes 8 servings.

Beets

Selecting: *Markets supply fresh garden beets year-round. Choose round, small-to-medium beets with a smooth, firm, deep red flesh and a slender tap root. Large beets may be woody. Spring beets are often sold in bunches with the tender, young tops still intact (to allow for weight of tops, buy about ½ pound more for each pound of beets needed). If fresh and reasonably unblemished, the tops make good eating (see Greens). You can store fresh beets with tops in the refrigerator crisper for a few days. Late-crop beets are usually sold without tops and can be stored for longer periods.*

Preparing: *Cut off all but 1 inch of stems and roots; wash. Leave whole beets unpeeled. Or, peel beets and slice, cube, or shred.*

Cooking: *In covered pan cook whole beets in boiling salted water till tender, 35 to 50 minutes. Cool slightly and slip off skins. Cook sliced or cubed beets in small amount of water for 15 to 20 minutes; shredded beets about 10 minutes.*

Serving: *Enjoy beets tossed with a little melted butter or heavy cream and seasoned with herbs.*

Borscht with Mushroom Dumplings

　1 **ounce** *dried* **mushrooms (¾ cup)**
3½ **cups boiling water**
　2 **pounds beets, peeled,**
　　　thinly sliced, and quartered
　4 **cups water**
　1 **cup chopped carrot**
　1 **cup chopped celery**
½ **cup chopped onion**
　2 **bay leaves**
　1 **teaspoon salt**
　2 **tablespoons vinegar**
　1 **teaspoon sugar**
　1 **teaspoon salt**
⅛ **teaspoon pepper**
　　Mushroom Dumplings

Combine mushrooms with boiling water. Let soak 2 hours at room temperature. Simmer, uncovered, till tender, 7 to 10 minutes. Drain; reserve liquid. Set mushrooms aside.

In large saucepan combine next 7 ingredients. Cover and cook till vegetables are tender, 40 to 45 minutes. Remove bay leaves. Stir in reserved mushroom liquid, vinegar, sugar, the 1 teaspoon salt, and pepper. Bring to boil. Ladle into bowls; add Mushroom Dumplings to each serving. Serves 10.

Mushroom Dumplings: Mix 1 cup all-purpose flour, 1 beaten egg, 2 to 3 tablespoons water, and ¼ teaspoon salt. Knead on floured surface till smooth and elastic. Cover; let stand 10 minutes. Cook 2 tablespoons chopped onion in 1 table-spoon butter. Chop reserved mushrooms; add to onion mixture with 1 tablespoon fine dry bread crumbs, 1 egg white, ¼ teaspoon salt, and dash pepper. Divide dough in half. Roll each half ⅛ inch thick; cut in 1½-inch squares. Top each with ½ teaspoon mushroom mixture; fold into triangle. Seal. Cook in large amount boiling salted water 5 minutes.

When it's too hot to cook, toss together this cool and colorful *Beet Supper Salad*. Sweet and juicy red beets and tender leaf lettuce contribute fresh-from-the-garden flavor.

Beet Supper Salad

1 **pound beets**
1 **small clove garlic, halved**
6 **cups leaf lettuce**
¼ **cup sliced green onion with tops**
1 **6½- or 7-ounce can tuna, chilled and well drained**
½ **cup sliced celery**
2 **hard-cooked eggs, chopped**
½ **cup mayonnaise or salad dressing**
½ **teaspoon salt**
  Dash pepper
  Sliced green onion with tops (optional)

Cook fresh whole beets as directed on page 216. Drain, peel, and slice cooked beets. Chill. Just before serving, rub a salad bowl with halved garlic. Combine leaf lettuce and the ¼ cup green onion in salad bowl. Arrange beets, tuna, celery, and hard-cooked eggs atop. Combine mayonnaise or salad dressing, salt, and pepper; dollop in center of salad. Garnish with additional sliced green onion, if desired. To serve, gently toss mayonnaise mixture with the salad ingredients. Makes 6 to 8 servings.

Harvard Beets

1 8¼-ounce can sliced beets
1 tablespoon sugar
1 teaspoon cornstarch
⅛ teaspoon salt
2 tablespoons vinegar
1 tablespoon butter *or* margarine

Drain beets, reserving ¼ cup liquid. In saucepan combine sugar, cornstarch, and salt. Stir in reserved beet liquid, the vinegar, and butter. Cook, stirring constantly, till mixture is thickened and bubbly. Stir in beets. Cook until heated through. Makes 2 servings.

Microwave cooking directions: Drain beets; reserve ¼ cup liquid. In a 2-cup glass measure combine sugar, cornstarch, and salt. Stir in reserved liquid, vinegar, and butter. Cook, uncovered, in countertop microwave oven till thick and bubbly, about 1 minute; stir every 15 seconds. Stir in beets. Micro-cook, covered, till hot, about 2 minutes.

Beet and Pineapple Mold

1 16-ounce can diced *or*
   shoestring beets
1 8¼-ounce can crushed pineapple
1 6-ounce package lemon-flavored
   gelatin
2 cups boiling water
3 tablespoons lemon juice
   Dash salt
½ cup chopped celery

Drain beets and pineapple, reserving liquids. Combine liquids and add water to make 1½ cups. Dissolve gelatin in boiling water; stir in reserved liquid mixture, lemon juice, and salt. Chill till partially set. Fold in drained beets, pineapple, and chopped celery. Pour gelatin mixture into a 6½-cup mold. Chill till firm. Makes 8 to 10 servings.

Beets with Sour Cream

1 pound beets
½ cup dairy sour cream
2 tablespoons milk
1 tablespoon sliced green onion
   with tops
1 tablespoon vinegar
1 teaspoon sugar
¼ teaspoon salt
   Dash cayenne

Peel and slice beets; halve slices. Cook beets as directed on page 216. Drain. Meanwhile, in small saucepan combine sour cream, milk, green onion, vinegar, sugar, salt, and cayenne. Heat through over low heat, but *do not boil*. Turn beets into serving dish; spoon sour cream mixture atop. Stir to combine, if desired. Makes 4 servings.

Beet-Apple Relish

3 pounds beets, cooked,
   peeled, and cut up (6 cups)
6 large apples, peeled, cored,
   and quartered
2 large onions, cut up
4 inches stick cinnamon, broken
1½ cups sugar
1½ cups vinegar
½ cup water
1 tablespoon salt

Put beets, apples, and onions through a food grinder, using coarse blade. In large kettle or Dutch oven combine ground mixture, cinnamon, sugar, vinegar, water, and salt. Bring to boiling; reduce heat. Cover and simmer 20 minutes, stirring often. Remove cinnamon. Ladle hot relish into hot, clean half-pint jars, leaving ½-inch headspace.

Prepare lids according to manufacturer's directions. Wipe jar rim. Adjust lid on jar. Process jars in boiling water bath for 15 minutes. (Start timing when water returns to boiling.) Makes 11 half-pints.

Broccoli

Selecting: Broccoli grows year-round, but the supply is smallest during the hot summer months. Look for firm, tender stalks bearing small, crisp leaves. The dark green or purplish-green buds should be tightly closed, showing no signs of flowering. You can store broccoli in the refrigerator crisper in a plastic bag for a few days.

Preparing: Wash broccoli; remove the outer leaves and tough part of stalks. Cut broccoli stalks lengthwise into uniform spears, following the branching lines.

Cooking: In covered pan cook spears in 1 inch of boiling salted water till crisp-tender, 10 to 15 minutes. For cut-up broccoli, cut off the buds and set aside. Cut the remaining part of spears into 1-inch pieces; in covered pan cook in boiling salted water 5 to 8 minutes. Add the reserved broccoli buds and cook about 5 minutes longer.

Serving: A variety of sauces complements the flavor of cooked broccoli. Try hollandaise, cheese, mayonnaise, or mustard sauce over individual servings.

Broccoli-Egg Bake

1 pound broccoli *or* 2 10-ounce packages frozen broccoli spears
6 hard-cooked eggs
½ cup finely chopped fully cooked ham
2 tablespoons butter, softened
1 tablespoon finely chopped onion
½ teaspoon Worcestershire sauce
¼ teaspoon dry mustard
¼ cup butter *or* margarine
¼ cup all-purpose flour
¼ teaspoon salt
2½ cups milk
1 cup shredded sharp American cheese (4 ounces)
1½ cups soft bread crumbs
¼ cup butter, melted

Cut fresh broccoli stalks into spears and cook as directed above. (Or, cook frozen broccoli according to package directions.) Drain. Halve the hard-cooked eggs. Remove egg yolks; set egg whites aside. Mash egg yolks; stir in chopped ham, the 2 tablespoons softened butter, onion, Worcestershire sauce, and dry mustard. Fill egg whites with yolk mixture. Arrange cooked broccoli in a 12x7½x2-inch baking dish; top with the filled eggs.

In saucepan melt ¼ cup butter. Blend in flour and salt. Stir in milk; cook quickly, stirring constantly, till mixture is thickened and bubbly. Add shredded American cheese; stir till melted. Pour sauce mixture over broccoli and eggs. Toss bread crumbs with ¼ cup melted butter; sprinkle over casserole. Bake at 350° till heated through, about 25 minutes. Makes 6 servings.

Whether your meal is simple or formal, *Broccoli-Onion Deluxe* is an excellent choice
for entertaining. This colorful casserole features two popular vegetables in a creamy sauce.

Broccoli-Onion Deluxe

1 **pound broccoli** *or* **2 10-ounce**
  packages frozen cut broccoli
2 **cups frozen small whole onions**
  or **3 medium onions,**
  quartered
¼ **cup butter** *or* **margarine**
2 **tablespoons all-purpose flour**
¼ **teaspoon salt**
1 **cup milk**
1 **3-ounce package cream cheese**
½ **cup shredded sharp American**
  cheese (2 ounces)
1 **cup soft bread crumbs**

Cut up fresh broccoli and cook as directed on page 219. (Or, cook frozen broccoli according to package directions.) Drain. Cook frozen or fresh onions in boiling salted water till tender. Drain. In saucepan melt *half* of the butter or margarine. Blend in flour, salt, and dash pepper. Add milk. Cook, stirring constantly, till thickened and bubbly. Reduce heat; blend in cream cheese till smooth.

Place vegetables in a 1½-quart casserole. Pour sauce mixture over and mix lightly. Top with American cheese. Melt the remaining butter; toss with bread crumbs. Sprinkle atop casserole. Bake at 350° till heated through, 40 to 45 minutes. Makes 6 servings.

Broccoli Soufflé

2 **cups chopped broccoli** *or*
  1 10-ounce package frozen
  chopped broccoli
2 **tablespoons butter** *or*
  margarine
2 **tablespoons all-purpose flour**
½ **teaspoon salt**
½ **cup milk**
4 **egg yolks**
¼ **cup grated Parmesan cheese**
4 **egg whites**

In covered pan cook fresh chopped broccoli in boiling salted water 8 to 10 minutes. (Or, cook frozen broccoli according to package directions.) Drain well. Chop any large pieces. Melt butter; blend in flour and salt. Add milk. Cook and stir till bubbly; remove from heat. Beat egg yolks till thick and lemon-colored. Slowly stir half of hot mixture into yolks; return to hot mixture. Stir rapidly. Stir in cheese and broccoli. Beat egg whites till stiff peaks form; fold into broccoli mixture. Turn into *ungreased* 1-quart soufflé dish. Bake at 350° till knife inserted off-center comes out clean, 35 to 40 minutes. Serve at once. Serves 4.

Lemon Broccoli

1½ **pounds broccoli** *or* **3 10-ounce**
  packages frozen broccoli spears
½ **cup chopped green onion**
  with tops
½ **cup chopped celery**
6 **tablespoons butter**
2 **tablespoons lemon juice**
½ **teaspoon finely shredded lemon**
  peel

Cut fresh broccoli stalks into spears and cook as directed on page 219. (Or, cook frozen broccoli spears according to package directions.) Drain well. In small saucepan cook green onion and celery in butter till tender but not brown. Stir in lemon juice; heat through. To serve, layer broccoli and butter mixture in a serving dish. Sprinkle with shredded lemon peel. Makes 8 servings.

Curried Broccoli Salad

½ **pound broccoli**
1 **cup dairy sour cream**
¼ **cup milk**
½ **teaspoon curry powder**
¼ **teaspoon seasoned salt**
¼ **teaspoon dry mustard**
3 **medium tomatoes, cut in wedges**
  Lettuce

Remove the broccoli buds; use stalks another time. In covered pan cook broccoli buds in boiling salted water till crisp-tender, about 5 minutes. Drain well. Cool.

Combine sour cream, milk, curry powder, seasoned salt, dry mustard, and dash pepper. Pour over broccoli buds, stirring to coat. Cover and chill for 2 to 3 hours. To serve, arrange broccoli buds and tomato wedges on a bed of lettuce. Makes 5 or 6 servings.

Brussels Sprouts

Selecting: *These dense, compact buds resembling miniature cabbages receive their name from their area of origin, the Belgian city of Brussels. They're at their best between October and March. Select small-to-medium sprouts of a vivid green color with tight-fitting outer leaves. Store, unwashed, in a plastic bag in the refrigerator crisper. Sprouts keep for one or two days.*

Preparing: *Trim stems slightly, remove wilted or discolored leaves, and wash. Cut any large sprouts in half lengthwise.*

Cooking: *In covered pan cook sprouts in small amount boiling salted water till crisp-tender, 10 to 15 minutes.*

Serving: *An especially popular way to serve this nutty-flavored winter vegetable is "à la Polonaise"—in the Polish style. Cook 2 pints (about 1 pound) Brussels sprouts and drain well. Meanwhile, lightly brown 2 tablespoons butter or margarine. Blend in ¼ cup fine dry bread crumbs, 2 tablespoons snipped parsley, and 1 hard-cooked egg, finely chopped. Spoon the crumb mixture over the hot sprouts and toss together lightly.*

Saucy Brussels Sprouts

2 pints Brussels sprouts
½ cup chopped onion
2 tablespoons butter
1 tablespoon all-purpose flour
1 tablespoon brown sugar
½ teaspoon dry mustard
½ cup milk
1 cup dairy sour cream

Cook fresh Brussels sprouts as directed above; drain well. Meanwhile, in 8-inch skillet or medium saucepan cook chopped onion in butter till tender but not brown. Blend in flour, brown sugar, dry mustard, and 1 teaspoon salt. Stir in milk. Cook, stirring constantly, till thickened and bubbly. Blend in sour cream. Add cooked Brussels sprouts; stir gently to combine. Cook till heated through, but *do not boil.* Makes 6 to 8 servings.

Marinated Brussels Sprouts Appetizers

2 10-ounce packages frozen
   Brussels sprouts, cooked
   Tangy Marinade
2 tablespoons thinly sliced
   green onion with tops

Drain sprouts; toss with Tangy Marinade and onion. Cover; chill 8 hours or overnight, stirring often. Drain to serve.
   Tangy Marinade: Combine ½ cup tarragon vinegar; ½ cup cooking oil; 1 small clove garlic, minced; 1 tablespoon sugar; 1 teaspoon salt; and dash bottled hot pepper sauce.

Cabbage

Selecting: *Popular cabbage varieties, available year-round, include the smooth-leafed green cabbage, crinkle-leafed Savoy green cabbage, and red cabbage. Look for firm, solid heads that feel heavy for their size. The leaves should be bright and free of blemishes. Store cabbage in a plastic bag in refrigerator crisper. Most varieties keep at least a week.*

Preparing: *Remove any wilted outer leaves; wash cabbage. Cut into wedges; remove center core. For shredded cabbage, hold wedge firmly and cut into even shreds with a sharp knife. To make short, fine shreds for a juicy slaw, finely chop shredded cabbage or use a shredder.*

Cooking: *In uncovered pan cook cabbage in small amount of boiling salted water for the first few minutes, then cover pan and cook till crisp-tender. Cook wedges 10 to 12 minutes; shredded cabbage 5 to 7 minutes. When cooking red cabbage, add a little lemon juice or vinegar to the water to prevent discoloring.*

Serving: *Use raw cabbage in coleslaw or any tossed salad. Cook cabbage with corned beef and other vegetables for the traditional New England boiled dinner.*

Coleslaw

3 cups shredded cabbage
⅓ cup chopped green pepper
⅓ cup mayonnaise *or* salad
    dressing
1 tablespoon vinegar
1 teaspoon sugar
½ teaspoon caraway seed

Combine shredded cabbage and chopped green pepper. Blend together mayonnaise or salad dressing, vinegar, sugar, caraway seed, and ¼ teaspoon salt. Toss mayonnaise mixture with vegetables. Cover and chill. Makes 6 servings.

Pennsylvania Red Cabbage

2 tablespoons bacon drippings
¼ cup packed brown sugar
¼ cup vinegar
½ teaspoon caraway seed
4 cups shredded red cabbage
2 cups cubed unpeeled apple

Heat bacon drippings in a skillet. Stir in brown sugar, vinegar, caraway seed, ¼ cup water, 1¼ teaspoons salt, and dash pepper. Add red cabbage and apple, stirring to coat. Cover and cook over low heat, stirring occasionally. For crisp cabbage, cook 15 minutes; for tender cabbage, cook 25 to 30 minutes. Makes 4 or 5 servings.

A superb variation of a cherished old-time recipe, *Cabbage and Ham Slaw* is sure to become a family favorite. The hollowed-out cabbage shell makes an eye-catching serving bowl.

Cabbage and Ham Slaw

2 tablespoons all-purpose flour
2 tablespoons sugar
1 teaspoon salt
1 teaspoon dry mustard
½ teaspoon celery seed
1 cup milk
2 slightly beaten egg yolks
3 tablespoons vinegar
2 tablespoons lemon juice
1 large head cabbage
2 cups cubed fully cooked ham
1 apple, cored and cut in thin
   wedges
¼ cup chopped green pepper
¼ cup sliced radish

In saucepan combine flour, sugar, salt, dry mustard, and celery seed; gradually blend in milk. Cook, stirring constantly, till thickened and bubbly. Stir half of the hot mixture into egg yolks; return to hot mixture in saucepan. Cook, stirring constantly, over low heat for 1 minute more. Stir in vinegar and lemon juice; cool.

Spread apart outer leaves of cabbage. Carefully cut out the center, leaving a ½-inch-thick shell to form a "bowl." Shred the removed cabbage to make 4 cups; toss with ham, apple, green pepper, and radish. Toss with cooked mixture; serve in cabbage shell. Makes 6 servings.

Rice-Stuffed Cabbage Rolls

½ **cup chopped onion**
2 **tablespoons butter**
3 **cups cooked rice**
¼ **cup snipped parsley**
12 **large cabbage leaves**
1 **24-ounce can vegetable juice
    cocktail**
1 **tablespoon sugar**
  Dairy sour cream
  Snipped parsley *or* **crumbled,
    crisp-cooked bacon**

Cook onion in butter till tender. Combine with rice and the ¼ cup parsley. Cut about 2 inches of heavy center vein out of cabbage leaves. Immerse leaves in boiling water just till limp, about 3 minutes; drain. Sprinkle generously with salt. Place about ¼ *cup* of the rice mixture in center of *each* leaf; fold in sides. Fold ends so they overlap atop rice. Place, seam side down, in 12x7½x2-inch baking dish. Combine vegetable juice cocktail and sugar; pour over cabbage rolls. Bake, covered, at 350° for 1 hour. Before serving, garnish with sour cream. Sprinkle with the additional parsley or the crumbled bacon. Makes 6 servings.

Perfection Salad

1 **6-ounce package lemon-flavored
    gelatin**
⅓ **cup white vinegar**
2 **tablespoons lemon juice**
2 **cups finely shredded cabbage**
1 **cup chopped celery**
½ **cup chopped green pepper**
¼ **cup sliced pimiento-stuffed
    green olives**
  Lettuce

Combine lemon gelatin and ¾ teaspoon salt. Add 3¼ cups boiling water; stir to dissolve gelatin. Stir in vinegar and lemon juice. Chill till mixture is partially set.

Fold in shredded cabbage, celery, green pepper, and olives. Turn mixture into a 5½-cup mold or ten ½-cup molds. Chill till set. Unmold salad onto lettuce. Serve with mayonnaise or salad dressing, if desired. Makes 10 servings.

Mustard-Sauced Cabbage Wedges

1 **small head cabbage**
2 **tablespoons finely chopped
    onion**
2 **tablespoons butter**
1 **tablespoon all-purpose flour**
1 **5⅓-ounce can evaporated milk**
1 **tablespoon prepared mustard**
2 **teaspoons prepared horseradish**

Cut cabbage into 4 wedges; cook as directed on page 223. Drain well. Meanwhile, in small saucepan cook onion in butter till tender. Blend in flour, ¼ teaspoon salt, and dash pepper. Add evaporated milk and ½ cup water. Cook and stir till thickened and bubbly. Stir in mustard and horseradish. Spoon sauce over cabbage wedges. Sprinkle with snipped parsley, if desired. Makes 4 servings.

Sauerkraut

5 **pounds fully matured cabbage,
    quartered, cored, and finely
    shredded**
3½ **tablespoons salt**
  Cold water

Sprinkle cabbage with salt; mix well. Let stand 30 to 60 minutes. Firmly pack into clean, room-temperature jars; leave 2-inch headspace. Fill with cold water; leave ½-inch headspace. Prepare lids according to manufacturer's directions. Adjust lid on jar; screw band tight. Place jars on pan to catch brine that overflows. Set in cool place. Keep cabbage covered with brine. If necessary, open jars and add more brine made by dissolving 1½ tablespoons salt in 1 quart water. Sauerkraut is ready to can in 6 to 8 weeks.

Wipe jar rim; replace lid if sealer appears damaged. Screw band tight. Set jars in water bath canner filled with cold water (should extend 2 inches above jars). Bring slowly to boil. Process pints or quarts for 30 minutes. Makes 7 pints.

Carrots

Selecting: Look for firm, well-shaped, bright golden carrots. Avoid carrots that are shriveled, soft, or cracked. Cut off any tops, then store carrots in refrigerator crisper in a plastic bag for as long as four weeks.

Preparing: Wash and trim carrots. If desired, scrub with a stiff brush, or peel. Leave tiny carrots whole. For larger carrots, dice, slice, shred, or cut into strips.

Cooking: Place carrots in a saucepan containing 1 inch of boiling salted water. Cover pan and cook till just tender (allow about 5 minutes for shredded carrots; 10 to 20 minutes for carrot strips or sliced, diced, or tiny whole carrots).

Serving: Crisp raw carrots are perfect vegetable dippers and enhance tossed and gelatin salads and relish trays. Shredded raw carrots and raisins tossed with mayonnaise or salad dressing make a delicious salad. For an easy vegetable dish, glaze cooked carrots with melted orange marmalade or a granulated or brown sugar-butter mixture.

Sunshine Carrots (pictured on page 229)

7 or 8 medium carrots
1 tablespoon granulated sugar *or* brown sugar
1 teaspoon cornstarch
¼ teaspoon ground ginger
¼ cup orange juice
2 tablespoons butter

Bias-slice carrots crosswise about ½ inch thick. Cook as directed above; drain. Meanwhile, in small saucepan combine sugar, cornstarch, ginger, and ¼ teaspoon salt. Add orange juice; cook, stirring constantly, till thickened and bubbly. Boil 1 minute; remove from heat. Stir in butter. Pour over hot carrots, tossing to coat evenly. Garnish with parsley and orange twist, if desired. Makes 6 servings.

Zesty Vegetable Salad

3 medium carrots
3 medium turnips
½ small head cauliflower, broken into flowerets (1½ cups)
1 small green pepper, cut into strips (½ cup)
½ cup vinegar
⅓ cup sugar
¼ cup salad oil
2 teaspoons curry powder

Peel and slice carrots and turnips; halve turnip slices. In saucepan combine carrots, turnips, cauliflower, green pepper, 2 cups water, and 1 teaspoon salt. Bring to boiling; reduce heat. Cover and simmer till crisp-tender, about 5 minutes. Drain and cool vegetables.

In screw-top jar combine vinegar, sugar, oil, curry, 1 teaspoon salt, and ¼ teaspoon pepper. Cover and shake vigorously. Pour vinegar mixture over vegetables; toss lightly. Refrigerate several hours or overnight, stirring vegetable mixture occasionally. Makes 8 servings.

Carrot Cake

2 cups all-purpose flour
2 cups granulated sugar
1 teaspoon baking powder
1 teaspoon baking soda
1 teaspoon ground cinnamon
3 cups finely shredded carrot
1 cup cooking oil
4 eggs
Cream Cheese Frosting
¼ cup chopped nuts

Stir together flour, sugar, baking powder, soda, cinnamon, and 1 teaspoon salt. Add carrot, oil, and eggs. Mix till moistened; beat at medium speed of electric mixer for 2 minutes. Pour into greased and floured 13x9x2-inch baking pan. Bake at 325° for 50 to 60 minutes. Cool thoroughly. Spread with Cream Cheese Frosting. Top with nuts.

Cream Cheese Frosting: Soften one 3-ounce package cream cheese and ¼ cup butter *or* margarine; beat together till fluffy. Slowly beat in 2 cups sifted powdered sugar till smooth. Stir in 1 teaspoon vanilla.

Garden Gold Soup

6 medium carrots, cut up
   (1 pound)
3 medium potatoes, peeled and
   cubed
3 ribs celery with leaves,
   cut up
2 medium onions, quartered
4 cups water
2 teaspoons instant chicken
   bouillon granules
¼ teaspoon dried dillweed
1 cup milk
¼ cup butter *or* margarine

Place ¼ of the vegetables and *1 cup* of the water in a blender container. Cover and blend till coarsely chopped. Transfer mixture to a large kettle. Repeat process 3 times, using remaining vegetables and water. Stir in bouillon granules, dillweed, 2½ teaspoons salt, and ¼ teaspoon pepper. Cover; simmer till tender, 45 to 60 minutes.

Place *half* of the cooked mixture in blender container. Cover; blend till smooth, about 1 minute. Repeat process with remaining mixture. (*Or,* force the hot cooked mixture through a food mill.) Return pureed mixture to kettle; stir in milk and butter. Cover; heat through. Serves 8.

Crockery cooker directions: Blend vegetables and water as above; transfer to an electric slow crockery cooker. Stir in bouillon and seasonings as above. Cover; cook on low-heat setting 10 to 12 hours. Blend cooked mixture as above. Return to cooker; turn to high-heat setting. Stir in milk and butter. Cover; heat through, 30 minutes.

Golden Carrot Bake

3 cups shredded carrot (1 pound)
⅔ cup long grain rice
½ teaspoon salt
2 cups shredded American cheese
1 cup milk
2 beaten eggs
2 tablespoons instant minced
   onion

In saucepan combine carrot, rice, salt, and 1½ cups water. Bring to boiling. Reduce heat and simmer, covered, 25 minutes. *Do not drain.* Stir in 1½ cups of the shredded cheese, milk, eggs, onion, and ¼ teaspoon pepper. Turn into 1½-quart casserole. Bake, uncovered, at 350° about 1 hour. Top with remaining ½ cup shredded cheese. Return to oven to melt cheese, about 2 minutes. Makes 6 servings.

Pickled Carrots

6 medium carrots (1 pound)
¾ cup sugar
¾ cup vinegar
¾ cup water
1 tablespoon mustard seed
2½ inches stick cinnamon, broken
3 whole cloves

Cut carrots into 3-inch lengths. Simmer in small amount of boiling water for 5 minutes. Drain; cut into thin sticks. Combine sugar, vinegar, water, and mustard seed. Tie cinnamon and cloves in cheesecloth bag; add to vinegar mixture. Simmer 10 minutes. Pour over carrots; cool. Cover and refrigerate for 8 hours or overnight. Remove cheesecloth bag and drain before serving. Makes 2 cups.

Cauliflower

Selecting: *Cauliflower's peak season is September through November, but it is available in most areas year-round. Appearance is the most helpful indicator for selecting cauliflower. Choose a heavy, compact, white or creamy white head that has bright green leaves. Sprinkle leaves with water, cover tightly, and store in refrigerator crisper up to a week.*

Preparing: *Wash cauliflower head and remove leaves and woody stem. If desired, break the head into flowerets.*

Cooking: *In covered pan cook in a small amount of boiling salted water till just tender when tested with a fork (allow 10 to 15 minutes for flowerets; about 20 minutes for the whole head). Overcooking, even for only a few minutes, causes cauliflower to turn dark and become strong-flavored, so test frequently.*

Serving: *Raw cauliflower is a tasty addition to tossed salads, relish trays, or a platter of vegetable dippers. For a crisp relish, marinate cooked cauliflowerets in a vinegar-and-herb mixture. Serve cooked cauliflower with a cheese sauce.*

Cauliflower Polonaise

1 medium head cauliflower
1 hard-cooked egg
1 tablespoon butter *or* margarine
¼ cup fine dry bread crumbs
1 tablespoon snipped parsley

Cook whole cauliflower as directed above, or break into flowerets and cook as directed above. Drain well. Finely chop hard-cooked egg. Heat butter till lightly browned; stir in crumbs, snipped parsley, and chopped egg. Spoon over cooked cauliflower. Makes 5 or 6 servings.

Italian-Dressed Cauliflower

1 tablespoon chopped onion
1 small clove garlic, minced
2 tablespoons Italian salad dressing
3 cups small cauliflowerets
2 tablespoons chopped green pepper
⅛ teaspoon dried basil, crushed
1 cup cherry tomatoes, halved

In 1½-quart saucepan cook onion and garlic in salad dressing till onion is tender, about 2 minutes. Add cauliflowerets, ¼ cup water, and ½ teaspoon salt. Cook, covered, over low heat for 10 minutes. Add green pepper; cook till cauliflower is tender, about 5 minutes more. Stir in basil. Add tomatoes; heat through. Makes 6 servings.

Carrot and cauliflower favorites include *Sunshine Carrots* (see recipe, page 226), colorful
Italian-Dressed Cauliflower, and *Cauliflower with Cheese-Mushroom Sauce* (see recipe, page 230).

Cauliflower with Cheese-Mushroom Sauce (pictured on page 229)

1 medium head cauliflower
1½ cups sliced fresh mushrooms
(4 ounces) *or* 1 4-ounce can
sliced mushrooms, drained
2 tablespoons butter
2 tablespoons all-purpose flour
Dash white pepper
1 cup milk
1 cup shredded American
cheese (4 ounces)
1 teaspoon prepared mustard
1 tablespoon snipped parsley

Cook whole cauliflower as directed on page 228, or break into flowerets and cook as directed on page 228. Drain cauliflower thoroughly; keep warm.

Meanwhile, cook fresh mushrooms in butter till tender, about 4 minutes. (Or, if using canned mushrooms, set them aside and melt butter.) Blend flour, white pepper, and ¼ teaspoon salt into butter. Add milk all at once. Cook and stir till thickened and bubbly. Stir in cheese and mustard. If using canned mushrooms, stir them into sauce. Heat till cheese melts. Place head of cauliflower on platter; spoon some sauce over. Pass remaining sauce. Or, pour sauce over flowerets. Sprinkle with parsley. Serves 6.

Cauliflower-Ham Chowder

2 cups sliced cauliflowerets
1 13¾-ounce can chicken broth
1 cup milk *or* light cream
1 10¾-ounce can condensed cream
of potato soup
2 tablespoons cornstarch
⅛ teaspoon white pepper
2 cups diced fully cooked ham

In large covered saucepan cook cauliflower in chicken broth till almost tender, about 10 minutes. *Do not drain;* set aside. In bowl gradually add milk to soup; mix well. Slowly blend ¼ cup cold water into cornstarch and white pepper; stir into soup mixture. Pour soup mixture over cauliflower; cook and stir till thickened and bubbly. Stir in ham; simmer till hot, about 10 minutes. Garnish with sliced green onion with tops, if desired. Serves 5 or 6.

Cauliflower Scallop

1 10¾-ounce can condensed cream
of celery soup
½ cup milk
2 slightly beaten eggs
1 cup shredded Cheddar cheese
¾ cup soft bread crumbs
¼ cup snipped parsley
¼ cup chopped pimiento
1 tablespoon instant minced
onion
2 10-ounce packages frozen cauliflower, cooked and drained

Combine soup, milk, and eggs; stir in *half* of the cheese, bread crumbs, parsley, pimiento, onion, ½ teaspoon salt, and dash pepper. Chop cauliflower; stir into soup mixture. Turn into 10x6x2-inch baking dish. Bake at 350° for 35 minutes. Top with remaining shredded Cheddar cheese; bake 5 minutes more. Makes 6 to 8 servings.

Cauliflower-Onion Bake

1 10-ounce package frozen
cauliflower, thawed
2 9-ounce packages frozen
onions with cream sauce
2 tablespoons butter
¾ cup shredded American cheese
¼ cup toasted slivered almonds
1 tablespoon snipped parsley
½ cup canned French-fried
onions, crumbled

Cut up any large pieces of cauliflower; set aside. In saucepan combine frozen onions, butter, and 1½ cups water. Cover; bring to boiling. Reduce heat and simmer for 4 minutes, stirring occasionally. Remove from heat; stir till sauce is smooth. Stir in cauliflower, cheese, almonds, and parsley. Turn mixture into a 1½-quart casserole.

Bake at 350° till bubbly, about 35 minutes. Top with crumbled French-fried onions; bake 5 minutes more. Makes 8 servings.

Celery & Celeriac

Selecting: *The well-known celery is a stalk consisting of individual ribs, but the less familiar celeriac (celery root) is grown for its turnip-like root. Look for celery stalks with crisp, solid, medium-sized ribs. Avoid stalks that are blemished, discolored, or have wilted leaves. When shopping for celeriacs, choose small roots, since large ones tend to be woody and hollow.*

Preparing: *Separate celery ribs and trim leaves. Peel celeriacs before using.*

Cooking: *In covered pan cook sliced celery or celeriac in a small amount of boiling salted water till just tender (10 to 15 minutes for celery; about 10 minutes for celeriac).*

Serving: *Raw celery ribs are a favorite vegetable dipper or, when stuffed with a cheese or peanut butter mixture, a popular relish tray addition. Try cooked celery creamed or use it to add texture to dishes. Cooked celeriacs are flavorful substitutes for potatoes. The French serve strips of raw celeriac with a sharp-flavored rémoulade sauce as an appetizer.*

Celeriac Sauté

2 small celeriacs (about 1 pound)
2 tablespoons butter *or* margarine
1 tablespoon snipped parsley

Peel celeriacs; cut into julienne strips. Cook as directed above; drain thoroughly.

In small saucepan heat butter till brown. Pour over cooked celeriac. Season to taste with salt and pepper. Sprinkle with snipped parsley. Makes 4 servings.

Celeriac Toss

2 small celeriacs (about 1 pound)
2 medium carrots, cut into julienne strips (about 1 cup)
1 large avocado, pitted, peeled, and chopped
⅔ cup French salad dressing
Lettuce cups

Peel and coarsely chop celeriacs; cook as directed above. Drain. In deep bowl combine celeriacs, carrots, and avocado. Pour French salad dressing over and toss to coat. Refrigerate 2 to 3 hours, stirring occasionally. Drain vegetables and spoon into lettuce cups. Makes 6 to 8 servings.

Celery Slaw

3 cups very thinly sliced celery
1 tablespoon sugar
1 tablespoon salad oil
1 tablespoon white vinegar
1 tablespoon finely chopped
    onion
½ teaspoon salt
¼ teaspoon paprika
⅛ teaspoon pepper
½ cup dairy sour cream
½ cup shredded carrot (1 medium)
    Lettuce

In covered pan cook celery in small amount of boiling water till crisp-tender, about 5 minutes; drain well. In medium bowl combine sugar, salad oil, vinegar, onion, salt, paprika, and pepper. Blend in sour cream. Add celery and shredded carrot; toss lightly to mix. Chill. Serve in lettuce-lined bowl. Makes 6 servings.

Crisp Dilled Celery

3 cups celery bias-sliced ¾
    inch thick
1 medium green pepper, cut in
    strips
⅓ cup water
2 tablespoons chopped onion
1 teaspoon instant chicken
    bouillon granules
½ teaspoon dried dillweed
¼ teaspoon salt
2 tablespoons butter *or*
    margarine

In saucepan combine sliced celery, green pepper strips, water, chopped onion, chicken bouillon granules, dillweed, and salt. Cover tightly; simmer till celery is crisp-tender, 8 to 10 minutes. Drain. Add butter or margarine, stirring till melted. Makes 6 servings.

Baked Celery with Almonds

1 stalk celery
2 cups boiling water
½ teaspoon salt
3 tablespoons butter
3 tablespoons all-purpose flour
1⅓ cups milk
3 tablespoons toasted slivered
    almonds
¼ cup fine dry bread crumbs
1 tablespoon butter, melted

Cut celery ribs into ½-inch slices (5 cups), reserving tops. Combine sliced celery, tops, boiling water, and salt. Cook till celery is tender, 12 to 15 minutes. Discard tops; drain, reserving ½ cup cooking liquid. Melt the 3 tablespoons butter. Blend in flour, ½ teaspoon salt, and ¼ teaspoon pepper. Add milk and reserved liquid. Cook and stir till thickened. Remove from heat. Stir in celery and *half* of the nuts. Turn into 1-quart casserole. Top with remaining nuts. Toss crumbs with melted butter; sprinkle atop. Bake at 350° till heated through, 20 to 25 minutes. Makes 4 servings.

Cream of Celery Soup

1½ cups chopped celery
⅓ cup chopped onion
1 cup water
3 cups milk
3 tablespoons all-purpose flour
⅛ teaspoon white pepper
2 tablespoons butter *or*
    margarine

In 2-quart saucepan combine celery, onion, and ½ teaspoon salt; add water. Cover and cook till vegetables are tender, about 15 minutes. *Do not drain.* Add 2½ cups of the milk. Blend the remaining ½ cup milk, the flour, white pepper, and ½ teaspoon salt; add to celery mixture. Cook, stirring constantly, till thickened and bubbly. Stir in butter or margarine. Season to taste with salt and pepper. If desired, garnish with snipped parsley. Makes 6 servings.

Corn

Selecting: *The peak season for fresh sweet corn is during the summer. Choose ears of corn that are well filled with even rows of plump, milky kernels. Look for fresh, green husks and avoid ears that are wormy. For best flavor, use fresh corn right after picking or purchasing. If corn can't be used immediately, store it, unhusked, in the coolest part of the refrigerator. If storage space is limited, you may husk the ears and place them in a plastic bag before refrigerating.*

Preparing: *Remove husks; scrub with a stiff brush to remove silks; rinse. For cut corn, use a sharp knife to cut off just the kernel tips, then scrape the cob with dull edge of knife.*

Cooking: *Cook ears of corn in a covered pan in a small amount of boiling salted water till just done, 6 to 8 minutes. Or, cook in uncovered pan in enough boiling salted water to cover ears. For foil-baked corn, spread ears with butter and sprinkle with salt and pepper. Wrap corn in foil; bake at 450° about 25 minutes. Turn several times during baking. For cut corn, cook in a covered pan in a small amount of boiling salted water or milk till done, 12 to 15 minutes.*

Green Corn Pudding

4 **fresh ears of corn**
3 **egg yolks**
2 **tablespoons sugar**
2 **tablespoons butter, melted**
2 **cups milk**
3 **stiffly beaten egg whites**

With sharp knife, make cuts *through center* of kernels. Scrape cob. Measure 1¾ cups corn. Beat egg yolks till thick and lemon-colored. Stir in corn, sugar, butter, and 1 teaspoon salt. Slowly beat in milk. Fold in egg whites. Bake in 8x8x2-inch baking dish at 350° till knife inserted off-center comes out clean, 45 to 50 minutes. Serves 6 to 8.

Baked Corn with Chive Sauce

2 **12-ounce cans whole kernel corn, drained**
1 **4-ounce container whipped cream cheese with chives**

In a 1-quart casserole combine whole kernel corn, cream cheese with chives, ¼ teaspoon salt, and dash pepper. Cover and bake at 325° about 45 minutes. Serve baked corn in sauce dishes. Makes 6 servings.

Swiss Corn Bake (see recipe, page 236) is equally delicious made with commercially-canned corn as with *Home-Canned Whole Kernel Corn. Home-Canned Cream-Style Corn* is another vegetable favorite.

Two-Corn Bread

1 **cup all-purpose flour**
1 **cup yellow cornmeal**
2 **tablespoons sugar**
1 **tablespoon baking powder**
3 **eggs**
1 **cup cream-style cottage cheese**
1 **8-ounce can cream-style corn**

Stir together flour, cornmeal, sugar, baking powder, and ¼ teaspoon salt. Beat eggs and cottage cheese till smooth; stir in corn. Add to dry ingredients; stir just till blended. Turn into greased 9x9x2-inch baking pan. Bake at 375° for 30 to 35 minutes. Serve warm. Makes 9 servings.

Home-Canned Whole Kernel Corn

Fresh ears of corn (allow 3 to 6 pounds for each quart)
Salt (¼ teaspoon for each pint; ½ teaspoon for each quart)
Boiling water

Cut corn from cob at ⅔'s depth; do not scrape cob. For *raw pack,* pack corn loosely into hot, clean jars; leave 1-inch headspace. Add salt. Cover corn with boiling water; leave 1-inch headspace. For *hot pack,* add 2 cups boiling water per 1 quart corn; bring to boil. Pack loosely into hot, clean jars; leave 1-inch headspace. Add salt and boiling cooking liquid; leave 1-inch headspace. Prepare lids according to manufacturer's directions. Wipe jar rim. Adjust lid on jar. Process raw or hot pack corn in *pressure canner* at 10 pounds pressure for 55 minutes for pints; 85 minutes for quarts. Boil corn 20 minutes *before* tasting or using.

Home-Canned Cream-Style Corn

Fresh ears of corn (allow 1½ to 3 pounds for each pint)
Salt (¼ teaspoon for each pint)
Boiling water

Cut corn from cob, cutting only about half the kernel; then scrape cob. For *raw pack,* pack corn loosely into hot, clean pint jars, leaving 1-inch headspace. Add salt. Fill jars with boiling water, leaving 1-inch headspace. For *hot pack,* cover corn with boiling water; bring to a boil. Pack loosely into hot, clean pint jars, leaving 1-inch headspace. Add salt. Prepare lids according to manufacturer's directions. Wipe off rim of jar. Adjust lid on jar.

Process raw pack corn in *pressure canner* at 10 pounds pressure for 95 minutes for pints. *Process hot pack* corn in *pressure canner* at 10 pounds pressure for 85 minutes for pints. Boil corn 20 minutes *before* tasting or using.

Pressure Canning is Essential

All vegetables—except tomatoes or those made into pickles, relishes, or sauerkraut—are susceptible to botulism. They *must be pressure-canned* to reach the high temperature needed to destroy botulism-causing organisms. When using a pressure canner, read and follow the manufacturer's directions thoroughly. At 10 pounds pressure, the temperature reaches 240° at sea level (versus 212° in a boiling water bath). The processing time in the recipe ensures adequate heat penetration. In high-altitude areas, over 2,000 feet, check with a county extension agent for corrections. *Never* serve home-canned vegetables cold from the jar. Boil corn or spinach 20 minutes (others at least 10 minutes) before tasting or using.

Swiss Corn Bake (pictured on page 234)

1 pint Home-Canned Whole Kernel
Corn (see page 235) *or*
1 16-ounce can whole kernel
corn, drained
1 5⅓-ounce can evaporated milk
1 cup shredded process Swiss
cheese (4 ounces)
2 beaten eggs
2 tablespoons finely chopped
onion
1 cup soft bread crumbs
2 tablespoons butter, melted

Boil home-canned corn, uncovered, 20 minutes *before* tasting or using. Drain well. Combine corn, evaporated milk, ¾ *cup* of the shredded cheese, eggs, chopped onion, and dash pepper. Turn mixture into a 10x6x2-inch baking dish or a 1-quart casserole. Toss bread crumbs with the melted butter and the remaining ¼ cup shredded cheese. Sprinkle over corn mixture. Bake at 350° for 25 to 30 minutes. Garnish with green pepper rings, if desired. Makes 4 to 6 servings.

Corn Medley

1 10-ounce package frozen whole
kernel corn
½ cup chopped celery
1 teaspoon instant chicken
bouillon granules
1 2½-ounce jar sliced mushrooms
1 medium tomato

In saucepan combine corn, celery, bouillon granules, and ⅓ cup water. Bring to boiling; reduce heat. Cover and simmer till vegetables are tender, 5 to 7 minutes. Drain mushrooms. Cut tomato into thin wedges. Stir mushrooms and tomato wedges into corn mixture; heat through. Season to taste with salt and pepper. Makes 6 servings.

Roasted Corn on the Cob

½ cup butter *or* margarine,
softened
1 teaspoon salt
½ teaspoon dried rosemary,
crushed
½ teaspoon dried marjoram,
crushed
6 fresh ears of corn in husks

Cream together butter and salt till fluffy. Combine herbs and blend into butter. Keep butter at room temperature for 1 hour to mellow. Turn back husks of corn; remove silks with a stiff brush. Place each ear on a piece of heavy-duty foil. Spread corn with about *1 tablespoon* of the butter mixture. Lay husks back in position. Wrap corn securely with foil. Roast ears directly on *hot* coals; turn frequently till corn is tender, 12 to 15 minutes. Or, if you have a covered grill with an elevated rack, roast corn according to manufacturer's directions. Makes 6 servings.

Corn Relish

1 10-ounce package frozen whole
kernel corn
½ cup sugar
1 tablespoon cornstarch
½ cup vinegar
2 tablespoons finely chopped
celery
2 tablespoons finely chopped
green pepper
2 tablespoons chopped pimiento
1 tablespoon minced onion
1 teaspoon ground turmeric
½ teaspoon dry mustard

Cook corn according to package directions; drain. In saucepan combine sugar and cornstarch; stir in vinegar and ⅓ cup cold water. Stir in corn, celery, green pepper, pimiento, onion, turmeric, and dry mustard. Cook, stirring constantly, till thickened and bubbly; cook and stir 3 to 4 minutes more. Cover and chill thoroughly. Makes 2 cups.

Scalloped Corn

1 beaten egg
1 cup milk
1 cup coarsely crushed saltine
   crackers (22 crackers)
¾ teaspoon salt
   Dash pepper
1 17-ounce can cream-style corn
¼ cup finely chopped onion
3 tablespoons chopped pimiento
1 tablespoon butter, melted

Combine egg, milk, ⅔ *cup* of the cracker crumbs, salt, and pepper. Stir in corn, onion, and pimiento; mix well. Turn into 1-quart casserole. Toss melted butter with the remaining ⅓ cup cracker crumbs; sprinkle atop corn mixture. Bake at 350° for 65 to 70 minutes. Makes 6 servings.

Parsley Buttered Corn

6 fresh ears of corn
½ cup butter *or* margarine,
   softened
1 tablespoon snipped parsley
1 teaspoon lemon juice
⅛ teaspoon salt
⅛ teaspoon dried savory, crushed
   Dash pepper

Cook ears of corn in boiling salted water as directed on page 233. Cream butter. Blend in parsley, lemon juice, salt, savory, and pepper. Serve with corn. Makes 6 servings.
   Microwave cooking directions: Wrap each ear of corn in waxed paper; twist ends of paper to seal. Arrange corn on paper toweling, allowing at least 1 inch between ears. Cook corn in countertop microwave oven for 8 to 10 minutes for six ears. (Allow 2 minutes for one ear; 3 to 4 minutes for two ears; and 6 to 7 minutes for four ears.) Halfway through cooking, rearrange corn and turn over. Prepare butter mixture as above and serve with corn.

Fresh Creamed Corn

5 fresh ears of corn
2 slices bacon
½ cup milk
½ teaspoon sugar
½ teaspoon salt
   Dash pepper
½ cup light cream
1½ teaspoons all-purpose flour
1 tablespoon butter *or* margarine

Cut corn from cob; set aside. In an 8-inch skillet cook bacon till crisp; remove and crumble, reserving drippings. Add corn, milk, sugar, salt, and pepper to reserved drippings. Cover and cook 15 to 20 minutes, stirring occasionally. In screw-top jar shake together light cream and flour till combined; stir into corn mixture. Add butter or margarine. Cook, stirring constantly, till thickened and bubbly. Garnish with crumbled bacon. Makes 6 servings.

Fresh Corn Chowder

6 fresh ears of corn
⅓ cup water
¼ cup chopped onion
½ teaspoon salt
4 cups milk
2 tablespoons butter
1 teaspoon salt
¼ teaspoon white pepper
3 tablespoons all-purpose flour
1 beaten egg

With sharp knife, make cuts *through center* of kernels. Cut corn off cob; scrape cob. In saucepan combine corn, water, onion, and the ½ teaspoon salt. Bring to a boil. Reduce heat and simmer, covered, 15 minutes, stirring occasionally. Stir in 3½ *cups* of the milk, butter, the 1 teaspoon salt, and white pepper. Blend together remaining ½ cup milk and flour; stir into corn mixture. Cook and stir till thickened and bubbly. Gradually stir about 1 cup of the hot mixture into egg; return to hot mixture in saucepan. Cook over low heat, stirring constantly, for 2 minutes more. Garnish with snipped chives and paprika, if desired. Makes 6 servings.

Cucumbers

Selecting: Choose firm, bright or dark green, well-shaped cucumbers. Pass up those that have an overgrown, puffy appearance and yellowing rind. Cucumbers 6 to 9 inches in length are best suited for slicing and recipe use. Smaller 1- to 4-inch cucumbers are preferred for pickles. Cucumbers keep fresh up to two weeks stored in the refrigerator.

Preparing: Scrub cucumbers. The cucumber peel is edible and adds color to most recipes, but this vegetable may be peeled if desired. For pretty frilled slices, run the tines of a fork lengthwise along the unpeeled cucumber before slicing.

Tip: To keep the cucumber crisp, very thinly slice the vegetable and place in ice water immediately after cutting.

Serving: Add cucumbers to tossed salads, molded salads, and relish trays, or combine them with onion slices in a vinegar or sour cream dressing. Whether your preference is dill or sweet, cucumber pickles are an all-time favorite.

Cucumbers in Sour Cream

2 medium cucumbers, thinly
  sliced
1 medium onion, thinly sliced
½ cup dairy sour cream
1 tablespoon sugar
1 tablespoon vinegar

Combine the cucumbers and onion. Stir together sour cream, sugar, vinegar, and ½ teaspoon salt; toss with vegetables. Cover and chill, stirring occasionally. Makes 3 cups.

Quick Mustard Pickles

2½ to 3 pounds cucumbers
1½ cups vinegar
1 cup water
1 cup sugar
1 4-ounce jar prepared mustard
  (½ cup)
2 teaspoons salt
1 teaspoon prepared horseradish

Cut cucumbers into ½-inch chunks or ¼-inch slices. Measure 8 cups. In large saucepan mix vinegar, water, sugar, mustard, salt, and horseradish; bring to boil. Pack cucumbers into hot, clean pint jars; pour boiling liquid over cucumbers, leaving ½-inch headspace. (Liquid will be cloudy due to mustard.) Prepare lids according to manufacturer's directions. Wipe jar rim. Adjust lid on jar. Process in boiling water bath 5 minutes. (Start timing when water returns to boil.) Mustard may settle during standing. Makes 4 pints.

Refreshing *Cucumber Ring Supreme* wreathed with fresh watercress and garnished with colorful cherry tomatoes is the perfect salad choice for a summer buffet or luncheon menu.

Cucumber Ring Supreme

  1 **tablespoon sugar**
1½ **teaspoons unflavored gelatin**
  ½ **teaspoon salt**
  2 **tablespoons lemon juice**
  ½ **cucumber, thinly sliced**
  2 **tablespoons sugar**
  1 **envelope unflavored gelatin**
  ¾ **teaspoon salt**
  2 **tablespoons lemon juice**
  1 **8-ounce package cream cheese, cubed and softened**
   About 6 medium cucumbers, peeled
  1 **cup mayonnaise** *or* **salad dressing**
  ¼ **cup snipped parsley**
  3 **tablespoons finely chopped onion**

In small saucepan combine the 1 tablespoon sugar, the 1½ teaspoons unflavored gelatin, and the ½ teaspoon salt. Stir in ¾ cup water; stir over low heat till gelatin and sugar are dissolved. Stir in 2 tablespoons lemon juice. Pour into 6½-cup ring mold. Chill till partially set. Overlay the thinly sliced cucumber atop gelatin mixture in mold; press into gelatin. Chill till *almost* firm.

Meanwhile, in saucepan mix the 2 tablespoons sugar, the 1 envelope unflavored gelatin, and the ¾ teaspoon salt. Add ⅔ cup water; stir over low heat till gelatin and sugar are dissolved. Stir in 2 tablespoons lemon juice. Gradually beat hot gelatin mixture into softened cream cheese with rotary beater till mixture is smooth.

Halve the 6 cucumbers and scrape out seeds; grind using fine blade, or finely shred. Measure 2 cups drained ground cucumber. Fold ground cucumber, mayonnaise, parsley, and onion into cream cheese mixture. Pour over almost firm gelatin in mold. Chill till firm. Makes 8 servings.

Dill Pickles

For each quart:
½ pound 4-inch cucumbers
    (5 or 6 cucumbers)
3 or 4 heads fresh dill
1 teaspoon mustard seed
2 cups water
1 cup cider vinegar
1 tablespoon pickling salt

Pack cucumbers loosely in hot, clean quart jars, leaving ½-inch headspace. Add dill and mustard seed to each quart. Make a brine by combining water, vinegar, and salt. Bring to boiling. Slowly pour hot brine over cucumbers, leaving ½-inch headspace. Prepare lids according to manufacturer's directions. Wipe jar rim. Adjust lid on jar. Process in boiling water bath for 20 minutes (start timing as soon as jars are placed in water).

Kosher Dill Pickles: Pack cucumbers in quart jars as above. Add dill to each quart; *omit* the mustard seed. Add 1 clove garlic and 1 small piece hot red pepper (optional) to each quart. Prepare a brine using 2¼ cups water, ¾ cup vinegar, and 1 tablespoon pickling salt. Bring to boiling. Slowly pour hot brine over cucumbers, leaving ½-inch headspace. Prepare lids and process as above.

Crisp Pickle Slices

4 quarts sliced cucumbers
6 medium onions, sliced
    (6 cups)
2 green peppers, sliced
    (1⅔ cups)
3 cloves garlic
⅓ cup pickling salt
    Cracked ice
5 cups sugar
3 cups cider vinegar
2 tablespoons mustard seed
1½ teaspoons ground turmeric
1½ teaspoons celery seed

Combine sliced cucumbers, onions, green peppers, garlic (speared on wooden picks for easy removal), and pickling salt. Cover with cracked ice; mix well. Let cucumber mixture stand for 3 hours; drain well. Remove garlic. Combine sugar, cider vinegar, mustard seed, turmeric, and celery seed; pour over cucumber mixture. Bring to boiling. Pack cucumbers and liquid into hot, clean pint jars, leaving ½-inch headspace. Prepare lids according to manufacturer's directions. Wipe jar rim. Adjust lid on jar. Process jars in boiling water bath for 5 minutes. (Start timing when water returns to boiling.) Makes 8 pints.

Pickle-making Pointers

- Choose a cucumber variety developed just for pickling.
- Make pickles out of cucumbers within 24 hours of harvesting. Cucumbers that are held longer may produce a hollow or soft pickle.
- Use pure granulated pickling salt or uniodized table salt. Iodized table salt causes pickles to darken.
- Choose a high-grade vinegar of 4- to 6-percent acid (40 to 60 grain). Never dilute the vinegar more than specified in the recipe.
- Use herbs and spices from newly opened packages.
- Use soft water for pickles. Minerals in hard water settle in the bottom of the jar after processing.
- Choose utensils made of stoneware, aluminum, glass, or stainless steel.
- Pack pickles in standard canning jars.
- Process pickles in water bath canner. The processing destroys organisms that cause spoilage.

Eggplant

Selecting: This pear-shaped vegetable is most plentiful in August and September, although it's available in most supermarkets throughout the year. Look for a firm, heavy eggplant with a dark, shiny, smooth skin and a fresh-looking, green cap. Avoid those that have dark spots, which indicate decay, or feel spongy. Store in refrigerator up to two weeks.

Preparing: Wash, cut off the cap, and, if desired, peel the eggplant.

Cooking: For freshest flavor, sauté eggplant in oil, bake it, broil it, or cook in a small amount of boiling salted water. Avoid boiling in a large amount of water. A well-cooked eggplant has a tender and moist interior that's not wet or soggy.

Serving: For a tasty main dish, stuff eggplant with a meat filling or use sliced or cubed eggplant in casseroles. Serve sautéed eggplant with a rich tomato sauce for a delicious vegetable dish. Team cubed eggplant and your favorite meat for special kabobs. Or, try deep-fat fried eggplant strips as an unusual snack or appetizer.

Jackstraw Eggplant

- 1 **medium eggplant, peeled**
- 1 **cup all-purpose flour**
- 1 **cup ice water**
- 1 **slightly beaten egg**
- 2 **tablespoons cooking oil**
- ½ **teaspoon sugar**
  Fat for deep-fat frying
  Grated Parmesan cheese

Halve eggplant lengthwise; cut crosswise into ½-inch slices. Cut slices into ½-inch strips. Beat together flour, ice water, egg, oil, sugar, and ½ teaspoon salt. Dip eggplant strips in batter, allowing excess to drain off. Fry, a few at a time, in deep hot fat (365°) for 4 to 5 minutes. Drain on paper toweling. Sprinkle with additional salt. Serve hot with Parmesan cheese.

Pan-Fried Eggplant

- 1 **medium eggplant, peeled**
- 1 **slightly beaten egg**
- ½ **cup finely crushed rich round crackers**
- 2 **tablespoons snipped parsley**
- ½ **cup cooking oil**

Halve eggplant lengthwise, then cut crosswise into ½-inch slices. Combine egg and 1 tablespoon water. Combine crackers, parsley, ½ teaspoon salt, and ⅛ teaspoon pepper. Dip eggplant in egg mixture, then in cracker mixture. Cook eggplant in hot oil till tender and golden, 2 to 3 minutes per side. Drain on paper toweling. Serves 4 to 6.

The Greek specialty *Moussaka for a Crowd* features tender slices of eggplant nestled in a cinnamon-custard mixture. Layered beneath are more eggplant and wine-tomato sauced ground lamb or beef.

Moussaka for a Crowd

2 **large eggplants, peeled and cut into ½-inch slices**
¼ **cup cooking oil**
2 **pounds ground lamb** *or* **ground beef**
1 **cup chopped onion**
1 **clove garlic, minced**
1 **8-ounce can tomato sauce**
¾ **cup dry red wine**
2 **tablespoons snipped parsley**
¼ **teaspoon dried oregano, crushed**
¼ **teaspoon ground cinnamon**
1 **beaten egg**
¼ **cup butter** *or* **margarine**
¼ **cup all-purpose flour**
2 **cups milk**
3 **beaten eggs**
½ **cup grated Parmesan cheese**
  Ground cinnamon

Brush both sides of eggplant slices with the oil; sprinkle with salt. In large skillet brown eggplant slices, about 1½ minutes on each side. Drain and set aside. In same skillet cook lamb or beef, onion, and garlic till meat is brown and onion is tender; drain off excess fat. Stir in tomato sauce, wine, parsley, oregano, the ¼ teaspoon cinnamon, and 1 teaspoon salt. Simmer, uncovered, for 10 minutes. Gradually stir mixture into the 1 beaten egg.

Meanwhile, in a saucepan melt butter or margarine; stir in flour, 1 teaspoon salt, and dash pepper. Add milk all at once; cook and stir till thickened and bubbly. Gradually stir the hot sauce into the 3 beaten eggs.

In 13x9x2-inch baking dish arrange *half* the eggplant. Pour all the meat mixture over; top with remaining eggplant. Pour milk mixture over all. Top with Parmesan and additional cinnamon. Bake at 325° for 40 to 45 minutes. Top with more parsley, if desired. Makes 8 to 10 servings.

Eggplant Parmigiana

¼ **cup all-purpose flour**
½ **teaspoon salt**
1 **medium eggplant, peeled and cut into ½-inch slices**
1 **beaten egg**
½ **cup cooking oil**
⅓ **cup grated Parmesan cheese**
  Homemade Tomato Sauce
1 **6-ounce package sliced mozzarella cheese**

Combine flour and salt. Dip eggplant into beaten egg, then in flour mixture. In large skillet brown eggplant in hot oil; drain well on paper toweling. Place 1 layer of eggplant in 10x6x2-inch baking dish, cutting slices to fit. Sprinkle with *half* the Parmesan. Top with *half* the Homemade Tomato Sauce and *half* the mozzarella. Cut remaining mozzarella into triangles. Repeat eggplant, Parmesan, Homemade Tomato Sauce, and mozzarella layers. Bake at 400° till heated through, 15 to 20 minutes. Makes 6 servings.

Homemade Tomato Sauce: In saucepan cook ⅓ cup chopped onion; ¼ cup finely chopped celery; ½ clove garlic, minced; and 1 teaspoon dried parsley flakes in 2 tablespoons olive oil *or* cooking oil till onion and celery are tender but not brown. Stir in one 16-ounce can Italian tomatoes; ⅓ cup tomato paste; ½ teaspoon salt; ½ teaspoon dried oregano, crushed; ¼ teaspoon pepper; and 1 bay leaf. Simmer gently, uncovered, 45 to 50 minutes. Remove bay leaf.

Stuffed Eggplant

1 **large eggplant (1½ pounds)**
¼ **cup chopped onion**
1 **tablespoon butter** *or* **margarine**
1 **10¾-ounce can condensed cream of mushroom soup**
1 **tablespoon snipped parsley**
½ **teaspoon Worcestershire sauce**
1 **cup finely crushed rich round crackers (24 crackers)**

Cut a thin slice off one side of eggplant. Remove pulp to within ½-inch of skin. Cook pulp in small amount of boiling water till tender, about 10 minutes; drain well. Cook onion in butter till tender. Stir in eggplant pulp, soup, parsley, and Worcestershire. Set aside 2 tablespoons crushed crackers; stir remaining crackers into onion mixture. Fill eggplant shell with mixture. Place in 10x6x2-inch baking dish; sprinkle reserved crumbs over top. Carefully pour hot water in bottom of dish to depth of ½ inch. Bake at 375° till heated through, 50 to 60 minutes. Serves 4 to 6.

Greens

Selecting: *The green leaves and, sometimes, stems of plants have been used as vegetables for hundreds of years. Turnip greens, collard greens, mustard greens, beet greens, dandelion greens, kale, and chard or Swiss chard are all greens. Choose fresh-looking, crisp greens that are free of insect injury. For best quality, use greens the same day as purchased.*

Preparing: *Thoroughly wash greens in cool water to remove dirt and sand particles. Cut off any roots and remove damaged portions and large veins. Tear or cut up large leaves.*

Cooking: *Greens need to be cooked in covered pan in boiling salted water only till tender, but cooking time varies from 10 minutes to 75 minutes depending on the type and maturity of the greens. Considerably longer cooking is typical in many recipes.*

Serving: *Raw greens are flavorful additions to tossed salads. Salt pork, butter, vinegar, and lemon juice are popular seasonings for cooked greens.*

Sweet-Sour Swiss Chard

  6 **cups torn Swiss chard**
  6 **slices bacon**
 ½ **cup sliced green onion with tops**
  4 **teaspoons sugar**
  2 **teaspoons all-purpose flour**
 ⅓ **cup water**
 ¼ **cup vinegar**

Place chard in large salad bowl; set aside. In skillet cook bacon till crisp; drain, reserving ¼ cup bacon drippings. Crumble bacon; set aside. In same skillet cook onion in reserved drippings till tender but not brown. Blend in sugar, flour, and ½ teaspoon salt; stir in water and vinegar. Cook and stir till thickened and bubbly. Pour hot mixture over chard, tossing to coat. Sprinkle with bacon. Serve immediately. Makes 4 to 6 servings.

Salt Pork and Greens

 ½ **pound salt pork**
  8 **cups water**
1½ **pounds beet greens, turnip greens, Swiss chard, *or* mustard greens (about 16 cups)**

Cut salt pork into thin strips. Place pork and water in kettle or Dutch oven; simmer, covered, for 45 minutes. Prepare greens as directed above; add to pork and water. Simmer, covered, 1 hour. Drain greens, reserving liquid. Season greens and pork with salt and pepper to taste. If desired, serve cooking liquid over. Makes 6 servings.

Garden-fresh turnips become a hearty vegetable dish when you prepare a big kettle of
the flavorful Southern favorite, *Turnip Greens with Cornmeal Dumplings* (see recipe, page 246).

Turnip Greens with Cornmeal Dumplings (pictured on page 245)

4 ounces salt pork with rind
2 pounds turnip greens
1 pound turnips
10 cups water
1 teaspoon salt
1½ cups cornmeal
½ cup all-purpose flour
1 teaspoon baking powder
1 teaspoon sugar
½ teaspoon salt
3 tablespoons butter *or*
    margarine, melted
1 beaten egg

Chop salt pork, cutting to, but not through, rind. Discard stems of greens and any damaged portions. Tear up large leaves (should have about 12 cups greens). Peel and quarter turnips. In large kettle bring water to boil. Add salt pork, greens, turnips, and 1 teaspoon salt. Simmer, covered, 2 hours. Remove 1 cup broth; reserve for dumplings. Remove and discard salt pork. Season remaining broth to taste.

For dumplings, in mixing bowl combine cornmeal, flour, baking powder, sugar, and the ½ teaspoon salt; stir together thoroughly. Stir in melted butter or margarine and the reserved 1 cup broth. Stir in beaten egg. Spoon batter by rounded tablespoonfuls onto simmering greens to make 12 dumplings. Cover and simmer 25 to 30 minutes. To serve, ladle greens and broth into soup bowls; top each serving with 2 dumplings. Makes 6 servings.

Sweet-Sour Kale

½ pound kale, mustard greens, *or*
    collard greens *or* 1 10-ounce
    package frozen chopped kale
    or collard greens
2 slices bacon
4 teaspoons all-purpose flour
¾ cup hot water
1 tablespoon sugar
1 tablespoon cider vinegar
¼ teaspoon salt
    Dash pepper

Cut roots off fresh kale or greens and remove any damaged portions. Cut stems and leaves into small pieces. In covered saucepan cook fresh kale or greens in large amount of boiling salted water till tender, 60 to 75 minutes. Drain well. (Or, cook frozen chopped kale or collard greens according to package directions; drain well.)

In skillet cook bacon till crisp. Remove bacon, reserving drippings in skillet. Crumble bacon and set aside. Blend flour into drippings. Add hot water; cook and stir till thickened and bubbly. Stir in sugar, cider vinegar, salt, and pepper. Stir in drained cooked kale or greens; heat through. Garnish with crumbled bacon. Makes 4 servings.

Ham Hocks 'n Greens

1 pound mustard greens
½ pound turnip greens
½ pound collard greens
4 cups water
3½ pounds ham hocks
    Corn Bread
    Hard-cooked egg slices
    (optional)

Discard stems of greens and any damaged portions. Tear up large leaves. In large kettle combine water and ham hocks; bring to boiling. Add mustard, turnip, and collard greens; return to boiling. Reduce heat; simmer, covered, 1½ hours.

About ½ hour before greens are done, prepare Corn Bread. To serve, ladle greens and juices (pot liquor) into bowl; garnish with hard-cooked egg slices, if desired. Offer ham hocks in another bowl. Pass Corn Bread. Makes 4 servings.

Corn Bread: In mixing bowl stir together 1 cup all-purpose flour, 1 cup yellow cornmeal, ¼ cup sugar, 4 teaspoons baking powder, and ¾ teaspoon salt. Add 1 cup milk, 2 eggs, and ¼ cup cooking oil. Beat with rotary beater or electric mixer just till smooth, about 1 minute; do not overbeat. Bake in greased 9x9x2-inch baking pan at 350° for 20 to 25 minutes. Cut into squares.

Kohlrabi

Selecting: Although sometimes called cabbage turnip because of its appearance and flavor, kohlrabi is not a root vegetable; the edible globe forms above the ground. The plant grows well spring through fall, but marketable quantities are greatest in June and July. Choose globes that look fresh and unscarred. Those less than 3 inches in diameter are younger and usually milder in flavor. Leaves are edible too, but wilt quickly and are often trimmed off before sale. Kohlrabies will keep for several days in the refrigerator crisper.

Preparing: Peel off tough outer skin. Slice or chop the flesh according to planned use.

Cooking: In covered pan cook in small amount of boiling salted water till tender, about 25 minutes.

Serving: Serve raw on relish tray or in a salad. Serve cooked kohlrabi buttered or mashed with salt and pepper, or accented with other seasonings such as dry mustard, tarragon, or thyme.

Kohlrabi Slaw

6 **medium kohlrabies**
2 **apples, cored and chopped**
1 **tablespoon sliced green onion**
   with tops
½ **cup dairy sour cream**
¼ **cup creamy French salad**
   dressing

Peel and coarsely shred kohlrabies (should have about 3 cups). In medium bowl combine kohlrabies, apples, and green onion. Stir together sour cream and French salad dressing; stir into kohlrabi mixture. Chill. Serve in lettuce-lined bowl, if desired. Makes 6 servings.

Kohlrabi-Carrot Bake

3 **medium kohlrabies**
4 **medium carrots, bias-sliced**
¼ **cup chopped onion**
2 **tablespoons butter**
2 **tablespoons all-purpose flour**
½ **teaspoon salt**
1½ **cups milk**
¼ **cup snipped parsley**
1 **tablespoon lemon juice**
¾ **cup soft bread crumbs**
1 **tablespoon butter, melted**

Peel and slice kohlrabies. In covered saucepan cook kohlrabies in small amount of boiling salted water 15 minutes. Add carrots; cover and continue cooking till vegetables are tender, 10 to 12 minutes more. Drain. In saucepan cook onion in the 2 tablespoons butter till tender but not brown. Blend in flour, salt, and dash pepper. Add milk all at once. Cook and stir till thickened and bubbly. Stir in cooked vegetables, parsley, and lemon juice. Turn into 1-quart casserole. Combine bread crumbs and the 1 tablespoon melted butter; sprinkle around edge of casserole. Bake at 350° till heated through, 20 to 25 minutes. Makes 6 servings.

Lettuce

Selecting: *While bright, fresh-looking green leaves are signs of quality, each lettuce type has special characteristics. Shown clockwise: Iceberg lettuce, with a firm but not hard head, should give slightly when squeezed. Avoid heads with rust marks. Salad bowl and leaf lettuce have leaves clustered loosely around a stem. Some types are red-tipped. Look for soft, tender leaves free from wilt or decay. Bibb lettuce, a small cup-shaped head with soft textured leaves, is a butterhead variety. Its deep green outer leaves become almost white near the core. Romaine or Cos (shown cut lengthwise) has a long head of coarse, stiff leaves with heavy midribs. Select full, unblemished heads. Wash lettuce as below and store in a plastic bag in refrigerator crisper. Iceberg and romaine keep up to a week; others keep one or two days.*
Preparing: *Remove discolored or wilted leaves and the core. Rinse lettuce under cold running water and drain thoroughly.*
Tip: *To core iceberg lettuce, whack stem end on a counter. Twist the core and lift out.*

24-Hour Vegetable Salad

3 **cups torn romaine**
　Salt
　Pepper
　Sugar
1½ **cups shredded Swiss cheese
　　(6 ounces)**
4 **hard-cooked eggs, sliced**
½ **pound bacon, crisp-cooked,
　　drained, and crumbled
　　(10 or 11 slices)**
3 **cups torn leaf lettuce**
1 **10-ounce package frozen
　　peas, thawed (2 cups)**
¾ **cup mayonnaise *or* salad
　　dressing**
2 **tablespoons sliced green
　　onion with tops**

Place romaine in bottom of large bowl; sprinkle with salt, pepper, and sugar. Top with *1 cup* of the cheese. Layer eggs atop cheese, standing some slices on edge, if desired. Sprinkle generously with salt. Next, layer in order *half* of the bacon, the leaf lettuce, and the peas. Spread mayonnaise or salad dressing over top, sealing to edge of bowl. Cover and chill 24 hours or overnight. Garnish with remaining cheese, remaining bacon, and green onion. Toss before serving. Makes 10 to 12 servings.

Lettuce salads usually have to be made at the last minute. This *24-Hour Vegetable Salad* is an exception. A creamy layer of mayonnaise seals in the flavor, and chilling keeps it crisp.

Chili-Pepperoni Salad Bowl

1 medium head iceberg lettuce
3 cups corn chips
4 ounces pepperoni, thinly
   sliced
1 large tomato, chopped
½ cup shredded Cheddar cheese
   (2 ounces)
¼ cup sliced pitted ripe olives
1 15-ounce can chili with beans

Line salad bowl with outer lettuce leaves; cut remaining lettuce into bite-size chunks. Place lettuce chunks, chips, pepperoni, tomato, cheese, and olives in bowl. Heat chili; pour atop salad. Toss lightly. Makes 6 servings.

Braised Lettuce

2 tablespoons finely chopped
   onion
2 tablespoons finely chopped
   carrot
1 tablespoon butter *or* margarine
½ cup water
2 teaspoons sugar
½ teaspoon instant chicken
   bouillon granules
½ teaspoon salt
1 medium head iceberg lettuce,
   shredded (6 cups)
½ of an 8-ounce can water chestnuts,
   drained and sliced
   Snipped parsley
   Toasted slivered almonds
   (optional)

In medium saucepan cook onion and carrot in butter or margarine till tender but not brown. Stir in water, sugar, bouillon granules, and salt; heat and stir till bouillon granules are dissolved. Add shredded lettuce and water chestnuts. Cover and simmer over low heat for 5 to 8 minutes. *Do not overcook.* Drain; transfer to serving dish and top with parsley. Add toasted slivered almonds, if desired. Serve immediately. Makes 6 servings.

Original Caesar Salad

   Garlic Olive Oil
   Caesar Croutons
3 medium heads romaine, chilled
   and broken into 2- or 3-inch
   pieces (16 cups)
2 to 3 tablespoons wine vinegar
1 lemon, halved
2 1-minute coddled eggs*
   Dash Worcestershire sauce
   Whole black pepper
⅓ cup grated Parmesan cheese
   Rolled anchovy fillets
   (optional)

One or more days before serving prepare Garlic Olive Oil. Several hours before serving prepare Caesar Croutons. Chill salad bowl and dinner plates.

At serving time place romaine in *chilled* salad bowl. Drizzle with about ⅓ cup Garlic Olive Oil; drizzle with vinegar. Squeeze lemon over; break in eggs. Add Worcestershire; sprinkle with salt. Generously grind pepper over; sprinkle with cheese. Toss lightly till dressing is well combined and romaine is coated. Add Caesar Croutons; toss once or twice. Serve immediately on *chilled* dinner plates. Garnish with anchovies, if desired. Makes 6 to 8 servings.

Garlic Olive Oil: Slice 6 cloves garlic lengthwise into quarters; combine with 1 cup olive *or* salad oil. Store in covered jar in refrigerator. Remove garlic before using oil.

Caesar Croutons: Cut 3 slices bread into ½-inch cubes. Spread out on baking sheet; pour a little Garlic Olive Oil over bread. Heat at 250° about 1 hour. Sprinkle with grated Parmesan cheese. Store croutons in covered jar in refrigerator.

*To coddle eggs, place eggs in shell in boiling water; remove from heat and let stand 1 minute. Cool slightly.

Mushrooms

Selecting: Since mushrooms are cultivated indoors under controlled conditions, they are always in season. Freshness and shape come first when selecting mushrooms. Look for caps that are closed around the stem. Wilting and wide-open caps are signs of age. Color should be uniform, but depends on the mushroom variety; white, off-white, and tan are the most common. Size alone does not indicate tenderness; popular varieties range in diameter from ¾ inch to 3 inches. Highly perishable, mushrooms should be purchased for immediate use. If not used at once, refrigerate in the original covered carton or in a plastic bag up to two days.

Preparing: Rinse gently in cold water; pat dry. Slice through cap and stem, chop, or use whole.

Serving: Raw mushrooms are tasty in salads. Cooked mushrooms add flavor to soups, casseroles, and other main dishes. Serve sautéed mushrooms as a vegetable or as a topper for steaks or burgers. To sauté, sprinkle 2 cups sliced fresh mushrooms with 1 teaspoon all-purpose flour. Cover; cook slowly in 1 tablespoon butter; stir occasionally. Season to taste.

Mushroom-Sauced Eggs

2 cups fresh mushrooms (5 ounces)
4 teaspoons all-purpose flour
2 tablespoons butter *or* margarine
¾ cup milk
1½ teaspoons Worcestershire sauce
¾ teaspoon dry mustard
½ teaspoon paprika
¼ teaspoon salt
Dash pepper
Poached Eggs
2 English muffins, split and toasted

Chop mushrooms; sprinkle with flour. In 1½-quart saucepan cook mushrooms in butter, covered, for 5 minutes, stirring occasionally. Stir in next 6 ingredients. Cook, uncovered, stirring constantly, till thickened and bubbly; boil for 1 minute. Cover; keep warm. Prepare Poached Eggs. Place Poached Eggs on muffin halves. Spoon sauce over. Serves 4.

Poached Eggs: Add water to a medium skillet to depth of 2 inches; bring just to boiling. Reduce heat. Using 4 eggs, break eggs, one at a time, into a saucer. Slide egg into simmering water. Working quickly, repeat with remaining 3 eggs. Simmer, uncovered, till whites are firm, 3 to 5 minutes. Remove with slotted spoon.

Microwave cooking directions: Chop mushrooms; sprinkle with flour. In a 1-quart nonmetal casserole combine mushrooms and butter. Cook in countertop microwave oven about 3½ minutes, stirring after 2 minutes. Stir in next 6 ingredients. Micro-cook till thickened and bubbly, about 3 minutes, stirring every 30 seconds. Cover; keep warm. Prepare Poached Eggs and serve as above.

Pickled Mushrooms

1 **small onion, thinly sliced
   and separated into rings**
⅓ **cup dry white wine**
⅓ **cup white wine vinegar**
⅓ **cup salad oil**
2 **tablespoons snipped parsley**
1 **small clove garlic, minced**
1 **bay leaf**
1 **teaspoon salt**
¼ **teaspoon dried thyme, crushed
   Dash freshly ground pepper**
4 **cups small fresh whole
   mushrooms (10 ounces)** *or* **2
   8-ounce cans whole
   mushrooms, drained**

In saucepan combine onion, wine, vinegar, salad oil, parsley, garlic, bay leaf, salt, thyme, and pepper; bring to boiling. Add fresh or canned mushrooms and return to boiling. Simmer, uncovered, for 10 minutes. Cool. Transfer to covered container; chill at least 24 hours before serving. Store in refrigerator up to 2 weeks. Makes 2 cups.

Cream of Mushroom Soup

1 **cup sliced fresh mushrooms**
2 **tablespoons chopped onion**
2 **tablespoons butter** *or*
   margarine
2 **tablespoons all-purpose flour**
2 **cups chicken broth**
1 **cup whipping cream**
¼ **teaspoon salt**
¼ **teaspoon ground nutmeg**
⅛ **teaspoon white pepper**

Cook mushrooms and onion in butter or margarine till tender but not brown, about 5 minutes. Blend in flour; add chicken broth. Cook, stirring constantly, till slightly thickened and bubbly. Stir in whipping cream, salt, nutmeg, and white pepper. Heat through. Makes 4 to 6 servings.

Dill-Stuffed Mushrooms

24 **large fresh mushrooms**
2 **tablespoons sliced green onion
   with tops**
2 **tablespoons butter** *or*
   margarine
¼ **cup fine dry bread crumbs**
½ **teaspoon dried dillweed**
⅛ **teaspoon salt**
⅛ **teaspoon Worcestershire sauce**

Remove stems from mushrooms; chop stems. Cook stems and onion in butter till tender. Remove from heat. Stir in bread crumbs, dillweed, salt, and Worcestershire; fill mushroom crowns with bread crumb mixture. Bake on greased baking sheet at 425° for 6 to 8 minutes. Makes 24.

Mushroom Cocktail

⅓ **cup catsup**
1 **tablespoon vinegar**
¼ **teaspoon prepared horseradish
   Lettuce leaves**
1½ **cups shredded lettuce**
12 **medium fresh mushrooms, sliced**

In small bowl combine catsup, vinegar, and horseradish. Chill. Line 6 sherbets with lettuce leaves; top with shredded lettuce. Arrange about ¼ cup sliced mushrooms atop each. Chill. Just before serving, drizzle each with about 1 tablespoon catsup mixture. Makes 6 servings.

Okra

Selecting: *This podded vegetable, a standby with Southern cooks as an ingredient in Creole dishes, is now becoming available everywhere. Peak quantities of okra come to market from June to September. Choose fresh, tender pods, and avoid those that look dull, dry, or shriveled. Both smooth and ridged okra is grown. Depending on the variety, sizes range from thick 3-inch to slender 7-inch pods. Coloring, from deep to light green, also varies with type of okra. Store in a plastic bag in the refrigerator crisper up to two weeks.*

Preparing: *Wash okra pods and cut off stems.*

Cooking: *In covered pan cook in small amount of boiling salted water till tender, 8 to 15 minutes. (Do not use iron, copper, brass, or tin utensils; okra discolors and is unappetizing.)*

Serving: *Dip sliced okra in cornmeal and pan-fry quickly. Sliced into stews and gumbos, okra lends both flavor and thickening.*

Southern Vegetable Medley

4 ounces salt pork
4 fresh ears of corn
½ pound okra, sliced (2 cups)
1 cup water
½ cup chopped onion
1 to 2 teaspoons chili powder
1 teaspoon instant beef bouillon granules
4 medium tomatoes, peeled and cut up

Rinse and chop salt pork. In 10-inch skillet cook salt pork till crisp. Cut corn from cobs. Add corn, fresh okra, water, onion, chili powder, and beef bouillon granules to salt pork in skillet. Bring to boiling; reduce heat. Cover and simmer 20 minutes. Add tomatoes; cover and simmer 10 minutes longer. Makes 8 servings.

Garlic Okra Pickles

3 pounds okra
3 cups water
1 cup white vinegar
¼ cup pickling salt
2 cloves garlic, minced

Pack whole fresh okra into hot, clean pint jars. Combine remaining ingredients; bring to boiling. Slowly pour boiling liquid into jars, leaving ½-inch headspace. Prepare lids according to manufacturer's directions. Wipe jar rim. Adjust lid. Process jars in boiling water bath for 5 minutes (start timing when water returns to boil). Makes 4 pints.

You don't have to live on the Gulf Coast to enjoy flavorful *Creole Gumbo*. This savory
version of seafood-okra stew is made with fresh or frozen okra and canned shrimp and crab meat.

Brunswick Stew

1 6-pound ready-to-cook
   stewing chicken
3 potatoes, peeled and cubed
2 large onions, sliced
2 cups sliced okra *or* 1 10-ounce
   package frozen cut okra
2 17-ounce cans whole kernel
   corn, drained
1 28-ounce can tomatoes
1 10-ounce package frozen lima
   beans
1 tablespoon sugar

Cut up stewing chicken. In large kettle or Dutch oven combine cut-up chicken and 6 cups water. Bring to boiling. Reduce heat and simmer till chicken is tender, 1½ to 2 hours. Remove chicken from broth; cool chicken and broth. Remove meat from bones. Cube meat; discard skin and bones. Skim fat from broth. Add cubed chicken to broth. Add potatoes, sliced onions, fresh or frozen okra, corn, tomatoes, lima beans, sugar, 4 teaspoons salt, and ¼ teaspoon pepper. Cover and simmer till vegetables are tender and flavors are blended, about 30 minutes. Makes 16 servings.

Meatball-Okra Stew

1 slightly beaten egg
¼ cup fine dry bread crumbs
¼ cup milk
½ teaspoon dried oregano,
   crushed
1 pound lean ground beef
4 teaspoons instant beef
   bouillon granules
1 tablespoon Worcestershire
   sauce
1 clove garlic, minced
1 teaspoon chili powder
1½ cups coarsely chopped onion
4 potatoes, peeled and chopped
10 ounces okra, cut up (2 cups)

In mixing bowl combine egg, bread crumbs, milk, oregano, ½ teaspoon salt, and ⅛ teaspoon pepper. Add ground beef and mix well. Shape mixture into 48 small meatballs. In large saucepan combine bouillon granules, Worcestershire, garlic, chili powder, 4 cups water, and ⅛ teaspoon pepper. Bring to boiling; add meatballs and onion. Cover and simmer 20 minutes. Add potatoes and okra; simmer till vegetables are tender, about 10 minutes longer. Makes 8 servings.

Creole Gumbo

½ cup chopped onion
1 clove garlic, minced
3 tablespoons butter
3 tablespoons all-purpose flour
1 16-ounce can tomatoes, cut up
½ cup chopped green pepper
2 bay leaves
1 teaspoon dried oregano,
   crushed
1 teaspoon dried thyme, crushed
¼ to ½ teaspoon bottled hot
   pepper sauce
10 ounces okra, cut up
   (2 cups), *or* 1 10-ounce
   package frozen cut okra
2 4½-ounce cans shrimp, drained
1 7½-ounce can crab meat,
   drained, flaked, and
   cartilage removed
Hot cooked rice

In large saucepan cook onion and garlic in butter till onion is tender but not brown. Blend in flour. Cook, stirring constantly, till flour is golden brown. Stir in undrained tomatoes, green pepper, bay leaves, oregano, thyme, hot pepper sauce, 1½ cups water, and ½ teaspoon salt. Bring to boiling; reduce heat and simmer, covered, 20 minutes.

Remove bay leaves. Stir in the fresh or frozen okra; bring mixture to boiling. Simmer for 5 minutes. Cut up any large shrimp. Stir shrimp and crab meat into okra mixture and heat through, about 5 minutes. Serve the gumbo mixture over hot cooked rice in soup plates. (Traditionally, hot cooked rice is mounded in a heated soup plate and the gumbo spooned around it.) Makes 6 servings.

Onions, Leeks & Shallots

Selecting: *Most varieties of onions are in good supply year-round. Select dry onions or shallots for their bright, thin skins; the bulbs should be firm, thin-necked, and free of blemishes. Store in a cool, dry, well-ventilated area. Green onions and leeks should have firm, white bulbs and bright green tops. Refrigerate in a plastic bag up to a week.*

Preparing: *Peel dry onions and shallots. Leave small boiling onions whole, but cut off ends. Wash green onions and leeks to remove sand. Trim roots and tops, but save 2 to 3 inches of the green tops.*

Cooking: *In a covered pan cook quartered or small whole onions in boiling salted water till tender, 25 to 30 minutes; cook leeks 15 minutes.*

Serving: *Onions add flavor to many dishes. Shallots are usually chopped and used as a seasoning. Leeks and small onions are often served in cream sauce. Add raw mild onions and leeks to salads.*

French Onion Soup

1½ **pounds onions, thinly sliced
   (6 cups)**
 ¼ **cup butter** *or* **margarine**
 3 **10½-ounce cans condensed
   beef broth**
 1 **teaspoon Worcestershire sauce**
 ¼ **teaspoon salt**
 6 **to 8 slices French bread** *or*
   hard rolls, toasted
   Grated Parmesan cheese

In a covered 3-quart saucepan cook sliced onions in butter till tender, about 20 minutes. Add beef broth, Worcestershire sauce, salt, and dash pepper. Bring to boiling.

Sprinkle toast slices with grated Parmesan cheese; place under broiler till cheese is lightly browned. Ladle soup into bowls and float toast slices atop. (Or, place a toast slice on soup in each broiler-proof soup bowl; sprinkle with Parmesan cheese and place bowl under broiler till cheese is lightly browned.) Makes 6 to 8 servings.

Creamed Onions

 3 **medium onions**
 3 **tablespoons butter**
 2 **tablespoons all-purpose flour**
 ¼ **teaspoon salt**
   Dash white pepper
1⅓ **cups milk**
 1 **cup shredded Muenster cheese**

Cut onions into small wedges. In covered pan cook onions in boiling salted water till nearly tender, 8 to 10 minutes. Drain well. In saucepan melt butter; blend in flour, salt, and white pepper. Add milk all at once; cook and stir till thickened and bubbly. Add shredded Muenster cheese; stir till melted. Stir in drained onions; heat through. Garnish with parsley, if desired. Makes 6 to 8 servings.

There's no better way to start a meal than with steaming bowls of *French Onion Soup.*
Use canned beef broth to shortcut preparation without sacrificing any of the classic flavor.

Perfect French-Fried Onions

⅔ **cup milk**
1 **egg**
3 **Bermuda *or* mild white onions,**
   sliced ¼ inch thick and
   separated into rings
1 **cup all-purpose flour**
   Fat for deep-fat frying

In bowl combine milk and egg; beat well. Pour into shallow pan. Drop a few onion rings into pan. With fingers, turn rings till each is well coated. Lift out; drain off excess mixture. Then, drop rings into pan of flour, a few at a time; turn to coat well. Shake to remove excess flour.

Fill French-frying basket only ¼ full of onions. Set basket into deep hot fat (375°). Stir once with a fork to separate. When onion rings are golden brown, remove from fat and drain on paper toweling. To keep onions crisp, don't salt until just before serving. Makes 8 servings.

Oxtail-Leek Stew

⅓ **cup all-purpose flour**
5 **pounds oxtails, disjointed**
¼ **cup shortening**
1 **cup chopped onion**
¾ **cup chopped peeled tomato**
1 **large carrot, quartered**
1 **medium turnip, peeled**
   and quartered
2 **cloves garlic, minced**
   Few sprigs parsley
1 **bay leaf**
2 **10½-ounce cans condensed**
   beef broth
1¼ **cups port**
1 **cup water**
1½ **cups sliced carrots**
2 **cups sliced leeks**

Combine flour, 2 teaspoons salt, and dash pepper. Coat oxtails with flour mixture. In large Dutch oven brown oxtails in hot shortening, turning often; drain off fat. Add onion, tomato, the quartered carrot, turnip, garlic, parsley, and bay leaf. Stir in broth, ¼ *cup* of the port, and water. Bring to boiling; reduce heat. Cover and simmer till oxtails are almost tender, about 1½ hours.

Remove and discard the cooked carrot, turnip, parsley, and bay leaf. Skim off fat. Return mixture to boiling; reduce heat and stir in the remaining 1 cup port. Add 1 teaspoon salt and dash pepper. Simmer, covered, for 30 minutes. Add sliced carrots; simmer 10 minutes longer. Add leeks; simmer till vegetables are just tender, 10 to 15 minutes longer. If desired, serve with boiled potatoes and sprinkle with snipped parsley. Makes 6 to 8 servings.

Shallot Soufflé with Mushroom Sauce

1 **tablespoon butter *or* margarine**
2 **tablespoons grated Parmesan**
   cheese
¼ **cup finely chopped shallots**
¼ **cup butter *or* margarine**
¼ **cup all-purpose flour**
1 **cup milk**
½ **teaspoon salt**
2 **dashes bottled hot pepper**
   sauce
1 **cup shredded Cheddar cheese**
   (4 ounces)
4 **egg yolks**
4 **stiffly beaten egg whites**
   Mushroom Sauce

Spread the 1 tablespoon butter over bottom and sides of a 1½-quart soufflé dish. Sprinkle with the Parmesan cheese.

In saucepan cook shallots in the ¼ cup butter till tender but not brown; blend in flour. Add milk, salt, and hot pepper sauce; cook and stir till thickened and bubbly. Remove from heat. Stir in Cheddar cheese till melted.

Beat egg yolks on high speed of electric mixer till thick and lemon-colored, about 5 minutes. Slowly add cheese mixture, stirring constantly; cool slightly. Slowly pour yolk mixture over stiffly beaten egg whites; fold together well. Turn into prepared dish. Bake at 300° till knife inserted just off-center comes out clean, about 1¼ hours. Serve immediately with Mushroom Sauce. Makes 6 servings.

Mushroom Sauce: In medium skillet cook 2 cups sliced fresh mushrooms (5 ounces) and 2 tablespoons finely chopped shallots in 3 tablespoons butter till tender, 5 to 7 minutes. Add 4 teaspoons all-purpose flour, ⅛ teaspoon salt, and dash pepper; stir till smooth. Add ½ cup whipping cream all at once. Cook and stir till thickened and bubbly.

Oriental Vegetables

Selecting: *Vegetables commonly used in Oriental cooking are diverse. Bean sprouts have a delicate flavor and crunchy texture; look for crisp, plump, white sprouts. Pea pods (also known as sugar peas and snow peas) should be bright green and crisp. Fresh gnarled gingerroot has an ivory interior with a pungent, spicy flavor; select fresh-looking, firm roots. Look for Chinese cabbage, also known as celery cabbage, with a firm, compact head and fresh, crinkled, light green leaves. Bok choy has long white stems and large dark green leaves; look for leaves that are fresh and shiny.*

Preparing: *For bean sprouts, remove roots, if desired; rinse sprouts. Wash pea pods; remove tips and strings (do not shell). Peel gingerroot, if desired; grate, slice, or chop. For Chinese cabbage or bok choy, discard any tough outer stalks and rinse well.*

Serving: *Serve raw Oriental vegetables in salads. Or cook, but very briefly so crispness is retained.*

Oriental Garden Toss

6 ounces pea pods *or*
  1 6-ounce package frozen
  pea pods, thawed
½ cup salad oil
⅓ cup vinegar
2 tablespoons sugar
1 tablespoon soy sauce
¼ teaspoon ground ginger
½ teaspoon salt
⅛ teaspoon freshly ground pepper
3 cups sliced bok choy
3 cups torn leaf lettuce
1 cup bean sprouts
2 tablespoons chopped pimiento

Remove tips and strings from fresh pea pods. In covered pan cook fresh or frozen pea pods in 2 cups boiling salted water for 1 minute; drain well.

In screw-top jar combine oil, vinegar, sugar, soy sauce, ginger, salt, and pepper; cover and shake vigorously. Pour mixture over pea pods; cover and marinate in refrigerator for 1 to 1½ hours.

At serving time combine bok choy, leaf lettuce, bean sprouts, and pimiento in large salad bowl. Add pea pods and marinade. Toss to coat vegetables. Makes 6 to 8 servings.

Sukiyaki

½ **pound beef tenderloin**
6 **to 8 ounces bean curd (tofu)**
1 **cup bean sprouts** *or* **½ of a**
    16-ounce can bean sprouts
2 **ounces fresh water chestnuts,**
    peeled, *or* **½ of an 8-ounce**
    can water chestnuts, drained
½ **of a 5-ounce can bamboo shoots**
1 **tablespoon cooking oil**
1 **tablespoon sugar**
½ **teaspoon instant beef bouillon**
    granules
¼ **cup boiling water**
3 **tablespoons soy sauce**
1 **cup bias-sliced green onion**
    with tops
½ **cup bias-sliced celery**
3 **cups torn bok choy** *or* **small**
    spinach leaves
½ **cup thinly sliced fresh**
    mushrooms
    Hot cooked rice

Partially freeze beef. Slice beef very thinly across the grain. Cube bean curd. Drain canned bean sprouts. Thinly slice fresh or canned water chestnuts. Drain bamboo shoots.

Preheat a large skillet or wok; add oil. Add beef slices; cook quickly, turning meat over and over, just till browned, 1 to 2 minutes. Sprinkle with sugar. Dissolve bouillon granules in boiling water; add soy sauce. Pour over meat. Remove meat from skillet with a slotted spoon. Let soy mixture bubble. Add onion and celery. Continue cooking and toss-stirring over high heat about 1 minute. Add bean curd, bean sprouts, water chestnuts, bamboo shoots, bok choy or spinach, and mushrooms. Return meat to pan. Cook and stir just till heated through. Serve with hot cooked rice. Pass soy sauce, if desired. Makes 2 or 3 servings.

Hot Firepot

1 **2-ounce package** *dried*
    mushrooms
1 **pound beef flank steak**
½ **cup sesame oil** *or* **cooking oil**
¼ **teaspoon garlic salt**
1 **pound fresh** *or* **frozen shrimp,**
    shelled and deveined
½ **pound fresh** *or* **frozen white**
    fish
2 **cups spinach**
1 **head Chinese cabbage**
4 **to 6 cups chicken broth**
4 **ounces fresh whole bamboo**
    shoots, cut up, *or* **1 5-ounce**
    can bamboo shoots, drained
    Hong Kong Dip
1 **cup fine noodles**

Soak mushrooms in water according to package directions. Partially freeze beef. Slice beef across the grain into ¼-inch-wide strips. Combine oil and garlic salt; marinate meat in oil mixture for a few hours. Drain well. Thaw shrimp, if frozen. Sprinkle shrimp with 1 teaspoon salt. Let stand 10 minutes; rinse. Thaw fish, if frozen. Cut fish into ½-inch cubes; sprinkle lightly with salt. Cut fresh spinach and Chinese cabbage into 2-inch-wide strips; halve strips crosswise.

Pour broth into firepot till about half full; heat to boiling according to firepot manufacturer's directions. (Or, pour broth into metal fondue pot till about half full; heat to boiling on range top. Transfer to fondue burner.) Arrange all of the meats and vegetables in Oriental cooking baskets, or spear with fondue forks; cook in hot broth till done. Serve with Hong Kong Dip. Drop noodles into the remaining boiling broth. Cook till tender but still firm. Ladle soup into bowls. Serves 6.

Hong Kong Dip: In small saucepan heat 1 cup sesame oil *or* cooking oil. Remove from heat. Stir in 2 tablespoons soy sauce and ¼ teaspoon bottled hot pepper sauce.

Buttered Pea Pods

12 **ounces pea pods (4 cups)**
    or **2 6-ounce packages**
    frozen pea pods
½ **teaspoon sugar**
2 **tablespoons butter**

Remove tips and strings from fresh pea pods. In saucepan combine fresh or frozen pea pods, sugar, ½ cup water, and 1 teaspoon salt. Cover; bring to boiling. Boil 2 minutes; drain well. Heat and stir butter till light golden; toss with pea pods. Season with salt and pepper. Makes 6 to 8 servings.

Oriental vegetables contribute a variety of colors, flavors, and textures to Japanese
Sukiyaki. It takes only a few minutes to cook, so cut up meat and vegetables before you begin.

Parsnips

Selecting: You'll find parsnips in the market all year, but they're most plentiful during the fall and winter months. Buy firm, well-shaped vegetables that are free of major blemishes. The best ones to buy are small to medium in size, as larger roots tend to be woody. Wrap parsnips tightly and store in the refrigerator crisper up to two weeks.

Preparing: Wash parsnips, then scrape or peel to remove outer skin. Leave whole or cut in slices, julienne strips, or halves.

Cooking: In covered pan cook parsnips in a small amount of boiling salted water till tender, 25 to 40 minutes for whole parsnips; 15 to 20 minutes for strips, halves, or slices. For a menu variation, arrange a few cut-up parsnips around a beef pot roast during the last 40 to 60 minutes of cooking; baste the vegetables frequently with pan juices.

Serving: Serve hot cooked parsnips with butter and sprinkle with a little sugar, if desired. Serve with a cream sauce or a glaze sprinkled with nutmeg, or mash as you would potatoes. Add rich flavor to soups and stews with a few cut-up parsnips, or deep-fat fry thin slices for a snack that resembles potato chips.

Whipped Parsnips and Sweet Potatoes

1 pound parsnips
1 pound sweet potatoes
2 tablespoons butter
½ teaspoon salt
¼ teaspoon ground allspice
Milk (optional)

Peel and slice parsnips and potatoes. In covered pan cook vegetables in a small amount of boiling salted water till tender, about 15 minutes; drain. In mixer bowl combine hot vegetables, butter, salt, and allspice. Beat till smooth; add milk, if needed, to make fluffy. If desired, top with sliced green onion with tops and more butter. Serves 4 to 6.

Hawaiian-Style Parsnips

2 pounds parsnips (10 medium)
2 tablespoons brown sugar
1 tablespoon cornstarch
1 8¼-ounce can crushed pineapple
½ teaspoon shredded orange peel
½ cup orange juice
2 tablespoons butter

Peel and slice parsnips. Cook as directed above; drain well. In large saucepan blend brown sugar, cornstarch, and ¾ teaspoon salt; stir in undrained pineapple, orange peel, and orange juice. Cook and stir till thickened and bubbly. Add butter; stir till melted. Add parsnips to sauce. Cover and simmer 5 minutes. Makes 6 to 8 servings.

Peas

Selecting: *The peak season for fresh peas is May through August; look for bright green, crisp, well-filled pods. Choose fresh black-eyed peas with crisp, full pods. Refrigerate peas in their pods and use as soon as possible. Store all dry peas in a cool, dry place.*

Preparing: *Shell fresh peas; wash. Rinse dry peas. Split peas do not need to be soaked. Place dry whole or black-eyed peas in kettle with about 4 times as much water as peas. Cover pan; soak overnight. (Or, bring to boil; simmer 2 minutes. Remove from heat. Cover; soak 1 hour.) Do not drain.*

Cooking: *In covered pan cook fresh peas in small amount of boiling salted water till just tender, 10 to 12 minutes; cook fresh black-eyed peas till tender. In covered pan cook unsoaked split peas in about 4 times as much water as vegetables for 1½ to 2 hours. Cook soaked dry whole or black-eyed peas for 1 to 1½ hours.*

Serving: *Offer buttered peas with an herb for a fresh-tasting dish; try basil, marjoram, or sage. Creamed peas and new potatoes is a popular combination. Dry peas or black-eyed peas are tasty additions to soup.*

Deluxe Peas and Mushrooms

2 cups shelled peas *or* 1
    10-ounce package frozen peas
1 cup sliced fresh mushrooms
¼ cup chopped onion
2 tablespoons butter
1 teaspoon sugar
1 tablespoon chopped pimiento

Cook fresh peas as directed above. (Or, cook frozen peas according to package directions.) Drain well.

Cook mushrooms and onion in butter till tender. Stir in sugar, ½ teaspoon salt, and dash pepper. Add cooked peas and pimiento. Cover and heat through. Makes 4 servings.

Oven-Style Peas

1 20-ounce package frozen peas
1 2½-ounce jar sliced mushrooms,
    drained
¼ cup chopped onion
2 tablespoons butter
¼ teaspoon dried savory, crushed

In a 1½-quart casserole combine frozen peas, mushrooms, onion, butter, savory, 1 tablespoon water, ¼ teaspoon salt, and dash pepper. Cover and bake at 350° till peas are tender, 45 to 50 minutes, stirring after 20 minutes. Serves 8.

Pea-Cheese Salad (pictured on page 206)

2 cups shelled peas *or*
  1 10-ounce package frozen
  peas *or* 1 17-ounce can peas
1 cup cubed Cheddar cheese
2 hard-cooked eggs, chopped
¼ cup chopped celery
2 tablespoons chopped onion
2 tablespoons chopped pimiento
⅓ cup mayonnaise *or* salad
  dressing
½ teaspoon salt
¼ teaspoon bottled hot pepper
  sauce
⅛ teaspoon pepper
6 medium tomatoes
  Lettuce leaves

Cook fresh peas as directed on page 263. (Or, cook frozen peas according to package directions.) Thoroughly drain the cooked or canned peas. Cool cooked peas.

In large bowl combine peas, cheese cubes, hard-cooked eggs, celery, onion, and pimiento. Combine mayonnaise or salad dressing, salt, hot pepper sauce, and pepper. Add to pea mixture; toss to combine. Cover and refrigerate several hours or overnight. Stir mixture well.

Cut each tomato into 8 wedges, cutting to, but not through, bottom of tomato. On salad plates, place tomatoes atop lettuce leaves; fill with pea mixture. Makes 6 servings.

Creamed Peas and Onions (pictured on page 206)

2 cups shelled peas *or* 1
  10-ounce package frozen peas
1 cup whole pearl onions *or*
  frozen small whole onions
1 tablespoon butter *or* margarine
1 tablespoon all-purpose flour
½ teaspoon salt
  Dash white pepper
1 cup milk
  Grated Parmesan cheese

In a covered saucepan cook fresh peas and pearl or frozen onions in boiling salted water till tender, about 10 minutes. (If using frozen peas, add to onions only during the last 5 minutes.) Drain peas and onions well.

Meanwhile, melt butter or margarine in saucepan over low heat. Blend in flour, salt, and white pepper. Add milk all at once; cook and stir till thickened and bubbly. Pour over hot vegetables; stir to coat vegetables. Serve in sauce dishes. Pass Parmesan cheese. Makes 4 servings.

Springtime Peas

3 to 6 lettuce leaves
2 cups shelled peas *or* 1
  10-ounce package frozen peas
¼ cup sliced green onion
  with tops
1 teaspoon sugar
  Dash dried thyme, crushed
1 tablespoon butter *or* margarine

Moisten lettuce leaves, leaving a few drops of water clinging. Line bottom of a 10-inch skillet with lettuce leaves. Top with fresh or frozen peas and green onion. Sprinkle with sugar, thyme, ½ teaspoon salt, and dash pepper. Cover tightly and cook over low heat till peas are tender, 18 to 20 minutes. Remove lettuce. Drain peas well; dot with butter or margarine. Makes 4 servings.

Creole Peas

2 cups shelled peas *or*
  1 10-ounce package frozen
  peas *or* 1 17-ounce can peas
¼ cup chopped onion
¼ cup chopped green pepper
2 tablespoons butter
1 8-ounce can tomatoes, cut up
2 teaspoons cornstarch

Cook fresh peas as directed on page 263. (Or, cook frozen peas according to package directions.) Thoroughly drain the cooked or canned peas. In saucepan cook onion and green pepper in butter till tender but not brown. Drain tomatoes, reserving liquid. Add tomatoes to cooked onion. Stir in peas, ½ teaspoon salt, and dash pepper. Blend tomato liquid into cornstarch; stir into pea mixture. Cook and stir till thickened and bubbly. Makes 4 servings.

Quick Creamed Peas

2 10-ounce packages frozen
    peas
¼ cup milk
1 4-ounce carton whipped cream
    cheese with chives

Cook peas according to package directions; drain well. In saucepan stir milk into the cream cheese; heat and stir till warm. Add peas. Stir gently to coat. Serve in individual sauce dishes. Makes 6 to 8 servings.

Pea and Celery Bake

1 10-ounce package frozen
    peas
1 stalk celery, bias-cut in
    1-inch pieces (4½ cups)
½ cup chopped onion
2 teaspoons instant chicken
    bouillon granules
1 8-ounce can tomato sauce
2 tablespoons butter
½ teaspoon dried oregano,
    crushed
⅓ cup grated Parmesan cheese

In colander or strainer rinse peas with hot water to thaw. In saucepan mix celery, onion, bouillon granules, and ½ cup *water*. Cover; bring to boiling. Reduce heat and simmer till celery is tender, 12 to 15 minutes. Stir in peas, tomato sauce, butter, and oregano.

Turn mixture into 1½-quart casserole. Bake, uncovered, at 400° till done, about 30 minutes. Sprinkle with Parmesan cheese. Makes 6 to 8 servings.

Dutch Pea Soup

1 pound bulk pork sausage
1 pound dry green split peas
7 cups water
2 fresh pigs' feet (1¼ pounds)
1 cup finely chopped onion
1 large potato, peeled and
    shredded (1 cup)
2 teaspoons salt

Shape sausage into ¾-inch balls; brown on all sides in Dutch oven. Drain, reserving 2 tablespoons fat in pan. Rinse peas; add to pan. Stir in water, pigs' feet, onion, potato, and salt. Bring to boiling. Reduce heat; cover and simmer for 1½ hours. Remove pigs' feet; cut off any meat and return to soup. Discard bones. Heat soup; season to taste. Serves 8 to 10.

Chilled Pea Soup

2 cups shelled peas *or* 1 10-ounce
    package frozen peas
2 cups shredded lettuce
1 13¾-ounce can chicken
    broth
⅓ cup water
¼ cup tomato juice
¼ cup finely chopped green
    onion
1 tablespoon snipped parsley
½ teaspoon salt
¼ teaspoon white pepper
¼ teaspoon dried thyme,
    crushed
½ cup whipping cream

In 2-quart saucepan combine peas, lettuce, chicken broth, water, tomato juice, onion, parsley, salt, white pepper, and thyme. Bring to boiling. Reduce heat; cover and simmer 20 minutes. Turn into blender container; cover and blend till smooth. Cool slightly; stir in whipping cream. Cover and chill. If desired, garnish with sour cream and fresh mint. Makes 4 servings.

Minted New Peas

½ cup chopped green onion
   with tops
3 tablespoons butter
2 cups shelled peas *or* 1
   10-ounce package frozen peas
1 tablespoon finely chopped
   fresh mint leaves
1 teaspoon sugar
1 teaspoon lemon juice
¼ teaspoon salt
¼ teaspoon dried rosemary,
   crushed

Cook green onion in butter till tender. Add fresh or frozen peas, chopped fresh mint, sugar, lemon juice, salt, rosemary, and 2 tablespoons water. Cover and cook till peas are just tender, 10 to 12 minutes, adding a little more water as necessary. Garnish with lemon twist and fresh mint leaves, if desired. Makes 4 servings.

French Canadian Split Pea Soup

1 pound dry green split peas
1 meaty ham bone
1 cup chopped onion
1 teaspoon instant chicken
   bouillon granules
½ teaspoon salt
¼ teaspoon pepper
1 cup sliced carrot
1 cup chopped celery
2 slices bacon
½ cup light cream
2 tablespoons butter

Rinse peas. In kettle mix peas, ham bone, onion, bouillon granules, salt, pepper, and 8 cups water. Bring to boiling. Reduce heat; cover and simmer 1½ hours, stirring often.
   Remove ham bone; chop meat. Return meat to soup; add carrot and celery. Simmer 30 minutes. Cook bacon till crisp; drain and crumble. Stir bacon, light cream, and butter into soup; heat through. Makes 8 servings.

Ham Hocks and Black-Eyed Peas

3 cups dry black-eyed peas
3 pounds ham hocks
1¼ cups chopped onion
1 cup chopped celery
1 bay leaf
1 teaspoon salt
⅛ teaspoon cayenne
10 ounces okra, cut up (2 cups),
   or 1 10-ounce package
   frozen cut okra

Place dry peas in a 6-quart kettle or Dutch oven and add 12 cups water. Soak as directed on page 263. *Do not drain.*
   Stir in ham hocks, onion, celery, bay leaf, salt, and cayenne. Bring to boiling. Reduce heat; cover and simmer till ham hocks are tender and peas are done, about 1½ hours. Stir in fresh or frozen okra; cook till okra is very tender, 10 to 15 minutes. Remove bay leaf. Season to taste with salt and pepper. Makes 6 servings.

Hoppin' John

1 cup dry black-eyed peas
8 cups water
6 slices bacon
¾ cup chopped onion
1 clove garlic, minced
1 cup regular rice
2 teaspoons salt
¼ teaspoon pepper

Soak dry peas, using 8 cups water, as directed on page 263. Drain mixture, reserving *6 cups* of the liquid.
   In heavy 3-quart saucepan cook bacon, onion, and garlic till bacon is crisp and onion is tender. Remove bacon; drain. Crumble and set aside. Stir peas, rice, salt, pepper, and reserved liquid into onion mixture. Bring to boiling; reduce heat. Cover; simmer 1 hour, stirring occasionally. To serve, stir in crumbled bacon. Makes 8 servings.

Peppers

Selecting: *This family ranges from the common sweet bell pepper to the extremely hot chili pepper. Although usually sold while still green, bell peppers will turn bright red if allowed to mature fully. Look for well-shaped, firm, unblemished vegetables that have a bright color. Store in refrigerator crisper, but plan to use within a few days.*

Preparing: *Remove the stems, seeds, and inner membranes of bell peppers before using. Fresh or dried hot peppers must be handled very carefully because the oil from the peppers can burn your eyes or skin. In fact, it's a good idea to wear rubber gloves and hold the peppers under cold running water during preparation. For hot peppers, remove the stems, seeds (these are very hot), and inner membranes.*

Cooking: *Precook bell peppers that are to be stuffed by immersing in boiling salted water for 3 to 5 minutes. Cook hot peppers as directed in specific recipes.*

Serving: *Green peppers are flavorful additions to salads, soups, dips, and casseroles. Hot peppers are particularly popular in Southwestern and Mexican dishes.*

Garden-Stuffed Peppers (pictured on page 268)

4 large green peppers
3 or 4 fresh ears of corn *or*
   1 12-ounce can whole kernel
   corn, drained
¼ cup chopped onion
2 tablespoons butter *or*
   margarine
1 cup shelled baby lima
   beans, cooked and drained,
   or 1 10-ounce package frozen
   baby lima beans, cooked and
   drained
1 large tomato, chopped
½ teaspoon dried rosemary,
   crushed
¾ cup soft bread crumbs
   (1 slice) (optional)
1 tablespoon butter *or* margarine,
   melted (optional)

Remove tops from green peppers. Cut peppers in half lengthwise and remove seeds. Cook peppers in boiling salted water for 3 to 5 minutes; invert to drain. If using fresh corn, cut off tips of corn kernels. Carefully scrape cobs with dull edge of knife; measure 1½ cups corn. In covered pan cook fresh corn in a small amount of boiling salted water till done, 12 to 15 minutes; drain.

Cook onion in the 2 tablespoons butter or margarine till tender but not brown. Stir in cooked or canned corn, lima beans, chopped tomato, and rosemary.

Season green pepper shells with salt and pepper. Fill peppers with vegetable mixture. If desired, toss soft bread crumbs with the melted butter or margarine; sprinkle atop peppers. Place in a 13x9x2-inch baking dish. Bake at 350° for 30 minutes. Makes 8 servings.

Garden-Stuffed Peppers are heaped with a corn-tomato-lima bean filling (see recipe, page 267). During the off-season, substitute canned corn and frozen limas for their fresh counterparts.

Chilies Rellenos Bake

2 4-ounce cans green chili
    peppers (6 chili peppers)
6 ounces Monterey Jack cheese
4 beaten eggs
⅓ cup milk
½ cup all-purpose flour
½ teaspoon baking powder
½ teaspoon salt
½ cup shredded Cheddar cheese

Drain peppers; halve lengthwise and remove seeds. Cut Monterey Jack cheese into strips to fit inside peppers. Wrap each pepper around a strip of Monterey Jack cheese; place in a greased 10x6x2-inch baking dish. Combine eggs and milk; beat in flour, baking powder, and salt till smooth. Pour over peppers. Sprinkle Cheddar cheese atop. Bake at 350° till golden, about 30 minutes. Makes 6 servings.

Home-Canned Red Pepper Relish

24 sweet red peppers, halved and
    seeded
7 medium onions, halved
3 cups sugar
3 cups vinegar
2 tablespoons salt

Thinly slice peppers and onions, or use coarse blade to grind peppers and onions. Reserve vegetable juices. In 4- to 6-quart kettle or Dutch oven combine reserved juices, peppers, onions, sugar, vinegar, and salt. Bring to boiling. Reduce heat; simmer 30 minutes. Pour into hot, clean half-pint jars, leaving ½-inch headspace. Prepare lids according to manufacturer's directions. Wipe jar rim. Adjust lid on jar. Process in boiling water bath 15 minutes (start timing as soon as jars are placed in water). Makes 10 half-pints.

Beef in Pepper Cups

6 medium green peppers
1 pound ground beef
½ cup chopped onion
¾ teaspoon salt
    Dash pepper
1 16-ounce can tomatoes, cut up
½ cup regular rice
½ cup water
1 teaspoon Worcestershire sauce
½ teaspoon chili powder
1 cup shredded sharp American
    cheese (4 ounces)

Remove tops and seeds from green peppers; chop enough of the tops to make ¼ cup. Cook whole green peppers in boiling salted water for 3 to 5 minutes; invert to drain. Sprinkle insides of peppers lightly with salt. In skillet cook beef, onion, and the ¼ cup chopped green pepper till meat is brown and vegetables are tender. Drain off excess fat. Season with the ¾ teaspoon salt and pepper. Add tomatoes, uncooked rice, water, Worcestershire, and chili powder. Cover and simmer till rice is tender, 15 to 20 minutes. Stir in *half* the cheese. Stuff peppers with meat mixture. Bake in 12x7½x2-inch baking dish at 350° for 25 to 30 minutes. Sprinkle with remaining cheese; return to oven till cheese melts, 2 to 3 minutes longer. Makes 6 servings.

Hot Pickled Peppers

1 pound red, green, or yellow
    hot peppers (8 cups)
4 heads fresh dill or 2 table-
    spoons dillseed (optional)
3 cups water
1 cup white vinegar
2 tablespoons pickling salt
1 tablespoon sugar
2 cloves garlic, minced
¼ teaspoon crushed dried red
    pepper

Make 2 small slits in each hot pepper (wear rubber gloves to prevent burning hands). Pack peppers into hot, clean pint jars, leaving ½-inch headspace. If desired, place *1 head* of the fresh dill *or 1½ teaspoons* of the dillseed in *each* jar. In saucepan combine water, white vinegar, pickling salt, sugar, garlic, and crushed red pepper; bring to boiling. Pour hot pickling liquid over peppers, leaving ½-inch headspace. Prepare lids according to manufacturer's directions. Wipe jar rim. Adjust lid on jar. Process jars in boiling water bath for 10 minutes (start timing when water returns to boiling). Makes 4 pints.

Potatoes

Selecting: *Potato varieties range in shape from oblong to round, and in skin color from creamy white to red and russet brown. Although there are some all-purpose varieties, many are best suited to a specific use. In general, round potatoes have firm, waxy interiors that are best for boiling. Long, oval potatoes usually have mealy interiors and are best for baking, frying, or mashing. New potatoes are simply tiny, immature potatoes. Choose firm, smooth potatoes with shallow eyes. Avoid cut, sprouted, or blemished vegetables and those with patches of green on the skin. Store potatoes in a cool (about 55°), dark place.*

Preparing: *Use a knife or vegetable peeler to peel potatoes. If baking or cooking potatoes with the skins on, scrub thoroughly with a vegetable brush and remove any sprouts and green areas. After cooking, the skins peel off easily. Be sure to prick the potato skins before baking.*

Cooking: *Baking and boiling are the most common ways to cook potatoes. Bake potatoes at 425° for 40 to 60 minutes. Bake foil-wrapped potatoes at 350° till done, about 1½ hours.*

In covered pan cook potatoes in boiling salted water till tender. Allow 25 to 40 minutes for whole potatoes, 20 to 25 minutes for quartered potatoes, 12 to 15 minutes for tiny new potatoes, and 10 to 15 minutes for cubed potatoes.

Hashed Brown Omelet

3 medium potatoes*
4 slices bacon
¼ cup chopped onion
¼ cup chopped green pepper
½ teaspoon salt
4 beaten eggs
¼ cup milk
¼ teaspoon salt
¼ teaspoon dried thyme, crushed
   Dash pepper
1 cup shredded Swiss cheese
   (4 ounces)

In covered pan cook whole potatoes in enough boiling salted water to cover till almost tender, 20 to 25 minutes; drain and chill. Peel potatoes; shred to make 3 cups. *(Or, substitute cooked packaged hashed brown potatoes.)

In 10-inch skillet cook bacon till crisp; drain, reserving 2 tablespoons drippings in skillet. Crumble bacon and set aside. Combine potatoes, onion, green pepper, and the ½ teaspoon salt; pat into skillet. Cook over low heat till underside is crisp and brown, about 20 minutes. Combine eggs, milk, the ¼ teaspoon salt, thyme, and pepper. Stir in bacon and cheese; pour over potatoes. Cover; cook over low heat till surface is set but still shiny, 8 to 10 minutes. Loosen edges of omelet; cut in wedges. Makes 4 servings.

Fresh Fries with Onion

4 cups sliced peeled potatoes
1 cup sliced onion
3 tablespoons bacon drippings

Combine potatoes and onion; season with salt and pepper. In skillet cook, covered, in drippings for 10 minutes. Uncover; turn and cook potatoes on the other side 5 to 10 minutes, loosening occasionally. Makes 6 to 8 servings.

Scalloped Potatoes

6 to 8 medium potatoes, peeled
  and thinly sliced (6 cups)
¼ cup finely chopped onion
⅓ cup all-purpose flour
1½ teaspoons salt
⅛ teaspoon pepper
2 cups milk

Place *half* the potatoes in a greased 2-quart casserole. Add *half* the onion. Sift *half* the flour over; sprinkle with *half* the salt and pepper. Repeat layers. Pour milk over all. If desired, sprinkle top with 3 tablespoons buttered fine dry bread crumbs. Cover and bake at 350° for 1¼ hours. Uncover; continue baking till potatoes are done, 15 to 30 minutes longer. Makes 6 servings.

Grilled Potato and Onion Bake

4 large baking potatoes, peeled
2 medium onions
⅓ cup grated Parmesan cheese
  Salt
  Pepper
2 tablespoons butter *or*
  margarine

Slice potatoes and onions onto a 24x18-inch sheet of buttered heavy-duty foil. Sprinkle with Parmesan cheese, salt, and pepper; mix lightly on foil. Slice the 2 tablespoons butter over all. Seal foil with double fold. Place on grill; cook over *slow* coals till vegetables are tender, 50 to 55 minutes, turning often. Makes 6 servings.

Vichyssoise

4 leeks, sliced (without tops)
1 medium onion, sliced
¼ cup butter *or* margarine
5 medium potatoes, peeled
  and thinly sliced
4 cups chicken broth
1 tablespoon salt
2 cups milk
2 cups light cream
1 cup whipping cream
  Snipped chives

In saucepan cook leeks and onion in butter or margarine till tender but not brown. Add potatoes, broth, and salt. Cook for 35 to 40 minutes. Rub through very fine sieve, or place in blender container; cover and blend till smooth.

Return to heat; add milk and light cream. Season to taste with salt and pepper. Bring to boiling. Cool. Stir in whipping cream. Chill thoroughly before serving. Garnish with snipped chives. Makes 8 servings.

Crunch-Top Potatoes

¼ cup butter *or* margarine,
  melted
2 16-ounce cans sliced potatoes,
  drained
1 cup shredded Cheddar
  cheese (4 ounces)
¾ cup crushed cornflakes
1 teaspoon paprika

Pour butter into 13x9x2-inch baking pan. Add potatoes in single layer; turn once in butter. Combine cheese, crushed cornflakes, and paprika; sprinkle over potatoes. Bake at 375° about 20 minutes. Makes 6 servings.

Potatoes and Eggs au Gratin

4 **medium potatoes (1½ pounds)**
¼ **cup chopped onion**
1 **tablespoon butter *or* margarine**
3 **tablespoons all-purpose flour**
1 **cup dairy sour cream**
¾ **cup shredded sharp American cheese (3 ounces)**
½ **cup milk**
2 **tablespoons snipped parsley**
1 **teaspoon salt**
⅛ **teaspoon paprika**
⅛ **teaspoon pepper**
4 **hard-cooked eggs, sliced**
1 **large tomato, peeled and cut in small wedges**
¾ **cup soft bread crumbs (1 slice)**
1 **tablespoon butter *or* margarine, melted**

In covered pan cook whole potatoes in enough boiling salted water to cover till almost tender, 20 to 25 minutes; drain. Peel and slice cooked potatoes (should have about 3 cups).

Meanwhile, in saucepan cook onion in 1 tablespoon butter or margarine till tender. Blend in flour. Stir in sour cream, shredded cheese, milk, parsley, salt, paprika, and pepper. Cook and stir over low heat till cheese melts. Combine sour cream mixture and sliced potatoes.

In 1½-quart casserole spread *half* the potato mixture. Top with egg slices and tomato wedges. Spoon remaining potato mixture atop. Toss bread crumbs with the melted butter; sprinkle atop. Bake at 350° for 45 to 50 minutes. Garnish with additional tomato wedges, hard-cooked egg wedges, and parsley, if desired. Makes 4 servings.

German-Style New Potato Salad

1 **pound tiny new potatoes**
2 **cups torn lettuce**
1 **cup torn curly endive**
2 **hard-cooked eggs, chopped**
¼ **cup thinly sliced radishes**
3 **tablespoons sliced green onion with tops**
6 **slices bacon**
⅓ **cup vinegar**
1 **teaspoon seasoned salt**
¼ **teaspoon celery seed**
⅛ **teaspoon pepper**

Peel strip around center of each potato. Cook potatoes in boiling water as directed on page 270. Drain. Halve any large potatoes. In bowl combine cooked potatoes, lettuce, curly endive, eggs, radishes, and green onion.

In skillet cook bacon till crisp. Drain, reserving ⅓ cup drippings. Crumble bacon; add to potato mixture. To reserved drippings in skillet add vinegar, seasoned salt, celery seed, and pepper. Heat to boiling; pour over potato mixture. Toss quickly; serve at once. Makes 4 to 6 servings.

Calico Potato Salad

7 **medium potatoes, cooked, peeled, and cubed**
½ **cup chopped cucumber**
½ **cup chopped onion**
¼ **cup chopped green pepper**
3 **tablespoons chopped pimiento**
1½ **teaspoons salt**
¾ **teaspoon celery seed**
¼ **teaspoon pepper**
2 **hard-cooked eggs**
⅓ **cup mayonnaise *or* salad dressing**
3 **tablespoons vinegar**
2 **tablespoons sugar**
1 **tablespoon prepared mustard**
½ **cup whipping cream**
Lettuce

Stir together cubed potatoes, cucumber, onion, green pepper, pimiento, salt, celery seed, and pepper. Reserve 1 hard-cooked egg yolk. Coarsely chop the white and remaining hard-cooked egg. Add chopped eggs to potato mixture; chill. Blend mayonnaise or salad dressing, vinegar, sugar, and mustard; whip cream and fold into mayonnaise mixture. About ½ hour before serving, toss with potato mixture. To serve, spoon into lettuce-lined bowl. Sieve the reserved egg yolk over salad. Makes 6 servings.

Vary the potato course of the menu with hearty, layered *Potatoes and Eggs au Gratin,* or *German-Style New Potato Salad* enhanced by bacon and lettuce and spiked with a zesty dressing.

French Fries

Baking potatoes, peeled
Fat for deep-fat frying
Salt

Cut potatoes lengthwise in ⅜-inch-wide strips. Fry potatoes, a few at a time, in deep hot fat (360°) till crisp and golden, 6 to 7 minutes. Drain on paper toweling. (For crisper French fries, fry potatoes at 360° till lightly browned, about 5 minutes. Drain on paper toweling and cool. Just before serving, return French fries to fat at 360° for 2 minutes more.) Sprinkle potatoes immediately with salt. Serve at once.

Potato Salad Roll

3 medium potatoes, peeled and
   quartered
⅓ cup mayonnaise
1 teaspoon salt
½ teaspoon paprika
3 hard-cooked eggs, finely
   chopped
½ cup chopped celery
2 tablespoons finely chopped
   onion
1 cup cream-style cottage cheese
2 tablespoons finely chopped
   green pepper
2 tablespoons chopped pimiento
2 tablespoons mayonnaise

Cook potatoes in boiling water as directed on page 270. Mash potatoes; *do not add liquid.* Combine mashed potatoes, the ⅓ cup mayonnaise, salt, and paprika; stir in eggs, celery, and onion. Chill thoroughly.

Pat potato mixture on foil to a 12x9-inch rectangle. Drain cottage cheese. Combine cottage cheese, green pepper, pimiento, and the 2 tablespoons mayonnaise; spread atop potato mixture to within 1 inch of edges. Beginning with narrow side, lift foil and gently roll up potato mixture jelly-roll fashion. Chill thoroughly. Cut well-chilled potato roll into slices. Makes 6 servings.

Twice-Baked Potatoes

4 medium baking potatoes
2 tablespoons butter *or*
   margarine
   Milk
1 2-ounce can chopped
   mushrooms, drained
2 slices American cheese,
   halved diagonally
   Paprika

Scrub potatoes thoroughly and prick with a fork. Bake potatoes as directed on page 270.

Cut a lengthwise slice from top of each potato; discard skin from slice. Reserving potato shells, scoop out the insides and add to potato portions from top slices; mash. Add butter. Beat in enough milk to make a stiff consistency. Season to taste with salt and pepper. Stir in mushrooms.

Pile mashed potato mixture into potato shells. Place in 10x6x2-inch baking dish. Return to oven; bake at 425° till lightly browned, 20 to 25 minutes. Place cheese atop potatoes; sprinkle with paprika. Bake till cheese melts, 2 to 3 minutes longer. Makes 4 servings.

Microwave cooking directions: Scrub potatoes; prick with fork. In countertop microwave oven arrange potatoes on paper toweling, leaving at least 1 inch between potatoes. Micro-cook, uncovered, till potatoes are done, 13 to 15 minutes for four potatoes. (Allow 6 to 8 minutes for two potatoes; 17 to 19 minutes for six potatoes.) Halfway through cooking time, rearrange potatoes and turn over.

Prepare potato shells and mashed potato mixture as above. Pile mashed potato mixture into potato shells. Place in 10x6x2-inch nonmetal baking dish. Micro-cook, uncovered, till potatoes are heated through, about 5 minutes, rearranging potatoes twice. Place cheese atop potatoes. Sprinkle with paprika. Micro-cook 30 seconds longer.

Spinach

Selecting: *Look for large, fresh-looking leaves, and avoid spinach that's wilted or yellowed. Store covered in the refrigerator crisper and plan to use soon after purchasing.*
Preparing: *It's important to wash spinach thoroughly to remove sand particles. Rather than washing each leaf separately under cold water, place the leaves in a pan of lukewarm water. After a few minutes, lift out and drain leaves; discard the water. Repeat until no sand collects in the pan. To crisp the leaves, add crushed ice to spinach and refrigerate about 1 hour.*
Cooking: *For best flavor, cook spinach with a very small amount of water. In fact, if you use a tightly covered saucepan, you can cook spinach with only the water that clings to the leaves. Reduce heat when steam begins to form, and cook 3 to 5 minutes longer. Turn leaves frequently while cooking.*
Serving: *Torn raw spinach is attractive and delicious in tossed salads. Add allspice, basil, cinnamon, or nutmeg to spinach while cooking.*

Chinese Spinach

1 pound spinach (12 cups)
2 tablespoons cooking oil
2 tablespoons soy sauce
½ teaspoon sugar
½ cup sliced water chestnuts
2 tablespoons chopped onion

Cut fresh spinach stems into 1-inch pieces; tear leaves into bite-size pieces. In large covered saucepan simmer spinach with a small amount of water for 3 minutes; drain well. Heat oil, soy, and sugar in skillet; add spinach, water chestnuts, and onion. Cook and toss till spinach is well-coated and heated through, 2 to 3 minutes. Makes 4 servings.

Scalloped Spinach

2 10-ounce packages frozen
    chopped spinach
¾ cup milk
¾ cup shredded American cheese
3 beaten eggs
3 tablespoons chopped onion
1 cup soft bread crumbs
1 tablespoon butter, melted

Cook spinach according to package directions; drain well. Mix with milk, ½ *cup* of the cheese, eggs, onion, ½ teaspoon salt, and dash pepper. Turn into greased 8x8x2-inch baking pan. Bake at 350° for 25 minutes. Combine crumbs, remaining cheese, and butter; sprinkle atop spinach. Bake till knife inserted off-center comes out clean, 10 to 15 minutes longer. Let stand 5 minutes before serving. Makes 6 servings.

Japanese Custard Soup

6 small raw shrimp, peeled and
   deveined
6 spinach leaves, cut into 1½-
   inch pieces
⅓ cup sliced fresh mushrooms
   (1 ounce)
6 water chestnuts, sliced
2 slightly beaten eggs
1 13¾-ounce can chicken broth
¼ teaspoon salt

Make small slit in each shrimp; pull tail through. Pour hot water over spinach to wilt; drain. Divide and arrange shrimp, spinach, mushrooms, and water chestnuts in six 6-ounce custard cups or Chawan-Mushi cups.

Combine eggs, broth, and salt; pour into cups. Cover each cup with foil; set on wire rack in Dutch oven or deep skillet. Pour hot water around cups to depth of 1 inch on cup sides; cover Dutch oven or skillet. Over medium heat bring water to simmering. Reduce heat; cook till knife inserted off-center comes out clean, about 10 minutes. Makes 6 servings.

Wilted Spinach Salad

½ pound spinach (6 cups)
¼ cup sliced green onion with
   tops
   Dash freshly ground pepper
2 or 3 slices bacon
1 tablespoon white wine vinegar
2 teaspoons lemon juice
½ teaspoon sugar
1 hard-cooked egg, chopped

Wash fresh spinach and pat dry on paper toweling; tear into a bowl. Add green onion; sprinkle with pepper. Chill. Cut bacon into small pieces. In large chafing dish or skillet cook bacon till crisp. Blend in vinegar, lemon juice, sugar, and ¼ teaspoon salt. Gradually add spinach and green onion, tossing just till spinach is coated and wilted slightly, 3 to 5 minutes. Turn into serving dish; sprinkle with chopped hard-cooked egg. Makes 4 servings.

Herbed Spinach Bake

1 10-ounce package frozen
   chopped spinach
2 tablespoons butter
1 cup cooked rice
1 cup shredded American cheese
⅓ cup milk
2 slightly beaten eggs
2 tablespoons chopped onion
½ teaspoon Worcestershire sauce
¼ teaspoon dried rosemary,
   crushed

Cook the spinach according to package directions; drain well. Stir in butter till melted. Stir in rice, shredded cheese, milk, eggs, onion, Worcestershire sauce, rosemary, and ½ teaspoon salt. Pour mixture into 10x6x2-inch baking dish. Bake at 350° till knife inserted halfway between center and edge comes out clean, 30 to 35 minutes. Cut into squares to serve. Makes 6 servings.

Cottage Cheese-Spinach Salad

½ cup dairy sour cream
2 tablespoons sugar
1 tablespoon prepared
   horseradish
½ teaspoon dry mustard
¼ teaspoon salt
3 tablespoons herb-flavored
   vinegar
10 ounces spinach (7 cups)
1½ cups cream-style cottage
   cheese
½ cup chopped walnuts

Stir together sour cream, sugar, horseradish, dry mustard, and salt. Gradually blend in vinegar. Cover and chill.

Tear fresh spinach into bite-size pieces. Arrange spinach in salad bowl; top with cottage cheese and chopped walnuts. Pour sour cream mixture over; toss lightly to coat spinach. Makes 6 to 8 servings.

Squash (winter)

Selecting: Winter squash is the common name for mature, hard-shelled varieties such as acorn, banana, butternut, turban, Hubbard, and buttercup squash. Choose squash that are heavy for their size, with hard rinds and good coloring and shaping for the variety. Large banana or Hubbard squash are sometimes cut into pieces and sold by the pound. Avoid pieces that are discolored or don't appear fresh.

Preparing: Although you can peel squash before cooking, it's much easier to cook it and then remove the peel. Unless very small, halve the squash and remove the seeds and strings before cooking. Cut the squash into serving-size pieces, rings, or cubes.

Cooking: For baked squash, place halves or serving-size pieces, cut side down, in baking pan. Cover with foil; bake at 350° for 30 minutes. Turn cut side up; bake, covered, till tender (20 to 30 minutes more for acorn, buttercup, or butternut squash; 45 to 50 minutes more for Hubbard or banana squash). Or, in covered pan cook squash in small amount of boiling salted water (allow 15 minutes for cubes).

Serving: For a hearty main dish, serve meat-stuffed squash pieces. To serve the other winter squash as a vegetable, simply fill the cavities with butter and brown sugar or honey.

Sausage-Stuffed Turban Squash

1 3-pound turban squash
Salt
1 pound bulk pork sausage
1 cup chopped celery
½ cup sliced fresh mushrooms
¼ cup chopped onion
1 slightly beaten egg
½ cup dairy sour cream
¼ cup grated Parmesan cheese
¼ teaspoon salt

Cut slice from stem end of squash so squash will stand upright. Cut out turban end; scoop out seeds. Lightly salt inside of squash. Place squash, scooped end down, in shallow baking pan. Bake at 375° till tender, about 1 hour.

Meanwhile, in skillet combine pork sausage, celery, mushrooms, and onion; cook till vegetables are tender and meat is brown. Drain well. Combine egg, sour cream, Parmesan cheese, and the ¼ teaspoon salt. Stir into sausage mixture. Turn squash scooped end up; fill with sausage mixture. Bake 20 to 25 minutes longer. Makes 6 servings.

Simple but delicious describes *Candied Squash Rings.* Acorn squash and an easy brown sugar-and-butter glaze are all you need for the conventional or microwave version of this recipe.

Candied Squash Rings

2 acorn squash
Salt
Pepper
½ cup packed brown sugar
¼ cup butter *or* margarine
2 tablespoons water

Cut squash crosswise into 1-inch slices; discard seeds. Arrange in single layer in shallow baking pan; season with salt and pepper. Cover and bake at 350° till almost tender, about 40 minutes. In saucepan combine brown sugar, butter, and water; cook and stir till bubbly. Spoon over squash. Continue baking, uncovered, till squash is tender, about 15 minutes more, basting often. Makes 4 to 6 servings.

Microwave cooking directions: Pierce squash with metal skewer in several places. Cook in countertop microwave oven till soft, 8 to 10 minutes. Let stand 5 minutes. Cut crosswise into 1-inch slices; discard seeds. Place squash in 12x 7½x2-inch nonmetal baking dish. Season with salt and pepper. In glass measuring cup combine remaining ingredients. Micro-cook 15 *seconds*. Spoon over squash. Cover with waxed paper. Micro-cook till hot, 3 to 5 minutes; baste once.

Squash Soufflé

3 cups mashed cooked winter
    squash
¼ cup butter *or* margarine
2 tablespoons brown sugar
½ teaspoon salt
½ teaspoon finely shredded
    orange peel
⅛ teaspoon ground nutmeg
    Dash pepper
4 egg yolks
4 stiffly beaten egg whites

In large mixing bowl combine squash, butter or margarine, brown sugar, salt, orange peel, nutmeg, and pepper. Beat till fluffy. Add egg yolks; beat well. Carefully fold squash mixture into stiffly beaten egg whites. Turn into 1½-quart soufflé dish. Bake soufflé at 350° till set, 55 to 60 minutes. Makes 8 to 10 servings.

Bean and Squash Soup

1 pound dry navy beans (2⅓ cups)
8 cups water
2 pounds winter squash, peeled,
    seeded, and cubed
    (about 4 cups)
1 meaty ham bone (about 1 pound)
1 cup chopped onion
1 cup chopped celery
1½ teaspoons salt
¼ teaspoon pepper

In 5-quart Dutch oven combine navy beans and water. Cover and soak overnight. (Or, bring to boiling; reduce heat and simmer 2 minutes. Remove from heat. Cover and let stand 1 hour.) *Do not drain.* Add *half* the winter squash, the ham bone, onion, celery, salt, and pepper. Bring to boiling. Reduce heat; cover and simmer 1½ hours. Remove ham bone; cool slightly. Partially mash beans with potato masher. Cut meat from ham bone. Chop meat; return to Dutch oven along with remaining winter squash. Simmer, covered, 20 minutes longer. Season to taste. Makes 8 to 10 servings.

Saucy Dilled Winter Squash

2 pounds winter squash,
    seeded and cubed (4 cups)
2 tablespoons sliced green onion
    with tops
1 tablespoon butter *or* margarine
½ cup dairy sour cream
2 tablespoons milk
¼ teaspoon salt
    Dash pepper
¼ teaspoon dried dillweed

Cook squash in boiling water as directed on page 277; drain well. Peel squash. Cook onion in butter till tender; blend in sour cream, milk, salt, and pepper. Heat through, but *do not boil.* Arrange squash on serving plate; top with sour cream mixture. Sprinkle with dillweed. Makes 6 servings.

Shaker Squash

1 2½- to 3-pound Hubbard squash,
    cut in large pieces
2 tablespoons maple *or*
    maple-flavored syrup
2 tablespoons butter
1 teaspoon salt
    Dash pepper
1 tablespoon snipped parsley *or*
    sliced green onion with tops

Place squash pieces in large baking pan. Bake, covered, at 350° till tender, about 1¼ hours. Remove pulp; press through sieve. Place pulp in saucepan; stir in syrup, butter, salt, and pepper. Heat through. (If thin, cook and stir till desired consistency.) Top with snipped parsley or sliced onion. Makes 6 to 8 servings.

Sweet Potatoes & Yams

Selecting: Sweet potatoes range in skin color from light yellow to orange to copper, and in flesh color from light yellow to red-orange. In this country, "yam" is used interchangeably with "sweet potato" and refers particularly to a sweet potato variety with copper skin and orange flesh. Uniform shape, uniform skin color, and firmness are characteristics to look for when selecting sweet potatoes. Don't choose decayed, soft, or shriveled vegetables. Store sweet potatoes in a cool (about 55°), dry place rather than in the refrigerator, and plan to use them within a few days.

Preparing: Scrub sweet potatoes; remove ends and woody portions. Peel sweet potatoes before or after cooking, depending on their use.

Cooking: Bake whole sweet potatoes at 375° for 40 to 45 minutes; allow a little less time for thickly sliced sweet potatoes. Or, in covered pan cook whole sweet potatoes in enough boiling salted water to cover till tender, 30 to 40 minutes.

Serving: Baked, mashed, or candied—sweet potatoes are a holiday tradition. Marshmallows are the perfect topping for a sweet potato casserole. Sweet potato pie, bread, and biscuits are also favorites, particularly in the South.

Sweet Potato-Cashew Bake

½ **cup packed brown sugar**
⅓ **cup broken cashews**
½ **teaspoon salt**
¼ **teaspoon ground ginger**
2 **pounds sweet potatoes (5 or 6 medium), cooked, peeled, and cut crosswise into thick pieces**
1 **8-ounce can peach slices, well drained**
3 **tablespoons butter *or* margarine**

Combine brown sugar, cashews, salt, and ginger. In 10x6x2-inch baking dish layer *half* the sweet potatoes, *half* the peach slices, and *half* the brown sugar mixture. Repeat layers. Dot with butter or margarine. Bake, covered, at 350° for 30 minutes. Uncover and bake mixture about 10 minutes longer. Spoon brown sugar syrup over before serving. Makes 6 to 8 servings.

Glazed sweet potatoes are enhanced by cashews and canned peach slices in golden
Sweet Potato-Cashew Bake. Include this recipe in your Thanksgiving menu. It's sure to be a hit.

Raisin-Filled Sweet Potatoes

1 17-ounce can sweet potatoes, drained
2 tablespoons butter, softened
1 egg
½ teaspoon salt
  Dash ground cinnamon
  Dash ground ginger
2 tablespoons butter, melted
¼ cup sugar
2 teaspoons cornstarch
1 teaspoon finely shredded orange peel
½ cup orange juice
½ cup raisins

Beat together drained sweet potatoes, the softened butter, egg, salt, cinnamon, and ginger. Spoon into 6 mounds on a greased baking sheet. Make depressions in centers with spoon. Brush with the melted butter. Bake at 350° for 15 to 20 minutes. In saucepan combine sugar, cornstarch, and peel. Stir in orange juice and raisins. Cook and stir till thickened and bubbly. To serve, spoon raisin mixture into depressions in potato mounds. Makes 6 servings.

Candied Sweet Potato Boats

4 small sweet potatoes
½ cup prepared mincemeat
3 tablespoons butter *or* margarine
1 tablespoon lemon juice
½ teaspoon salt
¼ cup chopped pecans

Scrub sweet potatoes with brush. Bake as directed on page 280. Remove from oven; reduce oven temperature to 325°. Cut potatoes in half lengthwise. Scoop out center of halves, leaving about ½-inch shell; set shells aside. In a mixing bowl mash centers; stir in mincemeat, butter, lemon juice, and salt. Sprinkle shells lightly with additional salt; spoon mashed potato mixture into potato shells. Sprinkle pecans over potatoes. Return to oven and bake at 325° till heated through, about 15 minutes longer. Makes 8 servings.

Apricot-Sauced Sweets

1 cup snipped dried apricots
¾ cup orange juice
½ cup water
3 tablespoons brown sugar
2 tablespoons honey
2 tablespoons butter
2½ pounds sweet potatoes, cooked, peeled, and cut crosswise into thick pieces
½ cup walnut halves

In saucepan combine apricots, orange juice, water, brown sugar, and honey. Bring to boiling. Reduce heat; cover and simmer till apricots are tender, 20 to 25 minutes. Remove from heat and stir in butter.

Arrange sweet potatoes in a 12-inch skillet; sprinkle with walnuts. Pour apricot sauce over. Cover and simmer till potatoes are heated through and glazed, about 15 minutes. Baste frequently. Makes 12 servings.

Sweet Potato Biscuits

1¼ cups all-purpose flour
1 tablespoon baking powder
2 teaspoons brown sugar
½ teaspoon salt
⅓ cup shortening
1 beaten egg
½ cup mashed cooked sweet potato
2 tablespoons milk

In mixing bowl stir together the flour, baking powder, brown sugar, and salt. Cut in shortening till mixture resembles coarse crumbs. Combine egg, mashed sweet potato, and milk; add all at once to dry mixture. Stir just till dough clings together. Knead gently on lightly floured surface (10 to 12 strokes). Roll or pat dough to ½-inch thickness. Cut with 2½-inch biscuit cutter, dipping cutter in flour between cuts. Place on ungreased baking sheet. Bake at 425° for 10 to 12 minutes. Makes 8 biscuits.

Tomatoes

Selecting: *Red tomatoes come in a variety of sizes and shapes, but in all cases look for ripe, firm tomatoes that are unblemished and well-shaped. Tomatoes that aren't quite ripe will ripen if left at 60° to 70° out of direct light. Store fully ripe tomatoes in the refrigerator crisper and use within a few days.*

Preparing: *Wash and remove stems. If a tomato has a large core, cut it out. Tomatoes peel easily by spearing with a fork and immersing in boiling water for about 30 seconds. Remove from boiling water and immediately place tomato in cold water. When cool, slip off the skin. Or, spear the tomato with a fork and rotate it over an open flame till the skin wrinkles slightly; then cool and peel.*

Cooking: *For stewed tomatoes, place peeled whole or cut-up tomatoes in saucepan. Tightly cover and cook over low heat till done, 10 to 15 minutes (do not add water). Season stewed tomatoes with salt, pepper, and a little sugar.*

Serving: *Whole raw tomato cups stuffed with a meat or seafood salad make a refreshing luncheon entrée. Tomato wedges are a favorite salad ingredient. Tomatoes are also delicious broiled, stewed, or scalloped. Green (unripe) tomatoes are sometimes fried, pickled, or used for pies.*

Huevos Rancheros

¼ cup cooking oil
6 frozen tortillas, thawed
½ cup chopped onion
1 small clove garlic, minced
2 tablespoons cooking oil
3 large tomatoes, peeled
    and finely chopped
2 canned green chili peppers,
    drained, seeded, and
    chopped (¼ cup)
¼ teaspoon salt
6 eggs
1 cup shredded Monterey Jack
    cheese (4 ounces)

Heat the ¼ cup oil in a small skillet. Dip tortillas in oil for a few seconds till softened but not brown. Keep warm. In medium skillet cook onion and garlic in the 2 tablespoons oil till onion is tender but not brown. Add tomatoes, chili peppers, and salt. Simmer 10 minutes.

Carefully break eggs, one at a time, into a small bowl. Slide each egg into tomato mixture, taking care not to break yolk. Season with salt and pepper. Cover skillet and cook eggs till desired doneness. Place an egg with some of the tomato mixture on each tortilla. Sprinkle shredded Monterey Jack cheese atop eggs. Makes 6 servings.

Scalloped Tomatoes

2 **pounds tomatoes, peeled
and cut up (6 medium),** *or*
**1 28-ounce can tomatoes,
cut up**
1 **cup sliced celery**
½ **cup chopped onion**
2 **tablespoons all-purpose flour**
1 **tablespoon sugar**
½ **teaspoon salt**
½ **teaspoon dried marjoram,
crushed**
Dash pepper
¼ **cup water**
2 **tablespoons butter**
4 **slices bread, toasted**
2 **tablespoons grated Parmesan
cheese**

In saucepan combine fresh or canned tomatoes, celery, and onion. Cover and bring to boiling; reduce heat. Simmer, covered, till celery is tender, about 10 minutes. Combine flour, sugar, salt, marjoram, and pepper. Blend in water; stir into tomatoes. Cook, stirring constantly, till thickened and bubbly. Stir in butter till melted.

Cut *3 slices* toast into cubes; stir into tomato mixture. Pour into a 1½-quart casserole or a 10x6x2-inch baking dish. Bake at 350° for 30 minutes. Cut the remaining slice of toast into 4 triangles. Arrange triangles down center of tomato mixture, overlapping slightly. Sprinkle with Parmesan cheese. Bake 20 minutes longer. Serve scalloped tomatoes in sauce dishes. Makes 6 servings.

Herbed Fresh Tomato Soup

2 **tablespoons butter**
2 **tablespoons olive oil** *or*
cooking oil
2 **medium onions, thinly sliced**
2 **pounds tomatoes, peeled and
quartered (6 medium)**
1 **6-ounce can tomato paste**
2 **tablespoons snipped fresh
basil** *or* **2 teaspoons dried
basil, crushed**
4 **teaspoons snipped fresh thyme**
or **1 teaspoon dried thyme,
crushed**
1 **tablespoon instant chicken
bouillon granules**
3 **cups water**
1 **teaspoon salt**
⅛ **teaspoon pepper**

In large saucepan heat butter and oil till butter melts. Add onions; cook till tender but not brown. Stir in tomatoes, tomato paste, basil, thyme, and bouillon granules; mash tomatoes slightly. Stir in water; bring to boiling. Reduce heat; cover and simmer for 40 minutes. Press through food mill. (*Or,* place a small amount at a time in blender; cover and blend till pureed. Repeat with remaining mixture.) Strain mixture. Return to saucepan; stir in salt and pepper. Heat through. Pour into soup tureen or ladle into individual soup bowls. Garnish with celery tops, if desired. Makes 8 servings.

Salsa

4 **medium tomatoes, peeled
and chopped**
½ **cup chopped onion**
½ **cup chopped celery**
¼ **cup chopped green pepper**
¼ **cup olive oil** *or* **cooking oil**
2 **to 3 tablespoons chopped
canned green chili peppers**
2 **tablespoons red wine vinegar**
1 **teaspoon mustard seed**
1 **teaspoon coriander seed,
crushed**

Combine tomatoes, onion, celery, green pepper, olive or cooking oil, green chili peppers, vinegar, mustard seed, coriander seed, 1 teaspoon salt, and dash pepper. Cover; refrigerate several hours or overnight, stirring occasionally. Garnish with green pepper strips, if desired. Serve as a relish. Makes about 3 cups.

The popular tomato crops up in a wide variety of tasty dishes. Old-fashioned *Scalloped Tomatoes, Herbed Fresh Tomato Soup*, and Mexican-style *Salsa* are three long-standing favorites.

Tomato Spaghetti Sauce

1 cup finely chopped onion
2 cloves garlic, minced
2 tablespoons cooking oil
    (conventional method only)
2 pounds tomatoes, peeled and
    cut up, *or* 1 28-ounce can
    tomatoes, cut up
1 6-ounce can tomato paste
1 tablespoon sugar
2 teaspoons instant beef
    bouillon granules
1 teaspoon dried oregano, crushed
½ teaspoon dried basil, crushed
1 large bay leaf
1 4-ounce can sliced mushrooms
2 tablespoons cornstarch
    (crockery cooker method only)
Hot cooked spaghetti

In 3-quart saucepan cook onion and garlic in oil. Add tomatoes, tomato paste, sugar, bouillon granules, oregano, basil, bay leaf, ½ teaspoon salt, and ⅛ teaspoon pepper. Stir in 1½ cups water. Bring to boiling. Reduce heat and simmer, uncovered, for 1¼ to 1½ hours, stirring occasionally. Remove bay leaf. Stir in mushrooms; simmer till desired consistency, 15 to 30 minutes more. Serve over spaghetti; pass grated Parmesan cheese, if desired. Makes 6 servings.

Crockery cooker directions: In electric slow crockery cooker combine onion, garlic, tomatoes, tomato paste, sugar, bouillon granules, oregano, basil, bay leaf, ½ teaspoon salt, and ⅛ teaspoon pepper (omit cooking oil). Stir in 1½ cups water. Cover; cook on low-heat setting for 10 to 12 hours. Turn to high-heat setting. Remove bay leaf; stir in mushrooms. Blend 2 tablespoons cold water into the 2 tablespoons cornstarch; stir into sauce. Cover; cook till thickened and bubbly, about 25 minutes. Serve as above.

Vera Cruz Tomatoes

3 slices bacon
¼ cup chopped onion
½ pound spinach, snipped
½ cup dairy sour cream
    Dash bottled hot pepper sauce
4 medium tomatoes
½ cup shredded mozzarella
    cheese (2 ounces)

Cook bacon till crisp. Drain; reserve 2 tablespoons drippings. Crumble bacon; set aside. Cook onion in drippings; stir in fresh spinach. Cover; cook till tender, 3 to 5 minutes. Remove from heat; stir in sour cream, pepper sauce, and bacon. Cut tops off tomatoes. Remove centers, leaving shells; drain. Sprinkle shells with salt; fill with spinach mixture. Bake in 8x8x2-inch baking pan at 375° for 20 to 25 minutes. Top with cheese; heat till cheese melts. Makes 4 servings.

Marinated Herbed Tomatoes

6 tomatoes
⅔ cup salad oil
¼ cup vinegar
¼ cup *each* snipped parsley and
    sliced green onion with tops
½ teaspoon dried marjoram,
    crushed

Peel tomatoes; place in a deep bowl. In a screw-top jar combine oil, vinegar, parsley, green onion, marjoram, 1 teaspoon salt, and ¼ teaspoon pepper. Shake well. Pour over tomatoes. Cover and refrigerate several hours or overnight, spooning herb mixture over tomatoes occasionally. At serving time, spoon herb mixture over tomatoes again. If desired, serve on lettuce-lined platter. Makes 6 servings.

Tomato Aspic

4 medium tomatoes
2 ribs celery, sliced
¼ small onion
2 tablespoons brown sugar
2 tablespoons lemon juice
½ teaspoon salt
½ teaspoon celery salt
    Dash bottled hot pepper sauce
2 envelopes unflavored gelatin

Peel and quarter tomatoes; place in blender container. Cover; blend till pureed. Add celery, onion, brown sugar, lemon juice, salt, celery salt, and hot pepper sauce. Cover; blend till vegetables are finely chopped.

In small saucepan soften gelatin in ¾ cup cold water. Place over low heat and stir till gelatin is dissolved. Stir in tomato mixture; chill till partially set. Turn into 4½-cup ring mold. Chill till firm. Makes 8 servings.

Canned Tomatoes

15 **pounds firm, ripe tomatoes**
   (select tomatoes of about
   the same size)
   Salt (¼ teaspoon for each
   pint; ½ teaspoon for each
   quart)

Peel tomatoes. Cut out stem ends and cores. Pack small or medium tomatoes whole; cut large tomatoes in quarters or eighths. Scrape out seeds with spoon, if desired. For *raw pack*, pack tomatoes into hot, clean jars, pressing gently; leave ½-inch headspace. Add salt. For *hot pack*, bring tomatoes to a boil; stir constantly but gently. Pack hot tomatoes into hot, clean jars; leave ½-inch headspace. Add salt.

Prepare lids according to manufacturer's directions. Wipe jar rim. Adjust lid on jar. *Process raw pack* tomatoes in boiling water bath 35 minutes for pints; 45 minutes for quarts. *Process hot pack* tomatoes in boiling water bath for 10 minutes for pints and quarts (start timing raw or hot pack when water returns to boil). Makes 6 quarts.

Canned Tomato Juice

9 **pounds firm, ripe tomatoes**
1 **tablespoon lemon juice**
   Salt (¼ teaspoon for each
   pint; ½ teaspoon for each
   quart)

Cut up tomatoes, discarding stem ends and cores. Measure about 20 cups. In covered 8- to 10-quart kettle slowly cook tomatoes till soft, about 15 minutes; stir often. Press through food mill or sieve to extract juice; measure 12 cups juice. Return juice to kettle; bring to boil. Stir in lemon juice. Pour hot juice into hot, clean jars; leave ½-inch headspace. Add salt. Prepare lids according to manufacturer's directions. Wipe jar rim. Adjust lid. Process jars in boiling water bath for 10 minutes for pints; 15 minutes for quarts (start timing when water returns to boil). Makes 6 pints.

Green Tomato Pickles

4 **pounds green tomatoes**
4 **medium onions, sliced**
1 **cup chopped green pepper**
8 **cups white vinegar**
5 **cups sugar**
¼ **cup mustard seed**
1 **tablespoon celery seed**
1 **teaspoon ground turmeric**

Core tomatoes and slice ¼ inch thick. Measure 16 cups. Combine tomatoes, onions, and green pepper; set aside. In saucepan combine remaining ingredients; bring to boil. Pack vegetables into hot, clean pint jars; leave ½-inch headspace. Pour hot liquid over vegetables; leave ½-inch headspace.

Prepare lids according to manufacturer's directions. Wipe jar rim. Adjust lid. Process jars in boiling water bath 15 minutes (start timing when water returns to boil). Makes 8 pints.

Water-bath Canning Tips

Process tomatoes and vegetables made into sauerkraut, relishes, and pickles (see tip, page 240) in a water-bath canner. The 212° temperature reached at sea level in the boiling water bath sufficiently destroys organisms that cause spoilage in tomatoes. Sauerkraut, relishes, and pickles are prepared with vinegar and/or brine to preserve the product. In high-altitude areas, check with the county extension agent for altitude corrections. *Do not can* overripe tomatoes or those with soft spots or decay. The acid content of overripe tomatoes is lower than that of firm, ripe tomatoes. This may interfere with the tomatoes' keeping quality.

Turnips & Rutabagas

Selecting: Turnips and rutabagas are most plentiful in the fall and winter. The best-known turnip variety is raised for its bulbous root, identified by a purple-collared white skin. Some varieties do not form an enlarged root, but are grown mainly for the leaves (see Greens). Rutabagas are larger than turnips and slightly elongated. The yellow-fleshed varieties are most common. Select smooth, firm turnips and rutabagas of small or medium size. An edible wax coating is sometimes applied to preserve freshness. Turnips and rutabagas keep best stored in the refrigerator.

Preparing: Wash turnips and rutabagas and peel off outer skin. Slice or cube.

Cooking: In covered pan cook vegetable in small amount of boiling salted water till just tender. Allow 10 to 20 minutes for turnips; 20 to 35 minutes for rutabagas.

Serving: Include turnips or rutabagas in soups, pot roasts, and side dishes. Or, mash cooked vegetable like potatoes.

Lemon Turnips

3 medium turnips, peeled and
   cut into strips
2 tablespoons butter
1 tablespoon snipped parsley
1 teaspoon chopped onion
1 teaspoon lemon juice

Cook turnips as directed above; drain well. Add butter, snipped parsley, chopped onion, and lemon juice. Toss to coat. Season with salt and pepper. Makes 4 servings.

Rutabaga and Apple

1 medium rutabaga (1 pound),
   peeled and cubed
1 medium apple, peeled, cored,
   and sliced
⅓ cup packed brown sugar
2 tablespoons butter *or*
   margarine

Cook rutabaga as directed above; drain well. Place *half* the rutabaga and *half* the apple in a 1-quart casserole. Sprinkle with *half* the brown sugar; dot with *half* the butter. Sprinkle with salt. Repeat layers of rutabaga, apple, brown sugar, butter, and salt. Bake, covered, at 350° for 30 minutes. Makes 4 to 6 servings.

Zucchini & other summer squash

Selecting: Soft-shelled varieties of squash—commonly called summer squash—include dark green zucchini, yellow crookneck, disk-shaped patty-pan, and spaghetti squash. Choose young squash that are firm, well-formed, glossy, and heavy for their size. Avoid hard or dull-rinded squash. You can store summer squash in refrigerator crisper one or two days.

Preparing: Usually the tender, thin rinds of summer squash are not removed. Wash squash and cut off ends. Slice, cube, or halve lengthwise.

Cooking: In covered pan cook squash in small amount of boiling salted water till crisp-tender, 5 to 10 minutes. Or, sauté in butter.

Serving: Mild-flavored summer squash combine well with tomatoes, corn, and other vegetables. Marinate uncooked slices in a tangy salad dressing, or use the raw pieces in salads or as vegetable dippers. Squash halves perform a dual role as vegetable and serving dish when filled with stuffing.

Summer Squash Casserole

2 **pounds crookneck** *or* **zucchini squash, sliced ⅜ inch thick (7 cups)**
¼ **cup chopped onion**
1 **10¾-ounce can condensed cream of chicken soup**
1 **cup dairy sour cream**
1 **cup shredded carrot**
¼ **cup butter** *or* **margarine**
2 **cups herb-seasoned stuffing mix (about ½ of an 8-ounce package)**

Cook summer squash with onion in boiling salted water as directed above. Drain well. Combine soup and sour cream; stir in carrot. Fold in drained squash and onion. Melt butter or margarine; toss with stuffing mix.

Spread *half* the stuffing mixture in a 12x7½x2-inch baking dish. Spoon vegetable mixture atop. Sprinkle with remaining stuffing mixture. Bake at 350° till heated through, 25 to 30 minutes. Makes 6 servings.

Microwave cooking directions: Combine squash and onion in a 12x7½x2-inch nonmetal baking dish. Add ¼ cup water. Cover and cook in countertop microwave oven till squash is crisp-tender, about 15 minutes; stir every 3 minutes. Drain well. Combine soup and sour cream; stir in carrot. Fold in squash and onion. In nonmetal bowl micro-melt butter about 30 seconds. Stir in stuffing mix. Spread *half* the stuffing mixture in same nonmetal baking dish. Continue assembling as above. Micro-cook, uncovered, till heated through, about 7 minutes; give dish a half-turn after 4 minutes.

Enliven an ordinary luncheon or supper with a distinctive entrée, *Egg-Stuffed Zucchini.*
Crisp-tender squash shells hold the colorful, rich-tasting scrambled egg and tomato mixture.

Egg-Stuffed Zucchini

4 medium zucchini squash
   (about 1½ pounds)
½ cup water
1 large tomato, chopped
2 tablespoons butter *or*
   margarine
3 beaten eggs
¼ teaspoon salt
   Dash pepper
½ cup shredded sharp American
   cheese (2 ounces)

Halve zucchini lengthwise. Scoop out pulp, leaving ¼-inch shell. Chop pulp to make 1 cup; set aside. Place zucchini shells, cut side down, in large skillet. Add the water. Simmer, covered, till just tender, 5 to 6 minutes. Drain; turn cut side up in same skillet. Sprinkle with a little salt.

Meanwhile, in medium skillet cook zucchini pulp and tomato in butter till squash is tender, about 3 minutes. Add eggs, the ¼ teaspoon salt, and pepper. Cook over low heat till just set, lifting with spatula so uncooked portion runs underneath. Spoon egg mixture into zucchini shells. Top with cheese. Cover; heat till cheese melts. Makes 4 servings.

Stuffed Pattypan Squash

6 pattypan squash
4 slices bacon
⅓ cup finely chopped onion
¾ cup seasoned fine dry bread
   crumbs
½ cup milk

Cook whole squash in boiling salted water till just tender, 15 to 20 minutes. Drain; cool. Cut a small slice from stem end of each squash. Scoop out pulp, leaving ½-inch shell. Finely chop pulp; set aside. Sprinkle shells with salt. Cook bacon till crisp. Drain, reserving 2 tablespoons drippings. Crumble bacon; set aside. Cook onion in reserved drippings till tender. Stir in crumbs, milk, and squash pulp. Fill shells; top with bacon. Bake, covered, in 12x7½x2-inch baking dish at 350° for 30 to 35 minutes. Makes 6 servings.

Zucchini Nut Loaf

1 cup grated zucchini squash
1 cup sugar
1 egg
¼ cup cooking oil
1½ cups all-purpose flour
1 teaspoon ground cinnamon
½ teaspoon baking soda
½ teaspoon ground nutmeg
¼ teaspoon baking powder
¼ teaspoon finely shredded lemon
   peel
½ cup chopped walnuts

In mixing bowl beat together zucchini, sugar, and egg. Add cooking oil; mix well. Stir together flour, cinnamon, baking soda, nutmeg, baking powder, lemon peel, and ½ teaspoon salt. Stir into zucchini mixture. Fold in walnuts. Pour into a greased 8½x4½x2½-inch loaf pan. Bake at 350° till done, 55 to 60 minutes. Cool in pan on rack for 10 minutes; remove from pan. Cool thoroughly on rack. Wrap and store overnight before slicing. Makes 1 loaf.

Zucchini Relish

4 to 4½ pounds zucchini squash
2 medium onions
1 sweet red pepper
2 tablespoons salt
2 cups sugar
1 cup vinegar
1 cup water
2 teaspoons celery seed
1 teaspoon ground turmeric
1 teaspoon ground nutmeg

Cut up vegetables; grind in food chopper, using coarse blade. Add salt. Cover; refrigerate overnight. Rinse in cold water. Drain well. In 4- to 5-quart kettle combine vegetable mixture, sugar, vinegar, water, celery seed, turmeric, nutmeg, and ⅛ teaspoon pepper. Bring to boil. Cover; boil gently for 10 minutes; stir often. Ladle hot mixture into hot, clean pint jars; leave ½-inch headspace. Prepare lids according to manufacturer's directions. Wipe jar rim. Adjust lid. Process jars in boiling water bath 15 minutes (start timing when water returns to boil). Makes 4 pints.

Vegetable Combinations

Old-Fashioned Fresh Vegetable-Beef Soup

3 pounds beef shank cross cuts
8 cups water
4 teaspoons salt
½ teaspoon dried oregano, crushed
¼ teaspoon dried marjoram, crushed
5 whole black peppercorns
2 bay leaves
4 fresh ears of corn *or* 1 10-ounce package frozen whole kernel corn
3 tomatoes, peeled and cut up
2 medium potatoes, peeled and cubed (2 cups)
1 cup fresh *or* ½ of a 9-ounce package frozen cut green beans
2 medium carrots, sliced (1 cup)
2 ribs celery, sliced (1 cup)
1 medium onion, chopped (½ cup)

In large kettle or Dutch oven combine beef cross cuts, water, salt, oregano, marjoram, peppercorns, and bay leaves. Bring mixture to boiling. Reduce heat; cover and simmer for 2 hours. Remove the beef. Cut meat from bones; chop meat. Strain broth; skim off excess fat. Return broth to kettle. Cut fresh corn from cobs. Add the chopped meat, fresh or frozen corn, tomatoes, potatoes, green beans, carrots, celery, and onion. Simmer, covered, for 1 hour. Season to taste with salt and pepper. Makes 10 to 12 servings.

Garden Row Salad

3 medium carrots, sliced
1 large cucumber, cut up
1 pint cherry tomatoes, halved
4 ribs celery, sliced
1½ cups croutons
4 ounces sharp Cheddar cheese
½ slice bread, torn in pieces
2 hard-cooked eggs, sliced
6 slices bacon, crisp-cooked
    Choice of salad dressing

Place carrots in blender; cover with *cold* water. Cover container; blend till coarsely chopped. Drain well. Place carrots in glass salad bowl. Discard cucumber seeds. Repeat above blending procedure for cucumber; drain and layer atop carrots. Place tomatoes atop cucumber. Repeat the blending procedure for celery; drain and layer atop tomatoes. Place croutons atop celery. Wipe blender dry. Cube cheese; place in blender with bread. Cover; blend till coarsely chopped. Layer with eggs atop salad. Crumble bacon; sprinkle atop. To serve, toss with dressing. Serves 10 to 12.

Succotash

2 cups fresh *or* 1 10-ounce package frozen baby lima beans
2 ounces salt pork (optional)
½ teaspoon sugar
4 fresh ears of corn *or* 1
    10-ounce package frozen
    whole kernel corn
⅓ cup light cream
1 tablespoon all-purpose flour

In saucepan combine lima beans, salt pork, sugar, ½ cup water, ½ teaspoon salt, and dash pepper. Cover and simmer till limas are almost tender, about 20 minutes. Cut fresh corn from cobs. Stir fresh or frozen corn into lima mixture. Cover and simmer till vegetables are tender, about 12 minutes more. Remove salt pork. Slowly blend light cream into the flour; stir into vegetable mixture. Cook and stir till thickened and bubbly. Makes 6 servings.

Vegetable Tempura

Assorted fresh vegetables such
    as asparagus spears, green
    onion, cauliflower, sweet
    potatoes, mushrooms, green
    beans, and zucchini squash
Cooking oil for deep-fat frying
1 cup all-purpose flour
1 slightly beaten egg
2 tablespoons cooking oil
½ teaspoon sugar
    Condiments

Wash and dry vegetables well. Slice or cut into strips or pieces, if desired. Using a skillet at least 3 inches deep, pour in cooking oil to depth of 1½ inches. Heat to 365°. For batter, combine flour, egg, the 2 tablespoons oil, sugar, 1 cup *ice* water, and ½ teaspoon salt. Beat just till moistened (a few lumps should remain). Stir in 1 or 2 ice cubes. *Use at once.* Dip vegetables into batter. Fry in hot oil, several at a time, till light brown; drain on paper toweling. Serve with *Condiments:* (1) grated gingerroot; (2) equal parts grated turnip and radish, mixed; (3) ½ cup prepared mustard mixed with 3 tablespoons soy sauce.

Louisiana Relish

10 fresh ears of corn
4 large onions
2 large green peppers, halved
2 sweet red peppers, halved
2 medium cucumbers
4 ribs celery
1 small head cabbage
2 small dried hot red peppers
1 clove garlic
2½ cups packed brown sugar
2 tablespoons all-purpose flour
3 cups vinegar

Cut corn from cobs; set aside. Using coarse blade of food grinder, grind onions, green and red peppers, cucumbers, celery, cabbage, hot peppers, and garlic. Combine ground vegetables with corn; stir in ¼ cup salt. Cover; chill overnight. Rinse and drain mixture. Combine brown sugar and flour; stir in vinegar and ½ cup water. Pour over vegetables. Bring mixture to boiling; boil gently 5 minutes. Ladle hot mixture into hot, clean pint jars; leave ½-inch headspace.

Prepare lids according to manufacturer's directions. Wipe off rim of jar. Adjust lid on jar. Process jars in boiling water bath for 15 minutes (start timing when water returns to boil). Makes 6 pints relish.

5 Salad favorites

Add to your list of salad favorites from this wide collection of popular recipes. These imaginative salads serve as a tantalizing accompaniment to an entrée or make up the main course for a satisfying, but light, meal.

Salads add fresh flavor to any meal—*Crab-Stuffed Avocado* (see recipe, page 344),
Potato Salad Nicoise (see recipe, page 307), and *Fruity Ginger Ale Mold* (see recipe, page 325).

Toss-it-together Greens

Spicy Italian Salad (pictured above)

½ cup salad oil
⅓ cup tarragon vinegar
1 tablespoon sugar
1 teaspoon dried thyme, crushed
½ teaspoon dry mustard
1 small clove garlic, minced
1 7-ounce can artichoke hearts, drained and halved
3 cups torn romaine
3 cups torn iceberg lettuce
1 small sweet red *or* green pepper, cut in strips
½ cup chopped summer sausage
¼ cup sliced pitted ripe olives
2 tablespoons grated parmesan cheese

In screw-top jar combine oil, vinegar, sugar, thyme, mustard, and garlic. Cover and shake well to mix. Pour over artichoke hearts. Cover; marinate in refrigerator 4 to 6 hours or overnight.

In salad bowl combine romaine, iceberg lettuce, red or green pepper, summer sausage, olives, and parmesan. Add artichokes with the dressing mixture. Toss to coat vegetables. Makes 6 servings.

Taos Salad Toss

1 medium head iceberg
  lettuce, chopped
1 15-ounce can dark red
  kidney beans, drained
½ cup sliced pitted ripe
  olives
1 large avocado, mashed
½ cup dairy sour cream
¼ cup Italian salad dressing
1 tablespoon chopped canned
  green chili peppers
1 teaspoon minced dried
  onion
¾ teaspoon chili powder
¼ teaspoon salt
1 medium tomato, cut into
  wedges
½ cup shredded sharp cheddar
  cheese (2 ounces)
½ cup tortilla chips

In salad bowl combine lettuce, beans, and olives; chill. To make dressing, blend avocado and sour cream. Stir in Italian dressing, green chili peppers, onion, chili powder, salt, and dash *pepper;* mix well. Chill. Spoon avocado dressing in center of salad. Arrange tomato wedges in circle atop salad. Top with shredded cheese. Trim edge of bowl with tortilla chips. To serve, toss salad. Makes 8 servings.

Spring Salad Toss

3 cups torn iceberg lettuce
3 cups torn romaine
2 cups thinly sliced
  zucchini
½ cup sliced radishes
½ cup sliced fresh mushrooms
3 green onions, sliced
  Salt
  Pepper
  Italian salad dressing
½ cup crumbled blue cheese

In large salad bowl combine lettuce, romaine, zucchini, radishes, mushrooms, and green onions. Season with salt and pepper. Toss lightly with Italian dressing to coat vegetables; sprinkle blue cheese atop. Makes 6 servings.

Marinated Vegetable Salad

2 cups thinly sliced
  cucumber
2 cups thinly sliced carrot
1 medium onion, sliced and
  separated into rings
½ cup chopped celery
1 cup vinegar
¾ cup sugar
¼ cup salad oil
1 teaspoon celery seed
1 teaspoon salt
¼ teaspoon pepper
  Lettuce

In large bowl combine cucumber, carrot, onion, and celery. To make dressing, in screw-top jar combine vinegar, sugar, salad oil, celery seed, salt, and pepper. Cover and shake to mix well. Pour over vegetables; stir gently. Cover and refrigerate several hours or overnight, stirring occasionally.

    To serve, drain the vegetables, reserving marinade. Mound vegetables in lettuce-lined bowl. Return any leftover vegetables to marinade; store in refrigerator. Makes 6 to 8 servings.

Asparagus Toss

1 **pound fresh asparagus,
cut into 2-inch pieces
(2 cups)**
½ **cup salad oil**
¼ **cup finely chopped
canned beets**
2 **tablespoons white wine
vinegar**
2 **tablespoons lemon juice**
1 **teaspoon sugar**
1 **teaspoon salt**
1 **teaspoon paprika**
½ **teaspoon dry mustard**
4 **drops bottled hot pepper
sauce**
5 **cups torn iceberg lettuce**
1 **cup sliced celery**
1 **hard-cooked egg, chopped**
¼ **cup sliced green onion**

Cook asparagus in boiling salted water 8 to 10 minutes or till just tender; drain. Chill.

To make dressing, in screw-top jar combine salad oil, beets, vinegar, lemon juice, sugar, salt, paprika, dry mustard, and hot pepper sauce. Cover and shake well to mix. Chill. In salad bowl combine chilled asparagus, lettuce, celery, egg, and green onion. Pour dressing over salad. Toss to coat vegetables. Garnish salad with additional sliced canned beets, if desired. Makes 6 servings.

South American Mixed Salad

1 **medium cucumber, peeled**
2 **large bananas, sliced**
2 **sweet red *or* green peppers,
cut in thin strips**
1 **avocado, seeded, peeled,
and sliced**
½ **small onion, sliced and
separated into rings**
⅓ **cup vinegar**
¼ **cup olive *or* salad oil**
½ **teaspoon salt**
¼ **teaspoon bottled hot
pepper sauce**

Halve cucumber lengthwise; remove seeds and slice crosswise. Arrange cucumber, bananas, peppers, avocado, and onion in salad bowl. To make dressing, in screw-top jar combine vinegar, oil, salt, and bottled hot pepper sauce. Cover and shake to mix well. Pour dressing over vegetable mixture; toss to coat. Cover and refrigerate 1 to 2 hours. Makes 8 servings.

Mushroom-Avocado Duo

½ **cup salad oil**
3 **tablespoons tarragon
vinegar**
2 **tablespoons lemon juice**
2 **tablespoons water**
1 **tablespoon snipped
parsley**
1 **clove garlic, minced**
¾ **teaspoon salt**
8 **ounces fresh mushrooms,
halved (3 cups)**
2 **avocados, seeded, peeled,
and sliced**

To make dressing, in screw-top jar combine salad oil, tarragon vinegar, lemon juice, water, snipped parsley, minced garlic, salt, and a dash *pepper*. Cover and shake well to mix. Pour dressing over mushrooms and avocados in shallow dish. Cover and refrigerate several hours; occasionally spoon over dressing. To serve, drain mushrooms and avocados and arrange on serving platter. Garnish with parsley sprigs, if desired. Makes 8 servings.

Raw Vegetable Antipasto (opposite, above)

1 **tomato, peeled and thinly
    sliced**
1 **cup cauliflowerets**
1 **cup broccoli buds**
1 **cucumber, sliced**
1 **zucchini, cut into sticks**
1 **carrot, cut into sticks**
1 **onion slice, separated
    into rings**
½ **cup olive oil**
3 **tablespoons wine vinegar**
1 **teaspoon dried oregano,
    crushed**
½ **teaspoon salt**
¼ **teaspoon pepper**
    Bibb lettuce leaves
½ **cup pitted ripe olives**

In shallow dish combine tomato, cauliflowerets, broccoli, cucumber, zucchini, carrot, and onion rings. To make dressing, in screw-top jar combine olive oil, wine vinegar, oregano, salt, and pepper. Cover and shake to mix well. Pour dressing over the vegetables in dish. Cover and refrigerate 2 to 3 hours, spooning dressing over vegetables occasionally. Drain. Arrange vegetables on lettuce-lined platter. Garnish the center of the salad with ripe olives. Makes about 8 to 10 appetizer servings or 4 to 6 salad servings.

Tomatoes Rosé (opposite, below left)

4 **large tomatoes, peeled and
    thinly sliced**
½ **cup rosé wine**
⅓ **cup salad oil**
3 **tablespoons wine vinegar**
¼ **cup finely chopped celery**
¼ **cup thinly sliced green onion**
1 **envelope Italian salad
    dressing mix**
    Celery leaves

Place tomatoes in shallow dish or deep bowl. To make dressing, in screw-top jar combine wine, salad oil, and vinegar. Stir in celery, green onion, and dressing mix. Cover and shake to mix well. Pour dressing over tomatoes. Cover; refrigerate several hours. Lift tomatoes from marinade. Arrange slices of tomato on platter. Spoon some of the dressing over; pass remaining. Garnish with celery leaves. Makes 6 servings.

Broccoli Vinaigrette (opposite, below right)

1 **pound fresh broccoli *or*
    2 10-ounce packages
    frozen broccoli spears**
¾ **cup Vinaigrette Dressing
    (see recipe, page 359)**
⅓ **cup finely chopped dill
    pickle**
⅓ **cup finely chopped green
    pepper**
3 **tablespoons snipped
    parsley**
2 **tablespoons capers,
    drained**
1 **hard-cooked egg, finely
    chopped**

Cut fresh broccoli stalks lengthwise into uniform spears, following branching lines. Cook fresh broccoli in small amount of boiling salted water 10 to 15 minutes, frozen broccoli 4 to 5 minutes, or just till crisp-tender. Drain. In screw-top jar combine *Vinaigrette Dressing*, dill pickle, chopped green pepper, snipped parsley, and capers. Cover and shake to mix well. Pour dressing over broccoli spears; refrigerate several hours or overnight. Drain off liquid. Arrange broccoli spears on serving plate; top with finely chopped egg. Garnish with additional sawtooth-cut, hard-cooked eggs filled with sieved egg yolks, if desired. Makes 6 to 8 servings.

Serve fresh-tasting *Raw Vegetable Antipasto* for pre-dinner snacking.
You can forget the plates and forks with a pick-up-and-munch assortment like this.

Italian salad dressing mix and wine
make the flavorful marinade for *Tomatoes Rosé*.

Dress up *Broccoli Vinaigrette*
with a fancy stuffed egg garnish.

Enjoy the sophisticated taste of anchovy-topped *Greek Salad*. Cubes of
sharp feta cheese and an herb, vinegar, and oil dressing blend for a distinctive flavor.

Greek Salad (opposite)

1 medium head iceberg
   lettuce, chopped
1 head curly endive, chopped
2 tomatoes, peeled and
   chopped (1 cup)
¾ cup cubed feta cheese
   (3 ounces)
¼ cup sliced pitted
   ripe olives
¼ cup sliced green onion
1 2-ounce can anchovy
   fillets, drained
⅔ cup olive *or* salad oil
⅓ cup white wine vinegar
¼ teaspoon dried oregano,
   crushed

In mixing bowl toss together chopped lettuce and endive; mound onto 6 individual salad plates. Atop greens arrange tomatoes, feta cheese, olives, green onion, and anchovies. To make dressing, in screw-top jar combine oil, vinegar, oregano, ½ teaspoon *salt,* and ⅛ teaspoon *pepper.* Cover and shake well to mix. Pour dressing over salads. Makes 6 servings.

Belgian Tossed Salad

1 10-ounce package frozen
   brussels sprouts
½ cup salad oil
⅓ cup vinegar
1 clove garlic, minced
1 teaspoon dried parsley
   flakes, crushed
¼ teaspoon dried basil,
   crushed
8 cups torn mixed salad
   greens
½ medium red onion, sliced
   and separated into rings
6 slices bacon, crisp-cooked,
   drained, and crumbled

Cook brussels sprouts in small amount of boiling salted water about 5 minutes or till barely tender; drain. To make dressing, in screw-top jar combine oil, vinegar, garlic, parsley, basil, ½ teaspoon *salt,* and ⅛ teaspoon *pepper.* Cover and shake well to mix. Cut brussels sprouts in half lengthwise; pour dressing over. Cover; chill 3 to 4 hours.

In salad bowl combine greens, onion rings, and bacon. Add brussels sprouts with dressing; toss to coat vegetables. Makes 8 servings.

Tossed Mixed Greens

3 cups torn iceberg lettuce
2 cups torn fresh spinach
1 cup watercress leaves
1 medium tomato, cut in wedges
¼ cup chopped celery
1 tablespoon snipped chives
¼ cup sugar
¼ cup white wine vinegar
1 tablespoon chopped onion
½ teaspoon dry mustard
¼ teaspoon worcestershire sauce
   Few drops bottled hot pepper
   sauce
⅓ cup salad oil

In salad bowl combine lettuce, spinach, watercress, tomato wedges, celery, and chives. To make dressing, in small mixer bowl combine sugar and white wine vinegar; blend in onion, dry mustard, worcestershire sauce, bottled hot pepper sauce, and ¼ teaspoon *salt.* Gradually add salad oil, beating with electric mixer about 2 minutes or till thick. Cover and chill. Pour dressing over salad. Toss to coat vegetables. Makes 6 servings.

Bermuda Salad Bowl (opposite, above)

1 small head cauliflower,
  broken into flowerets
½ large bermuda onion,
  sliced and separated
  into rings
½ cup sliced pimiento-
  stuffed olives
⅔ cup French salad dressing
1 small head iceberg lettuce,
  torn (4 cups)
½ cup crumbled blue cheese
  (2 ounces)

Slice the flowerets. In large salad bowl combine cauliflow-er, onion rings, and olives. Pour French dressing over salad. Toss to coat vegetables. Cover and refrigerate 30 minutes. Just before serving, add the lettuce and blue cheese; toss lightly. Pass extra French dressing, if desired. Makes 8 to 10 servings.

Curried Vegetable Salad (opposite, below)

3 medium turnips, peeled,
  halved, and thinly
  sliced
3 medium carrots, sliced
½ small head cauliflower, broken
  into flowerets
1 medium green pepper, cut
  in strips
½ cup vinegar
⅓ cup sugar
¼ cup salad oil
2 teaspoons curry powder
1 teaspoon salt
⅛ teaspoon pepper
  Romaine (optional)

In covered saucepan cook turnips, carrots, cauliflowerets, and green pepper in small amount boiling salted water about 5 minutes or till crisp-tender. Drain and cool. To make dressing, in screw-top jar combine vinegar, sugar, salad oil, curry powder, salt, and pepper. Cover and shake to mix well. Pour curry dressing over vegetables. Toss to coat vegetables. Cover and refrigerate 4 hours or overnight, stirring occasionally. To serve, lift vegetables from dressing with a slotted spoon. Serve in romaine-lined bowl, if de-sired. Makes 8 servings.

Piquant Cauliflower

1 medium head cauliflower,
  broken into flowerets
1 cup cherry tomatoes,
  halved
½ cup salad oil
⅓ cup vinegar
2 tablespoons sliced
  pimiento-stuffed
  olives
1 tablespoon sweet pickle
  relish
1 teaspoon sugar
1 teaspoon paprika
½ teaspoon salt
⅛ teaspoon pepper
  Lettuce

In covered saucepan cook cauliflowerets in small amount of boiling salted water 9 to 10 minutes or till crisp-tender. Drain. In deep bowl combine cauliflowerets and tomatoes. To make dressing, in screw-top jar combine salad oil, vinegar, olives, pickle relish, sugar, paprika, salt, and pepper. Cover and shake to mix well. Pour dressing over cauliflower and tomatoes. Cover and refrigerate 2 to 3 hours, stirring occasionally. To serve, lift vegetables from dressing with slotted spoon. Serve in lettuce-lined bowl. Makes 8 servings.

Deep red onion rings are the center of attention in this unusual combination of vegetables. Pour on bottled French dressing and spark *Bermuda Salad Bowl* with chunks of crumbled blue cheese.

Marinate part of your fall garden harvest in a zesty curry dressing. Make up a big batch—you can store *Curried Vegetable Salad* in the refrigerator and enjoy encores for up to one week.

Hearts of Palm Salad

2 tablespoons vinegar
⅛ teaspoon dried tarragon, crushed
⅛ teaspoon dried thyme, crushed
⅛ teaspoon dried basil, crushed
⅓ cup olive *or* salad oil
1 tablespoon dijon-style mustard
1 clove garlic, minced
½ teaspoon salt
½ teaspoon pepper
1 14-ounce can hearts of palm, drained
6 cups torn mixed salad greens
1 medium tomato, cut in wedges (optional)

To make dressing, in screw-top jar combine vinegar, tarragon, thyme, and basil; let stand for 1 hour. Add olive or salad oil, mustard, garlic, salt, and pepper. Shake well to mix. Cover and chill.

Cut hearts of palm into bite-size pieces. In large salad bowl combine hearts of palm and torn greens. Pour dressing over salad. Toss to coat vegetables. Garnish with tomato wedges, if desired. Makes 6 servings.

Zucchini Salad

1 cup white wine vinegar
⅔ cup olive oil
2 tablespoons sugar
1 clove garlic, minced
1 teaspoon salt
1 teaspoon dried basil, crushed
Few dashes pepper
4 cups sliced zucchini
Leaf lettuce
¼ cup sliced green onion
2 medium tomatoes, cut in thin wedges

To make dressing, in screw-top jar combine white wine vinegar, olive oil, sugar, garlic, salt, basil, and pepper. Cover and shake to mix well. Cook sliced zucchini in small amount of boiling salted water about 3 minutes or till crisp-tender. Drain. Arrange *half* the zucchini in single layer in 10×6×2-inch dish. Shake dressing; pour *half* over zucchini. Arrange remaining zucchini over first layer. Pour on remaining dressing. Cover and refrigerate several hours or overnight. To serve, drain zucchini, reserving ¼ cup dressing. Arrange zucchini on a lettuce-lined plate; top with sliced green onion. Arrange tomato wedges around zucchini; drizzle with the reserved dressing. Makes 8 servings.

Preparing Salad Greens

To prepare lettuce for use, remove and discard wilted outer leaves. For thorough rinsing, remove core from head lettuce; separate leafy lettuce. Rinse the greens in cold water. Drain. Place leafy greens in clean kitchen towel or paper toweling, and pat or toss gently to remove clinging water. Tear greens into bite-size pieces. (Tearing exposes the interior and allows dressing to be absorbed by the greens.) Place greens in salad bowl; cover with damp paper towel and refrigerate until serving time.

Tomato-Cucumber Salad

2 tomatoes, cut into wedges
1 cucumber, scored and
    sliced
¼ cup pitted ripe olives
¼ cup salad oil
3 tablespoons lemon juice
½ teaspoon salt
¼ teaspoon dry mustard
⅛ teaspoon garlic powder
    Freshly ground pepper
    Leaf lettuce (optional)

In bowl combine tomato wedges, sliced cucumber, and olives. To make dressing, in screw-top jar combine salad oil, lemon juice, salt, dry mustard, garlic powder, and pepper. Cover and shake well to mix. Pour dressing over vegetables. Cover and refrigerate several hours, spooning dressing over vegetables occasionally. Lift vegetables from dressing with slotted spoon. Serve on lettuce leaves, if desired. Makes 4 servings.

Marinated Relish Salad

1 16-ounce can bean sprouts,
    rinsed and drained
2 cups sliced fresh
    mushrooms
2 cups sliced cauliflower
1 medium cucumber, peeled
    and sliced
1 medium green pepper, cut
    in strips
⅓ cup sliced green onion
1⅓ cups vinegar
½ cup sugar
⅓ cup salad oil
1 clove garlic, minced
½ teaspoon salt
12 cherry tomatoes, halved

Combine bean sprouts, mushrooms, cauliflower, cucumber, green pepper, and onion. To make dressing, in screw-top jar combine vinegar, sugar, salad oil, garlic, and salt. Cover and shake well to mix. Pour dressing over vegetables. Toss to coat vegetables. Cover and refrigerate several hours or overnight. To serve, add cherry tomatoes; toss lightly. Makes 12 to 14 servings.

Hearts of Artichoke Versailles

3 large artichokes
3 or 4 lemon slices
3 ½-inch-thick tomato
    slices
½ cup French salad dressing
6 hard-cooked eggs,
    chopped
⅓ cup mayonnaise *or* salad
    dressing
½ teaspoon salt
    Dash pepper
3 lettuce cups
3 teaspoons caviar
    Thousand island dressing
    (optional)

Rinse artichokes. Cut off 1 inch of tops, stems, and tips of leaves. Pull off any loose leaves. Place artichokes and lemon slices in boiling salted water. Cover and simmer 25 to 30 minutes or till a leaf pulls out easily. Drain. Remove leaves and scoop out choke. In bowl combine tomato slices and artichoke bottoms. Pour French salad dressing over vegetables; refrigerate at least 1 hour. Combine eggs, mayonnaise or salad dressing, salt, and pepper. Cover and chill. To serve, place 1 of the tomato slices in a lettuce cup. Top with 1 artichoke bottom. Mound some of the egg mixture over artichoke. Top with *1 teaspoon* of caviar. Repeat to make remaining salads. Pass thousand island dressing, if desired. Makes 3 servings.

Home-style Salads

Creamy Potato Salad (pictured above)

1 tablespoon sugar
2 teaspoons all-purpose flour
1½ teaspoons dry mustard
¾ teaspoon salt
3 slightly beaten egg yolks
¾ cup milk
¼ cup vinegar
3 tablespoons butter *or* margarine
1 cup whipping cream
9 medium potatoes (3 pounds)
1 cup chopped celery
⅓ cup sliced green onion
¼ cup sweet pickle relish
1½ teaspoons salt
⅛ teaspoon pepper
½ cup sliced radishes
Hard-cooked egg slices
Parsley sprig

To make dressing, in saucepan combine sugar, flour, mustard, and the ¾ teaspoon salt. Add egg yolks and milk. Cook and stir over low heat till thickened. *(Do not boil.)* Blend in vinegar and butter or margarine. Cool. Whip cream to soft peaks; fold into cooked mixture.

Meanwhile, in covered saucepan cook potatoes in boiling salted water for 25 to 30 minutes or till tender; drain. Cool slightly. Peel and slice potatoes. In large bowl combine potatoes, celery, green onion, relish, 1½ teaspoons salt, and pepper. Stir in the cooked dressing. Toss lightly to coat vegetables. Cover and chill. Before serving, fold in radishes. Garnish with egg slices and parsley. Makes 12 to 16 servings.

Potato Salad Nicoise (pictured on page 294)

Vinaigrette Dressing (see
    recipe, page 359)
4 medium potatoes (1½ pounds)
1 7-ounce can artichoke
    hearts, drained and
    halved
1 small red onion, sliced and
    separated into rings
1 small green pepper, sliced
    into thin rings
1 cup cherry tomatoes
¼ cup pitted ripe olives
    Leaf lettuce
3 hard-cooked eggs, quartered
1 2-ounce can anchovy
    fillets, drained
¼ cup snipped parsley

Prepare *Vinaigrette Dressing*. In covered saucepan cook potatoes in boiling salted water for 25 to 30 minutes or till tender; drain. Peel and cube potatoes. Combine potatoes, artichokes, onion rings, green pepper, tomatoes, and olives; toss with dressing. Cover and chill several hours or overnight, stirring gently once or twice. To assemble salad, drain dressing from potato mixture; reserve dressing. Line salad bowl with lettuce. Spoon potato mixture onto lettuce. Arrange hard-cooked eggs and anchovies on top. Sprinkle with snipped parsley. Pass the reserved dressing. Makes 8 to 10 servings.

German Potato Salad

6 medium potatoes (2 pounds)
6 slices bacon
½ cup chopped onion
2 tablespoons all-purpose
    flour
2 tablespoons sugar
1½ teaspoons salt
1 teaspoon celery seed
    Dash pepper
1 cup water
½ cup vinegar
2 hard-cooked eggs, sliced

In covered saucepan cook potatoes in boiling salted water for 25 to 30 minutes or till tender; drain. Peel and slice potatoes. In large skillet cook bacon till crisp; drain and crumble, reserving ¼ cup drippings. Cook onion in the reserved drippings till tender but not brown. Blend in flour, sugar, salt, celery seed, and pepper. Add water and vinegar. Cook and stir till thickened. Stir in bacon and potatoes. Cook about 5 minutes or till heated through, tossing lightly. Add hard-cooked eggs; toss lightly just to mix vegetables. Makes 6 to 8 servings.

Potluck Potato Salad

3 tablespoons vinegar
2 teaspoons mustard seed
1½ teaspoons celery seed
9 medium potatoes (3 pounds)
1 cup chopped celery
½ cup thinly sliced green
    onion
3 hard-cooked eggs, chopped
2 cups mayonnaise *or* salad
    dressing
1 teaspoon salt
    Paprika

Combine vinegar, mustard seed, and celery seed; let stand several hours. In covered saucepan cook potatoes in boiling salted water for 25 to 30 minutes or till tender; drain. Peel and cube potatoes. In large bowl sprinkle potatoes with a little salt. Add celery, onion, and eggs; toss lightly. Combine mayonnaise, salt, and vinegar mixture. Add to potato mixture; toss to mix vegetables. Chill. Sprinkle with paprika. Makes 12 to 15 servings.

Bean and Carrot Salad (opposite, above)

1 16-ounce can (2 cups) cut
  green beans, drained
1 16-ounce can (2 cups)
  sliced carrots, drained
1 15½-ounce can (2 cups) red
  kidney beans, drained
1 small onion, thinly sliced
¼ cup chopped green pepper
¼ cup chopped celery
2 tablespoons snipped parsley
½ cup vinegar
⅓ cup sugar
2 tablespoons salad oil
1 teaspoon dry mustard
  Dash pepper

In deep bowl combine green beans, carrots, kidney beans, onion, green pepper, celery, and parsley. In a screw-top jar combine vinegar, sugar, oil, mustard, and pepper; cover and shake well to mix. Pour mixture over vegetables and stir to coat. Cover and refrigerate several hours or overnight, stirring occasionally. To serve, spoon vegetables into serving dish, arranging onion rings atop. Makes 10 to 12 servings.

Scandinavian Cucumbers (opposite, below right)

½ cup dairy sour cream
2 tablespoons snipped parsley
2 tablespoons tarragon vinegar
1 tablespoon sugar
1 tablespoon snipped chives
3 small unpeeled cucumbers,
  thinly sliced (3 cups)

Stir together sour cream, parsley, tarragon vinegar, sugar, and chives. Gently fold in cucumbers. Cover and chill. Makes 6 servings.

Dilly Macaroni Salad (opposite, below left)

1 cup elbow macaroni
1 cup cubed American cheese
  (4 ounces)
½ cup sliced celery
½ cup chopped green pepper
3 tablespoons chopped
  pimiento
½ cup mayonnaise *or* salad
  dressing
1 tablespoon vinegar
¾ teaspoon salt
½ teaspoon dried dillweed

Cook macaroni according to package directions; drain well. Cool. Combine macaroni, cheese cubes, celery, green pepper, and pimiento.
  Blend together mayonnaise or salad dressing, vinegar, salt, and dillweed; add to macaroni mixture. Toss lightly. Cover and chill well. Serve salad in lettuce-lined bowl, if desired. Makes 6 servings.

Toting
Picnic Salads

To keep salads chilled for patio buffets or summer picnic outings, pack cold prepared salads in an insulated ice bucket. Secure lid with masking tape. The container is easy to tote and doubles as an attractive serving dish.

Bean and Carrot Salad provides a refreshing twist to the popular
three-bean salad. A deviled dressing complements the colorful vegetable combination.

A sprinkling of dillweed gives *Dilly Macaroni Salad* a summer-fresh taste.

Seasoned sour cream accents the crisp vegetable in *Scandinavian Cucumbers*.

You're sure to find your favorite coleslaw among this cabbage-patch selection.
For *Tangy Coleslaw*, toss red and green cabbage with a spunky, home-cooked dressing.

Tangy Coleslaw (pictured above)

1 tablespoon butter *or*
   margarine
4 teaspoons all-purpose flour
2 tablespoons sugar
1 teaspoon dry mustard
½ teaspoon salt
   Dash white pepper
1½ cups milk
⅓ cup vinegar
2 tablespoons lemon juice
3 cups shredded green cabbage
1 cup shredded red cabbage
1 cup shredded carrot
¼ cup chopped green pepper

In saucepan melt butter over low heat. Blend in flour, sugar, mustard, salt, and white pepper. Add milk; cook and stir till thickened and bubbly. Stir in vinegar and lemon juice. Chill. Combine cabbages, carrot, and green pepper. Pour chilled dressing over vegetables; toss to coat vegetables. Garnish with carrot curls, if desired. Makes 6 to 8 servings.

Coleslaw Vinaigrette

2 cups shredded cabbage
⅓ cup sliced green onion
¼ cup snipped parsley
3 tablespoons vinegar
2 tablespoons sugar
2 tablespoons salad oil
1 teaspoon salt
2 hard-cooked eggs, chilled

Combine cabbage, onion, and parsley. Stir together vinegar, sugar, salad oil, and salt till sugar is dissolved. Pour vinegar mixture over vegetables; toss to coat vegetables. Cover and chill. Separate yolk from white of one hard-cooked egg. Cut up white; toss with cabbage. Slice remaining egg; arrange atop salad. Sieve yolk over the egg slices. Makes 4 servings.

Crunchy Garden Slaw

4 cups finely shredded
    cabbage
1 cup thinly sliced celery
1 cup chopped cucumber
½ cup chopped green pepper
½ cup mayonnaise *or* salad
    dressing
2 tablespoons vinegar
1 teaspoon prepared mustard
½ teaspoon sugar
¼ teaspoon salt
¼ teaspoon paprika
1 tablespoon chopped
    pimiento

Combine shredded cabbage, celery, cucumber, and green pepper. Stir together mayonnaise or salad dressing, vinegar, mustard, sugar, salt, and paprika. Pour mayonnaise mixture over vegetables; toss to coat vegetables. Cover and chill. Garnish with pimiento. Makes 8 servings.

Cabbage to Coleslaw

To make coleslaw the way you like it, follow these guides for cutting cabbage. (A) For long, coarse shreds, hold quarter head of cabbage firmly against cutting surface; slice with long-bladed knife. (B) For short, medium shreds, push quarter head of cabbage across coarse blade of vegetable shredder. (C) For fine, juicy shreds, cut cabbage into small wedges. Place half the wedges at a time in blender container; cover with cold water. Blend till chopped. Drain.

Macaroni-Cheddar Salad

3 cups medium shell macaroni
  (10 ounces)
1 cup dairy sour cream
1 cup mayonnaise *or* salad
  dressing
¼ cup milk
½ cup sweet pickle relish
2 tablespoons vinegar
2 teaspoons prepared mustard
¾ teaspoon salt
2 cups cubed cheddar cheese
  (8 ounces)
1 cup chopped celery
½ cup chopped green pepper
¼ cup chopped onion

Cook macaroni according to package directions; drain. Rinse with cold water. Drain and set aside. Combine sour cream, mayonnaise, and milk; stir in pickle relish, vinegar, mustard, and salt. Toss together cooled macaroni, cheese, celery, green pepper, and onion. Pour sour cream mixture over all; toss lightly to mix. (Salad will appear quite moist.) Chill several hours or overnight. Makes 12 servings.

Macaroni Salad

16 ounces shell macaroni
½ cup milk
2 teaspoons instant beef bouillon
  granules
2 tablespoons hot water
1½ cups mayonnaise *or* salad
  dressing
½ cup dairy sour cream
3 tomatoes, seeded and chopped
¾ cup finely chopped red onion
2 small green peppers, chopped
⅓ cup chopped sweet pickle
2 to 3 large shallots, chopped
2 teaspoons dried dillweed

Cook macaroni in boiling salted water till tender; drain. Toss with milk; cover and chill. Dissolve bouillon granules in the hot water. Stir together mayonnaise or salad dressing, sour cream, bouillon, 1½ teaspoons *salt,* and several dashes of *pepper.* Stir into macaroni. Reserve a *third* of the chopped tomato, a *fourth* of the chopped onion, and a *fourth* of the green pepper for garnish. Fold remaining tomato, onion, and green pepper, along with chopped pickle, shallots, and dillweed, into macaroni. Turn into serving bowl. Garnish with reserved tomato, onion, and green pepper. Makes 16 servings.

Hot Five-Bean Salad

8 slices bacon
⅔ cup sugar
2 tablespoons cornstarch
1½ teaspoons salt
  Dash pepper
¾ cup vinegar
½ cup water
1 16-ounce can dark red
  kidney beans
1 16-ounce can cut green
  beans
1 16-ounce can lima beans
1 16-ounce can cut wax beans
1 15-ounce can garbanzo
  beans

In large skillet cook bacon till crisp; drain, reserving ¼ cup drippings in skillet. Crumble bacon and set aside. Combine sugar, cornstarch, salt, and pepper; blend into reserved drippings. Stir in vinegar and water; cook and stir till boiling. Drain all beans; stir beans into the skillet. Cover and simmer for 15 to 20 minutes. Stir in crumbled bacon. Transfer to a serving dish. Makes 10 to 12 servings.

Creamy Lima Cups

1 10-ounce package frozen
   baby lima beans
¼ cup dairy sour cream
1 tablespoon milk
1 tablespoon vinegar
1 tablespoon salad oil
½ clove garlic, minced
½ teaspoon sugar
¼ teaspoon salt
   Dash paprika
½ cup thinly sliced celery
4 lettuce cups

Cook limas according to package directions; drain well. Cool. Blend together dairy sour cream, milk, vinegar, salad oil, garlic, sugar, salt, and paprika. Combine with beans and celery; cover and chill well. To serve, spoon the mixture into 4 lettuce cups. Sprinkle with additional paprika, if desired. Makes 4 servings.

Carrot-Pineapple Toss

½ cup raisins
1 8¼-ounce can pineapple
   slices, drained
2 cups coarsely shredded
   carrot
½ cup mayonnaise *or* salad
   dressing
1 teaspoon lemon juice
   (optional)

Place raisins in bowl; cover with boiling *water*. Let stand 5 minutes; drain well. Cut pineapple into small pieces; mix pineapple with shredded carrot and raisins. Cover and chill. Just before serving, blend in mayonnaise. Sprinkle with lemon juice, if desired. Makes 4 servings.

Sauerkraut Salad

1 16-ounce can sauerkraut
¼ cup finely chopped celery
¼ cup chopped onion
¼ cup shredded carrot
¾ cup sugar
¼ cup vinegar

Drain and snip sauerkraut, reserving liquid. Rinse sauerkraut under cold running water. Drain well. Combine sauerkraut, celery, onion, and carrot. In saucepan combine reserved sauerkraut liquid, sugar, and vinegar; bring to boil, stirring constantly. Remove from heat; pour over vegetable mixture. Toss to coat vegetables evenly. Chill several hours or overnight. Makes 6 servings.

Wilted Cabbage Salad

3 slices bacon
¼ cup chopped onion
2 tablespoons vinegar
2 tablespoons water
1 tablespoon sugar
½ teaspoon salt
⅛ teaspoon pepper
1 small head cabbage,
   shredded (about 4 cups)
1 apple, peeled, cored, and
   finely chopped (1 cup)

In skillet cook bacon till crisp; drain, reserving 3 tablespoons drippings. Set bacon aside. Add onion to drippings and cook till tender. Stir in vinegar, water, sugar, salt, and pepper; bring to boiling. Add cabbage and apple; toss to coat. Cover and cook over medium heat about 5 minutes or till cabbage is just wilted. Crumble bacon over top and serve. Makes 6 to 8 servings.

Spanish Vegetable Mold (pictured above)

1 6-ounce package lemon-
   flavored gelatin
1 12-ounce can (1½ cups)
   vegetable juice cocktail
¼ cup Italian salad dressing
3 tablespoons vinegar
1 8-ounce can red kidney beans
½ of a 15-ounce can (¾ cup)
   garbanzo beans
¾ cup tiny cauliflowerets
½ cup chopped, seeded tomato
½ cup chopped celery
⅓ cup chopped green pepper

In bowl dissolve gelatin in 1½ cups boiling *water*. Stir in vegetable juice cocktail, Italian salad dressing, and vinegar. Chill till partially set. Drain the kidney beans and garbanzo beans. Fold beans, cauliflowerets, tomato, celery, and green pepper into gelatin mixture. Turn into a 6½-cup mold. Chill till firm. Unmold onto serving plate. Garnish with curly endive and avocado slices, if desired. Makes 10 to 12 servings.

One Cup Cottage Ring

1 3-ounce package lime-
   flavored gelatin
1 cup mayonnaise *or* salad
   dressing
1 8-ounce carton cream-style
   cottage cheese
1 cup finely chopped celery
1 cup diced green pepper

Dissolve gelatin in 1 cup boiling *water*. Add mayonnaise or salad dressing and beat with rotary beater or electric mixer till smooth. Chill till partially set. Fold in cottage cheese, chopped celery, and diced green pepper. Pour into 4-cup ring mold. Chill till firm. Unmold onto serving plate. Makes 6 servings.

Garden-Fresh Tomato Aspic

8 **large tomatoes**
1 **3-ounce package lemon-flavored gelatin**
2 **tablespoons catsup**
1 **tablespoon lemon juice**
2 **teaspoons prepared horse-radish**
1½ **teaspoons worcestershire sauce**
½ **teaspoon salt**
   Dash pepper
¾ **cup finely chopped celery**
¼ **cup finely chopped onion**
¼ **cup finely chopped green pepper**
   Spinach leaves
   Mayonnaise *or* **salad dressing**

Cut off stems of tomatoes. Prepare tomato shells by scooping out pulp; reserve pulp. To drain, invert tomato shells on paper toweling. Place reserved pulp in blender container. Cover; blend till pureed. Sieve to remove seeds. Measure 2 cups puree. In saucepan combine puree and gelatin. Bring to boiling; stir to dissolve gelatin. Remove from heat; stir in catsup, lemon juice, horseradish, worcestershire, salt, and pepper. Chill till partially set. Fold celery, onion, and green pepper into gelatin mixture. Sprinkle insides of tomato shells with salt; place upright on tray. Fill with gelatin mixture. Chill till firm. Serve on spinach leaves with mayonnaise, if desired. Makes 6 servings.

Tomato Soup Salad

1 **10¾-ounce can condensed tomato soup**
1 **envelope unflavored gelatin**
¼ **teaspoon salt**
1 **cup cream-style cottage cheese**
¼ **cup mayonnaise** *or* **salad dressing**
1 **cup chopped celery**
1 **cup chopped radishes**
½ **cup chopped cucumber**
2 **tablespoons sliced green onion**

In medium saucepan stir together soup, gelatin, and salt; let stand 10 minutes to soften gelatin. Stir over low heat till gelatin dissolves. With rotary beater or electric mixer, beat in cottage cheese and mayonnaise or salad dressing. Chill mixture till partially set. Fold in celery, radishes, cucumber, and green onion. Pour into 4-cup mold. Chill till firm. To serve, unmold onto serving platter. Makes 6 to 8 servings.

Cheesy Coleslaw Mold

1 **3-ounce package lime-flavored gelatin**
1½ **cups boiling water**
2 **tablespoons vinegar**
⅓ **cup mayonnaise** *or* **salad dressing**
½ **teaspoon salt**
   Dash pepper
1 **cup chopped cabbage**
½ **cup shredded carrot**
½ **cup shredded sharp American cheese (2 ounces)**
⅛ **teaspoon celery seed**

Dissolve gelatin in boiling water; stir in vinegar. Add mayonnaise, salt, and pepper; beat smooth with rotary beater. Chill till partially set. Fold cabbage, carrot, cheese, and celery seed into gelatin. Pour into 6 individual molds. Chill till firm. To serve, unmold salads onto lettuce-lined plates, if desired. Makes 6 servings.

Like your Italian salad chilled? All the makings for the traditional tossed version go into this refreshing *Italian Salad Mold.*

Creamy Vegetable Mold gets a rich, smooth taste from sour cream sauce mix, a tangy bite from lemon juice, and a delightful herb flavor from dillweed.

Italian Salad Mold (opposite, above)

1 6-ounce package lemon-
    flavored gelatin
½ of a 0.6-ounce envelope (2½
    teaspoons) Italian
    salad dressing mix
1½ cups boiling water
2 cups cold water
¼ cup vinegar
1 cup chopped iceberg
    lettuce
1 cup quartered and thinly
    sliced zucchini
½ cup shredded carrot
¼ cup sliced radishes
    Curly endive

In bowl combine gelatin and salad dressing mix. Add boiling water, stirring to dissolve gelatin. Stir in cold water and vinegar. Chill till partially set. Fold chopped lettuce, zucchini, carrot, and radishes into gelatin. Pour mixture into 5½-cup mold. Chill till firm. To serve, unmold and garnish with curly endive, if desired. Makes 8 servings.

Creamy Vegetable Mold (opposite, below)

2 1.25-ounce packages sour
    cream sauce mix
1 6-ounce package lemon-
    flavored gelatin
2 cups boiling water
½ cup cold water
2 tablespoons lemon juice
¾ teaspoon dried dillweed
2 small carrots, cut up
1 medium green pepper, seeded
    and cut up
1 medium cucumber, peeled,
    seeded, and cut up

Prepare sour cream sauce mixes according to package directions; let stand 10 minutes. Dissolve gelatin in boiling water. Stir in the prepared sour cream sauce, cold water, lemon juice, and dillweed. Beat with rotary beater till blended. Chill till partially set. Put carrots in blender container; cover with cold water. Cover; blend a few seconds or till coarsely chopped. Drain well. Repeat with green pepper and cucumber. Fold chopped vegetables into gelatin mixture. Turn into 5½-cup mold. Chill till firm. To serve, unmold and fill center with assorted fresh vegetables, if desired. Makes 8 servings.

Imperial Garden Salad

⅓ cup sugar
2 envelopes unflavored
    gelatin
1 14-ounce can beef broth
2 cups cold water
2 tablespoons lemon juice
2 tablespoons soy sauce
1 tablespoon vinegar
¼ teaspoon salt
1 16-ounce can fancy mixed
    Chinese vegetables,
    drained
¼ cup diced green pepper
½ cup dairy sour cream
1 tablespoon milk
2 teaspoons soy sauce

In saucepan combine sugar and gelatin. Add beef broth; bring to boiling, stirring to dissolve gelatin. Remove from heat; add cold water, lemon juice, 2 tablespoons soy sauce, vinegar, and salt. Chill till partially set. Fold in Chinese vegetables and green pepper. Pour mixture into 5-cup mold. Chill till firm. To make dressing, combine sour cream, milk, and 2 teaspoons soy sauce. To serve, unmold salad; serve with the dressing. Makes 6 servings.

Fabulous Fruit Bowls

Tossed Fruit Salad

½ cup sugar
¼ cup tarragon vinegar
2 tablespoons water
1 teaspoon celery salt
1 teaspoon paprika
1 teaspoon dry mustard
1 cup salad oil
2 medium oranges, chilled
1 medium grapefruit,
   chilled
1 ripe medium banana
4 cups torn iceberg lettuce
2 cups torn escarole
1 avocado, peeled and thinly
   sliced
1 cup red grapes, halved
   and seeded

To make dressing, in saucepan combine sugar, vinegar, and water. Heat and stir just till sugar dissolves; cool. Stir in celery salt, paprika, and mustard. Add oil in slow stream, beating with electric mixer till thick. Cover and chill.

Peel and section oranges and grapefruit, reserving juices. Peel and slice banana; brush with reserved citrus juices. Set aside. In large salad bowl combine iceberg lettuce and escarole. Arrange orange and grapefruit sections, banana, avocado slices, and grapes in a circle atop lettuce. Pour on chilled dressing. Toss to coat fruit and vegetables. Makes 6 to 8 servings.

Fruit Salad Platter (opposite)

1 pineapple
1 pint strawberries
1 papaya
¼ cup orange juice
2 cups honeydew melon balls
1 cantaloupe, peeled, seeded, and sliced
Lettuce
Honey-Lime Dressing
Spicy Nectar Dressing
Strawberry-Cheese Dressing

Rinse pineapple. Twist off the crown and cut off the base. Slice off strips of rind lengthwise, then cut out and discard eyes. Slice the fruit in spears; cut off hard core. Cover spears; chill. Rinse strawberries; drain and chill. Peel and slice papaya; dip in orange juice. Chill. Thoroughly chill honeydew balls and cantaloupe.

On large lettuce-lined platter arrange fruit. Serve with *Honey-Lime Dressing*, *Spicy Nectar Dressing*, and *Strawberry-Cheese Dressing*. Makes 8 servings.

Honey-Lime Dressing: In small mixer bowl blend together ½ cup *honey*, ¼ teaspoon finely shredded *lime peel*, ¼ cup *lime juice*, ¼ teaspoon *salt*, and ¼ teaspoon ground *mace*. Gradually add ¾ cup *salad oil*, beating with electric mixer or rotary beater till mixture is thickened. Beat in 2 drops green food coloring. Cover; chill. Makes 1½ cups.

Spicy Nectar Dressing: In small mixer bowl combine 1 cup dairy *sour cream*, ½ cup *apricot nectar*, ½ cup *salad oil*, 3 tablespoons *sugar*, ½ teaspoon ground *cinnamon*, ½ teaspoon *paprika*, and dash *salt*. Beat ingredients together with electric mixer or rotary beater till mixture is smooth. Cover dressing and chill thoroughly. Makes 1¾ cups.

Strawberry-Cheese Dressing: In small mixer bowl beat together one 3-ounce package *cream cheese*, softened; ½ of a 10-ounce package (½ cup) frozen *strawberries*, thawed; 1 tablespoon *sugar*; 1 tablespoon *lemon juice*; and dash *salt*. Gradually add ½ cup *salad oil*, beating till mixture is thickened. Beat in 1 or 2 drops *red food coloring*. Cover and chill thoroughly. Makes 1⅓ cups.

Pineapple-Berry Boat

2 medium pineapples
2 pints raspberries *or* strawberries
⅓ cup raspberry preserves
1 3-ounce package cream cheese, softened
1 tablespoon milk
½ teaspoon finely shredded lemon peel
2 teaspoons lemon juice
½ cup whipping cream

Halve pineapples lengthwise. Using a sharp knife, cut out the pineapple meat, leaving shell intact. Cut off the hard core and cut pineapple into chunks. Combine pineapple chunks and raspberries or strawberries; mound into pineapple shells. To make dressing, gradually blend the preserves into softened cream cheese. Stir in the milk, lemon peel, and lemon juice. Whip cream just till soft peaks form; fold into cream cheese mixture. Chill. Spoon dressing over pineapple-filled shells. Serve fruit salad from shells. Makes 8 servings.

Strawberry-Melon Salad

2 small honeydew melons
Leaf lettuce
1½ cups cream-style cottage cheese
1 cup strawberries

Cut melons in half and remove seeds. Use a melon baller to scoop out pulp. Line melon shells with leaf lettuce. Divide melon balls among lined shells. Mound a generous ⅓ cup cottage cheese in center of each. Place ¼ cup strawberries around each mound. Makes 4 servings.

Waldorf Salad is one of the easiest fruit salads to prepare, and one of the most popular. Just combine apples, celery, grapes, and walnuts, then stir in the creamy dressing.

When it comes to a tasty fruit combination, you can't top *Rainbow Compote.* Fresh strawberries, honeydew melon cubes, blueberries, and orange slices team well with a candied ginger-fruit syrup.

Waldorf Salad (opposite, above)

4 **medium apples, cored and
   chopped (3 cups)**
½ **cup chopped celery**
½ **cup red grapes, halved and
   seeded**
½ **cup chopped walnuts
   Romaine**
½ **cup mayonnaise *or* salad
   dressing**
1 **tablespoon sugar**
½ **teaspoon lemon juice**
½ **cup whipping cream
   Ground nutmeg**

Combine apples, celery, grapes, and walnuts. Turn fruit mixture into a romaine-lined salad bowl; chill. Combine mayonnaise or salad dressing, sugar, and lemon juice. Whip cream till soft peaks form; fold into mayonnaise mixture. Spoon the dressing over the chilled apple mixture. Sprinkle lightly with nutmeg. To serve, fold dressing into fruit mixture. Makes 6 servings.

Rainbow Compote (opposite, below)

½ **cup honey**
2 **tablespoons lemon juice**
1 **tablespoon finely snipped
   candied ginger (optional)**
1 **teaspoon finely shredded
   orange peel**
4 **oranges, peeled and sliced
   crosswise**
1½ **cups blueberries**
2 **cups cubed honeydew melon**
1½ **cups halved strawberries
   Whole strawberries**

Combine honey, lemon juice, candied ginger, and orange peel. Pour dressing over orange slices in bowl; cover and refrigerate for several hours or overnight. Chill the remaining fruits. Drain oranges, reserving dressing. Arrange orange slices in bottom of compote. Top with a layer of blueberries, a layer of melon cubes, and a layer of halved strawberries. Pour the reserved dressing over fruit. Garnish with additional whole strawberries, if desired. Makes 10 servings.

Tropical Fruit Salad

¼ **cup mayonnaise *or* salad
   dressing**
1 **tablespoon sugar**
½ **teaspoon lemon juice
   Dash salt**
½ **cup whipping cream**
1 **large red apple,
   chopped (1 cup)**
1 **large yellow delicious
   apple, chopped (1 cup)**
1 **large banana, sliced**
1 **cup sliced celery**
½ **cup broken walnuts
   Lettuce**
½ **cup toasted flaked coconut
   Unpeeled apple slices**

Blend together mayonnaise or salad dressing, sugar, lemon juice, and salt. Whip the cream till soft peaks form; fold into the mayonnaise mixture. Gently fold in the red and yellow apple, banana, celery, and walnuts. Chill.

Line salad bowl with lettuce; spoon in the chilled fruit mixture. Garnish with toasted coconut. Top with additional apple slices, if desired. Makes 6 servings.

24-Hour Fruit Salad

1 20-ounce can pineapple
   chunks
3 slightly beaten egg yolks
2 tablespoons sugar
2 tablespoons vinegar
1 tablespoon butter *or*
   margarine
   Dash salt
1 17-ounce can pitted light
   sweet cherries, drained
3 oranges, peeled, sectioned,
   and drained
2 cups tiny marshmallows
1 cup whipping cream

Drain pineapple; reserve 2 tablespoons syrup. To make custard, in small heavy saucepan combine reserved syrup, egg yolks, sugar, vinegar, butter or margarine, and salt. Cook and stir over low heat about 6 minutes or till mixture thickens slightly and coats a metal spoon. Cool to room temperature. In large bowl combine pineapple, cherries, oranges, and marshmallows. Pour custard over; mix fruit mixture gently. Whip the whipping cream till soft peaks form. Fold whipped cream into fruit mixture. Turn into serving bowl. Cover and refrigerate 24 hours or overnight. Makes 10 to 12 servings.

5-Cup Salad

1 11-ounce can mandarin
   orange sections, drained
1 8¼-ounce can pineapple
   chunks, drained
1 cup flaked *or* shredded
   coconut
1 cup tiny marshmallows
1 cup dairy sour cream

In bowl combine mandarin orange sections, pineapple chunks, coconut, marshmallows, and sour cream. Cover and refrigerate for several hours or overnight. Makes 6 to 8 servings.

Orange-Cream Fruit Salad

1 20-ounce can pineapple
   chunks, drained
1 16-ounce can peach slices,
   drained
1 11-ounce can mandarin orange
   sections, drained
3 medium bananas, sliced
2 medium apples, cored and
   chopped
1 3½- *or* 3¾-ounce
   package *instant* vanilla
   pudding mix
1½ cups milk
½ of a 6-ounce can (⅓ cup)
   frozen orange juice concentrate, thawed
¾ cup dairy sour cream
   Lettuce cups

In large bowl combine pineapple chunks, peaches, orange sections, bananas, and apples; set aside. In small bowl combine dry pudding mix, milk, and orange juice concentrate. Beat with rotary beater 1 to 2 minutes or till well blended. Beat in sour cream. Fold into the fruit mixture. Cover and refrigerate several hours.

Serve the salad in lettuce cups on individual serving plates. Makes 10 servings.

Cinnamon-Apple Salads

½ cup red cinnamon candies
2 cups water
6 small tart apples, peeled
    and cored
1 3-ounce package cream cheese,
    softened
2 tablespoons milk
1 teaspoon lemon juice
1 8¼-ounce can crushed
    pineapple, drained
⅓ cup snipped pitted dates
2 tablespoons chopped
    walnuts
    Lettuce

In 3-quart saucepan cook and stir cinnamon candies in water till dissolved. Add apples and cook slowly, uncovered, for 15 to 20 minutes or just till tender, turning once during cooking. Chill apples in syrup several hours, turning once. Blend together cream cheese, milk, and lemon juice till smooth. Stir in pineapple, dates, and walnuts. Drain apples; stuff center of each apple with some of the cream cheese mixture. Serve on lettuce-lined plates. Makes 6 servings.

Ambrosia Salad

1 15¼-ounce can pineapple
    chunks
3 medium oranges, peeled
    and sectioned
½ cup maraschino
    cherries, halved and
    drained
½ cup flaked or shredded
    coconut
    Fresh mint leaves

Drain pineapple chunks, reserving ¼ cup of the syrup. Combine pineapple chunks, the ¼ cup reserved pineapple syrup, orange sections, and maraschino cherries. Cover; chill thoroughly. Just before serving, fold in coconut. Garnish with fresh mint leaves, if desired. Makes 6 servings.

Sunshine Salad

½ of 21-ounce can (1 cup)
    apricot pie filling
½ of 14-ounce can (⅔ cup)
    sweetened condensed
    milk
½ of 4½-ounce carton frozen
    whipped dessert topping,
    thawed
¼ cup lemon juice
2 11-ounce cans mandarin
    orange sections, drained
1 15¼-ounce can pineapple
    chunks, drained
½ cup tiny marshmallows
½ cup chopped walnuts
¼ cup flaked or shredded
    coconut

In large bowl combine pie filling, condensed milk, whipped topping, and lemon juice. Reserve several mandarin orange sections. Fold remaining mandarin oranges into apricot mixture along with pineapple, marshmallows, chopped walnuts, and coconut. Cover and refrigerate several hours or overnight. Garnish salad with reserved oranges and sprinkle with additional coconut, if desired. Makes 8 to 10 servings.

Molded Fruit Salads

Harvest Fruit Mold (pictured above)

1 12-ounce package mixed dried
   fruits
¼ cup sugar
1 6-ounce package orange-
   flavored gelatin
2 cups boiling water
½ cup dry sherry
   Leaf lettuce
   Frosted Grapes
   Preserved kumquats, halved
   lengthwise

In saucepan combine dried fruit and enough water to cover the fruit. Simmer gently, covered, for 25 minutes. Add sugar; simmer 5 to 10 minutes more. Drain fruit, reserving syrup. Add water to syrup to make 1½ cups liquid. Dissolve gelatin in boiling water. Stir in reserved syrup mixture and sherry. Chill till partially set.

Pit prunes; cut up all cooked fruit. Fold into gelatin mixture. Pour into 6-cup ring mold. Chill till firm. Unmold on lettuce-lined platter. Fill center of mold with *Frosted Grapes*. Garnish with kumquat halves. Serves 8 to 10.

Frosted Grapes: Dip 1½ pounds *green grapes* into 2 lightly beaten *egg whites*. Drain. Dip grapes in ½ cup *sugar.* Place on rack to dry for 2 hours.

Grape and Grapefruit Mold

2 envelopes unflavored gelatin
½ cup sugar
1 cup boiling water
1 16-ounce can sweetened
   grapefruit sections
   Unsweetened grapefruit juice
   (about 1¼ cups)
¼ cup lemon juice
   Several drops yellow food
   coloring
2 cups seedless green grapes
   Lettuce

Dissolve gelatin and sugar in boiling water. Drain grapefruit, reserving syrup. Add enough unsweetened grapefruit juice to reserved syrup to make 2¼ cups. Add to gelatin mixture with lemon juice and food coloring. Chill till partially set. Fold grapefruit and grapes into gelatin. Carefully pour into 6-cup mold. Or, arrange a few of the grapes in bottom of mold; add gelatin to cover. Chill till almost set. Repeat with remaining grapes, the grapefruit, and gelatin, arranging fruit along sides of mold. Chill till firm. Unmold on lettuce-lined platter. Makes 10 to 12 servings.

Jubilee Salad Mold

1 **10-ounce package frozen red raspberries, thawed**
1 **6-ounce package red raspberry-flavored gelatin**
1¾ **cups boiling water**
½ **cup cream sherry**
¼ **cup lemon juice**
1 **16-ounce can pitted dark sweet cherries, drained and halved**

Drain raspberries, reserving syrup. In large mixing bowl dissolve gelatin in boiling water. Stir in sherry, lemon juice, and reserved raspberry syrup. Chill till partially set. Fold in raspberries and cherries. Pour into a 5- or 6-cup ring mold. Chill till firm. Unmold on lettuce-lined platter, if desired. Makes 8 servings.

Fruity Ginger Ale Mold (pictured on page 294)

1 **3-ounce package lemon-flavored gelatin**
1 **cup boiling water**
1 **cup ginger ale, chilled**
1 **medium apple, cored and cut in wedges**
1 **8¼-ounce can pineapple slices, cut up**
1 **small apple, cored, peeled, and chopped**
½ **cup halved seedless green grapes**

Dissolve gelatin in boiling water. Cool to room temperature. Slowly add ginger ale.

Arrange apple wedges in 4½-cup mold. Pour in *¾ cup* of the gelatin mixture. Chill till almost firm. Meanwhile, chill remaining gelatin till partially set. Fold in pineapple, chopped apple, and halved grapes. Pour over first layer. Chill till firm. Unmold on lettuce-lined platter, if desired. Makes 5 or 6 servings.

Unmolding a Gelatin Salad

Tower or ring gelatin salads aren't tricky to unmold if you follow these steps and helpful hints. With the tip of a small paring knife, loosen edge of gelatin from the mold (and around center of ring mold). (A) Dip the mold just to the rim in warm water for a *few seconds*. Tilt slightly to ease gelatin away from one side and let air in. Tilt and rotate mold so air can loosen gelatin all the way around. (B) Center an upside-down serving plate over the mold. Holding tightly, invert plate and mold. Shake mold gently. (C) Lift off the mold, being careful not to tear the gelatin. If the salad doesn't slide out easily, repeat the process, beginning with step A. Garnish serving plate, if desired.

Pear-Limeade Molds (opposite, above)

2 envelopes unflavored gelatin
½ cup cold water
2 pears, peeled, halved, and
   cored
2 cups water
¼ cup sugar
1 6-ounce can frozen limeade
   concentrate
Dash salt
Green food coloring
Whole maraschino cherries
Endive
Mayonnaise *or* salad
   dressing
Chopped pecans

Soften gelatin in cold water; set aside. In saucepan combine pear halves, the 2 cups water, and the sugar. Bring mixture to boil; reduce heat. Cover and simmer 5 to 6 minutes or till pears are tender. With slotted spoon, remove pears to a bowl; cover and refrigerate. Stir softened gelatin into hot pear liquid, stirring till dissolved. Add limeade concentrate, salt, and a few drops of food coloring. Pour ⅓ *cup* of the gelatin mixture into each of 4 flared water goblets or tall individual molds. Chill till almost firm. Chill the remaining gelatin till partially set. Add a pear half, narrow end down, to each goblet, tucking a maraschino cherry into each. Cover the pears with remaining gelatin. Chill till firm. Unmold on plates, flared end down. Garnish with endive. Spoon some mayonnaise or salad dressing atop and sprinkle with chopped pecans, if desired. Makes 4 servings.

Lemon-Frosted Plum Squares (opposite, below left)

1 6-ounce package strawberry-
   flavored gelatin
Dash salt
2½ cups boiling water
1 cup lemon-lime
   carbonated beverage
2 tablespoons lemon juice
2 cups plums, pitted and cut in
   wedges (9 plums)
1 3½- *or* 3¾-ounce package
   instant lemon pudding mix
1¼ cups cold milk
½ cup dairy sour cream
Bibb lettuce
Apple slices

Dissolve gelatin and salt in boiling water. Cool to room temperature. Slowly pour in carbonated beverage and lemon juice; stir gently. Chill till partially set. Fold in plums. Pour into 8×8×2-inch pan. Chill till almost firm. In mixer bowl combine pudding mix and milk; beat till smooth. Blend in sour cream. Spread pudding mixture atop gelatin. Chill till firm. Cut into squares and serve on lettuce-lined plates. Garnish with apple slices atop each square, if desired. Makes 6 to 8 servings.

Apricot Soufflé Salad (opposite, below right)

1 3-ounce package orange-
   flavored gelatin
1 cup boiling water
½ cup cold water
2 tablespoons lemon juice
⅓ cup mayonnaise *or* salad
   dressing
2 tablespoons finely chopped
   celery
4 *or* 5 apricots, peeled
   and sliced (1 cup)
1 medium apple, thinly sliced

Dissolve gelatin in boiling water. Stir in cold water and lemon juice. Chill till partially set; whip till fluffy. On low speed of mixer, beat in mayonnaise or salad dressing. Fold in celery. Arrange apricot and apple slices in a 5 to 5½ cup mold; carefully spoon in gelatin. Chill till firm. Makes 4 to 6 servings.

Tall, shimmering, and definitely fancy describe *Pear-Limeade Molds*. To make
this graceful tower salad, use a stemmed water goblet to mold the pear half and gelatin.

For a fast make-ahead salad,
fix *Lemon-Frosted Plum Squares*.

Treat your guests to the rich
flavor of *Apricot Soufflé Salad*.

Cherry-Cider Salad (opposite, above)

2 cups apple cider *or* apple
   juice
1 6-ounce package cherry-
   flavored gelatin
1 16-ounce can pitted dark
   sweet cherries
½ cup thinly sliced celery
½ cup chopped walnuts
1 3-ounce package cream
   cheese, softened
1 8½-ounce can (1 cup)
   applesauce
  Leaf lettuce

Bring apple cider or juice to boiling. Dissolve gelatin in boiling cider. Drain cherries, reserving syrup. Halve cherries and set aside. Add enough water to reserved syrup to measure 1½ cups liquid; stir into gelatin. Set aside 2 cups of the gelatin mixture; keep at room temperature. Chill remaining gelatin till partially set. Fold cherries, celery, and walnuts into partially set gelatin. Pour into 6½-cup ring mold. Chill till almost firm. Gradually add reserved gelatin to softened cream cheese, beating till smooth. Stir in applesauce. Spoon cream cheese mixture over cherry layer in mold. Chill till firm. Unmold on lettuce-lined platter. Serve with mayonnaise or salad dressing and sprinkle with additional walnuts, if desired. Makes 10 to 12 servings.

Strawberry Soufflé Salads (opposite, below)

1 10-ounce package frozen
   sliced strawberries,
   thawed
1 3-ounce package strawberry-
   flavored gelatin
1 cup boiling water
2 tablespoons lemon juice
¼ cup mayonnaise *or*
   salad dressing
¼ cup chopped walnuts
  Romaine
  Canned pineapple slices

Drain strawberries, reserving syrup. Add enough water to syrup to make ¾ cup liquid. Dissolve gelatin and ¼ teaspoon *salt* in boiling water. Stir in reserved syrup and lemon juice. Beat in mayonnaise or salad dressing. Chill till partially set. With electric mixer whip gelatin mixture till fluffy. Fold in strawberries and nuts. Pour into 4 to 6 individual molds. Chill till firm. Unmold onto a lettuce-lined platter, setting each salad atop a pineapple slice. Serve with additional mayonnaise or salad dressing, if desired. Makes 4 to 6 servings.

Minted Pear Salad

1 14-ounce can *or* jar mint-
   flavored pear halves
1 3-ounce package lime-
   flavored gelatin
1 cup boiling water
1 8-ounce carton plain yogurt

Drain pears, reserving ½ cup of the syrup. Dissolve gelatin in boiling water; stir in reserved pear syrup. Chill till partially set. Beat into yogurt. Chop pear halves; fold into gelatin. Pour into 9×5×3-inch loaf pan. Chill till firm. Cut in rectangles to serve. Makes 6 servings.

Gooseberry-Banana Salad

1 16-ounce can gooseberries
1 3-ounce package lime-
   flavored gelatin
1 3-ounce package lemon-
   flavored gelatin
1 pint lime sherbet
2 bananas, sliced
½ cup thinly sliced celery

Drain gooseberries, reserving syrup; add enough water to syrup to make 2 cups liquid. Heat gooseberry liquid to boiling; add lime and lemon gelatin and stir to dissolve. Stir in lime sherbet by tablespoonfuls. Chill till partially set. Stir gooseberries, bananas, and celery into gelatin mixture. Turn into 9×9×2-inch pan. Chill till firm. Cut in squares. Makes 12 servings.

This two-layered gelatin salad is a natural favorite for your fall menu. *Cherry-Cider Salad* offers a flavorful combination of sweet cherries, apple cider, cream cheese, and applesauce.

Individually molded *Strawberry Soufflé Salads* begin with frozen strawberries and strawberry-flavored gelatin. Pineapple slices form the base for these serving-size salads, and lemon juice adds a pleasant, flavorful accent.

Lemon-Papaya Salad

1 3-ounce package lemon-
   flavored gelatin
1 cup boiling water
1 3-ounce package cream cheese,
   softened
1 egg yolk
⅛ teaspoon salt
½ cup dairy sour cream
¼ teaspoon finely shredded
   lemon peel
1½ teaspoons lemon juice
1 stiffly beaten egg white
1 medium papaya, seeded,
   peeled, and diced
   Leaf lettuce

Dissolve gelatin in boiling water; cool to room temperature. In a large mixing bowl combine cream cheese, egg yolk, and salt; mix thoroughly. Stir in sour cream, lemon peel, and lemon juice. Stir cooled gelatin mixture into sour cream mixture. Chill till partially set. Gently fold in egg white and papaya. Chill till amost firm. Turn into a 4-cup ring mold. Chill till firm. Unmold salad on lettuce-lined platter. Makes 6 servings.

Cherry-Orange Squares

3 large oranges
1 6-ounce package cherry-
   flavored gelatin
1 cup boiling water
1 21-ounce can cherry pie
   filling
1 3-ounce package lemon-
   flavored gelatin
1 cup boiling water
½ cup cold water
1 8-ounce carton lemon yogurt
½ cup chopped toasted almonds

Section oranges over a bowl to catch juice; add enough water to juice to make ½ cup liquid. Dice oranges. Dissolve cherry-flavored gelatin in 1 cup boiling water; stir in orange juice. Chill till partially set. Fold in cherry pie filling and oranges. Pour into 12×7×2-inch dish. Chill till almost firm. Meanwhile, dissolve lemon-flavored gelatin in 1 cup boiling water; stir in cold water. Beat in yogurt. Spoon over the cherry layer. Sprinkle with toasted almonds. Chill till firm. Cut in squares to serve. Makes 10 to 12 servings.

Cran-Raspberry Ring

1 3-ounce package
   raspberry-flavored
   gelatin
1 3-ounce package lemon-
   flavored gelatin
1¼ cups boiling water
1 10-ounce package frozen
   red raspberries
1 14-ounce jar cranberry-
   orange relish
1 cup lemon-lime carbonated
   beverage
   Lettuce

Dissolve raspberry- and lemon-flavored gelatin in boiling water. Stir in frozen raspberries, breaking up large pieces with fork. Stir in cranberry-orange relish.

   Slowly pour in lemon-lime carbonated beverage; stir gently. Turn into a 6- or 6½-cup ring mold. Chill till firm. Unmold on lettuce-lined platter. Makes 8 to 10 servings.

Cider Waldorf Mold

2 **cups apple cider** *or* **apple juice**
1 **3-ounce package lemon-flavored gelatin**
1 **cup finely chopped apple**
¼ **cup finely chopped celery**
¼ **cup finely chopped pecans**
Lettuce
Mayonnaise *or* **salad dressing**

Bring *1 cup* apple cider or juice to boiling. Dissolve gelatin in boiling cider. Stir in remaining cider or juice. Chill till partially set. Fold in apple, celery, and pecans. Pour into a 3-cup mold or spoon into 6 individual molds. Chill till firm. Unmold on lettuce-lined plates. Serve with mayonnaise or salad dressing. Makes 6 servings.

Spicy Orange-Fig Mold

1 **cup water**
2 **inches stick cinnamon**
10 **whole cloves**
1 **3-ounce package orange-flavored gelatin**
1 **cup orange juice**
1 **large apple, peeled, cored, and diced (1 cup)**
½ **cup chopped dried figs**
Lettuce

In small saucepan combine water, stick cinnamon, and cloves; cover and simmer 5 minutes. Remove cinnamon and cloves. Measure liquid; add more boiling water, if necessary, to measure 1 cup. Add gelatin, stirring till dissolved. Stir in orange juice. Chill till partially set. Fold in apple and figs. Pour into 3½-cup mold. Chill till firm. Unmold on lettuce-lined platter. Makes 4 or 5 servings.

Note: If desired, soften dried figs before using. Place figs in strainer; pour boiling water over fruit. Drain well.

Terms to Know about Gelatin

Recipes for gelatin salads frequently refer to different "jellying" stages. Each step in preparing the salad (blending, folding, beating, and layering) should be done while the gelatin is the proper consistency or thickness. Because the consistency of gelatin changes as it chills, it's important to recognize each stage as it occurs. We've listed the terms used to describe the different stages, plus some helpful hints on how to recognize them.

Chill till partially set: The gelatin is the consistency of unbeaten egg whites. At this stage ingredients such as fruit and nuts are folded in. The solid ingredients will neither sink nor float, but remain evenly distributed. If whipped at this stage, the mixture will become fluffy and will mound.

Chill till almost firm: The gelatin mixture appears set, but will tend to flow if tipped to one side and is sticky to the touch. The mixture mounds when dropped from a spoon. This is the desired consistency when preparing a layered salad.

Chill till firm: The gelatin mixture can now hold a distinctive cut and doesn't move when tilted in the mold. The gelatin is completely set and ready to unmold.

Frozen Salad Favorites

Frozen Lime-Mint Salads (pictured above)

1 29½-ounce can crushed
   pineapple
1 3-ounce package lime-
   flavored gelatin
1 6½-ounce package tiny
   marshmallows
1 cup butter mints, crushed
1 9-ounce container frozen
   whipped dessert topping,
   thawed
   Grape leaves *or* lettuce

In large bowl combine *undrained* pineapple, *dry* lime gelatin, marshmallows, and crushed mints. Cover and refrigerate for several hours or till marshmallows soften and melt. Fold in dessert topping. Spoon mixture into 16 paper bake-cup-lined muffin pans. Cover and freeze till firm. Peel off paper and serve on grape leaf or lettuce-lined plates. Garnish with fresh mint sprigs, if desired. Makes 16.

Orange-Apricot Freeze

2 8-ounce cartons orange
   yogurt
½ cup sugar
1 17-ounce can unpeeled
   apricot halves, drained
⅓ cup coarsely chopped pecans
   Lettuce

In mixing bowl stir together yogurt and sugar till blended. Cut up apricots. Fold apricots and nuts into yogurt mixture. Spoon into 8 to 10 paper bake-cup-lined muffin pans. Cover and freeze till firm. Peel off paper from salads. Serve on lettuce-lined plates. Makes 8 to 10 servings.

Fruited Avocado Freeze

1 large avocado
2 tablespoons lemon juice
¼ cup mayonnaise *or* salad dressing
1 3-ounce package cream cheese, softened
2 tablespoons sugar
¼ teaspoon salt
1 16-ounce can pear halves, drained and chopped
¼ cup chopped maraschino cherries
½ cup whipping cream
Lettuce

Halve, seed, peel, and chop avocado; sprinkle with *1 table-spoon* of the lemon juice. Blend together the remaining lemon juice, mayonnaise or salad dressing, cream cheese, sugar, and salt. Add chopped avocado, pears, and chopped maraschino cherries. Whip the cream till soft peaks form. Fold into cream cheese mixture. Pour mixture into 7½×3½×2-inch junior loaf pan. Cover and freeze till firm.

To serve, let stand at room temperature about 10 minutes. Unmold. Slice and serve atop lettuce-lined salad plates. Makes 6 to 8 servings.

Frozen Orange-Date Molds

1 8-ounce package cream cheese, softened
¼ cup orange juice
1 8¼-ounce can crushed pineapple, drained
½ cup finely snipped pitted dates
½ cup chopped pecans
¼ cup maraschino cherries, halved
½ teaspoon finely shredded orange peel
1 cup whipping cream
Lettuce

Beat together cream cheese and orange juice till fluffy. Stir in drained pineapple, dates, nuts, cherries, and orange peel. Whip the cream till soft peaks form. Fold whipped cream into cream cheese mixture. Spoon into 9 individual molds or one 8×4×2-inch loaf dish. Cover and freeze till firm. Let stand at room temperature 10 to 15 minutes before serving. Unmold onto lettuce-lined plates. Garnish with orange slices, if desired. Makes 9 servings.

Frozen Lemon Salad

1 8-ounce package cream cheese, softened
¼ cup mayonnaise *or* salad dressing
1 pint lemon sherbet
1 11-ounce can mandarin orange sections, drained and cut up
1 8-ounce can peach slices, drained and chopped
¼ cup slivered almonds, toasted
Lettuce

In large bowl beat together cream cheese and mayonnaise or salad dressing till smooth. Stir sherbet to soften; quickly stir into cream cheese mixture. Stir in orange sections, peaches, and almonds. Turn cream cheese-fruit mixture into 8×8×2-inch dish. Cover and freeze till firm.

To serve, let stand at room temperature for 10 to 15 minutes. Cut into squares. Serve on lettuce-lined salad plates. Makes 9 to 12 servings.

Frozen Cheesecake Salads

1 10¾- *or* 11-ounce pack-
    age cheesecake mix
1 8¼-ounce can crushed pine-
    apple
1 cup milk
1 cup cranberries, chopped
½ cup chopped walnuts
½ cup snipped pitted dates

Set aside graham cracker crumb portion of cheesecake mix for another use. (For example, follow package directions to make a graham cracker crust.) In small mixing bowl blend together dry cheesecake mix, *undrained* pineapple, and milk. Beat till slightly thickened. Fold in chopped cranberries, nuts, and dates. Spoon the mixture into 8 to 10 paper bake-cup-lined muffin pans. Cover and freeze till firm. Peel off paper and serve. Makes 8 to 10 servings.

Frozen Strawberry-Banana Salads

1 21-ounce can strawberry pie
    filling
1 pint vanilla ice cream,
    softened
1 tablespoon lemon juice
3 medium bananas, chopped
¼ cup coarsely chopped toasted
    almonds
    Lettuce

Stir together pie filling, softened ice cream, and lemon juice. Stir in bananas and nuts. Turn mixture into 8 individual molds. Cover and freeze till firm. To serve, let stand at room temperature 10 minutes. Unmold onto lettuce-lined plates. Makes 8 servings.

Frozen Fruitcake Salad

1 cup dairy sour cream
½ cup sugar
½ of 4½-ounce container frozen
    whipped dessert topping,
    thawed
2 tablespoons lemon juice
1 teaspoon vanilla
½ cup red candied cherries
½ cup green candied cherries
1 13¼-ounce can crushed
    pineapple, drained
2 medium bananas, chopped
½ cup chopped walnuts
    Lettuce

In mixing bowl blend together sour cream, sugar, dessert topping, lemon juice, and vanilla. Slice the red and green candied cherries. Fold cherries, the drained pineapple, bananas, and nuts into sour cream mixture. Turn mixture into a 4½-cup ring mold. Cover and freeze till firm.

To serve, let stand at room temperature 10 minutes. Unmold onto lettuce-lined plate. Garnish with additional candied cherries, if desired. Slice to serve. Makes 8 servings.

Frozen Cherry Salad

1 4½-ounce container frozen
    whipped dessert topping,
    thawed
1 4-ounce container whipped
    cream cheese, softened
1 21-ounce can cherry pie
    filling
2 11-ounce cans mandarin
    orange sections, drained

Stir together whipped dessert topping and cream cheese. Fold in pie filling. Set aside 2 or 3 orange sections for garnish; fold remaining oranges into cherry mixture. Line bottom of a 9×5×3-inch loaf pan with waxed paper; pour in cherry mixture. Cover; freeze till firm. To serve, let stand at room temperature 10 minutes. Unmold onto serving platter; discard waxed paper. Garnish with reserved oranges. Slice to serve. Makes 8 to 10 servings.

Frosty Fruit Cubes

1 3½- *or* 3¾-ounce package
    instant vanilla pudding
    mix
1 4½-ounce container frozen
    whipped dessert topping,
    thawed
¼ cup mayonnaise *or* salad
    dressing
2 tablespoons lemon juice
2 8¼-ounce cans crushed
    pineapple, drained
2 large bananas, chopped
½ cup toasted slivered
    almonds
    Lettuce

Prepare instant pudding mix according to package directions. Stir in dessert topping, mayonnaise *or* salad dressing, and lemon juice. Combine pineapple, bananas, and almonds. Fold into pudding mixture. Turn mixture into 11×7×1½-inch pan. Cover and freeze till firm.

To serve, let stand at room temperature 10 minutes. Cut into 1-inch cubes; serve on lettuce-lined salad plates. If desired, top with additional toasted almonds. Makes 12 servings.

Frosty Pear Squares

1 4-ounce container whipped
    cream cheese
½ cup dairy sour cream
½ of a 6-ounce can (⅓ cup)
    frozen limeade concentrate,
    thawed
2 tablespoons sugar
    Few drops green food coloring
½ cup whipping cream
1 29-ounce can pear halves,
    drained and diced
½ cup flaked coconut
    Lettuce

Blend together cream cheese, sour cream, limeade concentrate, sugar, and food coloring. Whip cream till soft peaks form; fold into cream cheese mixture along with pears and coconut. Spread in 8×8×2-inch pan. Cover and freeze till firm. To serve, let stand at room temperature for 10 minutes. Cut in squares; serve on lettuce-lined salad plates. Garnish with additional whipped cream and coconut, if desired. Makes 9 servings.

Frozen Cranberry Salads

⅓ cup sugar
2 tablespoons cornstarch
    Dash salt
1¼ cups cranberry-apple drink
2 slightly beaten egg yolks
1 10-ounce package frozen
    cranberry-orange relish,
    partially thawed
2 egg whites
⅓ cup instant nonfat dry milk
    powder
    Lettuce

In medium saucepan combine sugar, cornstarch, and salt; stir in *1 cup* of the cranberry-apple drink. Cook and stir over medium-high heat till thickened and bubbly. Remove from heat. Gradually stir about ½ of the hot mixture into egg yolks; return mixture to saucepan. Cook and stir 2 minutes more; stir in cranberry-orange relish. Cool mixture to room temperature.

In small mixer bowl combine egg whites, nonfat dry milk powder, and the remaining ¼ cup cranberry-apple drink. Beat till stiff peaks form; fold into egg yolk mixture. Spoon into 8 individual molds or paper bake-cup-lined muffin pans. Cover and freeze till firm. To serve, let stand at room temperature 10 minutes. Unmold, or peel off paper. Serve on lettuce-lined salad plates. Makes 8 servings.

Hearty Main Dish Salads

Chef's Bowl (pictured above)

1 pound fresh asparagus
1 clove garlic, halved
1 medium head iceberg
   lettuce, torn (6 cups)
1 10-ounce package frozen
   peas, cooked, drained,
   and chilled
1 8-ounce package Swiss
   cheese, cut in julienne
   strips (2 cups)
5 to 8 ounces fully cooked
   ham, cut in julienne
   strips (1 to 1½ cups)
¾ cup sliced radishes
   Salt
   Pepper
   Creamy French dressing
   (see recipe, page 358)

Prepare asparagus according to directions in tip box on page 337. Drain and chill. Rub six individual salad bowls with cut garlic clove. Fill bowls with lettuce. Arrange asparagus, peas, cheese, ham, and radishes in bowls. Season to taste with some salt and pepper. Serve with *Creamy French Dressing*. Makes 6 servings.

Pepper Steak Salad

1 pound cooked roast beef
2 small tomatoes
1 large green pepper
1 cup sliced celery
⅓ cup sliced green onion
⅓ cup sliced fresh mushrooms
½ cup bottled teriyaki sauce
⅓ cup dry sherry
⅓ cup salad oil
3 tablespoons white vinegar
½ teaspoon ground ginger
1 cup bean sprouts (see
   Sprouting Mini Garden recipe,
   page 364)
4 cups shredded Chinese
   cabbage

Cut cooked beef into thin strips; they should measure about 3 cups. Cut tomatoes into wedges and green pepper into strips. In mixing bowl combine beef, tomatoes, green pepper, celery, onion, and mushrooms. To make marinade, in screw-top jar combine teriyaki sauce, sherry, oil, vinegar, and ginger; shake well. Pour over beef mixture. Toss to coat well. Cover and refrigerate 2 to 3 hours. Add bean sprouts; toss again. Drain, reserving marinade. Place shredded Chinese cabbage in large salad bowl; top with marinated meat and vegetables. Pass reserved marinade for dressing. Makes 6 servings.

Asparagus and Shrimp Salad

3 medium tomatoes
1 medium lemon
16 ounces fresh or frozen
   shrimp, shelled and
   cleaned
1 to 1½ pounds fresh
   asparagus
¼ cup sliced green onion
2 tablespoons snipped
   parsley
   Fresh Herb Dressing (see
   recipe, page 357)
   Lettuce

Cut tomatoes into wedges and lemon into thin slices; set aside. Cook fresh shrimp in large amount of boiling salted water for 1 to 3 minutes. (Cook frozen shrimp according to package directions.) Drain and set aside. Prepare asparagus according to tip box below, cutting spears into 1½-inch pieces. In mixing bowl combine shrimp, asparagus, lemon slices, onion, and parsley. Pour *Fresh Herb Dressing* over shrimp and vegetables. Cover and chill, stirring once or twice. To serve, drain vegetables and toss with tomato wedges; pile into lettuce-lined bowl. Makes 4 servings.

Fresh Asparagus: Buying, Storing, and Using

You'll find fresh asparagus available in most markets from mid-February through June. Frozen asparagus can be substituted during the off-season. Choose firm, straight stalks with tight, compact tips. Wrap stem ends in moist paper toweling; place in plastic bag or covered container and refrigerate. Use within 1 to 2 days.

To prepare asparagus, wash stalks and scrape off scales. Break off woody bases at point where stalks snap easily.

To cook, place whole spears in small amount of boiling salted water. To avoid overcooking, prop tips out of water with crumpled foil. Cook, covered, 10 minutes or till crisp-tender. Cook cut-up asparagus 8 to 10 minutes. Drain.

Beef and Caesar Salad (opposite, above)

1 egg
⅔ cup salad oil
1 3-ounce package cream
    cheese, softened
¼ cup dairy sour cream
2 tablespoons crumbled
    blue cheese
1 tablespoon lemon juice
2 teaspoons anchovy paste
¼ teaspoon garlic salt
8 ounces cooked roast beef
1 cup cherry tomatoes
4 cups torn romaine
2 cups torn fresh spinach
2 cups torn bibb lettuce
1 cup Garlic Croutons (see
    recipe, page 365)

To make dressing, in small mixer bowl beat egg slightly. Gradually add oil, beating at medium speed of electric mixer. Add cream cheese, sour cream, blue cheese, lemon juice, anchovy paste, and garlic salt; beat smooth. Cover and chill.

Cut beef into thin strips; season with a little salt. Halve cherry tomatoes. In large salad bowl combine romaine, spinach, bibb lettuce, *Garlic Croutons,* tomatoes, and beef; spoon about 1 cup dressing atop. Top with additional crumbled blue cheese, if desired. Toss to coat vegetables. Makes 6 servings.

Chili Salad (opposite, below)

1 medium head lettuce, cut
    in chunks
3 cups corn chips
1 large tomato, chopped
4 ounces pepperoni, thinly
    sliced
¼ cup pitted ripe olives
½ cup shredded cheddar
    cheese (2 ounces)
1 15-ounce can chili con
    carne with beans

In salad bowl combine lettuce, corn chips, chopped tomato, pepperoni, olives, and cheese. Meanwhile, in saucepan heat canned chili till bubbly. Immediately pour atop salad, tossing lightly to coat. Makes 6 servings.

Peachy Beef Toss

8 ounces cooked roast beef
4 cups torn romaine
3 cups torn fresh spinach
3 medium peaches,
    peeled, pitted, and
    sliced (1½ cups)
1 avocado, peeled, pitted,
    and sliced
12 cherry tomatoes, halved
½ cup salad oil
3 tablespoons vinegar
1 tablespoon prepared
    horseradish
½ teaspoon worcestershire
    sauce
    Few drops bottled hot
    pepper sauce

Cut beef into julienne strips, according to directions in tip box on page 341. In salad bowl combine romaine, spinach, peaches, avocado, tomatoes, and roast beef strips. To make dressing, in screw-top jar combine salad oil, vinegar, horseradish, worcestershire sauce, bottled hot pepper sauce, ½ teaspoon *salt,* and ⅛ teaspoon *pepper.* Cover and shake well to mix. Pour dressing atop salad; toss to coat meat and vegetables. Makes 6 servings.

Top this great combo of salad greens and roast beef strips with a tangy dressing, cherry tomatoes, and croutons. *Beef and Caesar Salad* is a delicious meal in itself.

Quick-fixin' *Chili Salad* tastes like a meal-size taco in a bowl. Gently toss the salad with hot chili con carne to get that zesty, south-of-the-border taste.

Start with julienne strips of ham and chicken atop lettuce and vegetables for hearty
Mexican Chef's Salad. Then pour a zesty, hot cheese sauce atop and sprinkle with corn chips.

Mexican Chef's Salad (opposite)

6 **ounces cooked chicken**
5 **ounces fully cooked ham**
1 **medium head iceberg let-**
   tuce, torn (6 cups)
1 **cup shredded carrot**
1 **cup chopped celery**
2 **medium tomatoes, chopped**
3 **tablespoons sliced green**
   onion
2 **cups shredded sharp**
   American cheese
   (8 ounces)
⅔ **cup milk**
3 **tablespoons chopped canned**
   green chili peppers
3 **tablespoons sliced pitted**
   ripe olives
2 **cups corn chips**

Cut cooked chicken and ham into julienne strips, according to directions in tip box below (makes about 1 cup each of cut-up meat). In large salad bowl combine lettuce, carrot, and celery. Arrange tomatoes, green onion, chicken, and ham atop. In heavy saucepan combine cheese and milk. Cook over low heat, stirring constantly, till cheese is melted and mixture is smooth. Stir in chopped chilies and sliced olives. To serve, pour cheese mixture over salad. Toss lightly. Pass corn chips to sprinkle atop each serving. Makes 6 servings.

Chicken and Ham Supreme

6 **ounces cooked chicken**
5 **ounces fully cooked ham**
2 **medium tomatoes**
1 **medium green pepper**
1 **medium head iceberg**
   lettuce, torn (6 cups)
1 **cup sliced cucumber**
3 **hard-cooked eggs, sliced**
½ **cup salad oil**
3 **tablespoons vinegar**
1 **tablespoon prepared horse-**
   radish
½ **teaspoon worcestershire**
   sauce
   Few drops bottled hot
   pepper sauce
½ **teaspoon salt**
⅛ **teaspoon pepper**

Cut cooked chicken and ham into julienne strips, according to directions in tip box below (makes about 1 cup each of cut-up meat). Cut tomatoes into wedges; cut green pepper into narrow strips. Fill four individual salad bowls with the lettuce. Arrange cucumber, eggs, chicken, ham, tomatoes, and green pepper in each bowl. To make dressing, in screw-top jar combine oil, vinegar, horseradish, worcestershire sauce, hot pepper sauce, salt, and pepper. Cover and shake well to mix. Pass dressing with salads. Makes 4 servings.

How to "Julienne"

"Julienne" meats and vegetables by cutting into long thin strips. First cut a thin slice off one side of the meat or vegetable, if necessary, to make it lie flat on the cutting board. Placing flat side down, cut into thin lengthwise slices. Then cut each slice into narrow strips about ⅛- to ¼-inch thick.

Tuna Salad in Tomato Cups (opposite, above)

1   6½- *or* 7-ounce can tuna,
     drained and flaked
½   cup sliced celery
¼   cup sliced pimiento-
     stuffed olives
¼   cup sliced green onion
1   tablespoon lemon juice
¼   teaspoon salt
     Dash pepper
2   hard-cooked eggs, chopped
½   cup mayonnaise *or* salad
     dressing
4   medium tomatoes
     Lettuce

In mixing bowl combine tuna, celery, olives, green onion, lemon juice, salt, and pepper. Gently stir in chopped egg and mayonnaise or salad dressing; cover and chill.

Prepare tomato cups according to directions in tip box on page 355. To serve, place chilled tomatoes on individual lettuce-lined plates; sprinkle with salt. Fill each tomato cup with about ½ cup of the tuna mixture. Garnish with parsley, olives, or additional hard-cooked egg slices, if desired. Makes 4 servings.

Avocado Egg Salad (opposite, below left)

4   hard-cooked eggs, chopped
4   slices bacon, crisp-
     cooked, drained, and
     crumbled
1   tablespoon finely chopped
     green onion
2   large avocados, halved
     and seeded
     Lemon juice
2   tablespoons mayonnaise
     or salad dressing
2   teaspoons lemon juice
1   teaspoon prepared mustard
½   teaspoon salt
     Dash pepper
     Lettuce

In small mixing bowl combine eggs, bacon, and onion. Carefully scoop out avocado halves, leaving firm shells; brush shells with a little lemon juice to prevent browning. Mash avocado pulp. In mixing bowl stir together the mayonnaise, 2 teaspoons lemon juice, mustard, salt, and pepper. Add mashed avocado and the egg mixture; spoon avocado-egg salad mixture into avocado shells. Place filled avocados on individual lettuce-lined serving plates. Garnish with bacon curl, if desired. Makes 2 servings.

Lobster in Orange Cups (opposite, below right)

4   large oranges
1   5-ounce can lobster *or*
     1¼ cups cooked lobster,
     broken into pieces
1   cup thinly sliced celery
¼   cup mayonnaise *or* salad
     dressing
¼   teaspoon salt
     Leaf lettuce
2   teaspoons thinly sliced
     green onion

Cut slice from top of each orange. Remove fruit from oranges, leaving shells. Discard orange tops. Chop fruit. Cut top edge of each orange shell in sawtooth fashion. Place orange shells in plastic bag and refrigerate. In mixing bowl combine chopped orange, lobster, and celery; chill.

Stir together mayonnaise or salad dressing and salt. Drain lobster mixture; add to mayonnaise mixture and toss. Line 4 orange shells with lettuce; spoon in lobster mixture. Place filled orange cups on lettuce-lined plates. Garnish orange cups with sliced green onion. Makes 4 servings.

Tuna Salad in Tomato Cups, nestled on a bed of frilly leaf lettuce, is an easy
way to dress up everyday ingredients. For added color, garnish with pimiento-stuffed olive slices.

Add avocado and bacon to the popular salad
sandwich filling for elegant *Avocado Egg Salad.*

For the light appetite, citrus and
seafood team up in *Lobster in Orange Cups.*

Crab-Stuffed Avocados (pictured on page 294)

1 pound crab legs, cooked,
   chilled, and shelled
   (½ pound crab meat), *or* 1
   7-ounce can crab meat,
   chilled and drained
2 hard-cooked eggs, chopped
¼ cup chopped celery
¼ cup mayonnaise *or* salad
   dressing
1 teaspoon dry mustard
¼ teaspoon salt
   Dash worcestershire sauce
4 medium avocados

Break crab meat into pieces; set aside several larger segments of meat. Combine remaining crab meat with eggs, celery, mayonnaise or salad dressing, mustard, salt, and worcestershire sauce. Chill. Prepare avocado shells according to directions in tip box below. Fill avocados with crab mixture. Top with pieces of reserved crab meat. Serve on lettuce-lined plates, if desired. Makes 4 servings.

Chicken Salad a l'Orange

12 ounces cooked chicken,
   cubed (2 cups)
1 cup sliced celery
½ cup sliced pitted ripe
   olives
3 tablespoons frozen orange
   juice concentrate,
   thawed
3 tablespoons salad oil
1 tablespoon sugar
1 tablespoon vinegar
⅛ teaspoon dry mustard
   Few drops bottled hot
   pepper sauce
¼ cup mayonnaise *or* salad
   dressing
1 medium avocado
1 medium orange

In mixing bowl combine chicken, celery, and olives; cover and chill. To make dressing, stir together orange juice concentrate, oil, sugar, vinegar, dry mustard, hot pepper sauce, and dash *salt*. Fold in mayonnaise or salad dressing. Pour over chicken mixture and toss lightly to coat. Cover and chill. Pit, peel, and slice avocado according to tip box below. Peel and section orange. Arrange avocado slices and orange sections on individual serving plates. Mound chicken mixture in center. Makes 3 or 4 servings.

cAvocados

Avocados range in color from green to almost black, but the ripeness test is the same for all varieties. The fruit should yield to gentle pressure when ready to eat. Store firm avocados at room temperature to ripen quickly; refrigerate to ripen slowly.

To prepare avocados, cut fruit in half lengthwise; twist gently and separate. Tap seed with sharp edge of knife; twist and lift or gently pry out seed. Use a knife to loosen and strip skin from fruit. (The peel may be left on for filled avocado shells.)

To make avocado rest firmly, trim a thin slice from bottom of each half. Fill avocado half with salad mixture or slice to use in tossed salads. Brush cut surface of avocado with lemon juice to prevent darkening.

Polynesian Shrimp Bowl

1 15¼-ounce can pineapple
   chunks (juice pack)
2 teaspoons cornstarch
1½ teaspoons curry powder
2 teaspoons lemon juice
⅓ cup mayonnaise *or* salad
   dressing
⅓ cup dairy sour cream
2 cups medium noodles,
   cooked, drained,
   and chilled
2 4½-ounce cans shrimp,
   rinsed and drained
½ cup sliced water chestnuts
¼ cup chopped green pepper

Drain pineapple, reserving juice. Set pineapple aside. To make curry dressing; in small saucepan combine cornstarch, curry powder, reserved pineapple juice, and ¼ teaspoon *salt*. Cook and stir over medium heat till thick and bubbly; stir in lemon juice. Cool. Blend in mayonnaise and sour cream. In salad bowl combine pineapple chunks, noodles, shrimp, water chestnuts, and green pepper. Pour on curry dressing; toss gently to coat. Chill thoroughly. Makes 6 servings.

Chicken and Brown Rice Toss

3 cups cooked brown rice
12 ounces cooked chicken,
   cubed (2 cups)
½ cup sliced celery
¼ cup sliced pitted ripe
   olives
2 tablespoons sliced green
   onion
½ cup mayonnaise *or* salad
   dressing
¼ cup Italian salad dressing
½ cup coarsely chopped
   cashew nuts
   Lettuce

In mixing bowl combine cooked brown rice, chicken, celery, olives, and green onion. Stir together mayonnaise and Italian dressing; add to chicken mixture. Toss gently to coat. Cover and chill. Just before serving, add cashews and toss again. Turn into lettuce-lined salad bowl. Makes 4 or 5 servings.

Quick Tuna-Macaroni Salad

1 16-ounce can macaroni and
   cheese
1 8-ounce can peas, drained
1 6½- *or* 7-ounce can tuna,
   drained and flaked
2 hard-cooked eggs, chopped
¼ cup mayonnaise *or* salad
   dressing
1 tablespoon finely chopped
   green pepper
1 teaspoon prepared mustard
1 teaspoon minced dried
   onion
6 medium tomatoes
   Lettuce
   Paprika

In mixing bowl combine macaroni and cheese, peas, tuna, eggs, mayonnaise or salad dressing, green pepper, mustard, onion, ¼ teaspoon *salt,* and dash *pepper*. Cover and chill. Prepare tomato cups according to directions on page 355. To serve, place tomato cups on individual lettuce-lined plates; fill with tuna mixture. Sprinkle with paprika. Makes 6 servings.

Sausage Supper Salad (opposite)

4 cups torn iceberg lettuce
8 ounces assorted dry and
    semi-dry sausages
2 hard-cooked eggs, cut in
    wedges
½ of a 15-ounce can (1 cup)
    garbanzo beans, drained
1 cup sliced celery
½ cup chopped onion
½ cup mayonnaise
2 tablespoons milk
1½ teaspoons prepared
    horseradish
½ teaspoon dry mustard

Place lettuce in a large bowl. Cut sausages in thin slices, then in bite-size pieces. Arrange sausages, egg wedges, beans, celery, and onion atop lettuce. To make dressing, blend together mayonnaise, milk, horseradish, and mustard; pour over salad. Toss to coat vegetables and sausages. Makes 4 to 6 servings.

Salami-Cheese Salad

1 medium head iceberg
    lettuce, torn (6 cups)
5 ounces salami, sliced
    and quartered (1 cup)
4 ounces Swiss cheese, cut
    in strips
½ cup sliced pitted ripe
    olives
3 tablespoons chopped
    pimiento
¾ cup Italian Dressing (see
    recipe, page 357)

In salad bowl combine lettuce, salami, cheese, olives, and pimiento. Pour *Italian Dressing* over salad and toss lightly. Makes 4 servings.

Cassoulet Salad

2 16-ounce cans red kidney
    beans, drained
1 16-ounce can pinto beans,
    drained
1 15-ounce can garbanzo
    beans, drained
¼ cup sliced green onion
1 2-ounce jar (¼ cup)
    pimiento, chopped
½ of a 15½-ounce jar (1 cup)
    spaghetti sauce
⅓ cup white wine vinegar
2 tablespoons salad oil
    Few dashes bottled hot
    pepper sauce
6 cups torn mixed salad
    greens
4 ounces thuringer sausage,
    sliced

In large bowl combine kidney beans, pinto beans, garbanzo beans, onion, and pimiento. To make dressing, in small bowl combine spaghetti sauce, wine vinegar, salad oil, and hot pepper sauce; pour over bean mixture. Cover; refrigerate several hours or overnight, stirring occasionally. In salad bowl combine torn greens, sausage, and bean mixture. Toss. Makes 12 servings.

An assortment of sausages such as salami, pepperoni, and mortadella add variety to
Sausage Supper Salad. This main dish salad gets added protein from garbanzo beans and eggs.

Caesar's Chicken Salad (opposite, above)

3 anchovy fillets
¼ cup salad oil *or* olive oil
½ teaspoon dry mustard
2 tablespoons lemon juice
1 teaspoon worcestershire
   sauce
1 egg
12 ounces cooked chicken
1 7-ounce can artichoke
   hearts, drained
4 cups torn romaine
½ cup Garlic Croutons (see
   recipe, page 365)
2 tablespoons grated par-
   mesan cheese

To make dressing, cream together anchovies, *1 tablespoon* of the oil, dry mustard, and a dash *pepper*. Blend in lemon juice, worcestershire, and remaining oil; set aside. To coddle egg, place whole egg in small saucepan of boiling water; immediately remove from heat and let stand 1 minute. Remove egg from water; cool slightly. Break egg into dressing mixture. Beat till dressing becomes creamy. Cut chicken in julienne strips according to directions in tip box on page 341. Halve artichoke hearts. In large salad bowl combine chicken, artichokes, romaine, *Garlic Croutons*, and parmesan. Pour dressing over and toss to coat. Makes 6 servings.

Curried Chicken Salad (opposite, below)

1 large orange
1 medium banana
4 cups torn mixed salad
   greens
12 ounces cooked chicken,
   cubed (2 cups)
½ of an 8-ounce can (½ cup)
   jellied cranberry sauce,
   chilled and cut in ½-
   inch cubes
¼ cup light raisins
¼ cup salted peanuts
½ cup mayonnaise *or* salad
   dressing
½ of an 8-ounce carton (½
   cup) orange yogurt
½ to 1 teaspoon curry powder

Section orange over bowl to catch juice. Slice banana diagonally and dip in reserved orange juice. Place salad greens in large salad bowl. Arrange orange sections, banana, chicken, the cranberry cubes, raisins, and peanuts atop salad greens. Chill. To make dressing, combine mayonnaise or salad dressing, yogurt, and curry; chill. Pass dressing with salad. Makes 4 servings.

Imperial Chicken Salad

12 ounces cooked chicken,
   cut in strips (2 cups)
4 medium potatoes, cooked,
   peeled, and sliced
3 hard-cooked eggs, sliced
½ cup chopped dill pickle
½ cup chopped celery
1 tablespoon grated onion
1 tablespoon capers, drained
   and rinsed
¾ cup mayonnaise *or* salad
   dressing
1 tablespoon lemon juice

In large bowl combine chicken, potatoes, sliced eggs, pickle, celery, onion, capers, and 1 teaspoon *salt*. Blend together mayonnaise or salad dressing and lemon juice; stir mayonnaise mixture into salad. Chill. To serve, mound salad on plate. Garnish top with sieved hard-cooked egg, if desired. Makes 6 servings.

The traditional anchovy-egg Caesar dressing is tossed with romaine, chicken, and artichoke hearts for an upbeat main dish, *Caesar's Chicken Salad.*

Orange, banana, cranberry sauce cubes, raisins, peanuts, and a spicy yogurt dressing give an exotic flavor to *Curried Chicken Salad.*

Calorie-counted Salads

Marinated Tuna and Vegetables (pictured above)

2 large carrots, cut in
  julienne strips
1½ cups cauliflowerets
1 10-ounce package frozen
  peas
1 6½- or 7-ounce can tuna
½ cup thinly sliced celery
¼ cup sliced green onion
¾ cup Zesty Salad Dressing
  (see recipe, page 362)

Cook carrots and cauliflower together, uncovered, in small amount of boiling salted water for 10 minutes. Add peas. Cook 5 minutes more or till all vegetables are crisp-tender. Drain. Drain tuna well. In mixing bowl combine cooked vegetables, celery, and green onion. Add tuna and *Tomato Salad Dressing;* toss gently to coat. Cover and chill. Serve on lettuce leaf, if desired. Makes 3 servings (224 calories per serving).

Confetti Chicken Salad

12 ounces cooked chicken
  white meat, diced
  (2 cups)
1 cup chopped celery
½ cup shredded carrot
½ cup alfalfa sprouts (see
  Sprouting Mini Garden recipe,
  page 364)
½ cup Diet Salad Dressing
  (see recipe, page 363)
1 tablespoon lime juice

In bowl combine chicken, celery, carrot, and alfalfa sprouts. Stir together the *Diet Salad Dressing* and lime juice; pour over chicken mixture, tossing to coat. Makes 4 servings (124 calories per serving).

Salmon-Stuffed Tomatoes

1 9-ounce package frozen
   artichoke hearts
1 16-ounce can salmon,
   drained, boned, and
   broken into chunks
3 hard-cooked eggs, chopped
1 cup sliced fresh mushrooms
¼ teaspoon salt
6 large tomatoes
1 cup dairy sour cream
¼ cup diced cucumber
¼ cup milk
1 tablespoon lemon juice
2 teaspoons snipped fresh
   dillweed or ½ teaspoon
   dried dillweed
¼ teaspoon salt

Cook frozen artichoke hearts according to package directions; drain and chop. In mixing bowl combine chopped artichoke hearts, salmon, eggs, mushrooms, ¼ teaspoon salt, and dash *pepper;* cover and chill. Prepare tomato cups according to directions in tip box on page 355. Place tomato cups on serving plate; fill with salmon mixture. To make dressing combine sour cream, cucumber, milk, lemon juice, dill, and ¼ teaspoon salt. Pour dressing over filled tomato. Makes 6 servings (274 calories per serving).

Meatless Meal-in-a-Bowl

1 cup cherry tomatoes
4 cups torn fresh spinach
1 15-ounce can garbanzo
   beans, drained
1 cup cauliflowerets
1 cup sliced fresh mushrooms
1 small cucumber, sliced
½ small red onion, thinly
   sliced and separated
   into rings
½ cup coarsely chopped
   walnuts
1 small avocado
1 8-ounce carton (1 cup)
   plain yogurt
¼ cup milk
1 tablespoon honey
¼ teaspoon garlic salt

Halve cherry tomatoes. In salad bowl combine tomatoes, spinach, beans, cauliflower, mushrooms, cucumber, onion rings, and walnuts.

To make dressing peel, seed, and cut up avocado (see tip box on page 344). In blender container combine avocado, yogurt, milk, honey, and garlic salt. Cover and blend till mixture is smooth. Add additional milk if needed to make desired consistency. Pour dressing over salad; toss to coat. Makes 4 servings (316 calories per serving).

Chicken Pineapple Boat

12 ounces cooked chicken,
   cubed (2 cups)
1 15¼-ounce can pineapple
   chunks (juice pack), chilled
   and drained
1 medium green pepper, cut
   in strips
½ cup sliced water chestnuts
¾ cup Zesty Salad Dressing
   (see recipe, page 362)

In salad bowl combine chicken, pineapple, green pepper, and water chestnuts. Pour *Zesty Salad Dressing* over chicken mixture; toss lightly. Makes 4 servings (201 calories per serving).

Turkey in Aspic (opposite, above)

12 ounces cooked turkey white meat, cut in 6 slices
4 hard-cooked eggs, sliced
¾ pound fresh *or* 1 8-ounce package frozen asparagus spears, cooked and drained
6 pimiento strips
2 envelopes unflavored gelatin
2 13¾-ounce cans chicken broth
½ cup water
1 thin slice onion
2 tablespoons lemon juice
2 teaspoons prepared horse-radish
1 sprig parsley

Trim turkey slices to uniform shapes; arrange in 13×9×2-inch pan. Top each with 4 egg slices, about 3 asparagus spears, and a pimiento strip. In medium saucepan soften gelatin in chicken broth and water. Add onion, lemon juice, horseradish, and parsley. Bring to boiling, stirring frequently. Remove from heat and strain through cheesecloth. Chill just till syrupy. Spoon a little of the broth mixture over each salad in pan. Chill till almost set; keep remaining broth mixture at room temperature and stir occasionally. Repeat, spooning room-temperature broth mixture over turkey slices and chilling till a thin glaze of gelatin forms. Pour remaining broth mixture around salads in pan. Chill till set. To serve, trim around each turkey slice and transfer to serving plates. Break up remaining gelatin in pan with a fork and arrange around salads on serving plates. Makes 6 servings (206 calories per serving).

Shrimp Tomato Vinaigrette (opposite, below left)

2 cups cleaned cooked shrimp
1 6-ounce package frozen pea pods, thawed
2 tablespoons sliced green onion
¼ cup salad oil
2 tablespoons dry white wine
2 tablespoons white vinegar
1 0.6-ounce envelope Italian salad dressing mix
1 to 2 teaspoons capers, drained
Dash pepper
4 tomatoes

In mixing bowl combine shrimp, pea pods, and onion. To make dressing, in screw-top jar combine oil, wine, vinegar, Italian salad dressing mix, capers, and pepper; cover and shake well to mix. Pour dressing over shrimp mixture. Cover and refrigerate several hours. Prepare tomato cups according to directions on page 355. To serve, drain shrimp mixture; spoon into tomato cups. Place on lettuce-lined plates, if desired. Makes 4 servings (210 calories per serving).

Salmon Potato Salad (opposite, below right)

3 medium potatoes, cooked, peeled, and cubed (3 cups)
1 hard-cooked egg, chopped
½ cup sliced celery
½ cup shredded carrot
2 tablespoons chopped green onion
Cottage Dressing
1 16-ounce can salmon, drained, boned, and broken into chunks
Green pepper rings

In large bowl combine potatoes, egg, celery, carrot, and onion. Add Cottage Dressing to potato mixture, tossing lightly to coat. Gently fold in salmon. Cover and chill thoroughly. Place atop green pepper rings on individual salad plates; garnish with carrot curls and additional green pepper, if desired. Makes 6 servings (285 calories per serving).

Cottage Dressing: Blend together 1 cup cream-style *cottage cheese*, ½ cup *mayonnaise or salad dressing*, 2 tablespoons *milk*, 2 tablespoons *lemon juice*, 1 teaspoon dried *dillweed*, ¼ teaspoon *salt*, and a dash *pepper*.

For special luncheon menus, prepare individual servings of *Turkey in Aspic*.
These elegant, gelatin-glazed salad entrées go easy on calories but not on flavor.

A light vinegar-and-oil dressing flavors
the filling for *Shrimp Tomato Vinaigrette*.

For a low-calorie supper, turn a summer side
dish into protein-packed *Salmon Potato Salad*.

Salad Burritos

1 8-ounce can garbanzo *or* red kidney beans
½ small onion, sliced and separated into rings
½ cup sliced pitted ripe olives
½ cup salad oil
½ of a 1.25-ounce envelope (3 tablespoons) taco seasoning mix
3 tablespoons vinegar
½ teaspoon sugar
4 cups torn iceberg lettuce
8 ounces monterey jack cheese, cut in strips
1 small sweet red *or* green pepper, cut in strips
12 8-inch flour tortillas

Drain beans. In mixing bowl combine beans, onion rings, and olives. To make dressing, in screw-top jar combine salad oil, taco seasoning mix, vinegar, and sugar. Cover and shake well. Pour over bean mixture. Cover and chill. Just before serving, add lettuce, cheese, and pepper strips to marinated bean mixture. Toss gently to coat. Spoon about ½ cup salad atop each tortilla; roll up, folding in sides. Makes 6 servings (458 calories per serving).

Slim Ham Slaw

2 tablespoons all-purpose flour
2 tablespoons sugar
1 teaspoon dry mustard
½ teaspoon celery seed
1 cup skim milk
2 slightly beaten egg yolks
3 tablespoons vinegar
2 tablespoons lemon juice
6 cups coarsely shredded cabbage
10 ounces fully cooked ham, cubed (2½ cups)
1 medium apple, cored and chopped (1 cup)
¼ cup chopped green pepper

For dressing, in small saucepan combine flour, sugar, dry mustard, celery seed, and 1 teaspoon *salt;* gradually blend in milk. Cook and stir over medium heat till thickened and bubbly. Stir a moderate amount of hot mixture into egg yolks; return all to saucepan. Cook and stir over low heat 1 to 2 minutes more or till thickened. Stir in vinegar and lemon juice; cool. Combine cabbage, ham, apple, and green pepper. Toss with dressing mixture; cover and chill. Makes 4 servings (260 calories per serving).

Dieter's Chef Salad

1 12-ounce package frozen scallops, thawed
1 clove garlic, halved
4 ounces mozzarella cheese
3 cups torn lettuce
2 cups torn romaine
2 cups torn spinach
3 hard-cooked eggs, quartered
1 cup diced celery
12 cherry tomatoes, halved
⅓ cup Diet Thousand Island Dressing (see recipe, page 363)

Cook scallops over low heat in small amount boiling salted water for 3 minutes; drain and chill. Rub salad bowl with cut side of garlic; discard. Cut cheese in thin strips. In bowl, combine lettuce, romaine, spinach, the hard-cooked eggs, celery, tomatoes, scallops, and cheese. Pour the Diet Thousand Island Dressing over; toss to coat. Makes 6 servings (181 calories per serving).

Sprout Salad

2 cups alfalfa sprouts
   (see Sprouting Mini
   Garden recipe,
   page 90)
1 medium tomato
¼ cup sliced green onion
¼ cup snipped parsley
2 tablespoons chopped green
   pepper
   Garlic Dressing
1 cup cubed cheddar cheese

Cook sprouts, uncovered, in small amount of boiling water for 3 minutes; drain and cool. Peel and chop the tomato. In mixing bowl combine sprouts, tomato, onion, parsley, and green pepper. Pour Garlic Dressing over sprouts mixture and toss gently to coat. Cover and chill 30 minutes. Add cheese and mix lightly. Serve in lettuce cups, if desired. Makes 4 servings (316 calories per serving).

Garlic Dressing: In screw-top jar combine 3 tablespoons *salad oil,* 2 tablespoons *wine vinegar,* ⅛ teaspoon *garlic salt,* and a dash freshly ground *pepper.* Cover; shake well.

Grapefruit-Seafood Salad

1 7-ounce can water-pack tuna
2 grapefruit, peeled
4 cups shredded lettuce
½ cup chopped celery
½ cup Tomato Salad Dressing
   (see recipe, page 89)

Drain tuna; break into chunks. Section grapefruit. Combine tuna, grapefruit, lettuce, and celery. Toss with *Tomato Salad Dressing.* Makes 4 servings (122 calories per serving).

Cottage Cheese Bean Sprout Salad

2 medium tomatoes
1 cup cream-style cottage
   cheese
1 cup mung bean sprouts
   (see Sprouting Mini
   Garden recipe, page 90)
½ cup chopped cucumber
2 tablespoons sliced green
   onion
¼ teaspoon salt

Prepare tomato cups according to instructions in tip box below.

In mixing bowl combine cottage cheese, bean sprouts, chopped cucumber, green onion, and salt. To serve, place chilled tomato cups on individual salad plates. Fill each tomato with *half* the cottage cheese mixture. Makes 2 servings (277 calories per serving).

Tomato Cups

Fresh, red-ripe tomatoes make attractive containers for individual servings of main dish salads. To make decorative petal cups as shown at left, place tomatoes, stem end down, on cutting surface. With sharp knife, cut tomato into 4 to 6 wedges, cutting to, but not through, the stem end of the tomato. Spread the wedges apart slightly; sprinkle lightly with salt. Cover and chill. When ready to serve, spread the wedges apart and spoon in the salad mixture.

To make plain cups, cut a small slice from the top of the tomato. Remove core, if present. Use a spoon to scoop out the seeds, leaving a ½-inch-thick shell. Sprinkle with salt. Invert and chill. Fill with salad at serving time.

Shake-it-together Dressings

Tomato Soup Dressing (pictured above)

  1 10¾-ounce can condensed
      tomato soup
  ¾ cup vinegar
  ½ cup salad oil
  2 tablespoons sugar
  2 teaspoons grated onion
  2 teaspoons dry mustard
1½ teaspoons salt
1½ teaspoons worcestershire
      sauce
  ½ teaspoon paprika
  ¼ teaspoon garlic powder
      Dash cayenne

In blender container combine soup, vinegar, oil, sugar, grated onion, dry mustard, salt, worcestershire, paprika, garlic powder, and cayenne. Cover and blend till smooth. Transfer to storage container. Cover and chill. Shake again just before serving. Makes about 2⅓ cups.

Fresh Herb Dressing

¼ **cup salad oil**
3 **tablespoons dry white wine**
2 **tablespoons lemon juice**
1 **tablespoon sugar**
1 **tablespoon snipped fresh**
    basil *or* **1 teaspoon**
    dried basil, crushed
1 **teaspoon salt**
    Several dashes bottled
    hot pepper sauce

In screw-top jar combine oil, wine, lemon juice, sugar, basil, salt, bottled hot pepper sauce, and ¼ teaspoon *pepper*. Cover and shake to mix well. Chill. Shake again before serving. Makes ½ cup.

Red Wine Dressing

1 **cup salad oil**
⅓ **cup vinegar**
⅓ **cup dry red wine**
1 **teaspoon sugar**
1 **teaspoon dried thyme,**
    crushed
½ **teaspoon dried oregano,**
    crushed
1 **clove garlic**

In screw-top jar combine oil, vinegar, wine, sugar, thyme, oregano, garlic, and ¼ teaspoon *salt*. Cover and shake to mix well. Chill. Remove garlic clove; shake again just before serving. Makes 1⅔ cups.

Italian Dressing

1⅓ **cups salad oil**
½ **cup vinegar**
¼ **cup grated parmesan cheese**
1 **tablespoon sugar**
2 **teaspoons salt**
1 **teaspoon celery salt**
½ **teaspoon white pepper**
½ **teaspoon dry mustard**
¼ **teaspoon paprika**
1 **clove garlic, minced**

In screw-top jar combine oil, vinegar, parmesan cheese, sugar, salt, celery salt, white pepper, dry mustard, paprika, and garlic. Cover and shake to mix well. Chill. Shake again just before serving. Makes 1¾ cups.

Russian Dressing

⅔ **cup salad oil**
½ **cup catsup**
¼ **cup sugar**
3 **tablespoons lemon juice**
2 **tablespoons worcestershire**
    sauce
2 **tablespoons vinegar**
2 **tablespoons water**
1 **tablespoon grated onion**
½ **teaspoon salt**
½ **teaspoon paprika**

In screw-top jar combine oil, catsup, sugar, lemon juice, worcestershire, vinegar, water, onion, salt, and paprika. Cover and shake to mix well. Chill. Shake again just before serving. Makes 1¾ cups.

Tangy Tomato Dressing

1 8-ounce can tomato sauce
1 tablespoon vinegar
1 teaspoon worcestershire sauce
1 teaspoon sugar
1 teaspoon grated onion
½ teaspoon prepared horseradish
½ teaspoon salt
Few drops bottled hot pepper sauce

In screw-top jar combine tomato sauce, vinegar, worcestershire, sugar, onion, horseradish, salt, hot pepper sauce, and ⅛ teaspoon *pepper.* Cover and shake to mix well. Chill. Shake again just before serving. Makes 1 cup.

Zesty Blue Cheese Dressing

¾ cup salad oil
¼ cup lemon juice
2 tablespoons sliced green onion
2 tablespoons snipped parsley
1 tablespoon dijon-style mustard
1 teaspoon sugar
¼ teaspoon garlic salt
⅓ cup crumbled blue cheese

In screw-top jar combine oil, lemon juice, onion, parsley, mustard, sugar, garlic salt, and a dash *pepper.* Cover and shake well to mix. Chill. Add blue cheese and shake again just before serving. Makes 1½ cups.

Creamy French Dressing

1 tablespoon paprika
2 teaspoons sugar
1 teaspoon salt
Dash cayenne
¼ cup vinegar
1 egg
1 cup salad oil

In small mixer bowl combine paprika, sugar, salt, and cayenne. Add vinegar and egg; beat well. Add salad oil in slow, steady stream, beating constantly with electric mixer or rotary beater till thick. Transfer to storage container. Cover and chill. Makes about 1⅔ cups.

Chili Dressing

½ cup salad oil
3 tablespoons vinegar
3 tablespoons lemon juice
3 tablespoons chili sauce
1 tablespoon grated onion
2 teaspoons sugar
1½ teaspoons chili powder
¾ teaspoon dry mustard
½ teaspoon salt
⅛ teaspoon paprika
Few dashes bottled hot pepper sauce

In screw-top jar combine oil, vinegar, lemon juice, chili sauce, grated onion, sugar, chili powder, dry mustard, salt, paprika, and hot pepper sauce. Cover and shake well to mix. Chill. Shake again just before serving. Makes 1 cup.

Vinaigrette with Variations

This classic French dressing is a thin, clear vinegar and oil mixture used to dress or marinate vegetables, salads, meats, or fish. Create a flavor to suit your taste by varying the oil, acid, and seasonings used. Here's the basic formula for

Vinaigrette Dressing: In screw-top jar combine oil, acid, sweetener, salt, and choice of seasonings. Cover and shake well to mix. Chill. Shake again just before serving. Makes about 1½ cups. Store unused dressing in refrigerator up to one month.

OIL	(salad oil, olive oil, or a combination of both)	1 cup
ACID	(vinegar, lemon or lime juice, or combination)	⅔ cup
SWEETENER	(sugar, corn syrup, or honey)	1 to 2 teaspoons
SALT		1½ teaspoons
DRY MUSTARD	(optional)	1½ teaspoons
PAPRIKA	(optional)	1½ teaspoons
HERBS	(thyme, oregano, basil, tarragon, dillweed, chives)	2 to 3 teaspoons snipped fresh *or* ½ to 1 teaspoon dried, crushed

Tailored for Fruit Salads

This smooth, sweet dressing is the perfect topper for fresh or canned fruits and is especially good with the tart contrast of citrus fruit salads. Vary the ingredients to suit your taste, following the chart below for Sweet Seed Dressing: In small mixer

bowl combine sweetener, paprika, dry mustard, and salt. Stir in acid. Add oil in slow, steady stream, beating constantly with electric mixer or rotary beater till thick. Beat in choice of seed. Cover and chill. Makes 1¾ cups.

SWEETENER	(sugar, corn syrup, or honey)	⅔ cup
PAPRIKA		1 teaspoon
DRY MUSTARD		1 teaspoon
SALT		¼ teaspoon
ACID	(vinegar, lemon or lime juice, or combination)	⅓ cup
SALAD OIL		1 cup
SEED	(celery, poppy, or toasted sesame seed)	1 to 2 teaspoons

Dairy Salad Dressings

Cucumber Cream Dressing (pictured above)

½ cup finely chopped unpeeled
  cucumber
2 tablespoons finely chopped
  green pepper
2 tablespoons thinly sliced
  green onion
2 tablespoons thinly sliced
  radishes
1 cup dairy sour cream
2 tablespoons milk
½ teaspoon salt
  Dash pepper

In mixing bowl combine cucumber, green pepper, onion, and radishes. Stir in sour cream, milk, salt, and pepper; mix well. Transfer to storage container. Cover and chill. Garnish with additional radish slices and a sprig of fresh watercress, if desired. Makes 1½ cups.

Green Goddess Dressing

¾ cup snipped parsley
½ cup mayonnaise *or* salad
    dressing
½ cup dairy sour cream
1 green onion, cut up
2 tablespoons tarragon
    vinegar
1 tablespoon anchovy paste
½ teaspoon dried basil,
    crushed
¼ teaspoon sugar

In blender container combine parsley, mayonnaise or salad dressing, sour cream, green onion, vinegar, anchovy paste, basil, and sugar. Cover and blend till smooth. Transfer to storage container. Cover and chill. Makes 1¼ cups.

Blue Cheese Salad Dressing

1 cup mayonnaise *or* salad
    dressing
1 small onion, cut up
⅓ cup salad oil
¼ cup catsup
2 tablespoons sugar
2 tablespoons vinegar
1 teaspoon prepared mustard
½ teaspoon paprika
¼ teaspoon celery seed
1 cup crumbled blue cheese

In blender container combine mayonnaise or salad dressing, onion, salad oil, catsup, sugar, vinegar, mustard, paprika, celery seed, ½ teaspoon *salt,* and dash *pepper.* Cover and blend till smooth. Transfer dressing to storage container; stir in blue cheese. Cover and chill. Makes 2½ cups.

Buttermilk Dressing

½ cup mayonnaise *or* salad
    dressing
½ cup chive-style sour cream dip
½ cup buttermilk
¼ cup tomato juice
2 tablespoons grated parmesan
    cheese
½ teaspoon dry mustard
¼ teaspoon paprika
¼ teaspoon celery seed
⅛ teaspoon garlic powder

In a bowl blend mayonnaise or salad dressing, sour cream dip, buttermilk, tomato juice, parmesan cheese, dry mustard, paprika, celery seed, garlic powder, ⅛ teaspoon *salt,* and ⅛ teaspoon *pepper.* Transfer to storage container. Cover and chill. Makes 1¾ cups.

Creamy Garlic Dressing

½ cup mayonnaise *or* salad
    dressing
½ cup Italian salad dressing
2 tablespoons finely shredded
    cheddar cheese
1 tablespoon anchovy paste

In mixing bowl blend together mayonnaise or salad dressing, Italian dressing, cheddar cheese, and anchovy paste; mix well. Transfer to storage container. Cover and chill. Makes 1 cup.

Waist-watcher Dressings

Zesty Salad Dressing (above, left)

- 1 tablespoon cornstarch
- 1 teaspoon sugar
- 1 teaspoon dry mustard
- 1 cup cold water
- ¼ cup vinegar
- ¼ cup catsup
- 1 teaspoon prepared horseradish
- 1 teaspoon worcestershire sauce
- ½ teaspoon salt
- ½ teaspoon paprika
  Dash bottled hot pepper sauce
- 1 clove garlic, halved

In a small saucepan combine the cornstarch, sugar, and the dry mustard; gradually stir in water. Cook, stirring constantly, over medium heat till thick and bubbly. Remove from heat. Cover surface with waxed paper. Cool 10 to 15 minutes. Remove waxed paper; stir in the vinegar, catsup, horseradish, worcestershire, salt, paprika, and hot pepper sauce; beat till smooth. Add garlic. Transfer to storage container; cover and chill.

Remove garlic before using. Makes 1⅓ cups (6 calories per tablespoon).

Diet Blue Cheese Dressing (opposite, center)

1 8-ounce carton plain yogurt
2 tablespoons crumbled blue
   cheese
2 teaspoons sugar
½ teaspoon celery seed
   Dash bottled hot pepper
   sauce

In a small mixer bowl combine yogurt, *half* the blue cheese, the sugar, celery seed, and hot pepper sauce. Beat with rotary beater till smooth. Stir in the remaining blue cheese. Transfer to storage container. Cover and chill. Makes 1 cup (13 calories per tablespoon).

Diet Salad Dressing

1 tablespoon all-purpose
   flour
1 tablespoon sugar
1 teaspoon dry mustard
½ teaspoon salt
   Dash cayenne
¾ cup skim milk
2 slightly beaten egg yolks
3 tablespoons vinegar

In saucepan combine flour, sugar, dry mustard, salt, and cayenne; stir in milk. Cook and stir till thick and bubbly. Gradually stir hot mixture into egg yolks. Return mixture to saucepan; cook and stir 2 minutes more. Place a piece of waxed paper over surface; cool 10 to 15 minutes. Remove waxed paper; stir in vinegar. Transfer to storage container; cover and chill. Makes ¾ cup (18 calories per tablespoon).

Diet Thousand Island Dressing (opposite, right)

½ cup Diet Salad Dressing
   (see recipe above)
1 tablespoon sliced green
   onion
1 tablespoon chopped green
   pepper
1 tablespoon catsup *or* chili
   sauce
1 tablespoon chopped pimiento
1 teaspoon prepared
   horseradish

In a small mixing bowl stir together *Diet Salad Dressing*, green onion, green pepper, catsup or chili sauce, pimiento, and horseradish. Transfer to storage container. Cover and chill. Makes ⅔ cup (16 calories per tablespoon).

Tomato Salad Dressing

1 8-ounce can tomato sauce
2 tablespoons tarragon
   vinegar
1 teaspoon worcestershire
   sauce
½ teaspoon salt
½ teaspoon dried dillweed
½ teaspoon dried basil,
   crushed
½ teaspoon onion juice

In screw-top jar combine tomato sauce, vinegar, worcestershire sauce, salt, dried dillweed, basil, and onion juice. Cover and shake to mix well. Chill thoroughly. Shake again just before serving. Makes 1 cup (4 calories per tablespoon).

Salad Toppers

Sprouting Mini Garden (pictured above, front to back: lentils, cress, and alfalfa)

Lentils
Alfalfa seed
Curly cress seed
Radish seed
Mustard seed
Mung beans
Garbanzos
Dried peas
Lima beans
Pinto beans

You can find some of these in the dried bean section of your supermarket. Shop a health food shop for the less common seeds. (Don't buy seeds that have been chemically treated for farming. Some treated seeds can be poisonous.)

In separate small bowls soak seeds in water (use four times as much water as seeds) till seeds swell to double in size, about 3 hours. Place three layers of paper toweling on divided plate; top with single layer of cheesecloth. Drain seeds; place in single layer atop cheesecloth. (Curly cress will develop a gelatinous coating; don't remove it.) Spray thoroughly with a fine water spray. (Towels should be wet but seeds shouldn't be standing in water.) Prick holes in a sheet of foil large enough to cover plate. Cover plate loosely with the foil. Place plate in a warm dark place. Spray with water 4 to 5 times a day at first, then 2 or 3 times daily after sprouts reach ¼ inch, keeping moist at all times. Sprouts grow in 2 to 3 days. Leaves appear on the third or fourth day. After sprouts appear, remove foil and set plates in sunny place for several hours to let the leaves turn green. Keep paper toweling wet. To harvest sprouts, snip off tops; use on tossed salads.

Garlic Croutons

8 ½-inch-thick slices French
  bread
1 large clove garlic, halved
¼ cup salad oil
¼ cup butter *or* margarine
  softened

Rub both sides of bread slices with the cut clove of garlic; discard garlic. Gradually blend oil into softened butter or margarine; spread both sides of bread with oil-butter mixture. Cut bread into ½-inch cubes. Spread out on baking sheet. Bake in 300° oven for 20 to 25 minutes or till croutons are dry and crisp. Cool. Store in covered container in refrigerator. To serve, sprinkle over tossed salads. Makes 3 cups croutons.

Rye Croutons

5 slices rye bread
3 tablespoons butter *or*
  margarine, softened

Brush both sides of rye bread slices with butter or margarine; cut bread into ½-inch cubes. Spread out on baking sheet. Bake in 300° oven for 20 to 25 minutes or till croutons are dry and crisp. Cool. Store in covered container in refrigerator. To serve, sprinkle over tossed salads. Makes 2 cups croutons.

Salad Garnishes

Radish Roses
Carrot Curls

To make Radish Roses, rinse radishes well; cut off tops and roots. Using tip of paring knife, cut 4 or 5 thin petal-shaped pieces around the outside of each radish (leave each petal attached at bottom).

To make Carrot Curls, rest peeled carrot on flat surface. Using vegetable peeler, shave thin wide strips the full length of carrot. Roll up; secure with wooden pick. Place vegetables in ice water to crispen.

Sprout Gardening in a Jar

You can easily set up a sprout garden in the dark corner of a kitchen shelf. All you need is a quart jar, cheesecloth, and seeds (see suggested seeds in recipe at left). Wash and sort ½ cup of seeds, discarding damaged seeds. Soak seeds overnight in 2 cups water (seeds will swell to twice their size). Drain and rinse. Place ¼ cup of soaked seeds in each quart jar. Cover tops of jars with two layers of cheesecloth as shown; fasten each with rubber band or string. Place jars on their sides so seeds form shallow layer. Store in warm (68° to 75° F), dark place. Rinse seeds once daily in lukewarm water. Harvest sprouts in 3 to 5 days. You can eat the whole sprout: seed, root, stem, and outer hull. If you prefer to remove hulls, place sprouts in bowl; cover with water and stir vigorously, skimming away husks as they rise to the top. Drain. Pat dry with paper toweling. Sprinkle sprouts over tossed salads.

6 Bread specialties

Whether you're a beginning bread baker or an old hand, you'll find that this chapter is geared for you. Try the loaves, rolls, biscuits, and coffee cakes on the following pages and you'll have new favorites to add to your list.

Whole Wheat Rolls, French Chocolate Coffee Cake, miniature *Cornmeal Loaves,* and *Bacon Bread.* (See index for pages.)

Yeast Breads

Perfect White Bread (conventional method)

1 package active dry yeast
¼ cup warm water (110° to 115°)
2 cups milk
2 tablespoons sugar
1 tablespoon shortening
2 teaspoons salt
5¾ to 6¼ cups all-purpose flour

Soften yeast in warm water. In saucepan heat milk, sugar, shortening, and salt till sugar dissolves; cool to lukewarm (105° to 110°). Turn into a large mixing bowl. Stir in *2 cups* of the flour; beat well. Add softened yeast; stir till smooth. Stir in as much remaining flour as you can mix in using a spoon. Turn out onto lightly floured surface. Knead in enough remaining flour to make a moderately stiff dough. Continue kneading till smooth and elastic (8 to 10 minutes). Shape into ball. Place in lightly greased bowl, turning once.

Cover; let rise in warm place till double (about 1¼ hours). Punch down; turn out onto lightly floured surface. Divide in half. Shape into 2 smooth balls. Cover; let rest 10 minutes. Shape each into a loaf. (Or, roll each into a 12x8-inch rectangle; roll from one of the shorter ends to make a loaf.) Place in 2 greased 8x4x2-inch loaf pans. Cover; let rise in warm place till double (45 to 60 minutes). Bake at 375° till done, about 45 minutes. Remove from pans; cool on wire rack. Makes 2 loaves.

Perfect White Bread (easy-mix method)

5¾ to 6¼ cups all-purpose flour
1 package active dry yeast
2¼ cups milk
2 tablespoons sugar
1 tablespoon shortening
2 teaspoons salt

In large mixer bowl combine *2½ cups* of the flour and the yeast. In saucepan heat milk, sugar, shortening, and salt just till warm (115° to 120°) and shortening is almost melted; stir constantly. Add to flour mixture. Beat at low speed of electric mixer for ½ minute, scraping sides of bowl. Beat 3 minutes at high speed. Stir in as much of the remaining flour as you can mix in using a spoon. Turn out onto a lightly floured surface. Knead in enough of the remaining flour to make a moderately stiff dough. Continue kneading till smooth and elastic (5 to 8 minutes). Shape into a ball. Place in lightly greased bowl, turning once. Cover; let rise in a warm place till double (about 1¼ hours). Punch dough down.

Divide dough in half. Cover; let rest 10 minutes. Shape or roll each half into a loaf. Place in 2 greased 8x4x2-inch loaf pans. Cover; let rise in warm place till double (45 to 60 minutes). Bake at 375° till done, about 45 minutes. Remove from pans; cool on wire rack. Makes 2 loaves.

Refrig-A-Rise White Bread

Begin breadmaking ahead of time, then bake the loaves at your convenience. Prepare *Perfect White Bread* using either method. Place loaves in loaf pans. Brush with melted butter. Cover loosely with clear plastic wrap. Refrigerate for 3 to 24 hours. When ready to bake, remove from refrigerator. Uncover; let stand till nearly double, about 20 minutes. Just before baking, puncture any surface bubbles with a wooden pick. Bake at 375° till done, about 45 minutes. After 30 minutes of baking, brush tops with melted butter.

Basic Rolls (conventional method)

2 **packages active dry yeast**
½ **cup warm water (110° to 115°)**
½ **cup sugar**
½ **cup shortening**
½ **cup milk**
2 **teaspoons salt**
4½ **to 5 cups all-purpose flour**
3 **eggs**

Soften yeast in warm water. In saucepan heat sugar, shortening, milk, and salt till sugar dissolves; cool to lukewarm (105° to 110°). Place in large mixing bowl. Stir in *1 ½ cups* of the flour; beat well. Add softened yeast and eggs; beat till smooth. Stir in as much of the remaining flour as you can mix in using a spoon. Turn out onto lightly floured surface. Knead in enough of the remaining flour to make a moderately stiff dough. Continue kneading till smooth and elastic (5 to 8 minutes). Shape into a ball. Place in lightly greased bowl, turning once. Cover; let rise in warm place till double (1 to 1½ hours).

Punch dough down; turn out onto lightly floured surface. Cover; let rest 10 minutes. Shape dough into desired rolls. Cover and let rise in warm place till double (30 to 45 minutes). If desired, carefully brush with melted butter or margarine. Bake at 400° till done, 10 to 12 minutes. Remove from pans. Makes 2 to 3 dozen rolls.

Basic Rolls (easy-mix method)

4½ **to 5 cups all-purpose flour**
2 **packages active dry yeast**
1 **cup milk**
½ **cup sugar**
½ **cup shortening**
2 **teaspoons salt**
3 **eggs**

In large mixer bowl combine *2 cups* of the flour and the yeast. In saucepan heat milk, sugar, shortening, and salt just till warm (115° to 120°) and shortening is almost melted, stirring constantly. Add to flour mixture in mixer bowl; add eggs. Beat at low speed of electric mixer for ½ minute, scraping sides of bowl constantly. Beat 3 minutes at high speed. Stir in as much of the remaining flour as you can mix in using a spoon. Turn out onto lightly floured surface. Knead in enough of the remaining flour to make a moderately stiff dough. Continue kneading till smooth and elastic (5 to 8 minutes). Shape into a ball. Place in lightly greased bowl; turn once to grease surface. Cover; let rise in warm place till double (1 to 1½ hours).

Punch down; turn out onto lightly floured surface. Cover; let rest 10 minutes. Shape into desired rolls. Cover; let rise in a warm place till double (30 to 45 minutes). If desired, carefully brush with melted butter. Bake at 400° till done, 10 to 12 minutes. Makes 2 to 3 dozen rolls.

No-Knead Refrigerator Rolls

3½ **to 3¾ cups all-purpose flour**
1 **package active dry yeast**
1¼ **cups milk**
¼ **cup sugar**
¼ **cup shortening**
1 **teaspoon salt**
1 **egg**

In large mixer bowl combine *1 ½ cups* of the flour and the yeast. In saucepan heat milk, sugar, shortening, and salt just till warm (115° to 120°) and shortening is almost melted, stirring constantly. Add to flour mixture; add egg. Beat at low speed of electric mixer for ½ minute, scraping bowl. Beat 3 minutes at high speed. By hand, stir in enough remaining flour to make a soft dough.

Cover and refrigerate dough at least 2 hours or till needed. (Use within 3 to 4 days.) About 1½ to 2 hours before serving time, shape dough into desired rolls. Cover; let rise in warm place till double (1 to 1¼ hours). Bake at 400° till done, 9 to 10 minutes. Makes 2 to 3 dozen rolls.

Two-Tone Bread

5¼ to 5½ cups all-purpose flour
  2 packages active dry yeast
  3 cups milk
 ⅓ cup sugar
 ⅓ cup shortening
  1 tablespoon salt
  3 tablespoons dark molasses
2¼ cups whole wheat flour

In large mixer bowl combine *3 cups* of the all-purpose flour and the yeast. In saucepan heat milk, sugar, shortening, and salt just till warm (115° to 120°) and shortening is almost melted, stirring constantly. Add to flour mixture in mixer bowl. Beat at low speed of electric mixer for ½ minute, scraping sides of bowl constantly. Beat 3 minutes at high speed. Divide dough in half. To one half, stir in as much of the remaining all-purpose flour as you can mix in using a spoon. Turn out onto lightly floured surface. Knead in enough of the remaining all-purpose flour to make a moderately stiff dough. Continue kneading till smooth and elastic (5 to 8 minutes). Shape into ball. Place in well-greased bowl, turning once to grease surface; set aside.

To remaining dough, stir in molasses. Stir in the whole wheat flour. Turn out onto lightly floured surface. Knead in enough additional all-purpose flour (about 3 tablespoons) to make a moderately stiff dough. Continue kneading till smooth and elastic (5 to 8 minutes). Shape into ball. Place in well-greased bowl, turning once to grease surface.

Cover and let both doughs rise till double (1 to 1¼ hours). Punch down. Divide doughs in half; cover and let rest 10 minutes. Roll out *half* the light dough and *half* the dark dough, each to a 12x8-inch rectangle. Place dark dough atop light; roll up tightly into a loaf, starting at short side. Repeat with remaining doughs. Place in 2 greased 8x4x2-inch loaf pans. Cover; let rise till double (45 to 60 minutes). Bake at 375° for 30 to 35 minutes. Remove; cool. Makes 2 loaves.

Grandma's Oatmeal Bread

5¾ to 6¼ cups all-purpose flour
  2 packages active dry yeast
1¾ cups water
  1 cup quick-cooking rolled
     oats
 ½ cup light molasses
 ⅓ cup shortening
  1 tablespoon salt
  2 eggs
    Quick-cooking rolled oats
  1 beaten egg white (optional)
  1 tablespoon water (optional)

In large mixer bowl combine *2 cups* of the flour and the yeast. Heat the 1¾ cups water, 1 cup rolled oats, molasses, shortening, and salt just till warm (115° to 120°) and shortening is almost melted; stir constantly. Add to flour mixture; add eggs. Beat at low speed of electric mixer for ½ minute, scraping bowl. Beat 3 minutes at high speed. Stir in as much of the remaining flour as you can mix in using a spoon. Turn out onto a lightly floured surface. Knead in enough of the remaining flour to make a moderately soft dough. Continue kneading till smooth and elastic (5 to 8 minutes). Shape into a ball.

Place in lightly greased bowl, turning once to grease surface. Cover and let rise in warm place till double (about 1½ hours). Punch dough down; turn out onto lightly floured surface. Divide dough in half. Cover and let rest 10 minutes. Coat two well-greased 9x5x3-inch loaf pans with about 3 tablespoons rolled oats for each pan. Shape dough into loaves; place in prepared pans.

Cover and let rise in warm place till double (45 to 60 minutes). If desired, brush loaves with mixture of egg white and 1 tablespoon water; sprinkle tops lightly with rolled oats. Bake at 375° till done, 40 to 45 minutes. Cover loosely with foil the last 15 minutes if tops are browning rapidly. Remove from pans; cool. Makes 2 loaves.

Bacon Bread (pictured on page 366)

3½ to 3¾ cups all-purpose flour
1 package active dry yeast
10 slices bacon
1¼ cups milk
1 tablespoon sugar
1 teaspoon salt
   Melted butter *or* margarine

In large mixer bowl combine *1 cup* of the flour and the yeast. Cook bacon till crisp; drain, reserving 2 tablespoons drippings. Finely crumble bacon; set aside.

In saucepan heat the reserved bacon drippings, milk, sugar, and salt just till warm (115° to 120°), stirring constantly. Add to flour mixture in mixer bowl. Beat at low speed of electric mixer for ½ minute, scraping sides of bowl constantly. Beat 3 minutes at high speed.

Stir in the crumbled bacon and as much of the remaining flour as you can mix in using a spoon. Turn out onto a lightly floured surface. Knead in enough of the remaining flour to make a moderately stiff dough. Continue kneading till smooth and elastic (8 to 10 minutes).

Shape into a ball. Place in lightly greased bowl, turning once. Cover and let rise in a warm place till double (about 1¾ hours). Punch down; turn out onto lightly floured surface. Cover and let rest 10 minutes.

Shape dough into a loaf; place in greased 8x4x2-inch loaf pan. Cover and let rise in a warm place till double (35 to 40 minutes). Bake at 375° till done, about 35 minutes. Brush with melted butter or margarine. Remove from pan; cool on wire rack. Makes 1 loaf.

Cornmeal Loaves (pictured on page 366)

6 to 6½ cups all-purpose flour
2 packages active dry yeast
2¼ cups milk
⅓ cup sugar
⅓ cup shortening
1 tablespoon salt
2 eggs
1 cup yellow cornmeal
   Milk
   Yellow cornmeal

In large mixer bowl combine *3 cups* of the flour and the yeast. In saucepan heat the 2¼ cups milk, sugar, shortening, and salt just till warm (115° to 120°) and shortening is almost melted, stirring constantly. Add to flour mixture in mixer bowl; add eggs. Beat at low speed of electric mixer for ½ minute, scraping sides of bowl constantly. Beat 3 minutes at high speed.

Stir in the 1 cup yellow cornmeal and as much of the remaining flour as you can mix in using a spoon. Turn out onto a lightly floured surface. Knead in enough remaining flour to make a soft dough. Continue kneading till smooth and elastic (5 to 8 minutes). Shape into a ball. Place in lightly greased bowl, turning once. Cover and let rise in a warm place till double (1 to 1½ hours).

Punch dough down; turn out onto a lightly floured surface. Divide dough into eighths. Cover and let rest 10 minutes. Shape dough into 8 small loaves and place in 8 greased 6x3x2-inch loaf pans. (Or, divide dough in half; cover and let rest 10 minutes. Shape into 2 loaves and place in 2 greased 9x5x3-inch loaf pans.) Cover loaves and let rise in a warm place till double (45 to 60 minutes).

Carefully brush tops with a little milk; sprinkle with a little yellow cornmeal. Bake small loaves at 400° about 25 minutes. (Bake large loaves at 375° about 45 minutes.) Remove from pans; cool. Makes 8 small or 2 large loaves.

Old-Time Whole Wheat Bread

5 cups all-purpose flour
2 packages active dry yeast
2¾ cups water
½ cup packed brown sugar
¼ cup shortening
1 tablespoon salt
3 cups whole wheat flour

Combine 3½ cups all-purpose flour and the yeast. Heat water, sugar, shortening, and salt just till warm (115° to 120°) and shortening is almost melted; stir constantly. Add to flour mixture. Beat at low speed of electric mixer for ½ minute, scraping bowl. Beat 3 minutes at high speed.

Stir in whole wheat flour and as much remaining all-purpose flour as you can mix in using a spoon. Knead in enough remaining flour to make a moderately stiff dough. Knead till smooth and elastic (10 to 12 minutes). Place in greased bowl; turn once. Cover; let rise till double (about 1 hour).

Punch down; turn out onto lightly floured surface. Divide in half. Cover; let rest 10 minutes. Shape each half into loaf; place in 2 greased 8x4x2-inch loaf pans. Cover; let rise till almost double (about 45 minutes). Bake at 375° for 40 to 45 minutes. Cover loosely with foil the last 20 minutes if tops brown too quickly. Makes 2 loaves.

Pumpernickel Bread

2¾ to 3 cups all-purpose flour
3 packages active dry yeast
1 tablespoon caraway seed
1½ cups warm water (115° to 120°)
½ cup light molasses
2 tablespoons cooking oil
1 tablespoon salt
2 cups rye flour
   Cornmeal

Combine 2 cups all-purpose flour, yeast, and caraway. Blend water, molasses, oil, and salt; add to flour mixture. Beat at low speed of electric mixer for ½ minute, scraping bowl. Beat 3 minutes at high speed. Stir in rye flour and as much remaining all-purpose flour as you can mix in using a spoon. Knead in enough remaining flour to make a moderately stiff dough. Knead till smooth (5 to 8 minutes). Place in greased bowl; turn once. Cover; let rise till double (about 1½ hours). Punch down; turn out onto lightly floured surface.

Divide in half. Cover; let rest 10 minutes. Shape into two 6-inch round loaves; place on greased baking sheet sprinkled with cornmeal. Cover; let rise till double (30 to 45 minutes). Bake at 350° till well browned, 35 to 40 minutes. Cover loosely with foil the last 15 minutes if tops brown too quickly. For shiny crust, brush with warm water several times the last 10 to 15 minutes. Makes 2 loaves.

Rye Bread

3¼ to 3¾ cups all-purpose flour
2 packages active dry yeast
1 tablespoon caraway seed
2 cups warm water (115° to 120°)
½ cup packed brown sugar
1 tablespoon cooking oil
1 teaspoon salt
2½ cups rye flour

In large mixer bowl combine 2½ cups of the all-purpose flour, the yeast, and caraway. In mixing bowl blend water, brown sugar, oil, and salt. Add to flour mixture. Beat at low speed of electric mixer for ½ minute, scraping bowl. Beat 3 minutes at high speed. Stir in rye flour and as much remaining all-purpose flour as you can mix in using a spoon. Knead in enough remaining flour to make a moderately stiff dough. Continue kneading till smooth (about 5 minutes); dough will be sticky. Place in greased bowl, turning once.

Cover; let rise in warm place till double (about 1½ hours). Punch down; turn out on floured surface. Divide in half. Cover; let rest 10 minutes. Shape into two 4½-inch round loaves on greased baking sheet (or shape into loaves and place in 2 greased 8x4x2-inch loaf pans). Cover; let rise till double (about 40 minutes). Bake at 350° for 40 to 45 minutes. Makes 2 loaves.

Cinnamon Swirl Loaf

7 to 7½ cups all-purpose flour
2 packages active dry yeast
2 cups milk
½ cup sugar
½ cup shortening
2 teaspoons salt
2 eggs
½ cup sugar
2 teaspoons ground cinnamon
Confectioners' Icing

In large mixer bowl combine 3½ *cups* of the flour and the yeast. Heat milk, ½ cup sugar, shortening, and salt just till warm (115° to 120°) and shortening is almost melted; stir constantly. Add to flour mixture; add eggs. Beat at low speed of electric mixer for ½ minute, scraping bowl. Beat 3 minutes at high speed. Stir in as much remaining flour as you can mix in using a spoon. Knead in enough remaining flour to make a moderately soft dough. Continue kneading till smooth and elastic (5 to 8 minutes). Shape into ball. Place in greased bowl; turn once.

Cover; let rise till double (about 1 hour). Punch down; divide in half. Cover; let rest 10 minutes. Roll each half into a 15x7-inch rectangle. Brush with water.

Combine ½ cup sugar and cinnamon. Sprinkle half the mixture over each rectangle. Roll up jelly-roll style, starting with short side. Seal long edge and ends. Place, seam side down, in 2 greased 9x5x3-inch loaf pans. Cover; let rise till almost double (35 to 45 minutes). Bake at 375° till done, 35 to 40 minutes. Cover loosely with foil the last 15 minutes if tops brown too quickly. Remove; cool. Drizzle with Confectioners' Icing. Makes 2 loaves.

Confectioners' Icing: Combine 1 cup sifted *powdered sugar*, ¼ teaspoon *vanilla*, and enough *milk* to make of drizzling consistency (about 1½ tablespoons).

Easy Dill-Onion Bread

3 cups all-purpose flour
1 package active dry yeast
1¼ cups milk
2 tablespoons sugar
2 tablespoons butter *or* margarine
2 teaspoons dried dillseed
2 teaspoons instant minced onion
1 teaspoon salt
1 egg

In small mixer bowl combine 1½ *cups* of the flour and the yeast. Heat milk, sugar, butter, dillseed, onion, and salt just till warm (115° to 120°) and butter is almost melted; stir constantly. Add to flour mixture; add egg. Beat at low speed of electric mixer for ½ minute, scraping bowl. Beat 3 minutes at high speed. By hand, stir in remaining flour.

Cover; let rise till double (30 to 45 minutes). Stir down. Spread evenly in greased 9x5x3-inch loaf pan. Cover; let rise till nearly double (about 30 minutes). Bake at 350° for 25 to 30 minutes. Cover loosely with foil the last 10 minutes if bread browns too quickly. Remove; cool. Makes 1 loaf.

Garden Batter Bread

3 cups all-purpose flour
1 package active dry yeast
2 teaspoons salt
1¼ cups warm water (110° to 115°)
¼ cup light molasses
2 tablespoons cooking oil
1 egg
1 cup wheat germ
1 cup finely shredded carrot
¼ cup snipped parsley

In large mixer bowl combine 2 *cups* of the flour, the yeast, and salt. Add water, molasses, oil, and egg. Beat at low speed of electric mixer for ½ minute, scraping sides of bowl constantly. Beat 3 minutes at high speed. By hand, stir in the remaining flour, wheat germ, carrot, and parsley. Turn batter into a greased 2-quart casserole.

Cover; let rise in warm place till nearly double (45 to 60 minutes). Bake at 350° for 50 to 60 minutes. Cover loosely with foil after the first 20 minutes of baking. Remove from casserole as soon as done. Brush top crust with melted butter or margarine, if desired. Cool. Makes 1 loaf.

Make the swirl in *Cinnamon Swirl Loaf* by rolling up a mixture of sugar
and spice in the dough. After baking, drizzle Confectioners' Icing over the top.

Onion Buns

1¼ cups finely chopped onion
2 tablespoons butter *or* margarine
2½ to 3 cups all-purpose flour
1 package active dry yeast
¾ cup milk
¼ cup shortening
2 tablespoons sugar
¾ teaspoon salt
2 eggs
1 tablespoon milk
⅛ teaspoon salt
Poppy seed (optional)

Cook onion in butter till tender. Remove 2 tablespoons; set remainder aside. Combine *1½ cups* flour and yeast. Heat ¾ cup milk, shortening, sugar, and ¾ teaspoon salt just till warm (115° to 120°) and shortening is almost melted; stir constantly. Add to flour mixture; add 1 of the eggs and the 2 tablespoons onion. Beat at low speed of electric mixer for ½ minute. Beat 3 minutes at high speed. Stir in as much remaining flour as you can mix in using a spoon. Knead in enough remaining flour to make a soft dough. Knead till smooth (5 to 8 minutes). Place in greased bowl; turn once. Cover; let rise till double (about 1¼ hours).

Beat remaining egg slightly. Add 1 tablespoon beaten egg to remaining onion; stir in 1 tablespoon milk and ⅛ teaspoon salt. Punch dough down; divide in half. Divide each half into 6 portions. Cover; let rest 10 minutes. Shape into round buns. Place on greased baking sheet. Make large indentation in centers; spoon about 2 teaspoons onion mixture into each indentation. Brush tops with remaining beaten egg. Sprinkle with poppy seed, if desired. Cover; let rise till double (about 45 minutes). Bake at 375° about 20 minutes. Makes 12 rolls.

Crusty Water Rolls

1 package active dry yeast
¼ cup warm water (110° to 115°)
¾ cup boiling water
2 tablespoons shortening
1 tablespoon sugar
1½ teaspoons salt
3¼ to 3½ cups all-purpose flour
2 slightly beaten egg whites

Soften yeast in warm water. Combine boiling water, shortening, sugar, and salt; stir till shortening is melted. Cool to lukewarm (105° to 110°). Stir in *1 cup* of the flour; beat well. Add softened yeast and egg whites; beat till smooth. Stir in as much remaining flour as you can mix in using a spoon. Knead in enough remaining flour to make a moderately soft dough. Knead till smooth (8 to 10 minutes). Place in greased bowl; turn once. Cover; let rise till double (about 1 hour). Punch down. Cover; let rest 10 minutes.

Shape into 18 round rolls. Place 2½ inches apart on greased baking sheet. Cover; let rise in warm place till double (about 45 minutes). Place a large shallow pan on lower oven rack; fill with boiling water. Bake rolls on rack above water at 450° for 10 to 12 minutes. Makes 18 rolls.

Batter Rolls

3¼ cups all-purpose flour
1 package active dry yeast
1¼ cups milk
½ cup shortening
¼ cup sugar
1 teaspoon salt
1 egg
Milk (optional)
1 tablespoon poppy seed *or* sesame seed (optional)

Combine *2 cups* flour and yeast. Heat milk, shortening, sugar, and salt just till warm (115° to 120°) and shortening is almost melted; stir constantly. Add to flour mixture; add egg. Beat at low speed of electric mixer for ½ minute, scraping bowl. Beat 3 minutes at high speed. At low speed, beat in remaining flour till smooth, about 2 minutes, pushing batter away from beaters.

Cover; let rise till double (about 1 hour). Stir down; beat well with wooden spoon. Let rest 5 minutes. Drop by tablespoonfuls into greased muffin pans, filling half full. Cover; let rise till double (about 30 minutes). If desired, brush tops lightly with milk and sprinkle with poppy or sesame seed. Bake at 375° for 15 to 18 minutes. Makes 18 rolls.

Whole Wheat Rolls (pictured on page 366)

3 to 3½ cups all-purpose flour
2 packages active dry yeast
2 cups milk
½ cup sugar
3 tablespoons shortening
1 tablespoon salt
2 eggs
3½ cups whole wheat flour

In large mixer bowl combine 2½ cups of the all-purpose flour and the yeast. Heat milk, sugar, shortening, and salt just till warm (115° to 120°) and shortening is almost melted, stirring constantly. Add to flour mixture; add eggs. Beat at low speed of electric mixer for ½ minute, scraping bowl. Beat 3 minutes at high speed. Stir in whole wheat flour and as much remaining all-purpose flour as you can mix in using a spoon. Knead in enough remaining all-purpose flour to make a moderately stiff dough.

Knead till smooth and elastic (5 to 8 minutes). Place in greased bowl; turn once. Cover; let rise till double (about 1½ hours). Punch down; cover and let rest 10 minutes. Shape into desired rolls. Cover; let rise till almost double (about 45 minutes). Bake at 400° for 15 to 20 minutes. Makes 2 to 3 dozen.

Refrigerated Herb Rolls

3¼ to 3½ cups all-purpose flour
1 package active dry yeast
2 teaspoons celery seed
1 teaspoon dried thyme, crushed
1¼ cups milk
¼ cup sugar
¼ cup shortening
1 teaspoon salt
1 egg
Butter, melted

In large mixer bowl combine 1½ cups of the flour, the yeast, celery seed, and thyme. In saucepan heat milk, sugar, shortening, and salt just till warm (115° to 120°) and shortening is almost melted, stirring constantly. Add to flour mixture; add egg. Beat at low speed of electric mixer for ½ minute, scraping bowl. Beat 3 minutes at high speed. By hand, stir in enough remaining flour to make a moderately soft dough. Place in greased bowl, turning once to grease surface. Cover and chill at least 2 hours.

Shape dough into 1¼-inch balls. Place 3 balls in each greased muffin pan. Brush with melted butter. Cover; let rise till double (about 1 hour). Bake at 400° for 12 to 15 minutes. Makes 18 rolls.

Italian Breadsticks

2 to 2¼ cups all-purpose flour
1 package active dry yeast
1 tablespoon sugar
1½ teaspoons salt
¾ cup warm water (110° to 115°)
2 tablespoons olive oil or cooking oil
1 egg yolk
1 egg white
1 tablespoon water
Coarse salt (optional)

In large mixer bowl combine 1 cup of the flour, the yeast, sugar, and salt. Combine ¾ cup warm water, oil, and egg yolk; add to flour mixture. Beat at low speed of electric mixer for ½ minute, scraping bowl. Beat 3 minutes at high speed. Stir in as much remaining flour as you can mix in using a spoon. Knead in enough remaining flour to make a moderately soft dough. Continue kneading till smooth and elastic (5 to 8 minutes). Shape into ball. Place in greased bowl; turn once. Cover; chill 3 to 4 hours or overnight.

Turn out onto a very lightly floured surface; divide into 16 pieces. Cover; let rest 10 minutes. Roll each piece into a rope 14 inches long. Place on greased baking sheet. Brush with mixture of egg white and 1 tablespoon water. Cover; let rise till double (45 to 60 minutes). Brush again with egg white mixture. Sprinkle with coarse salt, if desired. Bake at 425° about 10 minutes. Makes 16.

French Chocolate Coffee Cake (pictured on page 366)

4 to 4¼ cups all-purpose flour
2 packages active dry yeast
¾ cup sugar
⅔ cup water
½ cup butter *or* margarine
⅓ cup evaporated milk
½ teaspoon salt
4 egg yolks
¾ cup semisweet chocolate
    pieces
⅓ cup evaporated milk
2 tablespoons sugar
½ teaspoon ground cinnamon
¼ cup all-purpose flour
¼ cup sugar
1 teaspoon ground cinnamon
¼ cup butter *or* margarine
¼ cup chopped nuts

In large mixer bowl combine 1½ *cups* of the flour and the yeast. In saucepan heat ¾ cup sugar, water, ½ cup butter or margarine, ⅓ cup evaporated milk, and salt just till warm (115° to 120°) and butter is almost melted, stirring constantly. Add to flour mixture in mixer bowl; add egg yolks. Beat at low speed of electric mixer for ½ minute, scraping sides of bowl constantly. Beat 3 minutes at high speed. Using the remaining 2½ to 2¾ cups flour, stir in as much of this flour as you can mix in using a spoon. Turn out onto a lightly floured surface. Knead in enough of this remaining flour to make a moderately soft dough. Continue kneading till smooth and elastic (3 to 5 minutes). Shape into a ball. Place in lightly greased bowl, turning once to grease surface. Cover; let rise in warm place till double (about 2 hours).

Punch down; turn out onto floured surface. Cover; let rest 10 minutes. Meanwhile, combine semisweet chocolate pieces, ⅓ cup evaporated milk, 2 tablespoons sugar, and ½ teaspoon ground cinnamon. Heat and stir over low heat till chocolate is melted; cool. Roll dough to an 18x10-inch rectangle. Spread with chocolate mixture; roll up jelly-roll style, starting from long side. Join and seal ends. Place in greased 10-inch tube pan.

Combine ¼ cup flour, ¼ cup sugar, and 1 teaspoon ground cinnamon. Cut in ¼ cup butter or margarine till crumbly; stir in chopped nuts. Sprinkle over dough. Cover; let rise in warm place till double (about 1¼ hours). Bake on lower oven rack at 350° for 45 to 50 minutes. Cool 15 minutes; remove from pan. Makes 1 large coffee cake.

Bubble Wreath

3½ to 3¾ cups all-purpose flour
1 package active dry yeast
1¼ cups milk
¼ cup sugar
¼ cup shortening
1 teaspoon salt
1 egg
    Sugar-Fruit Topping
    Melted butter *or* margarine
½ cup sugar
1 teaspoon ground cinnamon

In large mixer bowl combine 2 *cups* of the flour and the yeast. In saucepan heat milk, ¼ cup sugar, shortening, and salt just till warm (115° to 120°) and shortening is almost melted, stirring constantly. Add to flour mixture in mixer bowl; add egg. Beat at low speed of electric mixer for ½ minute, scraping sides of bowl. Beat 3 minutes at high speed. Stir in as much of the remaining flour as you can mix in using a spoon. Turn out onto lightly floured surface. Knead in enough of the remaining flour to make a soft dough. Continue kneading till smooth and elastic.

Shape into a ball. Place in lightly greased bowl, turning once to grease surface. Cover; let rise in warm place till double (about 2 hours). Grease a 10-inch tube pan; spread bottom with Sugar-Fruit Topping. Shape dough into 48 small balls. Roll in melted butter or margarine, then in mixture of ½ cup sugar and cinnamon. Place in rows in pan. Cover; let rise till double. Bake at 400° about 35 minutes. Loosen sides; turn out quickly. Makes 1 coffee cake.

Sugar-Fruit Topping: Melt 2 tablespoons *butter or margarine;* stir in ½ cup packed *brown sugar* and 2 tablespoons light *corn syrup*. Spread in pan. Place ½ cup halved *candied cherries,* cut side up, and ¼ cup sliced *almonds* atop sugar mixture in pan.

Swedish Tea Ring

4 to 4½ cups all-purpose flour
1 package active dry yeast
1 cup milk
⅓ cup sugar
⅓ cup shortening
1 teaspoon salt
2 eggs
2 tablespoons butter *or*
　　margarine, melted
　Raisin Filling
　Confectioners' Icing (see
　　recipe, page 372)

In large mixer bowl combine *2 cups* of the flour and the yeast. In saucepan heat milk, sugar, shortening, and salt just till warm (115° to 120°) and shortening is almost melted, stirring constantly. Add to flour mixture in mixer bowl; add eggs. Beat at low speed of electric mixer for ½ minute, scraping sides of bowl constantly. Beat 3 minutes at high speed. Stir in as much of the remaining flour as you can mix in using a spoon. Turn out onto a lightly floured surface. Knead in enough of the remaining flour to make a moderately soft dough. Continue kneading till smooth and elastic (3 to 5 minutes). Shape into a ball. Place in lightly greased bowl, turning once to grease surface. Cover and let rise in a warm place till double (1 to 1½ hours). Punch dough down; turn out onto a lightly floured surface. Divide dough in half. Cover; let rest 10 minutes.

Roll each half into a 13x9-inch rectangle. Spread each with 1 tablespoon melted butter; spread each with half the Raisin Filling. Roll up jelly-roll style, starting from long side; seal edge. Shape each into a ring, seam side down, on foil-lined baking sheet. Pinch to seal ends together. With scissors, snip ⅔ of the way to center at 1½-inch intervals. Turn each section slightly to one side. Cover and let rise in warm place till double (about 45 minutes). Bake at 350° for 20 to 25 minutes. Drizzle with Confectioners' Icing. Makes 2 coffee cakes.

Raisin Filling: Combine ¾ cup *raisins,* ⅓ cup *sugar,* and 2 teaspoons ground *cinnamon.*

Streusel Coffee Cake

2½ to 3 cups all-purpose flour
1 package active dry yeast
½ cup milk
⅓ cup sugar
⅓ cup butter *or* margarine
¾ teaspoon salt
1 egg
1 tablespoon finely shredded
　　lemon peel
½ teaspoon vanilla
　Streusel Topping

In large mixer bowl combine *1¼ cups* of the flour and the yeast. In saucepan heat milk, sugar, butter or margarine, and salt just till warm (115° to 120°) and butter is almost melted, stirring constantly. Add to flour mixture in mixer bowl; add egg, lemon peel, and vanilla. Beat at low speed of electric mixer for ½ minute, scraping sides of bowl constantly. Beat 3 minutes at high speed.

Stir in as much of the remaining flour as you can mix in using a spoon. Turn out onto a lightly floured surface. Knead in enough of the remaining flour to make a soft dough. Continue kneading till smooth and elastic (8 to 10 minutes). Shape dough into a ball. Place in a lightly greased bowl, turning once to grease surface.

Cover and let rise in a warm place till double (1½ to 2 hours). Punch dough down; turn out onto lightly floured surface. Divide dough in half. Cover; let rest 10 minutes. Pat each half evenly into a greased 8x1½-inch round baking pan. Sprinkle half of the Streusel Topping over each coffee cake. Cover; let rise in warm place till double (30 to 45 minutes). Bake at 375° about 20 minutes. Serve warm. Makes 2 coffee cakes.

Streusel Topping: Combine ½ cup all-purpose *flour,* ⅓ cup packed *brown sugar,* and 1 teaspoon ground *cinnamon.* Cut in ⅓ cup *butter or margarine* till crumbly. Add 2 tablespoons finely chopped *nuts.* Mix well.

Cinnamon Crescents

3½ to 4 cups all-purpose flour
  1 package active dry yeast
  ¾ cup milk
  ⅓ cup sugar
  6 tablespoons butter *or*
      margarine
  ½ teaspoon salt
  3 eggs
  1 cup raisins
  ½ cup sugar
  ½ cup chopped walnuts
  2 tablespoons butter *or*
      margarine, melted
  1 teaspoon ground cinnamon
    Confectioners' Icing (see
    recipe, page 372)

In large mixer bowl combine *1½ cups* of the flour and the yeast. In saucepan heat milk, ⅓ cup sugar, 6 tablespoons butter or margarine, and salt just till warm (115° to 120°) and butter is almost melted, stirring constantly. Add to flour mixture in mixer bowl; add eggs. Beat at low speed of electric mixer for ½ minute, scraping sides of bowl constantly. Beat 3 minutes at high speed. Stir in as much of the remaining flour as you can mix in using a spoon. Turn out onto a lightly floured surface. Knead in enough of the remaining flour to make a moderately soft dough. Continue kneading till smooth and elastic (3 to 5 minutes).

Shape into a ball. Place in lightly greased bowl, turning once to grease surface. Cover and let rise in a warm place till double (about 1 hour). Punch dough down; turn out onto lightly floured surface. Divide dough in half. Cover; let rest 10 minutes. Roll each half into a 12x10-inch rectangle; brush with water. Combine raisins, ½ cup sugar, walnuts, 2 tablespoons melted butter or margarine, and cinnamon; sprinkle half of the mixture over each rectangle. Roll up jelly-roll style, starting from long side; seal edge.

Place, seam side down, on greased baking sheet, curving to form crescent and pinching ends to seal. Cover and let rise in warm place till double (about 30 minutes). Bake at 350° till golden brown, about 25 minutes. Cover with foil last 15 minutes to prevent overbrowning. Frost with Confectioners' Icing. Sprinkle with additional chopped walnuts, if desired. Makes 2 crescents.

Cherry Lattice Coffee Cake

  ½ cup milk
  1 package active dry yeast
  6 tablespoons butter *or*
      margarine
  3 tablespoons sugar
  ½ teaspoon salt
  2 eggs
  2 cups all-purpose flour
    Cherry Filling
  2 tablespoons all-purpose
      flour
  1 teaspoon water

In small saucepan heat milk just till warm (110° to 115°). Add to yeast, stirring to dissolve. Set aside. In small mixer bowl cream together butter or margarine, sugar, and salt. Add 1 egg and 1 egg yolk (reserve 1 egg white); beat well. By hand, stir in the 2 cups flour alternately with the softened yeast mixture. Do not overbeat. Set aside ½ cup of the dough. Spread the remaining dough in a well-greased 9x9x2-inch baking pan. Spoon Cherry Filling over dough in pan, spreading the filling to edges of pan.

For lattice top, blend the 2 tablespoons flour into the reserved ½ cup dough. Roll out on a floured surface to a 9x4-inch rectangle. Cut dough into eight 9x½-inch strips. Arrange strips in a lattice pattern over the filling in pan. Combine the reserved egg white and the water; brush over strips of dough. Cover and let rise in a warm place till double (about 1 hour). Bake at 375° for 25 to 30 minutes. Serve coffee cake warm. Makes 1 coffee cake.

Cherry Filling: In small mixing bowl combine ½ cup *cherry preserves,* ¼ cup softened *butter or margarine,* ¼ cup *sugar,* and ¼ cup chopped *almonds.* Mix well.

Impress morning coffee friends with rich-tasting *Cherry Lattice Coffee Cake.*
Another time try apricot, pineapple, or strawberry preserves instead of cherry preserves.

Basic Sweet Roll Dough

3½ **to 4 cups all-purpose flour**
1 **package active dry yeast**
1 **cup milk**
¼ **cup sugar**
¼ **cup shortening**
1 **teaspoon salt**
2 **eggs**

In large mixer bowl combine *2 cups* of the flour and the yeast. In saucepan heat the milk, sugar, shortening, and salt just till mixture is warm (115° to 120°) and shortening is almost melted, stirring constantly. Add to flour mixture in mixer bowl; add the eggs.

Beat at low speed of electric mixer for ½ minute, scraping sides of bowl constantly. Beat 3 minutes at high speed. Stir in as much of the remaining flour as you can mix in using a spoon. Turn out onto a lightly floured surface. Knead in enough of the remaining flour to make a moderately stiff dough. Continue kneading till smooth and elastic (8 to 10 minutes). Shape into a ball.

Place ball of dough in a lightly greased bowl, turning once to grease surface. Cover; let rise in a warm place till double (45 to 60 minutes). Punch dough down; turn out onto lightly floured surface. Divide dough in half. Cover; let rest 10 minutes. Continue as directed in recipes below.

Cinnamon Rolls

Basic Sweet Roll Dough
¼ **cup butter *or* margarine, melted**
½ **cup sugar**
2 **teaspoons ground cinnamon**
¾ **cup raisins (optional)**
Confectioners' Icing (see recipe, page 372)

Roll each half of Basic Sweet Roll Dough into a 12x8-inch rectangle. Brush each piece with half the melted butter or margarine. Combine sugar and cinnamon; sprinkle over dough. Sprinkle with raisins, if desired. Roll up each piece jelly-roll style, starting from long side; seal seam. Slice each into 12 rolls. Place rolls, cut side down, in 2 greased 9x1½-inch round baking pans. Cover and let rise in a warm place till double (about 35 minutes). Bake at 375° for 18 to 20 minutes. Drizzle Confectioners' Icing over warm rolls. Makes 24.

Caramel-Pecan Rolls

Basic Sweet Roll Dough
3 **tablespoons butter *or* margarine, melted**
½ **cup granulated sugar**
1 **teaspoon ground cinnamon**
⅔ **cup packed brown sugar**
¼ **cup butter *or* margarine**
2 **tablespoons light corn syrup**
½ **cup chopped pecans**

Roll each half of Basic Sweet Roll Dough into a 12x8-inch rectangle. Brush each piece with half of the 3 tablespoons melted butter or margarine. Combine granulated sugar and cinnamon; sprinkle over dough. Roll up each piece jelly-roll style, starting from long side; seal seam. Slice each into 12 rolls.

In saucepan combine brown sugar, ¼ cup butter or margarine, and light corn syrup. Cook, stirring constantly, just till butter is melted and mixture is blended. Distribute the mixture evenly in two 9x1½-inch round baking pans. Sprinkle with chopped pecans.

Place rolls, cut side down, in prepared baking pans. Cover and let rise in a warm place till double (about 30 minutes). Bake at 375° for 18 to 20 minutes. Cool about 30 seconds; invert onto racks and remove pans. Makes 24 rolls.

Cinnamon Crisps

3½ cups all-purpose flour
1 package active dry yeast
1¼ cups milk
¼ cup granulated sugar
¼ cup shortening
1 teaspoon salt
1 egg
½ cup granulated sugar
½ cup packed brown sugar
¼ cup butter *or* margarine,
    melted
½ teaspoon ground cinnamon
¼ cup butter *or* margarine,
    melted
1 cup granulated sugar
½ cup chopped pecans
1 teaspoon ground cinnamon

In large mixer bowl combine *2 cups* of the flour and the yeast. In saucepan heat milk, ¼ cup granulated sugar, shortening, and salt just till warm (115° to 120°) and shortening is almost melted, stirring constantly. Add to flour mixture in mixer bowl; add egg. Beat at low speed of electric mixer for ½ minute, scraping sides of bowl constantly. Beat 3 minutes at high speed.

Stir in as much of the remaining flour as you can mix in using a spoon. Turn out onto a lightly floured surface. Knead in enough of the remaining flour to make a moderately soft dough. Shape into a ball. Place dough in a lightly greased bowl, turning once to grease surface. Cover and let rise in a warm place till double (1½ to 2 hours). Punch dough down; turn out onto lightly floured surface. Divide dough in half. Cover; let rest 10 minutes.

Roll out one portion of dough at a time to a 12-inch square. Combine ½ cup granulated sugar, brown sugar, ¼ cup melted butter, and ½ teaspoon ground cinnamon. Spread half the mixture over dough. Roll up jelly-roll style, starting from long side; pinch to seal edge. Slice into 12 rolls. Place at least 3 inches apart on greased baking sheets. Flatten each roll to about 3 inches in diameter. Repeat with the remaining dough and sugar mixture. Cover rolls and let rise in a warm place (about 30 minutes).

Cover with waxed paper. Roll over the tops with a rolling pin to flatten to ⅛-inch thickness. Carefully remove paper. Brush tops of rolls with ¼ cup melted butter or margarine. Combine 1 cup granulated sugar, pecans, and 1 teaspoon ground cinnamon. Sprinkle over rolls. Cover with waxed paper; roll flat again with a rolling pin. Remove paper. Bake at 400° for 10 to 12 minutes. Remove rolls immediately from baking sheets. Makes 24 rolls.

Peanut Butter-Jelly Twists

2¼ cups all-purpose flour
1 package active dry yeast
½ cup milk
¼ cup sugar
3 tablespoons butter *or*
    margarine
1 teaspoon salt
1 egg
⅓ cup peanut butter
⅓ cup red jam *or* preserves
1 tablespoon butter *or*
    margarine, melted

In large mixer bowl combine *1 cup* of the flour and the yeast. In saucepan heat milk, sugar, 3 tablespoons butter or margarine, and salt just till warm (115° to 120°) and butter is almost melted, stirring constantly. Add to flour mixture in mixer bowl; add egg.

Beat at low speed of electric mixer for ½ minute, scraping sides of bowl constantly. Beat 3 minutes at high speed. Stir in the remaining flour; beat well. Turn out onto a lightly floured surface. Cover and let rest for 30 minutes.

Roll dough into a 16x10-inch rectangle. Carefully spread the peanut butter lengthwise over half of the rectangle; spread jam or preserves over the peanut butter. Fold dough lengthwise to make a 16x5-inch rectangle; seal edges. Cut dough crosswise into sixteen 5x1-inch strips. Loosely twist each strip and arrange in a greased 11x7½x2-inch baking dish. Brush strips with 1 tablespoon melted butter. Cover and let rise in a warm place till double (about 1¼ hours). Bake at 375° for 15 to 20 minutes. Makes 16 rolls.

Doughnuts

3 to 3½ cups all-purpose flour
2 packages active dry yeast
¾ cup milk
⅓ cup sugar
¼ cup shortening
1 teaspoon salt
2 eggs
   Cooking oil *or* shortening
      for deep-fat frying
   Glaze *or* sugar (optional)

In large mixer bowl combine *1½ cups* of the flour and the yeast. In saucepan heat milk, ⅓ cup sugar, shortening, and salt just till warm (115° to 120°) and shortening is almost melted, stirring constantly. Add to flour mixture in mixer bowl; add eggs. Beat at low speed of electric mixer for ½ minute, scraping sides of bowl constantly. Beat 3 minutes at high speed. Stir in as much of the remaining flour as you can mix in using a spoon. Turn out onto a lightly floured surface. Knead in enough of the remaining flour to make a moderately soft dough. Continue kneading till smooth and elastic (5 to 8 minutes). Shape into a ball. Place in lightly greased bowl, turning once to grease surface.

Cover and let rise in a warm place till double (45 to 60 minutes). Punch dough down; turn out onto a lightly floured surface. Divide in half. Cover; let rest 10 minutes. Roll each half of dough to ½-inch thickness. Cut into doughnuts using floured doughnut cutter with hole in center. Cover and let rise in warm place till very light (30 to 45 minutes). Fry a few doughnuts at a time in deep hot fat (375°) till golden, about 1 minute on each side. Drain on paper toweling. If desired, dip warm doughnuts in Glaze or shake in bag of sugar. Makes 16 to 18 doughnuts.

Glaze: Combine 2 cups sifted *powdered sugar*, ¼ cup *milk*, and 1 teaspoon *vanilla*.

Chocolate Doughnuts: Prepare Doughnuts as above *except* heat two 1-ounce squares *semisweet chocolate* with the milk, ⅓ cup sugar, shortening, and salt. Cover and let dough rise 1 to 1½ hours the first time. Cut with floured doughnut cutter. Let rise. Fry in deep hot fat (365°) about 1 minute on each side. Dip warm doughnuts in *Chocolate Glaze,* then in ½ cup finely chopped *walnuts,* or shake in *sugar.*

Chocolate Glaze: In saucepan melt two 1-ounce squares *semisweet chocolate* and 2 tablespoons *butter or margarine* over low heat. Add 2 cups sifted *powdered sugar* and 1 teaspoon *vanilla.* Stir in ¼ cup *boiling water* till smooth.

Bismarcks

Doughnuts
Jam *or* jelly
Granulated *or* powdered sugar

Prepare Doughnuts, cutting with a round 2½-inch floured cookie cutter without hole in center. Let rise and fry as directed. Drain. With a sharp knife cut a wide slit in the side of each cooked doughnut. Insert 2 teaspoons jam or jelly into each. Or, make a narrow slit in the side of each doughnut and use a cake decorating tube with narrow point to insert jam or jelly. Roll bismarcks in granulated or powdered sugar. Makes 18 to 20 bismarcks.

Cream-Filled Bismarcks: Prepare Doughnuts, cutting with a round 2½-inch floured cookie cutter (no hole in center). With sharp knife cut cooked doughnuts in half crosswise. For filling, in mixer bowl cream together ½ cup *granulated sugar,* ¼ cup *butter or margarine,* ¼ cup *shortening,* and ½ teaspoon *vanilla.* Gradually beat in ½ cup *milk* (room temperature) till mixture is fluffy. Spoon about 1 tablespoon filling onto bottom half of each doughnut. Dip tops of remaining halves in *powdered sugar* and place on bottom halves of doughnuts.

Danish Pastry

1 cup butter
⅓ cup all-purpose flour
3¾ to 4 cups all-purpose flour
2 packages active dry yeast
1¼ cups milk
¼ cup sugar
1 teaspoon salt
1 egg
  Almond Filling
  Prune Filling
  Confectioners' Icing (see recipe, page 372)

Cream butter with the ⅓ cup flour. Roll into a 12x6-inch rectangle; chill. Combine 1½ cups of the flour and the yeast. Heat milk, sugar, and salt just till warm (115° to 120°). Add to flour mixture; add egg. Beat at low speed of electric mixer for ½ minute, scraping bowl. Beat 3 minutes at high speed. Stir in as much remaining flour as you can mix in using a spoon. Turn out onto lightly floured surface. Knead in enough remaining flour to make a soft dough. Knead till smooth (about 5 minutes). Cover; let rest 10 minutes. Roll into a 14-inch square. Place chilled butter mixture on half of dough. Fold over other half; seal. Roll into a 20x12-inch rectangle. Fold into thirds. Roll again to 20x12-inch rectangle. Repeat folding and rolling 2 more times. Chill 30 minutes. Divide dough into thirds. Return ⅔ to refrigerator.

To make *Almond Fans,* roll the unrefrigerated third of dough into a 12x8-inch rectangle. Cut into 4x2-inch rectangles; spoon 1 teaspoon Almond Filling down center of each. Fold each lengthwise; seal edges. Place on ungreased baking sheet. Curve rolls; snip side opposite sealed edge. To make *Bunting Rolls,* roll remaining ⅔ of dough into an 18x12-inch rectangle. Cut into 3-inch squares. Place on ungreased baking sheet. Spoon 1 teaspoon Prune Filling in center of each square. Bring opposite corners to center; seal.

Cover and let rolls rise till almost double (45 to 60 minutes). Bake at 450° about 8 minutes. Drizzle with Confectioners' Icing. Serve warm. Makes 36 rolls.

Almond Filling: Cream ¼ cup *sugar* and ¼ cup *butter or margarine.* Stir in ¼ cup chopped blanched *almonds.*

Prune Filling: Combine ½ cup cooked pitted dried *prunes,* ¼ cup *sugar,* 1 tablespoon all-purpose *flour,* 1 tablespoon *lemon juice,* and dash *salt.*

Lemon Puff Pillow Buns

3¼ cups all-purpose flour
1 package active dry yeast
¾ cup milk
6 tablespoons butter or margarine
¼ cup sugar
1 teaspoon salt
2 eggs
1 teaspoon finely shredded lemon peel
4 3-ounce packages cream cheese, softened
3 tablespoons sugar
1 egg yolk
1 teaspoon vanilla
1 beaten egg white

In large mixer bowl combine 1½ cups of the flour and the yeast. In saucepan heat milk, butter or margarine, ¼ cup sugar, and salt just till warm (115° to 120°) and butter is almost melted, stirring constantly. Add to flour mixture; add 2 eggs and lemon peel. Beat at low speed of electric mixer for ½ minute, scraping sides of bowl. Beat 3 minutes at high speed. By hand, stir in the remaining flour. Cover bowl lightly; chill dough at least 4 hours or overnight.

When ready to shape, blend together cream cheese, 3 tablespoons sugar, egg yolk, and vanilla. Divide dough into fourths. On well-floured surface roll each portion into a 12x8-inch rectangle. (Keep remaining dough chilled.) With floured knife cut into 4-inch squares. Place about 1 tablespoon cream cheese mixture in the center of each; bring opposite corners to center and pinch to seal. Place 2 inches apart on greased baking sheet. Brush with beaten egg white. Let rise, uncovered, in warm place till half again as large, not double (20 to 30 minutes). Bake at 400° till done, about 10 minutes. Serve warm. Makes 24.

Italian Bread

7¼ to 7¾ cups all-purpose flour
2 packages active dry yeast
2½ cups warm water (110° to
115°)
1 tablespoon salt
Yellow cornmeal
Boiling water
1 tablespoon water
1 slightly beaten egg white

In large mixer bowl combine *3 cups* of the flour and the yeast. Combine warm water and salt. Add to flour mixture. Beat at low speed of electric mixer for ½ minute, scraping bowl. Beat 3 minutes at high speed. Stir in as much remaining flour as you can mix in using a spoon. Turn out onto lightly floured surface. Knead in enough remaining flour to make a very stiff dough. Continue kneading till smooth and very elastic (15 to 25 minutes). Place in lightly greased bowl, turning once. Cover; let rise in a warm place till double (1¼ to 1½ hours). Punch down; divide in half. Cover; let rest 10 minutes. Shape into desired shape as directed below.

Place on greased baking sheets sprinkled with cornmeal. Cover; let shaped loaves rise till double (45 to 60 minutes). When ready to bake, place a large shallow pan on lower rack of oven and fill with boiling water. Add 1 tablespoon water to egg white; brush over top and sides of loaves.

Bake large loaves (round, long, or plump) at 375° about 20 minutes; brush again with egg white mixture. Bake about 20 minutes longer. Bake small breads (individual loaves or hard rolls) at 400° about 15 minutes. Brush again with egg white mixture. Bake 10 to 15 minutes more. Cool. Makes 2 Round Loaves, or 2 Long Loaves, or 2 Plump Loaves, or 8 Individual Loaves, or 16 Hard Rolls.

Round Loaves: Shape each half of dough into a round ball; place balls on large, greased baking sheet sprinkled with cornmeal. With sharp knife score loaves, making 3 shallow cuts, 1 inch apart, across top. Then, make 3 crosswise cuts. Follow recipe to brush, rise, and bake.

Long Loaves: Roll each half of dough to a 15x12-inch rectangle. Beginning at long side of rectangle, roll up dough tightly, sealing well as you roll. Taper ends of loaf. Place each loaf diagonally, seam side down, on greased baking sheet sprinkled with cornmeal. With sharp knife make diagonal cuts, 2½ inches apart (⅛ to ¼ inch deep), on tops of loaves. Follow recipe directions to brush, rise, and bake.

Plump Loaves: Roll each half of dough to a 15x8-inch rectangle. Beginning at short side of rectangle, roll dough up tightly, sealing well as you roll. Taper ends by rolling with hands till loaf measures 10 to 11 inches in length. Place loaves, seam side down, on greased baking sheet sprinkled with cornmeal. With sharp knife gently make lengthwise cut, ¼ to ½ inch deep, down center of each loaf. Follow recipe directions to brush, rise, and bake.

Individual Loaves: Cut each half of dough into quarters, making 8 pieces. Round each piece of dough into a ball. Cover and let rest 10 minutes. Shape each ball of dough into a small loaf, twisting and pulling ends to taper. (Loaf should measure about 6 inches in length.) Place 2 to 3 inches apart on greased baking sheet sprinkled with cornmeal. Press down ends of loaves. With sharp knife gently make 3 shallow cuts diagonally across top of each loaf. Follow recipe directions to brush, rise, and bake.

Hard Rolls: Divide each half of dough into eighths, making 16 pieces. Shape each piece into an oval or round roll; place about 2 inches apart on greased baking sheet sprinkled with cornmeal. With sharp knife cut shallow crisscross in top of each roll. Follow recipe to brush, rise, and bake.

Using the basic recipe for *Italian Bread*, you can mold the dough into any of these breads: *Round Loaves, Long Loaves, Plump Loaves, Individual Loaves,* or *Hard Rolls.*

Croissants

1½ **cups butter** *or* **margarine**
⅓ **cup all-purpose flour**
2 **packages active dry yeast**
½ **cup warm water (110° to**
115°)
¾ **cup milk**
¼ **cup sugar**
1 **teaspoon salt**
3¾ **to 4¼ cups all-purpose flour**
1 **egg**
1 **egg yolk**
1 **tablespoon milk**

Cream butter or margarine and the ⅓ cup flour. Roll mixture between two sheets of waxed paper into a 12x6-inch rectangle. Chill at least 1 hour.

Soften yeast in warm water. In saucepan heat ¾ cup milk, sugar, and salt till sugar dissolves; cool to lukewarm (105° to 110°). Turn into a large mixing bowl. Stir in *2 cups* of the flour; beat well. Add the softened yeast and 1 egg; stir till smooth.

Stir in as much of the remaining flour as you can mix in using a spoon. Turn out onto a lightly floured surface. Knead in enough of the remaining flour to make a moderately soft dough. Continue kneading till smooth and elastic (8 to 10 minutes). Shape dough into a smooth ball. Cover and let rest 10 minutes.

Roll dough into a 14-inch square. Place chilled butter on half of dough; fold over other half and seal edges. Roll into a 21x12-inch rectangle; seal edges. Chill. Fold into thirds; roll into a 21x12-inch rectangle; seal edges and chill. Fold and roll twice more; seal edges and chill after each rolling. Fold dough into thirds to a 12x7-inch rectangle. Chill several hours or overnight.

Cut dough crosswise into fourths. Roll each fourth into a 12-inch circle. Cut each into 12 wedges. Loosely roll up each wedge, starting from the side opposite the point.

Place on ungreased baking sheets, point down. Curve the ends. Cover and let rise in a warm place till double (30 to 45 minutes). Combine egg yolk and 1 tablespoon milk; brush over rolls. Bake at 375° for 12 to 15 minutes. Remove from baking sheets. Makes 48 rolls.

Brioche

1 **package active dry yeast**
¼ **cup warm water (110° to**
115°)
½ **cup butter** *or* **margarine**
⅓ **cup sugar**
½ **teaspoon salt**
4 **cups all-purpose flour**
½ **cup milk**
4 **eggs**
1 **tablespoon water**

Soften yeast in ¼ cup warm water. Cream butter or margarine, sugar, and salt. Add *1 cup* of the flour and the milk to creamed mixture. Separate one of the eggs; set egg white aside. Blend egg yolk with the remaining 3 eggs. Add eggs and softened yeast to creamed mixture; beat well. By hand, stir in the remaining flour till smooth. Turn into a lightly greased bowl. Cover and let rise in a warm place till double (about 2 hours). Refrigerate dough overnight.

Stir down. Turn out onto a lightly floured surface. Divide dough into quarters; set one quarter aside. Divide each of the remaining quarters into 8 pieces, making a total of 24. With floured hands, form each piece into a ball, tucking under cut edges. Place each in greased muffin cup. Divide the reserved dough into 24 pieces; shape into smooth balls.

With floured finger, make an indentation in each large ball. Press small balls into indentations. Cover and let rise in a warm place till double (40 to 45 minutes). Combine the reserved egg white and 1 tablespoon water; brush over rolls. Bake at 375° about 15 minutes, brushing again with egg white mixture after 7 minutes. Makes 24 rolls.

Kolache

1 package active dry yeast
¼ cup warm water (110° to 115°)
¾ cup milk
½ cup butter *or* margarine
¼ cup sugar
1 teaspoon salt
3½ to 4¼ cups all-purpose flour
¼ teaspoon ground cinnamon
2 eggs
1 teaspoon finely shredded lemon peel
Prune Filling
Sifted powdered sugar

Soften yeast in warm water. In saucepan heat milk, butter or margarine, sugar, and salt till sugar dissolves; cool to lukewarm (105° to 110°). Turn into a large mixing bowl. Stir in *2 cups* of the flour and the cinnamon; beat well. Add softened yeast, eggs, and lemon peel; stir till smooth. Stir in as much of the remaining flour as you can mix in using a spoon. Turn out onto a lightly floured surface. Knead in enough of the remaining flour to make a moderately soft dough. Continue kneading till smooth and elastic (8 to 10 minutes). Shape into a ball. Place in lightly greased bowl, turning once to grease surface. Cover and let rise in a warm place till double (1 to 1½ hours). Punch dough down; turn out onto lightly floured surface. Divide in half. Cover; let rest 10 minutes.

Shape each half into 9 balls. Place 3 inches apart on greased baking sheets. Flatten each to a 3-inch circle. Cover and let rise in a warm place till double (about 45 minutes). Make a depression in the center of each; fill with Prune Filling. Bake at 375° for 10 to 12 minutes. Remove from baking sheets; cool. Dust lightly with powdered sugar. Makes 18 rolls.

Prune Filling: In small saucepan combine 1 cup pitted dried *prunes* and enough *water* to come 1 inch above prunes. Simmer for 10 to 15 minutes; drain and chop prunes. Stir in ¼ cup *sugar* and ½ teaspoon ground *cinnamon.*

German Stollen

¾ cup raisins
½ cup chopped mixed candied fruits and peels
¼ cup dried currants
¼ cup rum
4 to 4½ cups all-purpose flour
2 packages active dry yeast
1 cup milk
½ cup butter *or* margarine
¼ cup sugar
1 teaspoon salt
2 eggs
2 tablespoons finely shredded orange peel
1 tablespoon finely shredded lemon peel
½ teaspoon almond extract
½ cup chopped blanched almonds
Confectioners' Icing (see recipe, page 372)

Combine raisins, mixed fruits, currants, and rum; set aside. In large mixer bowl combine *1½ cups* of the flour and the yeast. In saucepan heat milk, butter, sugar, and salt just till warm (115° to 120°) and butter is almost melted, stirring constantly. Add to flour mixture in mixer bowl; add eggs, orange peel, lemon peel, and almond extract.

Beat at low speed of electric mixer for ½ minute, scraping sides of bowl constantly. Beat 3 minutes at high speed. Stir in the fruit-rum mixture, the chopped almonds, and as much of the remaining flour as you can mix in using a spoon. Turn out onto a lightly floured surface. Knead in enough of the remaining flour to make a soft dough. Continue kneading till smooth and elastic (8 to 10 minutes). Shape into a ball. Place in lightly greased bowl, turning once to grease surface.

Cover and let rise in a warm place till double (about 1¼ hours). Punch dough down; turn out onto lightly floured surface. Divide dough in half. Cover and let rest 10 minutes. Roll each half into a 10x7-inch oval. Fold the long side of oval over to within ½ inch of the opposite side; seal edge. Place on greased baking sheets. Cover and let rise in a warm place till double (about 45 minutes). Bake at 375° till done, 15 to 20 minutes. While coffee cakes are warm, glaze with Confectioners' Icing. Garnish with candied fruits, if desired. Makes 2 coffee cakes.

Cracked Wheat Bread

4 to 4¼ cups all-purpose flour
1 cup cracked wheat
2 packages active dry yeast
1½ cups water
½ cup milk
3 tablespoons sugar
3 tablespoons butter *or*
   margarine
1 tablespoon salt
1 cup whole wheat flour

In large mixer bowl combine *2 cups* of the all-purpose flour, the cracked wheat, and yeast. In saucepan heat water, milk, sugar, butter or margarine, and salt just till warm (115° to 120°) and butter is almost melted, stirring constantly. Add to flour mixture in mixer bowl.

Beat at low speed of electric mixer for ½ minute, scraping bowl. Beat 3 minutes at high speed. Stir in whole wheat flour and as much remaining all-purpose flour as you can mix in using a spoon. Turn out onto lightly floured surface. Knead in enough remaining all-purpose flour to make a moderately stiff dough. Continue kneading till smooth and elastic (8 to 10 minutes). Shape into a ball. Place in lightly greased bowl, turning once to grease surface. Cover; let rise in warm place till double (45 to 60 minutes).

Punch down; turn out onto floured surface. Divide in half. Cover; let rest 10 minutes. Shape each half into a loaf and place in greased 8x4x2-inch loaf pans. Cover; let rise till double (30 to 45 minutes). Bake at 375° for 30 to 35 minutes. If loaves brown too quickly, cover loosely with foil the last 10 minutes. Remove from pans; cool. Brush tops with melted butter, if desired. Makes 2 loaves.

Whole Wheat Bread

4½ to 5 cups whole wheat flour
2 packages active dry yeast
1¾ cups milk
⅓ cup packed brown sugar
2 tablespoons shortening
2 teaspoons salt

In large mixer bowl combine *2 cups* of the flour and the yeast. In saucepan heat milk, brown sugar, shortening, and salt just till warm (115° to 120°) and shortening is almost melted, stirring constantly. Add to flour mixture. Beat at low speed of electric mixer for ½ minute, scraping sides of bowl. Beat 3 minutes at high speed. Stir in as much of the remaining flour as you can mix in using a spoon. Turn out onto lightly floured surface. Knead in enough of the remaining flour to make a moderately stiff dough.

Continue kneading till smooth and elastic (5 to 8 minutes). Shape into a ball. Place in lightly greased bowl, turning once to grease surface. Cover; let rise in warm place till double (1 to 1½ hours). Punch dough down; turn out onto lightly floured surface. Cover; let rest 10 minutes.

Shape into a loaf; place in greased 9x5x3-inch loaf pan. Cover and let rise in warm place till double (about 30 minutes). Bake at 375° for 35 to 40 minutes. Cover loosely with foil the last 20 minutes to prevent overbrowning. Remove from pan and cool on wire rack. Makes 1 loaf.

Rye Pretzels

1 package active dry yeast
1 tablespoon malted milk
   powder
1 tablespoon caraway seed
1 tablespoon molasses
4½ cups rye flour
   Coarse salt

Soften yeast in 1½ cups *warm water* (110° to 115°). Add milk powder, caraway, molasses, and 1 teaspoon *salt*. Stir in rye flour. Knead on floured surface till smooth (about 5 minutes). Cut into 12 portions; roll each into a rope 15 inches long. Shape into pretzels; place on greased baking sheet. Moisten lightly with water; sprinkle lightly with coarse salt. Bake at 425° till browned and crisp, 15 to 20 minutes. Makes 12.

Sourdough Starter

1 package active dry yeast
½ cup warm water (110° to 115°)
2 cups all-purpose flour
2 cups warm water (110° to 115°)
1 tablespoon sugar

Soften yeast in ½ cup warm water. Stir in flour, 2 cups warm water, and sugar. Beat till smooth. Cover with cheesecloth; let stand at room temperature till bubbly, 5 to 10 days, stirring 2 or 3 times a day. (Fermentation time depends on room temperature; a warmer room will hasten the process.) Store Starter, covered, in the refrigerator. To use, bring desired amount to room temperature.

To keep Starter going: After using some Starter, stir ¾ cup all-purpose *flour,* ¾ cup *water,* and 1 teaspoon *sugar* into remaining Starter. Cover with cheesecloth; let stand at room temperature till bubbly, at least 1 day. Refrigerate for later use. If not used within 10 days, stir 1 teaspoon *sugar* into Starter. Keep adding sugar every 10 days.

Sourdough Bread

1 package active dry yeast
1½ cups warm water (110° to 115°)
5½ to 6 cups all-purpose flour
1 cup Sourdough Starter (room temperature)
2 teaspoons sugar
2 teaspoons salt
½ teaspoon baking soda

In large mixing bowl soften yeast in warm water. Stir in 2½ *cups* of the flour, the Sourdough Starter, sugar, and salt. Combine 2½ *cups* of the flour and the baking soda; stir into flour-yeast mixture. Stir in as much of the remaining flour as you can mix in using a spoon. Turn out onto a lightly floured surface. Knead in enough of the remaining flour to make a stiff dough. Continue kneading till smooth and elastic (5 to 7 minutes). Shape into a ball. Place in lightly greased bowl, turning once. Cover and let rise in a warm place till double (1 to 1½ hours). Punch down; turn out onto lightly floured surface. Divide in half.

Cover; let rest 10 minutes. Shape into 2 round or oblong loaves. Place on lightly greased baking sheets. With sharp knife make parallel slashes across tops of loaves. Cover; let rise in warm place till double (1 to 1½ hours). Bake at 400° for 35 to 40 minutes. Remove from baking sheets; cool on wire racks. If desired, brush with melted butter or margarine. Makes 2 loaves.

Sourdough-Cheese Rolls

1 package active dry yeast
¾ cup warm water (110° to 115°)
4¼ to 4½ cups all-purpose flour
1 cup Sourdough Starter (room temperature)
¼ cup sugar
¼ cup butter *or* margarine, softened
1 egg
2 teaspoons salt
½ teaspoon baking soda
¾ cup shredded sharp cheddar cheese

In large mixer bowl soften yeast in warm water. Stir in 2 *cups* of the flour, the Sourdough Starter, sugar, softened butter, egg, and salt. Beat 3 to 4 minutes with electric mixer. Combine 1 *cup* of the flour and the baking soda; stir into flour-yeast mixture. Stir in cheese and as much of the remaining flour as you can mix in using a spoon. Turn out onto a lightly floured surface. Knead in enough of the remaining flour to make a soft dough. Continue kneading till smooth and elastic (5 to 8 minutes).

Place in greased bowl; turn once. Cover; let rise in warm place till double (1½ to 2 hours). Punch down; turn out onto floured surface. Cover; let rest 10 minutes. Divide into 24 pieces; shape into balls. Place on greased baking sheets. Cover; let rise in warm place till double (25 to 30 minutes). Bake at 375° about 20 minutes. Makes 24 rolls.

Quick Breads

Baking Powder Biscuits

2 cups all-purpose flour*
1 tablespoon baking powder*
½ teaspoon salt*
⅓ cup shortening
¾ cup milk

In bowl stir together flour, baking powder, and salt. Cut in shortening till mixture resembles coarse crumbs. Make a well in dry mixture; add milk all at once. Stir with fork just till dough clings together.

Knead gently on lightly floured surface (10 to 12 strokes). Roll or pat dough to ½-inch thickness. Cut with 2½-inch biscuit cutter; dip cutter in flour between cuts. Bake on ungreased baking sheet at 450° till golden, 10 to 12 minutes. Makes 10 biscuits.

*Note: When substituting self-rising all-purpose flour, omit the baking powder and salt.

Buttermilk Biscuits: Prepare Baking Powder Biscuits as above except add ¼ teaspoon baking soda to the flour mixture and substitute buttermilk for milk in recipe.

Bacon Biscuits: In skillet cook 6 slices bacon till crisp; drain, reserving 2 tablespoons drippings. Crumble bacon and set aside. Prepare Baking Powder Biscuits as above except decrease the shortening to ¼ cup. Add crumbled bacon, bacon drippings, and 2 teaspoons prepared horseradish to the dry mixture along with the milk.

Sour Cream Biscuits: Prepare Baking Powder Biscuits as above except substitute 1 cup dairy sour cream for the milk.

Biscuits Supreme

2 cups all-purpose flour
4 teaspoons baking powder
2 teaspoons sugar
½ teaspoon cream of tartar
½ teaspoon salt
½ cup shortening
⅔ cup milk

In mixing bowl stir together the flour, baking powder, sugar, cream of tartar, and salt. Cut in the shortening till mixture resembles coarse crumbs. Make a well in center of dry mixture; add the milk all at once. Stir with a fork just till dough clings together.

Knead gently on lightly floured surface (10 to 12 strokes). Roll or pat dough to ½-inch thickness. Cut with 2½-inch biscuit cutter; dip cutter in flour between cuts. Transfer to ungreased baking sheet. Bake at 450° till golden brown, 10 to 12 minutes. Makes 10 biscuits.

Cornmeal Biscuits

1½ cups all-purpose flour
½ cup yellow cornmeal
1 tablespoon baking powder
½ teaspoon salt
⅓ cup shortening
1 cup milk

In mixing bowl stir together flour, cornmeal, baking powder, and salt. Cut in the shortening till mixture resembles coarse crumbs. Make a well in center of dry mixture; add milk all at once. Stir with a fork just till dough clings together. (Dough will be very soft.)

Knead gently on well-floured surface (10 to 12 strokes). Roll or pat dough to ½-inch thickness. Cut with 2½-inch biscuit cutter; dip cutter in flour between cuts. Place on ungreased baking sheet. Bake at 450° till golden brown, 10 to 12 minutes. Makes 10 biscuits.

Nothing enhances a meal more than tall, flaky *Baking Powder Biscuits.*
Serve them piping hot with plenty of butter and the family's favorite preserves.

Drop Biscuits

2 **cups all-purpose flour**
1 **tablespoon baking powder**
½ **teaspoon salt**
⅓ **cup shortening**
1 **cup milk**

Stir together flour, baking powder, and salt. Cut in shortening till mixture resembles coarse crumbs. Make a well in dry mixture; add milk all at once. Stir just till dough clings together. Drop from tablespoon onto greased baking sheet. Bake at 450° about 12 minutes. Makes 12 to 14 biscuits.

Raisin Drop Biscuits

4 **cups all-purpose flour**
½ **cup sugar**
2 **tablespoons baking powder**
2 **teaspoons salt**
⅔ **cup shortening**
2 **cups raisins**
1 **teaspoon finely shredded orange peel**
2 **beaten eggs**
1½ **cups milk**
2 **tablespoons butter *or* margarine, melted**
3 **tablespoons sugar**
¼ **teaspoon ground cinnamon**
⅛ **teaspoon ground nutmeg**

Thoroughly stir together the flour, ½ cup sugar, baking powder, and salt. Cut in shortening till mixture resembles coarse crumbs. Stir in raisins and peel. Combine eggs and milk; add all at once to dry mixture. Stir quickly just till dough clings together. Drop from teaspoon into greased *1¾-inch muffin pans,* filling pans ⅔ full. Bake at 400° for 15 to 20 minutes. While biscuits are warm, dip tops in melted butter or margarine, then in a mixture of 3 tablespoons sugar, the cinnamon, and the nutmeg. Makes 48 biscuits.

Pecan Petal Biscuits

1⅔ **cups all-purpose flour**
¼ **cup granulated sugar**
2 **teaspoons baking powder**
½ **teaspoon baking soda**
½ **teaspoon cream of tartar**
½ **teaspoon salt**
⅓ **cup shortening**
½ **cup chopped pecans**
1 **beaten egg**
½ **cup buttermilk**
2 **tablespoons butter *or* margarine, melted**
½ **cup sifted powdered sugar**
½ **teaspoon vanilla**
Milk

Stir together the flour, granulated sugar, baking powder, soda, cream of tartar, and salt. Cut in shortening till mixture resembles coarse crumbs. Stir in pecans. Combine egg and buttermilk; add all at once to dry mixture. Stir just till dough clings together. Knead gently on lightly floured surface (10 to 12 strokes). Roll to 15x10-inch rectangle. Brush with melted butter. Cut crosswise into ten 10x1½-inch strips. Make 2 stacks of 5 strips each. Cut each stack into 6 pieces. Place biscuits, cut side down, in greased muffin pans. Bake at 400° about 22 minutes.

Meanwhile, in small bowl combine the powdered sugar and vanilla. Stir in enough milk (about 1½ teaspoons) till of drizzling consistency. Drizzle over warm biscuits. Makes 12.

Cinnamon Twists

1 **package refrigerated biscuits (8 biscuits)**
2 **tablespoons butter *or* margarine, melted**
¼ **cup sugar**
1 **teaspoon ground cinnamon**
1 **tablespoon chopped walnuts**

Roll each biscuit between hands to form a 9-inch rope. Pinch ends together to form a circle. Dip biscuit circles in melted butter, then in mixture of sugar and cinnamon. Twist each biscuit to form a figure 8. Place biscuits on ungreased baking sheet. Sprinkle with chopped walnuts. Bake at 425° for 8 to 10 minutes. Makes 8 twists.

Best-Ever Muffins

1¾ cups all-purpose flour*
¼ cup sugar
2½ teaspoons baking powder*
¾ teaspoon salt*
1 beaten egg
¾ cup milk
⅓ cup cooking oil *or* melted shortening

Stir together flour, sugar, baking powder, and salt; make a well in center. Combine egg, milk, and oil; add all at once to dry ingredients, stirring just till moistened. Fill greased or paper bake cup-lined muffin pans ⅔ full. Bake at 400° for 20 to 25 minutes. Makes 8 to 10 muffins.

Note: When substituting self-rising all-purpose flour, omit the baking powder and salt.

Enriched Best-Ever Muffins: Prepare Best-Ever Muffins as above *except* stir ⅓ cup nonfat *dry milk powder* in with the dry ingredients.

Low-Fat Best-Ever Muffins: Prepare Best-Ever Muffins as above *except* substitute *skim milk* for whole milk and reduce cooking oil to 1 tablespoon. If desired, substitute 1 *egg white* for the whole egg.

Nutty Muffins: Prepare Best-Ever Muffins as above *except* stir ½ cup chopped *peanuts, walnuts, pecans, or macadamia nuts* into dry ingredients.

Sweet Best-Ever Muffins

1¾ cups all-purpose flour
½ cup sugar
2½ teaspoons baking powder
¾ teaspoon salt
1 beaten egg
¾ cup milk
⅓ cup cooking oil *or* melted shortening

Stir together flour, sugar, baking powder, and salt; make a well in center. Combine eggs, milk, and oil; add all at once to dry ingredients, stirring just till moistened. Fill greased or paper bake cup-lined muffin pans ⅔ full. Bake at 375° for 18 to 20 minutes. Makes 8 to 10 muffins.

Pineapple-Pecan Muffins: Prepare Sweet Best-Ever Muffins as above *except* drain one 8-ounce can crushed *pineapple* (juice pack), reserving the juice; add enough milk to juice to equal ¾ cup. Combine the juice-milk mixture with egg, oil, and crushed pineapple. Stir this mixture into the dry ingredients just till moistened. Fill prepared muffin pans ⅔ full. Sprinkle ⅓ cup chopped *pecans* over tops. Bake as above. Makes 10 to 12 muffins.

Chocolate Chip Muffins: Prepare Sweet Best-Ever Muffins as above *except* add enough milk to juice of one *orange* to make ¾ cup. Combine orange-milk mixture with egg, oil, and 2 teaspoons finely shredded *orange peel*. Mix as directed, then carefully fold ½ cup semisweet *chocolate pieces* into muffin batter. Makes 10 to 12 muffins.

Cinnamon-Apple-Raisin Muffins: Prepare Sweet Best-Ever Muffins as above *except* stir ½ teaspoon ground *cinnamon* in with dry ingredients. Mix as directed, then carefully fold 1 cup chopped peeled *apple* and ⅓ cup *raisins* into batter. Bake for 20 to 25 minutes. Dip tops, while still warm, in melted *butter or margarine,* then in *sugar.* Makes 12 muffins.

Blueberry-Lemon Muffins: Prepare Sweet Best-Ever Muffins as above *except* combine ¾ to 1 cup *fresh blueberries or frozen blueberries,* thawed and drained, and 2 tablespoons *sugar;* fold into batter along with 1 teaspoon finely shredded *lemon peel.* Bake as above. Dip tops, while still warm, in melted *butter or margarine,* then in *sugar.* Makes 12 muffins.

Filled Corn Muffins

1 cup all-purpose flour
1 cup yellow cornmeal
2 tablespoons sugar
1 tablespoon baking powder
½ teaspoon salt
1 beaten egg
1 cup milk
3 tablespoons cooking oil
¼ cup strawberry preserves

Stir together flour, cornmeal, sugar, baking powder, and salt. Blend egg, milk, and oil; add to dry mixture. Beat just till smooth. Fill paper bake cup-lined or greased muffin pans ⅔ full. Top each with 1 teaspoon preserves. Bake at 425° for 20 to 25 minutes. Makes 12 muffins.

Bran Muffins

1½ cups whole bran cereal
1 cup buttermilk
1 cup all-purpose flour
2 teaspoons baking powder
½ teaspoon baking soda
½ teaspoon salt
⅓ cup packed brown sugar
1 beaten egg
¼ cup cooking oil *or* melted
    shortening
¾ cup raisins *or* snipped
    pitted dates (optional)

Combine bran and buttermilk; let stand till liquid is absorbed, about 3 minutes. In mixing bowl stir together flour, baking powder, baking soda, and salt; stir in brown sugar. Combine cereal-milk mixture, egg, and oil or melted shortening; add all at once to dry ingredients, stirring just till moistened. (Batter will be thick.) Fold in raisins or dates, if desired. Fill greased muffin pans ⅔ full. Bake at 400° for 20 to 25 minutes. Makes 10 to 12 muffins.

Two-Cheese Muffins

1½ cups all-purpose flour
½ cup yellow cornmeal
¼ cup sugar
1 tablespoon baking powder
¾ teaspoon salt
½ cup shredded sharp Cheddar
    cheese (2 ounces)
1 beaten egg
1 cup milk
½ cup cream-style cottage
    cheese
¼ cup cooking oil *or* melted
    shortening

Thoroughly stir together the flour, cornmeal, sugar, baking powder, and salt; stir in shredded cheese. Combine egg, milk, cottage cheese, and cooking oil or melted shortening; add all at once to dry ingredients, stirring just till moistened. Fill well-greased muffin pans ⅔ full. Bake at 400° for 20 to 25 minutes. Makes 12 muffins.

Carrot Muffins

1 cup all-purpose flour
¼ cup packed brown sugar
2 teaspoons baking powder
½ teaspoon salt
2 beaten eggs
1 cup finely shredded carrot
¼ cup cooking oil
1 tablespoon lemon juice

Thoroughly stir together flour, brown sugar, baking powder, and salt; make a well in center. Combine eggs, carrot, oil, and lemon juice; add all at once to dry ingredients, stirring just till moistened. Fill paper bake cup-lined or well-greased muffin pans ¾ full. Bake at 375° about 25 minutes. Makes 8 muffins.

Include wholesome *Bran Muffins* as the perfect mealtime accompaniment to round
out lunch, supper, or dinner. If you wish, add raisins or dates to further enhance the muffins.

Raspberry Coffee Cake

1 3-ounce package cream cheese
¼ cup butter *or* margarine
2 cups packaged biscuit mix
⅓ cup milk
½ cup raspberry preserves
  Confectioners' Icing (see recipe, page 372)

In mixing bowl cut cream cheese and butter or margarine into biscuit mix till crumbly. Blend in milk. Turn out onto lightly floured surface and knead 8 to 10 strokes. On waxed paper, roll dough to 12x8-inch rectangle. Turn onto a greased baking sheet; remove waxed paper. Spread preserves down center of dough. Make 2½-inch cuts at 1-inch intervals on long sides. Fold strips over preserves. Bake at 425° for 12 to 15 minutes. Drizzle warm coffee cake with Confectioners' Icing. Makes 1 coffee cake.

Cowboy Coffee Cake

2½ cups all-purpose flour
2 cups packed brown sugar
½ teaspoon salt
⅔ cup shortening
2 teaspoons baking powder
½ teaspoon baking soda
½ teaspoon ground cinnamon
½ teaspoon ground nutmeg
1 cup sour milk*
2 beaten eggs
⅓ cup chopped nuts

In mixing bowl stir together flour, sugar, and salt. Cut in shortening till mixture resembles coarse crumbs; reserve ½ cup for topping. To remaining crumbs add baking powder, soda, and spices; mix well. Add milk and eggs; mix well. Turn into 2 greased and floured 8x1½-inch or 9x1½-inch round baking pans. Combine the ½ cup reserved crumbs and nuts; sprinkle over batter. Bake at 375° for 20 to 25 minutes. Serve warm. Makes 2 coffee cakes.

Note: To make sour milk, combine 1 tablespoon lemon juice *or* vinegar and enough whole milk to make 1 cup. Let stand 5 minutes before using.

Peanut Butter Coffee Cake

½ cup packed brown sugar
½ cup all-purpose flour
¼ cup peanut butter
2 tablespoons butter, melted
½ cup peanut butter
¼ cup shortening
1 cup packed brown sugar
2 eggs
2 cups all-purpose flour
2 teaspoons baking powder
½ teaspoon baking soda
1 cup milk

Mix first 4 ingredients till crumbly; set aside. Cream together ½ cup peanut butter and shortening. Slowly beat in 1 cup brown sugar. Add eggs, one at a time, beating till fluffy. Thoroughly stir together 2 cups flour, baking powder, soda, and ½ teaspoon *salt.* Add alternately with milk to creamed mixture, beating after each addition. Spread in greased 13x9x2-inch baking pan. Top with crumbly mixture. Bake at 375° for 30 to 35 minutes. Makes 16 to 18 servings.

Quick Sally Lunn

2 cups all-purpose flour
⅓ cup granulated sugar
1 tablespoon baking powder
2 beaten eggs
¾ cup milk
½ cup cooking oil
¼ cup packed brown sugar
½ teaspoon ground cinnamon, ground cardamom, *or* aniseed, crushed

In mixing bowl thoroughly stir together flour, granulated sugar, baking powder, and ¼ teaspoon *salt;* make a well in center. Combine eggs, milk, and oil. Add all at once to dry ingredients; stir just till moistened. Pour into greased 9x9x2-inch baking pan. Combine brown sugar and spice; sprinkle over batter. Bake at 400° for 20 to 25 minutes. Serve hot with whipped butter or cream cheese, if desired. Serves 9.

Cranberry Relish Coffee Cake

  1 **cup all-purpose flour**
  ¼ **cup sugar**
1½ **teaspoons baking powder**
  ½ **teaspoon salt**
  ¼ **cup shortening**
  1 **beaten egg**
  ⅓ **cup milk**
  ½ **cup cranberry-orange relish**
  2 **tablespoons sugar**
  ¼ **cup sugar**
  ¼ **cup all-purpose flour**
  2 **tablespoons butter**

Stir together 1 cup flour, ¼ cup sugar, baking powder, and salt. Cut in shortening till mixture resembles coarse crumbs. Combine egg and milk. Add to dry ingredients, stirring just till moistened. Spread in greased 8x8x2-inch baking pan.
  Combine cranberry-orange relish and 2 tablespoons sugar; spoon over batter. Mix ¼ cup sugar and ¼ cup flour; cut in butter till crumbly. Sprinkle atop coffee cake. Bake at 400° for 30 to 35 minutes. Serve warm. Makes 9 servings.

Basic Coffee Cake

  2 **cups Quick Bread Mix**
    (see below)
  ¼ **cup granulated sugar**
  1 **beaten egg**
  ⅔ **cup milk**
  2 **tablespoons shortening**
  ¼ **cup packed brown sugar**
  2 **tablespoons Quick Bread Mix**
  1 **tablespoon butter** *or*
    margarine, melted
  ¼ **teaspoon ground cinnamon**

Combine 2 cups Quick Bread Mix and granulated sugar. Add egg, milk, and shortening. Beat with electric mixer till smooth. Spread in greased 8x8x2-inch baking pan. Combine remaining ingredients; mix well. Sprinkle atop batter. Bake at 375° for 25 to 30 minutes. Serve warm. Serves 9.
  Spicy Marble Coffee Cake: Prepare batter for Basic Coffee Cake. Divide batter in half. To one half, add 2 tablespoons light *molasses,* ½ teaspoon ground *cinnamon,* ¼ teaspoon ground *nutmeg,* and ⅛ teaspoon ground *cloves.* In a greased 8x8x2-inch baking pan, drop plain batter by teaspoons checkerboard fashion. Fill empty spaces with spiced batter. Swirl to marble. Add topping and bake as above.

Coconut-Jam Coffee Cake

  2 **cups Quick Bread Mix**
    (see below)
  ½ **cup flaked coconut**
  3 **tablespoons sugar**
  ½ **teaspoon ground cinnamon**
  1 **beaten egg**
  ½ **cup milk**
  ½ **cup apricot preserves**
  1 **tablespoon lemon juice**

In bowl stir together Quick Bread Mix, coconut, sugar, and cinnamon. Add egg; mix well. Reserve ½ cup mixture. To remaining mixture stir in milk. Spread in greased 8x8x2-inch baking pan. Combine apricot preserves and lemon juice; spread over dough. Sprinkle with the ½ cup reserved flour mixture. Bake at 350° for 35 to 40 minutes. Cool in pan; cut into squares. Makes 9 servings.

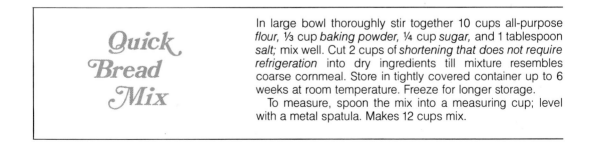

Quick Bread Mix

In large bowl thoroughly stir together 10 cups all-purpose *flour,* ⅓ cup *baking powder,* ¼ cup *sugar,* and 1 tablespoon *salt;* mix well. Cut 2 cups of *shortening that does not require refrigeration* into dry ingredients till mixture resembles coarse cornmeal. Store in tightly covered container up to 6 weeks at room temperature. Freeze for longer storage.
  To measure, spoon the mix into a measuring cup; level with a metal spatula. Makes 12 cups mix.

Banana Nut Bread

1¾ **cups all-purpose flour**
1¼ **teaspoons baking powder**
¾ **teaspoon salt**
½ **teaspoon baking soda**
⅔ **cup sugar**
⅓ **cup shortening**
2 **eggs**
2 **tablespoons milk**
1 **cup mashed ripe banana**
   (3 medium bananas)
¼ **cup chopped pecans** *or*
   walnuts

Stir together flour, baking powder, salt, and soda; set aside. In small mixer bowl cream sugar and shortening till light and fluffy. Add eggs, one at a time, and milk; beat well. Add flour mixture and mashed banana alternately to creamed mixture, beating smooth after each addition. Fold in nuts.

Turn into lightly greased 8x4x2-inch loaf pan. Bake at 350° till a wooden pick inserted near center comes out clean, 60 to 65 minutes. Cool 10 minutes; remove from pan. Cool on wire rack. Wrap and store overnight. Makes 1 loaf.

Orange Nut Bread

2 **cups all-purpose flour**
¾ **cup sugar**
½ **teaspoon salt**
½ **teaspoon baking soda**
1 **beaten egg**
1 **tablespoon finely shredded**
   orange peel
¾ **cup orange juice**
¼ **teaspoon finely shredded**
   lemon peel
2 **tablespoons lemon juice**
2 **tablespoons cooking oil**
½ **cup coarsely chopped walnuts**

In mixing bowl stir together flour, sugar, salt, and soda. Combine egg, orange peel, orange juice, lemon peel, lemon juice, and oil. Add to dry ingredients, stirring just till moistened. Fold in nuts. Turn into greased 8x4x2-inch loaf pan. Bake at 350° till done, 50 to 60 minutes. Cool in pan 10 minutes; remove from pan. Cool thoroughly. Wrap and store overnight before slicing. Makes 1 loaf.

Pumpkin Bread

1 **cup packed brown sugar**
⅓ **cup shortening**
2 **eggs**
1 **cup canned pumpkin**
¼ **cup milk**

● ● ●

2 **cups all-purpose flour**
2 **teaspoons baking powder**
½ **teaspoon salt**
½ **teaspoon ground ginger**
¼ **teaspoon baking soda**
¼ **teaspoon ground cloves**
½ **cup coarsely chopped walnuts**
   or **pecans**
½ **cup raisins (optional)**

In mixing bowl cream together brown sugar and shortening till light and fluffy. Beat in eggs. Add pumpkin and milk; mix well. Stir together flour, baking powder, salt, ginger, baking soda, and cloves; add to creamed mixture, mixing well. Stir in nuts and raisins. Turn into greased 9x5x3-inch loaf pan. Bake at 350° till done, 55 to 60 minutes. Cool 10 minutes. Remove from pan; cool. Wrap and store overnight before slicing. Makes 1 loaf.

Pour steaming coffee and ice-cold milk to accompany refreshing slices of *Orange Nut Bread.* Tangy orange and lemon flavors mingle to make it the perfect breakfast bread.

Buttermilk Doughnuts

4 **cups all-purpose flour**
4 **teaspoons baking powder**
¾ **teaspoon salt**
¼ **teaspoon baking soda**
2 **beaten eggs**
1 **cup granulated sugar**
¼ **cup cooking oil**
1 **teaspoon vanilla**
1 **cup buttermilk**
　 Cooking oil *or* shortening
　　 for deep-fat frying
　 Sifted powdered sugar

In bowl stir together the flour, baking powder, salt, and baking soda. Beat eggs and granulated sugar together till thick and lemon-colored. Stir in oil and vanilla. Add dry ingredients and buttermilk alternately to egg mixture, beginning and ending with dry ingredients. Beat just till blended after each addition.

Roll out dough on lightly floured surface to ½-inch thickness. Cut with floured 2½-inch doughnut cutter. Fry in deep hot fat (375°) till golden brown, about 1½ minutes per side, turning once. Drain on paper toweling. Sprinkle with powdered sugar. Makes 24 doughnuts.

Orange Doughnuts

3¼ **cups all-purpose flour**
2 **teaspoons baking powder**
　 Dash salt
2 **beaten eggs**
⅔ **cup sugar**
1 **teaspoon vanilla**
1 **teaspoon finely shredded orange**
　　 peel
⅔ **cup orange juice**
¼ **cup butter *or* margarine,**
　　 melted
　 Cooking oil *or* shortening
　　 for deep-fat frying
　 Orange Glaze

Stir together flour, baking powder, and salt. Beat eggs, sugar, and vanilla together till thick and lemon-colored. Combine orange peel, orange juice, and melted butter. Add orange mixture and ¾ of the dry ingredients alternately to egg mixture. Beat with electric mixer just till blended after each addition. By hand, stir in the remaining dry ingredients. Cover; chill dough 2 hours.

Roll dough on lightly floured surface to ⅜-inch thickness. Cut with floured 2½-inch doughnut cutter. Fry in deep hot fat (375°) about 1 minute per side, turning once. Drain on paper toweling. While doughnuts are warm, drizzle with Orange Glaze. Makes 16 doughnuts.

Orange Glaze: In small mixing bowl stir together 2 cups sifted *powdered sugar,* 1 teaspoon finely shredded *orange peel,* and 3 tablespoons *orange juice.*

Chocolate-Cinnamon Doughnuts

4 **cups all-purpose flour**
⅓ **cup unsweetened cocoa powder**
4 **teaspoons baking powder**
1 **teaspoon ground cinnamon**
¾ **teaspoon salt**
¼ **teaspoon baking soda**
2 **beaten eggs**
1¼ **cups sugar**
¼ **cup cooking oil**
1 **teaspoon vanilla**
¾ **cup buttermilk**
　 Cooking oil *or* shortening
　　 for deep-fat frying
　 Cinnamon Glaze

In mixing bowl stir together the flour, unsweetened cocoa powder, baking powder, cinnamon, salt, and baking soda. Beat eggs and sugar together till thick and lemon-colored. Stir in ¼ cup cooking oil and vanilla. Add dry ingredients and buttermilk alternately to egg mixture, beginning and ending with dry ingredients. Beat just till blended after each addition. Cover and chill dough about 2 hours.

Roll dough, half at a time, on lightly floured surface to ½-inch thickness. (Keep remaining half of dough chilled as other half is rolled.) Cut with floured 2½-inch doughnut cutter. Fry in deep hot fat (375°) about 1½ minutes per side; turn once. Drain. Dip warm doughnuts in Cinnamon Glaze. Makes 24 doughnuts.

Cinnamon Glaze: In mixing bowl combine 4 cups sifted *powdered sugar,* 1 teaspoon *vanilla,* ½ teaspoon ground *cinnamon,* and enough *milk* to make of drizzling consistency.

Baked Doughnut Twists

2 **cups packaged biscuit mix**
2 **tablespoons sugar**
1 **teaspoon instant coffee**
granules
¼ **cup milk**
1 **beaten egg**
1 **teaspoon finely shredded**
orange peel
Melted butter or **margarine**
½ **cup sugar**
1 **teaspoon ground cinnamon**
¼ **teaspoon ground nutmeg**

In mixing bowl combine biscuit mix and 2 tablespoons sugar. Dissolve instant coffee granules in milk; stir in egg and orange peel. Add mixture to dry ingredients; stir just till moistened. Knead on well-floured surface (10 to 12 strokes). Roll to ½-inch thickness. Cut with floured 2½-inch doughnut cutter. Holding opposite sides of doughnut, stretch and twist to form a figure eight. Bake on ungreased baking sheet at 400° for 10 to 12 minutes. Brush liberally with melted butter; coat with a mixture of ½ cup sugar, cinnamon, and nutmeg. Serve warm. Makes 8 doughnuts.

Spicy Spud Doughnuts

4 **cups all-purpose flour**
2 **tablespoons baking powder**
½ **teaspoon ground cloves**
½ **teaspoon ground cinnamon**
3 **beaten eggs**
1 **cup packed brown sugar**
1½ **cups mashed cooked potatoes**
1 **5⅓-ounce can evaporated milk**
2 **tablespoons shortening,**
melted
Cooking oil or **shortening**
for deep-fat frying

Stir together flour, baking powder, cloves, cinnamon, and 1 teaspoon *salt*. Beat eggs and brown sugar till thick. Stir in cooled potatoes, evaporated milk, and melted shortening. Gradually add the dry ingredients to potato mixture, stirring till combined. Cover and chill at least 3 hours. Roll dough, half at a time, on well-floured surface to ⅜-inch thickness. (Keep remaining half of dough chilled as other half is rolled.) Cut with floured 2½-inch doughnut cutter; chill 15 minutes. Fry in deep hot fat (365°) for 1 to 1½ minutes per side, turning once. Drain. Makes 36 doughnuts.

Apple Fritter Rings

4 **large tart apples**
1 **cup all-purpose flour**
2 **tablespoons sugar**
1 **teaspoon baking powder**
1 **beaten egg**
⅔ **cup milk**
1 **teaspoon cooking oil**
¼ **cup sugar**
½ **teaspoon ground cinnamon**

Peel and core apples; cut into ½-inch-thick rings. In mixing bowl stir together flour, 2 tablespoons sugar, baking powder, and dash *salt*. Combine egg, milk, and cooking oil; add all at once to dry ingredients, stirring just till blended. Heat 1 inch of cooking oil to 375° in skillet that is at least 2 inches deep. Dip apple slices into batter one at a time. Fry in hot oil till brown, about 1½ minutes per side, turning once. Drain on paper toweling. Sprinkle fritters with a mixture of ¼ cup sugar and cinnamon. Serve hot. Makes 16 fritters.

Corn Fritters

1 **8¾-ounce can whole kernel**
corn
Milk
1½ **cups all-purpose flour**
1 **tablespoon baking powder**
¾ **teaspoon salt**
1 **beaten egg**
Cooking oil

Drain corn, reserving liquid. Add enough milk to reserved liquid to make 1 cup. Stir together flour, baking powder, and salt. Combine egg, corn, and reserved 1 cup liquid. Stir into dry ingredients; mix just till moistened. Heat 1½ inches of oil to 375° in skillet that is at least 3 inches deep. Drop batter by tablespoonfuls into hot oil. Fry till golden brown, 1½ to 2 minutes per side; turn once. Drain. Serve with maple-flavored syrup, if desired. Makes 24.

Feather Pancakes

1 cup all-purpose flour*
2 tablespoons sugar
2 tablespoons baking powder*
½ teaspoon salt*
1 beaten egg
1 cup milk
2 tablespoons cooking oil

In mixing bowl thoroughly stir together flour, sugar, baking powder, and salt. Combine egg, milk, and cooking oil; add all at once to dry ingredients, beating till blended. Bake on hot, lightly greased griddle. Makes about 32 dollar-size pancakes or six to eight 4-inch pancakes.

Note: When substituting self-rising all-purpose flour, omit the baking powder and salt.

Peanut Butter Pancakes: Prepare Feather Pancakes as above *except* beat egg with ⅓ cup chunk-style *peanut butter* till blended; reduce cooking oil to 1 tablespoon.

Buttermilk Pancakes

1 cup all-purpose flour
1 tablespoon sugar
2 teaspoons baking powder
½ teaspoon baking soda
½ teaspoon salt
1 beaten egg
1 cup buttermilk *or* sour milk*
2 tablespoons cooking oil

In mixing bowl thoroughly stir together the all-purpose flour, sugar, baking powder, baking soda, and salt. In another bowl combine beaten egg, buttermilk or sour milk, and cooking oil; add to dry ingredients, beating till blended. Bake on hot, lightly greased griddle till golden. Makes eight 4-inch pancakes.

Note: To make sour milk, combine 1 tablespoon lemon juice *or* vinegar and enough whole milk to make 1 cup liquid. Let stand 5 minutes before using.

Oven Pancake

1 8-ounce package brown-and-serve sausage links
1 cup all-purpose flour
2 tablespoons sugar
1 tablespoon baking powder
½ teaspoon salt
1 beaten egg
¾ cup milk
3 tablespoons butter *or* margarine, melted
Maple-flavored syrup

Cut sausage links in half lengthwise. Brown the sausages in a skillet. Drain thoroughly and set aside. Thoroughly stir together flour, sugar, baking powder, and salt. Combine beaten egg, milk, and melted butter or margarine; add all at once to dry ingredients, beating till smooth. Turn batter into a greased and floured 15½x10½x1-inch baking pan, spreading the batter to edges of pan. Arrange the sausage halves, cut side down, atop batter in pan. Bake at 425° about 15 minutes. To serve, cut pancake into squares and pass maple syrup. Makes 6 servings.

Blender Bread Crumb Pancakes

2 slices dry bread
1½ cups buttermilk
2 eggs
2 tablespoons cooking oil
1½ cups all-purpose flour
1 teaspoon baking soda
½ teaspoon salt

Break dry bread slices into blender container; cover and blend till coarsely crumbled. Add remaining ingredients to bread in blender container. Cover; blend just to combine. Drop batter by tablespoonfuls onto hot, lightly greased griddle. Bake. (Small cakes are easier to turn.) Makes 24.

Everyday Waffles

1¾ cups all-purpose flour
1 tablespoon baking powder
½ teaspoon salt
2 beaten egg yolks
1¾ cups milk
½ cup cooking oil *or* melted
    shortening
2 stiffly beaten egg whites

In mixing bowl thoroughly stir together the flour, baking powder, and salt. Combine egg yolks, milk, and cooking oil or melted shortening. Add to dry ingredients all at once. Stir till blended but still slightly lumpy. Gently fold in stiffly beaten egg whites, leaving a few fluffs of egg white. *Do not overmix.* Bake in preheated waffle baker. Makes three 9-inch waffles.

Apricot-Sauced Pecan Waffles

2¼ cups all-purpose flour
1½ tablespoons sugar
4 teaspoons baking powder
¾ teaspoon salt
½ teaspoon finely shredded
    orange peel
2 beaten eggs
2¼ cups milk
½ cup cooking oil
1 cup chopped pecans
    Apricot Sauce

In mixing bowl thoroughly stir together the flour, sugar, baking powder, salt, and orange peel. Combine eggs, milk, and cooking oil; add all at once to dry ingredients, beating just till blended. Spread batter in preheated waffle baker; sprinkle with ⅓ of the pecans. Bake. Repeat. Serve with Apricot Sauce. Makes three 9-inch waffles.

Apricot Sauce: Drain one 8¾-ounce can unpeeled *apricot halves,* reserving the syrup. Chop fruit; set aside. In saucepan blend reserved syrup, ½ cup *maple-flavored syrup,* 2 tablespoons *cornstarch,* 2 tablespoons *honey,* 1 tablespoon *lemon juice,* and dash *salt.* Stir in 1 cup *apricot nectar.* Cook and stir over medium heat till mixture thickens and bubbles. Stir in apricots; heat through. Makes 2½ cups.

Chocolate Waffles

1 beaten egg
¾ cup milk
¼ cup chocolate-flavored syrup
2 tablespoons cooking oil
1 cup packaged buttermilk
    pancake mix
⅓ cup chopped pecans
¼ cup sifted powdered sugar
¼ cup butter *or* margarine
1 tablespoon unsweetened cocoa
    powder

Beat together egg, milk, chocolate syrup, and oil. Add to pancake mix, beating just till blended. Stir in nuts. Bake in preheated waffle baker. Meanwhile, cream together powdered sugar, butter, and cocoa powder till fluffy. Serve with hot waffles. Makes two 9-inch waffles.

Banana Waffles

2 cups packaged biscuit mix
2 tablespoons sugar
2 beaten egg yolks
1⅓ cups milk
1 large banana, mashed
2 tablespoons cooking oil
2 stiffly beaten egg whites

In mixing bowl stir together biscuit mix and sugar. Combine egg yolks, milk, banana, and cooking oil. Add to dry ingredients all at once, stirring till blended but still slightly lumpy. Carefully fold in egg whites, leaving a few fluffs of egg white. *Do not overmix.* Bake in preheated, lightly greased waffle baker. Makes three 9-inch waffles.

Buttermilk Corn Bread

1 cup all-purpose flour
1 cup yellow cornmeal
2 teaspoons baking powder
¾ teaspoon salt
½ teaspoon baking soda
2 beaten egg yolks
1 cup buttermilk
3 tablespoons butter *or*
    margarine, melted
2 stiffly beaten egg whites

In a mixing bowl thoroughly stir together the flour, cornmeal, baking powder, salt, and baking soda. Combine egg yolks, buttermilk, and melted butter or margarine; add to dry ingredients, beating till blended. Fold in stiffly beaten egg whites. Turn batter into greased 8x8x2-inch baking pan. Bake at 350° for 25 to 30 minutes. Makes 8 servings.

Molasses Corn Bread

1½ cups whole bran cereal
1 cup all-purpose flour
½ cup sugar
½ cup yellow cornmeal
1 tablespoon baking powder
2 eggs
1 cup milk
½ cup molasses
½ cup shortening

Stir together bran cereal, flour, sugar, cornmeal, baking powder, and ½ teaspoon *salt*. Add eggs, milk, molasses, and shortening. Beat with rotary beater just till blended (do not overbeat). Turn into greased 9x9x2-inch baking pan. Bake at 425° for 25 to 30 minutes. Serve warm. Serves 8 or 9.

Cheesy Corn Muffins

1 cup all-purpose flour
¾ cup yellow cornmeal
2 tablespoons sugar
1 tablespoon baking powder
½ teaspoon salt
1 beaten egg
1 cup shredded sharp American
    cheese (4 ounces)
1 cup milk
¼ cup cooking oil *or* melted
    shortening
    Poppy seed

In mixing bowl stir together the flour, cornmeal, sugar, baking powder, and salt. Combine egg, cheese, milk, and cooking oil; add to dry ingredients, stirring just till cornmeal mixture is moistened. Fill well-greased muffin pans ⅔ full. Sprinkle with poppy seed. Bake at 400° for 20 to 25 minutes. Makes 12 muffins.

Spoon Bread

1 cup yellow cornmeal
1½ cups water
1 cup milk
½ cup grated Parmesan cheese
2 tablespoons butter *or*
    margarine, melted
2 teaspoons sugar
2 teaspoons baking powder
½ teaspoon salt
3 beaten egg yolks
3 stiffly beaten egg whites

In saucepan combine cornmeal and water. Cook, stirring constantly, till mixture is the consistency of mush. Remove from heat; stir in milk, cheese, melted butter, sugar, baking powder, and salt. Stir in egg yolks; carefully fold in egg whites. (Batter will be thin.) Bake in greased 1½-quart casserole at 325° for 55 to 60 minutes. Serve immediately with additional butter. Makes 6 to 8 servings.

It's hard to resist big squares of freshly baked *Buttermilk Corn Bread*, especially
when the tender servings are spread with softened butter and drizzled with sweet honey.

Popovers

1½ **teaspoons shortening**
 2 **eggs**
 1 **cup milk**
 1 **tablespoon cooking oil**
 1 **cup all-purpose flour**
 ½ **teaspoon salt**

Grease six 6-ounce custard cups with ¼ teaspoon of the shortening per cup. Place custard cups in oven; preheat oven to 450°. Meanwhile, in mixing bowl beat eggs. Add milk and oil. Add flour and salt; beat till mixture is smooth. Fill the hot custard cups half full. Bake at 450° for 25 minutes. Reduce oven to 350° and bake till popovers are *very* firm, 15 to 20 minutes more. (If popovers brown too quickly, turn off oven and finish baking in the cooling oven till very firm.) A few minutes before removing from oven, prick each popover with a fork to let steam escape. Serve hot. Makes 6.

Company French Toast

 2 **beaten eggs**
 1 **cup orange juice**
 10 **slices raisin bread**
 1½ **cups finely crushed vanilla**
     wafers (33 wafers) *or*
     finely crushed graham
     crackers (21 crackers)
     Butter *or* **margarine**
     Maple-flavored syrup

Combine beaten eggs and orange juice. Dip bread into egg mixture and then into crumbs, coating both sides. Fry on both sides in 1 tablespoon butter till golden brown. Add additional butter each time more bread is added. Serve with butter and maple-flavored syrup. Makes 5 servings.

Frozen French Toast

 2 **eggs**
 1 **cup milk**
 1 **tablespoon sugar**
 ½ **teaspoon salt**
 12 **slices white bread**
     Butter *or* **margarine**
     Maple-flavored syrup

Beat together eggs, milk, sugar, and salt. Dip bread in egg mixture, coating both sides. Brown on both sides on hot, greased griddle or skillet. Serve at once. (Or, place on baking sheets and freeze. When firm, wrap in foil, using two slices per package and inserting waxed paper between slices. Return to freezer. To serve, place bread slice in toaster; toast.) Serve with butter and maple syrup. Serves 6.

Cinnamon-Graham Crackers

 2 **cups whole wheat flour**
 1 **cup all-purpose flour**
 1 **teaspoon baking powder**
 ½ **teaspoon baking soda**
 ¼ **teaspoon salt**
 ¾ **cup packed brown sugar**
 ½ **cup shortening**
 ⅓ **cup honey**
 1 **teaspoon vanilla**
 ½ **cup milk**
 3 **tablespoons granulated sugar**
 1 **teaspoon ground cinnamon**

Stir together whole wheat flour, all-purpose flour, baking powder, baking soda, and salt. Cream together brown sugar and shortening till light. Beat in honey and vanilla till fluffy. Add flour mixture alternately with milk to creamed mixture, beating well after each addition. Chill dough several hours or overnight. Divide chilled mixture into quarters. On well-floured surface roll each quarter to 15x5-inch rectangle. Cut rectangle crosswise into 6 small rectangles measuring 5x2½ inches. Place on ungreased baking sheet. Mark a line across center of each small rectangle with tines of fork and score a pattern of holes on squares with fork tines. Combine granulated sugar and ground cinnamon; sprinkle over crackers. Bake at 350° for 13 to 15 minutes. Remove from baking sheet immediately. Makes 24 crackers.

Shortcut Beer Bread

¾ cup dark *or* light beer
2 tablespoons butter *or*
    margarine
1 13¾-ounce package hot
    roll mix
1 egg
½ cup wheat germ
2 tablespoons sugar

In saucepan heat beer and butter just till warm. Pour into mixing bowl; add yeast from hot roll mix and dissolve. Add egg, wheat germ, sugar, and flour mixture from roll mix; mix well. Place in greased bowl. Cover and let rise till double (45 to 60 minutes). Punch down; knead and shape into loaf. Place in greased 8x4x2-inch loaf pan. Cover; let rise 35 minutes. Bake at 350° for 40 to 45 minutes. Makes 1 loaf.

Layered Parmesan Loaf

1 package refrigerated
    biscuits (10 biscuits)
2 tablespoons butter *or*
    margarine, melted
¼ cup grated Parmesan cheese

Separate biscuits; dip tops in melted butter, then in cheese. Arrange, cheese side up, overlapping in 2 rows on baking sheet. Bake at 450° about 12 minutes. Serve warm. Makes 10.

Thyme-Buttered Crescents

¼ cup butter, softened
1 teaspoon lemon juice
¼ teaspoon dried thyme,
    crushed
1 package refrigerated
    crescent rolls (8 rolls)

Cream butter or margarine till fluffy. Stir in lemon juice and thyme. Keep herb butter at room temperature for 1 hour to mellow before using. Unroll crescent rolls and separate; spread each with herb butter. Roll up dough, starting with wide end. Place on ungreased baking sheet, point side down. Bake at 350° about 15 minutes. Makes 8 rolls.

Orange Coffee Cake

2 tablespoons butter *or*
    margarine
⅓ cup sugar
1 tablespoon frozen orange
    juice concentrate, thawed
¼ teaspoon ground cinnamon
¼ cup chopped pecans
1 package refrigerated
    biscuits (10 biscuits)

Melt butter in 8x1½-inch round baking pan. Stir in sugar, orange juice concentrate, and cinnamon. Sprinkle with pecans. Separate biscuits; arrange biscuits atop nuts. Bake at 350° for 20 to 25 minutes. Cool 1 minute. Invert onto serving plate; serve warm. Makes 8 servings.

Brunch Cakes

1 3-ounce package cream cheese,
    softened
2 tablespoons sugar
1 egg yolk
¼ teaspoon vanilla
¼ cup crushed pineapple,
    drained
1 package refrigerated butter-
    flake rolls (12 rolls)

Beat together cheese, sugar, egg yolk, and vanilla; stir in pineapple. Flatten each biscuit on ungreased baking sheet to a 2½-inch circle, building up rim on sides. Spoon about 1 tablespoon filling in center of each. Bake at 375° for 10 to 12 minutes. Serve warm. Makes 12.

7 Dessert collection

You can turn dessert time into a memorable occasion with this tempting array of homemade favorites. Tender cakes, steaming fruit pies, cookies, creamy puddings, fruit desserts, and ice cream—all are featured in this section.

Few can resist the juicy goodness of fresh strawberries tucked inside flaky shortcake. Sweetened whipped cream complements *Strawberry Shortcake* (see recipe, page 411).

Cakes

Red Devil's Food Cake

- 1 **cup sugar**
- ½ **cup shortening**
- 3 **egg yolks**
- 1 **teaspoon vanilla**
- 2½ **cups sifted cake flour**
- ½ **cup unsweetened cocoa powder**
- 1½ **teaspoons baking soda**
- 1 **teaspoon salt**
- 1⅓ **cups cold water**
- 3 **egg whites**
- ¾ **cup sugar**
  Sea Foam Frosting
- 1 **1-ounce square unsweetened chocolate**
- ½ **teaspoon shortening**

In bowl cream together the 1 cup sugar and ½ cup shortening till light. Add egg yolks, one at a time, and vanilla, beating well after each addition. Sift together cake flour, cocoa powder, soda, and salt; add to creamed mixture alternately with cold water, beating well after each addition.

Beat egg whites to soft peaks; gradually add the ¾ cup sugar, beating till stiff peaks form. Fold into batter; blend well. Turn mixture into 2 greased and lightly floured 9x1½-inch round baking pans. Bake at 350° till wooden pick inserted in center comes out clean, 30 to 35 minutes. Cool on wire racks for 10 minutes. Remove from pans; cool thoroughly. Fill and frost with Sea Foam Frosting. Melt unsweetened chocolate with ½ teaspoon shortening, drizzle around edge of frosted cake.

Sea Foam Frosting: In top of double boiler combine 2 *egg whites,* 1½ cups packed *brown sugar,* ⅓ cup *cold water,* 2 teaspoons light *corn syrup or* ¼ teaspoon *cream of tartar,* and dash *salt.* Beat ½ minute at low speed of electric mixer. Place over hot, not boiling water. (Upper pan should not touch water.) Cook, beating constantly, till stiff peaks form, about 7 minutes *(do not overcook).* Remove from water. Beat in 1 teaspoon *vanilla.*

Busy-Day Cake

- ⅓ **cup shortening**
- 1½ **cups all-purpose flour**
- ¾ **cup sugar**
- 2½ **teaspoons baking powder**
- ½ **teaspon salt**
- ¾ **cup milk**
- 1 **egg**
- 1½ **teaspoons vanilla**

Place shortening in small mixer bowl. Add flour, sugar, baking powder, and salt. Add *half* the milk, the egg, and vanilla. Beat at low speed of electric mixer till blended. Beat 2 minutes at medium speed, scraping sides of bowl. Beat in remaining milk. Beat 2 minutes more at medium speed. Turn into a greased and lightly floured 9x9x2-inch baking pan. Bake at 375° till wooden pick inserted in center comes out clean, 25 to 30 minutes. Cool on wire rack. Frost cake with desired frosting.

White Cake Supreme

- 1½ **cups sugar**
- ¾ **cup shortening**
- 1½ **teaspoons vanilla**
- 2 **cups all-purpose flour**
- 1 **tablespoon baking powder**
- 1 **teaspoon salt**
- 1 **cup milk**
- 5 **egg whites**

In large mixer bowl cream sugar, shortening, and vanilla till light, scraping bowl frequently. Sift together flour, baking powder, and salt. Add flour mixture to creamed mixture alternately with milk, beating after each addition. In small mixer bowl beat egg whites till stiff peaks form. Gently fold into flour mixture. Turn into 2 greased and lightly floured 9x1½-inch round baking pans.

Bake at 375° till wooden pick inserted in center comes out clean, 18 to 20 minutes. Cool on wire racks for 10 minutes. Remove from pans. Cool thoroughly. Fill and frost with desired frosting.

Sweet Chocolate Cake

1 4-ounce bar sweet cooking
   chocolate
⅓ cup water
1 cup sugar
½ cup butter *or* margarine,
   softened
1 teaspoon vanilla
3 egg yolks
1⅔ cups all-purpose flour
1 teaspoon baking soda
½ teaspoon salt
⅔ cup buttermilk
3 egg whites
   Coconut Frosting

In small saucepan combine chocolate and water. Heat and stir over low heat till chocolate melts; cool thoroughly. In large mixer bowl cream sugar, butter, and vanilla till light and fluffy. Add egg yolks, one at a time, beating well after each addition. Beat in chocolate mixture.

Stir together flour, baking soda, and salt. Add flour mixture to creamed mixture alternately with buttermilk, beating after each addition. In small mixer bowl beat egg whites till stiff peaks form. Gently fold into flour mixture. Turn into 2 greased and lightly floured 8x1½-inch round baking pans.

Bake at 350° till wooden pick inserted in center comes out clean, 30 to 35 minutes. Cool cake in pans on wire racks for 10 minutes. Remove from pans. Cool thoroughly. Fill and frost top with Coconut Frosting.

Coconut Frosting: In saucepan beat 1 *egg* slightly. Stir in one 5⅓-ounce can *evaporated milk* (⅔ cup), ⅔ cup *sugar,* ¼ cup *butter or margarine,* and dash *salt.* Cook and stir over medium heat till thickened and bubbly, about 12 minutes. Stir in 1⅓ cups *coconut* and ½ cup chopped *pecans.* Cool.

Cake-making pointers

● To substitute all-purpose flour for cake flour, use the following formula: 1 cup minus 2 tablespoons sifted all-purpose flour equals 1 cup sifted cake flour.

● When a recipe calls for shortening, *do not* substitute butter, margarine, lard, or cooking oil. However, you can substitute margarine for butter.

● Eggs separate more readily when they are cold. However, egg whites whip up better if they are at room temperature.

● When beating egg whites, make sure the bowl and beater are completely clean. Any trace of fat or egg yolk will prevent the egg whites from reaching full volume.

● When adding dry ingredients alternately with liquid, begin and end with dry ingredients. Beat smooth after each addition.

● Preheat oven to correct temperature before mixing cake.

● For cakes made with shortening, grease and lightly flour bottoms of pans, or line bottoms with waxed or baking pan liner paper. Push batter to sides of pan. Tap pan lightly to remove air bubbles.

● Place pans as near center of oven as possible. Pans should not touch each other or oven sides. If necessary, stagger pans on two shelves; never place one pan directly under another.

● Test a cake for doneness in one or more of the following ways: cake is shrunk slightly from sides of pan, cake springs back when lightly pressed, or a wooden pick inserted in center comes out clean.

● Cool shortening layer cakes in pan 10 minutes; loaf cakes, 15 minutes. Loosen edges. Place inverted rack on cake; turn all over. Lift off pan. Put second rack on cake. Turn cake so top is up. Invert angel and sponge cakes in pan to cool.

● To split a cake layer, place wooden picks around sides of cake for a guide. Cut cake with a sharp, thin-bladed knife.

Nutmeg Feather Cake

¼ **cup butter** *or* **margarine**
¼ **cup shortening**
1½ **cups sugar**
3 **eggs**
½ **teaspon vanilla**
2 **cups all-purpose flour**
2 **teaspoons ground nutmeg**
1 **teaspoon baking soda**
1 **teaspoon baking powder**
¼ **teaspoon salt**
1 **cup buttermilk**
Toasted Meringue Topping
½ **cup flaked coconut**

In large mixer bowl cream together butter and shortening. Gradually add sugar, creaming till light. Add eggs, one at a time, and vanilla, beating well after each addition. Stir together flour, nutmeg, soda, baking powder, and salt. Add to creamed mixture alternately with buttermilk, beating after each addition. Turn into greased and lightly floured 13x9x2-inch baking pan. Bake at 350° till wooden pick inserted in center comes out clean, about 30 minutes.

Meanwhile, just before cake is removed from oven, prepare Toasted Meringue Topping. Carefully and quickly spread over *hot* cake. Sprinkle with coconut. Bake at 350° till meringue is golden, about 5 minutes. Store cake in refrigerator.

Toasted Meringue Topping: In small mixer bowl beat 2 *egg whites* and ½ teaspoon *vanilla* at medium speed of electric mixer till soft peaks form, about 2 minutes. Gradually add ¾ cup packed *brown sugar,* beating at high speed till stiff, glossy peaks form, about 4 minutes.

Orange-Strawberry Cake

1¼ **cups all-purpose flour**
⅓ **cup sugar**
6 **egg yolks**
1 **tablespoon finely shredded orange peel**
½ **cup orange juice**
⅔ **cup sugar**
¼ **teaspoon salt**
6 **egg whites**
1 **teaspoon cream of tartar**
½ **cup sugar**
1½ **cups whipping cream**
2 **cups fresh strawberries, sliced and sweetened lightly**

Combine flour and ⅓ cup sugar; set aside. Beat egg yolks till thick and lemon-colored, about 5 minutes. Add orange peel and juice; beat till very thick. Gradually add ⅔ cup sugar and salt, beating constantly. Sift flour mixture over yolk mixture, a little at a time, folding carefully just till blended.

Wash beaters. Beat egg whites and cream of tartar till soft peaks form. Gradually add ½ cup sugar, beating till stiff peaks form. Fold yolk mixture into whites. Turn into *ungreased* 10-inch tube pan. Bake at 325° till cake springs back and leaves no imprint when lightly touched, about 55 minutes. Invert cake in pan to cool.

Split cake into 3 layers. Whip cream. Stack cake layers, topping each with ⅓ of the whipped cream and sliced strawberries. Trim top with whole berries, if desired.

Strawberry Shortcake (pictured on page 408)

6 **cups fresh strawberries, sliced**
¼ **cup sugar**
4 **cups all-purpose flour**
¼ **cup sugar**
2 **tablespoons baking powder**
1 **teaspoon salt**
1 **cup butter** *or* **margarine**
2 **beaten eggs**
1⅓ **cups milk**
1 **cup whipping cream**
2 **tablespoons sugar**
Butter *or* **margarine, softened**

Stir together strawberries and ¼ cup sugar; set aside. Stir together flour, ¼ cup sugar, baking powder, and salt. Cut in 1 cup butter or margarine till mixture resembles coarse crumbs. Combine eggs and milk; add to dry ingredients, stirring just to moisten. Spread in 2 greased 8x1½-inch round baking pans; build up edges slightly. Bake at 450° for 15 to 18 minutes. Cool in pans 10 minutes; remove from pans. Whip cream and 2 tablespoons sugar till soft peaks form. Spread one layer with butter or margarine. Spoon whipped cream and berries between layers and on top.

Vanilla and Sour Cream Cake

1 cup **Vanilla Sugar**
6 tablespoons **butter** *or*
     margarine
1 teaspoon **vanilla**
1¾ cups **sifted cake flour**
1½ teaspoons **baking powder**
1 teaspoon **salt**
½ teaspoon **baking soda**
1 cup **dairy sour cream**
4 **stiffly beaten egg whites**
     Fluffy White Frosting
     Tinted coconut

Prepare Vanilla Sugar. Cream together 1 cup Vanilla Sugar and the butter or margarine; add vanilla. Sift together cake flour, baking powder, salt, and soda. Add to creamed mixture alternately with sour cream, beating just till mixed. Fold in beaten egg whites. Turn into 2 greased and lightly floured 8x1½-inch round baking pans. Bake at 350° till wooden pick inserted in center comes out clean, 30 to 35 minutes. Cool on wire racks for 10 minutes. Remove from pans; cool thoroughly. Fill and frost with Fluffy White Frosting. Sprinkle top and sides with tinted coconut.

Vanilla Sugar: Split 1 or 2 *vanilla beans* in half lengthwise; place in covered canister with 3 to 5 pounds *sugar.* Let age at least two weeks.

Fluffy White Frosting: In saucepan combine 1 cup *sugar,* ⅓ cup *water,* ¼ teaspoon *cream of tartar,* and dash *salt.* Bring to boiling, stirring till sugar dissolves. Very slowly add sugar mixture to 2 *unbeaten egg whites* in mixer bowl, beating constantly with electric mixer till stiff peaks form, about 7 minutes. Beat in 1 teaspoon *vanilla.*

Butter Pecan Cupcakes

1 cup **chopped pecans**
3 tablespoons **butter** *or*
     margarine
1¼ cups **sugar**
½ cup **butter** *or* **margarine**
2 teaspoons **vanilla**
2 **eggs**
2 cups **all-purpose flour**
1½ teaspoons **baking powder**
¼ teaspoon **salt**
⅓ cup **milk**
     Toasted Pecan Frosting

Place nuts in shallow baking pan; dot nuts with 3 tablespoons butter or margarine. Toast at 350° for 10 to 15 minutes, stirring often. Cool. Reserve ⅓ cup toasted pecans for frosting. Cream the sugar, ½ cup butter or margarine, and vanilla till light. Add eggs, one at a time, beating well after each. Stir together flour, baking powder, and salt; add to creamed mixture alternately with milk, beating well after each addition. Fold in the remaining ⅔ cup toasted pecans. Fill paper bake cup-lined muffin pans half full. Bake at 375° till wooden pick inserted in center comes out clean, 20 to 25 minutes. Cool on wire racks. Frost with Toasted Pecan Frosting. Makes 18 cupcakes.

Toasted Pecan Frosting: In mixing bowl combine 3 cups sifted *powdered sugar,* ¼ cup *milk,* 3 tablespoons *butter or margarine,* and ¼ teaspoon *vanilla.* Beat smooth with electric mixer. Stir in the reserved ⅓ cup toasted pecans.

Frosting a cake

Completely cool the cake before frosting. Use a pastry brush to brush loose crumbs from sides. Arrange strips of waxed paper around edge of serving plate. Position first cake layer, top side down, on the serving plate. Spread top of layer with about ¼ of the frosting. For a two-layer cake, position the second cake layer, top side up, over frosted layer. Spread sides of cake with a thin coat of frosting. Spread a thicker layer over the thin coat, swirling frosting decoratively. Spread remaining frosting over cake top, swirling decoratively and joining to frosted sides at edge. Carefully remove waxed paper strips.

Serve elegant *Vanilla and Sour Cream Cake* at the first sign of spring—
or anytime. *Vanilla Sugar,* a mixture of aged vanilla beans and sugar, enhances the flavor.

Marble Pound Cake

1¼ **cups sugar**
¾ **cup butter** *or* **margarine,**
   softened
½ **cup milk**
1 **teaspoon finely shredded**
   lemon peel
1 **tablespoon lemon juice**
2¼ **cups sifted cake flour**
1 **teaspoon baking powder**
1¼ **teaspoons salt**
3 **eggs**
2 **tablespoons boiling water**
1 **tablespoon sugar**
1 **1-ounce square unsweetened**
   chocolate, melted and
   cooled

Gradually beat 1¼ cups sugar into the butter or margarine; cream till light and fluffy, 8 to 10 minutes at medium speed of electric mixer. Beat in milk, lemon peel, and lemon juice. Sift together flour, baking powder, and salt. Add to creamed mixture; mix on low speed till smooth, about 2 minutes. Add eggs, one at a time, beating 1 minute after each. Beat 1 minute more, scraping sides of bowl frequently. Combine boiling water, 1 tablespoon sugar, and melted chocolate; stir into *half* of the batter.

Into a greased 9x5x3-inch loaf pan alternate spoonfuls of light and dark batters. With narrow spatula gently stir through batter to marble. Bake at 300° about 1 hour and 20 minutes. Cool 10 minutes in pan; remove from pan. Cool thoroughly. Sift powdered sugar atop, if desired.

Lemon Sponge Cake

8 **egg yolks**
¼ **cup water**
1 **teaspoon finely shredded**
   lemon peel
1 **tablespoon lemon juice**
1 **teaspoon vanilla**
¾ **cup sugar**
¾ **teaspoon salt**
1½ **cups all-purpose flour**
8 **egg whites**
1 **teaspoon cream of tartar**
¾ **cup sugar**

In small mixer bowl beat egg yolks at high speed till thick and lemon-colored, about 6 minutes. Combine water, lemon peel, lemon juice, and vanilla. Pour mixture into egg yolks. Beat at low speed till blended. Turn mixer to medium speed; beat till thick. Gradually add ¾ cup sugar and the salt, beating till sugar dissolves. Sprinkle about ¼ of the flour over yolk mixture. Gently fold in flour just till blended. Repeat with remaining flour, ¼ at a time.

Wash beaters thoroughly. In large mixer bowl beat egg whites and cream of tartar at medium speed till soft peaks form, about 1 minute. Gradually add ¾ cup sugar; continue beating till stiff peaks form. Stir about 1 cup of the beaten egg whites into yolks. Thoroughly fold yolk mixture into remaining whites. Turn into *ungreased* 10-inch tube pan. Bake at 325° till cake springs back and leaves no imprint when lightly touched, 60 to 65 minutes. Invert cake in pan; cool. Using a spatula, loosen cake from pan; remove.

Angel Cake

1½ **cups sifted powdered sugar**
1 **cup sifted cake flour** *or*
   sifted all-purpose flour
1½ **cups egg whites (11 or 12**
   large)
1½ **teaspoons cream of tartar**
1 **teaspoon vanilla**
¼ **teaspoon salt**
1 **cup granulated sugar**

Sift together powdered sugar and cake flour or all-purpose flour; repeat sifting twice. Set aside. In a large mixer bowl beat egg whites, cream of tartar, vanilla, and salt at medium speed of electric mixer till soft peaks form. Gradually add granulated sugar, 2 tablespoons at a time, beating till stiff peaks form.

Sift about ¼ of the flour mxiture over whites; fold in lightly by hand. Repeat, folding in remaining flour mixture by fourths. Turn into *ungreased* 10-inch tube pan. Bake at 350° till cake springs back and leaves no imprint when lightly touched, about 60 minutes. Invert cake in pan; cool. Using a spatula, loosen cake from pan; remove.

Golden Chiffon Cake

2¼ cups sifted cake flour
1½ cups sugar
1 tablespoon baking powder
1 teaspoon salt
½ cup cooking oil
5 egg yolks
¾ cup water
2 teaspoons finely shredded
lemon peel
1 teaspoon vanilla
8 egg whites (1 cup)
½ teaspoon cream of tartar

In a small mixer bowl sift together cake flour, sugar, baking powder, and salt; make a well in the center. Add cooking oil, egg yolks, water, lemon peel, and vanilla. Beat mixture at high speed of electric mixer till satin smooth, about 5 minutes.

Wash beaters thoroughly. In large mixer bowl combine egg whites and cream of tartar; beat at medium speed till very stiff peaks form. Pour batter in a thin stream over entire surface of egg whites; fold in gently. Pour into *ungreased* 10-inch tube pan. Bake at 325° till cake springs back and leaves no imprint when lightly touched, about 70 minutes. Invert cake in pan; cool. Using a spatula, loosen cake from pan; remove.

Golden Cupcakes

1 cup sugar
½ cup shortening
1 teaspoon vanilla
3 beaten egg yolks
2 cups all-purpose flour
2 teaspoons baking powder
¾ cup milk

In bowl cream together sugar, shortening, and vanilla till light. Add beaten egg yolks; beat well. Stir together flour, baking powder, and ½ teaspoon *salt.*

Add dry ingredients to creamed mixture alternately with milk, beating well after each addition.

Fill paper bake cup-lined muffin pans half full. Bake at 350° about 30 minutes. Makes 18 cupcakes.

Dark Fruitcake

3 cups all-purpose flour
2 teaspoons baking powder
2 teaspoons ground cinnamon
1 teaspoon salt
½ teaspoon ground nutmeg
½ teaspoon ground allspice
½ teaspoon ground cloves
1 16-ounce package diced mixed
candied fruits and peels
(2½ cups)
1 15-ounce package raisins
(3 cups)
1 8-ounce package whole
red candied cherries
(1½ cups)
1 8-ounce package pitted
dates, snipped (1⅓ cups)
1 cup slivered almonds
1 cup pecan halves
½ cup chopped candied
pineapple
4 eggs
1¾ cups packed brown sugar
1 cup orange juice
¾ cup butter *or* margarine,
melted and cooled
¼ cup light molasses

Stir together flour, baking powder, cinnamon, salt, nutmeg, allspice, and cloves. Add fruits and peels, raisins, cherries, dates, almonds, pecans, and pineapple; mix till well coated. Beat eggs till foamy. Gradually add brown sugar. Add orange juice, butter or margarine, and molasses; beat till blended. Stir into fruit mixture.

Grease one 6x3x2-inch loaf pan, one 8x4x2-inch loaf pan, and one 10x3½x2½-inch loaf pan.* Line bottom and sides of pans with brown paper; grease paper. (Brown paper prevents fruitcakes from overbrowning.) Turn batter into pans, filling each about ¾ full. Bake at 300° till a wooden pick inserted in center comes out clean, about 1½ hours for 6x3x2-inch pan and about 2 hours for two other pans. (Cover all pans with foil after 1 hour of baking.) Cool on wire racks; remove from pans. Wrap in wine-, brandy-, or fruit juice-moistened cheesecloth. Overwrap with foil. Store in refrigerator. Remoisten cheesecloth as needed if cakes are stored more than one week.

Note: If desired, use two 6x3x2-inch loaf pans and two 8x4x2-inch loaf pans instead of the three sizes suggested.

Date Cake

1 cup water
1 8-ounce package pitted
    dates, snipped (1⅓ cups)
1 cup sugar
½ cup shortening
2 eggs
1 teaspoon vanilla
1½ cups all-purpose flour
1 teaspoon baking soda
¼ teaspoon salt
¾ cup chopped walnuts
    Whipped cream (optional)

In saucepan bring water to boiling; stir in dates. Remove from heat; cool mixture to room temperature.

In large mixer bowl cream the sugar and shortening till light and fluffy. Add eggs and vanilla; beat well. Stir together flour, baking soda, and salt. Add dry ingredients to creamed mixture alternately with cooled date mixture; beat well after each addition. Stir in nuts. Spread in greased and lightly floured 13x9x2-inch baking pan.

Bake at 350° for 30 to 35 minutes. If desired, serve each piece with a dollop of whipped cream.

Chocolate-Date Cake: Prepare the Date Cake as above *except* omit the ¾ cup chopped walnuts. For topping combine 1 cup *semisweet chocolate pieces* and ½ cup chopped walnuts; mix well. Spread cake batter in prepared pan; sprinkle topping over batter. Bake as directed above.

Chocolate Cheesecake Torte

1 package 2-layer-size German
    chocolate cake mix
1 11-ounce can mandarin orange
    sections
1 envelope unflavored gelatin
1 8-ounce package cream
    cheese, softened
1 cup sugar
2 egg yolks
½ teaspoon finely shredded
    lemon peel
1 tablespoon lemon juice
2 egg whites
½ cup whipping cream
    Powdered sugar

Prepare cake mix according to package directions. Pour into 2 greased and lightly floured 9x1½-inch round baking pans. Bake at 350° till wooden pick inserted in center comes out clean, 25 to 30 minutes. Cool on wire racks for 10 minutes. Remove from pans; cool thoroughly.

Drain mandarin orange sections, reserving ¼ cup syrup. Chop orange sections; set aside. Soften unflavored gelatin in the reserved ¼ cup mandarin orange syrup. Place over hot water and stir to dissolve. Cool slightly.

Beat together cream cheese and sugar. Beat in egg yolks, lemon peel, and juice. Stir in cooled gelatin. Beat egg whites till stiff peaks form. Whip cream. Fold beaten egg whites, whipped cream, and chopped oranges into gelatin mixture. Turn into an 8x1½-inch round baking pan. Chill till set. Unmold onto bottom cake layer. Cover with second cake layer. Sift powdered sugar over top.

Applesauce Cake Roll

3 eggs
¾ cup granulated sugar
1 8-ounce can applesauce
1 cup all-purpose flour
½ teaspoon baking powder
½ teaspoon baking soda
½ teaspoon ground cinnamon
¼ teaspoon salt
¼ teaspoon ground cloves
    Powdered sugar
1 cup whipping cream
⅓ cup chopped walnuts

Beat eggs till thick; gradually add granulated sugar, beating well. Add ½ *cup* of the applesauce. Stir together flour, baking powder, soda, cinnamon, salt, and cloves. Fold into egg mixture. Spread in greased and lightly floured 15x10x1-inch jelly roll pan. Bake at 350° for 15 to 20 minutes. Immediately turn out onto towel sprinkled with powdered sugar. Roll up. Let cool on rack. Whip cream till soft peaks form. Fold in remaining applesauce and nuts. Unroll cake; spread with applesauce mixture. Roll up and chill:

Seven-Minute Frosting

1½ cups sugar
2 egg whites
2 teaspoons light corn syrup
  or ¼ teaspoon cream of
  tartar
  Dash salt
⅓ cup cold water
1 teaspoon vanilla

In top of double boiler combine sugar, egg whites, corn syrup or cream of tartar, and salt. Add cold water. Beat ½ minute at low speed of electric mixer to blend. Place over boiling water (water in bottom of double boiler should not touch top pan). Beating constantly with electric mixer on high setting, cook till frosting forms stiff peaks, about 7 minutes. Remove from heat; add vanilla. Beat till of spreading consistency and satiny in appearance, 2 to 3 minutes more. Frosts tops and sides of two 8- or 9-inch layers, or one 10-inch tube cake.

Butter Frosting

6 tablespoons butter
1 16-ounce package powdered
  sugar, sifted (4½ to 4¾
  cups)
¼ cup milk
1½ teaspoons vanilla

In mixer bowl cream butter till light and fluffy. Gradually add about half the powdered sugar, beating well. Beat in the ¼ cup milk and the vanilla. Gradually add remaining powdered sugar, beating constantly. Beat in additional milk, if necessary, to make frosting of spreading consistency. Frosts tops and sides of two 8- or 9-inch layers.

Chocolate Butter Frosting: Prepare Butter Frosting as above *except* add two 1-ounce squares unsweetened chocolate, melted and cooled, with the vanilla. Stir ¼ cup finely chopped nuts into frosting, if desired.

Mocha Butter Frosting: Prepare Butter Frosting as above *except* add ¼ cup unsweetened cocoa powder and 1 teaspoon instant coffee crystals to the butter; continue as directed.

Penuche Frosting

½ cup butter *or* margarine
1 cup packed brown sugar
¼ cup milk
3 cups sifted powdered sugar

In medium saucepan melt butter or margarine; stir in brown sugar. Bring to boiling, stirring constantly. Add milk; beat vigorously till smooth. Beat in enough powdered sugar to make of spreading consistency. Quickly frost cake. Frosts tops of two 8- or 9-inch layers or one 13x9x2-inch cake.

Three-Way Cream Cheese Frosting

1 3-ounce package cream
  cheese, softened
1 tablespoon butter *or*
  margarine, softened
1 teaspoon finely shredded
  orange peel *or* 1 teaspoon
  vanilla *or* 1 1-ounce
  square unsweetened chocolate, melted and cooled
2 cups sifted powdered sugar

Combine cream cheese, butter, and orange peel or vanilla or chocolate. Beat at low speed of electric mixer till light and fluffy. Gradually add powdered sugar, beating till fluffy. If necessary, add a little liquid (2 teaspoons milk or ½ teaspoon orange juice) to make of spreading consistency. Frosts a one-layer cake.

Pies

All-American Apple Pie

Pastry for Double-Crust Pie
(see recipe, page 427)
6 cups thinly sliced,
peeled cooking apples
(2 pounds)
1 tablespoon lemon juice
(optional)
1 cup sugar
2 tablespoons all-purpose
flour
½ to 1 teaspoon ground
cinnamon
Dash ground nutmeg
1 tablespoon butter or
margarine

Prepare and roll out pastry. Line a 9-inch pie plate with *half* of the pastry. Trim pastry to edge of pie plate.

If apples lack tartness, sprinkle with the 1 tablespoon lemon juice. In mixing bowl combine sugar, flour, cinnamon, and nutmeg. (For a very juicy pie, omit the flour.) Add sugar mixture to the sliced apples; toss to mix. Fill pastry-lined pie plate with apple mixture; dot with butter or margarine. Cut slits in top crust for escape of steam; place pastry atop filling. Seal and flute edge. Sprinkle some sugar atop, if desired. To prevent overbrowning, cover edge of pie with foil. Bake at 375° for 25 minutes. Remove foil; bake till crust is golden brown, 20 to 25 minutes more. Cool pie on rack before serving. Serve with vanilla ice cream, if desired.

Cherry Pie

2 16-ounce cans pitted tart
red cherries (water pack)
¾ cup sugar
⅓ cup cornstarch
Dash salt
¾ cup sugar
1 tablespoon butter or
margarine
3 or 4 drops almond extract
10 drops red food coloring
(optional)
Pastry for Double-Crust Pie
(see recipe, page 427)
Milk *and* sugar (optional)

Drain cherries, reserving 1 cup liquid. In a medium saucepan combine ¾ cup sugar, cornstarch, and salt; stir in reserved cherry liquid. Cook and stir over medium heat till thickened and bubbly. Cook and stir 1 minute more. Remove from heat. Stir in cherries, ¾ cup sugar, butter, and almond extract. If desired, stir in food coloring. Let stand while preparing pastry.

Prepare and roll out pastry. Line a 9-inch pie plate with *half* of the pastry. Trim to ½ inch beyond edge of pie plate. Turn cherry filling into pastry-lined pie plate. Cut remaining pastry into ½-inch-wide strips. Weave strips atop filling to make lattice crust; flute edge. Brush top of pastry with some milk and sprinkle with a little sugar, if desired. To prevent overbrowning, cover edge of pie with foil. Bake at 375° for 25 minutes. Remove foil; bake till crust is golden brown, 25 to 30 minutes more. Cool pie on rack before serving.

Rhubarb-Strawberry Pie

1¼ to 1½ cups sugar
3 tablespoons quick-cooking
tapioca
¼ teaspoon salt
¼ teaspoon ground nutmeg
3 cups rhubarb cut into ½-inch
pieces (1 pound)
2 cups sliced fresh
strawberries
Pastry for Double-Crust Pie
(see recipe, page 427)
1 tablespoon butter or
margarine

In large bowl stir together sugar, tapioca, salt, and nutmeg. Add rhubarb and strawberries; toss gently to coat fruit. Let mixture stand for 15 minutes.

Meanwhile, prepare and roll out pastry. Line a 9-inch pie plate with *half* of the pastry. Trim pastry to edge of pie plate. Pour fruit mixture into pastry-lined pie plate. Dot with butter. Cut slits in top crust for escape of steam; place pastry atop filling. Seal and flute edge.

To prevent overbrowning, cover edge of pie with foil. Bake at 375° for 25 minutes. Remove foil; bake till golden brown, 20 to 25 minutes more. Cool pie on rack before serving.

A juicy wedge of freshly baked *All-American Apple Pie* turns any
day into a special occasion. Serve a scoop of vanilla ice cream atop each slice.

Deep-Dish Apple Pie

**Pastry for Single-Crust Pie
(see recipe, page 427)**
1 **cup sugar**
⅓ **cup all-purpose flour***
1 **teaspoon ground cinnamon**
½ **teaspoon ground allspice**
¼ **teaspoon salt**
12 **cups thinly sliced, peeled
cooking apples (4 pounds)**
3 **tablespoons butter**
Milk *and* sugar
**Light cream *or* cheddar
cheese**

Prepare pastry. Roll out to a 13x8½-inch rectangle; cut slits in pastry. Combine sugar, flour, cinnamon, allspice, and salt; mix lightly with apples. Turn into a 12x7½x2-inch baking dish (apples will mound higher than sides). Dot with butter. Carefully place pastry atop apples; flute to the sides but not over the edge. Brush with milk and sprinkle with sugar. To prevent overbrowning, cover edge of pie with foil. Bake at 375° for 25 minutes. Remove foil; bake till crust is golden, 20 to 25 minutes more. Serve warm in dishes; pass cream or cheddar cheese.
Note: If you like a very juicy pie, use ¼ cup flour.

Strawberry Glacé Pie

Pastry for Single-Crust Pie
(see recipe, page 427)
6 cups fresh medium
strawberries
1 cup water
¾ cup sugar
3 tablespoons cornstarch
5 drops red food coloring
(optional)
Unsweetened whipped cream
(optional)

Prepare and roll out pastry. Line a 9-inch pie plate. Trim to ½ inch beyond edge of pie plate. Flute edge; prick pastry. Bake at 450° till golden, 10 to 12 minutes; cool.

To prepare strawberry glaze, in small saucepan crush 1 cup of the smaller berries; add the water. Bring to boiling; simmer 2 minutes. Sieve berry mixture. In saucepan combine sugar and cornstarch; stir in sieved berry mixture. Cook and stir over medium heat till glaze has thickened and is clear. Stir in food coloring, if desired.

Spread about ¼ cup glaze over bottom and sides of pastry shell. Arrange half of the whole berries, stem end down, in pastry shell. Carefully spoon half of the remaining glaze over berries, covering each berry. Arrange remaining berries, stem end down, atop first layer; spoon on remaining glaze, covering each berry. Chill pie at least 3 to 4 hours. If desired, garnish with whipped cream.

French Crunch Peach Pie

Pastry for Single-Crust Pie
(see recipe, page 427)
2 eggs
1 tablespoon lemon juice
⅓ cup sugar
1 29-ounce can *and* 1 16-ounce
can peach slices, drained
1 cup finely crushed vanilla
wafers (22 wafers)
½ cup chopped toasted almonds
¼ cup butter, melted

Prepare and roll out pastry. Line a 9-inch pie plate. Trim pastry to ½ inch beyond edge of pie plate. Flute edge; do not prick pastry. Bake at 450° for 5 minutes.

Beat eggs and lemon juice till blended; stir in sugar. Fold in peaches. Turn into pastry shell. Combine wafer crumbs, almonds, and butter; sprinkle over peach mixture. To prevent overbrowning, cover edge of pie with foil. Bake at 375° for 20 minutes. Remove foil; bake till filling is set in center, 20 to 25 minutes more. Cool on rack. Cover and chill to store. Serve with vanilla ice cream or cheddar cheese triangles, if desired.

Homemade Mincemeat Pie

1 pound beef stew meat
9 cups quartered, peeled
cooking apples (4 pounds)
4 ounces suet
2½ cups sugar
1 15-ounce package raisins
2 cups dried currants
½ cup chopped mixed candied
fruits and peels
1 teaspoon finely shredded
orange peel
1 cup orange juice
1 teaspoon finely shredded
lemon peel
¼ cup lemon juice
½ teaspoon ground nutmeg
¼ teaspoon ground mace
Pastry for Double-Crust Pie*
(see recipe, page 427)
Brandy Hard Sauce

Combine meat and enough water to cover. Simmer, covered, till tender, about 2 hours. Drain; cool. Using coarse blade of food grinder, grind meat, apples, and suet. In large kettle combine sugar, raisins, currants, candied fruits, orange peel, orange juice, lemon peel, lemon juice, nutmeg, mace, 2½ cups *water,* and 1 teaspoon *salt.* Stir in meat mixture. Cover; simmer 45 minutes. Stir frequently.

Prepare and roll out pastry. Line a 9-inch pie plate with *half* of the pastry. Trim to edge of pie plate. Fill with *4 cups* of the meat mixture. (Freeze remaining mincemeat in 4-cup portions.)* Cut slits in top crust; place atop filling. Seal and flute edge. Brush with a little milk, if desired. To prevent overbrowning, cover pie edge with foil. Bake at 375° for 20 minutes. Remove foil; bake till crust is golden, about 15 minutes more. Cool. Serve with Brandy Hard Sauce. Cover; chill to store.

Brandy Hard Sauce: Cream 2 cups sifted *powdered sugar,* ½ cup softened *butter,* and 1 teaspoon *brandy.* Stir in 1 beaten *egg yolk;* fold in 1 stiffly beaten *egg white.* Chill.

Note: This recipe makes enough mincemeat for 3 pies.

Lemon Meringue Pie

Pastry for Single-Crust Pie
(see recipe, page 427)
1½ cups sugar
3 tablespoons cornstarch
3 tablespoons all-purpose
flour
Dash salt
1½ cups water
3 eggs
2 tablespoons butter *or*
margarine
½ teaspoon finely shredded
lemon peel
⅓ cup lemon juice
Meringue for Pie

Prepare and roll out pastry. Line a 9-inch pie plate. Trim pastry to ½ inch beyond edge of pie plate. Flute edge; prick pastry. Bake at 450° for 10 to 12 minutes. Cool.

For filling, in medium saucepan combine sugar, cornstarch, flour, and salt. Gradually stir in water. Cook and stir over medium-high heat till thickened and bubbly. Reduce heat; cook and stir 2 minutes more. Remove from heat.

Separate egg yolks from whites; set whites aside for meringue. Beat egg yolks slightly. Stir about 1 cup of the hot mixture into the beaten yolks. Return mixture to saucepan. Bring to boil; cook and stir 2 minutes more. Remove from heat. Stir in butter or margarine and lemon peel. Gradually stir in lemon juice, mixing well. Turn into pastry shell.

Make Meringue for Pie using the 3 reserved egg whites. Spread over hot filling; seal to edge. Bake at 350° till golden, 12 to 15 minutes. Cool. Cover; chill to store.

Vanilla Cream Pie

Pastry for Single-Crust Pie
(see recipe, page 427)
1 cup sugar
½ cup all-purpose flour *or* ¼
cup cornstarch
¼ teaspoon salt
3 cups milk
4 eggs
3 tablespoons butter *or*
margarine
1½ teaspoons vanilla
Meringue for Pie

Prepare and roll out pastry. Line a 9-inch pie plate. Trim pastry to ½ inch beyond edge. Flute edge; prick pastry. Bake at 450° till golden, 10 to 12 minutes. Cool.

For filling, in medium saucepan combine the sugar, flour or cornstarch, and salt. Gradually stir in milk. Cook and stir till thickened and bubbly. Reduce heat; cook and stir 2 minutes more. Remove from heat.

Separate egg yolks from whites; set whites aside for meringue. Beat egg yolks slightly. Gradually stir 1 cup of the hot mixture into yolks. Return egg mixture to saucepan. Bring to boil; cook and stir 2 minutes more. Remove from heat. Stir in butter or margarine and the vanilla. Pour hot mixture into baked pastry shell.

Make Meringue for Pie using the 4 reserved egg whites. Spread over hot filling; seal to edge. Bake at 350° till golden, 12 to 15 minutes. Cool. Cover; chill to store.

Meringue for Pie

3 egg whites*
½ teaspoon vanilla
¼ teaspoon cream of tartar
6 tablespoons sugar

In a medium mixer bowl beat the egg whites, vanilla, and cream of tartar at medium speed of electric mixer till soft peaks form, about 1 minute.

Gradually add the sugar, about 1 tablespoon at a time, beating at high speed of electric mixer till mixture forms stiff, glossy peaks and sugar is dissolved, about 4 minutes more. Immediately spread over pie, carefully sealing to edge of pastry to prevent shrinkage. Bake as directed in individual pie filling recipe.

Note: Although the 3-egg-white recipe makes an adequate amount, you can use the extra egg white from a 4-egg-yolk pie for a more generous meringue. Follow the directions above, *except* use 4 *egg whites,* 1 teaspoon *vanilla,* ½ teaspoon *cream of tartar,* and ½ cup *sugar.* If necessary, beat slightly longer to achieve proper consistency.

Pumpkin Pie

Pastry for Single-Crust Pie (see recipe, page 427)
1 16-ounce can pumpkin
¾ cup sugar
1 teaspoon ground cinnamon
½ teaspoon salt
½ teaspoon ground ginger
½ teaspoon ground nutmeg
3 eggs
1 5⅓-ounce can evaporated milk (⅔ cup)
½ cup milk
Unsweetened whipped cream (optional)

Prepare and roll out pastry. Line a 9-inch pie plate. Trim pastry to ½ inch beyond edge of pie plate. Flute edge high; do not prick pastry.

In large mixing bowl combine pumpkin, sugar, cinnamon, salt, ginger, and nutmeg. Add eggs; lightly beat eggs into pumpkin mixture with a fork. Add the evaporated milk and milk; mix well. Place pie shell on oven rack; pour mixture into the pastry-lined pie plate. To prevent overbrowning, cover edge of pie with foil. Bake at 375° for 25 minutes. Remove foil; bake till knife inserted off-center comes out clean, 25 to 30 minutes more. Cool on rack. Garnish with whipped cream, if desired. Cover; chill to store.

Honey-Pumpkin Pie: Omit the ¾ cup sugar and add ½ cup *honey* to pumpkin mixture.

Molasses-Pumpkin Pie: Decrease sugar to ½ cup and add ⅓ cup *molasses* to pumpkin mixture.

Custard Pie

Pastry for Single-Crust Pie (see recipe, page 427)
4 eggs
½ cup sugar
½ teaspoon vanilla
¼ teaspoon salt
2½ cups milk
Ground nutmeg

Prepare and roll out pastry. Line a 9-inch pie plate. Trim to ½ inch beyond edge. Flute edge high; do not prick. Bake at 450° for 5 minutes. Cool on rack.

For filling, beat eggs slightly with rotary beater or fork. Stir in sugar, vanilla, and salt. Gradually stir in milk; mix well. Place pie shell on oven rack; pour filling into pastry shell. Sprinkle with nutmeg.

To prevent overbrowning, cover edge of pie with foil. Bake at 350° for 30 minutes. Remove foil; bake till knife inserted off-center comes out clean, 30 to 35 minutes more. Cool on rack before serving. Cover; chill to store.

Note: If desired, omit nutmeg and sprinkle ½ cup flaked *coconut* atop unbaked filling and bake as above.

Pecan Pie

Pastry for Single-Crust Pie (see recipe, page 427)
3 eggs
⅔ cup sugar
Dash salt
1 cup dark corn syrup
⅓ cup butter *or* margarine, melted
1 cup pecan halves

Prepare and roll out pastry. Line a 9-inch pie plate. Trim pastry to ½ inch beyond edge of pie plate. Flute edge; do not prick pastry.

For filling, in mixing bowl beat eggs slightly with rotary beater or fork. Add sugar and salt, stirring till dissolved. Stir in corn syrup and melted butter or margarine; mix well. Stir in pecan halves. Place pie shell on oven rack; pour filling into the pastry-lined pie plate. To prevent overbrowning, cover edge of pie with foil. Bake at 350° for 25 minutes. Remove foil; bake till knife inserted off-center comes out clean, about 25 minutes more. Cool on rack before serving. Cover; chill to store.

Cranberry-Pecan Pie: Prepare the pastry shell as above. Prepare the egg-corn syrup filling. Stir in 1 cup coarsely chopped fresh *cranberries* and the pecans. Bake as above.

Orange-Pecan Pie: Prepare pastry shell as above. Prepare filling. Stir in ½ teaspoon finely shredded *orange peel,* ½ cup finely chopped *orange,* and the pecans. Bake as above.

Strawberry Chiffon Pie

Pastry for Single-Crust Pie
(see recipe, page 427)
2½ **cups fresh strawberries**
¼ **cup sugar**
1 **tablespoon lemon juice**
¼ **cup sugar**
1 **envelope unflavored gelatin**
¾ **cup water**
2 **egg whites**
¼ **cup sugar**
½ **cup whipping cream**

Prepare and roll out pastry. Line a 9-inch pie plate. Trim pastry to ½ inch beyond edge. Flute edge; prick pastry. Bake at 450° till golden, 10 to 12 minutes. Cool on rack.

Reserve a few strawberries for garnish; set aside. In large mixing bowl crush enough of the remaining strawberries to measure 1¼ cups crushed berries. Stir in ¼ cup sugar and the lemon juice; let berry mixture stand 30 minutes.

Meanwhile, in small saucepan stir together ¼ cup sugar and the gelatin. Stir in the water; heat and stir till sugar and gelatin dissolve. Cool. Stir the cooled gelatin mixture into the strawberry mixture. Chill to the consistency of corn syrup, stirring occasionally. Remove from refrigerator (gelatin mixture will continue to set).

Immediately begin beating egg whites till soft peaks form. Gradually add ¼ cup sugar, beating till stiff peaks form. When gelatin is the consistency of unbeaten egg whites (partially set), fold in stiffly beaten egg whites.

Beat whipping cream till soft peaks form. Fold whipped cream into strawberry mixture. Chill till mixture mounds when spooned. Pile mixture into baked pastry shell. Chill pie 8 hours or till firm. Garnish with reserved strawberries. Serve with additional whipped cream, if desired.

Upside-Down Berry Pie

Pastry for Single-Crust Pie
(see recipe, page 427)
2 **egg whites**
½ **teaspoon vanilla**
¼ **teaspoon cream of tartar**
¼ **cup sugar**
3 **cups fresh strawberries**
½ **cup sugar**
3 **tablespoons cornstarch**
1 **cup whipping cream**
Sliced strawberries

Prepare and roll out pastry. Line a 9-inch pie plate. Trim to ½ inch beyond edge. Flute edge; prick pastry. Bake at 450° for 10 to 12 minutes. Cool. For meringue, beat whites, vanilla, and cream of tartar till soft peaks form. Gradually add ¼ cup sugar; beat till stiff peaks form. Spread on bottom and sides of pastry. Bake at 350° for 12 minutes; cool. Mash berries; add enough water to measure 2 cups mixture. Combine ½ cup sugar and cornstarch; add mashed berries. Cook and stir till bubbly. Cook and stir 2 minutes more. Cool; spread over meringue. Chill. Whip cream; spread over pie. Top with sliced strawberries. Cover; chill to store.

Pineapple Parfait Pie

Pastry for Single-Crust Pie
(see recipe, page 427)
1 **8¼-ounce can crushed**
pineapple
1 **3-ounce package**
lemon-flavored gelatin
1 **pint pineapple *or* lemon**
sherbet
Unsweetened whipped cream

Prepare and roll out pastry. Line a 9-inch pie plate. Trim pastry to ½ inch beyond edge of pie plate. Flute edge and prick bottom and sides of pastry with tines of a fork. Bake at 450° till golden, 10 to 12 minutes. Cool on rack.

Drain pineapple, reserving syrup. Add enough water to syrup to measure 1 cup liquid. In saucepan heat the 1 cup liquid to boiling; remove from heat. Add gelatin; stir till gelatin is dissolved. Add pineapple or lemon sherbet by spoonfuls, stirring after each addition till melted. Chill till mixture mounds when spooned. Fold in crushed pineapple. Turn into baked pastry shell. Chill several hours or overnight till set. Garnish with whipped cream. Cover; chill to store.

Lime Daiquiri Pie

**Pastry for Single-Crust Pie
(see recipe, page 427)**
⅔ cup sugar
1 envelope unflavored gelatin
¼ teaspoon salt
½ teaspoon finely shredded
lime peel (set aside)
⅓ cup lime juice
⅓ cup water
3 slightly beaten egg yolks
6 to 8 drops green food
coloring (optional)
¼ cup light rum
3 egg whites
⅓ cup sugar

Prepare and roll out pastry. Line a 9-inch pie plate. Trim to ½ inch beyond edge. Flute edge; prick pastry. Bake at 450° till golden, 10 to 12 minutes. Cool.

Combine ⅔ cup sugar, gelatin, and salt. Stir in lime juice, water, and egg yolks. Cook and stir over low heat till mixture thickens slightly. Remove from heat. Stir in lime peel; tint with food coloring, if desired. Cool slightly; stir in rum. Chill to the consistency of corn syrup, stirring occasionally. Remove from refrigerator. Immediately beat egg whites till soft peaks form. Gradually add ⅓ cup sugar, beating to stiff peaks. When gelatin is the consistency of unbeaten egg whites (partially set), fold in stiffly beaten egg whites. Chill till mixture mounds when spooned. Turn into baked pastry shell. Chill several hours or till set. If desired, garnish with unsweetened whipped cream, lime slices, and mint sprigs. Cover; chill to store.

High Citrus Pie

**Pastry for Single-Crust Pie
(see recipe, page 427)**
⅔ cup sugar
1 envelope unflavored gelatin
¼ teaspoon salt
½ teaspoon finely shredded
lemon peel (set aside)
½ cup lemon juice
1 teaspoon finely shredded
orange peel (set aside)
¼ cup orange juice
¼ cup water
5 slightly beaten egg yolks
5 egg whites
⅓ cup sugar

Prepare and roll out pastry. Line a 9-inch pie plate. Trim to ½ inch beyond edge. Flute edge; prick pastry. Bake at 450° till golden, 10 to 12 minutes. Cool.

In saucepan combine ⅔ cup sugar, gelatin, and salt. Stir in lemon juice, orange juice, water, and egg yolks. Cook and stir just till mixture thickens slightly. Remove from heat; stir in lemon and orange peels. Chill to the consistency of corn syrup, stirring occasionally. Remove from refrigerator.

Immediately beat egg whites till soft peaks form. Gradually add ⅓ cup sugar, beating to stiff peaks. When gelatin is the consistency of unbeaten egg whites (partially set), fold in stiffly beaten egg whites. Chill till mixture mounds when spooned. Turn into baked pastry shell. Chill several hours or overnight till set. If desired, garnish with orange slices and maraschino cherries. Cover and chill to store.

Peach Parfait Pie

**Gingersnap-Graham Crust
(see recipe, page 427)**
3½ cups sliced, peeled,
fresh peaches
¼ cup sugar
1 3-ounce package
lemon-flavored gelatin
1 pint vanilla ice cream
**Unsweetened whipped cream
Ground nutmeg**

Prepare Gingersnap-Graham Crust. Press crumb mixture onto bottom and sides of a buttered 9-inch pie plate. Bake at 375° till browned, 4 to 5 minutes. Cool on rack.

In mixing bowl combine peaches and sugar; toss gently to coat. Let the peaches stand about 15 minutes after mixing with sugar. Drain peaches, reserving the syrup. Add enough water to the reserved syrup to measure 1 cup liquid. Heat fruit liquid to boiling; remove from heat. Add gelatin; stir till gelatin is dissolved. Pour gelatin mixture into large mixing bowl. Add ice cream by spoonfuls, stirring till melted. Chill till mixture mounds when spooned. Set aside 10 peach slices. Fold remaining peaches into gelatin mixture. Turn peach mixture into baked crust. Chill pie several hours or overnight till set. Arrange the reserved peach slices spoke-fashion atop pie. Garnish with unsweetened whipped cream and sprinkle with nutmeg. Cover and chill to store.

Lime Daiquiri Pie, High Citrus Pie, and *Peach Parfait Pie* are a trio
of light, refreshing choices to top off summer meals—no matter what the occasion.

Fudge Ribbon Pie

Pastry for Single-Crust Pie
1 **5⅓-ounce can evaporated milk (⅔ cup)**
2 **1-ounce squares unsweetened chocolate**
1 **cup sugar**
2 **tablespoons butter** *or* **margarine**
1 **teaspoon vanilla**
1 **quart peppermint ice cream**
3 **egg whites**
½ **teaspoon vanilla**
¼ **teaspoon cream of tartar**
⅓ **cup sugar**
¼ **cup crushed peppermint candy**

Prepare and roll out pastry. Line a 9-inch pie plate. Trim pastry to ½ inch beyond edge. Flute edge; prick pastry. Bake at 450° for 10 to 12 minutes. Cool.

Combine evaporated milk and chocolate. Cook and stir over low heat till chocolate is melted. Stir in the 1 cup sugar and the butter or margarine. Cook over medium heat till thickened, 5 to 8 minutes more, stirring occasionally. Stir in the 1 teaspoon vanilla. Cool.

In mixing bowl soften ice cream using wooden spoon to stir and press against side of bowl. Soften till just pliable. Spoon *half* the ice cream into baked pastry shell. Return remaining ice cream to freezer. Cover with *half* the cooled chocolate sauce; freeze. Let remaining chocolate sauce stand at room temperature. Repeat layers with remaining ice cream and chocolate sauce, softening ice cream to spread, if necessary. Cover and freeze till firm.

Prepare meringue by beating egg whites, ½ teaspoon vanilla, and cream of tartar till soft peaks form. Gradually add ⅓ cup sugar, beating to stiff peaks. Fold 3 *tablespoons* of the crushed candy into meringue.

Remove pie from freezer. Spread meringue over chocolate layer, carefully sealing to edge of pastry. Swirl the meringue in a circular motion to make decorative peaks. Place on a baking sheet. Bake at 475° till meringue is golden, 3 to 5 minutes. Sprinkle with remaining 1 tablespoon crushed candy. Serve immediately.

Grasshopper Pie

Chocolate Wafer Crust
6½ **cups tiny marshmallows (about 11½ ounces)**
¼ **cup milk**
¼ **cup green crème de menthe**
2 **tablespoons white crème de cacao**
2 **cups whipping cream**
Unsweetened whipped cream
Chocolate curls

Prepare Chocolate Wafer Crust. Press crumb mixture onto bottom and sides of a 9-inch pie plate. Chill till firm.

For filling, in large saucepan combine marshmallows and milk. Cook over low heat, stirring constantly, till marshmallows melt. Remove from heat. Cool mixture, stirring every 5 minutes. Combine crème de menthe and crème de cacao; stir into marshmallow mixture. Whip 2 cups whipping cream till soft peaks form. Fold marshmallow mixture into the whipped cream; turn into chilled wafer crust. Freeze several hours or overnight till firm. Before serving, garnish pie with additional unsweetened whipped cream and chocolate curls.

Chocolate Wafer Crust

1½ **cups finely crushed chocolate wafers (25 wafers)**
6 **tablespoons butter** *or* **margarine, melted**

In mixing bowl combine crushed wafers and the melted butter or margarine. Turn the chocolate crumb mixture into a 9-inch pie plate. Spread the crumb mixture evenly in the pie plate. Press onto bottom and sides to form a firm, even crust. Chill till firm, about 1 hour.

Pastry for Single-Crust Pie

1¼ cups all-purpose flour
½ teaspoon salt
⅓ cup shortening *or* lard
3 to 4 tablespoons cold water

In medium mixing bowl stir together flour and salt. Cut in shortening or lard till pieces are the size of small peas. Sprinkle 1 tablespoon of the water over part of the mixture; gently toss with a fork. Push to side of bowl. Repeat till all is moistened. Form dough into a ball.

On lightly floured surface flatten dough with hands. Roll dough from center to edge, forming a circle about 12 inches in diameter. Wrap pastry around rolling pin. Unroll onto a 9-inch pie plate. Ease pastry into pie plate, being careful to avoid stretching pastry. Trim pastry to ½ inch beyond edge of pie plate. Flute edge.

For a baked pie shell, prick bottom and sides with tines of a fork. Bake at 450° for 10 to 12 minutes. (Or, for dishes such as quiches, line pastry with foil and fill with dry beans, or line the pastry with double thickness heavy-duty foil.) Bake at 450° for 5 minutes. Remove beans and foil or heavy-duty foil; bake til golden, 5 to 7 minutes more. Makes one 9-inch pastry shell.

Note: When you use commercial frozen pie crusts, remember that one of our pie filling recipes will fill two regular frozen pie crusts or one deep-dish frozen pie crust.

Pastry for Double-Crust Pie

2 cups all-purpose flour
1 teaspoon salt
⅔ cup shortening *or* lard
6 to 7 tablespoons cold water
Desired pie filling
Milk *and* sugar (optional)

In medium mixing bowl stir together flour and salt. Cut in shortening or lard till pieces are the size of small peas. Sprinkle 1 tablespoon water over part of mixture; gently toss with a fork. Push to side of bowl. Repeat till all is moistened. Form dough into 2 balls.

On lightly floured surface flatten 1 ball of dough with hands. Roll dough from center to edge, forming a circle about 12 inches in diameter. Ease pastry into pie plate, being careful to avoid stretching pastry. Trim pastry even with rim of pie plate. For top crust, roll out second ball of dough. Cut slits for escape of steam. Place desired pie filling in pie shell. Top with pastry for top crust. Trim top crust ½ inch beyond edge of pie plate. Fold extra pastry under bottom crust; flute edge. Using pastry brush, brush pastry with some milk; sprinkle with a little sugar, if desired. To prevent overbrowning, cover edge of pie with foil. Bake as directed in individual recipe. Remove foil after about half the baking time to allow crust to brown.

Gingersnap-Graham Crust

¾ cup fine gingersnap crumbs (12 cookies)
½ cup fine graham cracker crumbs (7 crackers)
¼ cup butter *or* margarine, melted
2 tablespoons sugar

In mixng bowl toss together gingersnap crumbs, graham cracker crumbs, melted butter or margarine, and sugar. Turn crumb mixture into a 9-inch pie plate. Spread the crumb mixture evenly in the pie plate. Press onto bottom and sides to form a firm, even crust. Bake at 375° for 4 to 5 minutes. Cool thoroughly on rack.

Cookies

Chocolate Chip Cookies

1 cup packed brown sugar
½ cup granulated sugar
½ cup butter *or* margarine, softened
½ cup shortening
2 eggs
1½ teaspoons vanilla
2½ cups all-purpose flour
1 teaspoon baking soda
½ teaspoon salt
1 12-ounce package semisweet chocolate pieces (2 cups)
1 cup chopped walnuts *or* pecans

In mixing bowl cream brown sugar, granulated sugar, softened butter, and shortening. Add eggs and vanilla; beat well. In a bowl stir together the flour, baking soda, and salt. Add to creamed mixture and stir till well blended. Stir in chocolate pieces and nuts. Drop from a teaspoon 2 inches apart onto an ungreased cookie sheet. Bake at 375° till done, 8 to 10 minutes. Remove from cookie sheet; cool on wire rack. Makes about 6 dozen cookies.

Peanut-Oatmeal Drops

¾ cup packed brown sugar
¾ cup shortening
½ cup granulated sugar
½ cup peanut butter
3 eggs
¼ cup milk
1 teaspoon vanilla
1½ cups all-purpose flour
1 teaspoon baking soda
½ teaspoon salt
1 cup quick-cooking rolled oats
1 cup chopped peanuts

Cream together brown sugar, shortening, granulated sugar, and peanut butter till light and fluffy. Add eggs, one at a time, beating well after each. Blend in milk and vanilla. Stir together flour, baking soda, and salt; stir into creamed mixture. Stir in oats and peanuts. Drop from teaspoon 2 inches apart onto greased cookie sheet. Bake at 350° for 10 to 12 minutes. Makes 6 dozen cookies.

Two-Tone Cookies

½ cup packed brown sugar
6 tablespoons butter *or* margarine, softened
¼ cup granulated sugar
1 egg
½ teaspoon vanilla
½ cup dairy sour cream
1¼ cups all-purpose flour
½ teaspoon salt
¼ teaspoon baking soda
¼ cup chopped walnuts
1 1-ounce square unsweetened chocolate, melted and cooled
Walnut halves (optional)

Cream together brown sugar, softened butter, and granulated sugar. Add egg and vanilla; beat well. Stir in sour cream. Stir together flour, salt, and soda. Gradually mix into creamed mixture; stir in chopped nuts. Divide dough in half; stir chocolate into one portion. Drop rounded teaspoonfuls of chocolate dough 2 inches apart onto ungreased cookie sheet. Drop rounded teaspoonfuls of plain dough next to chocolate mounds. (They will bake together as one.) If desired, press a walnut half atop each cookie. Bake at 375° for 12 to 15 minutes. Cool on rack. Makes 1½ to 2 dozen.

Coconut Macaroons

2 **egg whites**
½ **teaspoon vanilla**
   Dash salt
⅔ **cup sugar**
1 **3½-ounce can flaked coconut**
   (1⅓ cups)

Beat egg whites, vanilla, and salt till soft peaks form. Gradually add sugar, beating till stiff peaks form. Fold in coconut. Drop rounded teaspoonfuls onto greased cookie sheet. Bake at 325° about 20 minutes. Makes 1½ to 2 dozen.

Bran Puff Cookies

½ **cup granulated sugar**
½ **cup packed brown sugar**
½ **cup butter *or* margarine**
½ **cup dairy sour cream**
1 **egg**
1 **teaspoon vanilla**
1¾ **cups all-purpose flour**
½ **teaspoon baking soda**
½ **teaspoon salt**
1 **cup bran flakes**
½ **cup raisins**

In bowl cream together sugars and butter or margarine till light and fluffy. Beat in sour cream, egg, and vanilla. Stir together flour, baking soda, and salt; stir into creamed mixture. Fold in bran flakes and raisins. Drop rounded teaspoonfuls onto greased cookie sheet. Bake at 375° for 10 to 12 minutes. Cool on rack. Makes 4 dozen.

Sugar-Pecan Crisps

¾ **cup butter *or* margarine,**
   softened
⅔ **cup sugar**
1 **egg**
1 **teaspoon vanilla**
¼ **teaspoon salt**
1¾ **cups all-purpose flour**
½ **cup finely chopped pecans**

Cream together softened butter and sugar till light and fluffy. Add egg, vanilla, and salt; beat well. Gradually stir in flour. Cover and chill 30 minutes for easier handling. Shape dough into a 12-inch log; roll in chopped pecans to coat outside of log. Wrap in waxed paper or clear plastic wrap. Chill thoroughly. Cut into ¼-inch slices. Place on ungreased cookie sheet. Bake at 350° till lightly browned, 10 to 12 minutes. Makes 4 dozen cookies.

Date Pinwheels

   Date-Nut Filling
1 **cup packed brown sugar**
½ **cup shortening**
2 **eggs**
½ **teaspoon vanilla**
2⅓ **cups all-purpose flour**
½ **teaspoon baking powder**
¼ **teaspoon baking soda**
¼ **teaspoon salt**
¼ **teaspoon ground cinnamon**

Prepare Date-Nut Filling; chill. Cream together brown sugar and shortening. Add eggs and vanilla; beat well. Stir together flour, baking powder, soda, salt, and cinnamon; stir into creamed mixture. Cover and chill dough 30 minutes.

On waxed paper, roll dough to 18x10-inch rectangle. Spread with filling. Roll up jelly-roll fashion, beginning at long side; pinch edges together to seal. Cut roll in half crosswise. Wrap each roll in waxed paper or clear plastic wrap. Chill well. Carefully cut into ¼-inch slices.

Place on greased cookie sheet. Bake at 350° till lightly browned, 8 to 10 minutes. Makes 6 dozen cookies.

Date-Nut Filling: In small saucepan combine one 8-ounce package pitted *dates*, finely snipped (1⅓ cups); ⅓ cup *granulated sugar;* and ⅓ cup *water*. Bring to boiling. Cook and stir over low heat till thickened, about 4 minutes. Remove from heat; stir in ½ cup finely chopped *nuts* and ½ teaspoon *vanilla*.

Rich in heritage and design are two versions of German *Brown Sugar Spritz*,
wreath-shaped Norwegian *Berlinerkranser,* and chocolate-dipped *Finnish Chestnut Fingers*.

Finnish Chestnut Fingers

6 tablespoons butter, softened
¼ cup sugar
1 egg yolk
½ cup chestnut purée *or* canned
   chestnuts, drained and
   puréed
½ teaspoon vanilla
1 cup all-purpose flour
¼ teaspoon ground cinnamon
3 1-ounce squares semisweet
   chocolate *or* ½ cup semisweet chocolate pieces,
   melted

Cream butter and ¼ cup sugar. Add egg yolk; beat well. Beat in purée and vanilla. Stir together flour, cinnamon, and ¼ teaspoon *salt;* stir into creamed mixture.

Using a scant tablespoon dough for each cookie, roll into 2½-inch fingers. Place on lightly greased cookie sheet. Sprinkle with additional sugar. Bake at 350° till slightly browned, about 20 minutes. Remove from pan; cool on rack. Dip one end of each cookie in melted chocolate; place on waxed paper. Chill till set. Makes 2½ dozen cookies.

Berlinerkranser

1 cup butter *or* margarine,
   softened
½ cup sifted powdered sugar
1 hard-cooked egg yolk, sieved
1 raw egg yolk
1 teaspoon vanilla
2¼ cups all-purpose flour
1 slightly beaten egg white
⅓ cup crushed sugar cubes *or*
   granulated sugar

In bowl cream together butter and powdered sugar till light and fluffy. Add sieved egg yolk, raw egg yolk, and vanilla. Stir in flour. Cover and chill 1 hour.

Work with a small amount of dough at a time; keep remainder chilled. Using about 1 tablespoon dough for each cookie, shape into 6-inch ropes. Shape each rope into a wreath, overlapping about 1 inch from ends. Brush with egg white; sprinkle with crushed sugar cubes or granulated sugar. Place on ungreased cookie sheet. Bake at 325° till golden, 15 to 17 minutes. Let stand 1 minute before removing from cookie sheet. Makes 3 to 3½ dozen cookies.

Brown Sugar Spritz

Holiday Pineapple Filling*
1 cup butter *or* margarine,
   softened
½ cup packed brown sugar
1 egg
1 teaspoon vanilla
2⅔ cups all-purpose flour
1 teaspoon baking powder

Prepare Holiday Pineapple Filling; cool. Cream together butter and brown sugar; beat in egg and vanilla. Stir together flour and baking powder; add gradually to creamed mixture, mixing till smooth. Do not chill.

Place half of dough in cookie press.* Using ribbon plate, press dough in ten 10-inch strips on ungreased cookie sheets. Using star plate and remaining dough, press lengthwise rows of dough on top of each strip, making a rim along both edges. Spoon Holiday Pineapple Filling between rims. Bake cookies at 400° for 8 to 10 minutes. Cut hot strips into 1¼-inch diagonals. Cool. Makes about 6½ dozen.

Holiday Pineapple Filling: In saucepan stir together one 29½-ounce can *crushed pineapple,* drained, and 1 cup *granulated sugar;* bring to boiling. Simmer till very thick, 30 to 35 minutes, stirring often. Divide mixture in half. Using a few drops *food coloring,* tint half of the filling red and the other half green. Cool thoroughly.

Note: Or, omit Holiday Pineapple Filling and force all of dough through cookie press in desired shapes onto ungreased cookie sheet. In screw-top jar shake ground *almonds* with few drops red or green *food coloring;* sprinkle over cookies. Bake at 400° about 8 minutes. Makes about 5 dozen.

Rolled Sugar Cookies

¾ **cup sugar**
⅓ **cup shortening**
6 **tablespoons butter** *or*
   margarine, softened
1 **egg**
1 **tablespoon milk**
1 **teaspoon vanilla**
2 **cups all-purpose flour**
1½ **teaspoons baking powder**
¼ **teaspoon salt**

Cream sugar, shortening, and butter or margarine till fluffy. Add egg, milk, and vanilla; beat well. Stir together flour, baking powder, and salt; stir into creamed mixture. Cover and chill at least 3 hours. Working with half of the dough at a time, on lightly floured surface roll to ⅛-inch thickness. Cut with cookie cutters into desired shapes. Place on ungreased cookie sheet. Bake at 375° till set but not browned, about 8 minutes. Makes about 4 dozen cookies.

Almond Cookies

1¼ **cups sugar**
⅔ **cup shortening**
2½ **cups all-purpose flour**
1 **teaspoon baking soda**
1 **teaspoon salt**
2 **beaten eggs**
2 **tablespoons milk**
1 **teaspoon almond extract**
½ **teaspoon vanilla**

In mixer bowl cream together sugar and shortening till light and fluffy. Stir together flour, baking soda, and salt. Combine eggs, milk, almond extract, and vanilla. Add to creamed mixture alternately with flour mixture, beating well after each addition.

Cover and chill dough 1 to 2 hours or overnight. Roll dough on lightly floured surface to ¼-inch thickness. Cut with floured cookie cutters into desired shapes. Place on ungreased cookie sheet. Bake at 375° for 10 to 15 minutes. Cool on wire rack. Makes about 3 dozen cookies.

Jam-Filled Cookies

1 **cup granulated sugar**
1 **cup packed brown sugar**
1 **cup shortening**
2 **eggs**
¼ **cup buttermilk**
1 **teaspoon vanilla**
3½ **cups all-purpose flour**
1 **teaspoon baking powder**
1 **teaspoon baking soda**
1 **teaspoon ground nutmeg**
   Strawberry jam

In large bowl cream sugars and shortening. Add eggs, buttermilk, and vanilla; beat well. Stir together flour, baking powder, baking soda, nutmeg, and 1 teaspoon *salt;* stir into creamed mixture. Cover and chill.

On lightly floured surface roll dough to ⅛-inch thickness. Cut with cookie cutter into 1½-inch rounds. Place *1 teaspoon* jam on each of *half* of the rounds; top with remaining rounds. Lightly seal edges with fork. With knife cut crisscross slits in tops of cookies. Bake at 350° till golden, 10 to 15 minutes. Makes 5 dozen cookies.

Cream Cheese Pastries

1 **cup butter** *or* **margarine,**
   softened
1 **8-ounce package cream**
   cheese, softened
½ **cup sifted powdered sugar**
2 **cups all-purpose flour**
¼ **teaspoon salt**
⅓ **cup tart red jelly** *or* **jam**

Cream butter and cream cheese till fluffy; gradually blend in sugar. Stir together flour and salt; stir into creamed mixture. Cover; chill dough several hours or overnight.

Divide dough into thirds. On lightly floured surface roll each portion to 12½x10-inch rectangle. With fluted pastry wheel cut into 2½-inch squares. Place a dot of jelly or jam in center of each square; bring up two diagonal corners to center, pinching together to seal.

Place on ungreased cookie sheet. Bake at 375° till set but not brown, about 12 minutes. If desired, sift additional powdered sugar over slightly warm pastries. Makes 5 dozen.

Santa's Whiskers

1 cup sugar
1 cup butter **or** margarine,
   softened
2 tablespoons milk
1 teaspoon vanilla **or** rum
   flavoring
2½ cups all-purpose flour
1 cup finely chopped red **or**
   green candied cherries
½ cup finely chopped pecans
1 cup flaked coconut

In mixing bowl cream together sugar and butter or margarine till fluffy; blend in milk and vanilla or rum flavoring. Stir in flour, chopped candied cherries, and chopped pecans. Form dough into three 7-inch rolls. Roll in flaked coconut to coat outside.* Wrap dough in waxed paper or clear plastic wrap; chill thoroughly.

Cut into ¼-inch slices. Place on ungreased cookie sheet. Bake at 375° till edges are golden, about 12 minutes. Makes about 7 dozen cookies.

Note: If desired, stir the coconut into the dough instead of using it as a coating.

Double Peanut Cookies

1 cup granulated sugar
1 cup packed brown sugar
1 cup shortening
1 cup peanut butter
2 eggs
1 teaspoon vanilla
2¼ cups all-purpose flour
2 teaspoons baking soda
¼ teaspoon salt
1 cup coarsely chopped salted
   peanuts

Cream together sugars, shortening, and peanut butter. Add eggs and vanilla; beat well. Stir together flour, baking soda, and salt; stir into creamed mixture. Stir in nuts. Form dough into 1-inch balls. Place on ungreased cookie sheet; flatten slightly with fingers. Bake at 350° about 10 minutes. Makes 6 dozen cookies.

Chocolate Crinkles

1½ cups granulated sugar
½ cup cooking oil
4 1-ounce squares unsweetened
   chocolate, melted and
   cooled
2 teaspoons vanilla
3 eggs
2 cups all-purpose flour
2 teaspoons baking powder
   Sifted powdered sugar

In mixing bowl combine granulated sugar, oil, melted chocolate, and vanilla. Beat in eggs. Stir together flour and baking powder. Stir into chocolate mixture. Cover and chill. Using 1 tablespoon dough for each cookie, shape into balls; roll in powdered sugar. Place on greased cookie sheet. Bake at 375° for 10 to 12 minutes. Roll warm cookies again in powdered sugar. Makes 4 dozen cookies.

Lemon Rounds

1 cup butter **or** margarine,
   softened
½ cup sifted powdered sugar
1 teaspoon vanilla
½ teaspoon finely shredded
   lemon peel
1 tablespoon lemon juice
2½ cups all-purpose flour
½ cup finely chopped pecans
   Lemon Glaze

In mixing bowl cream butter or margarine, powdered sugar, and vanilla. Beat in lemon peel and lemon juice. Stir in flour, mixing well. Using one rounded teaspoon dough for each cookie, shape dough into balls; dip one side in chopped nuts. Place, nut side up, on ungreased cookie sheet. Flatten with bottom of a glass dipped in granulated sugar. Bake at 350° for 22 to 25 minutes. Cool; drizzle with Lemon Glaze. Makes 3½ dozen cookies.

Lemon Glaze: Combine 1 cup sifted *powdered sugar* and 3 to 4 teaspoons *lemon juice* till of drizzling consistency.

Chocolate Syrup Brownies

1 cup sugar
½ cup butter *or* margarine,
    softened
4 eggs
1 16-ounce can chocolate-
    flavored syrup (1½ cups)
1¼ cups all-purpose flour
1 cup chopped walnuts
    Chocolate Glaze

In mixing bowl cream together sugar and softened butter or margarine till light and fluffy. Add eggs; beat well. Stir in chocolate-flavored syrup and flour till blended (batter will look curdled). Stir in chopped walnuts. Pour mixture into greased 13x9x2-inch baking pan. Bake at 350° for 30 to 35 minutes. Cool slightly; top with Chocolate Glaze. Cool; cut into bars. Makes 32 brownies.

Chocolate Glaze: Combine ⅔ cup sugar, 3 tablespoons *milk,* and 3 tablespoons *butter or margarine.* Bring to boiling; boil for 30 seconds. Remove from heat; stir in ½ cup semisweet *chocolate pieces* till melted (mixture will be thin). Immediately pour atop brownies.

Buttermilk Brownies

1 cup butter *or* margarine
1 cup water
⅓ cup unsweetened cocoa
    powder
2 cups all-purpose flour
2 cups sugar
1 teaspoon baking soda
½ teaspoon salt
2 slightly beaten eggs
½ cup buttermilk
1½ teaspoons vanilla
    Cocoa-Buttermilk Frosting

In saucepan combine butter or margarine, water, and cocoa powder. Bring to boiling, stirring constantly. Remove from heat. In large mixing bowl stir together flour, sugar, baking soda, and salt; stir in eggs, buttermilk, and vanilla. Add cocoa mixture; mix till blended.

Pour mixture into one greased 15½x10½x1-inch baking pan, or two 11x7½x1½-inch baking pans, or two 9x9x2-inch baking pans. Bake at 375° about 20 minutes. Immediately pour Cocoa-Buttermilk Frosting over brownies; spread evenly. Cool; cut into bars. Makes 60 brownies.

Cocoa-Buttermilk Frosting: In saucepan combine ¼ cup *butter or margarine,* 3 tablespoons unsweetened *cocoa powder,* and 3 tablespoons *buttermilk.* Cook and stir till boiling; remove from heat. Beat in 2¼ cups sifted *powdered sugar,* ½ cup chopped *walnuts,* and ½ teaspoon *vanilla.*

Cheese-Marbled Brownies

1 6-ounce package semisweet
    chocolate pieces (1 cup)
6 tablespoons butter *or*
    margarine
⅓ cup honey *or* ½ cup sugar
2 beaten eggs
1 teaspoon vanilla
½ cup all-purpose flour
½ teaspoon baking powder
    Cheese Filling

In saucepan melt chocolate pieces and butter or margarine over low heat. Remove from heat. Add honey or sugar, eggs, and vanilla; stir just till blended. Stir together flour and baking powder. Add to chocolate mixture; stir just till dry ingredients are moistened.

Pour *half* of the batter into greased 9x9x2-inch baking pan. Bake at 350° for 10 minutes. Pour Cheese Filling over partially baked layer. Carefully spoon remaining half of brownie batter over filling. Swirl slightly with Cheese Filling, being careful not to touch bottom layer. Bake at 350° about 35 minutes. Cool; cut into bars. Store in refrigerator. Makes 24 brownies.

Cheese Filling: In mixing bowl cream together one 8-ounce package softened *cream cheese* and ½ cup *sugar;* beat in 1 *egg* and dash *salt.* Stir in ½ cup chopped *nuts.*

Saucepan Fudge Brownies

½ cup butter *or* margarine
2 1-ounce squares unsweetened
chocolate
1 cup sugar
2 eggs
1 teaspoon vanilla
¾ cup all-purpose flour
½ cup sliced almonds

In saucepan melt butter or margarine and chocolate. Remove from heat; stir in sugar. Blend in eggs, one at a time, beating well after each addition. Add vanilla. Stir in flour; mix well. Spread batter in a greased 8x8x2-inch baking pan. Sprinkle with almonds. Bake at 350° till wooden pick inserted in center comes out clean, about 30 minutes. Cool; cut into bars. Makes 8 to 12 brownies.

Lemon Bars

1 cup all-purpose flour
¼ cup sifted powdered sugar
½ cup butter *or* margarine
2 eggs
¾ cup granulated sugar
½ teaspoon finely shredded
lemon peel
3 tablespoons lemon juice
2 tablespoons all-purpose
flour
¼ teaspoon baking powder

Stir together 1 cup flour and ¼ cup powdered sugar; cut in butter till mixture clings together. Pat into ungreased 8x8x2-inch baking pan. Bake at 350° for 10 to 12 minutes.

In mixer bowl beat eggs; add granulated sugar, lemon peel, and juice. Beat till slightly thick and smooth, 8 to 10 minutes. Stir together 2 tablespoons flour and baking powder; add to egg mixture. Blend just till moistened. Pour over baked layer. Bake at 350° for 20 to 25 minutes. Sift more powdered sugar over top. Cool; cut into bars. Makes 20.

Apricot-Almond Bars

¾ cup butter *or* margarine,
softened
½ cup sifted powdered sugar
¼ teaspoon almond extract
1¾ cups all-purpose flour
½ cup finely chopped almonds
¼ teaspoon salt
1 12-ounce jar apricot preserves
½ cup finely chopped mixed
candied fruits and peels
½ teaspoon almond extract

Cream together butter or margarine, powdered sugar, and ¼ teaspoon almond extract. Stir together flour, chopped nuts, and salt; add to creamed mixture. Mix till crumbly. Reserve 1 cup for topping; pat remaining into ungreased 13x9x2-inch baking pan. Combine preserves, candied fruits, and ½ teaspoon almond extract; spread over crumb layer. Top with reserved 1 cup crumbs. Bake at 350° till golden, 30 to 35 minutes. Cut into bars while warm. Makes 32.

Chocolate Chip Bars

¾ cup packed brown sugar
½ cup butter *or* margarine,
softened
1 egg
1 tablespoon milk
1 teaspoon vanilla
1 cup all-purpose flour
½ teaspoon baking powder
⅛ teaspoon baking soda
1 6-ounce package semisweet
chocolate pieces (1 cup)

Cream together brown sugar and softened butter or margarine. Add egg, milk, and vanilla; beat well. Stir together flour, baking powder, baking soda, and ⅛ teaspoon *salt*. Add to creamed mixture; beat well. Stir in chocolate pieces. Spread in greased 9x9x2-inch baking pan. Bake at 350° for 30 to 35 minutes. Cool; cut into bars. Makes 32.

Cereal-Spice Bars

1 package 2-layer-size spice
   cake mix
½ cup quick-cooking rolled
   oats
¼ cup wheat germ
2 eggs
½ cup light molasses
¼ cup milk
¼ cup cooking oil
½ cup shredded coconut
   Powdered sugar

Thoroughly stir together cake mix, rolled oats, and wheat germ. Beat eggs; add light molasses, milk, and cooking oil. Mix well. Stir into dry mixture; blend just till moistened. Stir in shredded coconut. Spread in lightly greased 15½x10½x1-inch baking pan. Bake at 375° about 20 minutes. Cool; sift powdered sugar over top. Cut into bars. Makes 60.

Toffee Bars

½ cup sugar
½ cup butter *or* margarine,
   softened
½ teaspoon salt
1 cup all-purpose flour
1 14-ounce can *sweetened
   condensed* milk
2 tablespoons butter *or*
   margarine
¼ teaspon salt
2 teaspoons vanilla
   Fudge Frosting

Cream together sugar, ½ cup butter, and ½ teaspoon salt; stir in flour. Pat into ungreased 13x9x2-inch baking pan. Bake at 350° till lightly browned, about 15 minutes. In heavy saucepan cook and stir sweetened condensed milk, 2 tablespoons butter, and ¼ teapoon salt over low heat till butter melts. Cook and stir over medium heat for 5 minutes. (Mixture will thicken and become smooth.) Stir in vanilla. Spread over baked layer. Bake at 350° till golden, 12 to 15 minutes. Spread warm cookies with Fudge Frosting. While cookies are warm, cut into bars and remove from pan. Makes 48.

Fudge Frosting: In small saucepan melt one 1-ounce square *unsweetened chocolate* and 2 tablespoons *butter or margarine* over low heat, stirring constantly. Remove from heat; stir in 1½ cups sifted *powdered sugar* and 1 teaspoon *vanilla*. Blend in *hot water* (about 2 tablespoons) to make frosting of almost pourable consistency.

Chocolate Revel Bars

2 cups packed brown sugar
1 cup butter *or* margarine,
   softened
2 eggs
2 teaspoons vanilla
2½ cups all-purpose flour
1 teaspoon baking soda
1 teaspoon salt
3 cups quick-cooking rolled
   oats
1 14-ounce can *sweetened
   condensed* milk
1½ cups semisweet chocolate
   pieces
2 tablespoons butter *or*
   margarine
½ teaspoon salt
½ cup chopped walnuts
2 teaspoons vanilla

In large bowl cream together brown sugar and 1 cup butter till fluffy. Add eggs and 2 teaspoons vanilla; beat well. Stir together flour, soda, and 1 teaspoon salt; stir in oats. Stir into creamed mixture till blended. Set aside.

In heavy saucepan heat together sweetened condensed milk, chocolate, 2 tablespoons butter, and ½ teaspoon salt over low heat, stirring till smooth. Remove from heat; stir in nuts and 2 teaspoons vanilla.

Pat ⅔ of the oat mixture in bottom of ungreased 15½x10½x1-inch baking pan. Spread chocolate mixture over oat layer; dot with remaining oat mixture. Bake at 350° for 25 to 30 minutes. Cool; cut into bars. Makes 75.

Quick and nutritious *Cereal-Spice Bars* get a speedy start
with a spice cake mix. They're an especially good choice for busy cooks.

Puddings

Vanilla Pudding

½ cup sugar
2 tablespoons cornstarch
¼ teaspoon salt
2 cups milk
2 beaten egg yolks *or*
 1 beaten egg
2 tablespoons butter *or*
 margarine
1½ teaspoons vanilla

In medium saucepan combine the sugar, cornstarch, and salt. Stir in milk. Cook and stir over medium heat till thickened and bubbly. Cook and stir 2 minutes more. Remove from heat. Gradually stir about 1 cup of the hot mixture into egg yolks or egg. Return to mixture in saucepan. Bring to boil; cook and stir 2 minutes more. Remove from heat. Stir in butter or margarine and vanilla till butter melts. Pour into a bowl. Cover the surface with clear plastic wrap or waxed paper to prevent "skin" from forming. Chill without stirring. To serve, spoon into sherbet or dessert dishes. Makes 4 or 5 servings.

Chocolate Pudding: Prepare Vanilla Pudding as above *except* increase the sugar to ¾ cup. Add two 1-ounce squares *unsweetened chocolate,* chopped, with the milk.

Tapioca Fluff Pudding

½ cup sugar
¼ cup quick-cooking tapioca
¼ teaspoon salt
4 cups milk
3 slightly beaten egg yolks
1½ teaspoons vanilla
3 egg whites

In large saucepan combine sugar, tapioca, and salt. Stir in milk; let stand 5 minutes. Stir in egg yolks. Bring mixture to a full boil, about 10 minutes, stirring constantly. Remove from heat (mixture will be thin). Stir in vanilla.

Beat egg whites till stiff peaks form. Put ⅓ of the egg whites into a large bowl. Slowly stir in the tapioca mixture. Fold in the remaining egg whites, leaving little fluffs of egg white. Cover and chill. To serve, spoon into sherbet or dessert dishes. Makes 8 to 10 servings.

Baked Pineapple Tapioca

1 20-ounce can pineapple
 chunks (juice pack)
½ cup sugar
3 tablespoons quick-cooking
 tapioca
1 tablespoon lemon juice
½ teaspoon salt
 Dash ground nutmeg
 Frozen whipped dessert
 topping, thawed
½ cup chopped walnuts

In a bowl combine *undrained* pineapple, sugar, tapioca, lemon juice, salt, nutmeg, and ¾ cup *hot water*. Let stand 10 minutes. Pour into a 1-quart casserole. Bake, uncovered, at 325° till tapioca granules are clear and pudding is thick, 40 to 50 minutes; stir occasionally. Cool slightly. Serve topped with whipped dessert topping and sprinkled with chopped walnuts. Makes 6 servings.

Indian Pudding

3 cups milk
½ cup molasses
⅓ cup yellow cornmeal
½ teaspoon ground ginger
½ teaspoon ground cinnamon
1 tablespoon butter

In saucepan combine milk and molasses; stir in cornmeal, ginger, cinnamon, and ¼ teaspoon *salt*. Cook and stir till thick, about 10 minutes. Stir in butter. Turn into an ungreased 1-quart casserole. Bake, uncovered, at 300° about 1 hour. Makes 6 servings.

Pots de Crème

1 cup light cream
1 4-ounce package sweet
   cooking chocolate,
   coarsely chopped
1 tablespoon sugar
   Dash salt
3 beaten egg yolks
½ teaspoon vanilla
   Whipped cream (optional)

In small saucepan combine light cream, chocolate, sugar, and salt. Cook and stir over medium-low heat till blended, smooth, and *slightly thickened*. Gradually blend about half of the hot mixture into beaten egg yolks; return to saucepan. Cook and stir over medium-low heat 2 to 3 minutes more. Remove from heat; stir in vanilla. Pour into 4 to 6 pots de crème cups or *small* sherbet dishes. Cover and chill several hours or overnight till firm. Garnish with whipped cream, if desired. Makes 4 to 6 servings.

Saucepan Rice Pudding

3 cups milk
½ cup long grain rice
⅓ cup raisins
¼ teaspoon salt
1 tablespoon butter *or*
   margarine
¼ cup sugar
¼ teaspoon ground cinnamon

In medium heavy saucepan bring milk to boiling; stir in *un-cooked* rice, raisins, and salt. Cover and cook over low heat, stirring occasionally, till most of the milk is absorbed, 30 to 40 minutes. (Mixture may appear curdled.) Spoon into dessert dishes. Dot with butter and sprinkle with a mixture of the sugar and cinnamon. Makes 6 servings.

Baked Rice Pudding

2 cups milk
½ cup long grain rice
½ cup raisins
¼ cup butter *or* margarine
3 beaten eggs
2 cups milk
½ cup sugar
1 teaspoon vanilla
½ teaspoon salt
   Ground nutmeg *or* cinnamon
   Light cream

In medium heavy saucepan bring 2 cups milk, *uncooked* rice, and raisins to boiling; reduce heat. Cover and cook over very low heat till rice is tender, about 15 minutes. Remove from heat; stir in butter till melted. In mixing bowl combine eggs, 2 cups milk, sugar, vanilla, and salt.

Gradually stir rice mixture into egg mixture. Pour into 10x6x2-inch baking dish. Bake at 325° for 30 minutes. Stir well; sprinkle with nutmeg or cinnamon. Bake till knife inserted halfway between center and edge comes out clean, 15 to 20 minutes more. Serve warm or chilled with light cream. Makes 6 servings.

Bread Pudding

4 eggs
2 cups milk
⅓ cup sugar
½ teaspoon ground cinnamon
   or finely shredded orange
   peel
½ teaspoon vanilla
¼ teaspoon salt
2½ cups dry bread cubes
   (3½ slices)
⅓ cup raisins *or* snipped
   dried apricots

In mixing bowl beat together eggs, milk, sugar, cinnamon or orange peel, vanilla, and salt. Place bread cubes in an 8x1½-inch round baking dish. Sprinkle raisins or apricots over bread. Pour egg mixture over all. Bake at 325° till knife inserted off-center comes out clean, 40 to 45 minutes. Cool slightly. Makes 6 servings.

Dip your spoon into luscious *Butterscotch Crunch* and enjoy the
extraordinary flavor of chocolate-coated English toffee bars layered with creamy pudding.

Butterscotch Crunch

½ cup packed brown sugar
3 tablespoons cornstarch
¼ teaspoon salt
3 cups milk
3 beaten egg yolks
½ cup packed brown sugar
3 tablespoons butter *or*
    margarine
1½ teaspoons vanilla
3 1⅛-ounce chocolate-coated
    English toffee bars,
    crushed (about ¾ cup)
⅓ cup toasted coconut

In large saucepan combine ½ cup brown sugar, cornstarch, and salt. Stir in milk. Cook and stir over medium heat till thickened and bubbly. Gradually stir about 1 cup of the hot mixture into egg yolks. Return to saucepan. Bring to boil; cook and stir 2 minutes more. Remove from heat. Add remaining ½ cup brown sugar, butter or margarine, and vanilla, stirring gently just till combined. Cover surface of pudding with waxed paper or clear plastic wrap; cool without stirring. Combine crushed toffee bars and coconut. In 4 to 6 sherbet dishes or parfait glasses alternate layers of pudding and coconut mixtures. Repeat layers. Chill. Makes 4 to 6 servings.

Baked Custard

4 eggs
2 cups milk
½ cup sugar
1 teaspoon vanilla
¼ teaspoon salt
    Ground nutmeg (optional)

In a medium bowl beat eggs. Stir in milk, sugar, vanilla, and salt. Place six 6-ounce custard cups in a 13x9x2-inch baking pan. Divide egg mixture among the custard cups. Sprinkle mixture with ground nutmeg, if desired. Place on oven rack. Pour boiling water into pan around custard cups to depth of 1 inch. Bake at 325° till knife inserted near the center comes out clean, 30 to 40 minutes. Serve warm or chilled. To unmold chilled custard, first loosen edge with spatula or knife; slip point of knife down side to let in air. Invert onto serving plate. Makes 6 servings.

Stirred Custard

3 slightly beaten eggs
2 cups milk
¼ cup sugar
    Dash salt
1 teaspoon vanilla

In a heavy saucepan combine the eggs, milk, sugar, and salt. Cook and stir over medium heat till egg mixture coats a metal spoon, about 12 minutes. Pour custard mixture into a medium bowl; set inside a larger bowl filled with ice. Stir in the vanilla; stir gently 1 to 2 minutes. Cover surface of custard with clear plastic wrap; chill in refrigerator. Makes 6 servings.

Lemon Pudding Cake

¾ cup sugar
¼ cup all-purpose flour
    Dash salt
3 tablespoons butter *or*
    margarine, melted
1½ teaspoons finely shredded
    lemon peel
¼ cup lemon juice
3 beaten egg yolks
1½ cups milk
3 egg whites

In large mixing bowl combine sugar, flour, and salt. Stir in butter or margarine, lemon peel, and juice. In small bowl combine egg yolks and milk; add to flour mixture. Beat egg whites till stiff peaks form. Fold egg whites into flour mixture. Turn into ungreased 8x8x2-inch baking pan.

Place in larger baking pan on oven rack. Pour hot tap water into larger pan to depth of 1 inch. Bake at 350° till top is golden brown and cake springs back and leaves no imprint when lightly touched, 35 to 40 minutes. Serve warm or chilled in dessert dishes. Makes 6 to 9 servings.

Ginger-Lemon Pudding Cake

1⅓ **cups all-purpose flour**
½ **cup packed brown sugar**
1 **tablespoon baking powder**
1 **teaspoon ground cinnamon**
½ **teaspoon salt**
½ **teaspoon ground ginger**
½ **cup water**
¼ **cup light molasses**
¼ **cup cooking oil**
⅓ **cup chopped nuts**
1½ **cups water**
½ **cup packed brown sugar**
½ **of a 6-ounce can frozen**
   lemonade concentrate, thawed
   (6 tablespoons)
   Vanilla ice cream

Stir together flour, ½ cup brown sugar, baking powder, cinnamon, salt, and ginger. Combine the ½ cup water, molasses, and oil. Stir into dry ingredients till nearly smooth; fold in nuts. Turn into an ungreased 8x8x2-inch baking dish.

Bring 1½ cups water to boiling; stir in ½ cup brown sugar and lemonade concentrate. Pour carefully over batter in baking dish. Bake, uncovered, at 350° till done, 40 to 45 minutes. Serve warm with ice cream. Serves 6.

Baked Pumpkin Pudding

6 **tablespoons butter *or***
   margarine
¾ **cup packed brown sugar**
¼ **cup granulated sugar**
2 **eggs**
1½ **cups all-purpose flour**
½ **teaspoon salt**
½ **teaspoon baking soda**
½ **teaspoon ground cinnamon**
½ **teaspoon ground ginger**
¼ **teaspoon ground nutmeg**
¾ **cup mashed cooked pumpkin**
   ***or* canned pumpkin**
½ **cup buttermilk**
½ **cup chopped walnuts**
   Whipped cream (optional)

Cream butter and sugars together till light; beat in eggs. Stir together flour, salt, soda, cinnamon, ginger, and nutmeg. Combine pumpkin and buttermilk; add to creamed mixture alternately with dry ingredients, mixing well after each addition. Fold in chopped walnuts.

Spoon mixture into a greased and floured 6½-cup ring mold; cover tightly with foil. Bake at 350° for 1 hour. Let stand 10 minutes. Unmold. Serve with whipped cream, if desired. Makes 12 to 16 servings.

Apple Bread Pudding

3 **cups dry bread cubes**
   (4 slices)
1½ **cups applesauce**
⅛ **teaspoon ground cinnamon**
   Dash ground nutmeg
2 **tablespoons butter *or***
   margarine
2 **cups milk**
2 **beaten eggs**
½ **cup sugar**
½ **teaspoon vanilla**
   Dash salt
   Ground cinnamon

In a buttered 8x8x2-inch baking pan layer *half* the dry bread cubes. Combine applesauce, the ⅛ teaspoon cinnamon, and nutmeg. Spread applesauce mixture over bread cubes. Layer remaining bread cubes atop; dot with butter.

Combine milk, eggs, sugar, vanilla, and salt. Pour over bread mixture. Lightly sprinkle cinnamon over top. Bake, uncovered, at 350° till knife inserted just off-center comes out clean, 55 to 60 minutes. Makes 6 servings.

Fruit Desserts

Rumtopf

3 medium oranges
3 medium pears, cored and diced
1 cup maraschino cherries
1 cup sugar
1 cup rum

Peel, section, and cut up oranges over bowl to catch juice. In crock combine cut up oranges, pears, and maraschino cherries. Stir in sugar; pour in juice from sectioned oranges and rum. Cover. Refrigerate for 2 weeks. Serve as compote or over ice cream or cake. (*To keep Rumtopf going:* For every cup of fruit removed, add 1 cup of fruit, ⅓ cup sugar, and ⅓ cup rum. Keep refrigerated.)

Fruit Compote Supreme

1 16-ounce can peach slices
1 cup dried apricots
½ cup packed brown sugar
1 teaspoon grated orange peel
⅓ cup orange juice
½ teaspoon grated lemon peel
2 tablespoons lemon juice
1 16-ounce can pitted dark
   sweet cherries, drained

In 10x6x2-inch baking dish, combine peaches, apricots, brown sugar, orange peel, orange juice, lemon peel, and lemon juice. Cover; bake at 350° for 45 minutes. Stir in dark sweet cherries; bake, covered, 15 minutes more. Makes 6 to 8 servings.

Fruit Melange

1 16-ounce can pitted dark
   sweet cherries
1 pint fresh strawberries
1 medium cantaloupe, cut into
   balls (about 2½ cups)
1 15¼-ounce can pineapple
   chunks, drained
½ cup orange marmalade
¼ cup hot water
1 teaspoon finely chopped
   candied ginger
1 banana, sliced (1 cup)

Drain and halve cherries. Slice strawberries. Chill fruits; layer cherries, strawberries, cantaloupe, and pineapple in large glass bowl. Combine orange marmalade, hot water, and candied ginger. Drizzle over fruit. Chill.

Arrange banana atop fruit mixture. (To keep banana from darkening, dip in ascorbic acid color keeper or lemon juice mixed with a little water.) Makes 12 servings.

Cherries Jubilee

1 16-ounce can pitted dark
   sweet cherries
¼ cup sugar
2 tablespoons cornstarch
¼ cup brandy, kirsch, *or* cherry
   brandy
   Vanilla ice cream

Drain cherries, reserving syrup. Add enough cold water to syrup to make 1 cup. In saucepan combine sugar and cornstarch; gradually stir in syrup-water mixture, mixing well. Cook over medium heat, stirring constantly, till mixture has thickened and is bubbly. Remove from heat; stir in cherries. Turn mixture into blazer pan of chafing dish. Set pan over hot water (bain-marie).

Heat brandy or kirsch in small saucepan. Ignite and pour over cherry mixture. Stir to blend into sauce. Serve immediately over ice cream. Makes 6 to 8 servings.

Fresh Pear Dumplings

Pastry for Double-Crust Pie (see recipe, page 427)
6 **small pears, peeled and cored**
1 **3-ounce package cream cheese, softened**
2 **tablespoons chopped walnuts, toasted**
6 **teaspoons sugar**
1½ **cups water**
1¼ **cups sugar**
¼ **cup red cinnamon candies**
2 **tablespoons butter *or* margarine**

Prepare pastry according to recipe. On lightly floured surface roll pastry into 21x14-inch rectangle; cut into six 7-inch squares. Place one pear upright on each square. Stir together cream cheese and nuts. Fill center of *each* pear with about 1 tablespoon cheese mixture; sprinkle 1 teaspoon sugar over each. Moisten edges of pastry with water. Bring corners to center; overlap and pinch edges to seal. Place in 11x7½x1½-inch baking pan.

In saucepan combine the water, the 1¼ cups sugar, and candies; cook till candies dissolve. Bring to boiling; stir in butter or margarine. Pour over dumplings. Bake at 400° for 35 to 40 minutes. Serve warm; pass light cream, if desired. Makes 6 servings.

Nectarine Quick Shortcake

1½ **cups packaged biscuit mix**
½ **cup milk**
1 **egg**
2 **tablespoons granulated sugar**
½ **teaspoon grated lemon peel**
2 **nectarines**
2 **tablespoons butter *or* margarine**
⅓ **cup granulated sugar**
2 **tablespoons brown sugar**
½ **teaspoon ground cinnamon**
Dairy sour cream

In mixing bowl combine biscuit mix, milk, egg, the 2 tablespoons granulated sugar, and lemon peel; stir just till dry ingredients are moistened. Spread batter in greased 8x8x2-inch baking pan. Peel and pit nectarines; cut into ¼-inch thick slices. Arrange nectarine slices in rows atop batter. Melt butter or margarine; drizzle over nectarine slices. Mix the ⅓ cup granulated sugar, brown sugar, and cinnamon; sprinkle over nectarine slices. Bake at 400° for 18 to 20 minutes. Serve warm topped with sour cream. Makes 9 servings.

Citrus Crunch Dessert

1 **cup all-purpose flour**
⅓ **cup packed brown sugar**
½ **cup butter *or* margarine**
1 **cup quick-cooking rolled oats**
¼ **cup flaked coconut**
⅓ **cup granulated sugar**
1 **tablespoon cornstarch**
½ **of a 6-ounce can frozen orange juice concentrate, thawed (6 tablespoons)**
1 **16-ounce can orange and grapefruit sections**
Vanilla ice cream

Combine flour and brown sugar. Cut in butter or margarine till mixture resembles fine crumbs; stir in oats and coconut. Pat *half* the crumb mixture evenly into an 8x8x2-inch baking pan; set remaining crumb mixture aside.

In saucepan combine granulated sugar and cornstarch; blend in orange juice concentrate. Drain orange and grapefruit sections, reserving syrup. Add reserved syrup to cornstarch mixture. Cook and stir till thickened and bubbly; stir in orange and grapefruit sections.

Pour fruit mixture atop crumb mixture in pan; sprinkle with reserved crumbs. Bake, uncovered, at 350° for 30 to 35 minutes. Serve warm with ice cream. Makes 6 servings.

Fresh Strawberry Cobbler

Cobbler Topper (see page 446)
⅔ cup sugar
2 tablespoons cornstarch
1½ cups water
4 cups fresh strawberries
1 teaspoon vanilla
1 tablespoon sugar
Vanilla ice cream

Prepare Cobbler Topper; set aside. In saucepan combine the ⅔ cup sugar and cornstarch. Stir in water; cook and stir till thickened and bubbly. Cut any large berries in half. Add berries to mixture in saucepan; cook and stir till bubbly, about 5 minutes longer. Stir in vanilla.

Turn into a 2-quart casserole. Drop topper into 8 mounds atop *hot* fruit. Sprinkle with the 1 tablespoon sugar. Bake, uncovered, at 425° till lightly browned, about 25 minutes. Serve warm with ice cream. Makes 8 servings.

Apple and Raisin Cobbler

Cobbler Topper (see page 446)
½ cup packed brown sugar
2 tablespoons cornstarch
¼ teaspoon ground ginger
1¼ cups water
¼ cup raisins
6 cups sliced peeled apples
1 tablespoon lemon juice
1 tablespoon butter *or* margarine
1 tablespoon granulated sugar
Vanilla ice cream

Prepare Cobbler Topper; set aside. In saucepan combine the brown sugar, cornstarch, and ginger. Stir in water and raisins. Cook and stir till thickened and bubbly. Stir in apples, lemon juice, and butter. Cook till apples are hot, about 5 minutes. Turn into a 2-quart casserole.

Drop topper into 8 mounds atop *hot* fruit. Sprinkle with the granulated sugar. Bake, uncovered, at 425° till lightly browned, about 20 minutes. Serve warm with vanilla ice cream. Makes 8 servings.

Peach-Pecan Dessert

1 30-ounce can peach slices
¼ cup sugar
2 tablespoons cornstarch
¼ teaspoon salt
1 tablespoon lemon juice
Few drops almond extract
2 egg whites
¼ teaspoon cream of tartar
¼ teaspoon ground cinnamon
¼ cup sugar
2 egg yolks
¼ cup all-purpose flour
¼ cup chopped pecans

Drain peaches, reserving syrup. In saucepan stir together ¼ cup sugar, cornstarch, and salt. Stir in reserved syrup; cook and stir till thickened and bubbly. Remove from heat; stir in lemon juice and almond extract. Set aside a few peach slices for garnish; stir remaining into hot mixture. Set aside.

Beat egg whites with cream of tartar and cinnamon till soft peaks form, about 1 minute. Gradually add ¼ cup sugar, beating till stiff peaks form, about 3 minutes. Beat egg yolks till thick and lemon-colored, about 4 minutes. Fold yolks into whites; fold in flour.

Return peach mixture in saucepan to boiling; turn into a 1½-quart casserole. Immediately top *hot* fruit with batter, spreading evenly to edges. Sprinkle with pecans. Bake, uncovered, at 350° till done, about 40 minutes. Garnish with reserved peach slices. Makes 6 servings.

Elegant Fruit Combo

1 16-ounce can peach halves
1 cup fresh cranberries
¼ cup sugar
1 large banana, sliced
1 pint vanilla ice cream

Drain peaches, reserving syrup. Place peach halves in a bowl; cover and set aside. In a 1-quart casserole stir together reserved peach syrup, cranberries, and sugar. Bake, covered, at 350° for 1¼ hours.

To serve, stir reserved peach halves and banana slices into cranberry mixture. Top each serving with a scoop of vanilla ice cream. Makes 6 servings.

Cheese-Baked Apples

3 tablespoons granulated sugar
2 tablespoons brown sugar
2 tablespoons all-purpose flour
¾ teaspoon ground cinnamon
¼ teaspoon salt
⅓ cup water
1 tablespoon lemon juice
6 medium baking apples, peeled, cored, and cut into eighths
½ cup shredded Cheddar cheese (2 ounces)

In mixing bowl combine sugars, flour, cinnamon, and salt; stir in water and lemon juice. Add apples; stir to coat.

Arrange apples in a 9-inch pie plate; drizzle sugar mixture over all. Bake, covered, at 350° till apples are tender, 45 to 50 minutes. Uncover; sprinkle with cheese. Bake, uncovered, 5 minutes more. Makes 6 servings.

Cranberry-Peach Cobbler

Cobbler Topper (see below)
½ cup sugar
1 tablespoon cornstarch
1 cup cranberry juice cocktail
3 cups sliced peeled fresh *or* frozen peaches (6 medium)
½ cup fresh *or* frozen cranberries

Prepare Cobbler Topper; set aside. In saucepan combine sugar and cornstarch. Stir in juice; cook and stir till thickened and bubbly. Stir in peaches and cranberries. Cook, uncovered, till cranberry skins pop, about 5 minutes.

Turn into a 1½-quart casserole. Immediately spoon topper in 8 mounds atop *hot* fruit. Bake, uncovered, at 400° for 20 to 25 minutes. Serve warm with vanilla ice cream, if desired. Makes 8 servings.

Cobbler Topper

1 cup all-purpose flour
2 tablespoons sugar
1½ teaspoons baking powder
¼ teaspoon salt
¼ cup butter *or* margarine
1 beaten egg
¼ cup milk

Stir together flour, sugar, baking powder, and salt. Cut in butter till crumbly. Combine egg and milk; add all at once to dry ingredients. Stir just till all dry ingredients are moistened. Continue as directed in recipe.

Fresh Fruit Crisp

½ cup quick-cooking rolled oats
½ cup packed brown sugar
¼ cup all-purpose flour
½ teaspoon ground cinnamon
Dash salt
¼ cup butter *or* margarine
5 cups sliced peeled peaches, apples, *or* pears
Vanilla ice cream *or* light cream

Combine oats, brown sugar, flour, cinnamon, and salt; cut in butter till mixture is crumbly. Set aside.

Place fruit in a 10x6x2-inch baking dish. Sprinkle oat mixture over fruit. Bake, uncovered, at 350° till fruit is tender, about 40 minutes. Serve warm with ice cream or light cream. Makes 6 servings.

Fine examples of casserole desserts, *Cheese-Baked Apples* and *Cranberry-Peach Cobbler* are made with fresh fruits. These colorful meal-cappers go together with very little effort.

Ice Cream and Frozen Desserts

Marshmallow Ice Cream

2 eggs
¾ cup sugar
1 7-ounce jar marshmallow
   creme
3 cups milk
1 cup whipping cream
1½ teaspoons vanilla

In large mixing bowl beat eggs till thickened and lemon-colored; gradually add sugar, beating till mixture is thick. Stir in marshmallow creme; stir in milk, whipping cream, and vanilla. Freeze in 1-gallon ice cream freezer following manufacturer's directions. Makes 1½ quarts.

Vanilla Custard Ice Cream

1½ cups sugar
¼ cup all-purpose flour
½ teaspoon salt
4 cups milk
4 beaten eggs
4 cups whipping cream
3 tablespoons vanilla

In large saucepan stir together sugar, flour, and salt. Gradually stir in milk. Cook over medium-high heat, stirring constantly, till thickened and bubbly. Cook 1 minute more. Stir about 1 cup of the hot mixture into beaten eggs; return to remaining hot mixture in saucepan. Cook and stir 1 minute more. Cool; cover and chill at least 1½ hours. Stir in whipping cream and vanilla. Freeze in 1-gallon ice cream freezer following manufacturer's directions. Makes 3 quarts.

Fresh Strawberry Ice Cream

1 envelope unflavored gelatin
¼ cup cold water
2 well-beaten egg yolks
2 cups whipping cream
1 pint strawberries, crushed
   (1½ cups)
¾ cup sugar
1½ teaspoons vanilla
¼ teaspoon salt
10 to 12 drops red food
   coloring (optional)
2 egg whites
¼ cup sugar

In measuring cup soften gelatin in cold water. Place cup over hot water in saucepan; heat and stir till gelatin dissolves. Combine egg yolks, whipping cream, strawberries, the ¾ cup sugar, vanilla, salt, and food coloring. Add gelatin; mix well. Turn into 13x9x2-inch pan; freeze. Beat egg whites to soft peaks. Gradually add the ¼ cup sugar, beating to stiff peaks.
  Break frozen strawberry mixture into chunks; beat with electric mixer till fluffy. Fold in beaten egg whites. Return to pan; freeze. Makes 8 to 10 servings.

Peanut Butter and Jelly Freeze

6 eggs
2 cups sugar
2 cups whipping cream
2 cups light cream
1 cup peanut butter
4 teaspoons vanilla
  Jelly or preserves

In mixing bowl thoroughly beat eggs, sugar, whipping cream, light cream, peanut butter, and vanilla. Turn into 13x9x2-inch pan. Cover and freeze till partially frozen. Break partially frozen mixture into chunks. Beat with electric mixer till fluffy. Return to pan. Cover; freeze firm.
  To serve, scoop frozen mixture into sherbet dishes. Drizzle jelly or preserves over each serving. Makes about 2 quarts ice cream.

Peppermint Ice Cream Roll

4 egg yolks
¼ cup granulated sugar
½ teaspoon vanilla
4 egg whites
½ cup granulated sugar
⅔ cup sifted cake flour
¼ cup unsweetened cocoa
   powder
1 teaspoon baking powder
¼ teaspoon salt
   Powdered sugar
1 quart peppermint ice cream
¼ cup crushed peppermint candy
½ of a 4½-ounce container
   frozen whipped dessert
   topping, thawed
   Crushed peppermint candy

In mixer bowl beat egg yolks till thick and lemon-colored; gradually beat in the ¼ cup granulated sugar. Add vanilla. In mixer bowl beat egg whites till soft peaks form; gradually add the ½ cup sugar, beating to stiff peaks. Fold yolk mixture into whites. Sift together flour, cocoa powder, baking powder, and salt; fold into egg mixture. Spread batter evenly in greased and floured 15x10x1-inch jelly roll pan. Bake at 375° for 10 to 12 minutes.

Immediately loosen sides and turn out onto towel sprinkled with sifted powdered sugar. Starting at narrow end, roll cake and towel together; cool. Soften ice cream to spreading consistency. Unroll cake; spread ice cream over cake. Roll cake up; freeze. To serve, stir the ¼ cup crushed candy into dessert topping. Cut cake; top each serving with dollop of topping mixture. Garnish with additional crushed candy. Makes 10 servings.

Baked Alaska

2 pints or 1 quart brick-style
   ice cream
1 1-inch-thick piece sponge
   cake or layer cake
5 egg whites
1 teaspoon vanilla
½ teaspoon cream of tartar
⅔ cup sugar

If using pints, lay ice cream bricks side by side. Measure length and width of ice cream brick or bricks. Trim cake 1 inch larger on all sides than ice cream measurements. Place cake on a piece of foil. Center ice cream on cake. Cover; freeze till cake and ice cream are firm.

At serving time, beat together egg whites, vanilla, and cream of tartar to soft peaks. Gradually add sugar, beating till stiff peaks form. Transfer cake with ice cream to baking sheet. Spread with egg white mixture, sealing to edges of cake and of baking sheet all around. Swirl to make peaks. Bake at 500° till golden, about 3 minutes. Slice and serve immediately. Makes 8 servings.

Raspberry Sherbet

6 cups fresh or frozen
   raspberries
1 teaspoon finely shredded
   lemon peel
2 egg yolks
1 tablespoon lemon juice
1 tablespoon vanilla
⅛ teaspoon salt
2 cups sugar
4 cups buttermilk
2 egg whites

Thaw raspberries, if frozen. Place half of the berries in blender container or food processor. Cover; blend till smooth. Strain purée. Repeat with remaining berries. (Purée should total 2½ to 3 cups.) Stir in lemon peel. In large mixer bowl beat together egg yolks, lemon juice, vanilla, and salt. Gradually beat in ½ cup of the sugar. Stir in raspberry puree and 1 cup of the sugar, beating till sugar is dissolved. Stir in buttermilk. In small mixer bowl beat egg whites to soft peaks. Gradually add the remaining ½ cup sugar, beating till stiff peaks form. Fold egg whites into raspberry mixture. Freeze in 1-gallon ice cream freezer following manufacturer's directions. Makes 2 quarts.

Dessert Potpourri

Pink Parfaits

1 3-ounce package strawberry-
    flavored gelatin
¾ cup boiling water
1 10-ounce package frozen
    strawberries
1 cup strawberry ice cream

In blender container combine gelatin and boiling water. Cover and blend at high speed till gelatin is dissolved, about 20 seconds. Cut in half package of frozen strawberries; allow *half* to thaw for topping. Add remaining strawberries to gelatin; blend till nearly smooth. Add strawberry ice cream, a spoonful at a time, blending till smooth after each addition. Pour mixture into 4 parfait glasses; chill. To serve, garnish with thawed strawberries. Makes 4 servings.

Banana-Peanut Parfaits

2 bananas, sliced
1 18-ounce can vanilla
    pudding, chilled
¼ cup chopped milk chocolate
    pieces *or* milk chocolate
    candy bar
¼ cup chopped peanuts

Stir banana slices into vanilla pudding. Combine chopped milk chocolate and chopped peanuts. In parfait glasses alternate layers of pudding mixture and peanut-chocolate mixture, beginning with pudding mixture and ending with peanut-chocolate mixture. (Use about ½ cup pudding mixture and 1 tablespoon peanut-chocolate mixture in each parfait.) Makes 6 servings.

Pears in Chocolate Fluff

1 29-ounce can pear halves
½ cup semisweet chocolate
    pieces
¼ cup light corn syrup
½ teaspoon vanilla
½ of a 4½-ounce container
    frozen whipped dessert
    topping, thawed
¼ cup dairy sour cream
½ cup slivered almonds, toasted

Drain pear halves thoroughly; cut into large pieces and set aside. In small saucepan combine chocolate pieces and corn syrup. Heat, stirring constantly, just till chocolate is melted; stir in vanilla. Cool thoroughly.
    Stir together thawed whipped dessert topping and dairy sour cream; fold into cooled chocolate mixture. Add pear pieces and ⅓ *cup* of the slivered toasted almonds. Chill thoroughly. Spoon chilled chocolate mixture into dessert dishes; top with remaining almonds. Makes 6 servings.

Coffee Cheesecakes

1 tablespoon butter *or*
    margarine
½ cup crushed vanilla wafers
1 tablespoon sugar
4 egg whites
½ cup sugar
2 8-ounce packages cream
    cheese, softened
¼ cup coffee liqueur

Melt butter or margarine. Combine with the crushed wafers and the 1 tablespoon sugar. Press into bottom of six 6-ounce custard cups. In large mixer bowl beat egg whites to soft peaks; gradually add the ½ cup sugar, beating to stiff peaks. Beat together cream cheese and liqueur. Fold *half* of the egg white mixture into cheese mixture. Fold into remaining egg white mixture. Fill *each* prepared custard cup with about ⅔ cup filling. Bake at 350° for 20 minutes. (Cakes will puff, then fall when removed from oven.) Cool in cups. To serve, dip bottom of cup in warm water. Loosen sides of cake with knife; invert onto serving dish. Cover; chill. Drizzle with additional liqueur, if desired. Makes 6 servings.

Banana-Peanut Parfaits are so easy to make even the kids can make them. Keep a can of vanilla pudding in the refrigerator so you can make this tasty dessert anytime.

Praline Cheesecake

1¼ cups crushed graham
    crackers
¼ cup granulated sugar
¼ cup chopped pecans,
    toasted
¼ cup butter *or* margarine,
    melted
3 8-ounce packages cream
    cheese, softened
1 cup packed brown sugar
1 5⅓-ounce can evaporated
    milk (⅔ cup)
2 tablespoons all-purpose
    flour
1½ teaspoons vanilla
3 eggs
1 cup pecan halves, toasted
1 cup dark corn syrup
¼ cup cornstarch
2 tablespoons brown sugar
1 teaspoon vanilla

In small mixing bowl combine crushed crackers, the granulated sugar, and the chopped pecans. Stir in the melted butter or margarine. Press crumb mixture over the bottom and 1½ inches up the sides of a 9-inch spring-form pan. Bake at 350° for 10 minutes.

Meanwhile, beat together cream cheese, the 1 cup brown sugar, the evaporated milk, flour, and the 1½ teaspoons vanilla. Add eggs; beat just till blended. Pour into baked crust. Bake at 350° till set, 50 to 55 minutes. Cool in pan 30 minutes; loosen sides and remove rim from spring-form pan. Cool completely. Arrange nut halves atop cheesecake.

Before serving, combine corn syrup, cornstarch, and the 2 tablespoons brown sugar in a small saucepan. Cook and stir till thickened and bubbly. Remove from heat; stir in the 1 teaspoon vanilla. Cool slightly. To serve, spoon some of the warm sauce over the nuts on the cheesecake. Pass remaining sauce. Makes 12 to 16 servings.

Apricot Cream Fondue

1 30-ounce can unpeeled apricot
    halves, drained
⅓ cup sugar
1 tablespoon cornstarch
¾ cup whipping cream
1 tablespoon lemon juice
Pound cake cubes
Angel cake cubes
Apple slices
Banana slices

Blend apricots in blender till smooth, or press through a sieve or food mill. In saucepan combine sugar and cornstarch. Stir in apricot puree, whipping cream, and lemon juice. Cook, stirring constantly, till thickened and bubbly. Transfer to fondue pot; place over fondue burner. Spear cake cube or fruit piece with fondue fork and dip into fondue, swirling to coat. Makes 6 to 8 servings.

Chocolate Fondue

8 1-ounce squares semisweet
    chocolate
1 14-ounce can *sweetened
    condensed* milk
⅓ cup milk
Pound *or* angel cake cubes,
    banana *or* pineapple
    chunks, strawberries, and/or
    marshmallows

In heavy saucepan melt chocolate over *low* heat. Stir in sweetened condensed milk and milk till well blended. Heat through over low heat. Transfer to fondue pot; place over fondue burner. (If mixture becomes thick, stir in a little more milk.) Spear cake, fruit, or marshmallow with fondue fork; dip into fondue, swirling to coat. Makes 8 servings.

Coffee Fondue: Dissolve 2 tablespoons instant coffee crystals in the milk; blend into chocolate mixture.

Mint Fondue: Break up 4 ounces creme-filled mint patties (9 patties). Melt mint patties with chocolate; add sweetened condensed milk and milk.

Basic Eclairs

½ **cup butter** *or* **margarine**
1 **cup boiling water**
1 **cup all-purpose flour**
¼ **teaspoon salt**
4 **eggs**

In saucepan melt butter or margarine in boiling water. Add flour and salt all at once; stir vigorously. Cook and stir till mixture forms a ball that doesn't separate. Remove from heat; cool slightly. Add eggs, one at a time; beat after each addition till smooth. Shape on greased baking sheet as directed in recipe. Bake at 400° till golden and puffy, 30 to 35 minutes. Remove from oven; split. Cool on rack.

Vanilla Eclairs

Basic Eclairs
1 **3-** *or* **3¼-ounce package regular vanilla pudding mix**
1½ **cups milk**
1 **cup whipping cream**
¼ **teaspoon vanilla**
Sifted powdered sugar
1 **slightly beaten egg white**
Small multicolored decorative candies

Prepare Basic Eclair dough. Put dough through a pastry tube or spread with spoon, making strips 4x1½ inches on greased baking sheet. Bake and cool as directed in Basic Eclairs recipe.

For filling prepare pudding mix according to package directions, *except* use the 1½ cups milk instead of the liquid called for. Chill thoroughly. Whip cream to soft peaks. Beat pudding smooth; fold in whipped cream and vanilla. Fill eclairs with pudding mixture. Stir enough powdered sugar (about 1¼ cups) into egg white to make of spreading consistency; frost tops of eclairs. Sprinkle with candies. Chill till served. Makes 10.

Coffee and Ice Cream Eclairs

Basic Eclairs
1 **quart vanilla** *or* **coffee ice cream**
1 **cup light corn syrup**
1½ **cups water**
1 **tablespoon instant coffee crystals**
3 **tablespoons cornstarch**
2 **tablespoons butter** *or* **margarine**
1 **teaspoon vanilla**
½ **cup chopped pecans**

Prepare Basic Eclair dough. Using about ¼ cup dough for each eclair, onto greased baking sheet drop dough from spoon 2 inches apart, leaving 6 inches between rows. Shape each mound into a 4x1-inch rectangle, rounding sides and piling dough on top. Bake, cool, and split as directed in Basic Eclairs recipe.

Fill bottom halves of eclairs with vanilla or coffee ice cream; place on tops. Keep in freezer till serving time.

Meanwhile, to make sauce, measure corn syrup into saucepan. Combine water and coffee crystals; stir in cornstarch. Stir into syrup in pan. Cook, stirring constantly, till thickened and bubbly. Remove from heat; add butter or margarine and vanilla. Stir till butter melts; stir in pecans. Serve warm sauce over eclairs. Makes 10 to 12.

Cream puff tips

Eclairs and cream puffs are made from the same dough. They are just shaped differently. For cream puffs, prepare the Basic Eclair dough. Drop the dough by rounded tablespoons onto a greased baking sheet. Bake at 400° till golden brown and puffy, about 30 minutes. Split; cool on rack. Fill with your favorite filling. For a crisp, hollow puff, remove the excess center membrane from each puff before cooling.

Lemon Mousse

¾ **to 1 cup sugar**
1 **envelope unflavored gelatin**
1½ **teaspoons cornstarch**
2 **teaspoons finely shredded lemon peel**
1 **cup lemon juice**
4 **beaten egg yolks**
1½ **cups whipping cream**
2 **tablespoons orange liqueur**
6 **stiff-beaten egg whites**

In a 1½-quart saucepan combine sugar, gelatin, cornstarch, and lemon peel. Stir in lemon juice and egg yolks. Cook and stir till thickened and bubbly. Remove from heat; cover surface with clear plastic wrap. Cool, then chill. Beat whipping cream to soft peaks. Put chilled lemon mixture in blender container; add orange liqueur. Cover and blend till smooth. Pour mixture into large mixing bowl; fold in whipped cream. Fold in egg whites. Turn into serving bowl. Cover and chill 4 to 6 hours or overnight. Garnish with lemon slices, if desired. Makes 12 to 16 servings.

Soufflé Grand Marnier

Granulated sugar
¼ **cup all-purpose flour**
¼ **cup granulated sugar**
¼ **cup butter *or* margarine, softened**
1 **cup milk**
5 **egg yolks**
2 **tablespoons Grand Marnier**
5 **egg whites**
¼ **cup granulated sugar**
Sifted powdered sugar

Lightly butter a 1½-quart soufflé dish; dust with a little granulated sugar to coat. Add foil collar, if desired. (To make collar, measure foil to go around dish; fold into thirds lengthwise. Butter well; sprinkle with more granulated sugar. With sugared side toward center, put foil collar around top of dish, extending collar 2 inches above dish; fasten securely with tape.)

In small mixing bowl stir together flour, ¼ cup granulated sugar, and the ¼ cup softened butter or margarine till forms a smooth paste.

In saucepan heat milk to boiling; immediately remove from heat and add butter-flour mixture. Return to heat and cook and stir 2 minutes. Transfer mixture to mixing bowl. Add egg yolks, one at a time, beating well after each. Stir in Grand Marnier.

Beat egg whites till foamy; continue beating to stiff peaks, gradually adding ¼ cup granulated sugar. Fold yolk mixture into whites; turn into prepared soufflé dish. Dust top heavily with powdered sugar. Bake at 400° for 30 to 35 minutes. Makes 8 servings.

Fresh Orange Bavarian Cream

½ **cup sugar**
1 **3-ounce package orange-flavored gelatin**
1 **tablespoon finely shredded orange peel**
1 **cup orange juice**
⅔ **cup water**
1 **cup whipping cream**

In mixing bowl stir sugar into orange-flavored gelatin. In saucepan combine orange peel, orange juice, and water. Bring to boiling; add to gelatin mixture, stirring till gelatin dissolves. Chill mixture till partially set (consistency of unbeaten egg whites). Meanwhile, in small mixer bowl beat whipping cream till soft peaks form. In large mixer bowl beat partially set gelatin mixture till foamy; fold in whipped cream. Pour orange mixture into eight ½-cup molds *or* one 4-cup mold. Chill till firm, about 4 hours. Unmold on serving plates. Serves 8.

Whip up easy *Blueberry Sauce* to serve over tender angel or pound cake slices.
Everyone will enjoy this sweet berry sauce so much that the slices can be served without frosting.

Blueberry Sauce

**1 10-ounce package frozen
   unsweetened blueberries**
1 cup sugar
3 tablespoons cornstarch
1 cup boiling water
3 tablespoons lemon juice
   Angel *or* pound cake slices

Thaw frozen, unsweetened blueberries; drain. In small saucepan combine sugar and cornstarch; gradually stir in boiling water. Cook, stirring constantly, till thickened and bubbly; cook 2 minutes more. Remove from heat; stir in drained blueberries and lemon juice. Cool. Serve over angel or pound cake slices. Makes 3 cups sauce.

Lemon-Cheese Dessert Bombe

1 envelope unflavored gelatin
2 tablespoons water
1 cup milk
**1 3-ounce package cream
   cheese, softened**
½ cup sugar
1 cup lemon yogurt
   Fresh strawberries, halved

In small saucepan soften gelatin in the water; stir in milk. Cook and stir till gelatin is dissolved. Combine cream cheese and sugar; stir in yogurt. Gradually blend in gelatin mixture. Pour into six ½-cup molds. Chill till set. Unmold; garnish with halved fresh strawberries, if desired. Makes 6 servings.

Applesauce Topper

1 8½-ounce can applesauce
3 tablespoons red cinnamon
    candies
4 or 5 drops red food coloring
    (optional)
1 quart vanilla ice cream,
    softened
    Angel cake slices

In saucepan combine applesauce, cinnamon candies, and food coloring. Heat till candy is dissolved. Cool. Stir cooled applesauce mixture into softened ice cream. Spoon into 9x9x2-inch pan. Freeze applesauce mixture at least 6 hours or overnight. Serve scoops of applesauce mixture on angel cake slices. Makes about 4 cups.

Butter-Rum Sauce

1 cup packed brown sugar
3 tablespoons all-purpose
    flour
¼ teaspoon salt
½ cup water
1 5⅓-ounce can
    evaporated milk (⅔ cup)
¼ cup light corn syrup
½ cup coarsely chopped salted
    mixed nuts
2 tablespoons butter *or*
    margarine
2 teaspoons rum flavoring
    Vanilla ice cream *or* angel
    cake slices

In heavy saucepan combine brown sugar, flour, and salt; stir in water. Stir in evaporated milk and corn syrup. Cook, stirring constantly, till thickened. Stir in nuts, butter or margarine, and rum flavoring. Serve warm over scoops of vanilla ice cream or slices of angel cake. Makes 2 cups sauce.

Ambrosia Sauce

1 16-ounce can fruit cocktail
2 tablespoons sugar
2 teaspoons cornstarch
    Dash salt
2 tablespoons water
2 tablespoons frozen orange
    juice concentrate, thawed
1 orange, peeled and diced
½ cup flaked coconut
    Vanilla ice cream

Drain fruit cocktail, reserving 1 cup syrup. In saucepan combine sugar, cornstarch, and salt; blend in water. Add reserved syrup and orange juice concentrate. Cook, stirring constantly, till thickened and bubbly. Stir in fruit cocktail, diced orange, and coconut. Chill. Serve over vanilla ice cream. Makes 2½ cups sauce.

Orange Sauce

¼ cup sugar
1 tablespoon cornstarch
1 cup orange juice
1 tablespoon butter *or*
    margarine
2 teaspoons lemon juice
    Vanilla ice cream

In small saucepan combine sugar and cornstarch. Stir in orange juice; cook, stirring constantly, till thickened and bubbly. Remove from heat; stir in butter or margarine and lemon juice. Serve over vanilla ice cream. Makes about 1 cup sauce.

Mocha Steamed Pudding

3 slices white bread, torn
¾ cup milk
2 eggs
¾ cup granulated sugar
1 teaspoon instant coffee
   crystals
¼ cup cooking oil
1 cup all-purpose flour
¼ cup unsweetened cocoa
   powder
2 teaspoons baking powder
¼ teaspoon salt
1 cup raisins, chopped
½ cup chopped walnuts
2 cups sifted powdered sugar
½ cup butter *or* margarine
3 tablespoons coffee liqueur
1 teaspoon vanilla

In small mixer bowl combine bread and milk; let stand for 5 to 10 minutes. Beat smooth with electric mixer. Beat in eggs and granulated sugar. Dissolve coffee crystals in ¼ cup *hot water;* stir into bread along with oil. Stir together flour, cocoa powder, baking powder, and salt. Stir into bread mixture; fold in raisins and nuts. Pour into well-greased 1½-quart mold (not ring mold). Cover with foil; tie with string. Place on wire rack in deep kettle; add boiling water to kettle to depth of 1 inch. Cover kettle; steam 2 hours, adding more water if needed. Cool 10 minutes; unmold.

For sauce, thoroughly cream together powdered sugar and butter or margarine. Beat in coffee liqueur and vanilla. Serve with warm pudding. Makes 6 servings.

Steamed Carrot Pudding

2 medium carrots, cut up
2 medium apples, peeled, cored,
   and cut up
1 medium potato, peeled
   and cut up
4 ounces suet, cut up
1 cup sugar
⅓ cup orange juice
1 beaten egg
1 teaspoon vanilla
1½ cups all-purpose flour
1½ teaspoons baking soda
1 teaspoon ground cinnamon
1 teaspoon ground nutmeg
½ teaspoon ground cloves
½ teaspoon salt
1 cup snipped pitted dates
1 cup raisins
   Brown Sugar Sauce

Grease a 2-quart mold (not ring mold). Grind together carrots, apples, potato, and suet, using coarse blade of food grinder. Combine sugar, orange juice, egg, and vanilla. Stir into carrot mixture. Stir together flour, soda, cinnamon, nutmeg, cloves, and salt. Stir into carrot mixture; fold in dates and raisins. Pour batter into greased mold. Cover mold with foil. Add water to a deep kettle to a depth of 1-inch. Place mold on rack in kettle. Bring water to boiling. Cover kettle; steam 3½ hours, adding more water if needed. Remove mold from kettle. Cool 10 minutes. Unmold; serve warm with Brown Sugar Sauce. Makes 8 to 10 servings.

Brown Sugar Sauce: In small saucepan mix ½ cup packed *brown sugar* and 2 teaspoons *cornstarch;* stir in ⅓ cup *water* and 2 tablespoons *butter or margarine.* Cook and stir till thickened and bubbly. Gradually stir hot mixture into 1 beaten *egg;* return to saucepan. Cook and stir 1 minute more. Stir in 1 teaspoon *vanilla.*

Strawberry-Eggnog Shake

1 quart strawberry ice cream
1 cup fresh strawberries,
   mashed
2 cups canned eggnog, chilled
   Ground nutmeg

Soften ice cream in a large chilled mixer bowl. Add mashed berries; beat with electric mixer just to blend. Stir in eggnog. Serve in tall chilled glasses; sprinkle with nutmeg. Makes 4 (12-ounce) servings.

Basic Dessert Crepes

1 cup all-purpose flour
1½ cups milk
2 eggs
2 tablespoons sugar
1 tablespoon cooking oil
⅛ teaspoon salt

In mixing bowl combine flour, milk, eggs, sugar, oil, and salt; beat with a rotary beater till well mixed. Heat a lightly greased 6-inch skillet. Remove from heat. Spoon in 2 tablespoons batter; lift and tilt skillet to spread batter. Return to heat; brown on one side (do not turn). Invert pan over paper toweling; remove crepe. Repeat with remaining batter, greasing skillet as needed. Makes 16 to 18 crepes.

Classic Crepes Suzette

¼ cup butter *or* margarine
¼ cup orange liqueur
¼ cup orange juice
3 tablespoons sugar
8 Basic Dessert Crepes
2 tablespoons brandy

To make sauce, in skillet combine butter or margarine, orange liqueur, orange juice, and sugar; cook and stir till bubbly. (Or, make sauce and heat crepes in chafing dish over direct heat.)

Fold each Basic Dessert Crepe in half, browned side out; fold in half again, forming a triangle. Arrange crepes in sauce in skillet. Simmer till sauce thickens slightly, spooning sauce over crepes as they heat. In small saucepan heat the brandy over low heat just till hot. Ignite and pour flaming brandy over crepes and sauce. Makes 4 servings.

Red Raspberry Crepes

1 4-ounce container whipped cream cheese, softened
10 Basic Dessert Crepes
⅓ cup toasted slivered almonds
1 10-ounce package frozen red raspberries, thawed
Cranberry juice cocktail
⅓ cup sugar
4 teaspoons cornstarch
2 tablespoons butter
2 tablespoons orange liqueur (optional)
2 teaspoons lemon juice

Spread cream cheese over unbrowned side of each Basic Dessert Crepe, leaving ¼-inch rim around edge. Sprinkle each with some toasted almonds. Roll each crepe up as for jelly roll. Cover crepes and chill.

To make raspberry sauce, drain raspberries, reserving syrup. Add enough cranberry juice cocktail to syrup to make 1½ cups. In saucepan combine sugar, cornstarch, and dash *salt*. Stir in syrup mixture. Cook, stirring constantly, till bubbly. Stir in butter, orange liqueur, lemon juice, and raspberries. Keep warm.

Arrange crepes in chafing dish or skillet; spoon warm sauce over. Cover; heat through. Makes 5 servings.

Cherry-Topped Cheese Blintzes

1 beaten egg
1 12-ounce carton dry cottage cheese (1½ cups)
2 tablespoons sugar
½ teaspoon vanilla
Dash ground cinnamon
12 Basic Dessert Crepes
2 tablespoons butter
Canned cherry pie filling
Dairy sour cream

Beat together egg, cottage cheese, sugar, vanilla, and cinnamon till nearly smooth. Spoon some cheese mixture in center of unbrowned side of a crepe. Fold two opposite edges of crepe to overlap atop filling. Fold in remaining edges, forming a square packet; repeat with remaining cheese mixture and crepes. In a skillet cook filled crepes on both sides in hot butter till heated through. Heat cherry pie filling. Serve hot crepes with warm cherry pie filling and sour cream. Makes 6 servings.

For an impressive ending to a dinner party, serve *Classic Crepes Suzette.*
This traditional flaming dessert combines crepes, folded in quarters, and a delicate orange sauce.

Almond Fudge

3 **cups sugar**
1 **cup milk**
2 **tablespoons light corn**
  syrup
¼ **teaspoon salt**
3 **tablespoons butter** *or*
  margarine
½ **teaspoon vanilla**
¼ **teaspoon almond extract**
½ **cup coarsely chopped**
  toasted almonds

Butter an 8x8x2-inch baking pan. In heavy 3-quart saucepan combine sugar, milk, corn syrup, and salt. Cook and stir over medium heat till sugar is dissolved. Clip candy thermometer to side of pan. Gently boil, without stirring, till candy thermometer registers 236° (soft-ball stage). Remove from heat. Add the 3 tablespoons butter or margarine. Do not stir. Cool, without stirring, to 110°. Add vanilla and almond extract. Beat vigorously till fudge stiffens and begins to lose its gloss. Quickly stir in almonds. Pour into buttered 8x8x2-inch baking pan. Cool; cut into squares. Makes 3 dozen pieces.

Java Fudge

3 **cups sugar**
1½ **cups light cream**
3 **tablespoons light corn**
  syrup
2 **tablespoons instant coffee**
  crystals
  Dash salt
2 **tablespoons butter** *or*
  margarine
1 **teaspoon vanilla**

Butter an 8x8x2-inch baking pan and a 3-quart saucepan. In saucepan combine sugar, light cream, corn syrup, coffee crystals, and salt. Cook, stirring constantly, till boiling. Clip candy thermometer to side of pan. Gently boil, without stirring, till candy thermometer registers 234° (thread stage). Remove from heat. Add the 2 tablespoons butter or margarine and vanilla. Cool, without stirring, to 110°. Beat till fudge starts to lose its gloss, about 10 minutes. Pour into buttered 8x8x2-inch baking pan. Cool. Cut in squares. Makes 1¾ pounds.

Christmas Divinity

2½ **cups granulated sugar**
½ **cup light corn syrup**
½ **cup water**
2 **egg whites**
½ **teaspoon vanilla**
  Sifted powdered sugar
½ **cup creamy peanut butter**

In buttered 2-quart saucepan combine granulated sugar, corn syrup, and water. Bring to boiling. Clip candy thermometer to side of pan; cook, stirring constantly, till sugar dissolves. Continue cooking to 260° (hard-ball stage); remove from heat. In large mixer bowl immediately beat egg whites to stiff peaks. Gradually pour hot syrup over egg whites, beating constantly at high speed on electric mixer. Add vanilla and beat till candy holds its shape, 4 to 5 minutes.

On towel dusted generously with powdered sugar, quickly pat candy evenly with hands to a rectangle about 10x4 inches. Dust candy lightly with powdered sugar. Using rolling pin dusted with powdered sugar, roll candy to a 16x6-inch rectangle. Spread peanut butter over candy to within ½ inch of the sides. Roll up from long side, using towel to help roll. Wrap in towel; place on baking sheet. Chill till firm, about 1 hour. Cut in half crosswise; wrap in waxed paper. Store in refrigerator. To serve, cut into ¼ inch thick slices. Makes 1½ pounds.

No-Cook Fudge

½ cup butter *or* margarine
⅓ cup boiling water
4½ cups sifted powdered sugar
½ cup nonfat dry milk powder
½ cup unsweetened cocoa powder
    Dash salt

Butter an 8x8x2-inch baking pan. Stir the ½ cup butter or margarine into boiling water. Stir till butter or margarine is melted. Beat in powdered sugar, nonfat dry milk powder, cocoa powder, and salt. Pour into buttered 8x8x2-inch baking pan. Refrigerate several hours. Cut into squares. Makes 3 dozen pieces.

Brown Sugar Peanut Brittle

1 cup granulated sugar
1 cup packed brown sugar
1 cup light corn syrup
½ cup water
¼ cup butter *or* margarine
    Dash salt
2 cups raw peanuts
1½ teaspoons baking soda

Butter two baking sheets and sides of a heavy 3-quart saucepan. In the saucepan combine granulated sugar, brown sugar, corn syrup, water, butter or margarine, and salt. Bring to boiling, stirring to dissolve sugar. Clip candy thermometer to side of pan. Cook, over medium heat, with gentle boil over entire surface to 275° (syrup turns a deep golden color), stirring constantly. Stir in peanuts; continue cooking, stirring often, till thermometer registers 295° (syrup is a dark golden color). Remove from heat. Quickly stir in soda. Immediately pour hot mixture onto buttered baking sheets. If desired, pull with forks to stretch thin. Cool. Break into pieces. Makes about 2¼ pounds of candy.

Divinity

2½ cups sugar
½ cup light corn syrup
½ cup water
¼ teaspoon salt
2 egg whites
1 teaspoon vanilla

In heavy 2-quart saucepan stir together the sugar, corn syrup, water, and salt. Clip candy thermometer to side of pan. Cook, stirring constantly, till sugar dissolves. Continue cooking to 260° (hard-ball stage); remove from heat. Immediately beat the egg whites to stiff peaks. Remove candy thermometer from pan. Gradually pour syrup over egg whites, beating at high speed of electric mixer. Add the vanilla and continue beating till candy holds its shape, 4 to 5 minutes. Quickly drop candy from a teaspoon onto waxed paper. (Or, spread candy into a 10x6x2-inch dish and cut into squares.) Makes about 40 pieces.

Cherry Divinity: Prepare as above *except* fold in ½ cup chopped red *candied cherries* after beating candy.

Caramels

1 cup butter *or* margarine
1 16-ounce package brown sugar (2¼ cups packed)
    Dash salt
1 cup light corn syrup
1 14-ounce can *sweetened condensed* milk
1 teaspoon vanilla

Butter a 9x9x2-inch pan. Melt the 1 cup butter or margarine in a heavy 3-quart saucepan. Add brown sugar and salt; stir thoroughly. Stir in corn syrup. Gradually add the sweetened condensed milk, stirring constantly. Clip candy thermometer to side of pan. Cook and stir over medium heat to 245° (firm-ball stage). Remove from heat; stir in vanilla. Pour into buttered 9x9x2-inch pan. When cooled, cut into squares. Wrap pieces individually in clear plastic wrap. Makes about 2½ pounds.

Chocolate Torte

1 **frozen loaf pound cake**
4 **1-ounce squares semisweet chocolate**
1 **15-ounce container ricotta cheese**
½ **cup sugar**
1½ **teaspoons vanilla**
6 **tablespoons orange liqueur**
1 **cup sifted powdered sugar**
2 **tablespoons unsweetened cocoa powder**
1 **tablespoon butter, melted**
2 **to 3 tablespoons boiling water**
2 **tablespoons chopped walnuts**

Remove pound cake from freezer; let stand at room temperature. Meanwhile, finely chop chocolate squares. In bowl combine chopped chocolate, ricotta cheese, sugar, and vanilla. Slice pound cake horizontally into 3 equal layers. Drizzle *2 tablespoons* of the liqueur over *one* side of *each* cake layer. Set aside 2 tablespoons of the cheese filling. Divide remaining cheese filling in half; spread mixture evenly on the liqueur side of two of the cake layers. Stack one of the two cake layers with filling; on the other. Top with remaining cake layer. In mixing bowl stir together powdered sugar and cocoa. Add melted butter; stir in enough boiling water to make of glazing consistency. Spoon mixture over torte. Dollop the reserved cheese mixture atop cake; sprinkle with walnuts. Chill thoroughly. Makes 8 servings.

Praline Cheese Cups

1 **4-ounce container whipped cream cheese**
¼ **cup dairy sour cream**
2 **tablespoons sugar**
½ **teaspoon vanilla**
4 **cake dessert cups**
¼ **cup pecan halves**
½ **cup caramel ice cream topping**
1 **tablespoon brandy**

In mixing bowl combine whipped cream cheese, sour cream, sugar, and vanilla. With fork, remove small amount of center from each dessert cup. Fill centers with cheese mixture. Arrange pecans atop each. Chill. Before serving, heat together caramel topping and brandy. Spoon atop dessert cups. Garnish each with a maraschino cherry, if desired. Makes 4 servings.

Ginger Cupcakes

1 **8¼-ounce can crushed pineapple**
3 **tablespoons butter**
½ **cup packed brown sugar**
1 **14-ounce package gingerbread mix**

Drain pineapple, reserving syrup. In small saucepan melt butter. Remove from heat; stir in brown sugar and the drained pineapple. Spoon pineapple mixture into 18 muffin cups. Prepare gingerbread mix according to package directions *except* use pineapple syrup plus enough water to equal liquid called for in package directions. Divide batter among muffin cups, filling ⅔ full (do not overfill pans). Bake at 400° for 15 minutes. Let cool 5 minutes. Loosen and invert onto wire rack. Serve warm. Makes 18 cupcakes.

Caramel-Chocolate Fondue

1 **14-ounce can *sweetened condensed* milk**
1 **12-ounce jar caramel ice cream topping**
1 **6-ounce package semisweet chocolate pieces**
   Apples *or* bananas, cut into bite-size pieces

In medium saucepan combine sweetened condensed milk, caramel topping, and chocolate. Cook, stirring constantly, over low heat till chocolate melts. Transfer to fondue pot; place over fondue burner. To serve, dip fruit piece in chocolate mixture. Makes 3 cups.

Index

A-B

Acapulco Bean Casserole, 82
Alaska, Baked, 449
All-American Apple Pie, 418
Almond Bars, Apricot-, 435
Almond Cookies, 432
Almond Fudge, 460
Ambrosia Salad, 323
Ambrosia Sauce, 456
Angel Cake, 414
Antipasto, Raw Vegetable, 298
Appetizers
  Dill-Stuffed Mushrooms, 252
  Jackstraw Eggplant, 241
  Japanese Custard Soup, 276
  Marinated Brussels Sprouts
    Appetizers, 222
  Mushroom Cocktail, 252
  Sunburst Artichoke, 208
Apples
  All-American Apple Pie, 418
  Apple and Pork Casserole, 97
  Apple and Raisin Cobbler, 445
  Apple Bread Pudding, 442
  Apple Fritter Rings, 401
  Apple-Orange Stuffed Pork Chops,
    158
  Apple-Peanut Buttered Pork
    Steaks, 160
  Cheese-Baked Apples, 446
  Cider Waldorf Mold, 331
  Cinnamon-Apple Salads, 323
  Cottage Cabbage Apple Slaw, 355
  Deep-Dish Apple Pie, 419
  Pork and Apples with Stuffing, 91
  Waldorf Salad, 321
Applesauce Cake Roll, 416
Applesauce Topper, 456
Apricots
  Apricot-Almond Bars, 435
  Apricot Cream Fondue, 452
  Apricot Glazed Ribs, 162
  Apricot Lamb Kabobs, 185
  Apricot-Sauced Duckling, 58
  Apricot-Sauced Pecan Waffles, 403
  Apricot-Sauced Sweets, 282
  Apricot Soufflé Salad, 326
  Orange-Apricot Freeze, 332
Armenian Herb Marinade, 194
Armenian-Italian Lamb Chops, 187
Armenian Pilaf, 128
Artichokes
  Artichoke-Crab Entrée, 207
  Artichokes Parmesan, 208
  Artichokes with Lemon Butter
    Sauce, 208

Artichokes (continued)
  Hearts of Artichoke Versailles, 305
  Italian-Dipped Artichokes, 208
  Jerusalem Artichokes with Parslied
    Cream Sauce, 208
  Sunburst Artichoke, 208
A Soup for All Seasons, 45
Asparagus
  Asparagus and Shrimp Salad, 337
  Asparagus Omelet Tarragon, 209
  Asparagus Toss, 297
  Asparagus Vinaigrette, 210
  Asparagus with Orange
    Hollandaise Sauce, 211
  Chef's Bowl, 336
  Chilled Asparagus Soup, 211
  Sesame Asparagus, 211
  Stir-Fry Beef with Asparagus, 211
Aspic, Garden-Fresh Tomato, 315
Aspic, Tomato, 286
Aspic, Turkey in, 352
Au Gratin, Potatoes and Eggs, 272
Avocados
  Avocado Egg Salad, 342
  Crab-Stuffed Avocados, 344
  Fruited Avocado Freeze, 333
  Mushroom-Avocado Duo, 297
Bacon
  Bacon Bread, 370
  Bacon Burger Squares, 152
  Brunch Eggs Ranchero, 134
  Gold Rush Brunch, 118
  Quiche Lorraine, 129
  Shallot-Bacon Quiche, 117
  Steak and Bacon Tournedos, 137
  Yankee Bacon Bake, 73
Baked Alaska, 449
Baked Bean Cassoulet, 213
Baked Beans, Easy, 215
Baked Beans, New England, 214
Baked Celery with Almonds, 232
Baked Corn with Chive Sauce, 233
Baked Custard, 441
Baked Doughnut Twists, 401
Baked Eggs and Ham, 105
Baked Pineapple Tapioca, 438
Baked Pumpkin Pudding, 442
Baked Rice Pudding, 439
Baking Powder Biscuits, 390
Bananas
  Banana Nut Bread, 398
  Banana-Peanut Parfaits, 450
  Banana Waffles, 403
  Frozen Strawberry-Banana Salads,
    334
  Gooseberry-Banana Salad, 328
Barbecue Recipes, 136-205
  Barbecued Beans and Meatballs, 122

Barbecue Recipes (continued)
  Barbecued Beef Burgers, 152
  Barbecued Fish, 178
  Barbecued King Crab Legs, 182
  Barbecued Lemon Turkey, 168
  Barbecued Orange-Apricot Ribs,
    36
  Barbecued Shrimp Kabobs, 180
  Barbecued Spicy Chicken, 49
  Barbecue-Glazed Ham and
    Pineapple, 38
  Chili Barbecued Pork Chops, 33
  Fruit-Turkey Kabobs, 49
  Grilled Potato and Onion Bake,
    271
  Roasted Corn on the Cob, 236
Basic Broiled Chicken, 48
Basic Coffee Cake, 397
Basic Dessert Crepes, 458
Basic Eclairs, 453
Basic Grilled Burgers, 152
Basic Rolls (conventional method),
  368
Basic Rolls (easy-mix method), 368
Basic Sweet Roll Dough, 380
Batter Rolls, 374
Bavarian Cream, Fresh Orange, 454
Bavarian Supper, 17
Beans
  Acapulco Bean Casserole, 82
  Baked Bean Cassoulet, 213
  Barbecued Beans and Meatballs,
    122
  Bean and Carrot Salad, 308
  Bean and Squash Soup, 279
  Beef and Bean Ragout, 146
  Cassoulet Salad, 346
  Creamy Lima Beans, 213
  Creamy Lima Cups, 313
  Easy Baked Beans, 215
  Easy Cassoulet, 117
  Frank and Bean Skillet, 184
  Garden-Stuffed Peppers, 267
  Green Bean Bake with Onion, 214
  Green Beans Amandine, 214
  Green Beans Supreme, 212
  Hot Five-Bean Salad, 312
  Maple-Glazed Meat and Beans, 90
  Marinated Three-Bean Salad, 215
  Mexican Lima Beans, 215
  Mustard Beans, 213
  New England Baked Beans, 214
  Oven-Baked Beef-Lima Stew, 76
  Spanish String Beans, 215
  Spanish Vegetable Mold, 314
  Succotash, 293
  Taos Salad Toss, 296
  Two-Bean Fritters, 213

Bean Sprouts
  Oriental Garden Toss, 259
  Pork Chop Suey, 34
  Sukiyaki, 260
Beef (See also Corned Beef)
  Armenian Pilaf, 128
  Beef and Bean Pot Roast, 10
  Beef and Bean Ragout, 146
  Beef and Caesar Salad, 338
  Beef and Carrot Burgers, 150
  Beef and Mushroom Kabobs, 147
  Beef Bourguignonne, 27
  Beef-Broccoli Pie, 119
  Beef Burgundy Pies, 120
  Beef in Pepper Cups, 269
  Beef-Macaroni Italiano, 98
  Beef-Noodle Bake, 86
  Beef Stew Bake, 74
  Beef Stroganoff, 27
  Beef-Stuffed Acorn Squash, 105
  Beef-Yam Kabobs, 148
  Beefy Onion Pie, 99
  Brisket of Beef with Horseradish
    Sauce, 13
  Chicken and Beef Kabobs, 175
  Cider Stew, 29
  Cipâte, 130
  Curried Beef Bake, 120
  Delicatessen Casserole, 110
  Fruited Beef Stew, 111
  Hawaiian Kabobs, 149
  Mexican-Style Hash, 99
  Old-Fashioned Fresh Vegetable-
    Beef Soup, 292
  Oven-Baked Beef Stew, 29
  Oven Beef Hash, 99
  Oven Stew for Two, 106
  Peachy Beef Toss, 338
  Pepper Steak, Oriental, 28
  Pepper Steak Salad, 337
  Rainbow Beef, 28
  Sherried Beef Stroganoff, 120
  Skewered Beef Bundles, 149
  Smoked Beef and Cheese Soup,
    146
  Smoked Short Ribs, 144
  Sukiyaki, 260
  Tyrolean Alps Ragout, 27
  Wine-Basted Short Ribs, 144
  Zippy Mostaccioli, 74
Beef, Ground
  Bacon Burger Squares, 152
  Barbecued Beans and Meatballs,
    122
  Barbecued Beef Burgers, 152
  Basic Grilled Burgers, 152
  Beef and Carrot Burgers, 150
  Beef-Broccoli Pie, 119

Beef, Ground *(continued)*
  Beef in Pepper Cups, 269
  Beef-Noodle Bake, 86
  Beef-Stuffed Acorn Squash, 105
  Bull's-eye Burgers, 19
  Burgers Extravaganza, 150
  Burgers O'Brien, 150
  Burrito Burgers, 153
  Cheeseburger Chowder, 23
  Cheese-Stuffed Patties, 153
  Chili Burger Patties, 152
  Chili Meat Loaf, 155
  Dinner in a Pepper, 24
  Enchiladas Dos, 108
  Enchilada Squares, 84
  Everyday Meat Loaf, 20
  Giant Stuffed Grillburger, 155
  Grilling Hamburgers Outdoors, 19
  Hamburger-Noodle Bake, 122
  Hamburger Pie, 77
  Layered Supper, 122
  Macaroni and Meatballs, 86
  Manicotti, 24
  Meat and Potato Pie, 84
  Meatball Meal-in-One, 107
  Meatball-Okra Stew, 255
  Meatballs Oriental-Style, 22
  Meat Loaf Puff, 21
  Mini Pineapple Meat Loaves, 154
  Moussaka, 132
  Moussaka for a Crowd, 243
  Olive Spaghetti Sauce, 23
  Oven-Baked Beef-Lima Stew, 76
  Pan Pizza, 26
  Party Eggplant Parmesan, 119
  Pastel de Chocolo, 134
  Pasticchio, 131
  Planked Chopped Steak, 19
  Porcupine Meatballs, 22
  Sausage and Beef Chili, 23
  Sicilian Meat Roll, 20
  Skewered Cherry Tomato
    Meatballs, 149
  Sour Cream-Chili Bake, 84
  Spaghetti Pie, 77
  Stroganoff Sandwich, 26
  Stuffed Cabbage Rolls, 76
  Taco Salad, 20
  Texas Beef Skillet, 24
  Tostada Pizza, 26
  Vegetable-Beef Rolls, 137
  Vegetable Burgers, 153
Beef, Roasts
  Beef and Bean Pot Roast, 10
  Brazilian Barbecued Beef, 143
  Golden Beef Pot Roast, 10
  Horseradish-Stuffed Rump Roast,
    144

Beef, Roasts *(continued)*
  Hot-Style Eye of Round, 141
  Lemon-Marinated Chuck Roast,
    138
  Marinated Hickory-Smoked Chuck
    Roast, 141
  Pot Roast Dip Sandwiches, 9
  Preparing Beef Roasts, 8
  Rib Roast Barbecue, 141
  Rump Roast Supreme, 9
  Rump Roast with Vegetables, 7
  Sauerbraten, 9
  Spit-Roasted Châteaubriand, 140
  Standing Rib Roast with Yorkshire
    Pudding, 7
  Stuffed Rolled Rib Roast, 7
  Swedish Pot Roast, 11
  Wined-and-Dined Beef Roast, 143
Beef, Steaks
  Bavarian Supper, 17
  Beef Steaks Wellington, 15
  Broiling Beef Steaks, 14
  Budget Steak Diane, 16
  Cheese-Stuffed Beef Rounds, 16
  Chicken-Fried Round Steak, 18
  Deviled Swiss Steak, 18
  Grilling Steaks Outdoors, 15
  Lemon Pepper Flank Pinwheels,
    137
  Marinated Beef Broil, 18
  Onion-Stuffed Steak, 140
  Oven Swiss Steak, 18
  Peppy Chuck Steak Grill, 138
  Quick Garlic Cubed Steaks, 146
  Rice-Stuffed Flank Steak, 140
  Rice-Stuffed Steaks, 14
  Rolled Beef Italian-Style, 17
  Round Steak Louisiana, 76
  Smoked French Pepper Steak, 138
  Steak and Bacon Tournedos, 137
  Steak and Kidney Pie, 130
  Steak and Shrimp Kabob Dinner,
    147
  Steaks Bertrand, 16
  Steak with Lobster Tail, 14
  Stir-Fry Beef with Asparagus, 211
  Stuffed Steak Sandwiches, 155
  Vegetable-Stuffed Cubed Steaks, 17
Beer, Bratwursts in, 157
Beer Bread, Shortcut, 407
Beets
  Beet and Pineapple Mold, 218
  Beet-Apple Relish, 218
  Beet Supper Salad, 217
  Beets with Sour Cream, 218
  Borscht with Mushroom Dumplings,
    216
  Harvard Beets, 218

Belgian Tossed Salad, 301
Berlinerkranser, 431
Bermuda Salad Bowl, 302
Best-Ever Muffins, 393
Big-Batch Barbecue Sauce, 191
Biscuits
    Bacon Biscuits, 390
    Baking Powder Biscuits, 390
    Biscuits Supreme, 390
    Biscuit-Topped Stew, 103
    Buttermilk Biscuits, 390
    Cornmeal Biscuits, 390
    Drop Biscuits, 392
    Pecan Petal Biscuits, 392
    Raisin Drop Biscuits, 392
    Sour Cream Biscuits, 390
Bismarcks, 382
Bismarcks, Cream-Filled, 382
Black-Eyed Peas
    Ham Hocks and Black-Eyed Peas,
    266
    Hoppin' John, 266
Blender Bread Crumb Pancakes, 402
Blueberry Sauce, 455
Blue Cheese
    Blue Cheese Salad Dressing, 361
    Diet Blue Cheese Dressing, 363
    Zesty Blue Cheese Dressing, 358
Bologna Kabobs, Mustard-Brushed,
    183
Borscht with Mushroom Dumplings,
    216
Bouillabaisse, 62
Braised Lettuce, 250
Brandy Hard Sauce, 420
Bran-Flake Chicken and Peaches, 46
Bran Muffins, 394
Bran Puff Cookies, 429
Bratwurst Melt, Swiss, 43
Bratwursts in Beer, 157
Bratwurst, Skewered, 184
Brazilian Barbecued Beef, 143
Bread and Butter Stuffing, 60
Bread Pudding, 439
Bread Pudding, Apple, 442
Breads, Quick
    Apple Fritter Rings, 401
    Apricot-Sauced Pecan Waffles, 403
    Bacon Biscuits, 390
    Baked Doughnut Twists, 401
    Baking Powder Biscuits, 390
    Banana Nut Bread, 398
    Banana Waffles, 403
    Basic Coffee Cake, 397
    Best-Ever Muffins, 393
    Biscuits Supreme, 390
    Blender Bread Crumb Pancakes,
    402

Breads, Quick *(continued)*
    Blueberry-Lemon Muffins, 393
    Bran Muffins, 394
    Buttermilk Biscuits, 390
    Buttermilk Corn Bread, 404
    Buttermilk Doughnuts, 400
    Buttermilk Pancakes, 402
    Carrot Muffins, 394
    Cheesy Corn Muffins, 404
    Chocolate Chip Muffins, 393
    Chocolate-Cinnamon Doughnuts,
    400
    Chocolate Waffles, 403
    Cinnamon-Apple-Raisin Muffins,
    393
    Cinnamon-Graham Crackers, 406
    Cinnamon Twists, 392
    Coconut-Jam Coffee Cake, 397
    Company French Toast, 406
    Corn Fritters, 401
    Cowboy Coffee Cake, 396
    Cranberry Relish Coffee Cake, 397
    Drop Biscuits, 392
    Enriched Best-Ever Muffins, 393
    Everyday Waffles, 403
    Feather Pancakes, 402
    Filled Corn Muffins, 394
    Frozen French Toast, 406
    Low-Fat Best-Ever Muffins, 393
    Molasses Corn Bread, 404
    Nutty Muffins, 393
    Orange Doughnuts, 400
    Orange Nut Bread, 398
    Oven Pancake, 402
    Peanut Butter Coffee Cake, 396
    Peanut Butter Pancakes, 402
    Pecan Petal Biscuits, 392
    Pineapple-Pecan Muffins, 393
    Popovers, 406
    Pumpkin Bread, 398
    Quick Sally Lunn, 396
    Raisin Drop Biscuits, 392
    Raspberry Coffee Cake, 396
    Sour Cream Biscuits, 390
    Spicy Marble Coffee Cake, 397
    Spicy Spud Doughnuts, 401
    Spoon Bread, 404
    Sweet Best-Ever Muffins, 393
    Sweet Potato Biscuits, 282
    Two-Bean Fritters, 213
    Two-Cheese Muffins, 394
    Two-Corn Bread, 235
    Zucchini Nut Loaf, 291
Bread Stuffing, Old-Fashioned, 60
Breads, Yeast
    Bacon Bread, 370
    Basic Rolls, 368
    Basic Sweet Roll Dough, 380

Breads, Yeast *(continued)*
    Batter Rolls, 374
    Bismarcks, 382
    Brioche, 386
    Bubble Wreath, 376
    Caramel-Pecan Rolls, 380
    Cherry Lattice Coffee Cake, 378
    Chocolate Doughnuts, 382
    Cinnamon Crescents, 378
    Cinnamon Crisps, 381
    Cinnamon Rolls, 380
    Cinnamon Swirl Loaf, 372
    Cornmeal Biscuits, 390
    Cornmeal Loaves, 370
    Cracked Wheat Bread, 388
    Croissants, 386
    Crusty Water Rolls, 374
    Danish Pastry, 383
    Doughnuts, 382
    Easy Dill-Onion Bread, 372
    French Chocolate Coffee Cake,
    376
    Garden Batter Bread, 372
    German Stollen, 387
    Grandma's Oatmeal Bread, 369
    Italian Bread, 384
    Italian Breadsticks, 375
    Kolache, 387
    Lemon Puff Pillow Buns, 383
    No-Knead Refrigerator Rolls, 368
    Old-Time Whole Wheat Bread, 371
    Onion Buns, 374
    Peanut Butter-Jelly Twists, 381
    Perfect White Bread, 367
    Pumpernickel Bread, 371
    Refrigerated Herb Rolls, 375
    Rye Bread, 371
    Rye Pretzels, 388
    Sourdough Bread, 389
    Sourdough-Cheese Rolls, 389
    Streusel Coffee Cake, 377
    Swedish Tea Ring, 377
    Two-Tone Bread, 369
    Whole Wheat Bread, 388
    Whole Wheat Rolls, 375
Brioche, 386
Brisket of Beef with Horseradish
    Sauce, 13
Broccoli
    Beef-Broccoli Pie, 119
    Broccoli-Egg Bake, 219
    Broccoli-Onion Deluxe, 221
    Broccoli Soufflé, 221
    Broccoli Vinaigrette, 298
    Curried Broccoli Salad, 221
    Ham and Broccoli Bake, 124
    Lemon Broccoli, 221
    Salmon-Broccoli Crepes, 121

Broccoli *(continued)*
    Tuna-Broccoli Bake, 64
    Turkey-Broccoli Bake, 101
Broiled Chicken, Basic, 48
Broiled Crab-Chicken Rolls, 50
Broiled Fish, 62
Brownies
    Buttermilk Brownies, 434
    Cheese-Marbled Brownies, 434
    Chocolate Syrup Brownies, 434
    Saucepan Fudge Brownies, 435
Brown Rice Toss, Chicken and, 345
Brown Sauce, 27
Brown Sugar Peanut Brittle, 461
Brown Sugar Sauce, 457
Brown Sugar Spritz, 431
Brunch Cakes, 407
Brunch Eggs Ranchero, 134
Brunswick Stew, 255
Brussels Sprouts Appetizers,
    Marinated, 222
Brussels Sprouts, Saucy, 222
Bubble Wreath, 376
Budget Steak Diane, 16
Buffet Chicken Scallop, 127
Bull's-eye Burgers, 19
Burgers Extravaganza, 150
Burgers O'Brien, 150
Burrito Burgers, 153
Burritos, Salad, 354
Busy-Day Cake, 409
Buttered Pea Pods, 260
Butter Frosting, 417
Buttermilk
    Buttermilk Brownies, 434
    Buttermilk Corn Bread, 404
    Buttermilk Doughnuts, 400
    Buttermilk Dressing, 361
    Buttermilk Pancakes, 402
Butter Pecan Cupcakes, 412
Butter-Rum Sauce, 456
Butterscotch Crunch, 441

C

Cabbage
    Cabbage and Ham Slaw, 224
    Cheesy Coleslaw Mold, 315
    Coleslaw, 223
    Coleslaw Vinaigrette, 311
    Cottage Cabbage Apple Slaw, 355
    Crunchy Garden Slaw, 311
    Jiffy Frank and Cabbage Skillet,
        184
    Mustard-Sauced Cabbage
        Wedges, 225
    Pennsylvania Red Cabbage, 223
    Perfection Salad, 225

Cabbage *(continued)*
    Rice-Stuffed Cabbage Rolls, 225
    Sauerkraut, 225
    Slim Ham Slaw, 354
    Stuffed Cabbage Rolls, 76
    Tangy Coleslaw, 310
    Wilted Cabbage Salad, 313
Caesar Salad, Beef and, 338
Caesar Salad, Original, 250
Caesar's Chicken Salad, 348
Cakes
    Angel Cake, 414
    Applesauce Cake Roll, 416
    Busy-Day Cake, 409
    Butter Pecan Cupcakes, 412
    Carrot Cake, 227
    Chocolate Cheesecake Torte, 416
    Chocolate-Date Cake, 416
    Dark Fruitcake, 415
    Date Cake, 416
    Ginger Cupcakes, 462
    Golden Chiffon Cake, 415
    Golden Cupcakes, 415
    Lemon Sponge Cake, 414
    Marble Pound Cake, 414
    Nutmeg Feather Cake, 411
    Orange-Strawberry Cake, 411
    Red Devil's Food Cake, 409
    Strawberry Shortcake, 411
    Sweet Chocolate Cake, 410
    Vanilla and Sour Cream Cake, 412
    White Cake Supreme, 409
Calico Potato Salad, 272
Candied Squash Rings, 278
Candied Sweet Potato Boats, 282
Candies
    Almond Fudge, 460
    Brown Sugar Peanut Brittle, 461
    Caramels, 461
    Christmas Divinity, 460
    Divinity, 461
    Java Fudge, 460
    No-Cook Fudge, 461
Canning
    Beet-Apple Relish, 218
    Canned Tomatoes, 287
    Canned Tomato Juice, 287
    Crisp Pickle Slices, 240
    Dill Pickles, 240
    Garlic Okra Pickles, 253
    Green Tomato Pickles, 287
    Home-Canned Cream-Style Corn,
        235
    Home-Canned Red Pepper Relish,
        269
    Home-Canned Whole Kernel Corn,
        235
    Hot Pickled Peppers, 269

Canning *(continued)*
    Kosher Dill Pickles, 240
    Louisiana Relish, 293
    Quick Mustard Pickles, 238
    Sauerkraut, 225
    Zucchini Relish, 291
Caramel-Chocolate Fondue, 462
Caramel-Pecan Rolls, 380
Caramels, 461
Caraway-Cheese Spread, 192
Carolina Chicken Pie, 67
Carrots
    Bean and Carrot Salad, 308
    Beef and Carrot Burgers, 150
    Carrot Cake, 227
    Carrot Muffins, 394
    Carrot-Pineapple Toss, 313
    Garden Gold Soup, 227
    Golden Carrot Bake, 227
    Kohlrabi-Carrot Bake, 247
    Pickled Carrots, 227
    Steamed Carrot Pudding, 457
    Sunshine Carrots, 226
Casserole Recipes, 66-135
    Baked Bean Cassoulet, 213
    Baked Celery with Almonds, 232
    Broccoli-Egg Bake, 219
    Broccoli-Onion Deluxe, 221
    Casserole Chop Suey, 125
    Chicken and Stuffing Scallop, 53
    Chicken-Noodle Casserole, 51
    Chilies Rellenos Bake, 269
    Chili-Spaghetti Dinner, 44
    Choucroute Garni, 43
    Corn and Sausage Scallop, 44
    Eggplant Parmigiana, 243
    Golden-Sauced Franks, 45
    Green Bean Bake with Onion, 214
    Green Beans Supreme, 212
    Green Corn Pudding, 233
    Herbed Spinach Bake, 276
    Individual Chicken Pies, 51
    Kohlrabi-Carrot Bake, 247
    Manicotti, 24
    Moussaka for a Crowd, 243
    Pork Stroganoff for a Crowd, 35
    Potatoes and Eggs au Gratin,
        272
    Rutabaga and Apple, 288
    Scalloped Corn, 237
    Scalloped Potatoes, 271
    Scalloped Spinach, 275
    Shrimp and Tuna Bake, 64
    Summer Squash Casserole, 289
    Sweet Potato-Cashew Bake, 280
    Swiss Corn Bake, 236
    Tuna-Broccoli Bake, 64
Cassoulet Salad, 346

Cauliflower
Cauliflower-Ham Bake, 118
Cauliflower-Ham Chowder, 230
Cauliflower-Onion Bake, 230
Cauliflower Polonaise, 228
Cauliflower Scallop, 230
Cauliflower with Cheese-
  Mushroom Sauce, 230
Italian-Dressed Cauliflower, 228
Piquant Cauliflower, 302
Celery
Baked Celery with Almonds, 232
Celeriac Sauté, 231
Celeriac Toss, 231
Celery Slaw, 232
Cream of Celery Soup, 232
Crisp Dilled Celery, 232
Cereal-Spice Bars, 436
Charcoaled Halibut Steaks, 180
Charcoal-Grilled Shrimp, 180
Chard, Sweet-Sour Swiss, 244
Charts
Baking Smoked Pork, 39
Broiling Beef Steaks, 14
Grilling Hamburgers Outdoors, 19
Grilling Over the Coals, 202
Grilling Steaks Outdoors, 15
Preparing Beef Roasts, 8
Roasting Domestic Birds, 56
Roasting Fresh Pork, 32
Rotisserie Specialties, 204
Smoker Cooking, 204
Châteaubriand, Spit-Roasted, 140
Cheese
Beef in Pepper Cups, 269
Broccoli-Egg Bake, 219
Caraway-Cheese Spread, 192
Cauliflower Scallop, 230
Cauliflower with
  Cheese-Mushroom
  Sauce, 230
Cheese-Baked Apples, 446
Cheeseburger Chowder, 23
Cheese Filling, 434
Cheese-Marbled Brownies, 434
Cheese Soufflé, 129
Cheese-Stuffed Beef Rounds, 16
Cheese-Stuffed Patties, 153
Cheesy Coleslaw Mold, 315
Cheesy Corn Muffins, 404
Cheesy Hash-Spinach Pie, 75
Chilies Rellenos Bake, 269
Classic Cheese Strata, 82
Creamed Onions, 256
Crunch-Top Potatoes, 271
Delicatessen Casserole, 110
Dilly Macaroni Salad, 308
Frankfurter-Cheese Casserole, 70

Cheese (continued)
Garden Row Salad, 293
Golden Carrot Bake, 227
Grilled Crab and Cheese Rolls, 157
Herbed Spinach Bake, 276
Huevos Rancheros, 283
Macaroni and Cheese, 82
Macaroni and Cheese for Two, 107
Macaroni-Cheddar Salad, 312
Manicotti, 24
Mexican Chef's Salad, 341
Pan Pizza, 26
Pea-Cheese Salad, 264
Red-Ribbon Cheese Casserole, 92
Salad Burritos, 354
Salami-Cheese Pie, 72
Salami-Cheese Salad, 346
Sicilian Pizza Supreme, 44
Smoked Beef and Cheese Soup,
  146
Spinach and Cheese Soufflé, 119
Sprout Salad, 355
Stroganoff Sandwich, 26
Tostada Pizza, 26
Triple-Cheese Pie, 92
24-Hour Vegetable Salad, 248
Two-Cheese Muffins, 394
Cheesecake, Praline, 452
Cheesecakes, Coffee, 450
Chef's Bowl, 336
Chef's Salad, Mexican, 341
Cherries
Cherries Jubilee, 443
Cherry-Cider Salad, 328
Cherry Lattice Coffee Cake, 378
Cherry-Orange Squares, 330
Cherry Pie, 418
Cherry-Topped Cheese Blintzes,
  458
Fruit Compote Supreme, 443
Fruit Melange, 443
Chestnut Fingers, Finnish, 431
Chicken
Baked Bean Cassoulet, 213
Barbecued Spicy Chicken, 49
Basic Broiled Chicken, 48
Bran-Flake Chicken and Peaches,
  46
Broiled Crab-Chicken Rolls, 50
Brunswick Stew, 255
Buffet Chicken Scallop, 127
Caesar's Chicken Salad, 348
Carolina Chicken Pie, 67
Chicken and Beef Kabobs, 175
Chicken and Brown Rice Toss, 345
Chicken and Dumplings, 54
Chicken and Ham Supreme, 341
Chicken and Onion Bake, 67

Chicken (continued)
Chicken and Stuffing Scallop, 52
Chicken and Vegetable Bundles,
  174
Chicken-Asparagus Divan, 113
Chicken Breasts Florentine, 111
Chicken Cacciatore, 54
Chicken Curry Soufflés, 112
Chicken Divan, 52
Chicken Enchiladas, 134
Chicken-Noodle Casserole, 51
Chicken Pineapple Boat, 351
Chicken Puff Casserole, 100
Chicken Salad a l'Orange, 344
Chicken-Spaghetti Bake, 68
Chicken Teriyaki, 172
Chicken with Zucchini Stuffing,
  173
Cipâte, 130
Club Chicken Casserole, 112
Confetti Chicken Salad, 350
Corn-Stuffed Chicken Breasts, 172
Crab-Stuffed Chicken, 113
Creamy Chicken Casserole, 90
Crowd-Size Chicken Bake, 127
Curried Chicken Salad, 348
Curried Turkey Pie, 101
Curry Barbecued Chicken, 174
Deep-Dish Chicken Pie, 90
Foil-Wrapped Clambake, 181
Grilled Island Chicken, 172
Herb-Glazed Chickens, 173
Homemade Corn and Chicken
  Soup, 55
Imperial Chicken Salad, 348
Individual Chicken Pies, 51
Japanese-Style Chicken, 175
Lemonade Chicken, 175
Maryland Fried Chicken, 48
Mexican Chef's Salad, 341
Oven-Easy Chicken Croquettes, 49
Oven-Fried Chicken, 48
Paella Casserole, 132
Pan-Fried Chicken, 46
Pastel de Chocolo, 134
Pineapple Hawaiian Chicken, 50
Popover Chicken Tarragon, 53
Roasting Domestic Birds, 56
Roast Sweet-Sour Chickens, 58
Saucy Turkey Manicotti, 112
Sausage-Stuffed Chicken
  Roll-Ups, 172
Southern-Style Fried Chicken, 48
Spiced Orange Chicken, 51
Spicy Barbecued Chicken, 174
Stewed Chicken, 54
Sunday Chicken-Rice Bake, 67
Tetrazzini Crepes, 121

Chicken *(continued)*
  Turkey Chowder, 55
  Turkey Soufflé, 100
  Two-Step Fried Chicken, 46
  Wild Rice-Chicken Casserole, 113
Chicken-Fried Round Steak, 18
Chiffon Cake, Golden, 415
Chiffon Pie, Strawberry, 423
Chili
  Chili Barbecued Pork Chops, 33
  Chili Barbecue Sauce, 191
  Chili Burger Patties, 152
  Chili Dressing, 358
  Chili Manicotti, 107
  Chili Meat Loaf, 155
  Chili-Pepperoni Salad Bowl, 250
  Chili Salad, 338
  Chili-Spaghetti Dinner, 44
  Sausage and Beef Chili, 23
Chilies Rellenos Bake, 269
Chilled Asparagus Soup, 211
Chilled Pea Soup, 265
Chinese Smoked Ribs, 162
Chinese Spinach, 275
Chocolate
  Buttermilk Brownies, 434
  Caramel-Chocolate Fondue, 462
  Cheese-Marbled Brownies, 434
  Chocolate Butter Frosting, 417
  Chocolate Cheesecake Torte, 416
  Chocolate Chip Bars, 435
  Chocolate Chip Cookies, 428
  Chocolate-Cinnamon Doughnuts,
    400
  Chocolate Crinkles, 433
  Chocolate Fondue, 452
  Chocolate Glaze, 434
  Chocolate Pudding, 438
  Chocolate Revel Bars, 436
  Chocolate Syrup Brownies, 434
  Chocolate Torte, 462
  Chocolate Wafer Crust, 426
  Chocolate Waffles, 403
  French Chocolate Coffee Cake,
    376
  Fudge Ribbon Pie, 426
  Pots de Crème, 439
  Saucepan Fudge Brownies, 435
  Sweet Chocolate Cake, 410
Choucroute Garni, 43
Christmas Divinity, 460
Cider Basting Sauce, Tarragon-, 191
Cider Stew, 29
Cider Waldorf Mold, 331
Cinnamon
  Cinnamon-Apple Salads, 323
  Cinnamon Crescents, 378
  Cinnamon Crisps, 381

Cinnamon *(continued)*
  Cinnamon-Graham Crackers, 406
  Cinnamon Rolls, 380
  Cinnamon Swirl Loaf, 372
  Cinnamon Twists, 392
Cipâte, 130
Citrus Crunch Dessert, 444
Clambake, Foil-Wrapped, 181
Clam Chowder Pie, 79
Classic Cheese Strata, 82
Classic Crepes Suzette, 458
Club Chicken Casserole, 112
Cobbler
  Apple and Raisin Cobbler, 445
  Cobbler Topper, 446
  Cranberry-Peach Cobbler, 446
  Fresh Strawberry Cobbler, 445
Cocoa-Buttermilk Frosting, 434
Coconut Frosting, 410
Coconut-Jam Coffee Cake, 397
Coconut Macaroons, 429
Coffee Cakes
  Basic Coffee Cake, 397
  Bubble Wreath, 376
  Cherry Lattice Coffee Cake, 378
  Cinnamon Crescents, 378
  Coconut-Jam Coffee Cake, 397
  Cowboy Coffee Cake, 396
  Cranberry Relish Coffee Cake, 397
  French Chocolate Coffee Cake,
    376
  Orange Coffee Cake, 407
  Peanut Butter Coffee Cake, 396
  Quick Sally Lunn, 396
  Raspberry Coffee Cake, 396
  Spicy Marble Coffee Cake, 397
  Streusel Coffee Cake, 377
  Swedish Tea Ring, 377
Coffee Cheesecakes, 450
Coffee and Ice Cream Eclairs, 453
Coffee-Soy Glaze, 192
Coleslaws
  Coleslaw, 223
  Coleslaw Vinaigrette, 311
  Sandwich Coleslaw, 193
  Tangy Coleslaw, 310
Company French Toast, 406
Company Pork Loin Roast, 160
Compote Supreme, Fruit, 443
Confetti Chicken Salad, 350
Contemporary Strata, 102
Cookies
  Almond Cookies, 432
  Apricot-Almond Bars, 435
  Berlinerkranser, 431
  Bran Puff Cookies, 429
  Brown Sugar Spritz, 431
  Buttermilk Brownies, 434

Cookies *(continued)*
  Cereal-Spice Bars, 436
  Cheese-Marbled Brownies, 434
  Chocolate Chip Bars, 435
  Chocolate Chip Cookies, 428
  Chocolate Crinkles, 433
  Chocolate Revel Bars, 436
  Chocolate Syrup Brownies, 434
  Coconut Macaroons, 429
  Cream Cheese Pastries, 432
  Date Pinwheels, 429
  Double Peanut Cookies, 433
  Finnish Chestnut Fingers, 431
  Jam-Filled Cookies, 432
  Lemon Bars, 435
  Lemon Rounds, 433
  Peanut-Oatmeal Drops, 428
  Rolled Sugar Cookies, 432
  Santa's Whiskers, 433
  Saucepan Fudge Brownies, 435
  Sugar-Pecan Crisps, 429
  Toffee Bars, 436
  Two-Tone Cookies, 428
Corn
  Baked Corn with Chive Sauce,
    233
  Corn and Sausage Scallop, 44
  Corn Fritters, 401
  Corn Medley, 236
  Corn Relish, 236
  Corn-Stuffed Chicken Breasts, 172
  Corn-Stuffed Pork Chops, 158
  Corn-Stuffed Whitefish, 61
  Fresh Corn Chowder, 237
  Fresh Creamed Corn, 237
  Garden-Stuffed Peppers, 267
  Green Corn Pudding, 233
  Home-Canned Cream-Style Corn,
    235
  Home-Canned Whole Kernel Corn,
    235
  Homemade Corn and Chicken
    Soup, 55
  Parsley Buttered Corn, 237
  Roasted Corn on the Cob, 236
  Scalloped Corn, 237
  Southern Vegetable Medley, 253
  Succotash, 293
  Swiss Corn Bake, 236
  Two-Corn Bread, 235
Corned Beef
  Cheesy Hash-Spinach Pie, 75
  Corned Beef Barbecue Dinner, 142
  Corned Beef-Macaroni Pie, 87
  Corned Beef-Turkey Heroes, 156
  Festive Hash and Eggs, 86
  Layered Corned Beef Bake, 74
  New England Boiled Dinner, 13

Corned Beef *(continued)*
  Peach-Glazed Corned Beef, 13
  Reuben Casserole, 104
Corn Bread, Buttermilk, 404
Corn Bread, Molasses, 404
Corn Bread Stuffing Loaf, 60
Corn Bread, Two-, 235
Cornish Hens, Cranberry-Stuffed, 58
Cornish Hens, Sweet-Sour, 170
Cornish Hens with Rice Stuffing, 170
Cornmeal Loaves, 370
Cornmeal Biscuits, 390
Cottage Cabbage Apple Slaw, 355
Cottage Cheese Bean Sprout Salad, 355
Cottage Cheese-Spinach Salad, 276
Country-Style Barbecued Ribs, 162
Cowboy Coffee Cake, 396
Crab
  Artichoke-Crab Entrée, 207
  Barbecued King Crab Legs, 182
  Broiled Crab-Chicken Rolls, 50
  Crab or Lobster Newburg, 65
  Crab-Stuffed Avocados, 344
  Crab-Stuffed Chicken, 113
  Curried Seafood Bake, 80
  Delaware Crab Cakes, 65
  Grilled Crab and Cheese Rolls, 157
  Hot Crab Bake, 117
  Seafood Lasagna, 126
Cracked Wheat Bread, 388
Cranberries
  Cranberry-Peach Cobbler, 446
  Cranberry-Pecan Pie, 422
  Cranberry-Pork Bake, 97
  Cranberry Relish Coffee Cake, 397
  Cranberry-Stuffed Cornish Hens, 58
  Cran-Raspberry Ring, 330
  Ham Slice with Cranberry Sauce, 165
Cream Cheese Frosting, Three-Way, 417
Cream Cheese Pastries, 432
Creamed Corn, Fresh, 237
Creamed Onions, 256
Creamed Peas and Onions, 264
Cream of Celery Soup, 232
Cream of Mushroom Soup, 252
Creamy Chicken Casserole, 90
Creamy French Dressing, 358
Creamy Garlic Dressing, 361
Creamy Lima Beans, 213
Creamy Lima Cups, 313
Creamy Potato Salad, 306
Creamy Vegetable Mold, 317
Creole Gumbo, 255
Creole Peas, 264

Crepes
  Basic Dessert Crepes, 458
  Classic Crepes Suzette, 458
  Crepes, 121
  Red Raspberry Crepes, 458
  Salmon-Broccoli Crepes, 121
  Tetrazzini Crepes, 121
Crisp Dilled Celery, 232
Crisp Pickle Slices, 240
Crispy-Grilled Fish Fillets, 178
Crockery Cooker Recipes
  Garden Gold Soup, 227
  New England Baked Beans, 214
  Tomato Spaghetti Sauce, 286
Croissants, 386
Croquettes, Oven-Easy Chicken, 49
Croquettes, Salmon, 62
Croutons, Garlic, 365
Croutons, Rye, 365
Crowd-Size Chicken Bake, 127
Crown Roast of Lamb with Rice Stuffing, 40
Crumb-Topped Tomatoes, 8
Crunch-Top Potatoes, 271
Crunchy Garden Slaw, 311
Crusty Water Rolls, 374
Cucumbers
  Crisp Pickle Slices, 240
  Cucumber Cream Dressing, 360
  Cucumber Relish, 193
  Cucumber Ring Supreme, 239
  Cucumbers in Sour Cream, 238
  Dill Pickles, 240
  Kosher Dill Pickles, 240
  Quick Mustard Pickles, 238
  Scandinavian Cucumbers, 308
  Tomato-Cucumber Salad, 305
Cupcakes, Butter Pecan, 412
Cupcakes, Ginger, 462
Cupcakes, Golden, 415
Curry
  Curried Beef Bake, 120
  Curried Broccoli Salad, 221
  Curried Chicken Salad, 348
  Curried Eggs with Shrimp, 114
  Curried Seafood Bake, 80
  Curried Turkey Pie, 101
  Curried Vegetable Salad, 302
  Curry Barbecued Chicken, 174
  Curry-Sauced Ham, 38
Custard, Baked, 441
Custard Pie, 422
Custard, Stirred, 441

D-F

Danish Pastry, 383
Dark Fruitcake, 415

Date Cake, 416
Date Molds, Frozen Orange-, 333
Date-Nut Filling, 429
Date Pinwheels, 429
Deep-Dish Apple Pie, 419
Deep-Dish Chicken Pie, 90
Delaware Crab Cakes, 65
Delicatessen Casserole, 110
Deluxe Peas and Mushrooms, 263
Desserts (See also Cakes, Cookies, Ice Cream, Pies, Puddings)
  Ambrosia Sauce, 456
  Apple and Raisin Cobbler, 445
  Applesauce Topper, 456
  Apricot Cream Fondue, 452
  Baked Alaska, 449
  Banana-Peanut Parfaits, 450
  Basic Dessert Crepes, 458
  Basic Eclairs, 453
  Blueberry Sauce, 455
  Butter-Rum Sauce, 456
  Caramel-Chocolate Fondue, 462
  Cheese-Baked Apples, 446
  Cherries Jubilee, 443
  Cherry-Topped Cheese Blintzes, 458
  Chocolate Fondue, 452
  Chocolate Torte, 462
  Citrus Crunch Dessert, 444
  Classic Crepes Suzette, 458
  Coffee Cheesecakes, 450
  Coffee Fondue, 452
  Coffee and Ice Cream Eclairs, 453
  Cranberry-Peach Cobbler, 446
  Elegant Fruit Combo, 445
  Fresh Fruit Crisp, 446
  Fresh Orange Bavarian Cream, 454
  Fresh Pear Dumplings, 444
  Fresh Strawberry Cobbler, 445
  Fruit Compote Supreme, 443
  Fruit Melange, 443
  Lemon-Cheese Dessert Bombe, 455
  Lemon Mousse, 454
  Mint Fondue, 452
  Mocha Steamed Pudding, 457
  Nectarine Quick Shortcake, 444
  Orange Sauce, 456
  Peach-Pecan Dessert, 445
  Pears in Chocolate Fluff, 450
  Peppermint Ice Cream Roll, 449
  Pink Parfaits, 450
  Praline Cheesecake, 452
  Praline Cheese Cups, 462
  Red Raspberry Crepes, 458
  Rumtopf, 443
  Soufflé Grand Marnier, 454

Desserts *(continued)*
Steamed Carrot Pudding, 457
Strawberry-Eggnog Shake, 457
Vanilla Eclairs, 453
Deviled Swiss Steak, 18
Diet Blue Cheese Dressing, 363
Dieter's Chef Salad, 354
Diet Salad Dressing, 363
Diet Thousand Island Dressing, 363
Dill
Dilled Lamb Ragout, 129
Dill Pickles, 240
Dill-Stuffed Mushrooms, 252
Dilly Macaroni Salad, 308
Easy Dill-Onion Bread, 372
Dinner in a Pepper, 24
Divinity, 461
Divinity, Christmas, 460
Double Peanut Cookies, 433
Doughnuts
Baked Doughnut Twists, 401
Buttermilk Doughnuts, 400
Chocolate-Cinnamon
Doughnuts, 400
Chocolate Doughnuts, 382
Doughnuts, 382
Orange Doughnuts, 400
Spicy Spud Doughnuts, 401
Drop Biscuits, 392
Duckling, Apricot-Sauced, 58
Duckling, Kowloon, 171
Dumplings, Borscht with
Mushroom, 216
Dumplings, Chicken and, 54
Durango Sauce, 189
Dutch Pea Soup, 265
Easy Baked Beans, 215
Easy Barbecue Sauce, 189
Easy Cassoulet, 117
Easy Dill-Onion Bread, 372
Eclairs, Basic, 453
Eclairs, Coffee and Ice Cream, 453
Eclairs, Vanilla, 453
Egg Noodles, Old-Fashioned, 55
Eggplant
Eggplant Parmigiana, 243
Jackstraw Eggplant, 241
Moussaka, 132
Moussaka for a Crowd, 243
Pan-Fried Eggplant, 241
Party Eggplant Parmesan, 119
Stuffed Eggplant, 243
Eggs
Avocado Egg Salad, 342
Baked Eggs and Ham, 105
Broccoli-Egg Bake, 219
Brunch Eggs Ranchero, 134
Curried Eggs with Shrimp, 114

Eggs *(continued)*
Egg-Stuffed Zucchini, 291
Festive Hash and Eggs, 86
Hashed Brown Omelet, 270
Huevos Rancheros, 283
Mushroom-Sauced Eggs, 251
Potatoes and Eggs au Gratin, 272
Elegant Fruit Combo, 445
Enchiladas, Chicken, 134
Enchiladas Dos, 108
Enchilada Squares, 84
Everyday Meat Loaf, 20
Everyday Waffles, 403
Feather Pancakes, 402
Festive Hash and Eggs, 86
Fiesta Salmon, 109
Fig Mold, Spicy Orange-, 331
Filled Corn Muffins, 394
Finnish Chestnut Fingers, 431
Firepot, Hot, 260
Fish
Barbecued Fish, 178
Beet Supper Salad, 217
Bouillabaisse, 62
Broiled Fish, 62
Charcoaled Halibut Steaks, 180
Corn-Stuffed Whitefish, 61
Crispy-Grilled Fish Fillets, 178
Fiesta Salmon, 109
Fish and Chip Bake, 78
Fish Florentine, 89
Fish in a Basket, 178
Foil-Wrapped Clambake, 181
Grilled Salmon Steaks, 182
Halibut Kabobs, 179
Halibut with Dill Topping, 64
Highbrow Haddock, 115
Marinated Tuna and
Vegetables, 350
Pan-Fried Fish, 61
Quick Tuna-Macaroni Salad, 345
Rice and Tuna Pie, 114
Salmon-Broccoli Crepes, 121
Salmon Croquettes, 62
Salmon-Macaroni Pie, 89
Salmon Potato Salad, 352
Salmon-Stuffed Tomatoes, 351
Shaker Fish Pie, 79
Shrimp and Tuna Bake, 64
Skillet-Fried Fish, 176
Soy-Marinated Perch Fillets, 178
Stuffed Smoked Salmon, 179
Trout Amandine, 61
Tuna-Broccoli Bake, 64
Tuna-Macaroni Casserole, 80
Tuna-Noodle Casserole, 79
Tuna-Rice Soufflé, 89
Tuna Salad Bake, 89

Fish *(continued)*
Tuna Salad in Tomato Cups, 342
Tuna with Rice for One, 109
Wild Rice-Stuffed Salmon, 179
Wine-Sauced Trout, 176
5-Cup Salad, 322
Fluffy White Frosting, 412
Foil-Barbecued Shrimp, 181
Foil-Wrapped Clambake, 181
Fondues
Apricot Cream Fondue, 452
Caramel-Chocolate Fondue, 462
Chocolate Fondue, 452
Coffee Fondue, 452
Mint Fondue, 452
Frankfurters
Frank and Bean Skillet, 184
Frank and Corn Crown, 87
Frankfurter-Cheese Casserole, 70
Frank-Stuffed Tomatoes, 105
Frank Tamale Pie, 70
Frank-Vegetable Bake, 70
Golden-Sauced Franks, 45
Hot Frank and Rice Salad, 72
Jiffy Frank and Cabbage Skillet,
184
Pizza-Frank Sandwiches, 156
Quick Frank Kabobs, 183
Savory Frank-Noodle Bake, 87
Tangy Barbecued Franks, 183
French Canadian Split Pea Soup, 266
French Chocolate Coffee Cake, 376
French Crunch Peach Pie, 420
French Dressing, Creamy, 358
French-Fried Onions, Perfect, 258
French-Fried Shrimp, 65
French Fries, 274
French Onion Soup, 256
French Toast, Company, 406
French Toast, Frozen, 406
Fresh Corn Chowder, 237
Fresh Creamed Corn, 237
Fresh Fries with Onion, 271
Fresh Fruit Crisp, 446
Fresh Herb Dressing, 357
Fresh Mint Sauce, 40
Fresh Orange Bavarian Cream, 454
Fresh Pear Dumplings, 444
Fresh Strawberry Cobbler, 445
Fresh Strawberry Ice Cream, 448
Fried Chicken, Maryland, 48
Fried Chicken, Oven-, 48
Fried Chicken, Pan-, 46
Fried Chicken, Southern-Style, 48
Fried Chicken, Two-Step, 46
Fried Fish, Pan-, 61
Fritter Rings, Apple, 401
Fritters, Corn, 401

Fritters, Two-Bean, 213
Frostings
  Butter Frosting, 417
  Chocolate Butter Frosting, 417
  Chocolate Glaze, 434
  Cinnamon Glaze, 400
  Cocoa-Buttermilk Frosting, 434
  Coconut Frosting, 410
  Confectioners' Icing, 372
  Cream Cheese Frosting, 227
  Fluffy White Frosting, 412
  Fudge Frosting, 436
  Lemon Glaze, 433
  Mocha Butter Frosting, 417
  Orange Glaze, 400
  Penuche Frosting, 417
  Sea Foam Frosting, 409
  Seven-Minute Frosting, 417
  Three-Way Cream Cheese
    Frosting, 417
  Toasted Meringue Topping, 411
  Toasted Pecan Frosting, 412
Frosty Fruit Cubes, 335
Frosty Pear Squares, 335
Frozen Cheesecake Salads, 334
Frozen Cherry Salad, 334
Frozen Cranberry Salads, 335
Frozen French Toast, 406
Frozen Fruitcake Salad, 334
Frozen Lemon Salad, 333
Frozen Lime-Mint Salads, 332
Frozen Orange-Date Molds, 333
Frozen Strawberry-Banana
  Salads, 334
Fruitcake, Dark, 415
Fruit Compote Supreme, 443
Fruited Avocado Freeze, 333
Fruited Beef Stew, 111
Fruit-Glazed Ham, 165
Fruit Melange, 443
Fruit Salad Platter, 319
Fruit Salads, 318-323
Fruit Salads, Frozen, 332-335
Fruit Salads, Molded, 324-331
Fruit-Turkey Kabobs, 49
Fruity Ginger Ale Mold, 325
Fudge, Almond, 460
Fudge Frosting, 436
Fudge, Java, 460
Fudge, No-Cook, 461
Fudge Ribbon Pie, 426

G-N

Garden Batter Bread, 372
Garden-Fresh Tomato Aspic, 315
Garden Gold Soup, 227
Garden Row Salad, 293
Garden-Stuffed Peppers, 267
Garlic Croutons, 365
Garlic Okra Pickles, 253
Garnishes, Salad, 365
German Potato Salad, 307
German Stollen, 387
German-Style New Potato Salad,
  272
Giant Stuffed Grillburger, 155
Ginger Ale Mold, Fruity, 325
Ginger Cupcakes, 462
Ginger Ham Grill, Orange-, 165
Ginger-Lemon Pudding Cake, 442
Gingersnap-Graham Crust, 427
Glazed Pork Kabobs, 163
Golden Beef Pot Roast, 10
Golden Carrot Bake, 227
Golden Chiffon Cake, 415
Golden Cupcakes, 415
Golden-Sauced Franks, 45
Gold Rush Brunch, 118
Gooseberry-Banana Salad, 328
Graham Crackers, Cinnamon-, 406
Grandma's Oatmeal Bread, 369
Grape and Grapefruit Mold, 324
Grapes, Frosted, 324
Grasshopper Pie, 426
Greek Salad, 301
Greek Spinach Pie, 131
Green Bean Bake with Onion, 214
Green Beans Amandine, 214
Green Beans Supreme, 212
Green Corn Pudding, 233
Green Goddess Dressing, 361
Green Tomato Pickles, 287
Grilled Crab and Cheese Rolls, 157
Grilled Island Chicken, 172
Grilled Potato and Onion Bake, 271
Grilled Rock Lobster Tails, 182
Grilled Salmon Steaks, 182
Gumbo, Creole, 255
Gypsy Pork Steaks, 160
Haddock, Highbrow, 115
Halibut Kabobs, 179
Halibut Steaks, Charcoaled, 180
Halibut with Dill Topping, 64
Ham
  Baked Eggs and Ham, 105
  Barbecue-Glazed Ham and
    Pineapple, 38
  Cabbage and Ham Slaw, 224
  Cauliflower-Ham Bake, 118
  Cauliflower-Ham Chowder, 230
  Chef's Bowl, 336
  Chicken and Ham Supreme, 341
  Curry-Sauced Ham, 38
  Easy Cassoulet, 117
  Fruit-Glazed Ham, 165

Ham (continued)
  Ham and Broccoli Bake, 124
  Ham and Mac Bake, 68
  Ham and Vegetables Mornay, 94
  Ham Hocks and Black-Eyed
    Peas, 266
  Ham Hocks 'n Greens, 246
  Ham-Potato Bake, 94
  Ham Potluck Supper, 126
  Ham Pot Pie, 96
  Ham Slice with Cranberry
    Sauce, 165
  Mandarin Ham Rolls, 111
  Mexican Chef's Salad, 341
  Orange-Ginger Ham Grill, 165
  Orange-Sauced Ham, 166
  Pizza Quiche, 118
  Potato-Ham Scallop, 68
  Skewered Ham and Fruit
    Kabobs, 166
  Slim Ham Slaw, 354
  Spiced Ham Patties, 156
  Spinach Squares Hollandaise, 126
  Stuffed Pepper Cups, 96
  Sweet-Sour Ham, 166
  Triple-Cheese Pie, 92
Hamburger-Noodle Bake, 122
Hamburger Pie, 77
Hard Sauce, Brandy, 420
Harvard Beets, 218
Harvest Fruit Mold, 324
Harvest Pot Roast, 30
Hashed Brown Omelet, 270
Hash, Mexican-Style, 99
Hash, Oven Beef, 99
Hawaiian Kabobs, 149
Hawaiian-Style Parsnips, 262
Hearts of Artichoke Versailles, 305
Hearts of Palm Salad, 304
Herb Dressing, Fresh, 357
Herbed Fresh Tomato Soup, 284
Herbed Lamb Kabobs, 41
Herbed Lamb-Vegetable Kabobs,
  187
Herbed Spinach Bake, 276
Herb-Glazed Chickens, 173
Herb Marinade, Armenian, 194
Herb Rolls, Refrigerated, 375
Herb-Seasoned Marinade, 194
Hickory-Smoked Royal Ribs, 161
Hickory-Smoked Stuffed Trout, 176
Hickory-Smoked Turkey, 168
Highbrow Haddock, 115
High Citrus Pie, 424
Hollandaise Sauce, Asparagus with
  Orange, 211
Home-Canned Cream-Style
  Corn, 235

Home-Canned Red Pepper
Relish, 269
Home-Canned Whole Kernel
Corn, 235
Homemade Corn and Chicken
Soup, 55
Homemade Mincemeat Pie, 420
Honey-Pumpkin Pie, 422
Hoppin' John, 266
Horseradish Sauce, Brisket of Beef
with, 13
Horseradish-Stuffed Rump
Roast, 144
Hot Crab Bake, 117
Hot Firepot, 260
Hot Five-Bean Salad, 312
Hot Frank and Rice Salad, 72
Hot Pickled Peppers, 269
Hot Smoky Potato Salad, 45
Hot-Style Eye of Round, 141
Hot Turkey Sandwiches, 50
Huevos Rancheros, 283
Ice Creams
Fresh Strawberry Ice Cream, 448
Marshmallow Ice Cream, 448
Peanut Butter and Jelly
Freeze, 448
Raspberry Sherbet, 449
Vanilla Custard Ice Cream, 448
Indian Pudding, 438
Individual Chicken Pies, 51
Individual Pot Pies, 102
Imperial Chicken Salad, 348
Imperial Garden Salad, 317
Italian Bread, 384
Italian Breadsticks, 375
Italian-Dipped Artichokes, 208
Italian-Dressed Cauliflower, 228
Italian Dressing, 357
Italian Salad Mold, 317
Jackstraw Eggplant, 241
Jam-Filled Cookies, 432
Japanese Custard Soup, 276
Japanese-Style Chicken, 175
Java Fudge, 460
Jerusalem Artichokes with Parslied
Cream Sauce, 208
Jiffy Frank and Cabbage Skillet, 184
Jubilee Salad Mold, 325
Kabobs
Apricot Lamb Kabobs, 185
Barbecued Shrimp Kabobs, 180
Beef and Mushroom Kabobs, 147
Beef-Yam Kabobs, 148
Chicken and Beef Kabobs, 175
Fruit-Turkey Kabobs, 49
Glazed Pork Kabobs, 163
Halibut Kabobs, 179

Kabobs (continued)
Hawaiian Kabobs, 149
Herbed Lamb-Vegetable
Kabobs, 187
Japanese-Style Chicken, 175
Korean Kabobs, 163
Mustard-Brushed Bologna
Kabobs, 183
Quick Frank Kabobs, 183
Skewered Beef Bundles, 149
Skewered Bratwurst, 184
Skewered Cherry Tomato
Meatballs, 149
Skewered Ham and Fruit
Kabobs, 166
Skewered Scallops and Bacon,
181
Steak and Shrimp Kabob
Dinner, 147
Vegetable-Meat Kabobs, 167
Kale, Sweet-Sour, 246
Kidney Pie, Steak and, 130
Kohlrabi-Carrot Bake, 247
Kohlrabi Slaw, 247
Kolache, 387
Korean Kabobs, 163
Kowloon Duckling, 171
Lamb
Apricot Lamb Kabobs, 185
Armenian-Italian Lamb Chops,
187
Armenian Pilaf, 128
Crown Roast of Lamb with Rice
Stuffing, 40
Dilled Lamb Ragout, 129
Herbed Lamb Kabobs, 41
Herbed Lamb-Vegetable
Kabobs, 187
Lamb-Lentil Stew, 73
Lemony Lamb Shoulder Chops, 41
Marinated Leg of Lamb, 185
Moussaka, 132
Moussaka for a Crowd, 243
Saucy Lamb Riblets, 187
Seasoned Leg of Lamb, 40
Spicy Lamb Stew, 41
Lasaga, Peppy, 124
Lasagna, Seafood, 126
Layered Corned Beef Bake, 74
Layered Parmesan Loaf, 407
Layered Supper, 122
Leeks
Oxtail-Leek Stew, 258
Vichyssoise, 271
Lemon
Barbecued Lemon Turkey, 168
Lemonade Chicken, 175
Lemon Bars, 435

Lemon (continued)
Lemon Broccoli, 221
Lemon-Cheese Dessert Bombe,
455
Lemon-Frosted Plum Squares, 326
Lemon Glaze, 433
Lemon-Marinated Chuck Roast,
138
Lemon Meringue Pie, 421
Lemon Mousse, 454
Lemon-Papaya Salad, 330
Lemon Pepper Flank Pinwheels,
137
Lemon Pudding Cake, 441
Lemon Puff Pillow Buns, 383
Lemon Rounds, 433
Lemon Sponge Cake, 414
Lemon Turnips, 288
Soy-Lemon Basting Sauce, 192
Lemony Lamb Shoulder Chops, 41
Lentil Stew, Lamb-, 73
Lettuce
Braised Lettuce, 250
Chili-Pepperoni Salad Bowl, 250
Original Caesar Salad, 250
24-Hour Vegetable Salad, 248
Lima Beans, Creamy, 213
Lima Beans, Mexican, 215
Lima Cups, Creamy, 313
Lime Daiquiri Pie, 424
Lobsters
Crab or Lobster Newburg, 65
Grilled Rock Lobster Tails, 182
Lobster in Orange Cups, 342
Steak with Lobster Tail, 14
Louisiana Relish, 293
Low-Calorie Salads, 350-355
Low-Calorie Salad Dressings,
362-363
Luau Spareribs, 161
Luncheon Meats
Meat and Potato Bake, 167
Mustard-Brushed Bologna
Kabobs, 183
Pineapple-Glazed Luncheon
Meat, 167
Super-Simple Skillet Supper, 167
Vegetable-Meat Kabobs, 167
Macaroni
Beef-Macaroni Italiano, 98
Corned Beef-Macaroni Pie, 87
Creamy Chicken Casserole, 90
Curried Seafood Bake, 80
Dilly Macaroni Salad, 308
Frankfurter-Cheese Casserole,
70
Ham and Mac Bake, 68
Macaroni and Cheese, 82

Macaroni *(continued)*
Macaroni and Cheese for Two, 107
Macaroni and Meatballs, 86
Macaroni-Cheddar Salad, 312
Macaroni Salad, 312
Pasticchio, 131
Red-Ribbon Cheese Casserole, 92
Salmon-Macaroni Pie, 89
Tuna-Macaroni Casserole, 80
Macaroons, Coconut, 429
Main Dish Salads, 336-349
Mandarin Ham Rolls, 111
Manicotti, 24
Manicotti, Chili, 107
Manicotti, Saucy Turkey, 112
Maple-Glazed Meat and Beans, 90
Marble Pound Cake, 414
Marinades
Armenian Herb Marinade, 194
Herb-Seasoned Marinade, 194
Savory Wine Marinade, 194
Teriyaki Marinade, 194
Marinated Beef Broil, 18
Marinated Brussels Sprouts
Appetizers, 222
Marinated Herbed Tomatoes, 286
Marinated Hickory-Smoked Chuck
Roast, 141
Marinated Leg of Lamb, 185
Marinated Pork Loin Roast, 160
Marinated Relish Salad, 305
Marinated Three-Bean Salad, 215
Marinated Tuna and Vegetables, 350
Marinated Vegetable Salad, 296
Marshmallow Ice Cream, 448
Maryland Fried Chicken, 48
Meat and Potato Bake, 167
Meat and Potato Pie, 84
Meat and Rice Bake, 103
Meatballs
Barbecued Beans and
Meatballs, 122
Macaroni and Meatballs, 86
Meatball Meal-in-One, 107
Meatball-Okra Stew, 255
Meatballs Oriental-Style, 22
Porcupine Meatballs, 22
Meatless Main Dishes
Cheese Soufflé, 129
Classic Cheese Strata, 82
Greek Spinach Pie, 131
Macaroni and Cheese, 82
Macaroni and Cheese for
Two, 107
Meatless Meal-in-a-Bowl, 351
Pizza Siciliana, 135
Quiche Lorraine, 129
Spinach and Cheese Soufflé, 119

Meat Loaf, Everyday, 20
Meat Loaf Puff, 21
Meat Roll, Sicilian, 20
Melon Salad, Strawberry-, 319
Meringue for Pie, 421
Mexican Chef's Salad, 341
Mexican Lima Beans, 215
Mexican-Style Hash, 99
Microwave Recipes
Acapulco Bean Casserole, 82
Beef-Stuffed Acorn Squash, 105
Candied Squash Rings, 278
Chicken and Onion Bake, 67
Curried Seafood Bake, 80
Frank-Stuffed Tomatoes, 105
Frank-Vegetable Bake, 70
Harvard Beets, 218
Meat and Rice Bake, 103
Meatball Meal-in-One, 107
Microwave Know-How, 93
Mushroom-Sauced Eggs, 251
Parsley Buttered Corn, 237
Pork Chop-Fried Rice
Casserole, 69
Sesame Asparagus, 211
Stuffed Pepper Cups, 96
Summer Squash Casserole, 289
Tuna-Noodle Casserole, 79
Tuna with Rice for One, 109
Twice-Baked Potatoes, 274
Wild Rice-Chicken Casserole, 113
Mincemeat Pie, Homemade, 420
Mini Pineapple Meat Loaves, 154
Minted New Peas, 266
Minted Pear Salad, 328
Mocha Butter Frosting, 417
Mocha Steamed Pudding, 457
Molasses Corn Bread, 404
Molasses-Orange Barbecue
Sauce, 190
Molasses-Pumpkin Pie, 422
Molded Vegetable Salads, 314-317
Mostaccioli, Zippy, 74
Moussaka, 132
Moussaka for a Crowd, 243
Mousse, Lemon, 454
Muffins
Best-Ever Muffins, 393
Blueberry-Lemon Muffins, 393
Bran Muffins, 394
Carrot Muffins, 394
Cheesy Corn Muffins, 404
Chocolate Chip Muffins, 393
Cinnamon-Apple-Raisin Muffins,
393
Enriched Best-Ever Muffins, 393
Filled Corn Muffins, 394
Low-Fat Best-Ever Muffins, 393

Muffins *(continued)*
Nutty Muffins, 393
Pineapple-Pecan Muffins, 393
Sweet Best-Ever Muffins, 393
Two-Cheese Muffins, 394
Mushrooms
Beef and Mushroom Kabobs, 147
Beef Stroganoff, 27
Cauliflower with Cheese-
Mushroom Sauce, 230
Cream of Mushroom Soup, 252
Deluxe Peas and Mushrooms, 263
Dill-Stuffed Mushrooms, 252
Mushroom-Avocado Duo, 297
Mushroom Cocktail, 252
Mushroom-Sauced Eggs, 251
Pepper Steak, Oriental, 28
Pickled Mushrooms, 252
Rainbow Beef, 28
Tyrolean Alps Ragout, 27
Mustard Beans, 213
Mustard-Brushed Bologna
Kabobs, 183
Mustard-Glazed Country Ribs, 36
Mustard-Sauced Cabbage
Wedges, 225
Nectarine Quick Shortcake, 444
Newburg, Crab or Lobster, 65
New England Baked Beans, 214
New England Boiled Dinner, 13
No-Cook Fudge, 461
No-Knead Refrigerator Rolls, 368
Noodles
Beef-Noodle Bake, 86
Crowd-Size Chicken Bake, 127
Curried Beef Bake, 120
Hamburger-Noodle Bake, 122
Old-Fashioned Egg Noodles, 55
Savory Frank-Noodle Bake, 87
Tuna-Noodle Casserole, 79
Shrimp and Noodle Bake, 80
Nutmeg Feather Cake, 411

O-R

Oatmeal Bread, Grandma's, 369
Okra
Brunswick Stew, 255
Creole Gumbo, 255
Garlic Okra Pickles, 253
Ham Hocks and Black-Eyed
Peas, 266
Meatball-Okra Stew, 255
Southern Vegetable Medley, 253
Old-Fashioned Bread Stuffing, 60
Old-Fashioned Egg Noodles, 55
Old-Fashioned Fresh Vegetable-Beef
Soup, 292

Old-Time Whole Wheat Bread, 371
Olive Spaghetti Sauce, 23
Omelet, Hashed Brown, 270
Omelet Tarragon, Asparagus, 209
One Cup Cottage Ring, 314
Onions
　Beefy Onion Pie, 99
　Broccoli-Onion Deluxe, 221
　Chicken and Onion Bake, 67
　Creamed Onions, 256
　Creamed Peas and Onions, 264
　French Onion Soup, 256
　Fresh Fries with Onion, 271
　Grilled Potato and Onion Bake, 271
　Onion Buns, 374
　Onion-Stuffed Steak, 140
　Perfect French-Fried Onions, 258
Oranges
　Apple-Orange Stuffed Pork
　　Chops, 158
　Cherry-Orange Squares, 330
　Chicken Salad a l'Orange, 344
　Fresh Orange Bavarian Cream,
　　454
　Frozen Orange-Date Molds, 333
　Lobster in Orange Cups, 342
　Molasses-Orange Barbecue
　　Sauce, 190
　Orange-Apricot Freeze, 332
　Orange Coffee Cake, 407
　Orange-Cream Fruit Salad, 322
　Orange Doughnuts, 400
　Orange-Ginger Ham Grill, 165
　Orange-Glazed Smoked Shoulder,
　　38
　Orange Nut Bread, 398
　Orange-Pecan Pie, 422
　Orange Sauce, 456
　Orange-Sauced Ham, 166
　Orange-Strawberry Cake, 411
　Pineapple-Orange Glaze, 191
　Spiced Orange Chicken, 51
　Spicy Orange-Fig Mold, 331
Oriental Garden Toss, 259
Oriental Pork Wrap-Ups, 157
Original Caesar Salad, 250
Oven-Baked Beef-Lima Stew, 76
Oven-Baked Beef Stew, 29
Oven-Baked Pork Stew, 35
Oven Beef Hash, 99
Oven-Easy Chicken Croquettes, 49
Oven-Fried Chicken, 48
Oven Pancake, 402
Oven Stew for Two, 106
Oven-Style Peas, 263
Oven Swiss Steak, 18
Oxtail-Leek Stew, 258
Paella Casserole, 132

Pancakes
　Blender Bread Crumb Pancakes,
　　402
　Buttermilk Pancakes, 402
　Feather Pancakes, 402
　Oven Pancake, 402
　Peanut Butter Pancakes, 402
Pan-Fried Eggplant, 241
Pan-Fried Chicken, 46
Pan-Fried Fish, 61
Pan Pizza, 26
Papaya Salad, Lemon-, 330
Parmesan Loaf, Layered, 407
Parmigiana, Eggplant, 243
Parsley Buttered Corn, 237
Parsnips and Sweet Potatoes,
　Whipped, 262
Parsnips, Hawaiian-Style, 262
Party Eggplant Parmesan, 119
Pastel de Chocolo, 134
Pasticchio, 131
Pastry for Double-Crust Pie, 427
Pastry for Single-Crust Pie, 427
Pastry, Plain, 72
Pattypan Squash, Stuffed, 291
Pea and Celery Bake, 265
Pea-Cheese Salad, 264
Pea Pods
　Buttered Pea Pods, 260
　Oriental Garden Toss, 259
　Pork Chop Suey, 34
　Rainbow Beef, 28
Peaches
　Cranberry-Peach Cobbler, 446
　French Crunch Peach Pie, 420
　Peach-Glazed Corned Beef, 13
　Peach Parfait Pie, 424
　Peach-Pecan Dessert, 445
　Peachy Beef Toss, 338
Peanut Brittle, Brown Sugar, 461
Peanut Butter and Jelly Freeze, 448
Peanut Butter Coffee Cake, 396
Peanut Butter-Jelly Twists, 381
Peanut Cookies, Double, 433
Peanut-Oatmeal Drops, 428
Pears
　Fresh Pear Dumplings, 444
　Frosty Pear Squares, 335
　Fruited Avocado Freeze, 333
　Minted Pear Salad, 328
　Pear-Limeade Molds, 326
　Pears in Chocolate Fluff, 450
Peas
　Chilled Pea Soup, 265
　Creamed Peas and Onions, 264
　Creole Peas, 264
　Deluxe Peas and Mushrooms, 263
　Dutch Pea Soup, 265

Peas *(continued)*
　Minted New Peas, 266
　Oven-Style Peas, 263
　Pea and Celery Bake, 265
　Pea-Cheese Salad, 264
　Quick Creamed Peas, 265
　Springtime Peas, 264
Pecans
　Caramel-Pecan Rolls, 380
　Cranberry-Pecan Pie, 422
　Orange-Pecan Pie, 422
　Pecan Petal Biscuits, 392
　Pecan Pie, 422
Pennsylvania Red Cabbage, 223
Penuche Frosting, 417
Peppermint Ice Cream Roll, 449
Peppers
　Beef in Pepper Cups, 269
　Dinner in a Pepper, 24
　Garden-Stuffed Peppers, 267
　Stuffed Pepper Cups, 96
Pepper Steak, Oriental, 28
Pepper Steak Salad, 337
Peppy Chuck Steak Grill, 138
Peppy Lasagna, 124
Perch Fillets, Soy-Marinated, 178
Perfect French-Fried Onions, 258
Perfection Salad, 225
Perfect White Bread (conventional
　method), 367
Perfect White Bread (easy-mix
　method), 367
Pickled Vegetables
　Hot Pickled Peppers, 269
　Mustard Beans, 213
　Pickled Carrots, 227
　Pickled Mushrooms, 252
Pickles
　Kosher Dill Pickles, 240
　Crisp Pickle Slices, 240
　Dill Pickles, 240
　Garlic Okra Pickles, 253
　Green Tomato Pickles, 287
　Quick Mustard Pickles, 238
Pies
　All-American Apple Pie, 418
　Cherry Pie, 418
　Chocolate Wafer Crust, 426
　Cranberry-Pecan Pie, 422
　Custard Pie, 422
　Deep-Dish Apple Pie, 419
　French Crunch Peach Pie, 420
　Fudge Ribbon Pie, 426
　Gingersnap-Graham Crust, 427
　Grasshopper Pie, 426
　High Citrus Pie, 424
　Homemade Mincemeat Pie, 420
　Honey-Pumpkin Pie, 422

Pies *(continued)*
  Lemon Meringue Pie, 421
  Lime Daiquiri Pie, 424
  Meringue for Pie, 421
  Molasses-Pumpkin Pie, 422
  Orange-Pecan Pie, 422
  Pastry for Double-Crust Pie, 427
  Pastry for Single-Crust Pie, 427
  Peach Parfait Pie, 424
  Pecan Pie, 422
  Pineapple Parfait Pie, 423
  Pumpkin Pie, 422
  Rhubarb-Strawberry Pie, 418
  Strawberry Chiffon Pie, 423
  Strawberry Glacé Pie, 420
  Upside-Down Berry Pie, 423
  Vanilla Cream Pie, 421
Pilaf, Armenian, 128
Pineapples
  Baked Pineapple Tapioca, 438
  Mini Pineapple Meat Loaves, 154
  Pineapple-Berry Boat, 319
  Pineapple-Glazed Luncheon Meat,
    167
  Pineapple Hawaiian Chicken, 50
  Pineapple-Orange Glaze, 191
  Pineapple Parfait Pie, 423
Pink Parfaits, 450
Piquant Cauliflower, 302
Pizza
  Pan Pizza, 26
  Pizza-Frank Sandwiches, 156
  Pizza Quiche, 118
  Pizza Siciliana, 135
  Sicilian Pizza Supreme, 44
  Tostada Pizza, 26
Plain Pastry, 72
Planked Chopped Steak, 19
Plantation Spareribs, 36
Plum Squares, Lemon-Frosted, 326
Polish Sausage-Krauters, 184
Polynesian Shrimp Bowl, 345
Popover Chicken Tarragon, 53
Popovers, 406
Porcupine Meatballs, 22
Pork
  Apple and Pork Casserole, 97
  Apple-Orange Stuffed Pork Chops,
    158
  Apple-Peanut Buttered Pork
    Steaks, 160
  Apricot Glazed Ribs, 162
  Baking Smoked Pork, 39
  Barbecued Orange-Apricot Ribs,
    36
  Casserole Chop Suey, 125
  Chili Barbecued Pork Chops, 33
  Chinese Smoked Ribs, 162

Pork *(continued)*
  Choucroute Garni, 43
  Cipâte, 130
  Company Pork Loin Roast, 160
  Corn-Stuffed Pork Chops, 158
  Country-Style Barbecued Ribs, 162
  Cranberry-Pork Bake, 97
  Glazed Pork Kabobs, 163
  Gypsy Pork Steaks, 160
  Harvest Pot Roast, 30
  Hickory-Smoked Royal Ribs, 161
  Korean Kabobs, 163
  Luau Spareribs, 161
  Marinated Pork Loin Roast, 160
  Mustard-Glazed Country Ribs, 36
  Orange-Glazed Smoked Shoulder,
    38
  Oriental Pork Wrap-Ups, 157
  Oven-Baked Pork Stew, 35
  Plantation Spareribs, 36
  Pork and Apples with Stuffing, 91
  Pork Chop-Fried Rice Casserole,
    69
  Pork Chop Suey, 34
  Pork Chop Supper, 109
  Pork Crown Roast with Apricot
    Stuffing, 30
  Pork Florentine, 97
  Pork in Sweet-Sour Sauce, 34
  Pork Steaks with Apple Stuffing, 33
  Pork Stroganoff for a Crowd, 35
  Roasting Fresh Pork, 32
  Roast Pork Chops, 158
  Smoky Pork Skillet, 33
  Stuffed Cabbage Rolls, 76
  Sweet-Sour Kraut and Chops, 69
  Tourtiére, 130
Potatoes
  Apple and Pork Casserole, 97
  Beef Stew Bake, 74
  Calico Potato Salad, 272
  Cipâte, 130
  Clam Chowder Pie, 79
  Creamy Potato Salad, 306
  Crunch-Top Potatoes, 271
  Fish and Chip Bake, 78
  French Fries, 274
  Fresh Fries with Onion, 271
  German Potato Salad, 307
  German-Style New Potato Salad,
    272
  Gold Rush Brunch, 118
  Grilled Potato and Onion Bake, 271
  Ham and Vegetables Mornay, 94
  Hamburger Pie, 77
  Ham-Potato Bake, 94
  Hashed Brown Omelet, 270
  Layered Corned Beef Bake, 74

Potatoes *(continued)*
  Layered Supper, 122
  Meat and Potato Pie, 84
  Meatball Meal-in-One, 107
  Mexican-Style Hash, 99
  Oven Beef Hash, 99
  Oven Stew for Two, 106
  Potatoes and Eggs au Gratin, 272
  Potato-Ham Scallop, 68
  Potato Salad Nicoise, 307
  Potato Salad Roll, 274
  Potluck Potato Salad, 307
  Puffed Potatoes and Sausage, 73
  Salami-Cheese Pie, 72
  Sauerkraut and Sausage Bake, 92
  Sausage au Gratin, 124
  Scalloped Potatoes, 271
  Sweet-Sour Kraut and Chops, 69
  Twice-Baked Potatoes, 274
  Vichyssoise, 123
Potluck Potato Salad, 307
Pot Roast Dip Sandwiches, 9
Pots de Crème, 439
Poultry
  Apricot-Sauced Duckling, 58
  Baked Bean Cassoulet, 213
  Barbecued Lemon Turkey, 168
  Barbecued Spicy Chicken, 49
  Basic Broiled Chicken, 48
  Bran-Flake Chicken and Peaches,
    46
  Broiled Crab-Chicken Rolls, 50
  Brunswick Stew, 255
  Buffet Chicken Scallop, 127
  Caesar's Chicken Salad, 348
  Carolina Chicken Pie, 67
  Chicken and Beef Kabobs, 175
  Chicken and Brown Rice Toss, 345
  Chicken and Dumplings, 54
  Chicken and Ham Supreme, 341
  Chicken and Onion Bake, 67
  Chicken and Stuffing Scallop, 53
  Chicken and Vegetable Bundles,
    174
  Chicken-Asparagus Divan, 113
  Chicken Breasts Florentine, 111
  Chicken Cacciatore, 54
  Chicken Curry Soufflés, 112
  Chicken Divan, 53
  Chicken Enchiladas, 134
  Chicken-Noodle Casserole, 51
  Chicken Pineapple Boat, 351
  Chicken Puff Casserole, 100
  Chicken Salad a l'Orange, 344
  Chicken-Spaghetti Bake, 68
  Chicken Teriyaki, 172
  Chicken with Zucchini Stuffing, 173
  Cipâte, 130

Poultry *(continued)*
　Club Chicken Casserole, 112
　Confetti Chicken Salad, 350
　Corned Beef-Turkey Heroes, 156
　Cornish Hens with Rice Stuffing, 170
　Corn-Stuffed Chicken, 113
　Corn-Stuffed Chicken Breasts, 172
　Cranberry-Stuffed Cornish Hens, 58
　Creamy Chicken Casserole, 90
　Crowd-Size Chicken Bake, 127
　Curried Chicken Salad, 348
　Curried Turkey Pie, 101
　Curry Barbecued Chicken, 174
　Deep-Dish Chicken Pie, 90
　Foil-Wrapped Clambake, 181
　Fruit-Turkey Kabobs, 49
　Grilled Island Chicken, 172
　Herb-Glazed Chickens, 173
　Hickory-Smoked Turkey, 168
　Homemade Corn and Chicken Soup, 55
　Hot Turkey Sandwiches, 50
　Imperial Chicken Salad, 348
　Individual Chicken Pies, 51
　Japanese-Style Chicken, 175
　Kowloon Duckling, 171
　Lemonade Chicken, 175
　Maryland Fried Chicken, 48
　Oven-Easy Chicken Croquettes, 49
　Oven-Fried Chicken, 48
　Paella Casserole, 132
　Pan-Fried Chicken, 46
　Pastel de Chocolo, 134
　Pineapple Hawaiian Chicken, 50
　Popover Chicken Tarragon, 53
　Roasting Domestic Birds, 56
　Roast Sweet-Sour Chickens, 58
　Rotisserie-Roast Turkey, 170
　Saucy Turkey Manicotti, 112
　Sausage-Stuffed Chicken Roll-Ups, 172
　Smoked Turkey Roast, 168
　Southern-Style Fried Chicken, 48
　Spiced Orange Chicken, 51
　Spicy Barbecued Chicken, 174
　Stewed Chicken, 54
　Sunday Chicken-Rice Bake, 67
　Sweet-Sour Cornish Hens, 170
　Tetrazzini Crepes, 121
　Turkey-Broccoli Bake, 101
　Turkey Chowder, 55
　Turkey in Aspic, 352
　Turkey Soufflé, 100
　Turkey with Fruited Stuffing, 127
　Two-Step Fried Chicken, 46
　Wild Rice-Chicken Casserole, 113

Pound Cake, Marble, 414
Praline Cheesecake, 452
Praline Cheese Cups, 462
Pretzels, Rye, 388
Puddings
　Apple Bread Pudding, 442
　Baked Custard, 441
　Baked Pineapple Tapioca, 438
　Baked Pumpkin Pudding, 442
　Baked Rice Pudding, 439
　Bread Pudding, 439
　Butterscotch Crunch, 441
　Chocolate Pudding, 438
　Ginger-Lemon Pudding Cake, 442
　Indian Pudding, 438
　Lemon Pudding Cake, 441
　Pots de Crème, 439
　Saucepan Rice Pudding, 439
　Stirred Custard, 441
　Tapioca Fluff Pudding, 438
　Vanilla Pudding, 438
Puffed Potatoes and Sausage, 73
Pumpernickel Bread, 371
Pumpkin Bread, 398
Pumpkin Pie, 422
Pumpkin Pie, Honey-, 422
Pumpkin Pie, Molasses-, 422
Pumpkin Pudding, Baked, 442
Quantity Recipes (for 10 or more)
　Barbecued Beans and Meatballs, 122
　Bean and Carrot Salad, 308
　Buffet Chicken Scallop, 127
　Casserole Chop Suey, 125
　Cassoulet Salad, 346
　Cherry-Cider Salad, 328
　Cherry-Orange Squares, 330
　Creamy Potato Salad, 306
　Crowd-Size Chicken Bake, 127
　Frosty Fruit Cubes, 335
　Frozen Lemon Salad, 333
　Frozen Lime-Mint Salads, 332
　Gooseberry-Banana Salad, 328
　Grape and Grapefruit Mold, 324
　Ham and Broccoli Bake, 124
　Hamburger-Noodle Bake, 122
　Ham Potluck Supper, 126
　Hot Five-Bean Salad, 312
　Layered Supper, 122
　Macaroni-Cheddar Salad, 312
　Marinated Relish Salad, 305
　Moussaka for a Crowd, 243
　Orange-Cream Fruit Salad, 322
　Peppy Lasagna, 124
　Pork Stroganoff for a Crowd, 35
　Potluck Potato Salad, 307
　Rainbow Compote, 321
　Sausage au Gratin, 124

Quantity Recipes *(continued)*
　Seafood Lasagna, 126
　Spanish Vegetable Mold, 314
　Spinach Squares Hollandaise, 126
　Turkey with Fruited Stuffing, 127
　24-Hour Fruit Salad, 322
Quiche Lorraine, 129
Quiche, Pizza, 118
Quiche, Shallot-Bacon, 117
Quick Creamed Peas, 265
Quick Frank Kabobs, 183
Quick Garlic Cubed Steaks, 146
Quick Mustard Pickles, 238
Quick Sally Lunn, 396
Quick Tuna-Macaroni Salad, 345
Rainbow Beef, 28
Rainbow Compote, 321
Raisin Drop Biscuits, 392
Raisin-Filled Sweet Potatoes, 282
Raspberries
　Cran-Raspberry Ring, 330
　Raspberry Coffee Cake, 396
　Raspberry Sherbet, 449
　Red Raspberry Crepes, 458
Ratatouille Relish, 193
Raw Vegetable Antipasto, 298
Red Cabbage, Pennsylvania, 223
Red Devil's Food Cake, 409
Red Pepper Relish, 193
Red Raspberry Crepes, 458
Red-Ribbon Cheese Casserole, 92
Red Wine Dressing, 357
Refrigerated Herb Rolls, 375
Relishes
　Beet-Apple Relish, 218
　Corn Relish, 236
　Cucumber Relish, 193
　Home-Canned Red Pepper Relish, 269
　Louisiana Relish, 293
　Ratatouille Relish, 193
　Red Pepper Relish, 193
　Salsa, 284
　Sandwich Coleslaw, 193
　Zesty Sauerkraut Relish, 192
　Zucchini Relish, 291
Reuben Casserole, 104
Rhubarb-Strawberry Pie, 418
Rib Roast Barbecue, 141
Rib Roast with Yorkshire Pudding, Standing, 7
Rice
　Baked Rice Pudding, 439
　Beef-Stuffed Acorn Squash, 105
　Buffet Chicken Scallop, 127
　Casserole Chop Suey, 125
　Chicken and Brown Rice Toss, 345
　Club Chicken Casserole, 112

Rice *(continued)*
    Golden Carrot Bake, 227
    Ham and Broccoli Bake, 124
    Hot Frank and Rice Salad, 72
    Mandarin Ham Rolls, 111
    Meat and Rice Bake, 103
    Paella Casserole, 132
    Pork Chop-Fried Rice Casserole, 69
    Rice and Tuna Pie, 114
    Rice and Vegetable Stuffing, 60
    Rice-Stuffed Cabbage Rolls, 225
    Rice-Stuffed Flank Steak, 140
    Rice-Stuffed Steaks, 14
    Saucepan Rice Pudding, 439
    Stuffed Pepper Cups, 96
    Sunday Chicken-Rice Bake, 67
    Tuna-Rice Soufflé, 89
    Tuna with Rice for One, 109
Roasted Corn on the Cob, 236
Roasting Domestic Birds, 56
Roast Pork Chops, 158
Roast Sweet-Sour Chickens, 58
Rolled Beef Italian-Style, 17
Rolled Sugar Cookies, 432
Rolls
    Basic Rolls, 368
    Basic Sweet Roll Dough, 380
    Batter Rolls, 374
    Brioche, 386
    Brunch Cakes, 407
    Caramel-Pecan Rolls, 380
    Cinnamon Crisps, 381
    Cinnamon Rolls, 380
    Croissants, 386
    Crusty Water Rolls, 374
    Danish Pastry, 383
    Kolache, 387
    Lemon Puff Pillow Buns, 383
    No-Knead Refrigerator Rolls, 368
    Onion Buns, 374
    Peanut Butter-Jelly Twists, 381
    Refrigerated Herb Rolls, 375
    Sourdough-Cheese Rolls, 389
    Thyme-Buttered Crescents, 407
    Whole Wheat Rolls, 375
Rotisserie-Roast Turkey, 170
Round Steak Louisiana, 76
Rump Roast Supreme, 9
Rump Roast with Vegetables, 7
Rumtopf, 443
Russian Dressing, 357
Rutabaga and Apple, 288
Rye Bread, 371
Rye Croutons, 365
Rye Pretzels, 388

S

Salad Burritos, 354
Salad Dressings
    Blue Cheese Salad Dressing, 361
    Buttermilk Dressing, 361
    Chili Dressing, 358
    Cottage Dressing, 352
    Creamy French Dressing, 358
    Creamy Garlic Dressing, 361
    Cucumber Cream Dressing, 360
    Diet Blue Cheese Dressing, 363
    Diet Salad Dressing, 363
    Diet Thousand Island Dressing, 363
    Fresh Herb Dressing, 357
    Green Goddess Dressing, 361
    Honey-Lime Dressing, 319
    Italian Dressing, 357
    Red Wine Dressing, 357
    Russian Dressing, 357
    Spicy Nectar Dressing, 319
    Strawberry-Cheese Dressing, 319
    Tailored for Fruit Salads, 359
    Tangy Tomato Dressing, 358
    Tomato Salad Dressing, 363
    Tomato Soup Dressing, 356
    Vinaigrette with Variations, 359
    Zesty Blue Cheese Dressing, 358
    Zesty Salad Dressing, 362
Salad Garnishes, 365
Salads, Fruit, 318-335
Salads, Low-Calorie, 350-355
Salads, Main Dish, 336-349
    Beet Supper Salad, 217
    Cabbage and Ham Slaw, 224
    Chili-Pepperoni Salad Bowl, 250
    Sausage Supper Salad, 346
    Taco Salad, 20
Salads, Vegetable, 295-317
    Asparagus Vinaigrette, 210
    Beet and Pineapple Mold, 218
    Calico Potato Salad, 272
    Celeriac Toss, 231
    Celery Slaw, 232
    Coleslaw, 223
    Cottage Cheese-Spinach Salad, 276
    Cucumber Ring Supreme, 239
    Curried Broccoli Salad, 221
    Garden Row Salad, 293
    German-Style New Potato Salad, 272
    Kohlrabi Slaw, 247
    Marinated Three-Bean Salad, 215
    Oriental Garden Toss, 259
    Original Caesar Salad, 250
    Pea-Cheese Salad, 264

Salads, Vegetable *(continued)*
    Perfection Salad, 225
    Potato Salad Roll, 274
    Sweet-Sour Swiss Chard, 244
    Tomato Aspic, 286
    24-Hour Vegetable Salad, 248
    Wilted Spinach Salad, 276
    Zesty Vegetable Salad, 226
Salami-Cheese Pie, 72
Salami-Cheese Salad, 346
Salmon
    Fiesta Salmon, 109
    Grilled Salmon Steaks, 182
    Salmon-Broccoli Crepes, 121
    Salmon Croquettes, 62
    Salmon-Macaroni Pie, 89
    Salmon Potato Salad, 352
    Salmon-Stuffed Tomatoes, 351
    Stuffed Smoked Salmon, 179
    Wild Rice-Stuffed Salmon, 179
Salsa, 284
Salt Pork and Greens, 244
Sandwich Coleslaw, 193
Sandwiches
    Bacon Burger Squares, 152
    Beef and Carrot Burgers, 150
    Bratwursts in Beer, 157
    Burgers Extravaganza, 150
    Burgers O'Brien, 150
    Burrito Burgers, 153
    Chili Burger Patties, 152
    Corned Beef-Turkey Heroes, 156
    Grilled Crab and Cheese Rolls, 157
    Hot Turkey Sandwiches, 50
    Pizza-Frank Sandwiches, 156
    Pot Roast Dip Sandwiches, 9
    Stroganoff Sandwich, 26
    Swiss Bratwurst Melt, 43
    Vegetable Burgers, 153
Santa's Whiskers, 433
Saucepan Fudge Brownies, 435
Saucepan Rice Pudding, 439
Sauces
    Ambrosia Sauce, 456
    Apricot Sauce, 403
    Big-Batch Barbecue Sauce, 191
    Blueberry Sauce, 455
    Brandy Hard Sauce, 420
    Brown Sauce, 27
    Brown Sugar Sauce, 457
    Butter-Rum Sauce, 456
    Chili Barbecue Sauce, 191
    Coffee-Soy Glaze, 192
    Cranberry-Claret Sauce, 49
    Durango Sauce, 189
    Easy Barbecue Sauce, 189
    Easy Mushroom Sauce, 53
    Fresh Mint Sauce, 40

Sauces *(continued)*
 Golden Tarragon Sauce, 209
 Homemade Tomato Sauce, 243
 Molasses-Orange Barbecue
  Sauce, 190
 Mushroom Sauce, 258
 Orange Sauce, 456
 Snappy Barbecue Sauce, 189
 Soy-Lemon Basting Sauce, 192
 Tarragon-Cider Basting Sauce, 191
 Western Hot Sauce, 189
 Wine Barbecue Sauce, 188
Saucy Brussels Sprouts, 222
Saucy Dilled Winter Squash, 279
Saucy Lamb Riblets, 187
Saucy Turkey Manicotti, 112
Sauerbraten, 9
Sauerkraut, 225
Sauerkraut and Sausage Bake, 92
Sauerkraut Relish, Zesty, 192
Sauerkraut Salad, 313
Sausages
 A Soup for All Seasons, 45
 Baked Bean Cassoulet, 213
 Barbecued Beans and Meatballs,
  122
 Bratwursts in Beer, 157
 Cassoulet Salad, 346
 Chili-Spaghetti Dinner, 44
 Choucroute Garni, 43
 Corn and Sausage Scallop, 44
 Delicatessen Casserole, 110
 Easy Cassoulet, 117
 Frank-Stuffed Tomatoes, 105
 Hot Smoky Potato Salad, 45
 Paella Casserole, 132
 Peppy Lasagna, 124
 Pizza-Frank Sandwiches, 156
 Pizza Quiche, 118
 Polish Sausage-Krauters, 184
 Puffed Potatoes and Sausage, 73
 Salami-Cheese Salad, 346
 Sauerkraut and Sausage Bake, 92
 Sausage and Beef Chili, 23
 Sausage au Gratin, 124
 Sausage-Stuffed Chicken
  Roll-Ups, 172
 Sausage-Stuffed Turban Squash,
  277
 Sausage Supper Salad, 346
 Sicilian Pizza Supreme, 44
 Skewered Bratwurst, 184
 Spaghetti Pie, 77
 Spicy Italian Salad, 295
 Stuffed Zucchini for One, 109
 Swiss Bratwurst Melt, 43
 Toad in the Hole, 129
Savory Frank-Noodle Bake, 87

Savory Wine Marinade, 194
Scalloped Corn, 237
Scalloped Potatoes, 271
Scalloped Spinach, 275
Scalloped Tomatoes, 284
Scallops and Bacon, Skewered, 181
Scallops Mornay, 108
Scandinavian Cucumbers, 308
Sea Foam Frosting, 409
Seafood (See also Shrimp)
 Bouillabaisse, 62
 Clam Chowder Pie, 79
 Crab or Lobster Newburg, 65
 Creole Gumbo, 255
 Curried Seafood Bake, 80
 Delaware Crab Cakes, 65
 Dieter's Chef Salad, 354
 Paella Casserole, 132
 Scallops Mornay, 108
 Seafood Lasagna, 126
Seasoned Butter Log, 192
Seasoned Leg of Lamb, 40
Sesame Asparagus, 211
Seven-Minute Frosting, 417
Shaker Fish Pie, 79
Shaker Squash, 279
Shallot-Bacon Quiche, 117
Shallot Souffle with Mushroom
 Sauce, 258
Sherbet, Raspberry, 449
Sherried Beef Stroganoff, 120
Shortcake, Nectarine Quick, 444
Shortcake, Strawberry, 411
Shortcut Beer Bread, 407
Shrimp
 Asparagus and Shrimp Salad, 337
 Barbecued Shrimp Kabobs, 180
 Charcoal-Grilled Shrimp, 180
 Curried Eggs with Shrimp, 114
 Foil-Barbecued Shrimp, 181
 French-Fried Shrimp, 65
 Hot Firepot, 260
 Japanese Custard Soup, 276
 Polynesian Shrimp Bowl, 345
 Shrimp and Noodle Bake, 80
 Shrimp and Tuna Bake, 64
 Shrimp Rockefeller, 108
 Shrimp Tartlets, 117
 Shrimp Tomato Vinaigrette, 352
 Steak and Shrimp Kabob Dinner,
  147
Sicilian Meat Roll, 20
Sicilian Pizza Supreme, 44
Skewered Beef Bundles, 149
Skewered Bratwurst, 184
Skewered Cherry Tomato Meatballs,
 149
Skewered Ham and Fruit Kabobs, 166

Skewered Scallops and Bacon, 181
Skillet-Fried Fish, 176
Slim Ham Slaw, 354
Smoked
 Chinese Smoked Ribs, 162
 Hickory-Smoked Royal Ribs, 161
 Hickory-Smoked Stuffed Trout, 176
 Hickory-Smoked Turkey, 168
 Kowloon Duckling, 171
 Marinated Hickory-Smoked Chuck
  Roast, 141
 Smoked Beef and Cheese Soup,
  146
 Smoked French Pepper Steak,
  138
 Smoked Short Ribs, 144
 Smoked Turkey Roast, 168
 Stuffed Smoked Salmon, 179
 Wild Rice-Stuffed Salmon, 179
Smoky Pork Skillet, 33
Snappy Barbecue Sauce, 189
Souffles
 Broccoli Souffle, 221
 Chicken Curry Souffles, 112
 Shallot Souffle with Mushroom
  Sauce, 258
 Souffle Grand Marnier, 454
 Spinach and Cheese Souffle, 119
 Squash Souffle, 279
 Tuna-Rice Souffle, 89
 Turkey Souffle, 100
Soups
 A Soup for All Seasons, 45
 Bean and Squash Soup, 279
 Borscht with Mushroom Dumplings,
  216
 Bouillabaisse, 62
 Cauliflower-Ham Chowder, 230
 Cheeseburger Chowder, 23
 Chilled Asparagus Soup, 211
 Chilled Pea Soup, 265
 Cream of Celery Soup, 232
 Cream of Mushroom Soup, 252
 Dutch Pea Soup, 265
 French Canadian Split Pea Soup,
  266
 French Onion Soup, 256
 Fresh Corn Chowder, 237
 Garden Gold Soup, 227
 Ham Hocks and Black-Eyed Peas,
  266
 Herbed Fresh Tomato Soup, 284
 Homemade Corn and Chicken
  Soup, 55
 Old-Fashioned Fresh
  Vegetable-Beef Soup, 292
 Sausage and Beef Chili, 23
 Turkey Chowder, 55

Soups *(continued)*
Turnip Greens with Cornmeal Dumplings, 246
Vichyssoise, 271
Sour Cream Cake, Vanilla and, 412
Sour Cream-Chili Bake, 84
Sourdough Bread, 389
Sourdough-Cheese Rolls, 389
Sourdough Starter, 389
South American Mixed Salad, 297
Southern-Style Fried Chicken, 48
Southern Vegetable Medley, 253
Soy-Lemon Basting Sauce, 192
Soy-Marinated Perch Fillets, 178
Spaghetti Bake, Chicken-, 68
Spaghetti Pie, 77
Spaghetti Sauce, Olive, 23
Spaghetti Sauce, Tomato, 286
Spanish String Beans, 215
Spanish Vegetable Mold, 314
Spiced Ham Patties, 156
Spiced Orange Chicken, 51
Spicy Barbecued Chicken, 174
Spicy Italian Salad, 295
Spicy Lamb Stew, 41
Spicy Orange-Fig Mold, 331
Spicy Spud Doughnuts, 401
Spinach
Cheesy Hash-Spinach Pie, 75
Chinese Spinach, 275
Cottage Cheese-Spinach Salad, 276
Greek Spinach Pie, 131
Herbed Spinach Bake, 276
Japanese Custard Soup, 276
Scalloped Spinach, 275
Spinach and Cheese Soufflé, 119
Spinach Squares Hollandaise, 126
Wilted Spinach Salad, 276
Spit-Roasted Châteaubriand, 140
Split Pea Soup, French Canadian, 266
Sponge Cake, Lemon, 414
Spoon Bread, 404
Spring Salad Toss, 296
Springtime Peas, 264
Spritz, Brown Sugar, 431
Sprouting Mini Garden, 364
Sprout Salad, 355
Squash
Bean and Squash Soup, 279
Beef-Stuffed Acorn Squash, 105
Candied Squash Rings, 278
Saucy Dilled Winter Squash, 279
Sausage-Stuffed Turban Squash, 277
Shaker Squash, 279
Squash Soufflé, 279

Standing Rib Roast with Yorkshire Pudding, 7
Steak and Bacon Tournedos, 137
Steak and Kidney Pie, 130
Steak and Shrimp Kabob Dinner, 147
Steaks Bertrand, 16
Steak with Lobster Tail, 14
Steamed Carrot Pudding, 457
Stewed Chicken, 54
Stews
Beef Stew Bake, 74
Biscuit-Topped Stew, 103
Brunswick Stew, 255
Cider Stew, 29
Dilled Lamb Ragout, 129
Fruited Beef Stew, 111
Lamb-Lentil Stew, 73
Meatball-Okra Stew, 255
Oven-Baked Beef-Lima Stew, 76
Oven-Baked Beef Stew, 29
Oven-Baked Pork Stew, 35
Oven Stew for Two, 106
Oxtail-Leek Stew, 258
Spicy Lamb Stew, 41
Stir-Fry Beef with Asparagus, 211
Stirred Custard, 441
Stollen, German, 387
Strata, Classic Cheese, 82
Strata, Contemporary, 102
Strawberries
Fresh Strawberry Cobbler, 445
Fresh Strawberry Ice Cream, 448
Fruit Melange, 443
Fruit Salad Platter, 319
Orange-Strawberry Cake, 411
Pineapple-Berry Boat, 319
Pink Parfaits, 450
Rhubarb-Strawberry Pie, 418
Strawberry Chiffon Pie, 423
Strawberry-Eggnog Shake, 457
Strawberry Glacé Pie, 420
Strawberry-Melon Salad, 319
Strawberry Shortcake, 411
Strawberry Soufflé Salads, 328
Upside-Down Berry Pie, 423
Streusel Coffee Cake, 377
Stroganoff, Beef, 27
Stroganoff Sandwich, 26
Stuffed Cabbage Rolls, 76
Stuffed Eggplant, 243
Stuffed Pattypan Squash, 291
Stuffed Pepper Cups, 96
Stuffed Rolled Rib Roast, 7
Stuffed Smoked Salmon, 179
Stuffed Steak Sandwiches, 155
Stuffed Zucchini for One, 109

Stuffings
Bread and Butter Stuffing, 60
Corn Bread Stuffing Loaf, 60
Old-Fashioned Bread Stuffing, 60
Rice and Vegetable Stuffing, 60
Succotash, 293
Sugar Cookies, Rolled, 432
Sugar-Pecan Crisps, 429
Sukiyaki, 260
Summer Squash Casserole, 289
Sunburst Artichoke, 208
Sunday Chicken-Rice Bake, 67
Sunshine Carrots, 226
Sunshine Salad, 323
Super-Simple Skillet Supper, 167
Swedish Pot Roast, 11
Swedish Tea Ring, 377
Sweet Best-Ever Muffins, 393
Sweet Chocolate Cake, 410
Sweet Potatoes
Apricot-Sauced Sweets, 282
Candied Sweet Potato Boats, 282
Raisin-Filled Sweet Potatoes, 282
Sweet Potato Biscuits, 282
Sweet Potato-Cashew Bake, 280
Whipped Parsnips and Sweet Potatoes, 262
Sweet-Sour Cornish Hens, 170
Sweet-Sour Ham, 166
Sweet-Sour Kale, 246
Sweet-Sour Kraut and Chops, 69
Sweet-Sour Swiss Chard, 244
Swiss Bratwurst Melt, 43
Swiss Corn Bake, 236
Swiss Steak, Deviled, 18
Swiss Steak, Oven, 18

T-Z

Taco Salad, 20
Tailored for Fruit Salads, 359
Tangy Barbecued Franks, 183
Tangy Coleslaw, 310
Tangy Tomato Dressing, 358
Taos Salad Toss, 296
Tapioca, Baked Pineapple, 438
Tapioca Fluff Pudding, 438
Tarragon-Cider Basting Sauce, 191
Tea Ring, Swedish, 377
Tempura, Vegetable, 293
Teriyaki Marinade, 194
Tetrazzini Crepes, 121
Texas Beef Skillet, 24
Thousand Island Dressing, Diet, 363
Three-Way Cream Cheese Frosting, 417
Thyme-Buttered Crescents, 407

Toad in the Hole, 129
Toasted Meringue Topping, 411
Toasted Pecan Frosting, 412
Toffee Bars, 436
Tomatoes
  Canned Tomatoes, 287
  Canned Tomato Juice, 287
  Crumb-Topped Tomatoes, 8
  Frank-Stuffed Tomatoes, 105
  Garden-Fresh Tomato Aspic, 315
  Green Tomato Pickles, 287
  Herbed Fresh Tomato Soup, 284
  Huevos Rancheros, 283
  Italian-Dressed Cauliflower, 228
  Marinated Herbed Tomatoes, 286
  Salmon-Stuffed Tomatoes, 351
  Salsa, 284
  Scalloped Tomatoes, 284
  Shrimp Tomato Vinaigrette, 352
  Southern Vegetable Medley, 253
  Tomato Aspic, 286
  Tomato-Cucumber Salad, 305
  Tomatoes Rosé, 298
  Tomato Salad Dressing, 363
  Tomato Soup Dressing, 356
  Tomato Soup Salad, 315
  Tomato Spaghetti Sauce, 286
  Tuna Salad in Tomato Cups, 342
  Vera Cruz Tomatoes, 286
Torte, Chocolate, 462
Torte, Chocolate Cheesecake, 416
Tossed Fruit Salad, 318
Tossed Mixed Greens, 301
Tossed Salads, 295-305
Tostada Pizza, 26
Tourtière, 130
Triple-Cheese Pie, 92
Tropical Fruit Salad, 321
Trout Amandine, 61
Tuna
  Beet Supper Salad, 217
  Marinated Tuna and Vegetables, 350
  Quick Tuna-Macaroni Salad, 345
  Rice and Tuna Pie, 114
  Shrimp and Tuna Bake, 64
  Tuna-Broccoli Bake, 64
  Tuna-Macaroni Casserole, 80
  Tuna-Noodle Casserole, 79
  Tuna-Rice Soufflé, 89
  Tuna Salad Bake, 89
  Tuna Salad in Tomato Cups, 342
  Tuna with Rice for One, 109
Turkey
  Barbecued Lemon Turkey, 168
  Buffet Chicken Scallop, 127
  Chicken Curry Soufflés, 112
  Chicken Puff Casserole, 100

Turkey *(continued)*
  Club Chicken Casserole, 112
  Corned Beef-Turkey Heroes, 156
  Crowd-Size Chicken Bake, 127
  Curried Turkey Pie, 101
  Fruit-Turkey Kabobs, 49
  Hickory-Smoked Turkey, 168
  Hot Turkey Sandwiches, 50
  Roasting Domestic Birds, 56
  Rotisserie-Roast Turkey, 170
  Saucy Turkey Manicotti, 112
  Smoked Turkey Roast, 168
  Tetrazzini Crepes, 121
  Turkey-Broccoli Bake, 101
  Turkey Chowder, 55
  Turkey in Aspic, 352
  Turkey Soufflé, 100
  Turkey with Fruited Stuffing, 127
  Wild Rice-Chicken Casserole, 113
Turnip Greens with Cornmeal Dumplings, 246
Turnips, Lemon, 288
24-Hour Fruit Salad, 322
24-Hour Vegetable Salad, 248
Twice-Baked Potatoes, 274
Two-Bean Fritters, 213
Two-Cheese Muffins, 394
Two-Corn Bread, 235
Two-Step Fried Chicken, 46
Two-Tone Bread, 369
Two-Tone Cookies, 428
Tyrolean Alps Ragout, 27
Upside-Down Berry Pie, 423
Vanilla Cream Pie, 421
Vanilla Custard Ice Cream, 448
Vanilla Éclairs, 453
Vanilla Pudding, 438
Vanilla and Sour Cream Cake, 412
Vanilla Sugar, 412
Veal
  Cipâte, 130
  Party Eggplant Parmesan, 119
  Veal Parmesan Casserole, 135
Vegetable-Beef Rolls, 137
Vegetable-Beef Soup, Old-Fashioned Fresh, 292
Vegetable Burgers, 153
Vegetable-Meat Kabobs, 167
Vegetable-Stuffed Cubed Steaks, 17
Vegetable Tempura, 293
Vera Cruz Tomatoes, 286
Vichyssoise, 271
Vinaigrette with Variations, 359
Waffles
  Apricot-Sauced Pecan Waffles, 403
  Banana Waffles, 403
  Chocolate Waffles, 403
  Everyday Waffles, 403

Waldorf Mold, Cider, 331
Waldorf Salad, 321
Wellington, Beef Steaks, 15
Western Hot Sauce, 189
Wheat Bread, Cracked, 388
Whipped Parsnips and Sweet Potatoes, 262
White Cake Supreme, 409
Whole Wheat Bread, 388
Whole Wheat Bread, Old-Time, 371
Whole Wheat Rolls, 375
Wild Rice-Chicken Casserole, 113
Wild Rice-Stuffed Salmon, 179
Wilted Cabbage Salad, 313
Wilted Spinach Salad, 276
Wine
  Artichoke-Crab Entrée, 207
  Beef and Bean Ragout, 146
  Beef Bourguignonne, 27
  Beef Stroganoff, 27
  Big-Batch Barbecue Sauce, 191
  Broiled Crab-Chicken Rolls, 50
  Budget Steak Diane, 16
  Charcoal-Grilled Shrimp, 180
  Chicken Cacciatore, 54
  Choucroute Garni, 43
  Cranberry-Claret Sauce, 49
  Harvest Fruit Mold, 324
  Jubilee Salad Mold, 325
  Moussaka for a Crowd, 243
  Olive Spaghetti Sauce, 23
  Peppy Chuck Steak Grill, 138
  Rolled Beef Italian-Style, 17
  Rump Roast Supreme, 9
  Savory Wine Marinade, 194
  Smoked Short Ribs, 144
  Steaks Bertrand, 16
  Tomatoes Rosé, 298
  Tyrolean Alps Ragout, 27
  Wine Barbecue Sauce, 188
  Wine-Basted Short Ribs, 144
  Wined-and-Dined Beef Roast, 143
  Wine-Sauced Trout, 176
Yam Kabobs, Beef-, 148
Yankee Bacon Bake, 73
Yorkshire Pudding, Standing Rib Roast with, 7
Zesty Blue Cheese Dressing, 358
Zesty Salad Dressing, 362
Zesty Sauerkraut Relish, 192
Zesty Vegetable Salad, 226
Zippy Mostaccioli, 74
Zucchini
  Egg-Stuffed Zucchini, 291
  Stuffed Zucchini for One, 109
  Zucchini Nut Loaf, 291
  Zucchini Relish, 291
  Zucchini Salad, 304